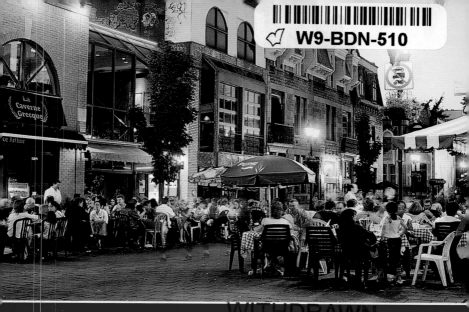

Frommer's®
Montréal & Québec City

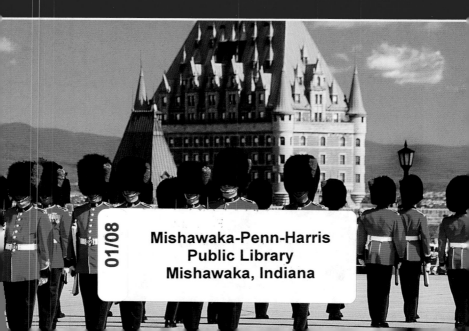

My Montréal & Québec City
by Herbert Bailey Livesey

ON MY FIRST VISIT TO QUÉBEC, HALF A LIFETIME AGO, I TOOK FULL advantage of the local sidewalk cafes. Nowhere else can a visitor more readily absorb the distinctive customs and rhythms of another culture. It was in just such a cafe, in Québec City, looking out over the silvered expanse of the St. Lawrence River and up to the peaked copper roofs of the Château Frontenac, that I began to understand what this singular province was all about. The couple at the next table was in deep conversation. She spoke only French, he only English, and yet they understood each other perfectly.

That's the key to Québec's self-labeled "distinct society." French and British traditions exist side by side, peppered with an internationalism that reflects Canada's liberal immigration policies. Old Francophones still play petanque in the parks on warm days, and in winter their grandchildren bobsled down the run from the capital's fortress to its grand château, the Frontenac. Unilingual Anglophones take high tea in Montréal's grand hotels of the privileged, while their progeny speak Franglish in *boîtes de nuit,* where the singers sound like Piaf and Azvanor. The two cities compete in mounting shoulder-to-shoulder festivals that celebrate everything from jazz to winter to comedy to film.

The photographs on the following pages are just a taste of the many reasons to put Montréal and Québec City on your list of must-see destinations.

MONTMORENCY FALLS (left) are higher than Niagara—as anyone is sure to be told, several times, upon visiting. Back in the 18th century, British and French forces lobbed cannonballs at each other from entrenchments on both banks. These days, fireworks, sometimes seen above the falls, are strictly for fun, and launched during annual festivals.

In this view from the east end of the **MONTREAL'S OLD PORT (above)**, the silver-domed 1847 Bonsecours building is in the foreground, with Colonial-era Vieux Montréal surrounding it, and modern-day office towers rising behind. In summer, the rehabilitated park in front hosts concerts, rollerbladers, cyclists, sunbathers, and others who enjoy *le pic-nic*.

The high altar of the **BASILIQUE NOTRE-DAME (left)**, easily the most beautifully embellished of Montréal's hundreds of churches, is richly carved linden wood, as is most of the interior. The bell in the tower weighs 12 tons, and the floor rumbles when it rings. Orchestras perform here, drawn by the magnificent acoustics. The church's Protestant Irish-American architect, James O'Donnell, was so stirred by what he had wrought that he converted to Catholicism.

Pedestrian-only **RUE DU TRESOR (above)** in Québec City is an obligatory stop on every stroll through the old Upper Town. Artists line both sides of the narrow lane, their watercolors, prints, and drawings on display. There's no pressure to buy. Subject matter is mostly various vistas and details of their city, but some artists set up easels beside nearby outdoor cafes and offer to do portraits.

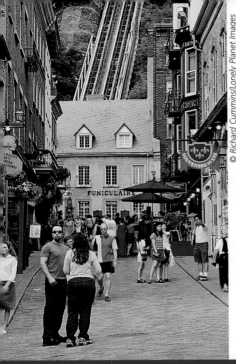

The historic district of Québec City is the only walled city north of Mexico. It's divided into two parts: Basse-Ville, the older part down by the river where the first European settlers built and farmed, and Haute-Ville, atop the steep-sided cliff to which the French citizens withdrew for greater safety from invaders. This **FUNICULAIRE (left)** connects the two, affording spectacular views and escape from the Breakneck Stairs, the other pedestrian route down the hill.

SUGARING-OFF (below) season is February through March, when sap is drawn from the vast stands of sugar maples with which the province is blessed. At first, the sap was merely processed, transformed into syrup and candies, and sent off to eager buyers. Then some canny Québecer decided to offer meals in his *cabane à sucre*—sugar shack. That evolved into an industry, and some sugar shacks stay open all year, providing gargantuan farm meals, live folkloric entertainment, simple lodgings, and even sleigh rides.

Boosters call Montréal the "City of Festivals," and justifiably so. Apart from a few bereft weeks here and there in the coldest months, it takes specific intent and careful planning to avoid celebratory events of one kind or another. Festivals throughout the year highlight comedy, film, cuisine, theater, cycling, motor racing, and fireworks. The greatest explosion of energy and talent, however, is during the annual **JAZZ FESTIVAL (above)**, with hundreds of performances in scores of venues, many of them free.

Montréal's **HÔTEL DE VILLE (right)** stands at the top of the Place Jacques-Cartier, which was the open-air market square of 19th-century Montréal. The extravagantly detailed French Second Empire style of the building is seen to best effect at night, and a dozen other impressive structures are similarly illuminated, constituting a rewarding—and safe—after-dark walking tour.

Few municipal symbols are as power-fully evocative as Québec's **CHATEAU FRONTENAC (above)**. In style, it is a Loire castle on steroids, one of a chain strung along the route of the Trans-Canada railway to encourage tourism at the start of the last century.

The long staircase leading down from the elevated La Citadelle to the promenade known as Terrace Dufferin is transformed into a **BOBSLED RUN (right)** during Québec City's annual winter carnival. No special skills or particular athleticism is required for the short but thrilling run, unless you count climbing up to the starting point.

Opposite page: © Walter Bibikow/Getty Images

Routinely designated the premier ski resort east of the Mississippi, **TREMBLANT** marches up the slopes of its namesake mountain. Active all year, Tremblant also offers water-sports on the town-mile lake at its base. Lodgings, dining, and nightlife range from economical to deluxe, and while kids are catered to, there are plenty of times and places for parents to get away for a few hours.

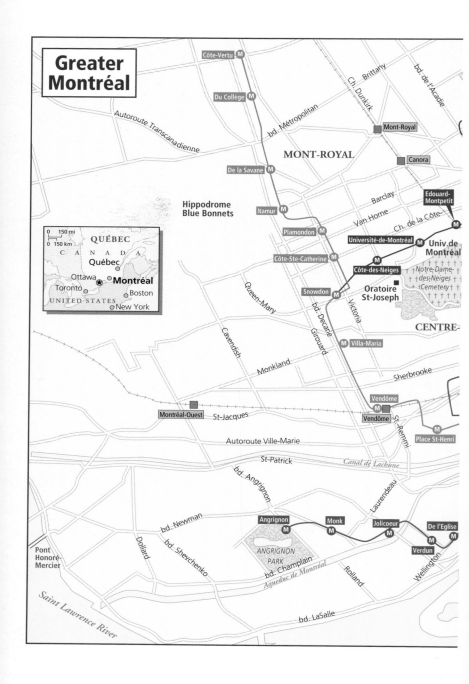

Greater Montréal

Côte-Vertu Ⓜ

Du Collège Ⓜ

Autoroute Transcanadienne

bd. Métropolitan

Ch. Brittany

bd. de l'Acadie

Ch. Dunkirk

Mont-Royal

MONT-ROYAL

Canora

De la Savane Ⓜ

Barclay

Edouard-
Montpetit Ⓜ

Hippodrome
Blue Bonnets

Namur Ⓜ

Van Horne

Ch. de la Côte

Plamondon Ⓜ

Université-de-Montréal Ⓜ

Univ.de
Montréal

Côte-Ste-Catherine Ⓜ

Côte-des-Neiges Ⓜ

Notre-Dame-
des-Neiges
Cemetery

QUÉBEC

150 mi
150 km

C A N A D A

Québec

Ottawa

Montréal

Toronto

Boston

UNITED STATES

New York

Snowdon Ⓜ

Oratoire
St-Joseph

CENTRE-

Queen-Mary

Cavendish

bd. Decarie

Girouard

Victoria

Villa-Maria Ⓜ

Monkland

Sherbrooke

Montréal-Ouest

St-Jacques

Vendôme Ⓜ
Vendôme

St-Remi

Place St-Henri Ⓜ

Autoroute Ville-Marie

St-Patrick

Canal de Lachine

bd. Angrignon

bd. Newman

Laurendeau

Dollard

bd. Shevchenko

Angrignon Ⓜ

Monk Ⓜ

Jolicoeur Ⓜ

De l'Eglise Ⓜ

ANGRIGNON
PARK

bd. Champlain

Verdun Ⓜ

Wellington

Pont
Honoré-
Mercier

Aqueduc de Montréal

Rolland

Saint Lawrence River

bd. LaSalle

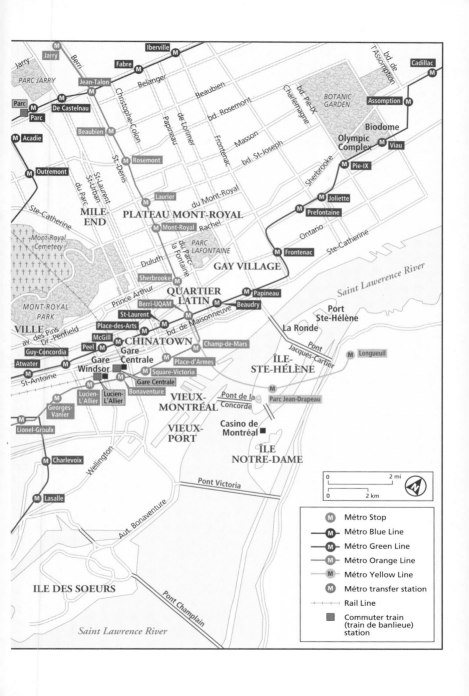

Jarry
Jarry
PARC JARRY
Berri
Iberville
Fabre
Jean-Talon
De Castelnau
Parc
Parc
Acadie
Beaubien
Outremont
Christophe-Colon
Belanger
Beaubien
bd.-Rosemont
Beaubien
de Lorimer
Papineau
Frontenac
Masson
bd. St-Joseph
bd. Pie-IX
Charlemagne
BOTANIC
GARDEN
bd. de l'Assomption
Cadillac
Assomption
Biodome
Olympic
Complex
Viau
St-Laurent
St-Urbain
du Parc
St-Denis
Rosemont
Laurier
du Mont-Royal
Sherbrooke
Pie-IX
Joliette
Prefontaine
MILE-
END
PLATEAU MONT-ROYAL
Ste-Catherine
Mont-Royal
Mont-Royal
Cemetery
Duluth
Rachel
Ontario
Ste-Catherine
Parc de
la Fontaine
PARC
LAFONTAINE
GAY VILLAGE
Frontenac
MONT-ROYAL
PARK
Sherbrooke
Prince Arthur
Berri-UQAM
Papineau
Beaudry
Saint Lawrence River
VILLE
av. des Pins
Dr.-Penfield
St-Laurent
Place-des-Arts
QUARTIER
LATIN
bd. de Maisonneuve
Port
Ste-Hélène
La Ronde
McGill
CHINATOWN
Champ-de-Mars
Pont
Jacques-Cartier
Longueuil
Guy-Concordia
Peel
Gare
Centrale
Place-d'Armes
ÎLE-
STE-HÉLÈNE
Atwater
Gare
Windsor
Square-Victoria
St-Antoine
Gare Centrale
Bonaventure
Lucien-
L'Allier
Lucien-
L'Allier
VIEUX-
MONTRÉAL
Pont de la
Concorde
Parc Jean-Drapeau
Georges-
Vanier
Lionel-Groulx
VIEUX-
PORT
Casino de
Montréal
ÎLE
NOTRE-DAME
Charlevoix
Wellington
Pont Victoria
Lasalle
Aut. Bonaventure

0   2 mi
0   2 km

N

ILE DES SOEURS
Pont Champlain
Saint Lawrence River

Métro Stop
Métro Blue Line
Métro Green Line
Métro Orange Line
Métro Yellow Line
Métro transfer station
Rail Line
Commuter train
(train de banlieue)
station

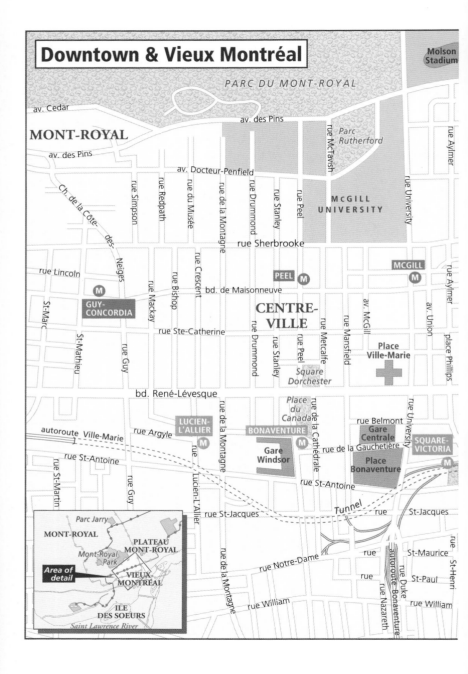

Downtown & Vieux Montréal

Molson Stadium

PARC DU MONT-ROYAL

av. Cedar

MONT-ROYAL

av. des Pins

av. des Pins

Parc Rutherford

rue McTavish

rue Aylmer

av. Docteur-Penfield

Ch. de la Côte- des- Neiges

rue Simpson

rue Redpath

rue du Musée

rue de la Montagne

rue Drummond

rue Stanley

rue Peel

rue University

McGILL UNIVERSITY

rue Sherbrooke

rue Lincoln

rue Crescent

PEEL Ⓜ

MCGILL Ⓜ

rue Aylmer

St-Marc

rue Bishop

rue Mackay

bd. de Maisonneuve

CENTRE-VILLE

av. McGill

av. Union

place Phillips

GUY-CONCORDIA Ⓜ

rue Ste-Catherine

St-Mathieu

rue Guy

rue Drummond

rue Stanley

rue Peel

rue Metcalfe

rue Mansfield

Place Ville-Marie

bd. René-Lévesque

Square Dorchester

autoroute Ville-Marie

rue Argyle

LUCIEN-L'ALLIER Ⓜ

rue de la Montagne

Place du Canada

rue de la Cathédrale

rue University

rue Belmont

Gare Centrale

SQUARE-VICTORIA Ⓜ

rue St-Antoine

rue Guy

rue Lucien-L'Allier

BONAVENTURE Ⓜ

Gare Windsor

rue de la Gauchetière

Place Bonaventure

rue St-Martin

rue St-Jacques

rue St-Antoine

Tunnel

rue

St-Jacques

rue St-Maurice

rue St-Henri

rue de la Montagne

rue Notre-Dame

rue

autoroute Bonaventure

rue Duke

St-Paul

rue Nazareth

rue William

rue William

Parc Jarry

MONT-ROYAL

PLATEAU MONT-ROYAL

Mont-Royal Park

Area of detail

VIEUX-MONTRÉAL

ILE DES SOEURS

Saint Lawrence River

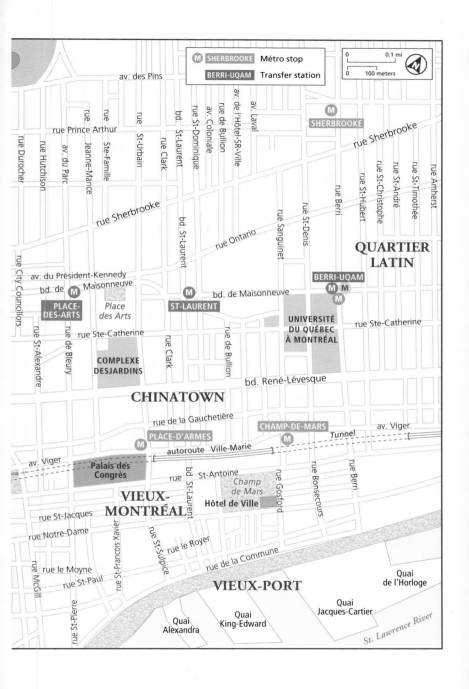

av. des Pins

rue Durocher
rue Hutchison
av. du Parc
rue Jeanne-Mance
Ste-Famille
rue St-Urbain
rue Clark
bd. St-Laurent
rue St-Dominique
av. Coloniale
av. de Bullion
av. de l'Hôtel-SR-Ville
av. Laval

rue Prince Arthur

Ⓜ SHERBROOKE

rue Sherbrooke

rue St-Hubert
rue Berri
rue St-Christophe
rue St-André
rue St-Timothée
rue Amherst

rue Sherbrooke

rue Ontario

rue Sanguinet
rue St-Denis

QUARTIER
LATIN

rue City Councillors

av. du Président-Kennedy

bd. de Ⓜ Maisonneuve

PLACE-
DES-ARTS

Place
des Arts

bd. St-Laurent

Ⓜ
ST-LAURENT

bd. de Maisonneuve

BERRI-UQAM
Ⓜ Ⓜ

rue St-Alexandre
rue de Bleury

rue Ste-Catherine

rue Clark

rue de Bullion

UNIVERSITÉ
DU QUÉBEC
À MONTRÉAL

rue Ste-Catherine

COMPLEXE
DESJARDINS

bd. René-Lévesque

CHINATOWN

rue de la Gauchetière

CHAMP-DE-MARS

av. Viger

PLACE-D'ARMES

Ⓜ

Tunnel

Ⓜ

autoroute Ville-Marie

av. Viger

Palais des
Congrès

rue St-Antoine

rue St-Jacques

bd. St-Laurent

Champ
de Mars

rue Gosford

rue Bonsecours

rue Berri

VIEUX-
MONTRÉAL

Hôtel de Ville

rue Notre-Dame

rue St-François Xavier

rue St-Sulpice

rue le Royer

rue McGill
rue le Moyne
rue St-Paul
rue St-Pierre

rue de la Commune

VIEUX-PORT

Quai
de l'Horloge

Quai
Alexandra

Quai
King-Edward

Quai
Jacques-Cartier

St. Lawrence River

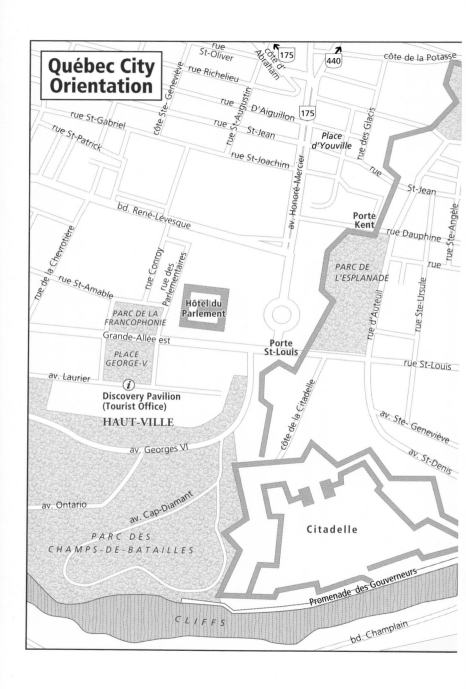

Québec City Orientation

rue St-Oliver

côte d'Abraham

175

440

côte de la Potasse

rue Richelieu

côte Ste-Geneviève

rue St-Gabriel

rue St-Patrick

rue St-Augustin

D'Aiguillon

175

rue St-Jean

St-Jean

rue des Glacis

Place d'Youville

rue St-Joachim

rue St-Jean

av. Honoré-Mercier

bd. René-Lévesque

Porte Kent

rue Dauphine

rue Ste-Angèle

rue de la Chevrotière

rue St-Amable

rue Conroy

rue des Parlementaires

Hôtel du Parlement

PARC DE L'ESPLANADE

rue d'Auteuil

rue Ste-Ursule

rue

PARC DE LA FRANCOPHONIE

Grande-Allée est

PLACE GEORGE-V

Porte St-Louis

rue St-Louis

av. Laurier

(i) Discovery Pavilion (Tourist Office)

côte de la Citadelle

av. Ste- Geneviève

HAUT-VILLE

av. St-Denis

av. Georges VI

av. Ontario

av. Cap-Diamant

Citadelle

PARC DES CHAMPS-DE-BATAILLES

Promenade des Gouverneurs

CLIFFS

bd. Champlain

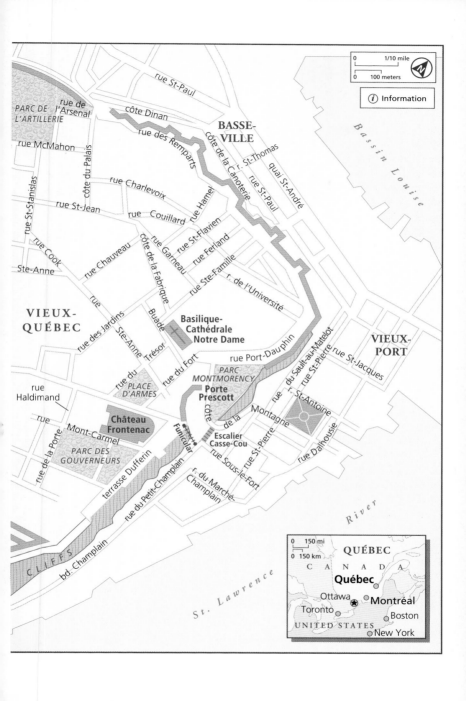

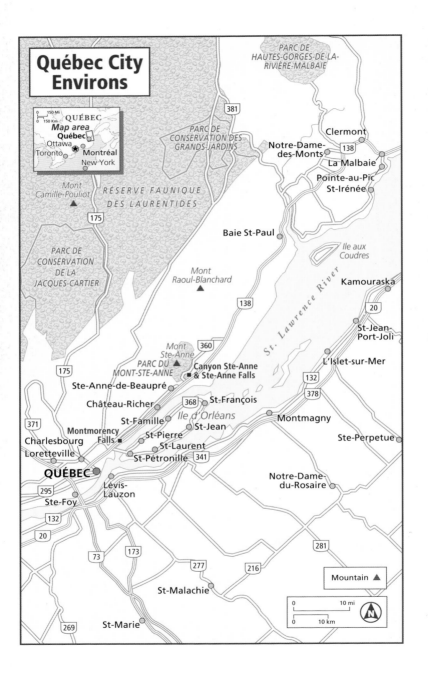

Québec City Environs

QUÉBEC

0   150 Mi
0   150 Km

Map area

Québec

Ottawa
Toronto
Montréal
New York

PARC DE HAUTES-GORGES-DE-LA-RIVIÈRE-MALBAIE

PARC DE CONSERVATION DES GRANDS-JARDINS

381

Clermont

Notre-Dame-des-Monts

138

La Malbaie

Pointe-au-Pic
St-Irénée

Mont Camille-Pouliot

RÉSERVE FAUNIQUE DES LAURENTIDES

175

Baie St-Paul

Ile aux Coudres

PARC DE CONSERVATION DE LA JACQUES-CARTIER

Mont Raoul-Blanchard

138

Kamouraska

20

St. Lawrence River

St-Jean-Port-Joli

Mont Ste-Anne
PARC DU MONT-STE-ANNE

360

L'Islet-sur-Mer

175

Canyon Ste-Anne & Ste-Anne Falls

132

Ste-Anne-de-Beaupré

378

Château-Richer

368

St-François

371

St-Famille

Ile d'Orléans

Montmagny

Montmorency Falls

St-Pierre

St-Jean

Charlesbourg

St-Laurent

Ste-Perpetue

Loretteville

St-Pétronille

341

QUÉBEC

Lévis-Lauzon

Notre-Dame-du-Rosaire

295

Ste-Foy

132

20

73

173

281

277

216

Mountain ▲

0   10 mi
0   10 km

St-Malachie

269

St-Marie

Frommer's®

Montréal & Québec City

2008

by Leslie Brokaw

Here's what the critics say about Frommer's:

"Amazingly easy to use. Very portable, very complete."
—*Booklist*

"Detailed, accurate, and easy-to-read information for all price ranges."
—*Glamour Magazine*

"Hotel information is close to encyclopedic."
—*Des Moines Sunday Register*

"Frommer's Guides have a way of giving you a real feel for a place."
—*Knight Ridder Newspapers*

Wiley Publishing, Inc.

About the Author

Leslie Brokaw is a frequent traveler to Montréal and Québec City from her home base in Boston. She teaches at Emerson College; writes a film column for *The Boston Globe;* and covers travel, business, and entertainment for a wide variety of other publications and websites. Brokaw spent her early career at *Inc.* magazine as a writer and Web editor.

Published by:

Wiley Publishing, Inc.

111 River St.
Hoboken, NJ 07030-5774

ISBN 978-0-470-17043-4
Editor: mcd editorial *with* Jennifer Reilly
Production Editor: Katie Robinson
Cartographer: Andrew Murphy
Photo Editor: Richard Fox
Anniversary Logo Design: Richard Pacifico
Production by Wiley Indianapolis Composition Services

Front cover photo: Place Jacques Cartier and Town Hall in Montréal
Back cover photo: Two waiters outside a Québec restaurant window

For information on our other products and services or to obtain technical support, please contact our Customer Care Department within the U.S. at 800/762-2974, outside the U.S. at 317/572-3993 or fax 317/572-4002.

Wiley also publishes its books in a variety of electronic formats. Some content that appears in print may not be available in electronic formats.

Manufactured in the United States of America

5   4   3   2   1

Contents

List of Maps

An Invitation to the Reader

In researching this book, we discovered many wonderful places—hotels, restaurants, shops, and more. We're sure you'll find others. Please tell us about them, so we can share the information with your fellow travelers in upcoming editions. If you were disappointed with a recommendation, we'd love to know that, too. Please write to:

Frommer's Montréal & Québec City 2008
Wiley Publishing, Inc. • 111 River St. • Hoboken, NJ 07030-5774

An Additional Note

Please be advised that travel information is subject to change at any time—and this is especially true of prices. We therefore suggest that you write or call ahead for confirmation when making your travel plans. The authors, editors, and publisher cannot be held responsible for the experiences of readers while traveling. Your safety is important to us, however, so we encourage you to stay alert and be aware of your surroundings. Keep a close eye on cameras, purses, and wallets, all favorite targets of thieves and pickpockets.

Acknowledgments

This edition of the book draws from over 10 years of earlier versions that were written by Herbert Bailey Livesey, the author's stepfather. She wishes to acknowledge her debt to The Geezer for his fine taste, keen research, and deft writing in those editions and the introductory essay. He writes about travel and food at www.geezerwisdom.blogspot.com.

Other Great Guides for Your Trip:

Frommer's Canada
Montréal & Québec City For Dummies
Montréal Day by Day

Frommer's Star Ratings, Icons & Abbreviations

Every hotel, restaurant, and attraction listing in this guide has been ranked for quality, value, service, amenities, and special features using a **star-rating system.** In country, state, and regional guides, we also rate towns and regions to help you narrow down your choices and budget your time accordingly. Hotels and restaurants are rated on a scale of zero (recommended) to three stars (exceptional). Attractions, shopping, nightlife, towns, and regions are rated according to the following scale: zero stars (recommended), one star (highly recommended), two stars (very highly recommended), and three stars (must-see).

In addition to the star-rating system, we also use **seven feature icons** that point you to the great deals, in-the-know advice, and unique experiences that separate travelers from tourists. Throughout the book, look for:

Finds	Special finds—those places only insiders know about
Fun Fact	Fun facts—details that make travelers more informed and their trips more fun
Kids	Best bets for kids and advice for the whole family
Moments	Special moments—those experiences that memories are made of
Overrated	Places or experiences not worth your time or money
Tips	Insider tips—great ways to save time and money
Value	Great values—where to get the best deals

The following **abbreviations** are used for credit cards:

AE	American Express	DISC	Discover	V	Visa
DC	Diners Club	MC	MasterCard		

Frommers.com

Now that you have this guidebook, to help you plan a great trip, visit our website at **www.frommers.com** for additional travel information on more than 3,600 destinations. We update features regularly, to give you instant access to the most current trip-planning information available. At Frommers.com, you'll find scoops on the best airfares, lodging rates, and car rental bargains. You can even book your travel online through our reliable travel booking partners. Other popular features include:

- Online updates of our most popular guidebooks
- Vacation sweepstakes and contest giveaways
- Newsletters highlighting the hottest travel trends
- Online travel message boards with featured travel discussions

What's New in Montréal & Québec City

Québec spent 2007 gearing up for its 400th anniversary party. New Year's Eve (Dec 31, 2007) is the official kickoff, but most events take place from June to September 2008. The waterfront has been spruced up, museums are mounting special anniversary-related exhibits, and shows featuring the Cirque du Soleil and other performers are in the works. The biggest days will be July 3 to July 6, so make plans now. **Espace 400ᵉ,** a new pavilion on the waterfront where the Centre d'Interprétation du Vieux-Port used to be, will be home base for the celebration, hosting special exhibits, performances, and conferences.

Meanwhile, is the quest for separatism fading in Québec? That's what many people across the province were wondering, with not a small sigh of relief, after provincial elections in March 2007. Jean Charest and the Liberal Party won a minority government to stay in power, but the big story was the second-place victory of the new, almost out-of-nowhere **Action démocratique du Québec** party and its young leader Mario Dumont, as well as the crushing defeat of the separatist Parti Québécois, which garnered just 28% of the vote. The election was perceived by many as the beginning of the end of the PQ's 40-year campaign for independence.

Also high on the political agenda has been cultural accommodation: How much Québec should bend its culture for newcomers to fit in has been a bigger topic of public discourse than separatism, with debates on things like whether the province's sugar shacks should restrict pork from the meals it serves to accommodate Islamic law. It's no coincidence that the most talked about television show of the year was the comedy *Little Mosque on the Prairie.*

PLANNING YOUR TRIP   Since January 2007, air travelers between the U.S. and Canada have been required to present a valid passport. The rule was temporarily relaxed until September 2007, with travelers required to show just a photo ID and proof that they had applied for a passport, but you should now plan to present your passport for entry.

If you're planning to travel between the U.S. and Canada by land or by sea, the rules are a little fuzzier. A passport or other document is *likely* to be required as of January 1, 2008. Concerns about the impact on tourism, though, have made that date a possibility instead of a certainty.

The Canadian tourism industry, in fact, is dealing with something of a triple whammy these days. In addition to the new passport requirements, the strength of Canadian dollar has sent Canadian tourists out of the country and kept U.S. visitors from spending as freely as they have in the past. Additionally, the federal Visitor Rebate Program that allowed nonresident guests to reclaim taxes they paid on purchases and lodging was eliminated in April 2007.

The upside for travelers? Hotels prices have held stable and, in some cases, declined from 2007 rates. While it's not quite a buyer's market, there may be extra opportunities to negotiate rates in 2008, as hotels scramble to fill rooms. This will be the case particularly in the off season.

GETTING TO KNOW MONTREAL In Montréal, the no. 2 Métro line has been extended into the north. The new end station is Montmorency, making that the train "direction" you'll see on platforms instead of Henri-Bourassa, the former end station.

WHERE TO STAY   Hotel openings in Montréal have slowed in the past year, perhaps because there have been proportionally more hotel rooms here than in other North American cities of similar size. Still, the plush **Hôtel Nelligan,** 106 rue St-Paul ouest (© 877/788-2040), in Vieux-Montréal, expanded from 63 to 105 units. An inexpensive entry is the downtown **Hôtel Le Dauphin,** 1025 rue de Bleury (© 888/784-3888). Its 72 rooms may be on the bland side, but every room is equipped with a computer terminal and free Internet access, and the introductory price of C$109 (US$95/£47) is low.

In Québec City's burgeoning arts and gastronomic community St-Roch, the new **Auberge Le Vincent,** 295 rue St-Vallier est (© 418/523-5000) has introduced sophisticated rooms with luxe features.

WHERE TO DINE   One of our favorite Montréal restaurants, **Les Chevres,** shut down in early 2007. On the plus side, the very good Spanish resto **Pintxo** has added a new, smaller outlet at 2 rue Sherbrooke est, at the corner of boulevard St-Laurent. **Nuances** (© 514/392-2708), the restaurant atop the city's casino, got a dazzling face-lift in 2007

and now looks as contemporary as the food on its plates. And in Vieux-Montréal, the new **Ora,** 394 rue St-Jacques (© 514/848-0202), seems primed to add some pop to the neighborhood with its neon-pink lighting, DJ booth, zesty food, and a 1am last call for food.

We've liked the restaurant **Cube** inside the sleek Hôtel St-Paul in Vieux-Montréal in the past, but it was undergoing renovations when we visited. It has reopened with the name Volver and an all-new Mediterranean menu with Spanish and Italian influences.

In Québec City, the total physical overhaul of **Laurie Raphaël,** 117 rue Dalhousie (© 418/692-4555), keeps it atop the local food pyramid: It's sophisticated *and* endlessly eclectic.

WHAT TO SEE & DO   A new discount ticket office for Montréal cultural events opened in summer 2007. Called **Vitrine culturelle de Montréal** ("cultural window of Montréal"; © 514/285-4545), it's in Place des Arts at 145 rue Sainte-Catherine ouest.

Both Montréal and Québec City now offer **museum cards.** The cards grant entry to dozens of museums and attractions as well as public transport.

In Montréal, the **Musée Marc-Aurèle Fortin,** which was dedicated to the art of French-Canadian landscape watercolorist Marc-Aurèle Fortin (1888–1970), donated its entire collection to the Musée des Beaux-Arts and shut down. Fortin's works are now in the Hornstein Pavilion with other Canadian art.

In Québec City, excavation in the epicenter of the tourist district—under the Terrasse Dufferin, the promenade alongside the Château Frontenac that overlooks the St. Lawrence—is still continuing. The Terrasse is expected to reopen for the 400th-anniversary parties, perhaps with some kind of Plexiglas viewing of the excavation below.

And in summer 2007, the Québec province officially inaugurated the new *Route verte* (**Green Route**), a 4,000km (2,485-mile) bike network that stretches from one end of the province to the other and links up all regions and cities. Accredited accommodations along the way have a *"Bienvenue cyclistes!"* sticker and provide safe bike storage, a bike pump and tools, information about where to make repairs nearby, and high-carb meals.

1

The Best of Montréal & Québec City

Just 10 years ago, something of a bleak mood prevailed in Québec province. It was driven by lingering recession and uncertainty over the future; it seemed possible that the province would choose to fling itself into independence from the rest of Canada.

Lately, though, something else is going on. Ripples of optimism have become waves. The Canadian dollar, as every traveler will discover, has strengthened against its U.S. counterpart. In Montréal, a billion-dollar building boom has been filling up vacant lots all over downtown. Montréal has become a modern city in every regard, with skyscrapers in unexpected shapes and bright, noncorporate colors; a historic district that has been beautifully preserved; and a large area of artists' lofts, boutiques, cafés, and miles of restaurants. Québec City, more traditional and more French, is replacing its former conservatism with an ever-expanding aura of sophistication.

American and European travelers will likely find Montréal an urban near-paradise. The subway system, called the Métro, is modern and swift. Streets are safe. Montréal's best restaurants are the equals of their south-of-the-border compatriots in every way, but 20% cheaper. Québec City, meanwhile, with its impressive location above the St. Lawrence River and its virtually unblemished Old Town of 18th- and 19th-century houses, looks French and is almost impossibly romantic and Continental-feeling—it's unlike any city in North America.

1 Unforgettable Travel Experiences in Québec

MONTREAL

- **Listen to Jazz:** Downtown, Old Town, the Latin Quarter, all over, this is a favorite pastime of locals and visitors alike, especially in late June and early July during the renowned Montréal Jazz Festival. See p. 15.
- **Savor Top-Notch Cuisine at Affordable Prices:** Experience all of French cuisine's permutations—traditional, haute, bistro, original Québécois—along with the city's fusion hybrids and ethnic restaurants the way the locals do: by ordering the table d'hôte specials. You'll get to indulge in three

or more courses for a fixed price that is only slightly more than the cost of an a la carte main course alone. Most full-service restaurants offer the option, if only at midday. See chapter 6.

- **Explore Vieux-Montréal:** The old quarter has an overwhelmingly European flavor. Wander Place Jacques-Cartier, the most engaging of the district's squares; explore museums and the stunning architecture of the churches; stroll or meander on a bike along the revitalized waterfront. See chapter 7, and the walking tour of Vieux-Montréal in chapter 8.

- **Shop:** Browse the shops of world-class domestic designers, from the up-and-coming to the well established; search for Inuit (Eskimo) sculptures of the highest order (with prices to match); and take in the scores of eclectic antiques shops along rue Notre-Dame between rue Guy and avenue Atwater. See chapter 9.

QUEBEC CITY

- **Admire the Skyline from the Lévis Ferry:** Approaching the city by car from the south, the ferry provides a grand view for little money. Passengers already in the city can start at the Vieux-Port side, and then stay onboard and come right back without disembarking.
- **Linger at an Outdoor Café:** Tables are set out at Place d'Armes in Upper Town, in the Quartier du Petit-Champlain in Lower Town, and along the Grande-Allée—a quality-of-life invention the French and their Québécois brethren have perfected. See chapter 14.
- **Soak Up the Blossoming Lower Town:** Once all but abandoned to shipping and grimy industry, the old riverside neighborhood of Basse-Ville/Vieux-Port has been reborn, with antiques shops, bistros, and boutique hotels filling its rehabilitated 18th- and 19th-century buildings. See chapter 15, and the walking tour of the Lower Town in chapter 16.
- **Relax in Battlefields Park (Parc des Champs-de-Bataille):** This park is beautifully situated, overlooking the St. Lawrence River, and is particularly lively on weekends, when families and lovers come to picnic and play. See p. 240.

2 The Best Splurge Hotels

MONTREAL

- **Hôtel Le St-James** (355 rue St-Jacques ouest; ✆ **866/841-3111**): Setting the standard against which any boutique hotel in town must measure itself, this former 19th-century bank in Vieux-Montréal lets no luxurious detail escape its attention. From its opulent main hall to the sybaritic subterranean spa to its immaculately trained staff, this is an experience that may well be the highlight of your visit. See p. 75.
- **W Montréal** (901 rue Square Victoria; ✆ **888/627-7081**): If you qualify as hip, aware, and on the fast track to somewhere good (or like to think you do), waste no time booking a suite at this local entry in the spreading chain. It won't hurt if your platinum card is paid up and you don't need much sleep, either. There are three bars and lounges, a hyper-chic restaurant, and a clientele composed of knockouts of both sexes. Also in Vieux-Montréal. See p. 76.

QUEBEC CITY

- **Auberge Saint-Antoine** (8 rue St-Antoine; ✆ **888/692-2211**): Sure, there's the Château Frontenac, looming up above, the very symbol of the city. But for a more intimate, less overwhelming visit, take the funicular down to the Basse-Ville. The auberge started as a stylish but largely unexceptional B&B and has grown in calculated phases into the most desirable lodging in town, now with a chic lounge and a top restaurant. See p. 219.
- **Dominion 1912** (126 rue Saint-Pierre; ✆ **888/833-5253**): Also a key player in the redevelopment of the once dreary Basse-Ville/Vieux-Port,

---

⟨Moments **Romantic Québec City**

"Romance" is Québec City's middle name. Every narrow street, leafy plaza, sidewalk café, horse-drawn *calèche*, pitched roof, and church spire breathes recollections of the provincial cities of the mother country. But to get the full Québec City treatment, amble those streets on a night of the full moon and find a bench on the **Terrasse Dufferin.** The river below will be the color of liquid mercury in the moon's glow, and there will be more stars than you can ever remember seeing. Streaks of comets and music faintly heard from the boîtes in Lower Town are possibilities. Romance is a certainty.

---

the Dominion has rooms so large and beds and bedding so cozily enveloping that you may not want to go out.

Do, though, at least for the fireplace, croissants, and café au lait in the lobby. See p. 220.

3 The Best Moderately Priced Hotels

MONTREAL

- **Auberge Bonaparte** (447 rue St-François-Xavier; © **514/844-1448**): The long-established restaurant on the ground floor was accorded a massive rehab and expansion a few years back, and now includes the comely inn upstairs. Rooms are simply furnished, but four out of the eight on each floor have whirlpool tubs and the rooftop terrace overlooks Vieux-Montréal's Basilique Notre-Dame. See p. 79.
- **Auberge Les Passants du Sans Soucy** (171 rue St-Paul oust; © **514/842-2634**): Just around the corner from Bonaparte, this charming little B&B helped pioneer the recovery of Vieux-Montréal to its current status as the must-see quarter of the city. The lobby is an art gallery with changing exhibits. Fireplaces and jet

tubs have been added to the nine bedrooms. See p. 80.

QUEBEC CITY

- **Hôtel Sainte-Anne** (32 rue Ste-Anne; © **877/222-9422**): Practically in the shadow of the Château Frontenac, this Euro-design hotel occupies a row house in the middle of the most touristy district of the Upper Town. Rooms are stripped to the minimum, but as equipped as can be reasonably expected with this location at these relatively gentle prices. See p. 216.
- **Château Laurier** (1220 Place Georges V ouest; © **800/463-4453**): There are now nine categories of rooms and suites in this Parliament Hill property, thanks to nearly continual expansion in recent years. The hotel is close to the Battlefields Park and Musée des Beaux-Arts. See p. 218.

4 The Most Unforgettable Dining Experiences

MONTREAL

- **Nuances** (1 av. du Casino, in the Casino de Montréal; © **514/392-2708**): This gourmet resto at the top of the city's casino got an impressive face-lift in early 2007 that made the

decor as contemporary and elegant as the food—all creamy walls, white linen, and pale-green leather banquettes. A room with real star power. See p. 106.

- **Toqué!** (900 Place Jean-Paul-Riopelle; ℂ **514/499-2084**): Superstar chef/owner Norman Laprise has been thrilling Montréal gourmands for years. In dishes of startling innovation, he brings together diverse ingredients that have rarely appeared before on restaurant plates. There's little point in describing individual dishes, for he moves on before any of his food achieves signature status. See p. 91.

QUEBEC CITY

- **Initiale** (54 rue St-Pierre; ℂ **418/694-1818**): From its gracious tone and subdued lighting to its carefully paced multi-course menus, Initiale exudes silky polish from greeting to adieu. You will dine gloriously. See p. 230.
- **Laurie Raphaël** (117 rue Dalhousie; ℂ **418/692-4555**): Dazzling. Given the growing local competition, the owners have utterly transformed their setting and shaken up the menu. Service is spot-on and the food creative and artfully presented. See p. 230.

5 The Best Museums

MONTREAL

- **Musée des Beaux-Arts** (1379–1380 rue Sherbrooke ouest; ℂ **514/285-2000**): Canada's first museum devoted exclusively to the arts started out in 1912 in a neoclassical space on the north side of Sherbrooke. A newer pavilion on the opposite side is connected by an underground series of galleries. Temporary exhibits are strong, and the permanent collection is largely devoted to international contemporary art and Canadian works. See p. 109.
- **Pointe-à-Callière/Montréal Museum of Archaeology and History** (350 Place Royale; ℂ **514/872-9150**): A first visit to Montréal might best begin here. This strikingly modernistic structure at the edge of Vieux-Montréal marks the spot where the first European settlement put down roots. It stands atop extensive excavations that unearthed not only remains of the French newcomers, but also the native bands that preceded them. Wind your way on the self-guided tour through the subterranean complex. See p. 114.

QUEBEC CITY

- **Musée de la Civilisation** (85 rue Dalhousie; ℂ **418/643-2158**): Here is that rarity among museums: a collection of cleverly mounted temporary and permanent exhibitions that both children and adults find engrossing, without talking down or metaphysical maunderings. Make sure to make time for *Memoires,* which charts the evolution of Québec from the first encounters between Native peoples and Europeans. See p. 235.

6 The Best Outdoor Activities

MONTREAL

- **Traverse the Lachine Canal:** The abandoned canal was first constructed to detour around the rapids of the same name. Falling into disuse after construction of the St. Lawrence Seaway, it was renovated in the last few years to serve as a recreational resource. Connecting the Vieux-Port with Atwater Market, a little over a mile away, it can be traveled by guided boat tour, on foot, or with bicycles or in-line skates rented at the Vieux-Port (p. 125).

- **Bike the City:** Montréalers' enthusiasm for bicycling has provided the impetus for the ongoing development of a network of bike-specific paths that wind through downtown areas and out to the countryside. Cyclists are allowed to take their bikes onto designated Métro cars and some taxis have special racks. Rentals can be arranged right at the waterfront park. See p. 128.

QUEBEC CITY

- **Take a Walking Tour:** Combine immersion in Québec's rich history with a good stretch of the legs among the battlements and along the cobble-stoned streets of the ancient city. Use the walking tours in chapter 16 or go on a group tour; information on meeting points, times, and routes is at the information kiosk on the Terrace Dufferin, opposite the Château Frontenac.
- **Visit Montmorency Falls:** Located a 15-minute ride by car or bus north of the city is this spectacular iron-tinged cascade—higher than Niagara Falls, as you will frequently be reminded. There are stairs and a cable car up and a footbridge directly over the plunging water. In summer, this is the site of an international fireworks festival. See chapter 19.

7 The Best Activities for Families

MONTREAL

- **Visit the Biodôme de Montréal:** Perhaps the most engaging attraction in the city for children—of any age. The Biodôme houses replications of four ecosystems: a Laurentian forest, the St. Lawrence marine system, a polar environment, and, most engagingly, a tropical rainforest. See p. 115.
- **Explore the Jardin Botanique and Insectarium:** Montréal's Botanical Garden has Chinese and Japanese gardens and greenhouses open all year long, while the Insectarium next door features praying mantises, tarantulas, a Butterfly House, and a gift shop that sells lollipops with scorpions inside. See p. 116.

QUEBEC CITY

- **Watch the Changing of the Guard:** La Citadelle is the fortress built by the British to repel an American invasion that never came. It's still an active military post, and the ceremonial changing of the guard and beating the retreat are colorful and not too long. See p. 238.
- **Thrill to the Canyon Ste-Anne:** About a half-hour drive from the city, the massive canyon and its thundering Ste-Anne waterfalls feature three footbridges that go directly across the water. See chapter 19.

8 The Best of Montréal & Québec City Online

There's lots of information on Montréal and Québec City on the Internet. Here are a few of our favorite planning and general information sites.

- **Bonjour Québec** (www.tourisme. gouv.qc.ca): The official site of the government of the Province of Québec endeavors to be a comprehensive information bank about all things Québec, and nearly succeeds. You'll find information on upcoming events and ongoing attractions, and you can search for hotels and reserve online.

- **A la Montréal** (www.tourisme-montreal.org): Another official tourism site, this one provides in-depth information on selected highlights. Check the "Traveler" section for feature stories, food highlights, "Sweet Deals" on lodging, and a "Montréal Gay to Z" section.
- **Hour** (www.hour.ca): *Hour* is a Montréal culture magazine that highlights local happenings, including entertainingly grumpy and often profane takes on current events, and regularly updated restaurant and arts reviews.
- **Québec** (www.quebecregion.com): Sponsored by the Québec City Tourism bureau, this site is full of detailed information about area accommodations, attractions, sports, shopping, dining, history, and culture.

2

Planning Your Trip to Montréal & Québec City

Montréal and Québec City have a stronger foreign flavor than other cities in Canada, and the first language of most residents is French. But pulling together information on getting there, crossing the border, exchanging money, and finding accommodations is almost as easy as finding information in your own country. The details below should help speed the process along.

1 Visitor Information & Maps

Tourism authorities for the Québec province produce detailed and highly useful publications, and they're easy to obtain by mail, by phone, or in person. To contact **Tourisme Québec,** write C.P. 979, Montréal, Québec H3C 2W3; e-mail info@bonjourquebec.com; call © **877/ 266-5687** or 514/873-2015; or visit **www. bonjourquebec.com**.

The Québec provincial government maintains offices in the United States and abroad, which provide specific tourism information about the region. In the U.S., there are offices in New York; Boston; Chicago; Los Angeles; Washington, D.C.; and Atlanta. To contact the main office, write **Québec Government Office in New York,** One Rockefeller Plaza, 26th Floor, New York, NY 10020-2102; call © **212/397-0200;** or visit **www.quebecusa.org**. To contact the main Québec office in the U.K., write **Québec Government Office in London,**

59 Pall Mall, London SW1Y 5JH, England; call © **(44) 207/766-5900;** or visit **www.quebec.org.uk**.

Tourist offices for the public in Montréal and Québec City are listed in the "Visitor Information" sections in chapters 4 and 12.

For more informal perceptions of the cities, the websites **www.realtravel.com**, **www.travelblog.com**, and **www.travel blog.org** feature a wide variety of real-people-real-advice travel blogs.

Good city maps are available for free from the tourist offices. The best detailed street guide of Montréal is the pocket-size atlas by JDM Géo. It's published by MapArt (**www.mapart.com**), which also makes good maps for all the regions outside Montréal and Québec City that are mentioned in this book. They're for sale online and in shops and gas stations in Canada.

2 Entry Requirements

PASSPORTS & PASS CARD

Since January 2007, all air travelers traveling between the U.S. and Canada have been required to present a valid passport.

This is a change from prior travel requirements and was implemented as part of The Intelligence Reform and Terrorism Prevention Act of 2004.

Destination Canada: Pre-Departure Checklist

- If you're flying, you'll need a passport to enter Canada. If you're driving or arriving by bus, train, or boat, a passport is a good idea, too, and may be required by early 2008 (see below).
- If you're driving and are a member of AAA, bring your card—it will be honored by CAA, the Canadian Automobile Association (p. 36).
- If you're flying, check with air transportation authorities about current rules for what you can bring in your carry-on bags. The Canadian Air Transport Security Authority, which oversees flights out of Canada, is at www.acsta.gc.ca. Rules about flights from the U.S. are overseen by the Transportation Security Administration, at www.tsa.gov.
- Make sure you know the PIN (personal identification number) for your credit card in addition to your bank card. Most Canadian banks only accept PINs of four digits.
- Confirm your daily ATM withdrawal limit.
- To check in at an airport kiosk with an e-ticket, make sure you have the credit card you bought your ticket with or frequent-flier card.
- If you purchased traveler's checks, record the check numbers and store them separately from the checks.
- Bring any ID cards that could entitle you to discounts, such as AARP cards and student IDs.

If you're traveling by land or by sea between the U.S. and Canada, the rules are a little fuzzier at press time. A passport or other document is likely to soon be required; implementation of this second stage was originally scheduled to take place on January 1, 2008, but concerns about tourism and subsequent legislative changes have made that date a possibility instead of a certainty.

The U.S. and Canada are developing a limited-use Passport Card, also called PASS Card, for land or sea travel between the two countries. At this writing the card is not available. Up-to-date information about passport requirements and the PASS Card is available at the U.S. State Department website at **http://travel.state.gov**.

Alien permanent residents of the U.S. must have their Alien Registration Cards (Green Cards) with them.

If you are driving into Canada, be sure to have your car's registration. U.S. citizens do not need an international driver's license; a U.S. license is fine. Note that if you have ever been convicted for driving while impaired, you may be denied entrance to the country. A waiver of exclusion may be obtained for a fee from a Canadian consulate in the U.S. Radar detectors are prohibited in Québec province and can be confiscated, even if they're not being used.

An important point for teenage travelers: Anyone under 18 and traveling without a parent needs a letter from a parent or guardian authorizing the trip to Canada. The letter must state the traveler's name and the duration of the trip. The teenager must have a photo ID—otherwise, the letter from Mom and Dad is useless at the border.

An important point for parents: Because of international concern about child abduction, if you are divorced, separated, or traveling without your spouse and are bringing your children to Canada, you will need proof of custody or a notarized letter from the other parent giving permission for foreign travel. Also note that passport requirements apply to children of all ages.

Citizens of Australia, New Zealand, the United Kingdom, and Ireland need only carry a valid passport. Citizens of many other countries must have visas.

For information on how to get a passport, go to **"Passports"** in the **"Fast Facts: Montréal & Québec City"** section at the end of this chapter—the websites listed provide downloadable passport applications as well as the current fees for processing passport applications.

VISAS

Citizens of the U.S., U.K., Australia, Ireland, and New Zealand do not need visas to enter Canada. Citizens of many other countries must have visas, applied for well in advance at their nearest Canadian embassy or consulate. Phone numbers and addresses are listed at the website **Citizenship and Immigration Canada** (www.cic.gc.ca).

CUSTOMS

For information on what you can bring into and take out of Canada, go to **"Customs"** in the **"Fast Facts: Montréal & Québec City"** section of this chapter.

3 When to Go

High season is late May through early September. Hotels are most likely to be full and charge their highest rates. Even then, though, weekends are cheaper and package plans reduce the bite, so advance planning has its rewards. The period from Christmas to New Year's is also busy (and more expensive), as are the days given to winter festivals in both Montréal and Québec City. **Low season** is during the least appealing months of March and April, when few events are scheduled and

winter sports start to be iffy, and the late fall months of October and November, which have all but empty calendars.

WEATHER

Temperatures are usually a few degrees lower in Québec City than in Montréal. Spring, short but sweet, arrives around the middle of May. Summer (mid-June through mid-Sept) tends to be humid in Montréal, Québec City, and other communities along the St. Lawrence River,

Montréal's Average Monthly Temperatures (°F/°C)

	Jan	Feb	Mar	Apr	May	June	July	Aug	Sept	Oct	Nov	Dec
High (°F)	21	24	35	51	65	73	79	76	66	54	41	27
(°C)	–6	–4	2	11	18	23	26	24	19	12	5	–3
Low (°F)	7	10	21	35	47	56	61	69	50	39	29	13
(°C)	–14	–12	–6	2	8	13	16	21	10	4	–2	–11

Québec City's Average Monthly Temperatures (°F/°C)

	Jan	Feb	Mar	Apr	May	June	July	Aug	Sept	Oct	Nov	Dec
High (°F)	18	21	32	46	63	72	77	73	64	52	37	23
(°C)	–8	–6	0	8	17	22	25	23	18	11	3	–5
Low (°F)	1	3	16	28	41	50	55	54	45	36	25	9
(°C)	–17	–16	–9	–2	5	10	13	12	7	2	–4	–13

Note: To convert Celsius to Fahrenheit, multiply the Celsius reading by 1.8 and then add 32. For example, 17°C X 1.8 is 30.6 + 32 is 62.6°F

and drier at the inland resorts of the Laurentides and the Cantons-de-l'Est. Intense, but usually brief, heat waves mark July and early August, but temperatures rarely remain oppressive in the evenings.

Autumn (Sept–Oct) is as short and changeable as spring, with warm days and cool or chilly nights. Canadian maples blaze with color for weeks.

Winter brings dependable snows for skiing in the Laurentides, the Cantons-de-l'Est, and Charlevoix. After a sleigh ride or a ski run in Parc Mont-Royal, Montréal's underground city is a climate-controlled blessing. February is the time for Québec City's robust Carnaval de Québec. Snow and slush are more or less constantly present from November to March.

For the current Canadian weather forecast, call ℭ **514/283-3010.**

MONTREAL & QUEBEC CITY CALENDAR OF EVENTS

Year-round, it's nearly impossible to miss a celebration of some sort in Montréal and Québec City. If something's not going on in one place, it's bound to be happening in the other, and it's easy to get between cities.

For an exhaustive list of events beyond those listed here, check **http://events.frommers.com**, where you'll find a searchable, up-to-the-minute roster of what's happening in cities all over the world.

January

La Fête des Neiges (Snow Festival), Montréal. Montréal's answer to Québec City's February winter carnival features outdoor events such as dogsled runs, a mock survival camp, street hockey, ice-skating, and tobogganing. The less athletically inclined can cheer from the sidelines and then inspect the snow and ice sculptures. The event has been condensed onto the Ile Ste-Hélène. Call ℭ **514/872-6120** or visit www.fetedesneiges.com for details. January 26 to February 10, 2008.

February

Carnaval de Québec, Québec City. Never mind that temperatures in Québec can plummet in January to minus 40 (fun fact: that's the point where Fahrenheit equals Celsius). Canadians are extraordinarily good-natured about eyeball-freezing cold and happily pack the family up to come out and play when the symbolic snowman called Bonhomme (Good Fellow) shuffles into town to preside over the merriment. Revelers descend upon the city to eddy around a monumental ice palace erected in front of Parliament Building, watch a dog-sledding race on the narrow streets of old town, play the table game of foosball on a human-size scale, fly over crowds on a zip-line, ride down snowy hills in rubber tubes, and dance in the evenings at outdoor concerts. There are even outdoor movies for the truly masochistic.

The party is family-friendly at every turn, even taking into consideration the wide availability of plastic trumpets and canes filled with a concoction called "Caribou," the principal ingredients of which are cheap liquor and sweet red wine. Try not to miss the canoe race that has teams rowing, dragging, and stumbling across the treacherous ice floes of the St. Lawrence. It's an homage to how the city used to break up the ice in order to keep a path open to Lévis, the town across the river.

A C$10 (US$8.70/£4.30) pass provides access to most activities over the 17 days. Hotel reservations must be made far in advance. Call ℭ **866/422-7628** or visit www.carnaval.qc.ca for details. February 1 to February 17, 2008.

Festival Montréal en Lumière (Montréal High Lights). Filling a hole in the yearly schedule, the self-dubbed City of

Festivals has created a winter celebration of somewhat disparate events including culinary competitions and wine tastings, multimedia light shows, classical and pop concerts, and a "Montréal All-Nighter" that ends with breakfast at dawn. Call ✆ **888/477-9955** or visit www.montrealhighlights.com. February 21 to March 2, 2008.

May

Montréal Museums Day. Open house for most of the city's museums, with free admission and free shuttle buses. Visit www.museesmontreal.org or call the tourism office (✆ **877/266-5687**) for details. Last Sunday in May.

Montréal Bike Fest, Montréal. Tens of thousands of enthusiasts converge on Montréal to participate in a variety of cycling competitions including a nocturnal bike ride ("Un Tour la Nuit") and the grueling Tour de l'Ile, a 50km (31-mile) race around the rim of the island that draws 30,000 cyclists, shuts down roads, and attracts over 100,000 spectators. The nonprofit biking organization Vélo Québec has details at **www.velo.qc.ca.** Eight days in late May into early June.

Festival Transamériques, Montréal. Formerly the Festival de Théâtre des Amériques, this avant-garde program was renamed and refocused in 2007, when it presented 20 contemporary theater works by companies from Canada and around the world. Sixteen days in late May into early June. Call ✆ **514/ 842-0704** or visit www.fta.qc.ca.

Mondial de la Bière, Montréal. Yes, beer fans, this is a 5-day festival devoted to your favorite beverage. More than 350 beers, including 100 new debuts, are showcased by both world brands and boutique microbreweries. They employ cooking demos, musical performances, and, of course, tastings, tastings, tastings. Details are available at

✆ **514/722-9640** or log onto www. festivalmondialbiere.qc.ca. May 28 to June 1, 2008.

June

Saint-Ambroise Montréal Fringe Festival. In performance spaces clustered along or near boulevard St-Laurent in Montréal's Plateau Mont-Royal neighborhood, this is 11 days of out-there theater: one-man *Star Wars* stand-up, clowns gone bad, drunken drag queens. Not everything's great, but, then, the festival does proclaim that it's "open to absolutely anybody to perform absolutely anything. As always, there will be no artistic restrictions whatsoever." Vive le fringe! Call ✆ **514/849-3378** or check www.montrealfringe.ca. June 12 to June 22, 2008.

Grand Prix du Canada, Montréal. The biggest tourist event of the year in Montréal, bar none. For 3 days, the only Formula 1 auto race in Canada roars around a year-round track on Ile Notre-Dame, the small island that's spitting distance from downtown Montréal. Hotel rates typically double during Grand Prix days (with 3-night minimums). Streets get shut down, gleaming race cars are put on display, and the city parties round-the-clock with much of the action on downtown rue Crescent. Details can be found at **www.grandprix.ca**.

Jean-Baptiste Day. Honoring Saint John the Baptist, the patron saint of French Canadians, this *fête nationale* on June 24 is marked by more festivities and far more enthusiasm throughout Québec province than Canada Day on July 1. It's Québec's own "national" holiday and is celebrated with fireworks, bonfires, music in parks, and parades.

L'International Des Feux Loto-Québec (International Fireworks Competition), Montréal. Held on nearly a dozen Wednesdays and Saturdays in June and July and pitting the shows of different countries against each other, this annual fireworks competition is a spectacular event on the city's calendar. Tickets are sold to watch from the open-air theater in La Ronde amusement park on Ile Ste-Hélène, although the pyrotechnics can be enjoyed for free from almost anywhere overlooking the river (tickets do include entrance to the amusement park). Kids, needless to say, love the whole explosive business. Call © **514/ 790-1245** for details.

July

Festival International de Jazz de Montréal. One of the monster events on the calendar. Montréal has a long tradition in jazz, and this enormously successful festival has been celebrating America's art form since 1979. Wynton Marsalis, Harry Connick, Jr., Keith Jarrett, and even Bob Dylan have been featured in recent years, but it costs serious money to hear stars of such magnitude, and tickets sell out months in advance. Fortunately, hundreds of other concerts are free during the late June/early July party, often right on the streets and plazas of downtown. For schedule and ticket information, call © **888/515-0515** or visit www. montrealjazzfest.com.

Festival d'Eté (Summer Festival), Québec City. The largest Francophone music festival in the world, or so its managers say. Held in the heart of Vieux-Québec and, since 2007, in the St-Roch neighborhood, the festival brings in artists from Africa, Asia, Europe, and North America for more than 500 programs showcasing theater, music, and dance. Over 900,000 people come to watch and listen for 11 days in July. Highlights include the free jazz and folk combos who perform

in an open-air theater next to City Hall. Call © **888/992-5200,** or check www.infofestival.com.

Festival International Nuits d'Afrique, Montréal. A 10-day world-beat music showcase in mid-July with musicians from the Caribbean, Africa, and the Americas. The festival also presents concerts year-round. Call © **514/499-9239** or check out www.festivalnuits dafrique.com.

Festival Juste pour Rire (Just for Laughs Festival), Montréal. This celebration strives to do for humor what the more famous jazz festival has done for that musical form. Well-known comics including Eddie Izzard, The Kids in the Hall, and Howie Mandel have been featured, while smaller name Francophone and Anglophone groups and stand-ups come from around the world to participate indoors and on the street. It's held mostly along rue St-Denis and elsewhere in the Latin Quarter. Call © **888/244-3155** for details or check www.hahaha.com.

Les Grands Feux Loto-Québec, Québec City. Overlapping with Montréal's fireworks competition, Québec's event uses the highly scenic Montmorency Falls 15 minutes north of city center as its setting. Pyrotechnical teams are invited from countries around the world in this international festival. Tickets get you admission to the base of the falls; there are 6,000 reserved bleacher seats and 22,500 general admission tickets. Call © **888/ 523-3473** for details; tickets online at www.quebecfireworks.com. Wednesdays and Saturdays from late July to mid-August.

Les FrancoFolies de Montréal. Around since 1988, this music fest features French-language pop, hip-hop, electronic, world-beat, and acoustic *chanteurs.* There are upwards of 150 free outdoor concerts along with for-fee stadium and club events. It's held in late July/early August. Check www.francofolies.com for the latest information.

Festival International de Courses de Bateaux-Dragons de Montréal. The annual dragon boat festival sees 200 teams pouring into the Olympic Basin on Ile Notre-Dame for 2 days in late July. It features a drawing contest for children and opportunities to try being a paddler on the ancient Chinese boats. Additional details can be found at www.montrealdragonboat.com.

August

Divers/Cité Festival, Montréal. Officially recognized by both government agencies and major corporate sponsors, Divers/Cité is one of the largest parties in North America for gay, lesbian, bisexual, and transgendered audiences. With dance, drag, art, and concerts on three stages, all shows are outdoor and free. Held in early August. Call ℂ **514/285-4011** or go to www.diverscite.org.

Festival des Films du Monde (World Film Festival), Montréal. This festival has been an international film event since 1977. A strong panel of actors, directors, and writers from around the world make up the jury each year, giving the event a weight that many festivals lack. Various movie theaters play host. Call ℂ **514/848-3883** or check www.ffm-montreal.org for details. Late August to early September.

September

Fall Foliage. Starting mid-month the maple trees blaze with color and a walk in the parks of Montréal and Québec City is a refreshing tonic. It's a perfect time to drive to the Laurentians or Cantons-de-L'Est (both near Montréal) or Ile d'Orléans or Charlevoix (easy drives from Québec City).

October

Black & Blue Festival, Montréal. One of the biggest gay festivals on the planet. Black & Blue was named the best international fest by France's gay and lesbian station Pink TV Awards, beating out even Carnival in Rio. It features a series of benefit parties such as the Military Ball for a week in early October. And when we say big we mean *big:* The main event for the 2007 fest was held at Olympic Stadium. Call ℂ **514/875-7026** or visit www.bbcm.org.

Festival du Nouveau Cinéma, Montréal. Screenings of new and experimental-edging-to-avant-garde films ignite controversy, and forums are held on the latest trends in film and video. Events take place at halls and cinemas throughout the city. Call ℂ **514/844-2172** or check www.nouveaucinema.ca for details. Twelve days in mid-October.

November

Festival d'Automne, Québec City. A relatively new event, the 3-day Autumn Festival is essentially an expanded Halloween celebration. There are ice-skating performances, concerts by the National League of Musical Improvisation of Québec, light-and-sound shows, and more. Check www.infofestival.com/faq. October 30 to November 1.

December/January

Christmas/New Year's, Québec City. Celebrating the holidays *a la Française* is a particular treat in Québec City, with its streets banked with snow and almost every ancient building sporting wreaths, decorated fir trees, and glittery white lights.

4 Getting There

Served by highways, transcontinental trains and buses, and several airports, Montréal and Québec City are easily accessible from any part of the United States and Europe.

BY PLANE

As of January 2007, all travelers traveling by plane between the U.S. and Canada are required to present a valid passport. This is a change from prior travel requirements. Even children under 18 need a passport to get into Canada and to return to the U.S. Have your passport at the ready to show at check-in, the security checkpoint, and sometimes even the gate.

TO MONTREAL Most of the world's major airlines fly into the **Aéroport International Pierre-Elliot-Trudeau de Montréal** (airport code YUL; ℂ 800/465-1213 and 514/394-7377; www.admtl.com), known more commonly as Montréal-Trudeau Airport. **Aéroport Mirabel,** farther from the city, is an all-cargo facility.

Visitors from the U.S. fly into Trudeau on **Air Canada** and its lower-cost sister carrier **Air Canada Jazz** (ℂ 888/247-2262; www.aircanada.ca); **American** (ℂ 800/433-7300; www.aa.com), **Continental** (ℂ 800/231-0856; www.continental.com), **Delta** (ℂ 800/221-1212; www.delta.com), **Northwest** (ℂ 800/225-2525; www.nwa.com), **United** (ℂ 800/241-6522; www.united.com), and **US Airways** (ℂ 800/432-9768; www.usairways.com).

Visitors from overseas fly in on a wide variety of carriers including **British Airways** (ℂ 800/247-9297; www.britishairways.com).

Your choice of airline and airplane will definitely affect your leg room. Find more about U.S. airlines at **www.seatguru.com**. For international airlines, the research firm Skytrax has posted a list of average seat pitches at **www.airlinequality.com**.

For details on getting from the airport to downtown and the city center, see p. 56.

TO QUEBEC CITY The small **Jean Lesage International Airport** in Québec City (airport code: YQB; ℂ 418/640-2700; www.aeroportdequebec.com) is served by a number of major airlines, notably **Air Canada** and **Air Canada Jazz** (ℂ 888/247-2262; www.aircanada.ca). Most air traffic comes by way of Montréal (see above), although there are direct flights from Boston on **Delta** (ℂ 800/221-1212; www.delta.com), from Detroit on **Northwest** (ℂ 800/225-2525; www.nwa.com), and from Newark, New Jersey, on **Continental** (ℂ 800/525-0280; www.continental.com).

The Québec City terminal is blissfully teeny: The length of the concourse can be walked in 1 minute, literally, and on a recent trip it took all of 3 minutes to get from the front door, through security, and to the gate. However, the terminal has been undergoing some renovations in hopes of attracting new carriers. Construction is expected to finish by May 2008.

For details on getting from the Lesage airport into Québec City, see p. 206.

FLYING FOR LESS: TIPS FOR GETTING THE BEST AIRFARE

- Passengers who can book their ticket either **long in advance or at the last minute,** or who **fly midweek** or **at less-trafficked hours** may pay a fraction of the full fare. If your schedule is flexible, say so, and ask if you can secure a cheaper fare by changing your flight plans.
- Search **the Internet** for cheap fares. The most popular online travel agencies are **Travelocity.com** (also at www.travelocity.co.uk); **Expedia.com** (also at www.expedia.co.uk and www.expedia.ca); and **Orbitz.com.** In the U.K., go to **Travelsupermarket** (ℂ 0845/345-5708; www.travelsupermarket.com), a flight search engine that offers flight comparisons for the budget airlines whose seats often end up in bucket-shop sales. Other websites for booking airline tickets online include **Cheapflights.com, Smarter Travel.com, Priceline.com,** and, in the U.K., **Opodo.co.uk.** Meta search

sites (which find and then direct you to airline and hotel websites for booking) include **Sidestep.com** and **Kayak.com**—the latter includes fares for budget carriers like Jet Blue and Spirit as well as the major airlines. **Site59.com** is a great source for last-minute flights and getaways. In addition, most **airlines** offer online-only fares that even their phone agents know nothing about. British travelers should check **Flights International** (© **0800/0187050;** www.flights-international.com) for deals on flights all over the world.

- Keep an eye on local newspapers for **promotional specials** or **fare wars,** when airlines lower prices on their most popular routes.
- **Consolidators,** also known as bucket shops, are wholesale brokers in the airline-ticket game. Consolidators buy deeply discounted tickets ("distressed" inventories of unsold seats) from airlines and sell them to online ticket agencies, travel agents, tour operators, corporations, and, to a lesser degree, the general public. Consolidators advertise in Sunday newspaper travel sections (often in small ads with tiny type), both in the U.S. and the U.K. They can be great sources for cheap international tickets. On the downside, bucket shop tickets are often rigged with restrictions, such as stiff cancellation penalties (as high as 50%–75% of the ticket price). And keep in mind that most of what you see advertised is of limited availability. Several reliable consolidators are worldwide and available online. **STA Travel** (www.statravel.com) has been the world's leading consolidator for students since purchasing Council Travel, but its fares are competitive for travelers of all ages. **Flights.com** (© **800/TRAV-800;** www.flights.com) has excellent fares worldwide.

- Join **frequent-flier clubs.** Frequent-flier membership doesn't cost a cent, but it does entitle you to free tickets or upgrades when you amass the airline's required number of frequent-flier points. But keep in mind that award seats are limited, seats on popular routes are hard to snag, and more and more major airlines are cutting their expiration periods for mileage points—so check your airline's frequent-flier program so you don't lose your miles before you use them. To play the frequent-flier game to your best advantage, consult the community bulletin boards on **Flyer-Talk** (www.flyertalk.com) or go to Randy Petersen's **Inside Flyer** (www.insideflyer.com).

BY CAR

U.S. citizens do not need an international driver's license to drive in Canada. A U.S. license is legal as long as you are a visitor and are actually resident in the U.S.

Passport rules may change on January 1, 2008, requiring a passport for all land travel between the U.S. and Canada. As of this writing, a passport is only required for air travel. The most up-to-date information is at the U.S. State Department website **http://travel.state.gov**.

See "Entry Requirements" on p. 11.

Highway distances and speed limits are given in kilometers (km) in Canada. The speed limit on the autoroutes (limited-access highways) is 100kmph (62 mph). In the unlikely event you are stopped, there is a stiff penalty for not wearing seatbelts. Passengers must buckle up in the back seat as well as in the driver's and passenger's seats up front. And if you possess a radar detector, it can be confiscated, even if it isn't connected, and you can be fined.

You cannot turn right on red on the island of Montréal. It is permitted in the rest of Québec and Canada.

Fill Up Before You Cross Over

Gasoline in Canada is expensive by U.S. standards. Although prices fluctuate as they do in the U.S., don't be surprised if you have to pay as much as 30% more than you're used to in the states. (Europeans will find the prices less of a shock.) Gas is sold by the liter, and 3.78 liters equals 1 gallon. Recent prices of C$1.15 a liter (US$1/49p) are the equivalent of about US$4.35 a gallon. If you're driving from the U.S., fill up just before you cross the border.

Members of the **American Automobile Association (AAA)** are covered by the **Canadian Automobile Association (CAA)** while traveling in Canada. See "AAA" in "Fast Facts: Montréal & Québec City" at the end of this chapter.

For details on road conditions and road repair, there is a 24-hour hot line (© **888/355-0511**).

TO MONTREAL Driving north from the U.S., the entire journey is on expressways. From New York City, all but the last 40 or so miles of the 603km (375-mile) journey are within New York state on Interstate 87. I-87 links up with Canada's Autoroute 15 at the border, which goes straight to Montréal. From Boston, I-93 north goes up through New Hampshire (and the beautiful Franconia Notch in the White Mountains) and merges into I-91 north to cross the tip of Vermont. At the border, I-91 becomes Autoroute 55. Signs lead to Autoroute 10 west to Montréal. From Boston to Montréal is about 518km (322 miles).

TO QUEBEC CITY Québec City is 867km (520 miles) from New York City and 644km (400 miles) from Boston. From New York, follow the directions to Montréal and then pick up Autoroute 20 to Québec. From Boston, follow the directions to Montréal, but at Autoroute 10 go east instead of west to stay on Autoroute 55. Pick up Autoroute 20 to Québec.

Coming into Québec City, follow signs for the bridge Pont Pierre-Laporte. Shortly after crossing the bridge, turn right onto boulevard Wilfrid-Laurier (Rte. 175). It changes names first to Boulevard Laurier and then to Grande-Allée, the grand boulevard that leads directly into the central Parliament Hill area and the Old City. Once the street passes through the ancient walls that ring the Old City it becomes rue St-Louis, which leads straight to the famed Château Frontenac on the cliff above the St. Lawrence river.

Another appealing option when you're approaching Québec City from the south is to follow Route 132 along the southern side of the St. Lawrence River to the town of Lévis. A car-ferry there, **Traverse Québec-Lévis** (© **418/644-3704**), provides a dramatic 10-minute ride across the river and is a dramatic way to view the city, especially for the first time. Although the schedule varies substantially according to time of day, week, and season, the ferry leaves at least every hour (more often during rush hours) from 6am to 2am. One-way, it costs C$5.95 (US$5.20/£2.55) for the car and driver, and C$2.65 (US$2.30/£1.15) for each additional adult. The ferry only takes cash, so if you arrive from the U.S. without Canadian money, there's an ATM in the small transport terminal next door.

BY TRAIN

TO MONTREAL Montréal is a major terminus on Canada's **VIA Rail** network (© **888/842-7245;** www.viarail.ca), with its station, **Gare Centrale,** at 895 rue de la Gauchetière ouest (© **514/989-2626**).

The VIA Rail trains are comfortable—all have Wi-Fi, some are equipped with dining cars and sleeping cars. **Amtrak** (© **800/ USA-RAIL** [872-7245]; www.amtrak. com) has one train a day to Montréal from New York that makes intermediate stops. Called the *Adirondack,* it is a no-frills, coach-only affair, and very slow, but its scenic route passes along the eastern shore of the Hudson River and west of Lake Champlain. The *Adirondack* is scheduled to take about 10½ hours from New York if all goes well, but delays aren't unusual.

TO QUEBEC CITY   Québec City's train station, the **Gare du Palais,** is in the Lower Town at 450 rue de la Gare-du-Palais. Like Montréal, it's served by VIA Rail (© **888/842-7245;** www.viarail.ca).

TRAVELING BETWEEN MONTREAL AND QUEBEC CITY

Train service between Montréal and Québec City is through **VIA Rail Canada** (© **888/842-7245;** www.viarail.ca). Travel time is about 3 hours. Round-trip prices start at about C$96 (US$84/£41) for supersaver economy class. Wi-Fi is available on board.

Air Canada's low-cost sister carrier **Air Canada Jazz** (© **888/247-2262;** www. flyjazz.ca) has frequent flights between Montréal and Québec City.

Buses run nearly hourly between the two cities on the **Orléans Express** (© **888/ 999-3977;** www.orleansexpress.com) and take 3 hours, 15 minutes. A one-way ticket is C$50 (US$44/£22) adult.

When driving between Québec City from Montréal, there are two main options: Autoroute 40, which runs along the north shore of the St. Lawrence, and Autoroute 20, on the south side (although not hugging the water at all). The trip takes less than 3 hours without stops.

5 Money & Costs

It's always advisable to bring money in a variety of forms on a vacation: a mix of cash, credit cards, and traveler's checks. You should also exchange enough petty cash to cover airport incidentals, tipping, and transportation to your hotel before you leave home, or withdraw money upon arrival at an airport ATM.

In many international destinations, ATMs offer the best exchange rates. Avoid exchanging money at commercial exchange bureaus and hotels, which often have the highest transaction fees.

CURRENCY

Canadian money comes in graduated denominations of **dollars and cents.** Aside from the $2 coin, Canadian coins are similar to their U.S. counterparts: 1¢, 5¢, 10¢, 25¢. Bills—$2, $5, $10, $20, $50, $100—are all the same size but have different colors, depending on the denomination. The gold-colored $1 coin (called a **Loonie** by Canadians because of the depiction of a loon on one side) has replaced the $1 bill. French speakers sometimes refer to a dollar as a *piastre.* A $2 coin, with a bronze center surrounded by a nickel disk, has replaced the old $2 bill. The $2 coin is sometimes called a "twonie," a reference to the next-smaller coin.

Prices in this book, unless otherwise indicated, are given in Canadian and U.S. dollars and British pounds. The Canadian dollar has been gathering strength in recent years, but at this writing the Canadian dollar is worth about 87¢ in U.S. currency, give or take a couple of points' daily variation. Put another way, one U.S. dollar buys about $1.15 in Canadian money. This is the exchange rate used to convert prices in this book.

Given the continued strength of the British pound in comparison to most other major currencies, including the U.S. and Canadian dollars, visitors from the U.K. will find Québec and the rest of Canada an almost unimaginable bargain. An exchange rate of one Canadian dollar to 43p in British currency is what's used here.

The website **www.xe.com/ucc** lists up-to-the-minute currency conversions.

ATMs are widely available both in the cities and in the villages. See "ATMs," below.

Visitors can bring in or take out any amount of money they wish, but if U.S. citizens import or export sums of US$10,000 or more, a report of the transaction must be filed with U.S. Customs.

CURRENCY EXCHANGE

Main branch banks and "caisses populaires" (Credit Union offices) will exchange most foreign currencies. In Québec City, **Caisse Populaire** at 19 rue des Jardins (© 418/522-6806) is open daily in the summer and Monday through Friday the rest of the year. Tourism offices can often exchange money or point you to a place that will.

ATMs

The easiest way to get cash away from home is from an ATM (automated teller machine), sometimes referred to as a "cash machine" or "cashpoint." As ubiquitous

in Québec province and the rest of Canada as in the U.S. or the U.K., ATMs in French are called GABs, or *guichet automatique bancaire*. They are found in most of the same places—outside or inside bank branches—but also at other locations, including, no surprise, the province's new casinos. Look for signs reading GUICHET AUTOMATIQUE or SERVICES AUTOMATISES.

Note: PINs (personal identification numbers) can only be four digits at many ATMs in Canada. If your PIN has more numbers, change it before departing. Your card may not work otherwise.

The **Cirrus** (© 800/424-7787; www.mastercard.com) and **PLUS** (© 800/843-7587; www.visa.com) networks span the globe. Go to your bank card's website to find ATM locations at your destination. Be sure you know your daily withdrawal limit before you depart. *Note:* Many banks impose a fee every time you use a card at another bank's ATM, and that fee can be higher for international transactions (up to $5 or more) than for domestic ones (where they're rarely more than $2). In addition, the bank from which you withdraw cash may charge its own fee. For international withdrawal fees, ask your bank.

Note: Banks that are members of the **Global ATM Alliance** charge no transaction fees for cash withdrawals at other Alliance member ATMs; these include Bank of America and Canadian-based Scotiabank.

What Things Cost in Québec Province	C$	US$	UK£
Moderate hotel room, summer	175.00	152.00	75.00
Montréal Métro ticket	2.75	2.40	1.15
Table d'hote 3-course dinner	25.00	21.75	10.75
Double espresso	3.25	2.80	1.40
Museum pass for 3 days	35.00 or	30.00 or	15.05 or
	45.00	39.00	19.35
Gasoline per liter	1.15	1.00	0.49
per gallon equivalent	5.00	4.35	2.15

The Canadian Dollar, the U.S. Dollar & the British Pound

The prices quoted in this guide are in Canadian dollars, with the U.S. and U.K. equivalents in parentheses. The exchange rate we've used is $1.00 Canadian to 87¢ U.S. to 43p U.K. For the most up-to-date exchange rates, visit **www.xe.com/ucc**. Here's a quick table of equivalents:

C$	US$	UK£
1.00	0.87	0.43
5.00	4.35	2.15
10.00	8.70	4.30
20.00	17.40	8.60
50.00	43.50	21.50
100.00	87.00	43.00

CREDIT CARDS

Credit cards are another safe way to carry money. They also provide a convenient record of all your expenses, and they generally offer relatively good exchange rates. You can withdraw cash advances from your credit cards at banks or ATMs but high fees make credit-card cash advances a pricey way to get cash. Keep in mind that you'll pay interest from the moment of your withdrawal, even if you pay your monthly bills on time. Also, note that many banks now assess a 1%-to-3% "transaction fee" on *all* charges you incur abroad (whether you're using the local currency or your native currency).

American Express, MasterCard, and Visa are most commonly accepted at hotels, restaurants, and shops in the province. Diners Club and Discover are listed less often.

TRAVELER'S CHECKS

Traveler's checks are accepted at venues throughout the Québec province.

You can buy traveler's checks at most banks. They are offered by **American Express, Thomas Cook, Visa,** and **MasterCard** in Canadian denominations and will be easier to use if you get them in Canadian dollars.

The most popular traveler's checks are offered by **American Express** (© **800/ 807-6233,** or © **800/221-7282** for card holders—this number accepts collect calls, offers service in several foreign languages, and exempts Amex gold and platinum cardholders from the 1% fee); **Visa** (© **800/732-1322**)—AAA members can obtain Visa checks for a $9.95 fee (for checks up to $1,500) at most AAA offices or by calling © **866/339-3378;** and **MasterCard** (© **800/223-9920**).

Be sure to keep a record of the traveler's checks serial numbers separate from your checks in the event that they are stolen or lost. You'll get a refund faster if you know the numbers.

Another option is the new prepaid traveler's check cards, reloadable cards that work much like debit cards but aren't linked to your checking account. The **American Express Travelers Cheque Card,** for example, requires a minimum deposit, sets a maximum balance, and has a one-time issuance fee of $15. You can withdraw money from an ATM (for a fee of $2.50 per transaction, not including bank fees), and the funds can be purchased in dollars, euros, or pounds. If you lose the card, your available funds will be refunded within 24 hours.

6 Insurance: Travel, Medical & Lost Luggage

Travel insurance covers everything from medical bills and collision insurance for rental cars to emergency evacuation costs and theft. The cost of travel insurance varies widely, depending on your destination, the cost and length of your trip, your age and health, and the type of trip you're taking, but expect to pay between 5% and 8% of the vacation itself. You can get estimates from various providers through **InsureMyTrip.com.** Enter your trip cost and dates, your age, and other information, for prices from more than a dozen companies.

U.K. citizens and their families who make more than one trip abroad per year may find an annual travel insurance policy works out cheaper. Check **www.money supermarket.com**, which compares prices across a wide range of providers for single- and multi-trip policies. **The Association of British Insurers** (✆ 020/7600-3333; www.abi.org.uk) gives advice by phone and publishes *Holiday Insurance,* a free guide to policy provisions and prices.

Most big travel agents offer their own insurance and will probably try to sell you their package when you book with them. Think before you sign.

You can also shop around for deals at **Columbus Direct** (✆ 0870/033-9988; www.columbusdirect.net).

TRIP-CANCELLATION INSURANCE

Trip-cancellation insurance will help retrieve your money if you have to back out of a trip or depart early, or if your travel supplier goes bankrupt. Trip cancellation traditionally covers such events as sickness, natural disasters, and State Department advisories. The latest news in trip-cancellation insurance is the availability of **expanded hurricane coverage** and the **"any-reason"** cancellation coverage—which costs more but covers cancellations

made for any reason. You won't get back 100% of your prepaid trip cost, but you'll be refunded a substantial portion. **Travel-Safe** (✆ 888/885-7233; www.travelsafe. com) offers both types of coverage. Expedia also offers any-reason cancellation coverage for its air-hotel packages.

For details, contact one of the following recommended insurers: **Access America** (✆ 866/807-3982; www.access america.com); **Travel Guard International** (✆ 800/826-4919; www.travel guard.com); **Travel Insured International** (✆ 800/243-3174; www.travel insured.com); and **Travelex Insurance Services** (✆ 888/457-4602; www.travelex-insurance.com).

MEDICAL INSURANCE

Check if your insurance policy covers you while traveling in Canada, especially for hospitalization abroad. Many policies require you to pay for services upfront and, if they reimburse you at all, will only do so after you return home. Carry details of your insurance plan with you, and leave a copy with a friend at home.

Medical treatment in Canada isn't free for foreigners, and hospitals make you pay your bills at the time of service. They may send you a refund after you've returned home and filed the necessary paperwork.

The U.S. Medicare and Medicaid programs do not provide coverage for hospital or medical costs outside the U.S.

U.K. nationals will have to pay for medical treatment in Canada. Details are at **www.dh.gov.uk/travellers**.

As a safety net, you may want to buy supplemental travel medical insurance. Options include **MEDEX Assistance** (✆ 410/453-6300; www.medexassist. com) and **Travel Assistance International** (✆ 800/821-2828; www.travel assistance.com; for general information on services, call the company's **Worldwide Assistance Services, Inc.,** at (℃ **800/ 777-8710**).

In a worst-case scenario, emergency evacuation is a particularly expensive service ($10,000 and up). If you're ever hospitalized more than 150 miles from home, **MedjetAssist** (℃ **800/527-7478;** www.medjetassistance.com) will pick you up and fly you to the hospital of your choice anywhere in the world in a medically equipped and staffed aircraft. Annual memberships are $225 individual, $350 family; you can also purchase short-term memberships.

LOST-LUGGAGE INSURANCE

On international flights (including U.S. portions of international trips), baggage coverage is limited to approximately $9.07 per pound, up to approximately $635 per checked bag. If you plan to check items more valuable than what's covered by the standard liability, see if your homeowner's policy covers your valuables, get baggage insurance as part of your comprehensive travel-insurance package, or buy Travel Guard's "BagTrak" product.

If your luggage is lost, immediately file a lost-luggage claim at the airport, detailing the luggage contents. Most airlines require that you report delayed, damaged, or lost baggage within 4 hours of arrival. The airlines are required to deliver luggage, once found, directly to your house or destination free of charge.

7 Health

STAYING HEALTHY

West Nile virus is an infection spread by the bite of an infected mosquito. In Canada, there were 226 cases and 12 deaths in 2005. To reduce the risk of mosquito bites, travelers should use an insect repellent and wear long-sleeve shirts and long pants at dawn and in the early evening.

During the 2003 SARS scare in Toronto, not a single case of SARS was reported in the province of Québec. Toronto and the province of Ontario were declared free of the disease by the World Health Organization later that year.

GENERAL AVAILABILITY OF HEALTHCARE

Before you go: No shots are required to enter Québec province.

Canada has a state-run health system. It is suffering a number of problems,

Avoiding "Economy Class Syndrome"

Deep vein thrombosis, or as it's known in the world of flying, "economy-class syndrome," is a blood clot that develops in a deep vein. It's a potentially deadly condition that can be caused by sitting in cramped conditions—such as an airplane cabin—for too long. During a flight (especially a long-haul flight), get up, walk around, and stretch your legs every 60 to 90 minutes to keep your blood flowing. Other preventative measures include frequent flexing of the legs while sitting, drinking lots of water, and avoiding alcohol and sleeping pills. If you have a history of deep vein thrombosis, heart disease, or another condition that puts you at high risk, some experts recommend wearing compression stockings or taking anticoagulants when you fly; always ask your physician about the best course for you. Symptoms of deep vein thrombosis include leg pain or swelling, or even shortness of breath.

including a nurse shortage, overcrowded emergency rooms, and budgetary difficulties. That said, Québec hospitals are modern and decently equipped, and staffs are well trained.

Contact the **International Association for Medical Assistance to Travelers (IAMAT)** (✆ **716/754-4883** or, in Canada, 416/652-0137; www.iamat.org) for tips on travel and health concerns in the countries you're visiting, and for lists of local, English-speaking doctors. The United States **Centers for Disease Control and Prevention** (✆ **800/311-3435;** www.cdc.gov) provides up-to-date information on health hazards by region or country and offers tips on food safety. You can find listings of reliable medical clinics overseas at the **International Society of Travel Medicine** (www.istm.org).

WHAT TO DO IF YOU GET SICK AWAY FROM HOME

Familiar over-the-counter medicines are widely available in Canada.

Hospitals and **drugstores** are listed under "Fast Facts: Montréal & Québec City," p. 36.

If there is a possibility you will run out of **prescribed medicines** during your visit, take along a prescription from your doctor. Carry the generic name of prescription medicines, in case a local pharmacist is unfamiliar with the brand name. Prescription drugs are usually cheaper in Canada than in the U.S.

Remember to pack your medications in your carry-on luggage, and have them in their original containers, with pharmacy labels—otherwise they may not make it through airport security. If you are entering Canada with syringes used for medical reasons, bring a medical certificate that shows they are for medical use and be sure to declare them to Canadian Customs officials.

If you suffer from a chronic illness, consult your doctor before your departure.

8 Safety

STAYING SAFE

Montréal and Québec City are far safer cities than their U.S. or European counterparts of similar size, but common sense insists that visitors stay alert to their surroundings and observe the usual urban precautions. It's best to stay out of the larger parks at night, for example, and to call for a taxi when returning from a late dinner or a club in a dicier area. Neighborhoods to avoid are well outside those of touristic interest.

There are reports of escalating road rage incidents, so expressions of impatience and anger with the actions of other drivers can be unwise.

Québec is one of the more liberal provinces in Canada and its residents often disagree strongly with U.S. policies, but mass demonstrations are rare and political violence is unusual.

Tolerance of others is a Canadian characteristic, and it is highly unlikely that visitors of ethnic, religious, and racial minorities will encounter even mild forms of discrimination. That applies to sexual orientation as well, especially in Montréal, which has one of the largest gay communities in North America.

9 Specialized Travel Resources

TRAVELERS WITH DISABILITIES

Most disabilities shouldn't stop anyone from traveling. There are more options and resources out there than ever before.

Québec regulations regarding accessibility for wheelchairs are similar to those in the U.S., including curb cuts, entrance ramps, designated parking spaces, and specially equipped bathrooms. However, access to the restaurants and inns housed in 18th- and 19th-century buildings, especially in Québec City, is often difficult or impossible.

Advice for travelers with physical limitations is provided in the French-language brochure *Le Québec Accessible* listing over 1,000 hotels, restaurants, theaters, and museums. It costs C$19.95 (US$17.35/£8.60) from **Kéroul** (© **514/ 252-3104;** www.keroul.qc.ca). Kéroul also offers English-language brochures in downloadable PDF form called *AccessiB— The Open Road,* with information about everything from how to get a handicapped parking sticker to which top attractions are most accessible inside and via public transport. The PDFs are online at www.keroul.qc.ca.

In Québec City, the Loews Le Concorde hotel (p. 218) touts spacious layout for easy wheelchair access, accessible safety bars throughout the room and bathroom, and accessible door handles, peep holes, and light switches.

When you're out and about, look for the **Tourist and Leisure Companion Sticker (T.L.C.S.)** at tourist sites; it designates that companions of travelers with disabilities can enter for free.

Organizations that offer a vast range of resources and assistance to disabled travelers include **MossRehab** (© **800/CALL-MOSS;** www.mossresourcenet.org); the **American Foundation for the Blind (AFB)** (© **800/232-5463;** www.afb.org); and **SATH** (Society for Accessible Travel & Hospitality; © **212/447-7284;** www. sath.org). **AirAmbulanceCard.com** is now partnered with SATH and allows you to preselect top-notch hospitals in case of an emergency.

Access-Able Travel Source (© **303/ 232-2979;** www.access-able.com) offers a comprehensive database on travel agents from around the world with experience in accessible travel; destination-specific access information; and links to such resources as service animals, equipment rentals, and access guides.

Flying with Disability (www.flying-with-disability.org) is a comprehensive information source on airplane travel. **Avis Rent a Car** (© **888/879-4273**) has an "Avis Access" program that offers services for customers with special travel needs. These include specially outfitted vehicles with swivel seats, spinner knobs, and hand controls; mobility scooter rentals; and accessible bus service. Be sure to reserve well in advance.

The "Accessible Travel" link at **Mobility-Advisor.com** (www.mobilityadvisor.com) offers a variety of travel resources to disabled persons.

The magazine *Emerging Horizons* (www.emerginghorizons.com), available by subscription ($16.95 year U.S.; US$21.95/£10.85 outside the U.S.), is another resource.

British travelers should contact **Holiday Care** (© **0845-124-9971** in the U.K. only; www.holidaycare.org.uk) for a wide range of travel information and resources for disabled and elderly people.

GAY & LESBIAN TRAVELERS

The Québec province has come far: Gay life here is generally open, accepted, and marketed to, especially in its two major cities. The official **Tourisme Montréal** website at **www.tourisme-montreal.org** has a special "Montréal Gay to Z" mini-site listing gay-friendly accommodations, links, and more; and travelers will find the rainbow flag prominently displayed on many hotel and restaurant doors and websites in all neighborhoods of the city. Since 2004, same-sex couples have been allowed to marry throughout the province.

In Montréal, many gay and lesbian travelers head straight to the **Gay Village** (or, simply, **The Village**), a neighborhood located primarily along rue Ste-Catherine est between rue St-Hubert and rue Papineau where there are antiques shops, bars, and clubs, clubs, clubs. The Beaudry Métro station is at the heart of the neighborhood and marked by the rainbow flag.

The Village Tourism Information Centre at 576 rue Ste-Catherine est, Suite 200 (℃ **888/595-8110** or 514-522-1885) is open daily in the summer and weekdays the rest of the year, and provides information on everything from where to find a wine bar to where to find a yoga class. **Gay Line** (℃ **888/505-1010** or 514/866-5090; www.gayline.qc.ca) answers questions by phone daily from 7 to 11pm and has an events listing page online.

The *Fugues* website at www.fugues.com is a leisure guide to gay life in Montréal and other Québec province cities; you can find the printed version in bars and hotels in and around the Village.

Try to visit Montréal during one of its several gay festivals. The August **Divers/Cité Festival** and October **Black & Blue Festival** are listed in the calendar earlier in this chapter.

In Québec City, the gay community in is smaller and centered in the Upper Town just outside the city walls, near Porte Saint-Jean. At the end of August, there's a 3-day gay fest, **Fête Arc-en-Ciel** (www.fetearcenciel.qc.ca).

Gay.com Travel (℃ **800/929-2268** or 415/644-8044; www.gay.com/travel) has a special section on Montréal, which it lists as one of its Top 20 destinations.

The International Gay and Lesbian Travel Association (IGLTA) (℃ **800/448-8550** or 954/776-2626; www.iglta.org) is the trade association for the gay and lesbian travel industry, and offers an online directory of gay- and lesbian-friendly travel businesses and tour operators.

Many agencies offer tours and travel itineraries specifically for gay and lesbian travelers. **Above and Beyond Tours** (℃ **800/397-2681;** www.abovebeyondtours.com) has a 12-day cruise that goes between Montréal and New York City.

These travel guides might be useful: *Spartacus International Gay Guide,* *35th Edition* (Bruno Gmünder Verlag; www.spartacusworld.com/gayguide); *Odysseus: The International Gay Travel Planner, 17th Edition* (www.odyusa.com); and the *Damron* guides (www.damron.com), with separate, annual books for men and women. The books are available at many bookstores, or you can order them from any online bookseller.

SENIOR TRAVEL

Mention the fact that you're a senior when you make your travel reservations. Although the major U.S. airlines have canceled their senior discount and coupon book programs, many Québec hotels offer discounts for seniors. Many theaters, museums, and other attractions offer reduced admission to people as young as 60.

Members of **AARP,** 601 E St. NW, Washington, DC 20049 (℃ **888/687-2277;** www.aarp.org), get discounts on hotels, airfares, and car rentals. Anyone over 50 can join.

And don't forget to flash your **AAA** card if you have one. Members of the American Automobile Association get the same discounts as members of the CAA. That means reduced rates at many museums, hotels, and restaurants.

Many reliable agencies and organizations target the 50-plus market. **Elderhostel** (℃ **800/454-5768;** www.elderhostel.org) arranges worldwide study programs for those aged 55 and over and offers a variety of trips to Québec and Montréal.

Publications with travel resources and discounts for seniors include the quarterly publication *Travel 50 & Beyond* (www.travel50andbeyond.com) and the best-selling paperback *Unbelievably Good Deals and Great Adventures That You Absolutely Can't Get Unless You're Over 50 2005–2006, 16th Edition* (McGraw-Hill), by Joann Rattner Heilman.

FAMILY TRAVEL

Montréal and Québec City offer an abundance of family-oriented activities, many of them outdoors, even in winter. Dog sledding, watersports, river cruises, fort climbing, and fireworks displays are among the many attractions. The walls and fortifications of Québec City are fodder for imagining the days of knights and princesses, and both cities have horse-drawn sightseeing carriages, a surefire hit with most youngsters. Many museums make special efforts to address children's interests and enthusiasms. For specific suggestions, see the "Especially for Kids" sections in chapters 7 and 15.

For family-friendly accommodations, restaurants, and attractions that are particularly kid-friendly, look for the "Kids" icon throughout this guide.

Recommended family travel websites include **Family Travel Forum** (www.familytravelforum.com), which offers customized trip planning; **TravelWith YourKids.com** (www.travelwithyourkids.com), a comprehensive site written by parents for parents offering sound advice for long-distance and international travel with children, and **Family Travel Network** (www.familytravelnetwork.com), an online magazine providing travel tips.

WOMEN TRAVELERS

Montréal and Québec City are among the safest cities in North America, so only the basic urban cautions about dark streets and care in giving out hotel room numbers need be observed.

Check out the award-winning website **Journeywoman** (www.journeywoman.com), a "real life" women's travel-information network where you can sign up for a free e-mail newsletter and get advice on everything from etiquette and dress to safety. The travel guide *Safety and Security for Women Who Travel* by Sheila Swan and Peter Laufer (Travelers' Tales Guides), offering common-sense tips on safe travel, was updated in 2004.

STUDENT TRAVEL

Both Montréal and Québec City have centrally located university areas filled with students, and both cities cater to the young adult crowd.

Always carry a university or similar ID card to obtain the many available discounts, especially at museums, theaters, and other attractions.

The **International Student Travel Confederation (ISTC)** (www.istc.org) was formed in 1949 to make travel around the world more affordable for students. Check out its website for comprehensive travel services information and details on how to get an **International Student Identity Card (ISIC),** which qualifies students for substantial savings on rail passes, plane tickets, entrance fees, and more. It also provides students with basic health and life insurance and a 24-hour helpline. The card is valid for a maximum of 18 months. You can apply for the card online or in person at **STA Travel** (© 800/781-4040 in North America; www.statravel.com), the biggest student travel agency in the world; check out the website to locate STA Travel offices worldwide.

If you're no longer a student but are still under 26, you can get an **International Youth Travel Card (IYTC),** which entitles you to some discounts. **Travel CUTS** (© 800/592-2887; www.travelcuts.com) offers similar services for both Canadians and U.S. residents. Irish students may prefer to turn to **USIT** (© 01/602-1904; www.usit.ie), an Ireland-based specialist in student, youth, and independent travel.

The Massachusetts-based tour company **MTL Vacations** (© **800/666-8732;** www.yescanada.com) sells package trips to students and young adults. Trips originate in New York; Boston; Springfield, Mass.; and Hartford, Conn.

SINGLE TRAVELERS

Many people prefer traveling alone, and for independent travelers, solo journeys offer infinite opportunities to explore a place deeply, meet locals, and even make friends.

The most frequent problem for solo travelers can be feelings of isolation, especially on Friday and Saturday nights, when everyone else seems to be out and about in numbers divisible by two. Check the sections in this book on popular local music clubs and bars (see chapters 10 and 18) where you might meet locals and engage in some lively conversation. Whether or not you feel like chatting with Québécois or not, jazz and folk music spots, especially those that charge no cover—and most in Montréal and Québec City do not—are also great places to visit if you're on your own.

Bed-and-breakfast inns can be a cozy way to travel on your own, and you can find them in both Montréal and Québec City. Guests come together over breakfast and might end up going out to explore together. Prices are often (but not always) lower than those at hotels, many of which charge the same rate for a room whether it's occupied by one or two people.

Guided walking tours are another excellent way to explore the cities and enjoy a couple of hours of social interaction at the same time.

Unfortunately, if you like resorts, tours, or cruises, you're likely to get hit with a "single supplement" to the base price. Single travelers can avoid these supplements, of course, by agreeing to room with other single travelers on the trip.

TravelChums (© **212/787-2621;** www.travelchums.com) is a travel-companion matching service with elements of online personals sites, hosted by the respected New York–based Shaw Guides travel service.

For more information, check out Eleanor Berman's classic *Traveling Solo: Advice and Ideas for More Than 250 Great Vacations, 5th Edition* (Globe Pequot), updated in 2005.

VEGETARIAN TRAVEL

In Montréal, Le Commensal is a down-town vegetarian restaurant and Aux Vivres a popular vegan spot in Mile End. Both are reviewed in chapter 6. Options are slimmer in Québec City, although both **Happy Cow's Vegetarian Guide to Restaurants & Health Food Stores** (www.happycow.net) and **VegDining.com** list vegetarian restaurants internationally including 24 in Montréal and Québec City.

TRAVELING WITH PETS

Pets with proper rabies vaccination records may be admitted to Canada, but review the necessary procedures with the **Canada Border Services Agency (CBSA),** at © **506/636-5064,** and online at **www.cbsa-asfc.gc.ca**.

To ensure a smooth border crossing on your return, check with **U.S. Customs and Border Protection** before leaving. The useful brochure "Pets and Wildlife" is available as a PDF from the U.S. Customs website at **www.customs.gov**.

Many hotels in the cities now accept pets, and some even offer walking services and little beds for dogs. There are often restrictions about the size of the animal, whether it can be in public areas, and whether it can be left alone in the hotel room. Most hotels charge an extra fee of C$25 (US$22/£11) or more.

10 Sustainable Tourism/Ecotourism

Each time you take a flight or drive a car CO_2 is released into the atmosphere. You can help neutralize this danger to our planet through "carbon offsetting"— paying someone to reduce your CO_2 emissions by the same amount you've added. Carbon offsets can be purchased in the U.S. from companies such as **Carbonfund.org** (www.carbonfund.org) and **TerraPass** (www.terrapass.org), and from **Climate Care** (www.climatecare.org) in the U.K.

Although one could argue that any vacation that includes an airplane flight can't be truly "green," you can go on holiday and still contribute positively to the environment. You can offset carbon emissions from your flight in other ways. Choose forward-looking companies that embrace responsible development practices, helping preserve destinations for the future by working alongside local people. An increasing number of sustainable tourism initiatives can help you plan a family trip and leave as small a "footprint" as possible on the places you visit.

Responsible Travel (www.responsible travel.com) contains a great source of sustainable travel ideas run by a spokesperson for responsible tourism in the travel industry. **Sustainable Travel International** (www.sustainabletravel international.org) promotes responsible tourism practices and issues an annual Green Gear & Gift Guide.

You can find eco-friendly travel tips, statistics, and touring companies and associations—listed by destination under "Travel Choice"—at the TIES website, www.eco tourism.org. Also check out **Conservation International** (www.conservation.org)— which, with *National Geographic Traveler,* annually presents **World Legacy Awards** (www.wlaward.org) to those travel tour operators, businesses, organizations, and places that have made a significant contribution to sustainable tourism. **Ecotravel. com** is part online magazine and part ecodirectory that lets you search for touring companies in several categories (water-based, land-based, spiritually oriented, and so on).

Frommers.com: The Complete Travel Resource

It should go without saying, but we highly recommend **Frommers.com**, voted Best Travel Site by *PC Magazine*. We think you'll find our expert advice and tips; independent reviews of hotels, restaurants, attractions, and preferred shopping and nightlife venues; vacation giveaways; and an online booking tool indispensable before, during, and after your travels. We publish the complete contents of over 128 travel guides in our **Destinations** section covering nearly 3,600 places worldwide to help you plan your trip. Each weekday, we publish original articles reporting on **Deals and News** via our free **Frommers.com Newsletter** to help you save time and money and travel smarter. We're betting you'll find our new **Events** listings (http://events. frommers.com) an invaluable resource; it's an up-to-the-minute roster of what's happening in cities everywhere—including concerts, festivals, lectures and more. We've also added weekly **Podcasts, interactive maps,** and hundreds of new images across the site. Check out our **Travel Talk** area featuring **Message Boards** where you can join in conversations with thousands of fellow Frommer's travelers and post your trip report once you return.

11 Staying Connected

TELEPHONES

The Canadian telephone system, operated by Bell Canada, closely resembles the U.S. model. All operators (dial ℂ 00 from Canada to get one) speak English as well as French, and respond in the appropriate language as soon as callers speak to them.

Pay phones in Québec province require C25¢ (US20¢/11p) for a 3-minute local call. Directory information calls (dial ℂ 411) are free of charge. Both local and long-distance calls usually cost more from hotels—sometimes a lot more, so check. As in the U.S., paper directories (annuaires des téléphones) come in White Pages (residential) and Yellow Pages (commercial).

When making a local call within Québec province, you must also dial the area code before the seven-digit number.

To call Québec province from the U.S.: Calls between Canada and the U.S. do not require the use of country codes. Simply dial the 3-digital area code and seven-digit number. Example: To call the Infotouriste Centre in Montréal, dial 514/873-2015.

To call Québec province from the U.K.: First dial the international access code 00 (from Australia, dial 0011). Follow that with the Canadian country code 1, then the area code, and the seven-digit number. Example: To call the Infotouriste Centre in Montréal, dial 00-1-514/873-2015.

To call U.S. from Québec province: Simply dial the three-digit area code and seven-digit number.

To call the U.K./Ireland/Australia/ New Zealand from Québec province: First dial 011, then the country code (U.K. 44, Ireland 353, Australia 61, New Zealand 64), then the number.

Directory assistance: Dial ℂ 411.

Toll-free numbers: Phone numbers that begin with 800, 888, 877, and 866 are toll-free. That means they're free to call within Canada and from the U.S. You need to dial 1 first. Remember that some hotels will charge you for all phone calls you make, including toll-free ones.

CELLPHONES

Visitors from the U.S. with newer cellphones should be able to get roaming service in Canada. Some wireless companies let you adjust your plan to get cheaper rates while traveling. Sprint, for instance, has an option for "Canadian roaming" for US$3 a month that reduces the per-minute rate from US65¢ to US30¢. Call your phone company and ask for options and pricing schedules.

Europeans and most Australians are on the **GSM** (Global System for Mobile Communications) network with removable plastic SIM cards in their phones. Call your wireless provider for information about traveling. You may be able to purchase pay-as-you-go SIM cards in Canada with local providers.

For many, **renting** a phone is a good idea. While you can rent a phone in many countries at airports or car-rental agencies, this is not a common practice in Canada, so we suggest renting the phone before you leave home. North Americans can rent one from **InTouch USA** (ℂ 800/872-7626; www.intouchglobal.com) or **RoadPost** (ℂ 888/290-1606 or 905/272-5665; www.roadpost.com). InTouch will also, for free, advise you on whether your existing phone will work in Canada; call ℂ **703/222-7161** between 9am and 4pm EST, or go to **http://intouch global.com/travel.htm**.

If you end up traveling without a cellphone, **online phone services** or **telephone cards** are your best option. With **OneSuite.com** (www.onesuite.com; ℂ **866/417-8483**) for instance, you prepay an online account for as low as US$10 and get a PIN. You then dial a toll-free or local access number wherever you're traveling, enter your PIN, and dial the number you're calling. Calls to the lower 48 states in the U.S. cost just US2.5¢ to US3.5¢. Calls to a U.K. landline cost 1p; calls to a U.K. mobile cost 9p.

Buying a phone can be economically attractive, as many nations have cheap prepaid phone systems. Stop by a local cellphone shop; you might pay less than C$100 (US$87/£43) for a phone and a starter calling card.

VOICE-OVER INTERNET PROTOCOL (VOIP)

If you have Web access while traveling, consider a broadband-based telephone service (in technical terms, **Voice-over Internet protocol,** or VoIP) such as Skype (www.skype.com) or Vonage (www.vonage.com). They allow you to make free international calls directly over your laptop or from a cybercafe. Check the sites for current details.

INTERNET/E-MAIL
WITHOUT YOUR OWN COMPUTER

Most large hotels have business centers with computers for use by guests or outsiders, and many of the smaller boutique hotels can arrange computer access for guests. Some hotels offer Internet access through in-room television systems.

Cybercafes seem to be fading from the Canadian scene with the rise of Wi-Fi hotspots, and new ones do not seem to be opening. In Québec City, though, **Centre Internet,** 52 Cote du Palais (© **418/ 692-3359**) was still doing good business in the Upper Town of Old Québec, just a block off of rue St-Jean.

For other options, check **www.cyber cafe.com**. Most major airports have **Internet kiosks** that provide basic Web access for a per-minute fee that's usually higher than cybercafe prices.

WITH YOUR OWN COMPUTER

It's getting easier to find hotels and cafés throughout the Québec province that offer **Wi-Fi** (wireless fidelity) "hotspots," though this is still a work in progress. Many of the hotels listed in this book had limited Wi-Fi in 2007 but plans for increased coverage in the future.

If your laptop has wireless capability (and most sold recently have it built-in), check **www.jiwire.com**; its Hotspot Finder holds the world's largest directory of public wireless hotspots.

For dial-up access, most business-class hotels throughout Québec offer dataports for laptop modems, and some have high-speed Internet access.

Wherever you go, bring a **connection kit** of the right power (110–120 volts AC

Hey, Google, did you get my text message?

It's bound to happen: The day you leave this guidebook back at the hotel for an unencumbered stroll through Vieux-Montréal or Québec City's port district, you'll forget the address of the lunch spot you had earmarked. If you're traveling with a mobile device, send a text message to © **466453 (GOOGLE)** for a lightning-fast response. For instance, type "chez l'epicier montreal" and within 10 seconds you'll receive a text message with the address and phone number. This nifty trick works in a range of search categories: Look up language translations ("translate asparagus in French"), currency conversions ("23 Canadian dollars in USD"), flight updates ("delta 5528") and more. For tips and search options, see www.google.com/intl/en_us/mobile/sms/. Regular text message charges apply.

Online Traveler's Toolbox

Veteran travelers usually carry some essential items to make their trips easier. Following is a selection of handy online tools to bookmark and use.

- **Airplane Food** (www.airlinemeals.net)
- **Airplane Seating** (www.seatguru.com and www.airlinequality.com)
- **ATM Locator** (Visa: www.visa.com and MasterCard: www.mastercard.com)
- **Foreign Languages for Travelers** (www.travlang.com)
- **Hotel reviews** (www.tripadvisor.com)
- **Maps** (www.mapquest.com and http://maps.google.com)
- **Montréal tourism** (www.tourisme-montreal.org)
- **Québec City tourism** (www.capitaleculture.com)
- **Restaurants in Montréal** (http://endlessbanquet.blogspot.com)
- **Subway Navigator** (www.subwaynavigator.com)
- **Time and Date** (www.timeanddate.com)
- **Travel Warnings** (http://travel.state.gov, www.fco.gov.uk/travel, www.voyage.gc.ca, and www.dfat.gov.au/consular/advice)
- **Universal Currency Converter** (www.xe.com/ucc)
- **Weather** (www.intellicast.com and www.weather.com)

[60 cycles] in Canada) and phone adapters, a spare phone cord, and a spare Ethernet network cable—or find out whether your hotel supplies them to guests. The electric current in Canada is the same as in the U.S.

12 Package Deals & Escorted Tours

Packages are simply a way to buy the airfare, accommodations, and other elements of your trip (such as car rentals, airport transfers, and sometimes even activities) at the same time and often at discounted prices.

One good source of package deals is the airlines themselves. Most major airlines offer air/land packages, including **American Airlines Vacations** (✆ 800/321-2121; www.aavacations.com), **Delta Vacations** (✆ 800/654-6559; www.deltavacations.com), **Continental Airlines Vacations** (✆ 800/301-3800; www.covacations.com), and **United Vacations** (✆ 888/854-3899; www.unitedvacations.com). Several big **online travel agencies**—Expedia, Travelocity, Orbitz, Site59, and Lastminute.com—also do a brisk business in packages.

Travel packages are also listed in the travel section of many Sunday newspapers. Or check ads in national travel magazines such as *Budget Travel Magazine, Travel + Leisure, National Geographic Traveler,* and *Condé Nast Traveler.*

Escorted tours are structured group tours, with a group leader. The price usually includes everything from airfare to hotels, meals, tours, admission costs, and local transportation. Many people derive security and peace of mind from the structure they offer. They're particularly convenient for people with limited mobility and they can be a great way to make new friends. On the downside, the tours can be jampacked with activities, leaving little room for individual sightseeing, whim, or adventure.

Cruising to Montréal & Québec City

Cruises from New York and New England up the St. Lawrence River to Montréal and Québec City are popular, especially from June through the foliage season. Among the lines offering cruises, which are usually 6 to 12 days long, are Crystal Cruises (✆ 888/722-0021; www.crystalcruises.com), **Holland America** (✆ 877/SAIL-HAL; www.hollandamerica.com), **Norwegian** (✆ 866/234-0292; www.ncl.com), **Princess** (✆ 800/PRINCESS; www.princess.com), and **Seabourn** (✆ 800/929-9391; www.seabourn.com).

If an escorted tour appeals to you, **Tauck World Discovery** (✆ 800/468-2825; www.tauck.com) offers a 10-day capital cities tour that includes Montréal, Québec City, Ottawa, and Toronto. Tours are offered May through October, providing the opportunity to view fall foliage in both countries.

Before you invest in a package deal or an escorted tour, ask a few important questions. Always check the **cancellation policy.** Ask about the **accommodations** choices and prices for each, then look up the hotels' reviews in a Frommer's guide and check their rates online for your specific dates of travel. For escorted tours, request a complete **schedule,** ask about the **size** and demographics of the group, and discuss what is included in the **price** (transportation, meals, tips, airport transfers). Finally, look for **hidden expenses:** Ask whether airport departure fees and taxes, for example, are included in the total cost (they rarely are).

13 Special-Interest Trips

Foodies have a number of options to **cook with some of the top chefs** in the Québec province during a trip. In the Laurentians, about 67km (42 miles) north of Montréal, chef and owner Anne Desjardins of the well-regarded **L'Eau à la Bouche** (✆ 888/828-2991; www.leaualabouche.com) offers a package that includes 2 days working alongside her in the kitchen, 1 night at the hotel, dinner, breakfast, and a kitchen vest, for C$525 (US$457/£226).

In Québec City, the famed restaurant **Laurie Raphaël** (✆ 418/692-4555; www.laurieraphael.com) underwent major renovation a few years ago that not only spiffed up its space but added a fancy public kitchen. Chef/owner Daniel Vézina gives cooking classes here on Wednesday nights and Saturday afternoons for C$150 (US$130/£64). The cost includes the meal that he cooks. Also in Québec City, **Les Artistes de la Table** (✆ 418/694-1056; www.lesartistesdelatable.com) offers 3- to 4-hour custom cooking classes in the first floor of a gorgeous neoclassical building from 1850. Serious cooks will want to walk by just to peek at the kitchen through the vast windows. Cost is about C$100 (US$87/£43) per person.

Bike touring is wildly popular and well-accommodated. In the summer of 2007, the Québec province inaugurated the new **Route verte (Green Route),** a 4,000km (2,485-mile) bike network. Many hotels and restaurants along the route put special focus on the nutritional, safety, and equipment needs of cyclists. See the "Biker's Paradise: The New 4,000km *Route Verte*" sidebar in chapter 11 on p. 180 for details and contact information.

EcoTours are offered in the gorgeous Charlevoix region just an hour north of

Québec City. Charlevoix was designated a protected UNESCO World Biosphere Reserve in 1988 and is subject to balanced development and cross-disciplinary research into conservation. Katabatik (© **800/453-4850** or 418/665-2332; www.katabatik.ca), based in La Malbaie, offers ecotouring that combines kayaking with information about the life of the capes and bays of the St-Lawrence estuary.

If you've got a car, the **route des vins wine route** 103km (64 miles) southeast of Montréal is pleasant vineyard tour. See "Cantons-de-l'Est: Wine (and *Cidre de Glace*) Country" on p. 195.

14 Tips on Accommodations

Both Montréal and Québec City are rich with the new category of boutique hotels, which combine high-end service with plush room accommodations and decor that ranges from Asian minimalist to country luxury. A good room in one of these smaller hotels could provide one of the best memories of your trip.

Because the region is so intensely cold so many months of the year, the tourist business is cyclical. That means that prices drop—sometimes steeply—for much of the October-through-April period. This is both a plus and a minus: Rooms are cheaper, but some of the essential vibrancy and *joie de vivre* is in hibernation.

SURFING FOR HOTELS

In addition to the online travel booking sites **Travelocity, Expedia, Orbitz, Priceline,** and **Hotwire,** you can book hotels through **Hotels.com; Quikbook** (www.quikbook.com); and **Travelaxe** (www.travelaxe.net).

HotelChatter.com is a daily webzine offering smart coverage and critiques of hotels worldwide. Go to **TripAdvisor.com** or **HotelShark.com** for helpful independent consumer reviews of hotels and resort properties.

It's a good idea to **get a confirmation number** and **make a printout** of any online booking transaction.

Most hotels in the Québec province offer online specials and package deals that bundle rooms with meals or sightseeing activities. In many cases this can result in rates significantly below what's quoted in this book. Always check hotel websites before calling to make a reservation.

SAVING ON YOUR HOTEL ROOM

The **rack rate** is the maximum rate that a hotel charges for a room. Hardly anybody pays this price, however, except in high season or on holidays. To lower the cost of your room:

- **Ask about special rates or other discounts.** You may qualify for corporate, student, military, senior, frequent flier, trade union, or other discounts.

- **Dial direct.** When booking a room in a chain hotel, you'll often get a better deal by calling the individual hotel's reservation desk rather than the chain's main number.

- **Book online.** In addition to offering Internet-only discounts, many hotels also supply rooms to Priceline, Hotwire, or Expedia at rates even lower than the ones you can get through the hotel itself.

- **Remember the law of supply and demand.** Business hotels in downtown Montréal and Québec City are busiest during the week, so you can expect big discounts over the weekend. Many hotels, especially in Québec City, the Laurentides, and the Cantons d' l'Est, have high-season and low-season prices, and booking just a day after "high season" ends can mean big discounts, even at luxury properties.

House-Swapping

House-swapping is becoming a more popular and viable means of travel; you stay in a stranger's home and they stay in yours. You both get a more authentic and personal view of a destination, the opposite of the escapist retreat many hotels offer. Three options: **HomeLink International** (Homelink.org), the largest and oldest home-swapping organization, founded in 1952, with more than 11,000 listings worldwide ($75 yearly membership). **HomeExchange.org** ($50 for 6,000 listings) and **InterVac.com** ($69 for over 10,000 listings) are also reliable.

- **Look into group or long-stay discounts.** If you come as part of a large group, you should be able to negotiate a bargain rate. Likewise, if you're planning a long stay (at least 5 days), you might qualify for a discount. As a general rule, expect 1 night free after a 7-night stay.
- **Sidestep excess surcharges and hidden costs.** Many hotels have adopted the unpleasant practice of nickel-and-diming their guests with opaque surcharges. When you book a room, ask what is included in the room rate, and what is extra. Avoid dialing direct from hotel phones, which can have exorbitant rates. And ignore the room's minibar offerings: Most hotels charge through the nose for water, soda, and snacks.
- **Carefully consider the options for hotel meal plans,** which are offered at many properties, especially in the Laurentians and Charlevoix. The **European Plan (EP)** is room alone, with no meals. The **Continental Plan (CP)** includes breakfast. The **Modified American Plan (MAP)** includes breakfast and one meal (usually dinner). The **American Plan (AP)** is a room plus all three meals.
- **Book an efficiency.** A room with a kitchenette allows you to shop for groceries and cook your own meals. This is a big money saver, especially for families on long stays.
- **Consider enrolling in hotel chains' "frequent-stay" programs,** which are upping the ante lately to win the loyalty of repeat customers. Perks are awarded not only by many chain hotels and motels (Hilton HHonors, Marriott Rewards, Wyndham ByRequest, to name a few), but individual inns and B&Bs.

FAST FACTS: Montréal & Québec City

AAA Members of the **American Automobile Association (AAA)** are covered by the **Canadian Automobile Association (CAA)** while traveling in Canada. Bring your membership card and proof of insurance. The 24-hour hot line for emergency service is ✆ **514/861-1313** in Montréal, ✆ **418/624-4000** in Québec City, and ✆ **800/222-4357** in the rest of Québec province and Canada. Most mobile phones can call ✆ ***CAA** (*222) to reach emergency road service. See www.caaquebec.com for more. The AAA card will also provide discounts at a wide variety of hotels and restaurants in Québec province.

American Express In Montréal, there are 10 travel agencies that are licensed to provide American Express Travel Services. One centrally located agency is Excellent

Travel at 383 rue St. Jacques (© **514/345-1121**) on the northern edge of Vieux-Montréal. To find other agencies and for general information, call © **800/668-2639.** There are no agencies in Québec City. For lost or stolen cards in either city, call © **800/869-3016.**

Area Codes The Montréal area code is **514,** and the Québec City code is **418.** Outside of Montréal, the southern part of the Laurentides is **450** and the northern part, from Val-David up, is **819.** The Cantons de l'Est are the same: **450** or **819,** depending on how close you are to Montréal. Outside Québec City, the area code for Ile d'Orléans and north into Charlevoix is **418,** the same as in the city. You need to dial the area code in addition to the seven-digit number even when calling within the city.

ATM Networks See "Money & Costs," p. 20.

Business Hours Most **stores** in the province are open from 9 or 10am to 6pm Monday through Wednesday, 9am to 9pm on Thursday and Friday, and 9am to 5pm on Saturday. Many stores are now also open on Sunday from noon to 5pm. **Banks** are usually open Monday through Friday from 8 or 9am to 4pm. Bankers' hours in Québec City are shorter, from 10am to 3pm.

Car Rentals See the "Getting Around" sections in chapters 4 and 12 for details about local transportation and about car rentals.

Currency See "Money & Costs," p. 20.

Customs **What You Can Bring Into Canada:** Regulations are flexible in most respects, but visitors can expect at least a probing question or two at the border or airport. Normal baggage and personal possessions should be no problem, but plants, animals, and their products may be prohibited or require additional documents before they're allowed entry. For specific questions about Canadian rules, check with the **Canada Border Services Agency** (© **506/636-5064** from outside the country or **800/461-9999** within Canada; **www.cbsa-asfc.gc.ca**).

Tobacco and alcoholic beverages face import restrictions. Individuals 18 years or over are allowed to bring in 200 cigarettes, 200 grams of loose tobacco, 50 cigars, and either 1.14 liters of liquor, 1.5 liters of wine, or a curiously generous case (24 cans or bottles) of beer. Additional amounts face hefty duties and taxes.

It is very important to keep in mind that if you do not declare goods or falsely declare them, they can be seized *along with the vehicle you brought them in.*

A car that is driven into Canada can stay for up to a year, but it must leave with the owner or a duty will be levied. Note that the use or even possession of a radar detector is prohibited, whether or not it is connected. Police officers can confiscate it and fine the owner C$500 to C$1,000 (US$435–US$870).

What You Can Take from Canada into the U.S.: For specifics on what you can bring back, download the invaluable free pamphlet *Know Before You Go* from the **U.S. Customs and Border Protection** website at **www.customs.gov**. It is a 56-page PDF. Or contact the agency at 1300 Pennsylvania Ave. NW, Washington, DC 20229 (© **877/CBP–5511**).

Returning **U.S. citizens** are allowed to bring back $800 duty-free as "accompanied baggage." Be sure to have your receipts handy. There are strict rules about the number of cigarettes and volume of alcoholic beverages you can count toward your exemption: 200 cigarettes, 100 cigars, 1 liter (33.8 fl. oz) of alcohol. You'll be charged a flat rate of 3% duty on the next $1,000 worth of purchases. Consider registering expensive items you're traveling with (laptops, musical equipment) before you leave the country to avoid challenges at the border on your return. If you try to bring back large amounts of alcohol you may be suspected of importing them for resale and be required to obtain a permit.

On mailed gifts, the duty-free limit is $200. With some exceptions, you cannot bring fresh fruits and vegetables into the United States. Large quantities of unpasteurized cheeses (*cru lait* in French) are likely to be confiscated, while small amounts for personal use are usually permitted.

U.K. citizens should check with **HM Customs & Excise** at ℂ **0845/010-9000** or 44-2920-501-261 from outside the U.K., or **www.hmce.gov.uk**. Citizens returning from **a non-E.U. country** have a Customs allowance of 200 cigarettes or 50 cigars or 250 grams of smoking tobacco; 2 liters of still table wine; 1 liter of spirits or strong liqueurs (over 22% volume) or 2 liters of fortified wine, sparkling wine, or other liqueurs; 60cc (ml) of perfume; 250cc (ml) of toilet water; and £145 worth of all other goods, including gifts and souvenirs. People under 17 cannot have the tobacco or alcohol allowance.

Australian citizens should get the helpful brochure *Know Before You Go*. It's available as a PDF online from the **Australian Customs Service** at **www.customs. gov.au**, or call ℂ **1300/363-263**. The duty-free allowance in **Australia** is A$900 (for those under 18, A$450). Citizens 18 and older can bring in 250 cigarettes or 250 grams of cigars or tobacco products, and 2.25 liters of alcohol. If you're planning to take over valuables such as computers or cameras, register them first by using the "Goods Exported in Passenger Baggage" form in the brochure.

New Zealand citizens can get most questions answered at the **New Zealand Customs Service** (ℂ **0800/428-786**) website at www.customs.govt.nz. The duty-free allowance is NZ$700. Citizens 17 and older can bring in 200 cigarettes, 50 cigars, or 250 grams of tobacco (or a mixture of all three if their combined weight doesn't exceed 250 grams); plus 4.5 liters of wine or beer and 1.125 liters of liquor. If you're planning to take over valuables such as computers or cameras, register them first by presenting them at a Customs office before leaving the country and filling out a Certificate of Export.

Dental Emergencies In Montréal: ℂ **514/721-6006**; www.carrefourdentaire.com. In Québec City: ℂ **418/524-2444** Monday through Friday, or ℂ **418/656-6080** on weekends.

Discount Theater Tickets In Montréal, a new discount ticket office for cultural events opened in summer 2007. Called **Vitrine culturelle de Montréal** ("cultural window of Montréal"), it's located at 145 rue Ste-Catherine ouest in Place des Arts (ℂ **514/285-4545**; www.vitrineculturelle.com). Along with last-minute deals, the central information office sells full-price tickets.

Driving Rules See "Getting Around," p. 62.

Drug Laws Note that penalties for possession, use, and dealing in illegal drugs are strict in Canada. If you have had a prior conviction, you may be denied permission to enter the country. A waiver of exclusion may be obtained from a

Canadian consulate in your home country for a fee. Expect several weeks for processing.

Drugstores A pharmacy is called a *pharmacie*, a drugstore is a *droguerie*. An important chain in Montréal is Pharmaprix. Its branch at 5122 Cote-Des-Neiges (℃ **514/738-8464;** www.pharmaprix.ca) is open 24 hours a day, 7 days a week, and has a fairly convenient location. In Québec City, **Caron & Bernier,** in the Upper Town, 38 Côte du Palais (at rue Charlevoix; ℃ **418/692-4252**), is open 8:15am to 8pm Monday through Friday, and 9am to 3pm on Saturday. **Pharmacie Brunet,** in the suburbs in Les Galeries Charlesbourg, 4250 av. Première, in Charlesbourg (℃ **418/623-1571**), is open 8:30am to 10:30pm 7 days a week.

Electricity As in the U.S., Canada uses 110–120 volts AC (60 cycles) compared to 220–240 volts AC (50 cycles) in most of Europe, Australia, and New Zealand. If your small appliances use 220–240 volts, you'll need a 110-volt transformer and a plug adapter with two flat parallel pins to operate them in Canada.

Embassies & Consulates All embassies are in Ottawa, the national capital. The U.S. has a consulate office in Montréal at 1155 rue St-Alexandre (℃ **514/ 398-9695**) and in Québec City, on Jardin des Gouverneurs at 2 Place Terrasse Dufferin (℃ **418/692-2095**). The United Kingdom has a consulate general in Montréal at 1000 rue de la Gauchetière ouest, Suite 4200 (℃ **514/866-5863**) and in Québec City in the St-Amable Complex, 1150 Claire-Fontaine, Suite 700 (℃ **418/521-3000**).

Emergencies Dial ℃ **911** for the police, firefighters, or an ambulance. Québec Poison Control Centre is at ℃ **800/463-5060.**

Holidays The important public holidays are New Year's Day (Jan 1); Good Friday and Easter Monday (late Mar or Apr); Victoria Day (the Mon preceding May 25); St-Jean-Baptiste Day, Québec's "national" day (June 24); Canada Day (July 1); Labour Day (first Mon in Sept); Canadian Thanksgiving Day (second Mon in Oct); and Christmas (Dec 25). For more information on holidays, see "Montréal & Québec City Calendar of Events," earlier in this chapter.

Hospitals In Montréal, hospitals with emergency rooms include **Hôpital Général de Montréal,** 1650 rue Cedar (℃ **514/934-8090**), and **Hôpital Royal Victoria,** 687 av. des Pins ouest (℃ **514/934-1934**), both of which are associated with McGill University. **Hôpital de Montréal pour Enfants,** 2300 rue Tupper (℃ **514/412-4400**), and **Centre Hospitalier Universitaire Sainte-Justine,** 3175 Chemin de la Côte-Sainte-Catherine (℃ **514/345-4931**), are children's hospitals.

In Québec City, go to the **Centre Hospitalier Hôtel-Dieu de Québec,** 11 côte du Palais (℃ **418/525-4444**).

Hot Lines **Alcoholics Anonymous** is at ℃ **514/376-9230** in Montréal and ℃ 418/ 529-0015 in Québec City. **Poison Control Centre** is at ℃ **800/463-5060** throughout the entire province. **Tel-Aide,** for emotional distress including anxiety and depression, is at ℃ **800/567-9699,** daily 7am to 2am. **Sexual Assault** victims can get bilingual help 24 hours a day at ℃ **514/934-4504.** U.S. Centers for Disease Control International Traveler's Hotline: ℃ **404/332-4559.**

Internet Access See "Staying Connected," earlier in this chapter.

Language Canada is officially bilingual, but Québec province has laws making the use of French mandatory in signage. Still, nearly 20% of Montréal's population has English as its first language (about 5% of Québec City's population does) and an estimated 4 out 5 Francophones speak at least some English as well. While hotel desk staff, sales clerks, and telephone operators nearly always greet people initially in French, they usually switch to English quickly. Outside of Montréal, visitors are more likely to encounter residents who do not speak English. If smiles and sign language don't work, look around for a young person—most of them study English in school.

Laundromats Found primarily in residential neighborhoods, laundromats aren't thick upon the ground in tourist districts. In Montréal, one option is **Baunderie Net-Net** in the Plateau Mont-Royal neighborhood at 310 rue Duluth est (© **514/844-8511**), which provides wash-and-fold services as well as self-operated machines. In Québec, try **Lavoir St-Ursule**, at 17B St-Ursule (no phone) in the Haute-Ville section of Vieux-Québec, or **Lavoir La Lavandière** at 625 rue St-Jean, near rue Ste-Marie (© **418/523-0345**), in the Parliament Hill area. Ask your hotel for options, too—many provide laundry service.

Legal Aid Your country's embassy or consulate can provide the names of attorneys who speak English. See "Embassies & Consulates," above. The U.S. Embassy information line © **888/840-0032** is available from either the U.S. or Canada and costs C$1.59/minute (US$1.40/minute).

Liquor Laws The legal drinking age in the province is 18. All hard liquor and spirits in Québec are sold through official government stores operated by the Québec Société des Alcools (look for maroon signs with the acronym SAQ). Wine and beer can be bought in grocery stores and convenience stores, called *dépanneurs.* Liquor is sold every day of the week in SAQ stores. Bars stop pouring drinks at 3am, but often stay open later.

Note that penalties for drunk driving in Canada are heavy.

Lost & Found Be sure to tell all of your credit card companies the minute you discover your wallet has been lost or stolen and file a report at the nearest police precinct. Your credit card company or insurer may require a police report number or record of the loss. Most credit card companies have an emergency toll-free number to call if your card is lost or stolen; they may be able to wire you a cash advance immediately or deliver an emergency credit card in a day or two.

For lost or stolen American Express cards, call © **800/869-3016.** For lost or stolen Visa cards, call © **800/847-2911.** For lost or stolen MasterCards, call © **800/307-7309.** If you need emergency cash over the weekend when all banks are closed, you can have money wired to you via **Western Union** (© **800/ 325-6000;** www.westernunion.com).

Mail All mail sent through **Canada Post** (© **866/607-6301;** www.canadapost.ca) must bear Canadian stamps. That might seem painfully obvious, but apparently large numbers of visitors, especially from the U.S., use stamps from their home countries. To mail within Canada, letters cost C52¢ (US45¢/22p). A letter or postcard to the U.S. is C93¢ (US81¢/40p]). A letter or postcard to anywhere else is C$1.55 (US$1.35/67p). **FedEx** offers service from Canada (⊘ **800/463-3339**; www.fedex.com/ca).

Newspapers & Magazines Montréal's primary English-language newspaper is the *Montréal Gazette* (www.montrealgazette.com). *The Globe and Mail* (www. theglobeandmail.com) is a national English-language paper. The leading French-language newspaper is *Le Soleil.* For information about current arts happenings in Montréal, pick up the Friday or Saturday edition of the *Gazette.* See p. 161 in chapter 10 for other local magazines. Most large newsstands and those in the larger hotels carry the *Wall Street Journal, The New York Times,* and the *International Herald Tribune.* Major newsstands include the multi-branch **Maison de la Presse Internationale,** in Montréal at 1166 rue Ste-Catherine ouest (at rue Stanley) and in Québec City at 1050 rue St-Jean inside the walls of Vieux-Québec.

Passports Allow plenty of time before your trip to apply for a passport; processing in the U.S. can take 10 weeks during busy periods (especially spring). And keep in mind that if you need a passport in a hurry, you'll pay a higher processing fee. If you lose your passport while traveling, contact your embassy or consulate.

For Residents of the United States: Whether you're applying in person or by mail, you can download passport applications from the U.S. State Department website at **http://travel.state.gov**. To find your regional passport office, either check the U.S. State Department website or call the **National Passport Information Center** toll-free number (⊘ **877/487-2778**) for automated information.

For Residents of the United Kingdom: To pick up an application for a standard 10-year passport (5-year passport for children under 16), visit your nearest passport office, major post office, or travel agency or contact the **United Kingdom Passport Service** at ⊘ **0870/521-0410** or search its website at www.ukpa.gov.uk.

For Residents of Australia: You can pick up an application from your local post office or any branch of Passports Australia, but you must schedule an interview at the passport office to present your application materials. Call the **Australian Passport Information Service** at ⊘ **131-232,** or visit the government website at www.passports.gov.au.

For Residents of Ireland: You can apply for a 10-year passport at the **Passport Office,** Setanta Centre, Molesworth Street, Dublin 2 (⊘ **01/671-1633**; www.irl gov.ie/iveagh). Those under age 18 and over 65 must apply for a 3-year passport. You can also apply at 1A South Mall, Cork (⊘ **021/272-525**) or at most main post offices.

For Residents of New Zealand: You can pick up a passport application at any New Zealand Passports Office or download it from their website. Contact the **Passports Office** at ⊘ **0800/225-050** in New Zealand or 04/474-8100, or log on to www.passports.govt.nz.

Pets In public areas, dogs must be kept on leash (maximum length 6 ft.). Dog owners must clean up after their pets. For emergency veterinary services 24 hours a day, 7 days a week, call ⊘ **418/872-5355.** See "Traveling with Pets" on p. 29.

Police Dial ℂ **911** for the police. There are three types of officers in Québec: **municipal police** in Montréal, Québec City, and other towns; **Sûreté de Québec officers,** comparable to state police or the highway patrol in the United States; and **RCMP** (Royal Canadian Mounted Police), who are similar to the FBI and handle cases involving infraction of federal laws. RCMP officers speak English and French. Other officers are not required to know English, though many do.

Restrooms Tourist offices are often the best place to find public restrooms. The addresses of tourist centers are listed on p. 57 and p. 206.

Safety See "Safety," earlier in this chapter.

Smoking Smoking was banned in the province's bars, restaurants, and some other public spaces in May 2006. Although enforcement is sometimes spotty, all restaurants, bars, clubs, and casinos are officially smoke-free.

Taxes Most goods and services in Canada are taxed 6% by the federal government (the GST, or Goods and Services Tax). On top of that, the province of Québec has an additional 7.5% tax (the TVQ). A 3% accommodations tax is also in effect in Montréal.

Nonresident visitors used to be able to apply for a rebate on the GST tax they paid on most items they purchased in Québec as well as on the taxes on lodging. No longer. The Visitor Rebate Program was eliminated in April 2007. A new Foreign Convention and Tour Incentive Program will provide limited rebates on the GST for services used during foreign conventions held in Canada, for nonresident exhibitors, and for the short-term accommodations portion of tour packages for nonresident individuals and tour operators. Details are at **www.cra-arc.gc.ca/visitors**.

Time Zone Montréal, Québec City, and all the regions listed in this book as side trips are all in the Eastern Time zone. Daylight saving time is observed by moving clocks ahead an hour on the second Sunday in March and back an hour on the first Sunday in November.

Tipping Practices are similar to those in the U.S.: 15% to 20% of restaurant bills, 10% to 15% for taxi drivers, C$1 (US87¢/43p) per bag for porters, C$5 (US$4.35/£2.15) per night for the hotel room attendant. Hairdressers and barbers expect 10% to 15%. Hotel doormen should be tipped for calling a taxi or other services.

Suggested Montréal & Québec City Itineraries

While Québec province is vast, most of its people live in the stretch immediately adjacent to the northern borders of the states of New York and New England. Its major cities and towns, including Montréal and the capital of Québec City, as well as most of its developed resort and scenic areas, lie within a 3-hour drive of either city (Montréal and Québec themselves are just 3 hr. apart). Many visitors, especially those who live in the northeastern U.S., choose to visit with their own cars.

While portions of the following itineraries are more readily accomplished with a car, there are intercity buses and shuttle services to reach major destinations in the outer districts. Public transportation in the cities is good to excellent, so there is little need for a personal vehicle while enjoying their attractions. Further, if you plan to combine visits to both Montréal and Québec City, train service between them is frequent, fairly priced, and of high quality. With a few adjustments, then, an entire Québec vacation can be completed without a personal or rental car. That's often desirable, especially when weather is variable, or when winter carnivals or skiing are prime reasons for going.

On the assumption that most visitors plan to visit either Montréal or Québec City but not both, the itineraries focus on each of those cities and their environs individually.

1 The Best of Montréal in 1 Day

This itinerary outlines a carefully paced exploration of this cosmopolitan city with ample time for random exploring, shopping, or simply lingering in sidewalk cafés. While many suggestions assume you are traveling in warm weather, there are periodic suggestions for the winter months. If you're staying only 1 night, do book a room in one of the new boutique hotels in Vieux-Montréal, the old quarter beside the port on the St. Lawrence River. Visitors find themselves drawn again and again to the plazas and narrow cobblestone streets of this 18th- and 19th-century neighborhood, so you might as well be based there. *Start: Vieux-Montréal.*

❶ Place d'Armes ✸✸✸

Begin the day in the heart of **Vieux-Montréal** ✸✸✸, at the place where the French settlers fought a bloody but decisive battle with the Iroquois in 1653. At the southeast corner of the plaza is the oldest building in the city, the **Vieux Séminaire de St-Sulpice** (p. 132), erected by Sulpician priests who arrived in 1657. Next to it is the **Basilique Notre-Dame** ✸✸✸ (p. 113), an 1824 church with a stunning interior of intricately gilded rare woods. Its acoustics are so clear that the late, famed opera star

Suggested Montréal Itineraries

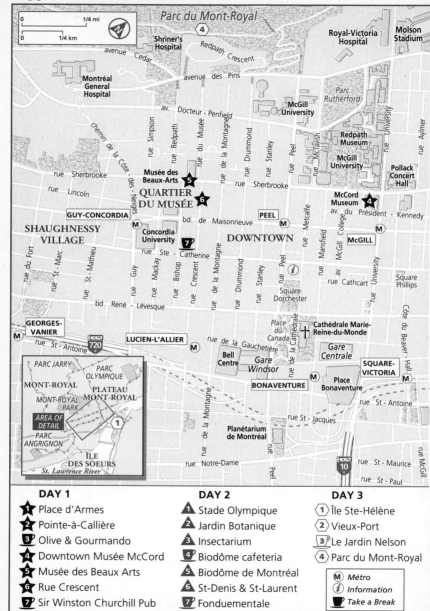

DAY 1

1. Place d'Armes
2. Pointe-à-Callière
3. Olive & Gourmando
4. Downtown Musée McCord
5. Musée des Beaux Arts
6. Rue Crescent
7. Sir Winston Churchill Pub

DAY 2

1. Stade Olympique
2. Jardin Botanique
3. Insectarium
4. Biodôme cafeteria
5. Biodôme de Montréal
6. St-Denis & St-Laurent
7. Fonduementale

DAY 3

1. Île Ste-Hélène
2. Vieux-Port
3. Le Jardin Nelson
4. Parc du Mont-Royal

Ⓜ Métro
ⓘ Information
Take a Break

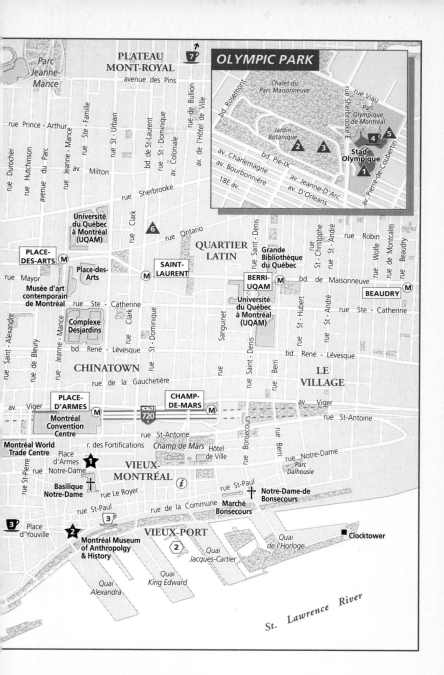

Parc Jeanne-Mance

PLATEAU
MONT-ROYAL

avenue des Pins

OLYMPIC PARK

Chalet du
Parc Maisonneuve

rue Viau

rue Sherbrooke E

Parc Olympique de Montréal

bd. Rosemont

Jardin Botanique

rue Prince - Arthur

rue Ste-Famille

rue St-Urbain

bd. de St-Laurent

rue St-Dominique

av. Coloniale

av. de l'Hôtel de Ville

rue de Bullion

rue Durocher

rue Hutchinson

avenue du Parc

rue Jeanne-Mance

av. Milton

rue Clark

rue Sherbrooke

2 3

bd. Pie-IX

av. Charlemagne

av. Bourbonnière

18E av.

av. Jeanne-D'Arc

av. D'Orleans

4 5

Stade Olympique

1

rue Pierre-de-Coubertin

Université du Québec à Montréal (UQAM)

6

rue Ontario

QUARTIER LATIN

rue Saint - Denis

Grande Bibliothèque du Québec

rue St - Christophe

rue St - André

rue Robin

rue Wolfe

rue de Montcalm

rue Beaudry

PLACE-DES-ARTS Ⓜ

Place-des-Arts

SAINT-LAURENT Ⓜ

BERRI-UQAM Ⓜ

bd. de Maisonneuve

BEAUDRY Ⓜ

rue Mayor

Musée d'art contemporain de Montréal

rue Ste - Catherine

Université du Québec à Montréal (UQAM)

rue St - Hubert

rue St - André

rue Ste - Catherine

rue Saint - Alexandre

rue de Bleury

Complexe Desjardins

rue Clark

rue St - Dominique

bd. René - Lévesque

Sanguinet

rue Saint - Denis

rue Berri

bd. René - Lévesque

CHINATOWN

rue de la Gauchetière

LE VILLAGE

PLACE-D'ARMES Ⓜ

Montréal Convention Centre

CHAMP-DE-MARS Ⓜ

720

av. Viger

rue St-Antoine

av. Viger

Montréal World Trade Centre

r. des Fortifications

rue St-Antoine

Champ de Mars

Hôtel de Ville

rue Bonsecours

rue Berri

rue Notre-Dame

Place d'Armes ★

Parc Dalhousie

rue St-Pierre

rue Notre-Dame

VIEUX-MONTRÉAL ℹ

Basilique Notre-Dame ✝

rue Le Royer

rue St-Paul

Notre-Dame-de-Bonsecours ✝

3️⃣ Place d'Youville

2️⃣

rue St-Paul

3️⃣

rue de la Commune

Marché Bonsecours

Montréal Museum of Anthropolgy & History

2️⃣

VIEUX-PORT

Quai Jacques-Cartier

Quai de l'Horloge

Clocktower ■

Quai Alexandra

Quai King Edward

St. Lawrence River

Luciano Pavarotti sang there several times. If it's still early, pick up "Walking Tour 1" in chapter 8, which will take you past every historic structure in Vieux-Montréal.

❷ Pointe-à-Callière 🕭🕭🕭

From the Basilique Notre-Dame, walk down the slope to the riverside edge of the district and **Pointe-à-Callière,** the Museum of Archaeology and History. After viewing the multimedia show above the ruins of the ancient city, descend below the streets to discover remnants of Amerindian camps and early French settlements unearthed and displayed where they were found. See p. 114.

---

❸ OLIVE ET GOURMANDO
A couple of cobblestone blocks away is Olive et Gourmando. It started out as a bakery, added prepared foods, and evolved into a full-service, French-feeling café. Eat in, or put together an appetizing picnic lunch to carry to the nearby park of the Vieux-Port. 351 rue St-Paul ouest (📞 514/350-1083). See p. 97.

---

❹ Musée McCord

After lunch, take the Métro to the Peel station and walk to the **Musée McCord,** opposite the campus of English-language McGill University. The somewhat eccentric collections of Canadian historical objects are the gifts of 19th-century benefactors—a kind of cataloged provisional attic—including objects gathered from Québec's Native peoples. See p. 112.

❺ Musée des Beaux-Arts 🕭🕭🕭

This is the city's most important fine-arts museum. The original building opened in 1912, and was augmented by the addition of a modern annex across the street in 1991. The ever-expanding permanent collection includes painting and sculpture from the Middle Ages to the 20th century, supplemented by displays from Oceania and Africa. An excellent art and gift shop is attached. See p. 109.

❻ Rue Crescent 🕭🕭

By now, you deserve a stroll and a sit-down, with a little shopping and people-watching. Walk south on rue Crescent. At first, it's lined with boutiques both hip and chic; soon it merges into downtown's primary nightlife district. By 5pm on a Thursday, at least when it's warm enough not to see your breath, the pedestrian traffic thickens and grows ever more intriguing.

---

❼ SIR WINSTON CHURCHILL PUB
Grab a sidewalk seat at the Sir Winston Churchill Pub. It's been an epicenter of the rue Crescent scene for ages, filled with chatty 20- and 30-somethings passing the time or seeking companionship for the coming weekend. The hamburgers look better than they are, so nurse a pint or two of cold beer instead while taking in the passing parade. 1459 rue Crescent near rue Ste-Catherine (📞 514/288-3814). See p. 168.

When it's time for dinner, there are several worthy restaurants on this and adjacent streets suggested in chapter 6.

2 The Best of Montréal in 2 Days

With the absolute essentials of historic Old Montréal and downtown Anglophone (English-speaking) cultural institutions under your belt, prepare to take a journey deep into French Montréal. When the Olympics were awarded to Montréal for 1976, municipal authorities erected some principal venues in the eastern, overwhelmingly Francophone precincts of the city, which is where we start. **Start:** *Take the Métro to the Viau station (it's at some distance, and a taxi would be expensive).*

---

❶ Stade Olympique

The controversial Olympic Stadium was long scorned as the "Big Owe" and then "Big Woe" due to cost overruns that provoked elevated taxes. Its fabric roof was meant to be retractable, but never did work to anyone's satisfaction. Nevertheless, it now houses a natatorium with five pools open to the public and has an inclined tower over 175m (574 ft.) high with a funicular that scoots to the observation level at the top in seconds. The vista afforded reaches as far as 56km (35 miles) past the city and into the mountains beyond. See p. 116.

A shuttle van can carry you from the Stade Olympique to the Jardin Botanique (Botanical Garden).

❷ Jardin Botanique ✦✦✦

The garden boasts 75 hectares (185 acres) of plants and flowers in dozens of specialized sections, including those sponsored by China and Japan. Ten large greenhouses assure that there are things to see all year, although May through September are the highlight months. A small train makes regular runs through the gardens. Plan to spend at least an hour or two. See p. 116.

❸ Insectarium ✦

Kids love the collection of more than 3,000 mounted and live bugs, beetles, spiders, and other sinister critters gathered in the two-story building on the grounds of the Jardin Botanique. Adults are more likely to enjoy the summer displays of gorgeous specimens in the adjacent Butterfly House.

Take the shuttle back to the Olympic Stadium and walk to the adjacent Biodôme.

❹ BIODÔME CAFETERIA

You might want to eat before you take on the Biodôme (below), which can easily occupy another hour or so, especially if you have youngsters in tow. The in-house cafeteria and casual restaurant won't soon win any gastronomic awards, but they're at least serviceable, and there's also an adjoining game room for kids, called Naturalia. 4777 av. Pierre-de-Coubertin (next to Olympic Stadium; ✆ 514/868-3000). See p. 115.

❺ Biodôme de Montréal ✦✦✦

Originally a velodrome (cycling track) built for the 1976 Olympics, this unique facility's four fascinating sections replicate four ecosystems, complete with tropical trees and animals, including golden lion tamarin monkeys that swing on branches only an arm's length away. See p. 115.

Take the Métro to Square Victoria or Place d'Armes.

❻ St-Denis & St-Laurent ✦✦

After all this, it might well be time to get back to your hotel for a recuperative lie-down. If you're ready to continue, take the path of generations of immigrants and walk from near the river in Vieux-Montréal due north on boulevard St-Laurent (French for Saint Lawrence). St-Laurent passes through the expanding **Quartier Chinois (Chinatown),** past the western edge of the **Gay Village** and the bohemian **Quartier Latin (Latin Quarter),** and into the lower precincts of the Plateau Mont-Royal neighborhood. Turn right along the pedestrian rue Prince Arthur, and reach rue St-Denis. Turn north (left). There are no must-see monuments or sights along this route, so surrender to the color and vitality of the heart of French Montréal. "Walking Tour 3" in chapter 8 (p. 142) provides guidance to some notable shops and restaurants along the way.

🥄 FONDUEMENTALE

If it's time for dinner, chapter 6 recommends at least a dozen likely restaurants along this route. But if you're just looking for a snack, it's hard to beat the longtime favorite, Fonduementale. Fondues and the related Swiss specialty raclette come in many guises, from snacks to full meals. There is a terrace in front and a garden in back. 4325 rue St-Denis (℡ **514/499-1446**).

You're in the right neighborhood if you want to follow dinner with a bit of bar- or club-hopping. The Main, as boulevard St-Laurent is known, is lined with both amiable and hard-driving places to bend an elbow and listen to music. The best stretch is from around avenue du Mont-Royal on the north to rue Sherbrooke on the south.

3 The Best of Montréal in 3 Days

Following these suggestions, you have now visited the primary must-see sights. On this third day, it's time to slack off a bit, combining a morning of re-created history with idylls in the park and a ride on the St. Lawrence—tranquil or thrilling, your choice. *Start: Take the Métro to the Parc Jean-Drapeau stop. Follow the signs to the Vieux Fort and Musée David M. Stewart, about a 15-minute walk.*

❶ Ile Ste-Hélène 𝕬

The island in the middle of the St. Lawrence was doubled in size with landfill for Expo '67, the World's Fair, to allow for the construction of national pavilions. A facility that dated from long before that event was the moated fortress ordered built by the duke of Wellington and completed in 1824. It is now the **Musée David M. Stewart** 𝕬, the original low stone barracks of the fort now housing a museum of military history from then until when the British left in 1870. There are parades and simulated military ceremonies from late June to late August. While the island is pleasant for strolling, with its views of the downtown skyline, there's no compelling reason to stay for more than an hour or two. See p. 120.

Take the Métro to Place d'Armes and walk down to the Vieux-Port.

❷ Vieux-Port 𝕬𝕬

A gray, ragged industrial/commercial harbor less than 20 years ago, the Old Port at the edge of Vieux-Montréal has been transformed into a broad linear park with frequent live concerts, abundant recreational activities, and several attractions of note. Principal among these is the **Centre des Sciences de Montréal** (p. 114), on King Edward Pier, which contains a popular IMAX cinema in addition to room after room of computer-driven interactive displays sure to enthrall your inner geek. At the east end of the park, near the old clock tower, is the departure point for **Les Sautes-Moutons** (℡ **514/284-9607**). The company entices adventurous spirits with special flat-bottomed boats that travel upriver in wet and wild challenges to the roiling Lachine Rapids. Other companies provide more sedate river cruises. It's also easy to rent bicycles and in-line skates by the hour or day here. See p. 115.

LE JARDIN NELSON

As you will already have noticed, Vieux-Montréal harbors a considerable number of eating places catering to most tastes and wallets. One of the most visible and popular is Le Jardin Nelson on the main square, Place Jacques-Cartier. Head for the garden in back if the weather is right, for on many days there are live musical performances at lunch hour. The menu has something for everyone, from soups, sandwiches, and pizzas to a delectable roster of stuffed main-course and dessert crepes. 407 Place Jacques-Cartier (© 514/861-5731).

④ Parc du Mont-Royal ☆☆

Montréalers choose to think of the hill that rises behind the spires of downtown office towers as "The Mountain" that gave the city its name, "Mont-Real." The rounded crest of the hill was made into a public park according to plans by Frederick Law Olmsted, the designer of New York's Central Park. It draws throngs of citizens to its woods, rolling lawns, and meadows throughout the year. If you still have the energy, join them with a hike up from the Peel Métro station (if you're in reasonably good shape) or take a taxi up to Lac des Castors (Beaver Lake).

In winter, horse-drawn calèches switch wheels for runners to tour the snow-covered top. However athletic or sedentary your appreciation of the terrain, though, by all means make your way to the southern edge of the mountain as dusk approaches. A building called Chalet du Mont-Royal provides a sweeping view of the city from its terrace—an unforgettable panorama. Take in the view; it's a fine way to end your stay in the Queen City of Québec.

4 The Best of Québec City in 1 Day

The capital of this singular province bears scant resemblance to Montréal. The oldest walled city north of Mexico sustains the look of a European provincial city that keeps watch over the powerful St. Lawrence River. Entrancing in both winter and summer, it lays out a yearlong banquet of festivals and celebrations. If you're visiting between May and October in 2008, check www.MyQuebec2008.com for the most up-to-date details about celebrations taking place for the city's 400th anniversary. To take greatest advantage of all that the city has to offer, book a hotel or B&B within the walls of the Haute-Ville (Upper Town) or in the revitalized Basse-Ville (Lower Town). *Start: Château Frontenac.*

❶ Terrasse Dufferin ☆☆☆

First thing after unpacking and a rest, get to the **Château Frontenac** ☆ (p. 242)—its peaked copper roofs can be seen from everywhere. In front of the hotel is a long promenade, the Terrasse Dufferin, which affords panoramic views of the old city's **Basse-Ville (Lower Town)** ☆☆☆ (p. 256) and the wide, wide river. In good weather, street performers entertain passersby; in the winter, an old-fashioned toboggan run is installed on the steep staircase at the south end.

❷ Funicular ☆

Take the funicular down from the north end of the Terrasse Dufferin. Traveling at a steep angle, it's enclosed in glass to take advantage of the views. (An alternative descent is via the Escalier Casse-Cou, which translates as "Breakneck Stairs" for reasons that are immediately apparent.) Both funicular and stairs wind up at rue

Suggested Québec City Itineraries

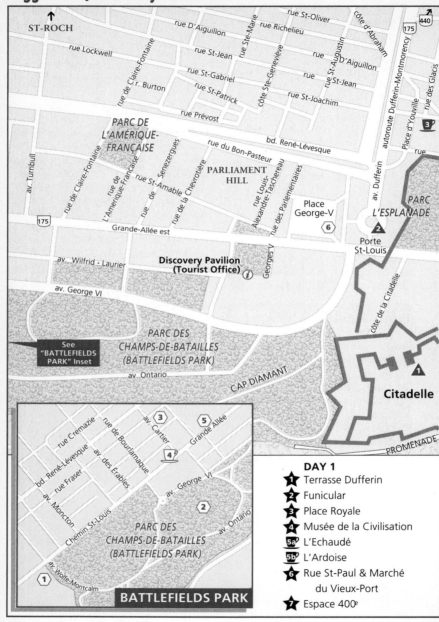

ST-ROCH

rue St-Oliver
côte d'Abraham
175
440

rue D'Aiguillon
rue Richelieu
rue Ste-Marie

rue Lockwell
rue St-Jean
rue D'Aiguillon

rue de Claire-Fontaine
rue St-Gabriel
rue St-Patrick
rue St-Augustin
rue St-Jean

rue de Cl. r. Burton
côte Ste-Geneviève
rue St-Joachim

rue Prévost

PARC DE L'AMÉRIQUE-FRANÇAISE
rue du Bon-Pasteur
bd. René-Lévesque

autoroute Dufferin-Montmorency
Place d'Youville
rue des Glacis

av. Turnbull
rue de Claire-Fontaine
rue de L'Amérique-Française
rue St-Amable
rue de Senezergues
rue de la Chevrotière
PARLIAMENT HILL
rue Louis-Alexandre-Taschereau
rue des Parlementaires

av. Dufferin

PARC L'ESPLANADE

175
Grande-Allée est
Place George-V
6
2
Porte St-Louis

av. Wilfrid - Laurier
Discovery Pavilion (Tourist Office) ℹ
Georges V

av. George VI

côte de la Citadelle

See "BATTLEFIELDS PARK" Inset

PARC DES CHAMPS-DE-BATAILLES (BATTLEFIELDS PARK)

av. Ontario
CAP DIAMANT

1
Citadelle

PROMENADE

rue Cremazie
av. Cartier
3
5
Grande Allée

bd. René-Lévesque
rue de Bourlamaque
av. des Érables
4

rue Fraser
av. Moncton
av. George VI

Chemin St-Louis
2

PARC DES CHAMPS-DE-BATAILLES (BATTLEFIELDS PARK)
av. Ontario

1
av. Wolfe-Montcalm

BATTLEFIELDS PARK

DAY 1
1 Terrasse Dufferin
2 Funicular
3 Place Royale
4 Musée de la Civilisation
5a L'Echaudé
5b L'Ardoise
6 Rue St-Paul & Marché du Vieux-Port
7 Espace 400ᵉ

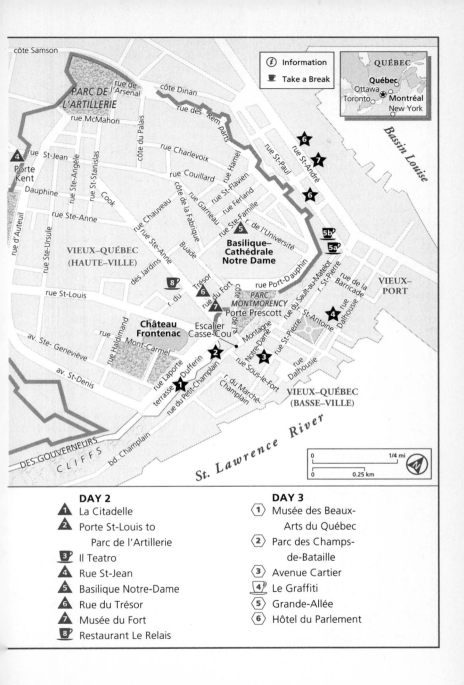

DAY 2

1. La Citadelle
2. Porte St-Louis to Parc de l'Artillerie
3. Il Teatro
4. Rue St-Jean
5. Basilique Notre-Dame
6. Rue du Trésor
7. Musée du Fort
8. Restaurant Le Relais

DAY 3

1. Musée des Beaux-Arts du Québec
2. Parc des Champs-de-Bataille
3. Avenue Cartier
4. Le Graffiti
5. Grande-Allée
6. Hôtel du Parlement

du Petit-Champlain, down to the right, a pedestrian street of shops and cafés populated largely by tourists. Save a visit to the street for later.

Continue straight ahead down rue Sous-le-Fort, and make the first left turn.

❸ Place-Royale 𝕲𝕲𝕲

This small but picturesque square was the site of the first European colony in Canada and is surrounded by restored 17th- and 18th-century houses. The church on one side is the Eglise Notre-Dame-des-Victoires, built in 1688. Walk straight ahead past the Centre d'Interprétation de Place-Royale, on the left. At the end of the block, turn around to view a *trompe l'oeil* mural depicting citizens of the early city. See p. 238.

Continue in the same direction, making the first right turn (Rue de la Barricade) down toward the river. Turn left on rue Dalhousie and follow for a couple of blocks until you get to:

❹ Musée de la Civilisation 𝕲𝕲𝕲

This ambitious museum, filled with fascinating exhibits, can easily fill 2 or 3 hours. At the least, take in the permanent exhibit, *Memoires,* but there are other reasons to linger, many involving interactive displays. See p. 235.

Leaving, turn left, then left again, and right on rue du Sainte-au-Matelot.

> **⑤ A BOUNTY OF BISTROS**
>
> Starting at the corner of rue St-Paul and rue Sault-du-Matelot is a continuous strand of bistros and casual eating places bending around to the left on rue St-Paul. Almost any of them will do for a snack or a meal, but our top choices are **⑤ᴬ L'Echaudé** 𝕲, 73 rue Sault-du-Matelot (𝄽 **418/692-1299**), and **⑤ᴮ L'Ardoise,** 71 rue St-Paul (𝄽 **418/694-0213**). Both offer excellent value for classic French dishes, and both have sidewalk tables in summer. The first has an edge in quality and wine list; the second is known for its mussel choices and is preferable for families.

After eating continue along St-Paul.

❻ Rue St-Paul 𝕲 and Marché du Vieux-Port

In the past decade, St-Paul has become the prime street for antiques and collectibles browsing. Turn right at rue St-Thomas and (carefully) cross busy rue St-André. Over to the left is the Marché du Vieux-Port (Old Port Market). Produce and other products of the farming island of Ile d'Orléans, seen downriver beyond the market, are sold here. See p. 266.

❼ Espace 400ᵉ

To the right (south) of the market is **Espace 400ᵉ,** a new pavilion on the waterfront where the Centre d'Interprétation du Vieux-Port used to be. For the last few years, Québec City has been sprucing itself up and planning blow-out celebrations for 2008 to commemorate its 400th anniversary, and the pavilion will be the celebration's hub, hosting special exhibits, performances, conferences, and shows from June to September. After 2008, it will become a Parks Canada discovery center.

Retrace your steps along rue Dalhousie, the Château Frontenac looming up to your right. Soon you'll see the dock for the ferry to Lévis, on the opposite shore. While it's intended for commuters, it makes an inexpensive, scenic trip. A round-trip takes under an hour. See p. 243.

From the dock, the funicular back to Upper Town is only a short walk away. After this day, you'll want to take it. Alternatively, you might want to stop in for dinner at one of the bistros you've passed along the way.

5 The Best of Québec City in 2 Days

During the repeated conflicts with the British during the 18th century, the residents of New France moved to the top of the cliffs of Cap Diamant that rise behind the Basse-Ville, which is down at river level. Over the years, they threw up fortifications with battlements and artillery emplacements that eventually encircled the city as it existed at that time. Most of them remain, albeit restored repeatedly over the years. Along with the narrow streets, leafy plazas, and leaning houses that compose the old town, they are the reason to spend the day within the walls. *Start: Return to the Terrasse Dufferin to begin the day. Bring your camera.*

❶ La Citadelle 🌟🌟

Today, start by walking south on the Terrasse. At the end, go onto the staircase that goes up to what's called the Promenade des Gouverneurs. Spread below is an extension of the views seen from the Terrasse, and to the right is La Citadelle, a partially star-shaped fortress built in anticipation of an American invasion that never happened. Walk around the rim. The fortress has a low profile, dug into the land rather than rising above it. At the far end is a courtyard where a ceremonial changing of the guard occurs at 10am every day in summer. It can be viewed from above, saving the admission fee and avoiding the rather boring guided tour. See p. 238.

Walk down the hill to avenue St-Denis, continuing as it drops down to the corner of rue St-Louis, the main road into the old town.

❷ Porte St-Louis to Parc de l'Artillerie

The main gate in the city walls is over to the left. Near it is a gathering place for some of the city's horse-drawn carriages. If you're in the mood and the fare (around C$75/US$65/£32) doesn't seem too expensive, take a ride. Otherwise, cross over to the long greenway known as the Parc l'Esplanade and continue along rue Ste-Ursule down a steep hill to the other main gate in the wall, Porte St-Jean (a 20th-c. re-creation). Next to it is the entrance to the Parc de l'Artillerie, recently reconstituted as a national park. On view are an officer's mess and their quarters, and an old iron foundry, shown by costumed guides.

Walk west on rue St-Jean through the gate and out of the walled city. This is **Place d'Youville**, a well-used space with hotels, a concert hall, vending stalls, and an open-air venue for the concerts of the city's many festivals.

Bear right around the plaza.

☕ ③ RISTORANTE IL TEATRO

A good bet for lunch, especially if you can snare a table out under the umbrellas on the sidewalk, is Il Teatro. It's part of the hotel-theater complex Le Capitole. Pasta is a specialty, as with duck ravioli and sausage and mushrooms with linguini in an earthy demi-glace. 972 rue St-Jean (€ 418/694-9996).

After lunch, walk back through the gate and down bustling rue St-Jean.

❹ Rue St-Jean

One of the liveliest of Vieux-Québec's Haute-Ville streets, rue St-Jean is lined with a great variety of shops, cafés, pubs, clubs, and restaurants. A stroll down its length can easily occupy an hour or two. See p. 262.

At the end, bear right up the Côte de la Fabrique. At the end is the:

❺ Basilique Notre-Dame ☆

What with bombardments, fires, and repeated rebuilding, this representative of the oldest Christian parish north of Mexico is nothing if not perseverant. Parts of it, including the bell tower, survive from the 1647 structure, but most of what remains is from a 1771 reconstruction. There is an organ concert the first Sunday of every month at 3:30pm. See p. 241.

When leaving the church, walk left along rue Baude until you reach, on your right:

❻ Rue du Trésor

This narrow pedestrian alley cuts up to the Place d'Armes. It's lined with the etchings, drawings, and watercolors of artists seeking tourist dollars. Nearly all the renderings are of Québec City scenes, and while they won't soon join the collections of major museums, they are competently done and make worthwhile souvenirs. See p. 264.

Turn left at the top of the alley.

❼ Musée du Fort

This daylong walk through history may have whetted your curiosity about the facts and figures of the city's past. While it is a commercial enterprise, the **Musée du Fort** stages a 25-minute multimedia show that outlines the battles and evolutionary changes of the capital using a 36-sq.-m (400-sq.-ft.) scale model of the city with film, light, and rousing music to tell the story. See p. 242.

---

❽ RESTAURANT LE RELAIS

If it's too early for dinner, see if you can cadge an outdoor table at the restaurant for the Auberge du Trésor, a red-roofed building with a mock-Tudor facade at 16 rue Ste-Anne, half a block from the Musée du Fort. Though meals are served, you might want to stick to coffee or a pint and save the calories for one of the superior restos described in chapter 14.

---

6 The Best of Québec City in 3 Days

While the romance of the capital is largely contained within the Lower and Upper Towns of Vieux-Québec, there is much to experience outside the old city. And though the suggested itineraries for the first 2 days can easily be extended over 3 days, especially if children and those with limited mobility are involved, do try to make time for at least one or two of the following attractions. *Start: Take a taxi ride to the Musée des Beaux-Arts (although it isn't too long a stroll, about 30 min., for those so inclined).*

---

❶ Musée des Beaux-Arts du Québec ☆☆

Standing at the southwestern end of the Parc des Champs-de-Bataille (Battlefields Park, also known as the Plains of Abraham), the capital's most important art museum focuses on the works of Québec-born painters and sculptors. Jean-Paul Riopelle, one of the best-known abstract expressionists, has his own permanent exhibition. Other galleries feature works of provincial artists from the earliest days of the colony to the present. The original

1933 museum is now connected to an adjacent structure by a glass-roofed pavilion that houses the reception area, museum shop, and café. Note the presence of the last, for you might wish to return for lunch as it is one of the better eateries in the area. See p. 240.

Walk outside and around back to:

❷ Parc des Champs-de-Bataille ☆☆

Get some fresh air with a stroll through the 108 hectares (267 acres) that is Canada's first national urban park and the city's playground. Within the park are two Martello towers, cylindrical stone defensive structures built between 1808 and 1812, as well as cycling and rollerblading paths, picnic grounds, and a bandstand called Kiosque Edwin-Bélanger where free concerts are given in the summer. See p. 240.

Go to the main street, Grand-Allée, near to the Musée, and cross over to the perpendicular street av. Cartier.

❸ Avenue Cartier

Opposite the museum, avenue Cartier is a street of intriguing shops and restaurants. Foodies will want to check out **Les Halles du Petit-Cartier,** 1191 av. Cartier, near rue Fraser. The indoor mall has shops that sell fish, meats, cheeses, produce, pâtés, and deli treats. It's open 7 days a week. Down the street is one of the largest **SAQ** outlets in the city, selling a wide selection of wines and spirits. See p. 227 and 266.

❹ RESTAURANT LE GRAFFITI

You could put together an entirely satisfying *pique-nique* at Les Halles, but if you'd prefer a sit-down lunch, a solid candidate is Graffiti. It's an ebullient neighborhood establishment, a mostly Italian trattoria with more than sufficient pastas on the card, but with forays into less-expected areas, such as roasted pike with leeks and toasted almonds. 1191 av. Cartier (📞 418/529-4949).

❺ Grande-Allée

Walk back toward Haute-Ville along the Grande-Allée. It's a lot easier this way, as it's mostly downhill. In about 3 blocks, the shoulder-to-shoulder rows of cafés and clubs begin, with one of the largest on the right, **Maurice** (p. 268). You might want to keep it in mind for this evening; it's a one-stop dining and entertainment emporium, with terrace bars, a good restaurant, **VooDoo Grill** ⦵ (p. 227), and a disco.

Continue on Grand-Allée until to the commanding Second Empire château on your left.

❻ Hôtel du Parlement

This august structure houses the legislative body that Québécois proudly proclaim their "National Assembly." The building can be toured on your own, but there are free 30-minute guided tours in both French and English (as well as Spanish and Italian). Among the best sights are the Assembly Chamber and the Room of the Old Legislative Council. See p. 243.

Exiting, the walls of the old city are directly in front of you.

4

Getting to Know Montréal

Getting oriented in Montréal is remarkably easy. The airport is only 23km (14 miles) away, and once you're in town, the Métro (subway) system is fast and efficient. Walking, of course, is the best way to enjoy and appreciate this vigorous, multidimensional city. Take it in, neighborhood by neighborhood.

1 Orientation

ARRIVING

BY PLANE The **Aéroport International Pierre-Elliot-Trudeau de Montréal** (© **800/465-1213** or 514/394-7377; www.admtl.com; airport code YUL), known less cumbersomely as Montréal-Trudeau Airport, is 23km (14 miles) southwest of downtown. A C$716-million (US$623-million/£308-million) expansion was completed in 2006, although work is currently underway to build a new area that will encompass U.S. Customs and a pre-boarding screening checkpoint. Wi-Fi is available throughout the airport. **Aéroport Mirabel,** 55km (34 miles) northwest of the city, is an all-cargo facility.

Montréal-Trudeau is served by the shuttle bus **L'Aérobus** (© **514/631-1856;** www.laerobus.qc.ca), which travels between the airport and four downtown stops, including Fairmont The Queen Elizabeth (Fairmont Le Reine Elizabeth) hotel at 900 bd. René-Lévesque ouest. One-way fares are C$14 (US$12/£6) for adults, C$13 (US$11/£5.60) for seniors, and C$11 (US$9.55/£4.75) for children. Free minibuses take passengers to 39 major hotels from the last stop at Station Centrale Berri (also known as the Station Centrale d'Autobus, the city's main bus terminal). Buses from Montréal-Trudeau run approximately every 20 to 30 minutes between 7am and 2am daily. The ride to the Fairmont stop is about 25 minutes if traffic isn't tangled.

A taxi trip to downtown Montréal is a flat fare of C$35 (US$30/£15) plus tip.

BY TRAIN Montréal has one intercity rail terminus, **Gare Centrale (Central Station)**, 895 rue de la Gauchetière ouest (© **514/989-2626**), below Fairmont The Queen Elizabeth hotel. The station is connected to the Métro subway system (Bonaventure Station).

BY BUS The central bus station, called **Station Centrale d'Autobus** (© **514/ 842-2281**), is at 505 bd. de Maisonneuve est. It has a bar, a cafeteria, and an information booth. Beneath the terminal is the Berri-UQAM Métro station, the junction of several important Métro lines and a good starting point for trips to most quarters of the city. (UQAM—pronounced "*Oo*-kahm"—stands for Université de Québec à Montréal.) Alternatively, taxis usually line up outside the terminal building.

BY CAR For driving directions to Montréal, see "Getting There," in chapter 2.

Tips   Montréal: Where the Sun Rises in the South

For the duration of your visit to Montréal, you'll need to accept local directional conventions, strange as they may seem. The city borders the St. Lawrence River, and as far locals are concerned, that's south, looking toward the United States. Never mind that the river, in fact, runs almost north and south at that point. For this reason, it has been observed that Montréal is the only city in the world where the sun rises in the south. Don't fight it: Face the river. That's south. Turn around. That's north. *Tout est clair?*

To ease the confusion, the directions given throughout the Montréal chapters conform to this local directional tradition. However, the maps in this book also have the true compass on them.

When examining a map of the city, note that prominent thoroughfares such as rue Ste-Catherine and boulevard René-Lévesque are said to run either "east" or "west," with the dividing line being boulevard St-Laurent, which runs "north" and "south." For streets that run east and west, the numbers start at St-Laurent and then *go in both directions.* They're labeled either *est,* for east, or *ouest,* for west. That means that an address at 500 *est* is actually very far from 501 *ouest,* as opposed to directly across the street.

VISITOR INFORMATION

The main information center for visitors in downtown Montréal is the large **Infotouriste Centre,** at 1255 rue Peel (© **877/266-5687** or 514/873-2015; Métro: Peel). It's open daily and the bilingual staff can provide suggestions for accommodations, dining, car rentals, and attractions.

In Vieux-Montréal (Old Montréal) there's a small **Tourist Information Office** at 174 rue Notre-Dame est, at the corner of Place Jacques-Cartier (Métro: Champ-de-Mars). It's open daily in warmer months, Wednesday through Sunday in winter, and has brochures, maps, and a helpful staff.

The city of Montréal maintains a terrific website at **www.tourisme-montreal.org,** and the Québec province an equally good one at **www.bonjourquebec.com.**

CITY LAYOUT

For a map of greater Montréal, please see the color insert at the front of this guide.

MAIN ARTERIES & STREETS   In **downtown Montréal,** the principal streets running east-west include boulevard René-Lévesque, rue Ste-Catherine (*rue* is the French word for "street"), boulevard de Maisonneuve, and rue Sherbrooke. The north-south arteries include rue Crescent, rue McGill, rue St-Denis, and boulevard St-Laurent, which serves as the line of demarcation between east and west Montréal. Most of the downtown areas in this book lie to the west of boulevard St-Laurent.

In **Plateau Mont-Royal,** northeast of the downtown area, major streets are avenue du Mont-Royal and avenue Laurier. In **Vieux-Montréal,** rue St-Jacques, rue Notre-Dame, and rue St-Paul are the major streets, along with rue de la Commune, the waterfront road that hugs the promenade bordering the Flueve Saint-Laurent (St. Lawrence River).

Impressions

You cannot fancy you are in America; everything about it conveys the idea of a substantial, handsomely built European town, with modern improvements of half English, half French architecture.

—Lt. Col. B. W. A. Sleigh, *Pine Forests and Hacmatack Clearings*, 1853

In addition to the maps in this book, neighborhood street plans are available online at www.tourisme-montreal.org and from the information centers listed above.

FINDING AN ADDRESS   Boulevard St-Laurent is the dividing point between east and west (*est* and *ouest*) in Montréal. There's no equivalent division for north and south (*nord* and *sud*)—the numbers start at the river and climb from there, just as the topography does. The odd numbers are on the east and the even numbers on the west.

For the streets that run east to west, it's a little trickier: The numbers start at boulevard St-Laurent and then go *in both directions*. That means, for instance, that 351 St-Paul ouest, where the café Olive & Gourmando sits, is blocks and blocks from 350 St-Paul est, the address for Marche Bonsecours—and not across the street. Make sure you know your east from your west, and confirm the cross street for all addresses.

In earlier days, Montréal was split geographically along ethnic lines. Those who spoke English lived predominantly west of boulevard St-Laurent, and French speakers were concentrated to the east. Things still do sound more French as you walk east: Street names and Métro station names change from Peel and Atwater to Papineau and Beaudry. The "ethnic split" is a little farther west from boulevard St-Laurent, roughly at rue de Bleury/avenue de Parc.

THE NEIGHBORHOODS IN BRIEF

Centre Ville/Downtown This area contains the most striking elements of the dramatic Montréal skyline and includes most of the city's large luxury and first-class hotels, principal museums, corporate headquarters, main railroad station, and department stores. The district is loosely bounded by rue Sherbrooke to the north, boulevard René-Lévesque to the south, boulevard St-Laurent to the east, and rue Drummond to the west. Within this neighborhood is the area formerly known as "The Golden Square Mile," an Anglophone district once characterized by dozens of mansions erected by the wealthy Scottish and English merchants and industrialists who dominated the city's politics and social life well into the 20th century. Many of those stately homes were torn down when skyscrapers began to rise here after World War II, but some remain. At the northern edge of the downtown area is the urban campus of prestigious McGill University, which retains its Anglophone identity.

Vieux-Montréal The city was born here in 1642, down by the river at Pointe-à-Callière, and today, especially in summer, activity centers around Place Jacques-Cartier, where café tables line narrow terraces and street performers, strolling locals, and tourists congregate. The area is larger than it might seem at first, bounded on the north by rue St-Antoine, once the "Wall Street" of Montréal and still home to some banks, and on the south by the Vieux-Port (Old Port), a waterfront promenade bordering rue de la

Commune that provides welcome breathing room for cyclists, in-line skaters, and picnickers. To the east, Vieux-Montréal is bordered by rue Berri and to the west, by rue McGill. Several small but intriguing museums are housed in historic buildings, and the architectural heritage of the district has been substantially preserved. Restored 18th- and 19th-century structures have been adapted for use as shops, boutique hotels, studios, galleries, cafés, bars, offices, and apartments. In the evening, many of the finer buildings are illuminated.

Plateau Mont-Royal Northeast of the downtown area, this may be the part of the city where Montréalers feel most at home—away from the chattering pace of downtown and the more touristed Vieux-Montréal. Bounded roughly by boulevard St-Joseph to the north, rue Sherbrooke to the south, avenue Papineau to the east, and rue St-Urbain to the west, the Plateau has a vibrant ethnicity that fluctuates with each new surge in immigration. Rue St-Denis (see below) runs the length of the district and is to Montréal what boulevard St-Germain is to Paris, while boulevard St-Laurent, running parallel, has a more polyglot flavor.

Known to all as "The Main," St-Laurent was the boulevard first encountered by foreigners tumbling off ships at the waterfront. They simply shouldered their belongings and walked north, peeling off into adjoining streets when they heard familiar tongues or smelled the drifting aromas of food they once cooked in the old country. New arrivals still come here to start their lives in Montréal. Without its gumbo of languages and cultures, St-Laurent would be another urban eyesore. But ground-floor windows here are filled with glistening golden chickens, collages of shoes and pastries

and aluminum cookware, curtains of sausages, and the daringly far-fetched garments of those designers on the forward edge of Montréal's active fashion industry. Many warehouses and former tenements have been converted to house this panoply of shops, bars, and high- and low-cost eateries, their often-garish signs drawing eyes away from the still-dilapidated upper stories above. (See chapter 8 for a walking tour of this fascinating neighborhood.)

Parc du Mont-Royal Not many cities have a mountain at their core. Okay, reality insists that Montréal doesn't either, and that what it calls a "mountain" most other people would call a "large hill." Still, Montréal is named for it—the "Royal Mountain"—and as a park, it's a soothing urban pleasure to drive, walk, or take a horse-drawn calèche to the top of for a view of the city and St. Lawrence River. The famous American landscape architect Frederick Law Olmsted, who created New York City's Central Park, designed Parc du Mont-Royal, which opened in 1876. On its far slope are two cemeteries, one that used to be Anglophone and Protestant, the other Francophone and Catholic—reminders of the linguistic and cultural division that persists in the city. With its trails for strolling, hiking, and cross-country skiing, the park is well used by Montréalers, who refer to it simply and affectionately as "The Mountain."

Rue Crescent One of Montréal's major dining and nightlife districts lies in the western shadow of the massed phalanxes of downtown skyscrapers. While a few streets on its northern end house luxury boutiques in Victorian brownstones, its southern end holds dozens of restaurants, bars, and clubs of all styles between Sherbrooke and René-Lévesque, centering on rue Crescent and spilling over onto neighboring streets. The Anglophone origins of the quarter are evident in the street names: Stanley, Drummond, Crescent, Bishop, and MacKay. The party atmosphere that pervades after dark never quite fades, and it builds to crescendos as weekends approach, especially in warm weather, when the quarter's largely 20- and 30-something denizens spill out into sidewalk cafés and onto balcony terraces.

The Village The city's gay and lesbian enclave, one of North America's largest, runs east along rue Ste-Catherine from rue St-Hubert to rue Papineau and onto side streets. A compact but vibrant district, it's filled with clothing stores, antiques shops, dance clubs, and cafés. A rainbow, symbolic of the gay community, marks the Beaudry Métro station, in the heart of the neighborhood. Two major annual festivals are Divers/Cité in July and Black & Blue in October.

St-Denis Rue St-Denis, running from the Latin Quarter downtown near rue Ste-Catherine est and continuing north into the Plateau Mont-Royal district, is the thumping central artery of Francophone Montréal, thick with cafés, bistros, offbeat shops, and lively nightspots. At the southern end of St-Denis, near the concrete campus of the Université du Québec à Montréal (UQAM), the avenue is decidedly student-oriented, with indie rock cranked up in the inexpensive bars and clubs, and kids in jeans and leather swapping philosophical insights and telephone numbers. It is rife with the visual messiness that characterizes student/ bohemian quarters.

Farther north, above Sherbrooke, a raffish quality persists along the facing rows of three- and four-story Victorian row houses, but the average age of residents and visitors nudges past 30. Prices are higher, too, and some of the city's better restaurants are located here. This is a district for taking the pulse of Francophone life, not for absorbing art and culture of the refined sort, for there are no museums or important galleries on St-Denis, nor is most of the architecture notable. But, then, that relieves visitors of the chore of obligatory sightseeing and allows them to take in the passing scene—just as the locals do—over bowls of café au lait at any of the numerous terraces that line the avenue.

Mile End Adjoining Plateau Mont-Royal at its upper west corner, this blossoming neighborhood is contained by rue St-Laurent on the east, avenue Du Parc on the west, rue Bernard in the north, and boulevard St-Joseph on the south. Although it is outside the usual tourist orbit, it has a growing number of retail attractions, including designer clothing and household goods. There has been a surge of worthwhile restaurants here in recent years, too, several of which are reviewed in chapter 6. The remnants of what some still call Greektown are found along avenue du Parc, largely in the form of social clubs and taverns.

Ile Ste-Hélène & Ile Notre-Dame St. Helen's Island in the St. Lawrence River was altered extensively to become the site of Expo '67, Montréal's very successful World's Fair. In the 4 years before the Expo opened, construction crews doubled its surface area with landfill and then went on to create beside it an island that hadn't existed before, Ile Notre-Dame. Much of the earth needed to do this was dredged up from the bottom of the St. Lawrence River, and 15 million tons of rock from the excavations for the Métro and the Décarie Expressway were carried in by truck. When Expo closed, the city government preserved the site and a few of the exhibition buildings. Parts were used for the 1976 Olympics, and today Ile Ste-Hélène is home to Montréal's popular casino and an amusement park, La Ronde. In June, the Grand Prix of Canada is held on the racing track on Ile Notre-Dame. The islands, connected by two bridges, now comprise the recently designated Parc Jean-Drapeau, almost entirely car-free and accessible by Métro.

Quartier International When the crosstown highway, Route 720, was constructed some years ago, it left behind a desolate swath of derelict buildings, parking lots, and empty spaces roughly located smack-dab between downtown and Vieux- Montréal. Bounded, more or less, by rue St-Antoine on the south, avenue Viger, under the highway, on the north, rue St-Urbain on the east, and rue University on the west, this no-man's land is slowly being spruced up with new parks, office buildings, and a recently expanded Palais des Congrès (Convention Center). A small plaza, opposite the west end of the Convention Center, is named for Jean-Paul-Piopelle, a prominent Québec artist of the latter half of the 20th century. One of his sculptures stands there. By some definitions, the Quartier incorporates the World Trade Center Montréal, a complex of brokerage houses, law firms, and import-export companies.

Chinatown Similarly tucked in just north of Vieux-Montréal, Montréal's pocket Chinatown is mostly restaurants and a tiny park, with the occasional grocery, laundry, church, and small business. Community spirit is strong— it has had to be to resist the bulldozers of commercial proponents of redevelopment—and Chinatown's inhabitants remain faithful to their traditions despite the encroaching modernism all around them. Bounded on the north by boulevard René-Lévesque and centered on the intersection of rue Clark and rue de la Gauchetière (pedestrianized at this point), there are fancy gates to the area on boulevard St-Laurent, guarded by white stone lions.

The Underground City During Montréal's long (long) winters, life slows on the streets of downtown as people escape into *la ville souterraine,* a parallel subterranean universe. Down there, in a controlled climate that's eternally spring, it's possible to arrive at the railroad station, check into a hotel, shop, go out for dinner, see a movie, attend a concert—all without donning an overcoat or putting on snow boots.

This underground "city" evolved when major building developments in the downtown—such as Place Ville-Marie (the city's first skyscraper), Place Bonaventure, Complexe Desjardins, Palais des Congrès, and Place des Arts—put their below-street-level areas to profitable use, leasing space for shops and other enterprises. Over time, in fits and starts and with no master plan in place, these spaces became connected with Métro stations and then with each other. It became possible to ride long distances and walk the shorter ones, through mazes of corridors, tunnels, and plazas. There are now more than 1,700 shops, hundreds of restaurants and food courts, and 40 cinemas and theaters down there.

Admittedly, the term "underground city" is not entirely accurate because of how some complexes funnel people through their own spaces. In Place Bonaventure, for instance, passengers may leave the Métro and wander on the same level only to find themselves peering out a window several floors above the street.

The city beneath the city has obvious advantages, including no threats of traffic accidents and avoidance of winter slush (or summer rain). Natural light is let in wherever possible, which drastically reduces the feeling of claustrophobia that some malls evoke. However, the underground city covers a vast area, without the convenience of a logical street grid, and can be confusing. There are plenty of signs, but it's wise to make careful note of landmarks at key corners along your route if you want to return to the same starting point. Expect to get lost anyway—but, being that you're in an underground maze, consider it part of the fun.

2 Getting Around

BY METRO

For speed and economy, nothing beats Montréal's Métro system for getting around. The stations are marked on the street by blue-and-white signs that show a circle enclosing a down-pointing arrow. Although starting to show its age (the system has run at a deficit in recent years), and recently afflicted with waves of graffiti, the Métro's relatively clean, quiet trains whisk passengers through an expanding network of underground tunnels. In April 2007, the orange line (no. 2 on our map) was extended three stops farther into the north. The new end station is Montmorency, making it the train "direction" you'll see on platforms (instead of Henri-Bourassa).

Fares are by the ride, not by distance. **Single rides** cost C$2.75 (US$2.40/£1.15), a **strip of six tickets** is C$12 (US$10/£5.05), and a **weekly pass,** good for unlimited rides, is C$19 (US$17/£8.15). Reduced fares are available to children and, with special Métro ID cards, seniors and students. **Tourist passes** are good for short visits: unlimited Métro rides for 1 day for C$9 (US$7.85/£3.85) or 3 days for C$17 (US$15/£7.30). Buy tickets at the booth in any station or from a convenience store.

To enter the system, slip your ticket into the slot in the turnstile or show your pass to the attendant in the booth. If you plan to transfer to a bus, take a transfer ticket *(correspondence)* from the machine just inside the turnstile; every Métro station has one, and it allows you a free transfer to a bus wherever you exit the subway. Remember to take the transfer ticket at the station where you *first* enter the system. If you start a trip by bus and intend to continue on the Métro, ask the driver for a transfer.

The Métro runs from about 5:30am to 12:30am. If you plan to be out late, check the website at www.stm.info or call © **514/786-4636** for the exact times of the last train on each line.

The Métro is not immune to transit strikes; an action in May 2007 led to reduced hours of operation for several days. And one caveat: Convenient as the Métro is, there can be substantial distances between stations, and accessibility is sometimes difficult for people with mobility problems. For example, to get from the lobby of the centrally located Fairmont The Queen Elizabeth hotel to the platform of the Bonaventure station "directly beneath" takes the equivalent of 3 city blocks and the use of 4 escalators.

BY BUS

Buses cost the same as Métro trains, and Métro tickets are good on buses, too. Exact change is required to pay bus fares in cash. Although they run throughout the city (and give riders the decided advantage of traveling aboveground), buses don't run as frequently or as swiftly as the Métro. If you start a trip on the bus and want to transfer to the Métro, ask the bus driver for a transfer ticket.

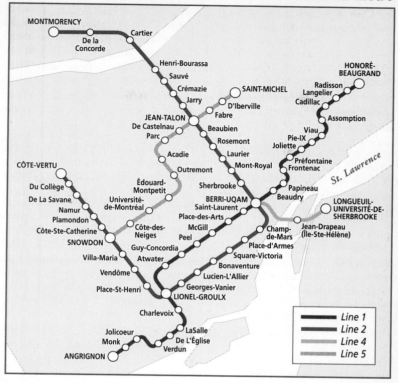

Montréal Métro

MONTMORENCY
De la Concorde
Cartier
Henri-Bourassa
Sauvé
Crémazie
Jarry
SAINT-MICHEL
D'Iberville
JEAN-TALON
De Castelnau
Parc
Fabre
Beaubien
Rosemont
HONORÉ-BEAUGRAND
Radisson
Langelier
Cadillac
Assomption
Viau
Pie-IX
Joliette
Acadie
Laurier
Mont-Royal
Préfontaine
Frontenac
CÔTE-VERTU
Outremont
Sherbrooke
Papineau
Beaudry
St. Lawrence
Du Collège
De La Savane
Namur
Plamondon
Côte-Ste-Catherine
SNOWDON
Édouard-Montpetit
Université-de-Montréal
BERRI-UQAM
Saint-Laurent
Place-des-Arts
McGill
Peel
LONGUEUIL-UNIVERSITÉ-DE-SHERBROOKE
Côte-des-Neiges
Guy-Concordia
Atwater
Champ-de-Mars
Place-d'Armes
Square-Victoria
Bonaventure
Jean-Drapeau (Île-Ste-Hélène)
Villa-Maria
Vendôme
Place-St-Henri
LIONEL-GROULX
Lucien-L'Allier
Georges-Vanier
Charlevoix
Jolicoeur
Monk
ANGRIGNON
LaSalle
De L'Église
Verdun

Line 1
Line 2
Line 4
Line 5

BY TAXI

There are plenty of taxis run by several different companies. Cabs come in a variety of colors and styles, so their principal distinguishing feature is the plastic sign on the roof. At night, the sign is illuminated when the cab is available. Fares continue to increase, largely due to hikes in gas prices, with an initial charge of C$3.15 (US$2.75) at the flag drop, C$1.45 (US$1.25) per kilometer (⅔ mile), and C55¢ (US48¢) per minute of waiting. A short ride from one point to another downtown usually costs about C$6 (US$5.20). Tip about 10% to 15%. Members of hotel and restaurant staffs can call cabs, many of which are dispatched by radio. They line up outside most large hotels or can be hailed on the street.

Montréal taxi drivers range in temperament from sullen cranks to the unstoppably loquacious. Some know their city well, others have sketchy knowledge and poor language skills, so it's a good idea to have your destination written down—with the cross street—to show your driver.

Cyclists will be glad to know that several taxi companies participate in the "Taxi+Vélo" (*vélo* means bicycle) program. Call one of them, specify that you have a bike to transport, and a cab with a specially designed rack arrives. Up to three bikes can be carried for an extra fee of C$3 (US$2.60/£1.30) each. The companies are listed at www.velo.qc.ca (search for "taxi"), or call ☎ 514/521-8356.

BY CAR

Montréal is an easy city to navigate by car. Visitors arriving by plane or train, however, will probably want to rely on public transportation and cabs. A rental car can come in handy, though, for trips outside of town or if you plan to drive to Québec City.

RENTALS Terms, cars, and prices for rentals are similar to those in the United States, and all the larger U.S. companies operate in Canada. Basic rates are about the same from company to company, although a little comparison shopping can unearth modest savings. A charge is usually levied when you return a car in a city other than the one in which it was rented.

All the companies listed here have counters at Trudeau Airport (the local numbers at the terminal are listed here). Major car-rental companies include **Avis** (🖉 800/437-0358 or 514/636-1902); **Budget** (🖉 800/268-8900 or 514/636-0052); **Hertz** (🖉 800/263-0600 or 514/636-9530); **National** (🖉 800/387-4747 or 514/636-9030); and **Thrifty** (🖉 800/367-2277 or 514/631-5567).

If you'll be doing much driving in Montréal, pick up the pocket-size atlas by JDM Géo. It's published by MapArt (**www.mapart.com**) and sold at gas stations throughout Canada. The company also sells good maps for the Laurentians and Cantons-de-l'Est regions, discussed in chapter 11.

GASOLINE Gasoline and diesel fuel are sold by the liter, and are significantly more expensive than in the United States (Europeans will find the prices less of a shock). With recent prices of C$1.15 a liter (US$1/49p), and 3.78 liters to 1 gallon, that comes out to about US$4.35 a gallon. It costs about C$40 (US$35/£17) to fill the tank of a small car with the lowest grade of unleaded gasoline.

PARKING It can be difficult to park for free on the heavily trafficked streets of downtown Montréal, but there are plenty of metered spaces. Look around before walking off without paying. Meters are set well back from the curb so they won't be buried by plowed snow in winter. Parking costs C$1 an hour, and meters are in effect weekdays until 9pm and weekends until 6pm. If there are no parking meters in sight, you're not off the hook. The city has started to install new black metal kiosks that serve a number of spaces on a street. Look for a column about 6 feet tall with a white "P" in a blue circle. Press the "English" button, enter the letter from the space where you are parked, then pay with cash or a credit card, following instructions on the screen.

In addition, check for signs noting restrictions, usually showing a red circle with a diagonal slash. The words LIVRAISON SEULEMENT, for example, mean "delivery only." Most downtown shopping complexes have underground parking lots, as do the big downtown hotels. Some of the hotels don't charge extra if you want to take your car in and out during the day—useful if you plan to do some sightseeing by car.

DRIVING RULES The limited-access expressways in Québec are called *autoroutes,* distances are given in kilometers (km), and speed limits are given in kilometers per hour (kmph). Because French is the official language of the province, some highway signs are in French only, although Montréal's autoroutes and bridges often bear dual-language signs.

One traffic signal function often confuses newcomers: Should you wish to make a turn and you know that the street runs in the correct direction, you may be surprised to initially see just a green arrow pointing straight ahead instead of a green light permitting the turn. The arrow is just to give pedestrians time to cross the intersection.

Fun Fact **July 1: Citywide Moving Day!**

Montréal is an island of renters, and close to 100,000 of them move from old apartments to new ones every July 1—that date, and only that date. It coincides with Canada's National Day, ensuring that separatist-minded Francophone Québécois won't have time to celebrate a holiday they have no intention of observing anyway.

All but certain to be miserably hot and humid, July 1 is a trial that can, nevertheless, be hilarious to observe. See families struggle to get bedroom sets and large appliances down narrow outdoor staircases! Watch sidewalks become obstacle courses of baby cribs, bicycles, and overflowing cardboard boxes! Hear the cacophony of horns as streets become clogged with every serviceable van, truck, and SUV!

Later in the day, hundreds of people get to their new digs and discover gifts of junk no longer desired by their predecessors—busted furniture, pantries of old food, pitiful plants.

No one can explain why reason didn't prevail long ago in the form of a mandated staggered schedule. One thing that doesn't take much thought, though, is that you'll want to either be someplace else on that day, or put on a strong backpack to walk around and do some good trash-picking.

After a few moments, the light will turn from an arrow to a regular green light and you can proceed.

Turning right on a red light is prohibited on the island of Montréal, except where specifically allowed by an additional green arrow. Outside the island of Montréal, it is now legal to turn right after stopping at red lights. The change has caused authorities to put up numerous signs at what they believe to be dangerous intersections specifically prohibiting that move.

Seat-belt use is required by law while driving or riding in a car in Québec province.

Note: Too many of the region's drivers take perverse pride in their reputation as dangerously fast at the wheel and are prone to such maneuvers as sudden U-turns or cutting across two lanes to snare a parking space. Growing indignation at such practices, with newspapers decrying excess speed and the accidents that result from it, doesn't seem to have curbed the behavior. Be aware.

Where to Stay in Montréal

Montréal hoteliers go the extra mile to make guests feel welcome, at least in part because there are proportionally more hotel rooms here than in other North American cities of similar size, still more are constructed every year, and all these hotels are hoping to have their rooms filled throughout the year. With high competition, the diminished exchange rate of the U.S. dollar, and the relative strength of the British pound, this is the place to step up in class.

Accommodations options range from soaring glass skyscrapers to grand boulevard hotels to converted row houses. Stylish inns and boutique luxury hotels appear in ever-increasing numbers, especially in Vieux-Montréal, and several of them are recommended in this chapter. Except in bed-and-breakfasts, visitors can almost always count on discounts and package deals, especially on weekends, when the hotels' business clients have packed their bags and gone home.

Though they don't usually offer discounts, B&Bs boast cozier settings than many hotels, often (but not always) at lower prices than comparable hotels. B&Bs also give visitors the opportunity to get to know a Montréaler or two. By the nature of the trade, bed-and-breakfast owners are among the most outgoing and knowledgeable guides one might want. For information about downtown B&Bs, contact **Bed & Breakfast Downtown Network,** 3458 av. Laval (at rue Sherbrooke), Montréal, PQ H2X 3C8 (© **800/ 267-5180** or 514/289-9749; www.bb montreal.qc.ca). As a referral agency for homeowners who have one or more rooms available for guests, this company represents about 30 properties with 46 guest rooms. Doubles range from C$65 to C$150 (US$57–US$130/£28–£65). Rooms with private bathrooms are more expensive than those that share facilities. Accommodations and the rules of individual homeowners vary significantly, so it's wise to ask all pertinent questions upfront, such as if children are welcome or if all guests share bathrooms. Deposits are usually required, with the balance payable upon arrival. American Express, MasterCard, and Visa are accepted.

See "Tips on Accommodations" in chapter 2 for suggestions on how to score the lodging of your dreams.

STAR SYSTEM   The tourist authorities in Québec province have a six-level rating system (zero to five stars) for all establishments offering six or more rooms to travelers. An ocher-and-brown shield bearing the assigned rating is found near the entrance to most hotels and inns. The Québec system is based on quantitative measures such as the range of services and amenities. No star is assigned to hotels or inns meeting only basic minimum standards, and five stars are reserved for establishments that are deemed exceptional. Most of the recommendations listed below have gotten at least three stars from the state system.

The stars you see in the reviews in this chapter are based on Frommer's *own* rating system, which assigns between zero and three stars. The Frommer's ratings are more subjective than the state's, taking into account such considerations as price-to-value ratios, quality of service, location, helpfulness of staff, and the presence of such facilities as spas and exercise rooms.

RATES   The rates quoted in the listings in this chapter are "rack rates"—the maximum rates that a hotel charges for rooms for double occupancy. The lowest room rate listed here is for off-season months, the highest for summer, major festivals, and holidays. These rates are used to divide the hotels into four price categories, ranging from "Very Expensive" to "Inexpensive," for easy reference. But rack rates are only guidelines, and most people end up paying less, often *much* less. See "Saving on Your Hotel Room" in chapter 2.

You'll find the highest hotel rates during the region's busiest times, from May to October, reaching a peak in July and August. High rates also pop up during the frequent summer festivals, annual holidays (Canadian or American), Grand Prix days in Montréal in June, and winter carnivals in January and February. (Festivals and dates are listed in chapter 2 on p. 13.) For those periods, reserve well in advance, especially if you're looking for special rates or packages. Most other times, expect to find plenty of available rooms.

CATEGORIES   The hotels listed below are near most city attractions, in downtown and Vieux-Montréal. The listings below are categorized first by neighborhood, then by price.

All rooms have private bathrooms unless otherwise noted. Many of the more luxurious hotels have stopped providing coffeemakers in their rooms, so check if this feature is important to you. Many hotels are also in the process of adding Wi-Fi to either parts of or all of their facilities; ask about availability when reserving a room.

Most of the hotels in Montréal are entirely nonsmoking. Those that aren't have a limited number of smoking rooms available; check with the hotel before booking.

TAXES   Unless specifically noted, prices given here do *not* include taxes. See "Taxes" in "Fast Facts: Montréal & Québec City" in chapter 2.

1 Best Hotel Bets

- **Best Historic Hotel:** No contest. The **Ritz-Carlton Montréal,** 1228 rue Sherbrooke ouest (© **800/363-0366** or 514/842-4212), has been around since 1913, giving it a half-century lead on the closest competition. See p. 73.
- **Best for Business Travelers:** A closer call, with several worthy candidates, but **Fairmont The Queen Elizabeth,** 900 bd. René-Lévesque ouest (© **800/441-1414** or 514/861-3511), gets the nod for its central location atop the railroad station, concierge floors, a fully equipped health club, and excellent bus connections to the airport. See p. 68.
- **Best New(ish) Luxury Hotel Downtown:** The nearby Omni, Ritz, and Vogue are challenged by the first Canadian branch of a pervasive French chain, the **Sofitel,** 1155 rue Sherbrooke ouest (© **514/285-9000**), which matches its rivals in every detail. See p. 69.
- **Best for a Romantic Getaway:** With ancient cut-stone walls, swags of velvet and brocade, and tilting floors that Benjamin Franklin once trod upon—not to mention a baronial dining room and stonewalled outdoor terrace, the **Hostellerie Pierre du Calvet,** 405 rue Bonsecours (© **866/544-1725** or 514/282-1725), provokes memories of lovers' hotels by the Seine. See p. 77.

- **Best Established Boutique Hotel:** When it opened, **Hôtel Le Germain,** 2050 rue Mansfield (© **877/333-2050** or 514/849-2050), brought a needed jolt of panache to the too-often-stodgy corps of downtown business hotels, and helped inspire a boom in similarly small, stylish hotels in Vieux-Montréal. See p. 69.

- **Best New Boutique Hotels (Posh Category):** The **Hôtel Le St-James,** 355 rue St-Jacques ouest, Vieux-Montréal (© **866/841-3111** or 514/841-3111), raises the bar to an almost impossibly high level, with a superbly sybaritic spa and gorgeous grand hall. See p. 75. The **Hôtel Nelligan,** 106 rue St-Paul ouest, Vieux-Montréal (© **877/788-2040** or 514/788-2040), which expanded from 63 to 105 units in 2007, counters with a great full-service restaurant and rooftop terrace. See p. 78.

- **Best New Boutique Hotels (Minimalist Category):** Also in Vieux-Montréal, **Hôtel St-Paul,** 355 rue McGill (© **866/380-2202** or 514/380-2222), softens its austere lines with pale cream walls and fur throws, while the **Hôtel Gault,** at 449 rue Ste-Hélène (© **866/904-1616** or 514/904-1616), leaves its raw concrete walls uncovered and uses candy-colored furniture that was startlingly modern in the 1950s. See p. 78 for Hôtel St-Paul and p. 77 for Hôtel Gault.

- **Best Lobby for Pretending That You're Rich:** A tie—the woody, hushed **Ritz-Carlton Montréal** (p. 73) exudes old money, while the newer **Hôtel Le St-James** (p. 75) caters to the international Bluetooth-using bespoked-suit-wearing set.

- **Best B&B:** Located in a 1723 house in Vieux-Montréal, **Auberge Les Passants du Sans Soucy,** 171 rue St-Paul ouest (© **514/842-2634**), is more upscale and stylish than most of its peers, and it's located near the top restaurants and clubs in the old town. See p. 80.

- **Best Service:** It's tough to choose among the troops at the **Hôtel Le St-James** (p. 75), the **Ritz-Carlton Montréal** (p. 73), and the **Hôtel InterContinental Montréal,** 360 rue St-Antoine ouest (© **514/987-9900;** see p. 78). All three teams display an almost equal amount of grace and care when it comes to tending to their guests.

- **Best Hotel Health Club: Hôtel Omni Mont-Royal,** 1050 rue Sherbrooke ouest (© **800/843-6664** or 514/284-1110), lays on yoga classes, free weights and weight machines, saunas, a steam room, whirlpools, a year-round heated outdoor pool, and massages to recover from the workout. See p. 74. A close second: **Fairmont The Queen Elizabeth** (see below).

2 Centre Ville/Downtown

VERY EXPENSIVE

Fairmont The Queen Elizabeth (Le Reine Elizabeth) ★★   Montréal's largest hotel—it has more than 1,000 rooms—has lent its august presence to the city since 1958. Its 21 floors sit atop VIA Rail's Gare Centrale (the main train station), with the Métro and popular shopping areas such as Place Ville-Marie and Place Bonaventure all accessible through underground arcades. This desirable location makes "the Queenie" a frequent choice for heads of state and touring celebrities, even though other hotels in town offer more luxurious pampering. The Fairmont Gold 18th and 19th floors (open to anyone willing to pay a premium) have a private concierge and reception and a lounge serving complimentary breakfasts and cocktail-hour canapés to go with the honor bar. Less exalted rooms on floors 4 through 17 are entirely satisfactory, furnished traditionally and featuring easy chairs, ottomans, and bright reading lamps.

The on-site spa was renovated in 2006. February 2009 will mark the 40th anniversary of John Lennon and Yoko Ono's weeklong "Bed-In for Peace" here—in suite no. 1742, if you're a fan.

900 bd. René-Lévesque ouest (at rue Mansfield), Montréal, PQ H3B 4A5. ✆ **800/441-1414** or 514/861-3511. Fax 514/954-2296. www.fairmont.com. 1,039 units. C$229–C$599 (US$199–US$521/£98–£258) double. Children 18 and under stay free in parent's room. Packages available. AE, DC, MC, V. Valet parking C$24 (US$21/£10). Métro: Bonaventure. Pets accepted. **Amenities:** 3 restaurants (French/International); 2 bars; heated indoor pool; exceptional health club and spa w/Jacuzzi, steam room, and instructors; concierge; business center; shopping arcade; 24-hr. room service; babysitting; laundry service; same-day dry cleaning; executive floors. *In room:* A/C, TV, high-speed Internet, minibar, coffeemaker, hair dryer, iron.

Hôtel Le Germain ✿✿✿

This undertaking by the owner of equally desirable boutique hotels in Québec City (Dominion 1912) and Toronto brought a big shot of panache to the downtown lodging scene, foretelling the explosion of similar hostelries in Vieux-Montréal. This one features a magical mix of Asian minimalism combined with all the Western comforts that international executives might anticipate—and a few they might not. Signature touches include the polished apples sitting in designated depressions on the shelves opposite the elevators, the big wicker chairs with fat cushions, and the beds with goose-down duvets and pillows that are so comfortable they can cure insomnia. Self-serve breakfasts feature perfect croissants, excellent café au lait fabricated by a magical machine, and newspapers in French and English, all set out on the mezzanine, near the lobby fireplace. A little too sophisticated for families, this gem of a hotel would be ideal for any other travelers. (Be careful, though: The hotel's marketing touts the venue for its "romance—a place to conceive babies.")

2050 rue Mansfield (at av. du President-Kennedy), Montréal, PQ H3A 1Y9. ✆ **877/333-2050** or 514/849-2050. Fax 514/849-1437. www.hotelgermain.com. 101 units. C$210–C$500 (US$183–US$435/£90–£215) double. Packages available. Rates include breakfast. AE, DC, MC, V. Valet parking C$23 (US$20/£9.90). Métro: Peel. Pets accepted. **Amenities:** Restaurant (eclectic); bar; exercise room; concierge; business center, limited room service; in-room massage; babysitting; dry cleaning. *In room:* A/C, TV, free Wi-Fi, CD player, minibar, hair dryer, iron, safe, umbrella.

Sofitel ✿✿

Creating a stir as the first downtown luxury hotel in many years, this representative of the French chain transformed a bland 1970s office tower into an instantly coveted destination for visiting celebrities and the power elite. It wows from the moment of arrival, from the light-filled stone-and-wood lobby to the universally warm welcome of the staff. The 100 standard rooms (called "Superior") make full use of current technology, and beds have Canadian goose-down duvets. Walls are painted a soothing oatmeal-cream and decorated with black-and-white photos of Montréal by local photographers and original paintings. Furnishings are made from Québec-grown cherrywood. Although chairs with right angled backs are a bit too over-designed for comfort, the thrust-desks attached to the wall are easy to use from either side. Bathrooms have an Asian-touch (bamboo spear in a vase, dimmer lights). Some floors are nonsmoking. The ambitious **Renoir** restaurant (p. 87) features a bar and outdoor terrace. Catering to international and business guests whose bodies are on different time zones, the exercise room is open 24 hours. In the early morning, towels and chilled water are put out in the lobby for joggers.

1155 rue Sherbrooke ouest (at Peel), Montréal, PQ H3A 2N3. ✆ **514/285-9000.** Fax 514/289-1155. www.sofitel. com. 258 units. C$195–C$405 (US$170–US$352/£84–£174) double; suites from C$295 (US$257/£127). Children under 12 stay free in parent's room. Packages available. AE, DC, MC, V. Valet parking C$26 (US$23/£11). Métro: Peel. Pets accepted. **Amenities:** Restaurant (French Provençal); bar; 24-hr. exercise room w/sauna; concierge; business center; Wi-Fi in lobby and restaurant; 24-hr. room service; in-room massage; babysitting; laundry service; same-day dry cleaning. *In room:* A/C, TV w/pay movies, high-speed Internet, CD player, minibar, hair dryer, iron, safe, telephone in bathroom.

Where to Stay in Downtown Montréal

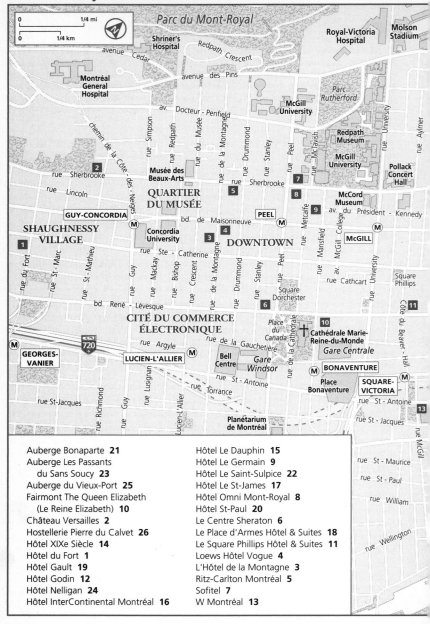

Auberge Bonaparte **21**
Auberge Les Passants
  du Sans Soucy **23**
Auberge du Vieux-Port **25**
Fairmont The Queen Elizabeth
  (Le Reine Elizabeth) **10**
Château Versailles **2**
Hostellerie Pierre du Calvet **26**
Hôtel XIXe Siècle **14**
Hôtel du Fort **1**
Hôtel Gault **19**
Hôtel Godin **12**
Hôtel Nelligan **24**
Hôtel InterContinental Montréal **16**

Hôtel Le Dauphin **15**
Hôtel Le Germain **9**
Hôtel Le Saint-Sulpice **22**
Hôtel Le St-James **17**
Hôtel Omni Mont-Royal **8**
Hôtel St-Paul **20**
Le Centre Sheraton **6**
Le Place d'Armes Hôtel & Suites **18**
Le Square Phillips Hôtel & Suites **11**
Loews Hôtel Vogue **4**
L'Hôtel de la Montagne **3**
Ritz-Carlton Montréal **5**
Sofitel **7**
W Montréal **13**

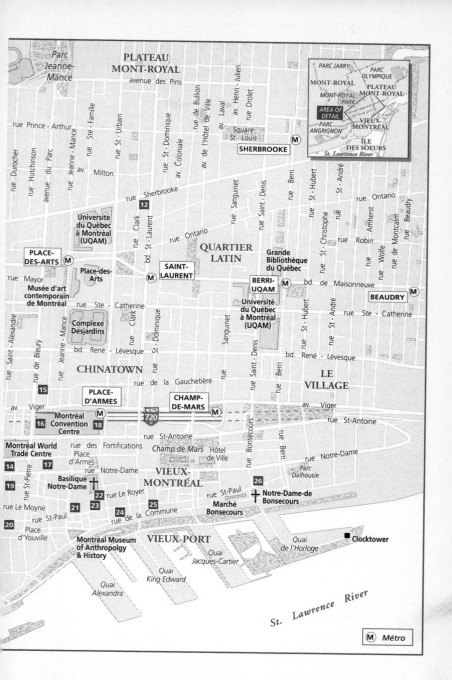

EXPENSIVE

Hôtel Godin ✦   The Godin projects the sort of voluptuous minimalism that characterizes forward-thinking design in Montréal. The owners previously launched four hot resto-lounges including **Buonanotte** (p. 99) and **Le Globe** (p. 100), both of which are a couple of blocks away. The high design works to both an advantage and a disadvantage: Decorated in a sea of gun-metal gray and chocolate brown colors and featuring low-flung beds with oversize pillows and duvets, rooms are cozy for hunkering in but maddeningly dark for anything else. Even with all the lights on, we're talking mood lighting at best. Any hopes to use the built-in wall-length desk for actual work are futile. On the other hand, the hotel's location directly at the base of the trendy boulevard St-Laurent and its fashionista restaurant and club action gives strong incentive to put down any books and pack away the computer, and indulge in eating, drinking, and then settling in for the night. A lounge adjacent to the reception serves free coffee and tea round-the-clock.

10 rue Sherbrooke ouest (at bd. St-Laurent), Montréal, PQ H2X 4C9. ⓒ 866/744-6346 or 514/843-6000. Fax 514/ 843-6810. www.hotelgodin.com. 136 units. C$159–C$299 (US$138–US$260/£68–£129) double. AE, DC, MC, V. Valet parking C$25 (US$22/£11). Packages available. Métro: St-Laurent. Pets accepted. **Amenities:** Restaurant (eclectic); 24-hr. exercise room; concierge; free Wi-Fi in lobby; in-room massage; laundry service; same-day dry cleaning. *In room:* A/C, TV w/Internet, minibar, hair dryer, safe.

L'Hôtel de la Montagne ✦   Two white lion sculptures stand sentinel at the front door, and the doorman has been known to wear a pith helmet. The fauna fixation continues in a crowded lobby that incorporates a pair of 1.8m (6-ft.) carved elephants, two gold-colored crocodile sculptures, and a nude female figure with stained-glass butterfly wings sitting atop a splashing fountain. Welcome to Montréal, Vegas-style! A French-style brasserie is the main restaurant. Lunches are available beside the pool on the roof, 20 stories up; in the evening, there's dancing under the stars. Off the lobby, a cabaret lounge featuring a piano player and jazz duos on weekends leads into **Thursday's** (p. 168), a singles bar and restaurant with a spangly disco and a terrace opening onto lively rue Crescent. After all that, the relatively serene bedrooms seem downright bland. Given all these inducements, a stay here is a genuine bargain, especially in contrast to other downtown options.

1430 rue de la Montagne (north of rue Ste-Catherine), Montréal, PQ H3G 1Z5. ⓒ 800/361-6262 or 514/288-5656. Fax 514/288-9658. www.hoteldelamontagne.com. 135 units. C$160–C$225 (US$139–US$196/£69–£97) double. Children up to 11 stay free in parent's room. Packages available. AE, DC, DISC, MC, V. Valet parking C$15 or C$30 for SUV (US$13/£6.45 or US$26/£13). Métro: Peel. Pets accepted. **Amenities:** 2 restaurants (French); 4 bars; heated outdoor pool; concierge; limited room service; laundry service; same-day dry cleaning. *In room:* A/C, TV w/pay movies, free Wi-Fi, minibar, coffeemaker, hair dryer.

Le Centre Sheraton ✦   Ever bustling, this sterling representative of the familiar brand goes about its business with efficiency and surety of purpose. That figures, since earnest people in suits make up most of the clientele. They gravitate toward the separate Club Rooms, which offers guests complimentary breakfast and a private lounge with expansive views and free evening hors d'oeuvres. The health club/spa includes an indoor pool, a sauna, a fully equipped fitness center, massage studio, and a landscaped terrace that is open in the summer. Near to the central Dorchester Square, Gare Centrale (the main train station), and the high-stepping rue Crescent dining and nightlife district, the hotel has as good a downtown location as any.

1201 bd. René-Lévesque ouest (between rue Drummond and rue Stanley), Montréal, PQ H3B 2L7. (C) **800/325-3535** or 514/878-2000. Fax 514/878-3958. www.sheraton.com/lecentre. 825 units. C$179–C$599 (US$156–US$521/£67–£258) double (club floor additional). Children under 17 stay free in parent's room. Packages available. AE, DC, DISC, MC, V. Valet parking C$26 (US$23/£11), self-parking C$19 (US$17/£8.15). Métro: Bonaventure. If you're driving, note that the entrance is on rue Drummond. Dogs accepted, but must be caged when owner is out. **Amenities:** Restaurant (international); bar; indoor pool; health club and spa; concierge (for Club floor); business center; shopping arcade; salon; limited room service; babysitting; laundry service; same-day dry cleaning; executive floors. *In room:* A/C, TV, high-speed Internet, video games, minibar, coffeemaker, hair dryer, iron, safe.

Loews Hôtel Vogue ✦✦ *(Kids)*

The Vogue created quite a stir when it opened in 1990, instantly joining the Ritz-Carlton at the top tier of the local luxury-hotel pantheon. While it is no longer the hip retreat it once was, confidence and capability resonates from every member of its staff, and luxury permeates the hotel from the lobby to the well-appointed guest rooms. Feather pillows and duvets dress the oversize beds, and all rooms feature "Ultimate Doeskin" robes by Chadsworth & Haig. Marble bathrooms are fitted with Jacuzzis—double-size in suites—and separate shower stalls. The hotel's **L'Opéra Bar** is a two-story room with floor-to-ceiling windows. For families, Loews goes beyond lending libraries of games and has special children's menus, Game Boys, and supervised recreational programs. A springtime "Sugar Season" package includes a private trip to a traditional sugar shack and advice from the hotel's executive chef, who doubles as a "syrup sommelier," about grades of maple syrup. An early morning joggers' station offers bottled water, towels, fruit, and maps to local jogging trails on nearby Mont Royal.

1425 rue de la Montagne (near rue Ste-Catherine), Montréal, PQ H3G 1Z3. (C) **866-LOEWSWB** (563-9792) or 514/285-5555. Fax 514/849-8903. www.loewshotels.com. 142 units. C$179–C$399 (US$156–US$347/£77–£172) double. Children under 18 stay free in parent's room. Packages available. AE, DC, DISC, MC, V. Valet parking C$30 (US$26/£13). Métro: Peel. Pets accepted. **Amenities:** Restaurant (international); bar; 24-hr. exercise room; children's programs; concierge; business center; 24-hr. room service; babysitting; laundry service; same-day dry cleaning. *In room:* A/C, TV w/pay movies, CD player, high-speed Internet, minibar, hair dryer, iron.

Ritz-Carlton Montréal ✦✦

In 1912, the Ritz-Carlton opened its doors to the carriage trade, and that clientele has remained faithful. Over the years, their Pierce-Arrows gave way to Rolls-Royces and Mercedes, and a few of these are always parked in readiness near the front door. A much-needed renovation restored the gloss and excellence of service that this hotel had long possessed. Rooms are large and traditional, most with tinkling glass chandeliers; some have marble fireplaces. Goose-down and non-allergenic foam pillows are standard, as are three phones and two telephone lines for each room and padded hangers. Marble bathrooms are equipped with robes and speakers carrying TV sound, and complimentary overnight shoeshine is available. The **Café de Paris** is favored for its high tea, weekend brunches, and weekday power breakfasts. Meals are served at **Le Jardin du Ritz** in summer, next to the garden's famous duck pond and its ducklings. The more hushed **Ritz Bar** has cocktails and dinner daily until 11pm.

1228 rue Sherbrooke ouest (at rue Drummond), Montréal, PQ H3G 1H6. (C) **800/363-0366** or 514/842-4212. Fax 514/842-3383. www.ritzmontreal.com. 229 units. C$180–C$239 (US$157–US$208/£77–£103) double; from C$248 (US$216/£107) and way up suite. Packages available. AE, DC, MC, V. Valet parking C$30 (US$26/£13). Métro: Peel. Pets accepted. **Amenities:** 2 restaurants (French, international); bar; small 24-hr. exercise room and access to off-site Club Sportif MAA pool and gym; concierge; 24-hr. business center; 24-hr. room service; in-room massage; babysitting; laundry service; same-day dry cleaning. *In room:* A/C, TV w/pay movies, high-speed Internet, minibar, hair dryer, iron, safe, umbrella.

MODERATE

Château Versailles ⚓ This long-popular facility underwent a remarkable transformation from a popular but dowdy inn to a full member of the growing local ranks of snappy boutique hotels. It began as a European-style pension in 1958, expanding into adjacent pre–World War I town houses. The spacious rooms have enjoyed the full decorator treatment, with navy, gold, and olive tones, fine modern furnishings with faint Deco tinges, and some Second Empire touches. Some have fireplaces. A buffet breakfast is served in the main living room, where you can sit at a small table or in an easy chair in front of a fireplace. Only one deficiency remains: the lack of an elevator to deal with the three floors. Because the hotel is the official lodging of the nearby **Musée des Beaux-Arts** (p. 109) and its price and location near rue Sherbrooke shopping are so competitive, reserve well in advance.

A modern tower across the street is the sister hotel **Le Meridien Versailles** (1808 rue Sherbrooke ouest; ℂ **888/933-8111** or 514/933-8111). It has 110 units, a fitness center, and the well-regarded restaurant **Brontë.** Rates there start at C$159 (US$138/ £68) with a variety of package deals.

1659 rue Sherbrooke ouest (at rue St-Mathieu), Montréal, PQ H3A 1E3. ℂ **888/933-8111** or 514/933-3611. Fax 514/933-8401. www.versailleshotels.com. 65 units. C$155–C$300 (US$135–US$261/£67–£129) double; suites from C$380 (US$330/£163). Rates include breakfast. Packages available. AE, DC, DISC, MC, V. Valet parking C$23 (US$20/£9.90). Métro: Guy-Concordia. Pets accepted. **Amenities:** 24-hr. exercise room w/sauna; business center; limited room service; babysitting; laundry service; same-day dry cleaning. *In room:* A/C, TV w/pay movies, high-speed Internet, Wi-Fi, CD player, minibar, coffeemaker, hair dryer, iron, safe, umbrella.

Hôtel du Fort *Kids* While hardly grand, this reliable hotel takes as its primary duty providing lodging to longer-term business travelers. That includes providing a fitness room (newly renovated) sufficient for a thorough morning workout, basic kitchenettes with fridges and microwave ovens in all rooms (the concierge can have groceries delivered), and an underground parking garage. Since all rooms are good-size and many have sofas with hide-a-beds, those same attributes are useful for small families, as well. There's even Nintendo for the kids. A buffet breakfast is served in the hotel's Louis XV Club Lounge and other meals can be taken at the Café Suprême in the adjoining Complexe du Fort mall, which also provides room service.

1390 rue du Fort (at rue Ste-Catherine), Montréal, PQ H3H 2R7. ℂ **800/565-6333** or 514/938-8333. Fax 514/938-2078. www.hoteldufort.com. 124 units. C$135–C$175 (US$117–US$152/£58–£75) double; suites from C$165 (US$144/£71). Children under 12 stay free in parent's room. AE, DC, MC, V. Métro: Guy-Concordia. **Amenities:** Exercise room; concierge; business center; limited room service; babysitting; laundry service; same-day dry cleaning. *In room:* A/C, TV w/pay movies and Nintendo, Internet, coffeemaker, hair dryer, iron, safe.

Hôtel Omni Mont-Royal ⚓⚓ *Kids* This Omni outpost is a worthy competitor to the nearby Ritz-Carlton, especially since an all-floors multimillion-dollar renovation. The coolly regal lobby, lined with marble, is softened by banks of plants and flowers. The hotel's health club, spa, and outdoor pool complex is the best in town, offering everything from Lifecyles to yoga classes to massages; nonguests can use it for C$25 (US$22/£11) adults and C$7 (US$6.10/£3) children. Rooms are large, with new-looking furnishings, and are offered in escalating categories of relative luxury. The hotel provides information for parents traveling with children at a special website, **www.omnikidsrule.com**, and special kids' meals and games. This is a great place for businesspeople, families, and honeymooners or lovebirds.

1050 rue Sherbrooke ouest (at rue Peel), Montréal, PQ H3A 2R6. ℂ **800/843-6664** or 514/284-1110. Fax 514/845-3025. www.omnihotels.com. 299 units. C$129–C$299 (US$112–US$260/£55–£129) double. Children under 17 stay free in parent's room. Packages available. AE, DC, DISC, MC, V. Valet parking C$23 (US$20/£9.90); self-parking C$15 (US$13/£6.45). Métro: Peel. Pets accepted. **Amenities:** 2 restaurants (Chinese, bistro/bar); year-round heated outdoor pool; impressive 24-hr. health club and spa; games for children; concierge; 24-hr. business center; shopping arcade; salon; 24-hr. room service; babysitting; laundry service; same-day dry cleaning. *In room:* A/C, TV w/pay movies, CD player, free Wi-Fi, minibar, coffeemaker, hair dryer, iron, safe.

Le Square Phillips Hôtel & Suites *Kids*   Originally designed as a warehouse by the noted Québec architect Ernest Cormier, the building was converted to its present use in 2003. The vaguely cathedral-like spaces were largely retained, making for capacious studio bedrooms and suites fully equipped for long stays and for vacationing families. Full kitchens in every unit come with all essential appliances—toasters, fridges, stoves, dishwashers, crockery, and pots and pans. There's an indoor pool on the roof adjoining an exercise room with exercise machines. A laundry room is available for guest use. The location is ideal, at the edge of the downtown shopping district and an easy walk to Vieux-Montréal and the rue Crescent nightlife district. Guests who like their mattresses firm will be delighted—on our last visit, the one we had was only slightly softer than a marble countertop.

1193 Square Phillips (south of rue Ste-Catherine), Montréal, PQ H3B 3C9. ✆ **866/393-1193** or 514/393-1193. Fax 514/393-1192. www.squarephillips.com. 160 units. C$132–C$277 (US$115–US$241/£57–£119) double; discounts for stays of 7 or more days. Rates include breakfast. AE, DC, DISC, MC, V. Métro: McGill. Pets accepted. **Amenities:** Heated indoor rooftop pool; exercise room; concierge; business center; coin-op laundry facilities; dry cleaning; babysitting. *In room:* A/C, TV w/pay movies, free high-speed Internet, coffeemaker, hair dryer, iron.

INEXPENSIVE

Hôtel Le Dauphin *Value*   This downtown location of the small Dauphin hotel chain opened in February 2007. Its nine floors are decorated in bland tans and putty, and room furnishings are just a step up from dorm-room functional. However, the bathrooms are sleek with black counters, slate floors, and glass-walled shower stalls, and—get this—every room is equipped with a computer terminal and free Internet access. Rooms also have large unstocked refrigerators. A key is required to access the elevator, for an added bit of safety. The introductory C$109 (US$95/£47) price might not last, but all in all, this is a good new option for travelers on a budget.

1025 rue de Bleury (near av. Viger), Montréal, PQ H2Z 1M7. ✆ **888/784-3888** or 514/788-3888. Fax 514/788-3889. www.hoteldauphin.ca. 72 units. C$109–C$140 (US$95–US$122/£47–£60) double. Rates include breakfast. AE, MC, V. Métro: Place d'Armes. **Amenities:** Access to gym; coin-op washers and dryers. *In room:* A/C, TV/DVD, computer w/free high-speed Internet, fridge, coffeemaker, hair dryer, iron, safe.

3 Vieux-Montréal (Old Montréal)

VERY EXPENSIVE

Hôtel Le St-James ✦✦✦   A triumph of the union of design and preservation. Montréal's surge of new designer hotels spans the spectrum from superminimalist to gentlemen's club posh, and Le St-James sits squarely in the gentlemen's club end of the range. It began life as a merchant's bank in 1870, and the opulence of that station of privilege has been both retained and upgraded. The richly paneled entry hall leads to a grand hall with potted palms, carved urns, bronze chandeliers, Corinthian columns, and balconies with gilded metal balustrades. Breakfast, lunch, afternoon tea, and dinner are served right in this "Banker's Hall," often accompanied by harp music. Rooms are furnished with entrancing antiques and impeccable reproductions. All have video screens that control lights, room temperature, and even the DO NOT DISTURB sign. The stone-walled, candlelit **Le Spa,** with both a regular massage table and full-body water therapy, has to be seen to be believed. The Rolling Stones have stayed here. Obviously they have excellent taste in lodging—perhaps the Terrace Apartment Suite with private elevator access at C$5,000 (US$4,350/£2,150) a night?

355 rue St-Jacques ouest, Montréal, PQ H2Y 1N9. ✆ 866/841-3111 or 514/841-3111. Fax 514/841-1232. www. hotellestjames.com. 60 units. C$350–C$400 (US$305–US$348/£150–£172) double; C$475 (US$413/£204) and way up suite. AE, DC, MC, V. Valet parking C$30 (US$26/£13). Métro: Square Victoria. Pets accepted. **Amenities:** Restaurant (international); bar; exercise room; high-end spa; concierge; laptop on loan; 24-hr. room service; babysitting; laundry service; same-day dry cleaning. *In room:* A/C, TV w/pay movies, high-speed Internet, CD player, minibar, hair dryer, iron, safe.

Hôtel Le Saint-Sulpice 🌟🌟 *Kids*   One of the wave of high-style boutique hotels that has washed across Vieux-Montréal, Le Saint-Sulpice impresses with an all-suites configuration, an ambitious restaurant, and courtly service. The hotel is a member of the international Concorde chain, and it easily meets the demanding standards of the chain. Suites come with myriad conveniences and gadgets, including a cordless phone, mini-kitchens with microwave ovens, stoves, and fridges. Children's services include gaming consoles in every room, board games, kid-friendly TV programming, a children's menu, and day-care service.

414 rue St-Sulpice (next to the Basilique Notre-Dame), Montréal, PQ H2Y 2V5. ✆ 877/785-7423 or 514/288-1000. Fax 514/288-0077. www.lesaintsulpice.com. 108 units. C$189–C$569 (US$164–US$495/£81–£245) suite. Children under 13 stay free in parent's room. AE, DC, DISC, MC, V. Valet parking C$25 or C$32 for SUV (US$22/£11 or US$28/£14). Métro: Place d'Armes. Pets accepted. **Amenities:** Restaurant (contemporary); bar; compact health club and spa; concierge; business center; 24-hr. room service; babysitting; laundry service; same-day dry cleaning. *In room:* A/C, TV w/pay movies, high-speed Internet, minibar, coffeemaker, hair dryer, iron, safe.

W Montréal 🌟🌟🌟   The high standards set in recent years by several of the city's boutique hotels were exceeded as soon as this exemplar of the growing W chain opened in late 2004 on the edge of where downtown meets Vieux-Montréal. "Whatever, whenever" is the shorthand motto of the staff, meaning that they endeavor to swiftly satisfy any guest request, however unusual. Said employees, male and female, are young and distractingly attractive, as are many of the guests. If it weren't for the reception and concierge desks at each end, the lobby would suggest an exclusive dance club, what with the ice-blue and fire-engine-red glow of the wall panels and the 12-foot waterfall. The hotel restaurant, **Otto,** drew instant approval from local gourmands, and it attracts a sleek crowd favoring black and Armani. Three bars cater to lovers of the night, from the intimate W Café/Bartini featuring specialty martinis to the Wunderbar lounge with DJs. Bedrooms follow through, with pillow-top mattresses, goose-down comforters, and 350-count Egyptian cotton sheets. That flatscreen TVs, DVD players, and high-speed Internet access are standard even in the basic (called "Cozy") rooms is only to be expected.

901 rue Square-Victoria, Montréal, PQ H2Z 1R1. ✆ 888/627-7081 or 514/395-3100. Fax 514/395-3150. www.whotels. com/montreal. 152 units. From C$255 (US$222/£110) double. Packages available. AE, DC, DISC, MC, V. Valet parking C$35 (US$30/£15). Métro: Square Victoria. Pets accepted. **Amenities:** Restaurant (fusion); 3 bars; exercise room and spa; concierge; business center; 24-hr. room service; in-room massage, babysitting, laundry service; same-day dry cleaning. *In room:* A/C, TV/DVD, high-speed Internet, minibar, hair dryer, iron, safe.

EXPENSIVE

Auberge du Vieux-Port 🌟🌟   This romantic luxury inn, housed in an 1882 building facing the waterfront, has an inviting cellar restaurant and a wine bar on the main floor. Polished hardwood floors, exposed brick and stone walls, massive beams, and the original windows define the hideaway bedrooms. Both snacks and full dinners are

served on the rooftop terrace, which has unobstructed views of the Vieux-Port—a particular treat during those summer nights when there are fireworks on the river. A complimentary glass of wine is served each afternoon in a sophisticated lounge off the lobby. Room-service meals are prepared by the same kitchen that serves the fine restaurant Les Remparts, one floor below. The auberge also runs the **Lofts du Vieux-Port** (www.loftsduvieuxport.com), rentals of suite-like lofts that have kitchenettes and other amenities for longer stays. This is a sister property to the equally esteemed **Hôtel Nelligan** (p. 78) and **Le Place d'Armes Hôtel & Suites** (p. 79).

97 rue de la Commune est (near rue St-Gabriel), Montréal, PQ H2Y 1J1. © 888/660-7678 or 514/876-0081. Fax 514/876-8923. www.aubergeduvieuxport.com. 27 units. C$180–C$295 (US$157–US$257/£77–£127) double. Rates include afternoon wine and cheese, and full breakfast. AE, DC, DISC, MC, V. Valet parking C$21 (US$18/£9.05). Métro: Champs-de-Mars. Pets accepted in certain loft rooms. **Amenities:** Restaurant (French contemporary); concierge; limited room service; in-room massage; babysitting; laundry service; dry cleaning; laptop and mobile phone rentals. *In room:* A/C, TV, CD player, free Wi-Fi, minibar, coffeemaker (upon request), hair dryer, iron, safe, umbrella.

Hostellerie Pierre du Calvet ✿

Step from cobblestone streets into an opulent 18th-century home, with broad dark-wood floors, stone walls, beamed ceilings, copious numbers of Oriental rugs, plush velvet curtains, gold-leafed writing desks, tapestry tablecloths, and four-poster beds made of teak mahogany. This wildly atmospheric inn transports guests to an elegant Breton manor in France, and if you've ever watched *Masterpiece Theatre* and thought "What I wouldn't give to live there!," this is for you. Public rooms are furnished with original antiques, not reproductions, and the voluptuous dining room, **Les Filles du Roy,** suggests a 19th-century hunting lodge. Some bedrooms have fireplaces and room no. 6 even has a stone-walled shower stall. New flatscreen TVs are as discordant as Victoria Beckham at Versailles but will be removed upon request. Door locks are awfully rickety; grin and bear it and imagine them as romantic period pieces. An outdoor courtyard with stone walls and a small fountain was converted in 2006 into a terrace for lunch and dinner; it's a wonderful little hideaway. At press time, plans were underway to turn the adjacent parking lot into a star-shaped vegetable garden just off the terrace.

405 rue Bonsecours (at rue St-Paul), Montréal, PQ H27 3C3. © 866/544-1725 or 514/282-1725. Fax 514/282-0456. www.pierreducalvet.ca. 9 units. C$265–C$295 (US$230–US$256/£114–£127). Rates include full breakfast. AE, MC, V. Métro: Champ-de-Mars. **Amenities:** Restaurant (French); laundry service; dry cleaning. *In room:* A/C, TV, free Wi-Fi, hair dryer, iron (on request).

Hôtel Gault ✿

This designer hotel explores the far reaches of minimalism, and guest responses vary from delight to dismay. Design aficionados will love it. With raw, monumental, concrete walls and brushed steel work surfaces, Gault's structural austerity is stark, but it's tempered by lollipop-colored reproductions of modern furniture from the 1950s to keep it more playful than chilly. The sleek lobby with massive arched windows doubles as a bar/café/breakfast area. The large bedrooms on the hotel's five floors are all loft-style to create a home-away-from-home feeling (they start at 310 sq. ft. and go up), and use curtains instead of walls to define spaces. Bedding comes from the high-end Italian company FLOU, and hypoallergenic pillows are available. The first floor "Existential"-category rooms feature the highest ceilings. Tubs aren't available in all rooms, but plush robes are.

449 rue Ste-Hélène, Montréal, PQ H2Y 2K9. © 866/904-1616 or 514/904-1616. Fax 514/904-1717. www.hotel gault.com. 29 units. C$200–C$299 (US$174–US$260/£86–£129) double. Rates include breakfast. AE, MC, V. Métro: Square Victoria. Pets accepted. **Amenities:** Bar; concierge; gym access; 24-hr. room service; laundry service; same-day dry cleaning. *In room:* A/C, TV/DVD, CD player, free high-speed Internet, minibar, safe.

Hôtel InterContinental Montréal ⭐⭐⭐   Only a few minutes' walk from the Basilique Notre-Dame and the restaurants and nightspots of Vieux-Montréal, this striking luxury hotel opened in 1991 and was instantly included in the coveted clique of top properties in town. The hotel's tower houses the sleek reception area and guest rooms, while the restored 1888 Nordheimer building contains a bar-bistro. (Take a look at the early-19th-c. vaults below.) Guest rooms are quiet, well lit, and decorated with photographs and lithographs by local artists. The turret suites are fun, with their round bedrooms and wraparound windows, and Club rooms have access to an exclusive lounge serving complimentary continental breakfast and afternoon hors d'oeuvres, beer, and wine.

360 rue St-Antoine ouest (near rue de Bleury), Montréal, PQ H2Y 3X4. ⓒ 514/987-9900. Fax 514/987-9904. www.montreal.intercontinental.com. 357 units. C$159–C$309 (US$138–US$269/£68–£133) double. Packages available. AE, DC, DISC, MC, V. Valet parking C$26 (US$23/£11) with in-out privileges or C$19 (US$17/£8.15) without. Métro: Square Victoria. **Amenities:** 2 restaurants (international); bar; small enclosed rooftop lap pool; health club w/sauna and steam rooms; concierge; substantial 24-hr. business center; 24-hr. room service; massage; laundry service; same-day dry cleaning; executive floors. *In room:* A/C, TV w/pay movies and video games, Internet, minibar, coffeemaker, hair dryer, iron, safe.

Hôtel Nelligan ⭐⭐⭐   Occupying adjoining 1850 buildings, the Nelligan opened in 2002 and spent C$8 million to expand in 2007, going from 63 to 105 units. Over half of the spaces are now suites. The staff performs its duties admirably, and the building has beautiful spaces, from the sun-splashed atrium and **Verses** restaurant (p. 95) on the ground floor to the rooftop terrace, where drinks and light meals are served in good weather. Get a room on the fifth floor and be steps away from both the terrace and the exercise room. Bedrooms are dark-wooded, masculine retreats you'll want to hide in for hours at a time, with puffy goose-down duvets and heaps of pillows. (You can re-create it at home: All the bedding and mattresses are for sale through the hotel's boutique). The one distraction is that because the hotel is built around a center atrium, noise from the bar, which can go until midnight, can filter up to the rooms; some might find this cheery. The Nelligan is named for the 19th-century Québécois poet Emile Nelligan, whose lines are excerpted on the walls of its rooms and suites. It is a sister property to the equally esteemed **Auberge du Vieux-Port** (p. 76) and **Le Place d'Armes Hôtel & Suites** (p. 79). Claiming an enveloping lobby chair facing the open front to the street, with a book and a cold drink at hand, is one definition of utter contentment.

106 rue St-Paul ouest (at rue St-Sulpice), Montréal, PQ H2Y 1Z3. ⓒ 877/788-2040 or 514/788-2040. Fax 514/788-2041. www.hotelnelligan.com. 105 units. C$235–C$260 (US$204–US$226/£101–£112) double; suites from C$335 (US$291/£144). Rates include afternoon wine and cheese, and breakfast. Packages available. AE, DC, DISC, MC, V. Valet parking C$24 (US$21/£10). Métro: Place d'Armes. **Amenities:** 2 restaurants (French contemporary); bar; exercise room; concierge; computer for guest use; limited room service; in-room massage; babysitting; laundry service; same-day dry cleaning. *In room:* A/C, TV, free high-speed Internet, Wi-Fi, CD player, minibar, hair dryer, iron, safe, umbrella.

Hôtel St-Paul ⭐⭐   Joining the laudable Vieux-Montréal ranks of worthwhile old buildings converted to hotels and other contemporary uses, the St-Paul was an instant front-runner. The exterior is a product of the Beaux Arts school, but minimalism prevails inside, with simple lines and muted tones. (Most of the guests are as trim and understated as the surroundings.) A floor-to-ceiling alabaster fireplace anchors one end of the long lobby, and similarly solid and linear lines are brought into each room. Elevators and hallways are hushed and dark, bordering on pitch black, and then open into bright rooms with walls and furnishings in various shades of cream, getting pops of texture from pelt rugs. Marble sinks are square, as are the clear plastic cubes covering the toiletries, and all rooms have plush robes and hypoallergenic duvets. Mobile phones and laptops are available upon request. Many rooms face the less touristed far western edge of Vieux-Montréal, with its mixture of stone and brick buildings in mid-conversion to modern condos and office space. The hotel's popular restaurant was under renovation when we visited in spring 2007; it has since reopened with a new name (Volver) and an all-new Mediterranean menu.

355 rue McGill (at rue St-Paul), Montréal, PQ H2Y 2E8. 𝓒 **866/380-2202** or 514/380-2222. Fax 514/380-2200. www.hotelstpaul.com. 120 units. C$189–C$279 (US$164–US$243/£82–£121) double; suites from C$339 (US$295/£146). Rates include breakfast. Children under 12 stay free in parent's room. Packages available. AE, DC, MC, V. Valet parking C$19 (US$17/£8.25). Pets accepted. Métro: Square Victoria. **Amenities:** Restaurant (eclectic); bar; 24-hr. exercise room; concierge; 24-hr. business center; free Wi-Fi in public areas; limited room service; in-room massage and yoga; babysitting; laundry service; same-day dry cleaning. *In room:* A/C, TV w/pay movies, fax, free high-speed Internet, CD player, minibar, coffeemaker, hair dryer, iron, safe.

Le Place d'Armes Hôtel & Suites 𝓡𝓡   This highly desirable property is housed in three cunningly converted adjoining buildings dating from the late 19th and early 20th centuries. The elaborate architectural details of that era are in abundant evidence inside, with high ceilings and richly carved capitals and moldings. Few desires are not catered to—a complimentary afternoon wine-and-cheese party is held in the ground-floor lounge of the original structure, which becomes a hugely popular gathering place in the evenings, and there's a rooftop sun deck. Many rooms have original brick walls and all are decorated in simple, contemporary fashion: slate floors in the bathrooms, deluxe bedding with down comforters, spotlight lighting. Many bathrooms feature downpour (rain-shower) shower heads. The hotel's acclaimed restaurant, **Aix Cuisine du Terroir** (p. 91), replaced a previous mediocrity lodged in the space below the lounge. A free morning shuttle service takes guests to several downtown business locations. On top of all that, the elaborate **Rainspa** incorporates a hammam—a traditional Middle Eastern steam bath—in addition to offering massages, microdermabrasions, French manicures, and body wraps. This is a sister property to the **Auberge du Vieux-Port** (p. 76) and **Hôtel Nelligan** (above).

55 rue St-Jacques ouest, Montréal, PQ H2Y 3X2. 𝓒 **888/450-1887** or 514/842-1887. Fax 514/842-6469. www.hotelplacedarmes.com. 135 units. From C$225 (US$196/£97) double; C$325 (US$283/£140) and up suite. Rates include complimentary wine and cheese, and breakfast. Packages available. AE, DC, DISC, MC, V. Valet parking C$24 (US$21/£10). Métro: Place d'Armes. **Amenities:** Restaurant (French contemporary); bar; exercise room; large spa; concierge; secretarial services; 24-hr. room service; babysitting; same-day laundry service; same-day dry cleaning. *In room:* A/C, TV, Wi-Fi, high-speed Internet, CD player, minibar, hair dryer, safe, umbrella.

MODERATE

Auberge Bonaparte 𝓡   The restaurant of the same name on the ground floor—romantic and faded in a Left Bank of Paris sort of way—has long been one of Vieux-Montréal's favorites (p. 92). It was accorded major renovations in 1999, and while they were at it, the owners transformed the overhead floors into this fashionable urban inn. The auberge continues the restaurant's romantic style; even the smallest rooms are surprisingly spacious, and they have a variety of combinations of furniture, including double beds, that are useful for families. Of the eight units on each floor, four have whirlpool tubs with separate showers. All guests can spend time on the rooftop terrace, which overlooks the Basilique Notre-Dame. The auberge's one suite is on the top floor and offers superb views of cobblestone streets and the basilica's cloistered gardens.

447 rue St-François-Xavier (north of rue St-Paul), Montréal, PQ H2Y 2T1. © **514/844-1448.** Fax 514/844-0272. www.bonaparte.com. 31 units. C$145–C$215 (US$126–US$187/£62–£92) double; C$305–C$355 (US$265–US$309/£131–£153) suite. Rates include full breakfast. AE, DC, MC, V. Parking C$15 (US$13/£6.45) per calendar day. Métro: Place d'Armes. **Amenities:** Restaurant (French); access to nearby health club; concierge; limited room service; in-room massage; babysitting; laundry service; same-day dry cleaning. *In room:* A/C, TV/VCR, Wi-Fi, hair dryer, iron.

Hôtel XIXe Siècle This tidy little hotel is worth seeking out for its central location and quiet demeanor. The building began life in 1870 as a bank in the Second Empire style, and the interior reflects these stately origins, with a lobby that looks like a Victorian library. Rooms are quite spacious, with tall 4.5m (15-ft.) ceilings throughout, and even the non-suite rooms have good-size areas for sitting and working at a desk. A handful of rooms have whirlpool tubs. Rooms facing the nondescript inner courtyard might not be scenic but are nearly silent and a dream for light sleepers. Three vaults remain from the building's original use as a bank, and one of them has been converted to a small bedroom. Despite its faintly aristocratic air, the hotel gives nods to green living, with energy-saving light bulbs and newspaper recycling buckets in each room.

262 rue St-Jacques ouest (at rue St-Jean), Montréal, PQ H2Y 1N1. © **877/553-0019** or 514/985-0019. Fax 514/985-0059. www.hotelxixsiecle.com. 59 units. C$145–C$260 (US$126–US$226/£62–£112) double. AE, DC, MC, V. Valet parking C$20 (US$17/£8.60). Métro: Place d'Armes. **Amenities:** Bar; concierge; laundry service; same-day dry cleaning. *In room:* A/C, TV, Wi-Fi, hair dryer, iron.

INEXPENSIVE

Auberge Les Passants du Sans Soucy ★ *Value* This cheery bed-and-breakfast in the heart of Vieux-Montréal is a former 1723 fur warehouse gracefully converted into an inn by the bilingual owners. The marble-floored front entry doubles as a gallery space, setting an immediately relaxed and urbane tone. Rooms feature mortared stone walls, beamed ceilings, wrought-iron or brass beds, buffed wood floors, and lace curtains (photos of all nine are posted online). All rooms now have jet tubs, flatscreen TVs, and electric fireplaces. A breakfast nook with skylight features two communal tables on either side of a fireplace brought over from Bordeaux, and the substantial morning meals include chocolate croissants and made-to-order omelets.

171 rue St-Paul ouest (at rue St-François-Xavier), Montréal, PQ H2Y 1Z5. © **514/842-2634.** Fax 514/842-2912. www.lesanssoucy.com. 9 units. C$115–C$185 (US$100–US$161/£49–£80) double; C$145–C$215 (US$126–US$187/£62–£92) suite. Rates include full breakfast. AE, MC, V. Self-parking C$13 (US$11/£5.50). Métro: Place d'Armes. *In room:* A/C, TV, free Wi-Fi, hair dryer, iron.

6

Where to Dine in Montréal

A generation ago, most restaurants in Montréal served only French cuisine. A few *temples de cuisine* delivered haute standards of gastronomy; numerous accomplished bistros served up humbler ingredients in less grand settings; and folksy places featured the hearty fare that long employed the ingredients available in New France—game such as caribou, maple syrup, and root vegetables. Everything else was considered "ethnic." The food crazes of the 1980s focusing on Cajun, Tex-Mex, and fusion didn't make much of a dent at the time: Québec province was French, and that was that.

Over the last 10 years, however, this attitude changed dramatically. A recession in the 1990s put many restaurateurs out of business and forced others to reexamine their operations. Immigration continued to increase, and along with it, the cooking styles of the world. Montréalers now routinely indulge in once-exotic edibles found in the storefront eateries all around them—Portuguese, Indian, Moroccan, Thai, Turkish, Mexican, Japanese.

An intermingling of styles, ingredients, and techniques was inevitable, and Montréal, long one of the world's elite gastronomic centers, is now as cosmopolitan in its offerings as any city on the continent. Indeed, in some eyes, it has taken Canada's leadership role in gastronomy. True, some of the silliness that attended culinary innovation elsewhere afflicted chefs here, too. But for most, novelty is still secondary to the freshness and appropriateness of ingredients.

The bottom line on dining in Montréal: A meal here can be the equal in every dimension to the best offered anywhere in the world.

THE DINING SCENE Deciding where to dine among the many tempting choices can be bewildering. We've highlighted the restaurants that are most honored, most special, or of the most value.

Restaurants—called "restos" in the colloquial—are often clustered together in certain neighborhoods. Many of this city's moderately priced bistros, cafés, and ethnic joints offer outstanding food, congenial surroundings, and amiable service at reasonable prices. Nearly all post menus outside, making it easy to do a little salivation-inducing reading and comparison shopping.

It's a good idea to make a reservation if you wish to dine at one of the city's top restaurants, especially on a weekend evening. Unlike in larger American and European cities, a day or two in advance is sufficient most places on most days. A hotel concierge can make the reservation, although nearly all restaurant hosts will switch immediately into English when they sense that a caller doesn't speak French.

Except in a handful of luxury restaurants, dress codes are all but nonexistent. But Montréalers are a fashionable lot, and manage to look smart even in casual clothes. Save the T-shirts and sneakers for another city.

Two insider websites featuring reviews and observations about the local dining scene are **www.montrealfood.com** and http://endlessbanquet.blogspot.com. The delightful essays and reviews of resto critic Lesley Chesterman of *The Montréal Gazette* can be found online at **www. montrealgazette.com**.

ON THE MENU   One thing to always look for are *table d'hôte* (fixed-price) meals. Entire two- to four-course meals, often with a beverage, can be had for little more than the price of an a la carte main course alone. Even the best restaurants offer them, so tables d'hôte can let you sample some excellent venues without breaking the bank. They're often offered at lunch, and are even cheaper then. Having your main meal at midday instead of in the evening is the most economical way to sample many of the top establishments.

Many higher-end establishments are offering tasting menus, with surprise menus equally popular—you don't know what you're getting until it's there in front of you. Remember that an *entrée* is an appetizer, not the main course, which is *le plat principal.* In fancier places, where a pre-appetizer nibble is proffered, it's called an *amuse-gueule* or *amuse-bouche.*

Be sure to try the inexpensive regional specialties. A Québécois favorite is *poutine:* french fries doused with gravy and cheese curds. It's especially ubiquitous in winter (see "*Poutine,* Smoked Meat & the World's Best Bagels" on p. 90). Numerous places serve sandwiches and snacks for only a few dollars and go by the generic name *casse-croûte*—literally, "break crust." You'll find a few stools at a counter and a limited number of menu items that might include soup and *chien chaud* (hot dog). As in Europe and the U.S., many Thai, Chinese, and Indian restaurants offer inexpensive all-you-can-eat lunch buffets.

It's becoming a little more common to find fine restaurants that offer wine pairings, where the sommelier selects a glass for each course. In general, though, alcohol is heavily taxed, and imported varieties even more so than domestic versions, so if you're looking to save a little, buy Canadian. That's not difficult when it comes to beer, for there are many breweries, from local powerhouse Molson to micro, that produce highly palatable products including Belle Gueule and Boréal. The sign BIERES EN FUT means "beers on draft." Wine is another matter. It is not produced in significant quantities in Canada due to a climate generally inhospitable to the essential grapes. But you might try bottles from the vineyards of the Cantons-de-l'Est region (just east of Montréal) or from British Columbia or the Niagara Frontier. And sample, too, the sweet "ice wines" and "ice ciders" made from fruit after the first frost. Many decent ones are made at vineyards and orchards just an hour from Montréal.

Québec cheeses deserve attention, and many can only be sampled in Canada because they are often unpasteurized—made of *lait cru* (raw milk)—and can't be exported. Better restaurants will offer them as a separate course. Of the more than 300 now available, you might look for Mimolette Jeune (firm, fragrant, orange in color), Valbert St-Isidor (similar to Swiss in texture), St-Basil de Port Neuf (buttery), Cru des Erables (soft, ripe), Oka (semisoft, made of cow's milk in a monastery), and Le Chèvre Noire (a sharp goat variety covered in black wax).

PRICES   The restaurants recommended here are categorized by neighborhood and then by the cost of an average dinner for one person. Prices listed for main courses in these entries are for dinner unless otherwise indicated (lunchtime prices are usually lower). Prices here *do not* include wine, tip, or the 7% federal tax and 8% provincial tax that are added to the restaurant bill.

PARKING   Because parking space is at a premium in most restaurant districts in Montréal, take the Métro or a taxi in the central districts. If you're driving, ask if valet parking is available when you call to make a reservation.

SMOKING Québec has long had a smoking culture, but smoking in bars and restaurants has been banned by law since 2006.

TIPPING Montréalers consider 15% of the check (before taxes) to be a fair tip, increased only for exceptional food and service. The easiest way to calculate the amount is to add together the federal and provincial taxes, separately listed on the check. They total 15%.

1 Best Dining Bets

- **Best Budget Restaurant:** The tapas phenomenon gave rise to the rampant small plates fashion, and **Pintxo,** in Plateau Mont-Royal at 256 rue Roy est, 2 blocks west of rue St-Denis (© **514/844-0222**), does its own variations on the Spanish Basque originals. It has a second, smaller resto at 2 rue Sherbrooke est, at the corner of boulevard St-Laurent. See p. 102.
- **Best Expensive Restaurant:** Among several candidates, this vote goes to Vieux-Montréal's **Version Laurent Godbout,** 295 rue St-Paul est (at rue St-Claude; © **514/871-9135**). This chef-entrepreneur has an astonishingly sure hand with the innovations he brings to the Mediterranean canon. See p. 95.
- **Best Restaurant, Period:** Ever-questing Normand Laprise and partner Christine Lamarche keep Vieux-Montréal's **Toqué!,** 900 Place Jean-Paul Riopelle, near rue St-Antoine (© **514/499-2084**), in a league of its own. Postmodern and dazzling. See p. 91.
- **Best Classic French Bistro:** Plateau Mont-Royal's most Parisian bistro, **L'Express,** 3927 rue St-Denis (at rue Roy; © **514/845-5333**), is where you come to see what the Francophone part of this city is all about. From the black-and-white checked floor to the grand, high ceilings, this is where Old France meets New France. See p. 101.
- **Best for a Low-Key Date Night:** The charming bistro **La Montée de Lait,** tucked in on a nondescript side street in Plateau Mont-Royal at 371 rue Villeneuve est (at the corner of rue Drolet; © **514/289-9921**), keeps you close to your honey—and puts you elbow-to-elbow with neighbors. See p. 100.
- **Best for a Celebration: Nuances,** 1 av. du Casino (© **514/392-2708**), got a dazzling face-lift in 2007 and now looks as contemporary as the food on its plates. A gracious, multi-starred *temple de cuisine* atop the Montréal casino on Ile Ste-Hélène. See p. 106.
- **Best Value:** Even the most expensive four-course table d'hôte dinner at **Le Bourlingueur,** in Vieux-Montréal at 363 St-François-Xavier (near rue St-Paul; © **514/845-3646**), comes in under C$17 (US$15/£7.30). See p. 97.
- **Best Guilty Treat:** *Poutine* is a plate of french fries—*frites*—drenched with gravy afloat with cheese curds, a bedrock Québec comfort food that's better than it sounds. Many say it should stay unadorned, but at **Au Pied de Cochon,** 536 rue Duluth, near rue St-Hubert in Plateau Mont-Royal (© **514/281-1114**), the dish is elevated to mid-haute levels with the addition of foie gras. See p. 99.
- **Best Smoked Meat:** There are other contenders, but **Chez Schwartz Charcuterie Hébraïque de Montréal,** known simply as Schwartz's, at 3895 bd. St-Laurent, north of rue Prince-Arthur in Plateau Mont-Royal (© **514/842-4813**), serves up the definitive version of regional brisket. See p. 102.

- **Best Seafood:** Few Montréal restos focus on fish, but **Ferreira Café,** 1446 rue Peel near boulevard Maisonnueve downtown (© **514/848-0988**), does extremely well by its repertoire of marine-focused Portuguese cuisine. See p. 87.
- **Best Burgers:** Local conviction is that the biggest, juiciest burgers are assembled at the Latin Quarter's **La Paryse,** 302 rue Ontario est, at rue Sanguinet (© **514/842-2040**). See p. 106. Nipping at its heels, though, is the young **MeatMarket,** 4415 bd. St-Laurent just south of avenue du Mont-Royal (© **514/223-2292**), a gourmet burger joint in Mile End. See p. 105.
- **Best Vegan:** A standard-bearer since 1997, Plateau Mont-Royal's **Aux Vivres** moved to new digs at 4631 bd. St-Laurent, near avenue du Mont-Royal (© **514/842-3479**) in 2006 and has been packing in vegans, vegetarians, and the meat-eaters who love them ever since. See p. 105.
- **Best Pizza:** The name says it all: **Pizzédélic,** 39 rue Notre-Dame ouest (near bd. St-Laurent; © **514/286-1200**), where they do anything from same-old tomato and cheese to designer concoctions with "shrimp satay ginger." See p. 98.
- **Best Bagels:** Even native New Yorkers have to give it up for Montréal's bagels, which are clearly superior to versions produced south of the border. Both **St-Viateur Bagel & Café,** at 1127 av. Mont-Royal est, near avenue Christophe-Colomb in Plateau Mont-Royal (© **514/528-6361**), and **Fairmont Bagel,** at 74 av. Fairmont ouest, near rue St-Urbain in Mile End (© **514/272-0667**), are the places to assess that claim. See p. 103.
- **Best Outdoor Terrace:** Serious food isn't the lure at **Le Jardin Nelson,** 407 Place Jacques-Cartier (© **514/861-5731**). Music—classical or jazz—is what draws the crowds to this central Vieux-Montréal locale to partake of crepes and pizzas under the crabapple tree in the garden. See p. 169.
- **Best Late-Night Eats:** If the bagels from **Fairmont Bagel** won't do the trick (the hole-in-the-wall shop is open 24 hr.), our heart is still with **L'Express** (p. 101). It's in the center of the Plateau neighborhood and serves until 3am. (Also see our list of "Late-Night Bites" on p. 107.)
- **Best Wine Bar: Aszú,** in Vieux-Montréal at 212 rue Notre Dame ouest near rue St-François-Xavier (© **514/845-5436**), features between 60 and 70 wines by the glass every night. See p. 168 in chapter 10.

2 Restaurants by Cuisine

BREAKFAST

Fairmont Bagel (Mile End, $, p. 105)
Café Cherrier (Plateau Mont-Royal, $, p. 102)
Cluny ArtBar (Vieux-Montréal, $, p. 96)
Eggspectation (Vieux-Montréal, $, p. 97)

DELI

Chez Schwartz Charcuterie Hébraïque de Montréal ⍟ (Plateau Mont-Royal, $, p. 102)

FRENCH BISTRO

L'Express ⍟ (Plateau Mont-Royal, $$, p. 101)

Key to Abbreviations: $$$$ = Very Expensive $$$ = Expensive $$ = Moderate $ = Inexpensive

The prices within each review refer to the cost in Canadian dollars of individual main courses, using the following categories: Very Expensive ($$$$), main courses at dinner average more than C$35; Expensive ($$$), C$25 to C$35; Moderate ($$), C$12 to C$25; and Inexpensive ($), C$12 and under. Restaurants are listed alphabetically at the end of the index in the back of this book.

La Montée de Lait ✦ (Plateau Mont-Royal, $$$, p. 100)

Le Bourlingueur (Vieux-Montréal, $, p. 97)

Leméac ✦ (Mile End, $$, p. 105)

FRENCH CONTEMPORARY

Aix Cuisine du Terroir ✦ (Vieux-Montréal, $$$, p. 91)

Café Méliès (Plateau Mont-Royal, $$, p. 101)

Europea ✦✦ (Downtown, $$$, p. 86)

Julien (Downtown, $$$, p. 87)

Nuances ✦✦ (Outer Districts, $$$$, p. 106)

Rosalie ✦ (Downtown, $$$, p. 87)

Toqué! ✦✦✦ (Vieux-Montréal, $$$$, p. 91)

Verses ✦ (Vieux-Montréal, $$$, p. 95)

FRENCH TRADITIONAL

Bonaparte ✦ (Vieux-Montréal, $$$, p. 92)

Chez Queux ✦ (Vieux-Montréal, $$$, p. 92)

Marché de la Villete ✦ (Vieux-Montréal, $, p. 97)

FUSION

Brunoise ✦✦ (Plateau Mont-Royal, $$$$, p. 98)

Chez l'Epicier ✦ (Vieux-Montréal, $$$, p. 92)

Jun-I ✦ (Mile End, $$$, p. 104)

La Chronique ✦✦ (Mile End, $$$$, p. 103)

Le Blanc ✦ (Plateau Mont-Royal, $$$, p. 100)

Le Club Chasse et Peche ✦ (Vieux-Montréal, $$$, p. 94)

Renoir (Downtown, $$$, p. 87)

ICE CREAM

Bilboquet ✦ (Mile End, $, p. 105)

INDIAN

Gandhi ✦ (Vieux-Montréal, $$, p. 96)

Le Taj (Downtown, $$, p. 90)

ITALIAN

BU (Mile End, $$, p. 104)

Buonanotte ✦ (Plateau Mont-Royal, $$$, p. 99)

Cavalli ✦✦ (Downtown, $$$, p. 86)

Le Globe ✦ (Plateau Mont-Royal, $$$, p. 100)

Otto (Vieux-Montréal, $$$, p. 95)

LEBANESE

Boustan (Downtown, $, p. 90)

LIGHT FARE

Café Cherrier (Plateau Mont-Royal, $, p. 102)

Claude Postel (Vieux-Montréal, $, p. 96)

Cluny ArtBar (Vieux-Montréal, $, p. 96)

Eggspectation (Vieux-Montréal, $, p. 97)

Fairmont Bagel (Mile End, $, p. 105)

MeatMarket Restaurant Café (Mile End, $$, p. 105)

Nocochi (Downtown, $, p. 91)

Olive et Gourmando ✦ (Vieux-Montréal, $, p. 97)

St-Viateur Bagel & Café ✦ (Plateau Mont-Royal, $, p. 103)

Titanic (Vieux-Montréal, $, p. 98)

Wilensky Light Lunch (Mile End, $, p. 106)

MEDITERRANEAN

Modavie ✦ (Vieux-Montréal, $$$, p. 94)

Ora (Vieux-Montréal, $$, p. 96)

Version Laurent Godbout ✦✦ (Vieux-Montréal, $$$, p. 95)

PIZZA

Pizzédélic (Vieux-Montréal, $, p. 98)

POLISH

Stash (Vieux-Montréal, $, p. 98)

QUEBECOIS

Au Pied de Cochon ✦✦ (Plateau Mont-Royal, $$$, p. 99)

SANDWICHES
La Paryse (Latin Quarter, $, p. 106)

SEAFOOD
Ferreira Café ✸ (Downtown, $$$, p. 87)
Joe Beef ✸ (Outer Districts, $$$, p. 107)
Le Garde Manger (Vieux-Montréal, $$$, p. 94)
Maestro S.V.P. (Plateau Mont-Royal, $$$, p. 101)

SPANISH
Pintxo ✸✸ (Plateau Mont-Royal, $$, p. 102)

STEAKHOUSE
Joe Beef ✸ (Outer Districts, $$$, p. 107)
Moishes ✸ (Plateau Mont-Royal, $$$$, p. 99)

THAI
Chao Phraya (Mile End, $$, p. 104)

VEGETARIAN/VEGAN
Aux Vivres (Mile End, $, p. 105)
Le Commensal (Downtown, $, p. 91)

3 Centre Ville/Downtown

EXPENSIVE

Cavalli ✸✸ ITALIAN   With a formula more common in the restaurants over on boulevard St-Laurent than here in the middle of the business district, the owners filled a glamorous space with striking young women in snug black dresses and hunky young men with requisite 4-day beards. It's like joining the after-party of a Hollywood premiere with 300 of the beautiful people. Being seen is top priority, but the food is noteworthy, too. Most dishes stick to four or five main ingredients, the better to appreciate the impeccably fresh components. Tempting as it is to simply make a meal of antipasti, that would mean ignoring such eminently worthwhile main events as the pine nut–crusted filet mignon or rack of lamb with oregano crust and black olive *jus*. Lighter appetites have several pastas to choose among. Prices are high, assuring a somewhat more prosperous crowd than usually found at similar emporia. The glowing pink bar is a heavy scene later in the evening; Thursday is the big night.

2040 rue Peel (at bd. de Maisonneuve). ✆ 514/843-5100. www.ristorantecavalli.com. Reservations recommended. Main courses C$25–C$42 (US$22–US$37/£11–£18); table d'hôte lunch C$29–C$31 (US$25–US$27/£12–£13). AE, MC, V. Mon–Fri noon–3pm and 6–10:30pm; Sat 6–10:30pm (bar open later). Métro: Peel.

Europea ✸✸ FRENCH CONTEMPORARY   When viewed from the outside, Europea doesn't particularly impress; it looks like any of the city's multitude of lowbrow cellar eateries. Even once inside, the low ceiling, bare wood floors, and brick walls are more simple than stunning. But then comes the food. The *amuse* (pre-appetizer) is in a three-segment dish with different tasty nibbles in each. It's followed by an unannounced "teaser," a demitasse of lobster bisque with a shot of truffle oil. Gaps in the procession are short, leading to the main event, maybe the roasted Alaska crab legs and warm lobster salad, or the beef filet. For the full treatment, order the 9-course *menu dégustation* for C$77 (US$67/£33). Europea don't court the family trade, and the average age of diners tends toward the far side of 40. Service is watchful and efficient.

1227 rue de la Montagne (at rue Ste-Catherine). ✆ 514/398-9229. www.europea.ca. Reservations strongly recommended. Main courses C$27–C$41 (US$23–US$35/£11–£17); table d'hôte dinner C$47 (US$40/£20), lunch C$27 (US$23/£11). AE, DC, MC, V. Mon–Fri noon–2pm; daily 6–10pm. Métro: Peel.

Ferreira Café ⚓ SEAFOOD   *Cataplana* is the name of both a venerated Portuguese recipe and the hinged copper clamshell-style pot in which it is cooked. Ingredients vary depending on the cook, but at this extremely popular downtown spot, that means a fragrant stew of mussels, clams, potatoes, *chouriço* sausage, and chunks of cod and salmon. Mostly middle-aged and dressed in business wear, customers fill every seat at lunchtime but go home at night, which is when to visit if you prefer a bit of tranquillity with your grilled squid or classic fried cod. Many dishes are priced according to the daily market, so they can be higher than outlined below.

1446 rue Peel (near bd. de Maisonnueve). ℂ 514/848-0988. www.ferreiracafe.com. Reservations recommended. Main courses C$28–C$45 (US$24–US$39/£12–£19). AE, MC, V. Mon–Fri 11:30am–3pm and 5:30–11pm; Sat 5:30–11:30pm. Métro: Peel.

Julien FRENCH CONTEMPORARY   A quiet downtown block in the financial district has been home to this relaxed Parisian-style bistro for over 15 years, hosting businesspeople at lunch and for cocktails after work and mostly tourists from nearby hotels in the evening. Much of the year diners have the option of tables in the heated terrace/garden. The chef isn't interested in being edgy, although he has been known to start out with a trendy amuse of marinated salt cod in porcelain Chinese spoon. Sautéed duck breast is served with armillaire mushrooms and potato purée, and grilled red tuna with parsnip purée. There's a gluten-free vegetarian pasta option. All is brought by an efficient staff working under the steady hand of the witty maitre d'. The cheese selection is good, as is the tiramisu. Solid food without the pyrotechnics.

1191 av. Union (at bd. René-Lévesque). ℂ 514/871-1581. www.restaurantjulien.com. Reservations recommended. Main courses C$21–C$35 (US$18–US$30/£9.05–£15); table d'hôte dinner from C$22 (US$19/£9.45), lunch from C$18 (US$16/£7.75). AE, DC, MC, V. Mon–Fri 11:30am–2:30pm; Mon–Sat 5:30–10pm. Métro: McGill.

Renoir FUSION   Lodged in the instantly popular **Sofitel** hotel (p. 69), this ambitious restaurant calls its food "inspired." Make that "cautiously creative"—not ostentatious enough to halt conversation in midsentence, but worth an approving comment *en passant*. Plates are beautifully presented, with main events including lamb rack and Chilean sea bass. Lunch is the busiest time, while dinner is quieter, populated mostly by hotel guests (yes, that was Halle Berry at the next table). A large terrace thrusts out toward busy Sherbrooke; in summer, jazz trios entertain diners and passersby and inside, a pianist plays Thursday through Saturday evenings.

1155 rue Sherbrooke ouest (in the Sofitel Hotel, at rue Stanley). ℂ 514/285-9000. www.restaurant-renoir.com. Reservations recommended. Main courses C$20–C$36 (US$17–US$31); table d'hôte lunch C$29 (US$25/£12), dinner C$47 (US$41/£20). AE, DC, MC, V. Daily 6am–10:30pm, with bar menu only 3–5pm. Métro: Peel.

Rosalie ⚓ FRENCH CONTEMPORARY   Big, boisterous, congenial—this eating-and-meeting spot in the midst of the rue Crescent hubbub is all of that. The original owner has moved on, opening **Joe Beef** (p. 107). But the bottomless source of great-looking young men and women he discovered still comprises the staff. They are very friendly, and good enough at their tasks, attending to throngs of people who look like they spend most of their evenings in places like this. Out front is an active terrace; inside, patrons draw leather-sling chairs up to the ranks of bare tables or perch along the long marble bar. Food is of the updated bistro style, including a pear, blue cheese and proscuitto tart, and tajine pot lamb shank *à la Provençale*. None of the food is too complicated, and most of it tasty. After 8pm, the lights go down and the decibel level shoots up.

Where to Dine in Downtown Montréal

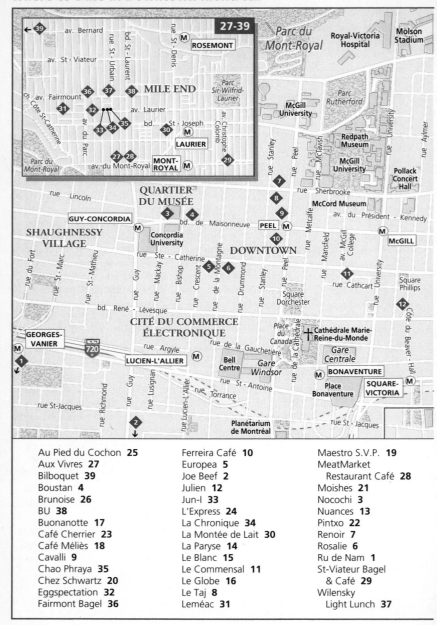

Au Pied du Cochon **25**	Ferreira Café **10**	Maestro S.V.P. **19**
Aux Vivres **27**	Europea **5**	MeatMarket
Bilboquet **39**	Joe Beef **2**	Restaurant Café **28**
Boustan **4**	Julien **12**	Moishes **21**
Brunoise **26**	Jun-I **33**	Nocochi **3**
BU **38**	L'Express **24**	Nuances **13**
Buonanotte **17**	La Chronique **34**	Pintxo **22**
Café Cherrier **23**	La Montée de Lait **30**	Renoir **7**
Café Méliès **18**	La Paryse **14**	Rosalie **6**
Cavalli **9**	Le Blanc **15**	Ru de Nam **1**
Chao Phraya **35**	Le Commensal **11**	St-Viateur Bagel
Chez Schwartz **20**	Le Globe **16**	& Café **29**
Eggspectation **32**	Le Taj **8**	Wilensky
Fairmont Bagel **36**	Leméac **31**	Light Lunch **37**

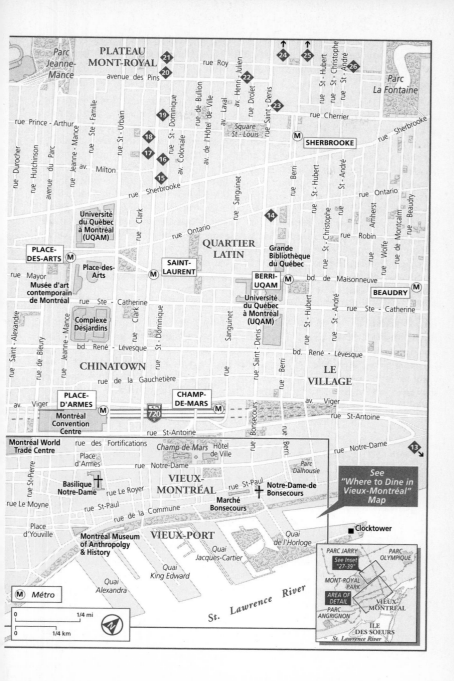

PLATEAU MONT-ROYAL

Parc Jeanne-Mance

avenue des Pins

rue Roy

rue Prince - Arthur

av. Milton

rue Sherbrooke

rue Durocher
rue Hutchinson
avenue du Parc
rue Jeanne - Mance
rue Ste - Famille
rue St-Urbain
rue Clark
av. Coloniale
rue St - Dominique
rue Bullion
av. de l'Hôtel de Ville
av. Laval
av. Henri- Julien
rue Drolet
rue Saint - Denis

Square St-Louis

rue Cherrier

rue St- Hubert
rue St - Christophe
rue St- André

Parc La Fontaine

rue Sherbrooke

SHERBROOKE

Université du Québec à Montréal (UQAM)

rue Ontario

QUARTIER LATIN

Grande Bibliothèque du Québec

PLACE-DES-ARTS Ⓜ

Place-des-Arts

Musée d'art contemporain de Montréal

rue Mayor

rue Ste - Catherine

SAINT-LAURENT

BERRI-UQAM Ⓜ

Université du Québec à Montréal (UQAM)

bd. de Maisonneuve

BEAUDRY Ⓜ

rue Ste - Catherine

rue Berri
rue St - Hubert
rue St - Christophe
rue St - André
rue Robin
rue Amherst
rue Wolfe
rue de Montcalm
rue Beaudry

Complexe Desjardins

bd. René - Lévesque

CHINATOWN

rue de la Gauchetière

bd. René - Lévesque

LE VILLAGE

rue Saint - Alexandre
rue de Bleury
rue Jeanne - Mance
rue Clark
rue St - Dominique
Sanguinet
rue Saint - Denis
rue Berri

PLACE-D'ARMES Ⓜ

CHAMP-DE-MARS Ⓜ

av. Viger

720

Montréal Convention Centre

rue St-Antoine

av. Viger

rue St-Antoine

rue Notre-Dame

Montréal World Trade Centre

rue des Fortifications

Champ de Mars

Hôtel de Ville

Place d'Armes

rue Notre-Dame

Parc Dalhousie

See "Where to Dine in Vieux-Montréal" Map

rue St-Pierre

Basilique Notre-Dame ✝

VIEUX-MONTRÉAL

rue St-Paul

Notre-Dame-de-Bonsecours ✝

rue Le Royer

rue St-Paul

rue Le Moyne

rue de la Commune

Marché Bonsecours

Place d'Youville

Montréal Museum of Anthropolgy & History

VIEUX-PORT

Quai de l'Horloge

■ Clocktower

Quai Jacques-Cartier

Quai King Edward

Quai Alexandra

Ⓜ Métro

0 ——— 1/4 mi
0 ——— 1/4 km

St. Lawrence River

PARC JARRY

PARC OLYMPIQUE

See Inset "27-39"

MONT-ROYAL PARK

AREA OF DETAIL

VIEUX-MONTRÉAL

PARC ANGRIGNON

ÎLE DES SOEURS

St. Lawrence River

1232 rue de la Montagne (south of rue Ste-Catherine). ✆ 514/392-1970. www.rosalierestaurant.com. Reservations recommended. Main courses C$14–C$36 (US$12–US$31/£6–£16). AE, DC, MC, V. Mon–Tues noon–11pm; Wed–Fri noon–midnight; Sat–Sun 5:30pm–midnight. Métro: Peel.

MODERATE

Le Taj *Value* INDIAN   This remains one of the tastiest bargains downtown. The price of the lunch buffet has barely changed since it opened in 1985, and the five-course dinner costs C$28 (US$24/£12). The kitchen specializes in the mughlai cuisine of the subcontinent. Seasonings tend more toward the tangy than the incendiary, but say you want your food spicy and you'll get it (watch out for the innocent-looking green coriander sauce.) Dishes are perfumed with turmeric, saffron, ginger, cumin, mango powder, and *garam masala* (a spice combination that usually includes cloves, cardamom, and cinnamon). For a real treat, order the marinated boneless lamb chops roasted in the tandoor; they arrive at the table sizzling and nested on braised vegetables. Vegetarians have ample choices, the chickpea-based *channa masala* among the most complex. Main courses are huge, arriving in a boggling array of bowls, saucers, cups, and dishes, all accompanied by *naan* (the pillowy flat bread) and basmati rice. Evenings are quiet, and lunchtimes are busy but not hectic.

2077 rue Stanley (near rue Sherbrooke). ✆ 514/845-9015. www.restaurantletaj.com. Main courses C$7.95–C$25 (US$6.90–US$22/£3.40–£11); lunch buffet C$12 (US$10/£5.15); table d'hôte dinner C$28 (US$24/£12). AE, DC, MC, V. Mon–Fri 11:30am–2:30pm and 5–10:30pm; Sat 5–11pm; Sun noon–2:30 and 5–10:30pm. Métro: Peel.

INEXPENSIVE

Boustan *Finds* LEBANESE   Completely non-descript and consistently top-of-the-line. In the middle of the hubbub among the bars and clubs on rue Crescent, this Lebanese pizza-parlor-style eatery gets lines out the door at 2pm (office workers) and again at 2am (late-night partiers), all jonesing for its famed falafel, shish taouk, or shawarma sandwiches. Yes, that's former Prime Minister Pierre Trudeau in the photo at the cash register; he was a regular.

Fun Fact **Poutine, Smoked Meat & the World's Best Bagels**

While you're in Montréal, be sure to indulge in at least a couple Québec standards. Although you'll find them dolled up on some menus, these are generally thought of as basic comfort foods:

- **Bagel:** The doughnut-shaped roll that in Montréal is smaller, chewier, and—it must be said—more deliciously sublime than its New York brethren.
- **Cretons:** A pâté of minced pork, allspice, and parsley.
- **Poutine:** French fries doused with gravy and cheese curds.
- **Queues de Castor:** Literally "beaver tail," a deep-fried pastry the size of a man's footprint served with chocolate or cinnamon.
- **Smoked meat:** A maddeningly tasty sandwich component that hovers in the neighborhood of pastrami and corned beef.
- **Tarte au sucre:** Maple sugar pie.
- **Tourtière:** Meat pie of beans and pork baked in maple syrup.

2020 rue Crescent (at bd. de Maisonneuve). ℂ **514/843-3576.** www.boustan.ca. Most items under C$10 (US$8.70/£4.30). AE, MC, V. Daily 11am–4am. Métro: Peel.

Le Commensal *(Value* VEGETARIAN   Come here for vegetarian fare buffet-style. Most of the dishes are so artfully conceived, with close attention paid to aroma, color, and texture that even avowed meat eaters won't feel deprived. The only likely complaint is that dishes that are supposed to be hot are too often lukewarm. There are more than 100 items, from appetizers to desserts. Patrons circle the table helping themselves, and then pay the cashier by weight—C$1.80 (US$1.55/75p) per 100 grams for the main buffet, C$2.05 (US$1.80/90p) for desserts. The second-floor location affords a view, which compensates for the utilitarian decor. Beer and wine are available. Additional branches include a location at 1720 rue St-Denis (Sherbrooke; ℂ **514/845-2627).**

1204 av. McGill College (at rue Ste-Catherine). ℂ **514/871-1480.** www.commensal.com. Pay by the weight; most meals under C$12 (US$10/£5.15). MC, V. Daily 11:30am–10pm Métro: McGill.

Nocochi LIGHT FARE   At a posh spot on the corner of rue Sherbrooke ouest next to the Musée des Beaux-Arts, this cute little café/patisserie is just the place for a panini or afternoon tea with sandwiches or scones after a few hours of power shopping or museum browsing. The all-white room is decorated with large close-up photos of the decadent pastries you can also indulge in.

2156 rue Mackay (at rue Sherbrooke). ℂ **514/989-7514.** Most meals under C$8 (US$6.95/£3.45). MC, V. Daily 9am–7pm. Métro: Guy-Concordia.

4 Vieux-Montréal (Old Montréal)
VERY EXPENSIVE

Toqué! ⭐⭐⭐ FRENCH CONTEMPORARY   Toqué! is a gem that single-handedly raised the gastronomic expectations of the entire city. A meal here is obligatory for anyone who admires superb food, dazzlingly presented. "Post-nouvelle" might be an apt description for the creations of Normand Laprise, for while presentations are eye-opening, the portions are quite sufficient and the singular combinations of ingredients are intensely flavorful. Asian and related Fusion influences are more evident these days, but the chef is still grounded in principles of the French contemporary kitchen. A short menu and top-of-the-bin ingredients, some of them rarely seen in combination—for example, cauliflower soup with foie gras shavings and milk foam—ensure that options are never set in stone. If you choose one of the two seven-course tasting menus—and on weekends, up to 80% of the crowd does—you can opt for a wine pairing with glasses selected to complement each preparation. Most diners are prosperous-looking men in suits and women who sparkle at throat and wrist, so while there is no stated dress code, you'll want to look your best. Service is efficient, helpful, and not a bit self-important. Allow at least 2 hours for dinner.

900 Place Jean-Paul-Riopelle (near rue St-Antoine). ℂ **514/499-2084.** www.restaurant-toque.com. Reservations required. Main courses C$32–C$45 (US$28–US$39/£14–£19); tasting menus C$92 (US$80/£40) or C$104 (US$90/£45). AE, DC, MC, V. Tues–Sat 5:30–10:30pm. Métro: Square-Victoria.

EXPENSIVE

Aix Cuisine du Terroir ⭐ FRENCH CONTEMPORARY   Replacing the less-than-mediocre resto once lodged beneath the **Place d'Armes Hôtel** (p. 79), this new addition received immediate critical plaudits and makes Vieux-Montréal dining even more attractive. *Terroir* refers to "soil" and a gastronomical allegiance to products of the immediate region, including wild boar from the Cantons de l'Est and caviar from New Brunswick. Contemplate the possibilities with a more generous martini than the (highly taxed) Canadian norm; an *amuse* of bits of grilled shrimp over seaweed drizzled with sesame oil helps. Among the appetizers might be house-smoked salmon with a buckwheat crepe and salmon roe. After that, perhaps pan-roasted red snapper with fiddleheads perked with the crunch of sea salt. Restful earth tones and soft lighting keep the mood subdued, especially in the evening. The restaurant is also open for breakfast daily and for lunch on the weekdays. Lighter appetites might wish to head upstairs to the even-newer **Suite 701** bar, with its small plates card of oysters, cheeses, and updated mac-'n'-cheese.

711 côte de la Place d'Armes (near rue St-Antoine). Ⓒ **514/904-1201.** www.aixcuisine.com. Main courses C$28–C$50 (US$24–US$44/£12–£21). AE, DC, DISC, MC, V. Daily 6:30–10:30am and 5:30–11pm; Mon–Fri 11:30am–2:30pm. Métro: Place d'Armes.

Bonaparte ⚜ FRENCH TRADITIONAL   In a city brimming with accomplished French restaurants, this is a personal favorite. The dining rooms run through the ground floors of two old row houses, and with rich maroon wallpaper and white tablecloths and china, the decorative details are suggestive of namesake Bonaparte's era. Adroit service is provided by schooled pros who manage to be knowledgeable without being stuffy. Recent highlights included salmon in a phyllo crust stuffed with leaks and a dash of vanilla, Dover sole filet with fresh herbs, and beef tartare with capers. Lunches cater to the upscale business crowd, and the restaurant offers an additional theater menu in the early evening.

447 rue St-François-Xavier (north of rue St-Paul). Ⓒ **514/844-4368.** www.bonaparte.ca. Main courses C$20–C$34 (US$17–US$30/£8.40–£15); table d'hôte lunch C$15–C$23 (US$13–US$20/£6.25–£9.70); 7-course tasting menu C$62 (US$54/£27). AE, DC, MC, V. Mon–Fri noon–2:30pm; daily 5:30–10:30pm. Métro: Place d'Armes.

Chez l'Epicier ⚜ FUSION   This crisp little eatery opposite the Marché Bonsecours does double-duty: It's both a high-end restaurant and a gourmet delicatessen with an abundance of tempting prepared foods, so remember it when you are planning a picnic down the hill in the Vieux-Port. When it started up, food here was often little more than workman-like, but over time, the kitchen took a welcome turn to more fashionable, extravagant preparations. Success nurtured ambition, and the chef-proprietor opened the **Version Laurent Godbout** (p. 95) restaurant a few doors away. If anything, that distraction energized this kitchen. While lunches are certainly well done, the dinner hour has seen creative flourishes equaled in only in a few other local establishments. Asian ingredients and techniques are part of the mix, as are witty surprises: Witness a humble turnip appetizer that the waiter injected with tomato confit . . . using a syringe!

331 rue St-Paul est (at rue St-Claude). Ⓒ **514/878-2232.** www.chezlepicier.com. Main courses C$26–C$34 (US$23–US$30/£11–£15), 6-course tasting menu C$80 (US$70/£34). AE, DC, MC, V. Mon–Fri 11:30am–2pm; daily 5:30–10pm. Métro: Champ-de-Mars.

Chez Queux ⚜ FRENCH TRADITIONAL   No fancy foams or nasturtiums on these plates. Chez Queux is a throwback to a time when the only cuisine was French, and that meant chateaubriand for two, showy tableside preparations, and flaming desserts—all the usual suspects that may be remembered from big nights out in the 1960s. Such a menu these days might result in tired renditions from chefs bored to tears with the weight of tradition. Not so here. A properly romantic mood is nurtured

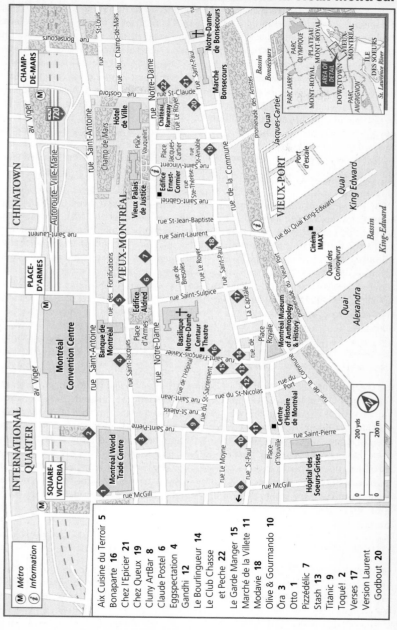

Aix Cuisine du Terroir **5**
Bonaparte **16**
Chez l'Epicier **21**
Chez Queux **19**
Cluny ArtBar **8**
Claude Postel **6**
Eggspectation **4**
Gandhi **12**
Le Bourlingueur **14**
Le Club Chasse et Peche **22**
Le Garde Manger **15**
Marché de la Villette **11**
Modavie **18**
Olive & Gourmando **10**
Ora **3**
Otto **1**
Pizzédélic **7**
Stash **13**
Titanic **9**
Toqué! **2**
Verses **17**
Version Laurent Godbout **20**

by the baronial setting of a mansion built for a mayor of the city in 1862. Deep paneling contrasts with exposed brick walls, fringed lampshades over the tables, wrought-iron chandeliers, weighty velvet drapes, a baby grand, and a two-sided gas fireplace that casts shadows over all. The waiters even wear tuxedos. The food is decidedly retro but the execution is superb. Shellfish bisque, Dover sole meunière, sweetbreads with morels, and even crêpes suzette are better than those of a certain age will recall and will be a revelation to those too young to remember rotary phones. A summer dining terrace adds views of the Vieux-Port to the experience. In short, this is a place to fire a new relationship or cement an old one.

158 rue St-Paul est (near Place Jacques Cartier). ℂ 514/866-5194. www.chezqueux.com. Reservations recommended. Main courses C$28–C$41 (US$24–US$36/£12–£18); table d'hôte C$25–C$40 (US$22–US$35/£11–£17). AE, DC, DISC, MC, V. Tues–Fri 11:30am–2:30pm; Tues–Thurs 5–10pm; Fri–Sat 5–10:30pm. Métro: Place d'Armes.

Le Club Chasse et Peche ⚜ FUSION   The name "Hunting and Fishing Club" doesn't suggest fine dining, but this restaurant received enthusiastic reviews after its 2005 opening and works hard to earn them. The short menu seems simple enough until the waiter comes, kneels beside the table, and describes all dozen or so items in considerable detail. Happily, the food is witty in combination. The recent version of what it calls the "new school surf and turf" is a combination of crisp sweetbread, "boulangères," mushrooms and bacon. Time can s-t-r-e-tch between courses, and the animated patrons at other tables underscore the caution that this isn't a place to go alone. Give it a try at lunch, when two courses run from C$20 to C$26 (US$17–US$23/£8.60–£11) and include homemade pasta with Kobe beef stew as a starter. The restaurant's website is a quirky blog of reviews, YouTube films, and other stuff the staff likes.

423 rue St-Claude (between rue St-Paul and rue Notre Dame). ℂ 514/861-1112. www.leclubchasseetpeche.com. Reservations recommended. Main courses C$27–C$35 (US$23–US$30/£11–£15). AE, DC, MC, V. Tues–Fri 11:30am–2pm; Tues–Sat 6–10:30pm. Métro: Champ-de-Mars.

Le Garde Manger SEAFOOD   Nothing delicate about this newcomer. From the moderately attentive baseball-capped servers to the dark roadhouse decor to the rowdy slip of a bar, this giddy, buzzing resto is a smackdown to its gentrified Vieux-Montréal neighbors. On the plus side, the food is pretty good and generously portioned. The menu changes nightly, but we liked the Chilean sea bass and beef cheeks with bok choy, although the General Tao's lobster was terrifically hot and heavy. At the next table the *assiette de fruits de mer* was served in a small wooden barrel perched sideways and looked fun—by the light of the Catholic saint candles, anyway. You'll need a lead stomach to survive a whole portion of the signature dessert, a fried Mars bar, unless deafening rock music helps you digest. When we last looked, there was no sign on the outside, just a blank, white cube.

408 rue St-François-Xavier (north of rue St-Paul). ℂ 514/678-5044. Reservations recommended. Main courses C$22–C$35 (US$19–US$30/£9.45–£15). AE, MC. Tues–Sun 6–11pm; bar open until 3am. Métro: Place d'Armes.

Modavie ⚜ MEDITERRANEAN   A highly visible location no doubt helps keep this wine bar/restaurant filled, but the management leaves little to chance. Arrayed around the handsome center bar are walls of shelves stacked with bottles of wine and single-malt scotches. Live jazz is presented nightly in summer, less often in winter. Candle flames flicker in river breezes that flow in through front and side windows flung wide on summer nights. The food doesn't disappoint, either in preparation or in portion. Lamb is the self-proclaimed specialty; in one version, it comes as deviled double chops with giant shrimps. There are options, however, such as bison or tiger shrimp in Grand Marnier sauce. The restaurant offers an early bird special from 4 to 6pm for C$16 (US$14/£6.85).

1 rue St-Paul ouest (corner of rue St-Laurent). (✆) **514/287-9582.** www.modavie.com. Reservations recommended on weekends. Main courses C$17–C$37 (US$15–US$32/£7.30–£16); table d'hôte dinner C$27–C$30 (US$23–US$26/£12–£13). AE, DC, MC, V. Mon–Wed 11:30am–10:30pm; Thurs 11:30am–11pm; Fri 11:30am–midnight; Sat–Sun noon–midnight. Métro: Place d'Armes.

Otto ITALIAN   The new upscale hotels opened in the city since the turn of the 21st century have made a point of creating desirable in-house restaurants, many of them recommended in these pages. This one, in the glossy **W Montréal** hotel (p. 76), hit the ground running. It was a proper reflection of the modish thrust of the building surrounding it, in design, clientele, and cuisine—hot, hot, hot. Now, mark it luke-warm. The chic Armani-clad crowd appears to have moved on, and there have been things you shouldn't see in a place of these pretensions—chipped china, film on table-tops, tears in upholstery. Fortunately, the food is still good. The largely Italian reper-toire is given fresh interpretation, from antipasti to *il dolce*. All the current Montréal faves are usually at hand, some with a special twist like the beef tartare topped with poached quail eggs. Among the dinner preparations you don't see everywhere else are black cod with shitake crust and pistachio sauce. None of the prices are a bargain, although the table d'hôte lunch comes close.

In the W Hôtel, 901 Square Victoria (near rue St-Antoine). (✆) **514/395-3180.** www.ristoranteotto.com. Reservations recommended. Main courses C$22–C$38 (US$19–US$33/£9.45–£16); table d'hôte lunch C$20–C$30 (US$17–US$26/£8.60–£13). AE, DC, MC, V. Daily 7am–3pm and 5–11pm. Métro: Square Victoria.

Verses (✦) FRENCH CONTEMPORARY   The flowering of boutique hotels has given multiple jolts of glamour to Old Montréal, joining daring design with the preservation of historic buildings. With it has come the creation of hotel restaurants that destroy the image of threadbare and bland dining rooms, including this snazzy space in the top-notch **Hôtel Nelligan** (p. 78). With its ancient stone-and-brick walls, high ceilings, and horseshoe bar, it's welcoming and clubby. The ambience contributes to the active bar scene toward week's end, especially when the weather is warm enough to open the doors at the front. Service is adroit and thankfully short on pretension, and the pace of a meal is sedate. Lunch can be a grilled beef with Pont-Neuf potatoes or seafood risotto, while dinner choices include lamb *osso buco,* duck breast with juniper berry demi-glace, and a 20-ounce Angus rib steak.

100 rue St-Paul ouest (at St-Sulpice). (✆) **514/788-4000.** www.hotelnelligan.com. Reservations recommended. Main courses C$28–C$38 (US$24–US$33/£12–£16), table d'hôte lunch C$19–C$29 (US$17–US$25/£8.20–£13), AE, DC, MC, V. Daily 6:30am–10:30pm (until 11pm Fri–Sat); bar until midnight Sun–Wed, 1am Thurs–Sat. Métro: Place d'Armes.

Version Laurent Godbout (✦✦) MEDITERRANEAN   Epicures will want to put this on their top-five list. Flush with the ongoing success of his **Chez L'Epicier** (p. 92), the chef-proprietor took on the challenge of this jinxed space on the ground floor of the 19th-century Hotel Rasco just down the block of Old Montréal's main rue St-Paul. There's nothing Victorian about his interior, splashed with crimson and furnished with thoroughly modern tables and sensibilities. Options include a surf and turf with braised pork, chorizo, clams, mussels, and saffron-flavored potatoes, or orzo au gratin with beet root and arugula. There are about 30 seats inside and more out on the terrace in back. If you love the aesthetic, an on-site boutique sells the glassware, plates, and wooden wine buckets so you can re-create the look at home.

295 rue St-Paul est (at rue St-Claude). © 514/871-9135. www.version-restaurant.com. Reservations strongly recommended. Main courses C$24–C$34 (US$21–US$30/£10–£15); lunch from C$14 (US$12/£6). AE, DC, MC, V. Tues–Fri 11:30am–2pm; Tues–Sat 5–10pm. Métro: Place d'Armes or Champ-d-Mars.

MODERATE

Gandhi ★ (Value) INDIAN   Classy but still inexpensive enough that both student and retiree budgets can afford it, Gandhi is so busy that the owners expanded into the adjacent building in 2007, doubling their seating space. Painted creamy yellow in one room and relaxing lavender in the other, the rooms are bright. Service is polite but brisk. The cooking is mostly to order and arrives fresh from the pot, pan, or oven. Flavors are delicate and subtle, but ask that they be ramped up to spicier levels and the kitchen will oblige. (Request "Madras hot" for medium heat.) Tandoori duck and lamb, and chicken tikka are popular, and vegetarian dishes fill a large section of the card.

230 rue St-Paul ouest (near rue St-François-Xavier). © 514/845-5866. www.restaurantgandhi.com. Reservations recommended. Main courses C$14–C$19 (US$12–US$16/£5.80–£7.95); table d'hôte dinner C$20–C$22 (US$17–US$19/£8.40–£9.45). AE, MC, V. Mon–Fri noon–2pm; daily 5–10:30pm. Métro: Place d'Armes.

Ora MEDITERRANEAN   When we visited in 2007, this bright spot in Vieux-Montréal was a few days from opening. We got a peek at the decor—white leather-like walls and banquettes, a neon-pink glow from recessed spots in the ceiling, a serious sound system with a corner DJ booth—and at the food, the brainchild of an Algerian-born wunderkind who most recently was sous chef at the acclaimed **Ferreira Café** (p. 87). He has a heavy hand with the cilantro and homemade mint oil, and his crab cakes were, simply, perfect (the secret: Japanese bread crumbs known as panko). Since we didn't see the kitchen working under the pressure of a full house this is a recommendation with an asterisk, but the preview was very promising. Plans called for the kitchen to be open until 1am.

394 rue St-Jacques (near rue St-Pierre). © 514/848-0202. www.restaurantora.com. Main courses C$11–C$26 (US$9.60–US$23/£4.75–£11). AE, DC, MC, V. Mon–Fri 11:30am–1am; Sat 6pm–1am. Métro: Square-Victoria.

INEXPENSIVE

Claude Postel LIGHT FARE   Starting out as a patisserie and chocolatier, they've added some tables and a short menu of three-course meals under C$12 (US$10). Most customers seem to go for other items, though, including salads, cheeses, pâtés, pastries, and ice cream. Clerks assemble a variety of sandwiches to order from an intriguing range of ingredients. Breads are chewy, crusty, and moist in proper proportion. It's a logical place for a snack or a treat in the midst of a stroll through Vieux-Montréal.

75 rue Notre-Dame ouest (near rue St-Sulpice). © 514/844-8750. www.claudepostel.com. Most items under C$12 (US$10/£5.15). AE, MC, V. Mon–Fri 7am–7pm; Sat–Sun 9am–5pm. Métro: Place d'Armes.

Cluny ArtBar (Finds) BREAKFAST/LIGHT FARE   The loft and factory district west of avenue McGill, at the edge of Vieux-Montréal, is showing signs of rebirth. Artists and high-tech businesses are moving in, although the streets are still quiet. Among the pioneers is the Darling Foundry, an avant-garde exhibition space in a vast, raw, former foundry. Room is provided for Cluny, which serves breakfasts and coffee and, at lunch, antipasti and sandwiches such as tuna melts and smoked salmon *panini*. Although it's called an ArtBar, its main hours are during the daylight, when the sun streams through mammoth industrial windows. It's open past 5pm only on Thursdays. Tables are topped with sections of bowling alley floors, just so you know. Wi-Fi is available.

257 rue Prince (near rue William). © 514/866-1213. www.cluny.info. Most items under C$10 (US$8.70/£4.30). MC, V. Daily 8am–5pm; Thurs until 10pm. Métro: Square Victoria.

Eggspectation BREAKFAST/LIGHT FARE Let the dopey name and punny-funny menu deter you and you'll miss a meal that may constitute one of your fondest food memories of Montréal, at least if you're of the breakfast-is-best school of gastronomy. Even if the dishes are tagged with names like *Eggsiliration* and *Oy Vegg*, prices are low and portions are huge. There are eight variations of Eggs Benedict alone, with sandwiches, burgers, and pastas options as well. In summer, the restaurant stays open into the evening. This is a chain ("constantly eggspanding," as they put it) with a half-dozen locations in the city.

213 rue St-Jacques (at rue St-François-Xavier). © 514/282-0119. www.eggspectation.ca. Most items under C$12 (US$10/£5.15). MC, V. Mon–Fri 6am–5pm; Sat–Sun 6am–6pm (later in summer). Métro: Place d'Armes.

Le Bourlingueur *Value* FRENCH BISTRO Although it doesn't look especially promising at first approach, this is a keeper. The restaurant charges almost unbelievably low prices for several four-course meals daily. The blackboard menu changes depending on what's available at the market that day, making it possible to dine here twice a day for a week without repeating anything, except the uninteresting salad. Roast pork with applesauce, glazed duck leg, and *choucroute garnie* (sauerkraut with meat) are likely to show up, but the specialty of the house is seafood—watch for the shrimp in Pernod sauce. Well short of chic, the interior doesn't make the most of the stone walls and old beams, but the decor hardly matters at these prices and relative quality. The crowd is diverse, with a wide range of ages and occupations.

363 rue St-François-Xavier (at rue St-Paul). © 514/845-3646. Reservations recommended on weekends. Main courses and table d'hôte lunch and dinner C$10–C$17 (US$8.85–US$15/£4.35–£7.30). MC, V. Daily 11:30am–9pm. Métro: Place d'Armes.

Marché de la Villete *Value* FRENCH TRADITIONAL Charming in its simplicity, and if you close your eyes you might convince yourself you're tucked into a shop in a quiet French village. While it started life as an atmospheric *boucherie* and *charcuterie* specializing in cheeses, meats, and breaks, the couple of tables in front multiplied quickly due to demand. Serving breakfast, snacks, and table d'hôte lunches costing as little as C$9.95 (US$8.65), Marché de la Villete packs in neighbors and office workers much of the day, especially between noon and 2pm. The changing tables d'hôte are sturdily satisfying, but the several available platters of merguez and Toulouse sausages, various cheeses, and smoked meats are as beguiling. Quiches, foie gras, sandwiches, and savory and sweet crepes are other possibilities. Wine is available.

324 rue St-Paul ouest (at rue St-Pierre). © 514/807-8084. Reservations not accepted. Most items under C$13 (US$11/£5.60). AE, MC, V. Mon–Sat 9am–6pm; Sun 9am–5pm. Métro: Square Victoria.

Olive et Gourmando LIGHT FARE This local favorite launched by chefs from **Toqué!** (p. 91) started out as an earthy bakery painted in reds, pinks, and gold curlicues, then added table service and transformed itself into a full-fledged café. It still sells near-perfect baguettes—a lot of the bread is out the door by midmorning—as well as many croissants, pastries, and specialty breads. Put your sandwiches together from the cheeses and sausages in the cold case, or choose from their interesting compositions, including a grilled portobello mushroom with a purée of olives and goat cheese, served on heavy, funky pottery or wood cutting board. The only pity is that this eminently appealing spot is not open Sundays, Mondays, or evenings.

351 rue St-Paul ouest (at rue St-Pierre). (℃ 514/350-1083). www.oliveetgourmando.com. Most items under C$10 (US$8.70/£4.30). No credit cards. Tues–Sat 8am–6pm. Métro: Square-Victoria.

Pizzédélic *Kids* PIZZA   Pizza here runs the gamut from traditional to wildly imaginative, with toppings such as your basic tomato sauce, fresh basil, and mozzarella to more startling concoctions involving Black Tiger shrimp and pickled ginger or seafood in a cream sauce. The base crusts are thin and not quite crispy, and the difference over ordinary pizzerias is the use of fresh, not canned, ingredients. Pastas, burgers, and salads are also available.

39 rue Notre-Dame ouest (near bd. St-Laurent). (℃ 514/286-1200. www.pizzedelic-montreal.com. Pizzas and pastas C$8.50–C$17 (US$7.40–US$15/£3.65–£6.35). MC, V. Daily 11am–midnight. Métro: Place d'Armes.

Stash *Value* POLISH   At this site for over a decade, this *restauracja polska* continues to draw throngs of enthusiastic returnees for its abundant offerings and low prices. The interior is composed of brick-and-stone walls, hanging lamps, and wood refractory tables and pews salvaged from an old convent. Roast wild boar has long been featured, along with *bigo*—a cabbage and meat stew—and *pirogis*—dumplings stuffed with meat and cheese—as to be expected in a Polish restaurant. Filling options and sides to these include potato pancakes and borscht with sour cream. A jolly tone prevails, with animated patrons and such menu admonitions as "anything tastes better with wodka, even wodka." An upright piano is played every night but Monday.

200 rue St-Paul oust (at rue St-François-Xavier). (℃ 514/845-6611. www.stashcafe.com. Main courses C$9.75–C$16 (US$8.50–US$14/£4.20–£6.75); table d'hôte dinner C$26–C$36 (US$23–US$31/£11–£16). AE, MC, V. Mon–Fri 11:30am–10:30pm; Sat–Sun noon–10:30pm. Métro: Place d'Armes.

Titanic *Finds* LIGHT FARE   Really good sandwiches aren't easy to locate, but they come to luscious life in these ramshackle rooms with overhead pipes. Freshly baked baguettes are split and filled with such savory combos as coarse country pâté with green peppercorns, or smoked ham and brie, or roast pork with chutney. There's a short cafeteria line of cold dishes, but go for the hot daily specials. Available extras include cornichons (gherkin pickles) and olive pesto. You can also stop in for a breakfast omelet, a meal-size antipasto plate, or an afternoon snack. No alcoholic beverages, but with good ol' Dad's Root Beer, who needs Chablis? Note that the restaurant closes at 4pm. There's free Wi-Fi on-site.

445 rue St-Pierre (near rue Le Moyne). (℃ 514/849-0894. http://titanic-mtl.ca. Reservations not accepted. Most items under C$12 (US$10/£5.15). MC, V. Mon–Fri 7am–4pm. Métro: Place d'Armes.

5 Plateau Mont-Royal

VERY EXPENSIVE

Brunoise ✦✦ FUSION   The kitchen half of this two-man partnership takes full advantage of his ingredients. His mussel-and-potato *bourride* (similar to bouillabaisse) starter, for instance, gives off a stronger aroma of saffron than from cooks who simply use it as coloring; vegetables are crunchy, the broth aromatic. Even the fairly short list of mains promotes indecision. The choices reveal many influences, as broad as Asian and Mediterranean and as focused as Catalan. In his zeal to innovate, the chef sometimes commits the sin of too many ingredients pushed and pulled into shape for presentation; a square of halibut filet resting on spinach and haricots vert, an artichoke purée to one side, with a tumble of olives and cherry tomatoes over all was one example. But choose the simpler preparations and you can expect sublime satisfaction. One other caveat: Their prices rank among the highest in town, and only prix-fixe menus are now offered. The owners expanded in 2007 with **La Brasserie Brunoise** next to the Bell Centre at 1012 rue de la Montagne, where most mains are under C$20 (US$17/£8.60).

3807 rue St-André (at rue Roy). ℭ **514/523-3885**. www.brunoise.ca. Reservations recommended. Prix-fixe and tasting menus C$48–C$70 (US$42–US$61/£21–£30). MC, V. Tues–Sat 5:30–10:30pm. Métro: Sherbrooke.

Moishes ⊛ STEAKHOUSE   Those who care to spend serious money for a slab of charred beef should take their credit ratings here. The oldest steak-and-seafood house in town is also arguably its finest, and less afflicted with tourists than the popular Gibby's in Vieux-Montréal. It used to be dark, musty, and populated with crusty waiters, although the addition of four windows has brightened things up and the venerable retainers who bring the food have eased up on the crabbiness. Moishes now gets the trim new breed of up-and-coming executives as well as those of the older generation who didn't know about triglycerides until it was too late. The former are more likely to go for the chicken teriyaki or Arctic char, perhaps, while the latter stick with the steak. The wine list is substantial, and the restaurant offers wine tasting evenings.

3961 bd. St-Laurent (north of rue Prince Arthur). ℭ **514/845-3509**. www.moishes.ca. Reservations recommended. Main courses C$27–C$52 (US$23–US$45/£12–£22). AE, DC, MC, V. Mon–Fri 11:30am–2:30pm and 5:30–11pm; Sat–Sun 5–11pm. Métro: Sherbrooke.

EXPENSIVE

Au Pied de Cochon ⊛⊛ QUEBECOIS   Packed to the walls 6 nights a week, this Plateau restaurant has become something of a cult, and we're all for it. Though it looks like another of the amiable-but-mediocre storefront restos that line most streets in the neighborhood, famed chef Normand Laprise of **Toqué!** (p. 91) and American chef Anthony Bourdain both love the place. As the name—"The Pig's Foot"—suggests, this is all about slabs of meat, especially pork. "The Big Happy Pig's Chop," weighing in at more than a pound, is emblematic. Meats are roasted to a falling-off-the-bone turn in the brick oven surviving from a previous pizza joint. Most dishes have only four or five easily identifiable ingredients, in balanced proportions. Chef Martin Picard does get clever with one pervasive product: foie gras. It comes in nearly a dozen combinations, including stuffed into a ham hock, with *poutine,* and in a goofy creation called "Duck in a Can" which does, indeed, come to the table with a can opener. When you feel like you another bite will send you into a cholesterol-induced coma, sugar pie is the only fitting finish.

536 rue Duluth est (near rue St-Hubert). ℭ **514/281-1114**. www.restaurantaupieddecochon.ca. Reservations strongly recommended. Main courses C$13–C$45 (US$11–US$39/£5.40–£19). MC, V. Tues–Sun 5pm–midnight. Métro: Sherbrooke.

Buonanotte ⊛ ITALIAN   This was closed for a month of renovations when we stopped by, so take this description with a grain of salt. In the past, though, with its high ceiling crowded with electric fans and heating ducts, Buonanotte resembled something out of New York's SoHo. Bass-heavy dance music, waitresses who look ready to depart to their next fashion shoots, everyone clad head to toe in black—it's all fabulous and dizzying. Although the food takes second place to the preening, the dishes have been surprisingly worthwhile in the past. Pastas prevail, tumbled with crunchy vegetables or any of eight other combinations. Service is stretched thin at dinner, especially on the weekends, and the noise level cranks up after 7pm. The active bar in back stays open until 3am. A principal component of the decor has been the collection of 300 plates painted by celebrity diners including Bono, supermodel Gisele Bündchen, and tennis vixen Maria Sharapova.

3518 bd. St-Laurent (near rue Sherbrooke). ℂ 514/848-0644. www.buonanotte.com. Reservations recommended. Main courses C$16–C$48 (US$14–US$42/£5.15–£21); table d'hôte lunch C$20–C$34 (US$17–US$30/£8.60–£15), dinner C$25–C$40 (US$22–US$35/£11–£17). AE, DC, MC, V. Mon–Sat 11:30am–midnight (until 1am Thurs–Sat); Sun 4pm–midnight; bar until 3am daily. Métro: St-Laurent.

La Montée de Lait 🌟 *Finds* FRENCH BISTRO   This compact bistro began life as a celebrator of dairy products (the "cheese and milk" of its name). When that proved too confining, the staff opened up their menu—quite successfully. Now the cramped corner space is filled nightly with neighborhood regulars, post-grads, and moneyed gourmands from upscale *quartiers*. They squeeze in around tipsy wood tables to partake of starters like red deer tartare (Québécois don't need euphemisms for their food) and such main dishes as scallops in a cream sauce touched with egg, buttery tuna over pencil asparagus and mushrooms, and crispy rectangles of pork belly with molasses and Brussels sprouts. Given the initial enthusiasm that inspired the resto, be certain to have cheese as one course. The selection is impeccable. Lunch is the best deal, for a fixed price of C$20 (US$17/£8.60).

371 rue Villeneuve est (corner rue Drolet). ℂ 514/289-9921. Reservations strongly recommended. Table d'hôte dinner C$40 (US$35/£17) for 4 courses, C$60 (US$52/£26) for 7 courses. MC, V. Tues–Sun 6–10pm; Wed–Fri noon–2pm. Métro: Mont-Royal.

Le Blanc 🌟 FUSION   Once a jinxed location that had seen three other restaurants crash in no time, this latest manifestation has lasted almost a decade, and 80-foot stretch limos regularly pull up to the door. Le Blanc shifted its formula in early 2007 to more of a club-and-lounge atmosphere, but office workers still take advantage of the inexpensive fixed-price lunches before moving aside for a 20- and 30-something crowd in the evening. The pleasingly Art Deco space has a few romantically secluded booths to one side and the front opens to the street in good weather. Food is of the globe-hopping sort, but none of it bizarre.

3435 bd. St-Laurent (north of rue Sherbrooke). ℂ 514/288-9909. www.restaurantleblanc.com. Main courses C$26–C$45 (US$23–US$39/£11–£19). AE, DC, MC, V. Mon–Fri 11am–3pm and 5:30pm–midnight (until 1am Thurs–Sat); Sat–Sun 5:30pm–midnight; bar until 3am daily. Métro: Sherbrooke.

Le Globe 🌟 ITALIAN   This isn't very different from a clutch of similar enterprises at this lively end of The Main north of Sherbrooke, including Buonanotte and Le Blanc. It's an erotically charged, high-end undertaking that starts with a hostess at the podium who looks like she just stopped by between runway gigs, continuing with waitresses bringing food that's better than it has to be, and ending with dancing at midnight and lots of hooking up. There's a bar where the activity intensifies after 9pm, and a DJ plays on Friday and Saturday nights. Meals, if that's why you're here, can begin with selections from an oyster bar listing as many as a dozen varieties, but other appetizers are as appealing. One is a thick disk incorporating layers of warm goat cheese, tomato confit, potatoes, and chives. After that, robust but uncomplicated helpings of beef, lamb, venison, ribs, and veal are the rule. A splurge for two is the *plateau de mer* for C$85 (US$74/£37) or C$145 (US$126/£62)—platters of iced seafood including clams, mussels, and crab legs.

3455 bd. St-Laurent (north of rue Sherbrooke). ℂ 514/284-3823. www.restaurantglobe.com. Reservations recommended. Main courses C$25–C$49 (US$22–US$43/£11–£21). AE, DC, MC, V. Daily 6:30–10pm (until 11pm Fri–Sat, with bar open until 3am). Métro: St-Laurent.

Maestro S.V.P. SEAFOOD Smaller and more relaxed than many of the other restaurants packed in the 2 blocks of The Main north of Sherbrooke, the highlight of this storefront bistro is its oysters. A typical night features 14 varieties from the Atlantic (New Brunswick, PEI, Nova Scotia) and Pacific (British Columbia, Japan), and Maestro claims it has the biggest selection 12 months a year of any city resto. The staff is happy to describe the differences and help you pick a few varieties to taste-test; the PEI Raspberry Point, for instance, is particularly salty when contrasted with the smooth and creamy BC Kusshi. Who knew? A wall of fame of signed oyster shells includes ones held by both the mayor of Montréal and scary guy Marilyn Manson. Mains course options, if you need them, include grilled shrimp with a fennel-and-spinach purée and Madagascar scallops, and the "Maestro Platter," an extravagant medley of clams, mussels, calamari, a half lobster, *and* king crab. There's a tapas menu weekdays until 5pm and Tuesday and Wednesday nights with 30 items under C$10 (US$8.70/£4.30).

3615 bd. St-Laurent (at rue Prince Arthur). ℂ 514/842-6447. www.maestrosvp.com. Reservations recommended. Main courses C$16–C$56 (US$14–US$49/£6.90–£24). AE, DC, MC, V. Mon–Fri 11am–11pm; Sat–Sun 5–11pm. Métro: Sherbrooke.

MODERATE

Café Méliès FRENCH CONTEMPORARY In a section of The Main that is almost bristling with hipness, hurray for the well-appointed but much lower-key Café Méliès, whose decor can best be described as "space-age submarine" (there are portholes throughout). Located inside the Ex-centris film center, this café-lounge has grown into a neighborhood favorite independent of its original function as an appendage to the cinema. Certainly it can be utilized as a quick dinner before a movie, but people drop in for light or bountiful breakfasts at week's end, a snack such as risotto with four mushrooms and truffle oil, or simply an espresso or a glass of wine. Single folks will feel comfortable here. Steel, chrome, and glass define the generous space, updating the traditional bistro concept.

3540 bd. St-Laurent (near av. des Pins). ℂ 514/847-9218. www.cafemelies.com. Main courses C$19–C$32 (US$17–US$28/£8.15–£14). AE, MC, V. Daily noon–10pm (until 11pm Fri–Sat); Sat–Sun brunch 8:30am–3pm. Métro: Sherbrooke.

L'Express ⭐ FRENCH BISTRO No obvious sign announces the presence of this restaurant, only its name discreetly spelled out in white tiles in the sidewalk. There's no need to call attention to itself, since *tout* Montréal knows exactly where this most classic of Parisian-style bistros is. While there are no table d'hôte menus, the food is fairly priced for such an eternally busy place and costs the same at midnight as at noon. After a substantial starter like quiche *jambon fromage* you may opt for one of the lighter main courses, such as the ravioli *maison,* round pasta pockets filled with a flavorful mixture of beef, pork, and veal. Or simply stop by for bowl of *soupe de poisson* or a simple croque-monsieur. This is honest, unpretentious food, thoroughly satisfying, and unlike the flossy new breed of bistro, it's open from breakfast until 3am. Although reservations are usually necessary for tables, single diners can often find a seat at the zinc-topped bar, where meals are also served.

3927 rue St-Denis (just north of rue Roy). © **514/845-5333**. Reservations recommended. Main courses C$13–C$21 (US$11–US$18/£5.50–£9.05). AE, DC, MC, V. Mon–Fri 8am–3am; Sat–Sun 10am–3am. Métro: Sherbrooke.

Pintxo ★★ *Value* SPANISH   Pronounced "Peent-choo," the Basque word for tapas, this tucked-away resto draws from the Spanish Basque tradition, going in for exquisitely composed dishes at fair prices in pleasant surroundings. The Mexican chef spent 5 years in kitchens of the País Vasco, the region in north-central Spain known for its gastronomical audacity. His performances take place in an open kitchen in the middle of a two-part room with antique wood floors and brick walls. Each *pintxo* is true tapa size, only three or four bites, so order recklessly. Some of our favorites: the braised beef cheek, the seared foie gras on a bed of lentils, and the white asparagus with Serrano ham and fried onion cut so fine it looked like tinsel. Diners aren't confined to meals composed solely of tapas presented on 4-inch tiles or slates, although that isn't a bad idea. For C$28 (US$24), the *menu dégustation* provides four pintxos and a main course of your choice, in considerably larger proportion. With the chef still ensconced, this is again accorded the honor of best budget resto in town. Recently, Pintxo opened a smaller resto at 2 rue Sherbrooke est at the corner of boulevard St-Laurent, open weekdays for lunch and Tuesday through Saturday for dinner.

256 rue Roy est (2 blocks west of St-Denis). © **514/844-0222**. Main courses C$18–C$21 (US$16–US$18/£7.75–£9); tapas from C$3 (US$2.60/£1.30). MC, V. Wed–Fri noon–2pm; Mon–Sat 6–11pm. Métro: Sherbrooke.

INEXPENSIVE

Café Cherrier BREAKFAST/LIGHT FARE   The tables on the terrace that wraps around this corner building are filled whenever there's even a slim possibility that a heavy sweater and a bowl of café au lait will fend off frostbite. In summer, the loyalists get to stay out until way past midnight. Brunch is popular even if the food is unexceptional, but do consider this place any time a snack or a meal is in order. Portions are ample and inexpensive. An easygoing atmosphere prevails; it's popular with musicians, actors, and artists, so contrive to look mysterious or celebrated.

3635 rue St-Denis (at rue Cherrier). © **514/843-4308**. Main courses C$7.50–C$20 (US$6.50–US$17/£3.25–£8.60); table d'hôte lunch C$12–C$18 (US$10–C$16/£5.15–£7.75). AE, MC, V. Mon–Fri 7:30am–10pm; Sat–Sun 8:30am–10pm. Métro: Sherbrooke.

Chez Schwartz Charcuterie Hébraïque de Montréal ★ DELI   French-first language laws turned this old-line delicatessen into a linguistic mouthful, but it's still known simply as Schwartz's to its ardent fans. Many are convinced it's the only place to indulge in the guilty treat of *viande fumée*—a kind of brisket that's called, simply, smoked meat. Housed in a long, narrow storefront, with a lunch counter and simple tables and chairs crammed impossibly close to each other, this is as nondescript a culinary landmark as you'll find. If there's not a line out the door, any empty seat is up for grabs. Sandwiches or plates are described either as small (meaning large) or large (meaning humongous), heaped with smoked meat, along with piles of rye bread. Most people also order sides of fries and mammoth garlicky pickles. There are a handful of alternative edibles, but leafy green vegetables aren't among them. Expect a wait. Schwartz's has no liquor license.

3895 bd. St-Laurent (just north of rue Roy). © **514/842-4813**. www.schwartzsdeli.com. Sandwiches C$4.25–C$4.95 (US$3.70–US$4.30/£1.85–£2.15); most other items under C$14 (US$12/£6). No credit cards. Sun–Thurs 8am–12:30am; Fri 8am–1:30am; Sat 8am–2:30am. Métro: Sherbrooke.

March of the Language Police (That Is, *Le Police de Langue*)

When the separatist Parti Québécois took power in the province in 1976, they wasted no time in attempting to make Québec unilingual. Bill 101 made French the sole official language of the provincial government and sharply restricted the use of other languages in education and commerce. The party's fortunes have fallen and risen and fallen in the years since (elections in 2007 saw their worst showing ever), but the primacy of French has remained.

In the early days, agents of *L'Office de la Langue Française* fanned out across the territory, scouring the landscape for linguistic insults to the state and her people. MERRY CHRISTMAS signs were removed from storefronts, and department stores had to come up with a new name for Harris Tweed. Because about 20% of the population had English as a primary language, one out of five Québécois felt instantly declared second-class citizens. Francophones responded that it was about time *les Anglais*—also known a *les autres* (the others)—knew what it felt like.

Affected, too, was the food world. By fiat and threat of punishment, hamburgers became *hambourgeois* and a hot dog was rechristened *le chien chaud*. And Schwartz's Montréal Hebrew Delicatessen, one of the city's fixtures since 1928? It became *Chez Schwartz Charcuterie Hébraïque de Montréal*.

St-Viateur Bagel & Café ⭑ LIGHT FARE   The bagel wars flare as hotly as Montréal's eternal smoked-meat battles once did, but this, an offshoot of the original bakery still located in on rue St-Viateur in the Mile End neighborhood, is among the top contenders (we're also partial to **Fairmont Bagel,** p. 105). At this café you can get bagels to go or to eat in—sesame and poppy seed choices only, thank you—with sandwiches, soup, and salad on the menu, too. Expect a short wait on weekends and not infrequently during the week.

1127 Mont-Royal est (at av. Christophe-Colomb). ② 514/528-6361. www.stviateurbagel.com. Most items under C$12 (US$10/£5.15). No credit cards. Daily 5:30am–midnight. Métro: Mont-Royal.

6 Mile End/Laurier
VERY EXPENSIVE

La Chronique ⭑⭑ FUSION   Montréal's top chefs have been recommending this modest-looking restaurant near Outremont for several years. It was feared that the resulting buzz might spoil the place, but it has only improved, unless you count the hefty increase in prices. You'll discover how remarkable traditional recipes can be in the hands of a master. Presentations are so impeccable that you hate to disturb them, and flavors are so eye-rolling that you want to scrape up every last smear of food. Even diners leery of organ meats will find the veal sweetbreads a silky revelation. The menu includes Mediterranean and Southwestern touches as well as expensive ingredients like foie gras and caviar. There's a price for that: Appetizers cost as much as C$45 (US$39/£19) and one tasting menu reaches C$200 (US$174/£86) per person, with wine. Good as it is, that's much too much, so stick to the available less costly routes. A small but judicious selection of cheeses can precede or replace the tantalizing desserts, which look as if they might take flight.

99 av. Laurier ouest (at rue St-Urbain). ℂ **514/271-3095**. www.lachronique.qc.ca. Reservations highly recommended. Main courses C$34–C$42 (US$30–US$37/£14–£18); table d'hôte dinner C$72 (US$63/£31). AE, DC, MC, V. Tues–Fri 11:30am–2:30pm; Tues–Sat 6–10pm. Métro: Laurier.

EXPENSIVE

Jun-I 👍 FUSION   At first glance, this looks like a standard sushi bar—effusive greetings from the chefs behind the counter, traditional-looking maki, and other bits of fish and rice. But the experienced eponymous chef, Junichi Ikematsu, has ideas that go far beyond the tired fabrications that first introduced us to edible raw seafood. We won't soon forget the unagi roll—thick rounds of sticky rice encasing grilled eel and avocado stood on end, sprinkled with flying fish roe and supporting a tiny grove of colorful micro-greens. Stick with the sushi and you won't go wrong, although there are options of more conventional, but precisely grilled meats and fish. Dessert includes non-Japanese but tasty tiramisu, chocolate cake, and cheesecake.

156 av. Laurier ouest (near rue St-Urbain). ℂ **514/276-5864**. Reservations recommended on weekends. Main courses dinner C$26–C$35 (US$23–US$31/£11–£13); table d'hôte lunch C$23–C$29 (US$20–US$25/£9.90–£12). AE, DC, MC, V. Tues–Fri 11:30am–2pm; Tues–Thurs 6–10pm; Fri–Sat 6–11pm. Métro: Laurier.

MODERATE

BU ITALIAN   Not just another award-winning designer bar, this place strikes an exquisite balance between wine and food. The eats in question are antipasti, which the manager stoutly contends are far superior to the currently fashionable variations on the tapas tradition ("one bite, gone," as he puts it). The Assiette BU is a satisfying assortment of meats, cheese, and grilled vegetables, and some people come just for BU's silky rendition of *vitello tonnato*—veal and crème of tuna. There are three hot dishes offered nightly, but the purpose of all the food is to complement, not do battle with, the wines. The long card of 500 selections eschews the same old bottlings, and even those who regard themselves as connoisseurs make delightful discoveries, guided by the knowledgeable staff. There are about 25 wines by the glass. The crowd gets younger as the night rolls on, and because the bar stays open late, off-duty chefs are often in the mix.

5245 bd. St-Laurent (at av. Fairmount). ℂ **514/276-0249**. Reservations recommended. Antipasti C$9–C$20 (US$7.85–US$17/£3.85–£8.60). AE, DISC, MC, V. Daily 5pm–1am. Métro: Laurier.

Chao Phraya *Finds* THAI   Contender for the title of best Thai in town, this spot boasts a panache that sets it a few notches above most of its rivals, which means that every table is filled on the weekends. Named for a river in Thailand, Chao Phraya brightens its corner on increasingly fashionable Laurier Avenue with white table linens and sprays of orchids on each table. The host helps with suggestions about the most popular items on the menu: dumplings in peanut sauce as an appetizer, and a mixed seafood composed of squid, scallops, shrimp, crab claws, mussels, and chunks of red snapper as a main. The food is tangy, and menu items are given one to three hot-pepper symbols grading hotness (two printed peppers are about right for most people). A cooling cucumber salad helps, and you'll want a side of sticky rice, too. There is a good selection of vegetarian options. Everything comes in attractive bowls and platters, and the atmosphere is warm and cozy.

50 av. Laurier ouest (1 block west of bd. St-Laurent). ℂ **514/272-5339**. Reservations recommended. Main courses C$9–C$19 (US$7.85–US$17/£3.85–£8.15). AE, DC, MC, V. Thurs–Sat 5–11pm; Sun–Wed 5–10pm. Métro: Laurier.

Leméac *⚜* FRENCH BISTRO   This sprightly member of the Laurier scene has a long tin-topped bar along one side, well-spaced tables, and, far from least, a crew of cheerful waitresses. While the bistro dishes sound conventional on the page, they are put together in freshly conceived ways. Two examples: A curried mussel soup was capped by a nicely browned pillow of puff pastry, and the salmon *pot-au-feu* was a perfectly cooked filet laid over a healthful selection of small potatoes, carrots, tender Brussels sprouts, and their collective broth. Food is different but not startlingly so, and served in an atmosphere that invites lingering. Weekend brunch is popular, as are the side terrace in warm weather and the C$22 (US$19/£9.45) appetizer-plus-main menu that kicks in at 10pm. The name comes from the publishing firm that used to occupy the building.

1045 av. Laurier ouest (corner of av. Durocher). *℗* 514/270-0999. www.restaurantlemeac.com. Reservations recommended on weekends. Main courses C$18–C$37 (US$15–US$32/£7.50–£16); table d'hôte lunch C$18–C$23 (US$15–US$20/£7.50–£9.90); late-night menu C$22 (US$19/£9.45). AE, DC, MC, V. Mon–Fri 11:45am–midnight; Sat–Sun 10:30am–midnight. Métro: Laurier.

MeatMarket Restaurant Café *Finds* LIGHT FARE   Neither a butcher shop nor a pickup joint, MeatMarket is actually a stylish gourmet sandwich and burger café, located on a nondescript block of Boulevard St-Laurent north of the fancier restaurant action. There are vegetarian and salad options, but if you can, go for one of the meats: maybe the Cuba Libre sandwich with grilled pork, plantain, Cuban marinade, and mint-and-mango ketchup, or one of five burgers. The Swiss Miss burger, with bacon, Swiss, caramelized onion, and mayo with pesto, was short of sublime, but only just. Led Zeppelin on the stereo added exactly the right kick.

4415 bd. St-Laurent (just south of av. du Mont-Royal). *℗* 514/223-2292. www.meatmarketfood.com. Main courses C$7.25–C$21 (US$6.30–US$18/£3.10–£9.05). AE, MC, V. Mon–Sat 11:30am–4pm; Tues–Sat 5–11pm. Métro: Mont-Royal.

INEXPENSIVE

Aux Vivres VEGAN   In business since 1997, this bright restaurant with white Formica tables, raw blonde walls, and pink Chinese lanterns has been humming and busy since moving into its current location in 2006. A large menu includes bowls of chili with guacamole and bok choi with grilled tofu and peanut sauce, as well as salads, sandwiches, desserts, and a daily chef special. All foods are vegan and the kitchen uses organic vegetables and local organic tofu and tempeh. In addition to inside tables, there is a juice bar off to one side and a back terrace that seats 25.

4631 bd. St-Laurent (at av. du Mont-Royal). *℗* 514/842-3479. Most items under C$11 (US$9.55/£4.75). No credit cards. Tues–Sun 11am–11pm. Métro: Mont-Royal.

Bilboquet *⚜* *Kids* ICE CREAM   You can get a good croque-monsieur here, but the reason to seek out this humble spot in the ritzy Outremont section of Mile End is the splendid ice creams and sorbets. This *artisan glacier* makes its own sweet stuff, rich with caramel, nuts, fruit . . . whatever is fresh and available and strikes the chef's fancy. Flavors include maple taffy, passion fruit, chocolate-orange, and vanilla-raspberry. In the warm weather there's always a line. With just a few tables inside and benches outside, prepare to stroll with your cone.

1311 rue Bernard ouest (at av. Outremont). *℗* 514/276-0414. Most items under C$8 (US$6.95/£3.45). No credit cards. Daily 7am–midnight. Closed Jan–Mar. Métro: Outremont.

Fairmont Bagel BREAKFAST/LIGHT FARE   Bagels in these parts are thinner, smaller, and crustier than the cottony monsters posing as the real thing south of the border. They're hand-rolled, twist-flipped into circles, and baked in big wood-fired ovens right on the premises. Fairmont was founded in 1919 and now offers 20 types, including unfortunate options like mueslix and (shudder) blueberry, but why opt for trendy odd-ball tastes when you can get a perfectly perfect sesame seed? A 24-hour hole in the wall, Fairmont sells its bagels and accouterments such as cream cheese and nova lox "to go" only, 7 days a week, even on Jewish holidays.

74 av. Fairmont ouest (near rue St-Urbain). ℂ **514/272-0667.** www.fairmountbagel.com. Under C$1 (US85¢/45p) per bagel. No credit cards. Open 24 hr. a day, 7 days a week, 365 days a year. Métro: Laurier.

Wilensky Light Lunch LIGHT FARE   Wilensky's has been a Montréal tradition since 1932, and has its share of regular pilgrims nostalgic for its grilled-meat sandwiches, low prices, curt service, and utter lack of decor. This is Duddy Kravitz/Mordecai Richler territory, and the ambience is Early Jewish Immigrant. There are nine counter stools, no tables. The house special is grilled salami and bologna, with mustard, thrown on a bun and squashed on a grill, and never, for whatever reason, cut in two. You can wash it down with an egg cream or Cherry Coke jerked from the rank of syrups—this place has drinks typical of the old-time soda fountain that it is. Enter Wilensky's to take a step back in time; we're talking tradition here, not cuisine.

34 rue Fairmount ouest (1 block west of bd. St-Laurent). ℂ **514/271-0247.** Most items under C$4 (US$3.50/£1.70). No credit cards. Mon–Fri 9am–4pm. Métro: Laurier.

7 Latin Quarter
INEXPENSIVE

La Paryse ⟨Value⟩ SANDWICHES   Only slightly larger than your basic hole in the wall, this Latin Quarter standby packs in students, profs, young execs, and middleagers. They come for the burgers, as much the consensus choice for best-in-town as Schwartz's is for smoked meat. Unless you possess a really large appetite and a capacious mouth to go with it, you certainly won't need the double burger or the *frites grosse* (big fries). Wines are available by the glass. The inevitable line moves quickly.

302 rue Ontario est (at rue Sanguinet). ℂ **514/842-2040.** All items under C$10 (US$8.70/£4.30). MC, V. Tues–Fri 11am–11pm; Sat 11:30am–11pm; Sun 11am–10pm. Métro: Berri-UQAM.

8 Outer Districts
VERY EXPENSIVE

Nuances 👒👒 FRENCH CONTEMPORARY   This is haute cuisine in a gambling casino, as unlikely as that seems. Ensconced atop four floors of blinking lights and the crash of cascading jackpots, this dazzling entry into Montréal's gastronomic sweepstakes got a face-lift in early 2007 that made the decor as contemporary and elegant as the food. A dramatic crystal chandelier may evoke the ghost of Liberace, but gone is the dark presidential decor and in are creamy walls, white linen, pale green leather banquettes, and Granny Smith–green candles. Every member of the staff is a sommelier and qualified to advise on appropriate wines from the extensive cellar. Recent triumphs have included loin of caribou (killed by arrow by an Inuit, we were told) with parsley gnocchi and caramelized squash, and Chilean sea bass with wine-butter emulsion. *Le fromage du Sommelier* is a selection of cheeses including admirable Québec options. Save room for the spiced Genoa cake, which is served with Mascarpone cream and fig chips, and an espresso, which comes with rock-candy sugar on a stick. Dress code is business attire, but women will feel equally comfortable in business dress or a little red dress. This is a room with real star power.

1 av. du Casino (in the Casino de Montréal, Ile Ste-Hélène). (514/392-2708. www.casino-de-montreal.com. Reservations strongly recommended. Main courses C$43–C$46 (US$37–US$40/£19–£20); 3 table d'hôte options C$65–C$110 (US$57–US$96/£28–£47). AE, DC, MC, V. Sun–Thurs 5:30–11pm; Fri–Sat 5:30–11:30pm. Métro: Parc Jean-Drapeau.

EXPENSIVE

Joe Beef SEAFOOD/STEAKHOUSE   Owner David McMillan used to ride the fast track, with interests in some of the most glamorous resto-clubs in town, packed with free-spending pretty people. He tired of that scene and opened this little beef-and-fish house far from the brightest lights in a neighborhood where the warehouses haven't all turned into high-end lofts yet. He minds the oyster bar and knows most of his customers and likes it that way. Housed in a narrow storefront that keeps diners elbow-to-elbow, the restaurant's menu and wine list are written on the big blackboard occupying one wall. Customary starters are oysters, including many rarely seen, such as Caraquets, Cortez Islands, and Marina Gems. The menu is written on the wall and might include *salade Joe Beef,* a tangy tangle of haricots vert, boiled potatoes, pickled beets, jicama straws, slices of duck breast, leaves of Parmesan . . . and a poached egg. Mains can include trout and suckling pig, but if you're only here once, how can it be anything but steak au poivre in a place with this name? The strip sirloin must be 14 ounces and 2 inches thick. McMillian is a wine connoisseur, as well, so seek his advice on a claret to go with the beef.

2491 rue Notre-Dame ouest (near av. Atwater). (514/935-6504. Reservations strongly recommended. Main courses C$24–C$36 (US$21–US$31/£10–£16). AE, MC, V. Tues–Sat 6–10pm. Métro: Lionel-Groulx.

Tips Late-Night Bites

Most Montréal restaurants serve until 10 or 11pm, but sometimes you need something else—a meal or just a snack—after midnight. Here are some places to keep in mind:

- **Boustan** (p. 90): In the middle of the late-night hubbub on downtown's rue Crescent, Boustan has lines out the door at 2am of partiers jonesing for a falafel or shawarma sandwich.
- **Buonanotte** (p. 99) and **Le Blanc** (p. 100): In the heart of the boulevard St-Laurent party action, Buonanotte serves until 1am Thursday through Saturday nights, and until midnight the rest of the week. Nearly across the street from Buonanotte, Le Blanc keeps the same hours.
- **Café Cherrier** (p. 102): The kitchen closes at 10pm, but on warm summer nights they will keep the terrace open to midnight or 1am.
- **Chez Schwartz** (p. 102): Schwartz's serves all your smoked meat needs until 12:30am every night, and until 1:30am on Fridays and 2:30am on Saturdays.
- **Leméac** (p. 105): This Mile End joint serves up bistro food on a terrace until midnight (until 1am Thurs–Sat nights).
- **L'Express** (p. 101): Not only is it a classic Parisian-style bistro, but it's open until 3am every day.
- **Ora** (p. 96): This newcomer plans to keep its kitchen going until 1am with pizzas, pastas, and super-tasty crab cakes.

9 Picnic Fare

If you're planning a picnic, bike ride, or simply an evening in, pick up supplies in Vieux-Montréal at any of three shops along rue St-Paul. On the west end of the street is **Olive et Gourmando** (p. 97) at no. 351 and, just across the street, the **Marché de la Villete** (p. 97) at no. 324. Both sell fresh breads, fine cheeses, sandwiches, salads, and pâtés. On the east end of rue St-Paul, a block and a half from the main plaza Place Jacques-Cartier, is **Chez l'Epicier** (p. 92), at no. 331. It's an ambitious restaurant with a gourmet delicatessen of takeout goodies.

Better still, use this as an excuse to make a short excursion by bicycle or Métro (the Lionel-Groulx stop) to **Marché Atwater,** the public farmer's market at 138 av. Atwater, which is open daily. The long interior shed is bordered by stalls of gleaming produce and flowers, the two-story center section given to wine purveyors, butchers, food counters, bakeries, and cheese stores. The **Boulangerie Première Moisson** (© 514/932-0328) fills the space with the tantalizing aromas of baskets of breads and cases of pastries—oh, the pastries!—and has a seating area for nibbling on toasted baguettes or sipping a bowl of café au lait. Two of the best cheese purveyors are the **Fromagerie du Deuxième** (© 514/932-5532), whose knowledgeable attendants know every detail of production of the scores of North American and European cheeses on offer, and the **Fromagerie du Marché Atwater** (© 514/932-4653), which has over 500 different cheeses, some 50 of them from Québec, and also sells pâtés and charcuterie. Marché Atwater is right on the revamped Lachine Canal, where you can stroll and find a picnic table.

7

Exploring Montréal

Montréal is a feast of choices, able to satisfy the desires of both physically active and culturally curious visitors. Hike up the city's mountain Mont-Royal in the middle of the city, cycle for miles beside 19th-century warehouses and locks on the Lachine Canal, take in artworks and ephemera at some 20 museums and as many historic buildings, attend a Canadiens hockey match, party until dawn on rue Crescent and The Main, or soak up the results, both concrete and spiritual, of some 400 years of conquest and immigration: It's all here for the taking.

Once you've decided what you want to do, getting from hotel to museum to attraction is pretty easy. Montréal has an efficient Métro system, a fairly logical street grid, wide boulevards, and a vehicle-free underground city that all aid in the swift, largely uncomplicated movement of people from place to place.

If you're planning to check out several museums, consider the Montréal Museums Pass (see the "Money Savers" box on p. 112).

For families with children, few cities assure kids of as good a time as this one. There are riverboat rides, the fascinating Biodôme—which replicates four distinct ecosystems—the creepy-crawlies of the Insectarium, a sprawling amusement park, the Vieux-Port Centre des Sciences de Montréal, and magical performances by the city's hometown Cirque du Soleil circus company. Recommended attractions are flagged with a "Kids" icon, and an "Especially for Kids" section is on p. 121.

When planning your visit, you might want to note which museums have restaurants or cafés so that you can plan a meal there. Most museums, although not all, are closed Mondays.

1 The Top Attractions

DOWNTOWN

If this is your first trip to Montréal, consider starting with the walking tour in chapter 8 (p. 138) for an overview of the neighborhood and its attractions. The downtown tour ends at the Musée des Beaux-Arts.

Musée des Beaux-Arts ★★★ Montréal's Museum of Fine Arts is the city's most prominent museum, opened in 1912 in Canada's first building designed specifically for the visual arts. The original neoclassical pavilion is on the north side of Sherbrooke. A striking new annex was built in 1991 directly across the street and tripled exhibition space, adding sub-street-level floors and underground galleries that connect to the old building. Art on display is nearly always dramatically mounted, carefully lit, and diligently explained in both French and English.

Our recommendation is to enter the annex on the south side of rue Sherbrooke, take the elevator to the top, and work your way down. The permanent collection,

Downtown & Vieux-Montréal Attractions

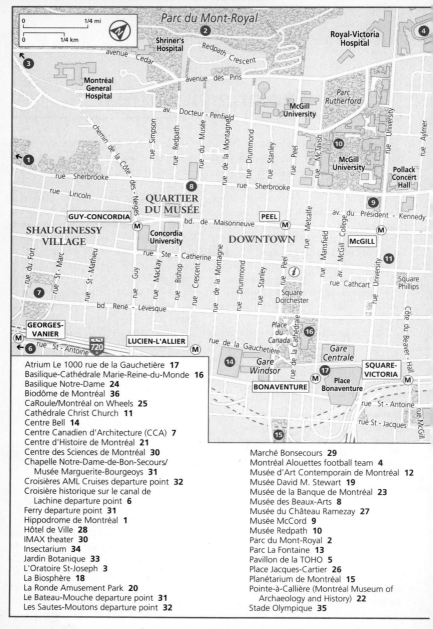

Atrium Le 1000 rue de la Gauchetière **17**
Basilique-Cathédrale Marie-Reine-du-Monde **16**
Basilique Notre-Dame **24**
Biodôme de Montréal **36**
CaRoule/Montréal on Wheels **25**
Cathédrale Christ Church **11**
Centre Bell **14**
Centre Canadien d'Architecture (CCA) **7**
Centre d'Histoire de Montréal **21**
Centre des Sciences de Montréal **30**
Chapelle Notre-Dame-de-Bon-Secours/
    Musée Marguerite-Bourgeoys **31**
Croisières AML Cruises departure point **32**
Croisière historique sur le canal de
    Lachine departure point **6**
Ferry departure point **31**
Hippodrome de Montréal **1**
Hôtel de Ville **28**
IMAX theater **30**
Insectarium **34**
Jardin Botanique **33**
L'Oratoire St-Joseph **3**
La Biosphère **18**
La Ronde Amusement Park **20**
Le Bateau-Mouche departure point **31**
Les Sautes-Moutons departure point **32**

Marché Bonsecours **29**
Montréal Alouettes football team **4**
Musée d'Art Contemporain de Montréal **12**
Musée David M. Stewart **19**
Musée de la Banque de Montréal **23**
Musée des Beaux-Arts **8**
Musée du Château Ramezay **27**
Musée McCord **9**
Musée Redpath **10**
Parc du Mont-Royal **2**
Parc La Fontaine **13**
Pavillon de la TOHO **5**
Place Jacques-Cartier **26**
Planétarium de Montréal **15**
Pointe-à-Callière (Montréal Museum of
    Archaeology and History) **22**
Stade Olympique **35**

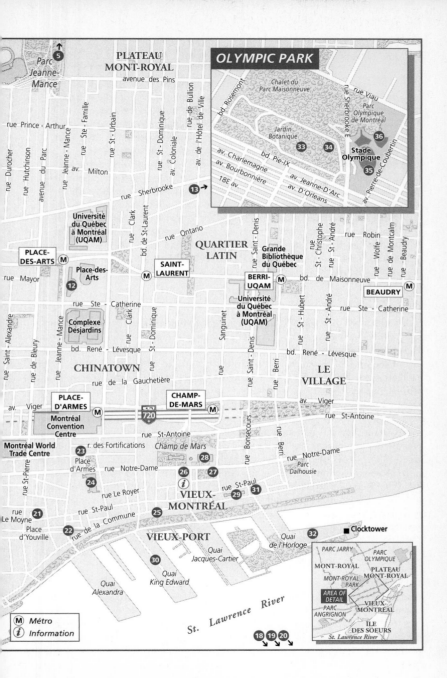

OLYMPIC PARK

Chalet du
Parc Maisonneuve

rue Viau

rue Sherbrooke E

Parc
Olympique
de Montréal

bd. Rosemont

Jardin
Botanique

33   34

36

Stade
Olympique

35

av. Charlemagne
av. Bourbonnière
18E av.

bd. Pie-IX

av. Jeanne-D'Arc
av. D'Orleans

av. Pierre-de-Coubertin

Parc
Jeanne-
Mance

5

PLATEAU
MONT-ROYAL

avenue des Pins

rue Prince - Arthur

rue Durocher
rue Hutchinson
avenue du Parc
av. Jeanne - Mance
rue Ste - Famille
rue St - Urbain
rue St - Dominique
av. Coloniale
rue de Bullion
av. de l'Hôtel de Ville

av. Milton

rue Sherbrooke

13

Université
du Québec
à Montréal
(UQAM)

rue Clark
bd. de St-Laurent

rue Ontario

QUARTIER
LATIN

rue Saint - Denis

Grande
Bibliothèque
du Québec

rue Robin

rue St - Christophe
rue St - André
rue Wolfe
rue de Montcalm
rue Beaudry

PLACE-
DES-ARTS M

rue Mayor

Place-des-
Arts

12

SAINT-
LAURENT M

BERRI-
UQAM M

bd. de Maisonneuve

BEAUDRY M

Université
du Québec
à Montréal
(UQAM)

rue St - Hubert
rue St - André

rue Ste - Catherine

rue Saint - Alexandre
rue de Bleury
av. Jeanne - Mance

Complexe
Desjardins

rue Clark
rue St - Dominique

rue Ste - Catherine

bd. René - Lévesque

rue Sanguinet

rue Saint - Denis
rue St - Hubert
rue Berri

bd. René - Lévesque

CHINATOWN

rue de la Gauchetière

rue

LE
VILLAGE

PLACE-
D'ARMES M

av. Viger

Montréal
Convention
Centre

Montréal World
Trade Centre

rue St-Pierre

23

24

rue
Le Moyne

21

Place
d'Youville

22

720

CHAMP-
DE-MARS M

rue St-Antoine

rue des Fortifications

Place
d'Armes

Champ de Mars

28

rue Notre-Dame

26   27

i

25

rue St-Paul

rue Le Royer

rue St-Paul

rue de la Commune

VIEUX-
MONTRÉAL

VIEUX-PORT

av. Viger

rue St-Antoine

rue Bonsecours

rue Berri

rue Notre-Dame

Parc
Dalhousie

rue St-Paul

29 31

32

Clocktower

Quai
de l'Horloge

Quai
Jacques-Cartier

30

Quai
King Edward

Quai
Alexandra

St. Lawrence River

M Métro
i Information

18 19 20

PARC JARRY

PARC
OLYMPIQUE

MONT-ROYAL

PLATEAU
MONT-ROYAL

MONT-ROYAL
PARK

AREA OF
DETAIL

PARC
ANGRIGNON

VIEUX-
MONTRÉAL

ÎLE
DES SOEURS

St. Lawrence River

Tips Money Savers

* **Time your trip to coincide with Montréal Museums Day.** On the last Sunday in May, over two dozen museums open their doors for free in a citywide open house. There are even free shuttle buses to get around.
* **Flash your AAA card.** Members of the American Automobile Association get the same discounts as members of its Canadian sister, the CAA. That includes reduced rates at many museums, hotels, and restaurants.
* **Buy the Montréal Museums Pass.** Good for 3 consecutive days, the pass gives entry to 32 museums and attractions, including most mentioned in this chapter. The price is C$45 (US$39/£19) for a pass that includes unlimited access to public transportation and C$35 (US$30/£15) for just the museums. There are no separate rates for seniors or children. The pass is available at all participating museums, many hotels, and the tourist offices at 174 rue Notre-Dame (in Vieux-Montréal) and 1255 rue Peel (downtown). To find out more, call © **877/266-5687** or visit www.montreal museums.org.

which totals more than 33,000 works, is largely devoted to international contemporary art and Canadian works created after 1960, and to European painting, sculpture, and decorative art from the Middle Ages to the 19th century. On the upper floors are many of the gems of the collection: paintings by 12th- to 19th-century artists Hogarth, Tintoretto, Bruegel, El Greco, Ribera, and portraitist George Romney; and works—representative, if not world-class—by more recent artists including Renoir, Monet, Picasso, Cézanne, and Rodin. French-Canadian landscape watercolorist Marc-Aurèle Fortin (1888–1970) is well represented; a separate museum that had been devoted just to him donated its entire collection to Beaux-Arts in 2007.

Temporary exhibitions can be dazzling: A recent show brought the treasures of Catherine the Great, including her spectacular Coronation Coach, from the Hermitage Museum of Saint Petersburg. An exhibition of art from Cuba is scheduled for 2008. The museum's street-level store on the south side of rue Sherbrooke has an impressive selection of quality books, games, and folk art. A good café is adjacent.

1379–1380 rue Sherbrooke ouest (at rue Crescent). © **514/285-2000.** www.mmfa.qc.ca. Free admission to the permanent collection (donations happily accepted). Admission to temporary exhibitions: C$15 (US$13/£6.45) adults, C$7.50 (US$6.50/£3.25) seniors and students, free for children 12 and under, C$30 (US$26/£13) family (1 adult and 3 children 16 and under, or 2 adults and 2 children 16 and under); half-price Wed 5–9pm. AE, MC, V. Tues 11am–5pm; Wed–Fri 11am–9pm; Sat–Sun 10am–5pm. Métro: Guy-Concordia. Bus: 24.

Musée McCord   Associated with McGill University, the McCord Museum of Canadian history showcases the eclectic—and not infrequently eccentric—collections of scores of benefactors from the 19th century through today. More than 16,600 costumes, 65,000 paintings, and 1,250,000 historical photographs documenting the history of Canada are rotated in and out of storage to be displayed. In general, expect to view furniture, clothing, china, silver, paintings, photographs, and folk art that reveal rural and urban life as it was lived by English-speaking immigrants of the past 3 centuries. A First Nations room displays portions of the museum's extensive collection of objects from Canada's Native population, including meticulous beadwork, baby carriers, and fishing implements. Exhibits are intelligently mounted, with texts in English and French. There's a popular café near the front entrance, and a shop that sells Native and Canadian arts and crafts, pottery, and more.

690 rue Sherbrooke ouest (at rue Victoria). (℃ 514/398-7100. www.mccord-museum.qc.ca. Admission C$12 (US$11/£5.15) adults, C$9 (US$7.85/£3.90) seniors, C$6 (US$5.20/£2.60) students, C$4 (US$3.50/£1.70) ages 6–12, free for children 5 and under; free admission on the first Sat of the month 10am–noon. Tues–Fri 10am–6pm; Sat–Sun 10am–5pm; summer and holiday weekends, also Mon 10am–5pm. Métro: McGill. Bus: 24.

Parc du Mont-Royal   Montréal is named for this 232m (761-ft.) hill that rises at its heart—the "Royal Mountain." Walkers, joggers, cyclists, dog owners, and skaters all use this largest of the city's green spaces throughout the year. In summer, **Lac des Castors (Beaver Lake)** is surrounded by sunbathers and picnickers (no swimming allowed, however). In winter, cross-country skiers follow miles of paths and snowshoers tramp along trails laid out for their use. The large, refurbished **Chalet du Mont-Royal** near the crest of the hill is a popular destination, providing a sweeping view of the city from its terrace and an opportunity for a snack. Up the hill behind the chalet is the spot where, tradition says, Paul de Chomedey, sieur de Maisonneuve (1612–76) erected a wooden cross after the colony survived a flood threat in 1643. The present incarnation of the steel **Croix du Mont-Royal** was installed in 1924 and is lit at night. It usually glows white, although it was lit red in the 1980s during a march against AIDS and purple in 2005 to announce the death of Pope John Paul II.

(℃ 514/843-8240 for the Maison Smith information center in the park's center. www.lemontroyal.qc.ca. Métro: Mont-Royal. Bus: 11; get off at Lac des Castors (Beaver Lake).

VIEUX-MONTREAL (OLD MONTREAL)

The central plaza of Vieux-Montréal is **Place Jacques-Cartier,** and it's the focus of much activity in the warm months. The plaza has two repaved streets bracketing a center promenade that slopes down from rue Notre-Dame to the Old Port, with venerable stone buildings from the 1700s along both sides. Horse-drawn carriages that gather at the plaza's base, outdoor cafés, street performers, and flower sellers recall a Montréal of a century ago. Montréalers insist they would never go to a place so overrun by tourists—which makes one wonder why so many of them do, in fact, congregate here. They take the sun and sip sangria on the bordering terraces just as much as visitors do, enjoying the unfolding pageant.

If this is your first trip to Montréal, consider starting with the walking tour in chapter 8 (p. 131) for an overview of the neighborhood and its attractions. The walk leads past most of the sites listed here and can help you get your bearings. For further information about this quarter, log on to its official website at **www.vieux.montreal.qc.ca**.

Basilique Notre-Dame ✸✸✸   Breathtaking in the richness of its interior furnishings and big enough to hold 4,000 worshipers, this magnificent structure was designed in 1824 by James O'Donnell, an Irish-American Protestant architect from New York. So profoundly was O'Donnell moved by the experience that he converted to Catholicism after the basilica was completed. The impact is understandable. Of the hundreds of churches on the island of Montréal, Notre-Dame's interior is the most stunning, with a wealth of exquisite detail, most of it carved from rare woods that have been delicately gilded and painted. O'Donnell, clearly a proponent of the Gothic revival style, is the only person honored by burial in the crypt.

The main altar was carved from linden wood, the work of Victor Bourgeau. Behind it is the **Chapelle Sacré-Coeur (Sacred Heart Chapel),** much of it destroyed by an arsonist in 1978 but rebuilt and rededicated in 1982. The altar has 32 bronze panels representing birth, life, and death, cast by Charles Daudelin of Montréal. A 10-bell carillon resides in the east tower, while the west tower contains a single massive bell nicknamed **"Le Gros Bourdon"** which weighs more than 12 tons and has a low, resonant rumble that vibrates right up through your feet.

Twenty-minute guided tours in English are offered throughout the day, beginning at 9am. Depending on his availability, the church's organist Pierre Grandmaison gives 90-minute tours of the organ on occasional Wednesday, Thursday, and Friday mornings. And a sound-and-light show called **"Et la lumière fut"** ("And then there was light")—advertised on garish banners in front of the church—is presented nightly Tuesday through Saturday.

110 rue Notre-Dame ouest (on Place d'Armes). ✆ 514/842-2925. www.basiliquenddm.org. Basilica C$4 (US$3.50/ £1.70) adults, C$2 (US$1.75/85p) ages 7–17. Light show C$10 (US$8.70/£4.30) adults, C$9 (US$7.85/£3.90) seniors, C$5 (US$4.35/£2.15) ages 7–17. MC, V. Basilica daily 8am–5pm; tours daily 9am–4pm; light shows Tues–Thurs 6:30pm, Fri 6:30 and 8:30pm, Sat 7 and 8:30pm. Métro: Place d'Armes.

Centre des Sciences de Montréal *(Kids*

Running the length of a central pier in Vieux-Port (Old Port), this ambitious complex occupies a steel-and-glass building along much of Quai King Edward. Focusing on science and technology, it has interactive displays and a cinema, as well as a popular **IMAX theater** (p. 121). Designed to make energy conservation, 21st-century communications, and life sciences vivid, in 2007 it hosted the touring Body Worlds exhibit. With its extensive use of computers and electronic visual displays, its displays are particularly appealing to youngsters. Admission fees vary according to combination of exhibits and movie showings you want. Pre-order tickets for special exhibits to avoid long lines. An outdoor terrace called **Origine Bistro,** offering light meals and drinks, opened in 2007 and joins an existing café selling sandwiches, salads, and sweets.

Vieux-Port, Quai King Edward. ✆ 514/496-4724. www.montrealsciencecentre.com. Admission from C$10 (US$8.70/£4.30) adults, C$9 (US$7.85/£3.90) seniors and ages 13–17, C$7 (US$6.10/£3) ages 4–12, free for children under 4. MC, V. Weekdays from 8:30am, weekends from 9am; closing hours vary. Métro: Place d'Armes or Champ-de-Mars.

Pointe-à-Callière (Montréal Museum of Archaeology and History) *(★★★*

A first visit to Montréal might best begin here. Built on the very site where the original colony was established in 1642 (Pointe-à-Callière), the modern Museum of Archaeology and History engages visitors in rare, beguiling ways. The triangular new building echoes the Royal Insurance building (1861) that stood here for many years. Go first to the 16-minute multimedia show in an auditorium that actually stands above exposed ruins of the earlier city. The show is accompanied by music and a playful bilingual narration that keeps the history slick and painless if a little chamber-of-commerce upbeat (children under 12 will likely find it a snooze).

Pointe-à-Callière was the spot where the St-Pierre River merged with the St. Lawrence. Evidence of the area's many inhabitants—from Amerindians to French trappers to Scottish merchants—was unearthed during archaeological digs that took more than a decade. Artifacts are on view in display cases set among the ancient building foundations and burial grounds below street level. Wind your way on the self-guided tour through the subterranean complex until you find yourself in the former Custom House, where there are more exhibits and a well-stocked gift shop. Allow at least an hour for a visit. The exhibit is wheelchair accessible.

New expansion has incorporated the Youville Pumping Station, across from the main building, into the museum. Dating from 1915, it has been restored to serve as an interpretation center. The main building contains **L'Arrivage café** and has a fine view of Vieux-Montréal and the Vieux-Port. Plan an hour and a half to visit.

350 Place Royale (at rue de la Commune). © 514/872-9150. www.pacmuseum.qc.ca. Admission C$13 (US$11/ £5.60) adults, C$8.50 (US$7.40/£3.65) seniors, C$7 (US$6.10/£3) students, C$5 (US$4.35/£2.15) children 6–12, free for under 6. Family rates available. AE, MC, V. July–Aug Mon–Fri 10am–6pm, Sat–Sun 11am–6pm; Sept–June Tues–Fri 10am–5pm, Sat–Sun 11am–5pm. Métro: Place d'Armes.

Vieux-Port ★★ *Kids*   Montréal's Old Port was transformed in 1992 from a dreary commercial wharf area into a 2km-long (1¼-mile), 53-hectare (131-acre) promenade and public park with bicycle paths, exhibition halls, and a variety of family activities, including the **Centre des Sciences de Montréal** (reviewed above). The area is most active from mid-May to October, when harbor cruises set out from here and bicycles, in-line skates and family-friendly Quadricycle carts are available for rent. The **Cirque du Soleil** raises its tents here for 2 months every spring, and warm months also bring information booths staffed by bilingual attendants and 45-minute guided tours in the open-sided La Balade tram. In the winter, things are quieter, but an outdoor ice-skating rink is an attraction. At the far eastern end of the port in the last of the old warehouses is a 1922 clock tower, **La Tour de l'Horloge,** with 192 steps leading past the exposed clockworks to observation decks overlooking the St. Lawrence River (admission is free). The Vieux-Port stretches along the waterfront parallel to rue de la Commune from rue McGill to rue Berri.

Information booth for the Vieux-Port area is at the Centre des Sciences de Montréal on Quai King Edward (King Edward pier). © 800/971-PORT. www.quaysoftheoldport.com. La Balade tram C$5 (US$4.35/£2.15) adults, C$3.50 (US$3.05/£1.50) seniors and teens (13–17), C$3 (US$2.60/£1.30) children 12 and under. Métro: Champ-de-Mars, Place d'Armes, or Square Victoria.

ELSEWHERE IN THE CITY

A 20-minute drive east on rue Sherbrooke or easy Métro ride from downtown is an area known as **Olympic Park,** which has four attractions: the Stade Olympique (Olympic Stadium), Biodôme de Montréal, Jardin Botanique (Botanical Garden), and Insectarium de Montréal. The first three are described below, and the Insectarium on p. 121. All four are walking distance from each other, and there's a free shuttle in summer. You could spend a day touring all four sites, and kids will especially love the Biodôme and Insectarium. Combination ticket packages are available, and the Biodôme, Jardin, and Insectarium are all included in the **Montréal Museum Pass** (see the "Money Savers" feature on p. 112). Underground parking at the Olympic Stadium is C$12 (US$10/£5.15) a day, with additional parking at the Jardin Botanique and Insectarium.

Biodôme de Montréal ★★★ *Kids*   Perhaps the most engaging attraction in the city for children of any age, the delightful Biodôme houses replications of four ecosystems: a tropical rainforest, a Laurentian forest, the St. Lawrence marine system, and a polar environment. Visitors walk through each and hear the animals, smell the flora, and, except in the polar region, which is behind glass, feel the changes in temperature. The rainforest area is the most engrossing (the subsequent rooms increasingly less so), so take your time here. It's a kind of "Where's Waldo" challenge to find all the critters, from the huge groundhog called a capybara to the golden lion tamarin monkeys that swing on branches only an arm's length away; only the bats, fish, and polar penguins and puffins are behind glass. A giant tank in the St. Lawrence region has Atlantic Stur-geon nearly 1.5m (5 ft.) long, while the open-air space features hundreds of shore birds whose shrieks can transport you to the beach. The building was originally the velodrome for cycling for the 1976 Olympics. The facility also has a game room for kids called Naturalia, a shop, a bistro, and a cafeteria.

4777 av. Pierre-de-Coubertin (next to Stade Olympique). © 514/868-3000. www.biodome.qc.ca. Admission C$16 (US$14/£6.90) adults, C$12 (US$10/£5.15) seniors and students, C$8 (US$6.95/£3.45) children 5–17, C$2.50 (US$2.20/£1.10) children 2–4. Binocular rentals available. AE, MC, V. Daily 9am–5pm (until 6pm late June to Aug). Closed most Mon Sept–Dec. Métro: Viau.

Jardin Botanique 🞵🞵🞵   Spread across 75 hectares (185 acres), Montréal's Botan-ical Garden is a fragrant oasis 12 months a year. Ten large conservatory greenhouses each have a theme: orchids, begonias and African violets, ferns, flora from the rainfor-est. Outdoors, spring is when things really kick in: lilacs in May, lilies in June, and roses from mid-June to the first frost. The **Chinese Garden,** a joint project of Mon-tréal and Shanghai, evokes the 14th- to 17th-century era of the Ming Dynasty and was built according to the Chinese landscape principles of yin and yang. It incorpo-rates pavilions, inner courtyards, ponds, and myriad plants indigenous to China. The serene **Japanese Garden** fills 6 hectares (15 acres) and includes a cultural pavilion with an art gallery, a tearoom where ancient tea ceremonies are performed, a stunning bonsai collection, and a Zen garden. A small train runs through the gardens from mid-May to October and is worth the small fee charged to ride it. The grounds are also home to the **Insectarium,** displaying some of the world's most beautiful and sinister insects (p. 121). Birders should bring along binoculars on summer visits to spot some of the more than 190 species that have been spotted here. An extensive website pro-vides great details on everything.

4101 rue Sherbrooke est (opposite Olympic Stadium). © **514/872-1400.** www.ville.montreal.qc.ca/jardin. Admis-sion includes access to the Insectarium. May 15–Oct C$16 (US$14/£6.90) adults, C$12 (US$10/£5.15) seniors and students, C$8 (US$6.95/£3.45) children 5–17, C$2.50 (US$2.20/£1.10) children 2–4. Rates drop about 15% rest of the year. MC, V. Daily 9am–5pm (until 6pm in summer, until 9pm mid-Sept to Nov). Closed Mon Nov to mid-May. No bicycles or dogs. Métro: Pie-IX, then walk up the hill; or take free shuttle bus from Olympic Park (Métro: Viau).

Stade Olympique *Overrated*   Centerpiece of the 1976 Olympic Games and looking not unlike a giant stapler, Montréal's controversial Olympic Stadium provides only moderate interest for visitors. The main event is the 175m (574-ft.) **inclined tower,** which leans at a 45-degree angle and does duty as an observation deck, with a funic-ular that whisks passengers to the top in 95 seconds. On a clear day, the deck bestows an expansive view over Montréal and into the neighboring Laurentian mountains, but at C$14 (US$12/£6), the admission price is as steep as the tower. It's worth a trip only if you've bought a combination ticket with the other attractions in this area.

The complex also includes a stadium that seats up to 56,000 for rock concerts and the like, and was home to the Montréal Expos baseball team before it relocated to Washington, D.C. in 2005. A **Sports Centre** houses five swimming pools open for public swims and classes, including a pool that's 15m deep (49 ft.) for scuba diving. Thirty-minute guided tours that describe the 1976 Olympic Games and current cen-ter are available daily for a fee.

The roof doesn't retract anymore—it never retracted well anyway. That's one reason that what was first known as "The Big O" was scorned as "The Big Woe" and then "The Big Owe" after cost overruns led to heavy increases in taxes. Plans for its future have run from total demolition to adding thousands of seats.

4141 av. Pierre-de-Coubertin ℂ 514/252-4141. www.rio.gouv.qc.ca. Tower admission C$14 (US$12/£6) adults, C$11 (US$9.15/£4.50) seniors and students, C$7 (US$6.10/£3) ages 5–17. Packages available that include guided tour. Public swims scheduled daily, with low admission rates. Tower daily 9am–7pm in summer; until 5pm in winter. Closed mid-Jan to mid-Feb. Métro: Viau.

2 More Attractions

DOWNTOWN

Basilique-Cathédrale Marie-Reine-du-Monde   No one who has seen both will confuse Montréal's "Mary Queen of the World" Cathedral with St. Peter's Basilica in Rome, but a scaled-down homage was the intention of Bishop Ignace Bourget, who oversaw its construction after the first Catholic cathedral burned to the ground in 1852. Construction lasted from 1875 to 1894, its start delayed by the bishop's desire to place it not in Francophone east Montréal but in the heart of the Protestant Anglophone west. The resulting structure covers less than a quarter of the area of its Roman inspiration. Most impressive is the 76m-high (249-ft.) dome, about a third of the size of the original. The statues standing on the roofline represent patron saints of the region, providing a local touch. The interior is less rewarding visually than the exterior, but the high altar is worth a look. Masses are held daily.

1085 rue de la Cathédrale (at rue Mansfield). ℂ 514/866-1661. www.cathedralecatholiquedemontreal.org. Free admission; donations accepted. Daily 7:30am–6pm. Métro: Bonaventure.

Cathédrale Christ Church   This Anglican cathedral, which is reflected in the shiny exterior of the pink-glassed postmodern Tour KPMG office tower, stands in glorious Gothic contrast to the city's downtown skyscrapers. Sometimes called the "floating cathedral" because of the many tiers of malls and corridors in the underground city beneath it and the way it was elevated during their construction, the building was completed in 1859. The original steeple was too heavy for the structure and replaced by a lighter aluminum version in 1940. The choirs of the cathedral offer music each Sunday at 10am and at Choral Evensong at 4pm, live and broadcast over the Internet. The church also hosts concerts throughout the year.

635 rue Ste-Catherine (at rue University). ℂ 514/843-6577, ext. 371 (recorded information about services and concerts). www.montreal.anglican.org/cathedral. Free admission; donations accepted. Daily 10am–6pm; services Sun 8am, 10am, and 4pm. Métro: McGill.

Musée d'Art Contemporain de Montréal ⚓   Montréal's Museum of Contemporary Art is the only museum in Canada devoted exclusively to contemporary art, "contemporary" defined here as since 1939. Much of the permanent collection of some 7,000 works is composed of the work of Québécois artists such as Jean-Paul Riopelle and Betty Goodwin, but it also includes examples of such international artists as Richard Serra, Bruce Nauman, Sam Taylor-Wood, and Nan Goldin. No single style prevails, so expect to see installations, video displays, and examples of pop, op, and abstract expressionism. That the works often arouse strong opinions signifies a museum that is doing something right. On "Friday Nocturnes"—the first Friday of the month—the museum is open until 9pm with live music, bar service, and tours of the exhibition galleries. The museum's restaurant, **La Rotonde,** serves such dishes as breast of duck in lavender honey, and has a summer dining terrace.

185 rue Ste-Catherine ouest. ℂ 514/847-6226. www.macm.org. Admission C$8 (US$6.95/£3.45) adults, C$6 (US$5.20/£2.60) seniors, C$4 (US$3.50/£1.70) students, free for children under 12, free to all Wed 6–9pm. Tues–Sun 11am–6pm (until 9pm Wed). Métro: Place des Arts.

VIEUX-MONTREAL (OLD MONTREAL)

Chapelle Notre-Dame-de-Bon-Secours/Musée Marguerite-Bourgeoys Just to the east of Marché Bonsecours, Notre Dame de Bon-Secours Chapel is called the Sailors' Church because of the special attachment that fishermen and other mariners have to it; their devotion is manifest in the several ship models hanging from the ceiling inside. There's an excellent view of the harbor from the church's tower.

The first building, which no longer stands, was the project of an energetic teacher named Marguerite Bourgeoys, and built in 1675. Bourgeoys had come from France to undertake the education of the children of Montréal; later on, she and several other teachers founded the Congregation of Notre-Dame, Canada's first nuns' order. The pioneering Bourgeoys was canonized in 1982 as the Canadian Church's first woman saint and in 2005, for the chapel's 350 birthday, her remains were brought to the church and interred in the left side altar.

A restored 18th-century crypt houses the museum. Part of it is devoted to relating Bourgeoys' life and work, while another section displays artifacts from the archaeological site under the chapel, including ruins and materials from the earliest days of the colony and an Amerindian fire pit dated to 400 B.C.

400 rue St-Paul est (at the foot of rue Bonsecours). ☎ **514/282-8670.** www.marguerite-bourgeoys.com. Free admission to chapel. Museum C$6 (US$5.20/£2.60) adults, C$4 (US$3.50/£1.70) seniors and students, C$3 (US$2.60/£1.30) children ages 6–12, free for children under 6; archaeological site and museum C$8 (US$6.95/£3.45). May–Oct Tues–Sun 10am–5pm; Nov to mid-Jan and Mar–Apr Tues–Sun 11am–3:30pm. Closed mid-Jan to Feb. Métro: Champ-de-Mars.

Hôtel de Ville City Hall, finished in 1878, is relatively young by Vieux-Montréal standards. It's still in use, with the mayor's office on the main floor. The French Second Empire design makes it look as though it was imported stone by stone from the mother country: balconies, turrets, and mansard roofs decorate the exterior. The details are seen particularly well when the exterior is illuminated at night. The Hall of Honour is made of green marble from Campagna, Italy, and houses Art Deco lamps from Paris and a bronze-and-glass chandelier, also from France, that weighs a metric ton. The hall also has a hand-carved ceiling and five stained-glass windows representing religion, the port, industry and commerce, finance, and transportation. It was from the balcony above the awning that, in 1967, an ill-mannered Charles de Gaulle, then president of France, proclaimed, "Vive le Québec Libre!"—a gesture that pleased his immediate audience but strained relations with the Canadian government for years.

275 rue Notre-Dame est (at the corner of rue Gosford). ☎ **514/872-3355.** Free admission. Mon–Fri 9am–4:30pm. Guided tours on weekdays May–Oct. Métro: Champ-de-Mars.

Marché Bonsecours Bonsecours Market, an imposing neoclassical building with a long facade, a colonnaded portico, and a silvery dome, was built in the mid-1800s—the Doric columns of the portico were cast of iron in England—and first used as the Parliament of United Canada and then as Montréal's City Hall. The architecture alone makes a brief visit worthwhile. For many years after 1878 it was the city's central market. Essentially abandoned for much of the 20th century, it was restored in 1964 to house city government offices and in 1992 became the information and exhibition center for the celebration of the city's 350th birthday. It continues to be used as an exhibition space and also houses three restaurants with terraces and over a dozen art galleries and high-end but affordable boutiques featuring Québécois products.

350 rue St-Paul est (at the foot of rue St-Claude). ☎ **514/872-7730.** www.marchebonsecours.qc.ca. Free admission. Daily 10am–6pm (until 9pm during peak seasons). Métro: Champ-de-Mars.

— I don't speak sign language.

A hotel can close for all kinds of reasons.
Our Guarantee ensures that if your hotel's undergoing construction, we'll let you know in advance. In fact, we cover your entire travel experience. See www.travelocity.com/guarantee for details.

travelocity
You'll never roam alone.

Musée du Château Ramezay ⭐ *Kids*   Benjamin Franklin was here. So, too, was Claude de Ramezay, the 11th governor of the colony, who built his residence at this site in 1705. The château became home to the city's royal French governors for almost 4 decades, until Ramezay's heirs sold it to a trading company in 1745. Fifteen years later it was taken over by British conquerors, and in 1775 an army of American revolutionaries invaded and held Montréal, using the château as their headquarters. For 6 weeks in 1776, Benjamin Franklin spent his days here, trying to persuade the Québécois to rise with the American colonists against British rule (he failed). After the American interlude, the house was used as a courthouse, a government office building, and headquarters for Laval University, before being converted into a museum in 1895.

Old coins and prints, portraits, furnishings, tools, a loom, Amerindian artifacts, and other memorabilia related to the economic and social activities of the 18th and first half of the 19th century fill the main floor. In the cellar are the vaults of the original house.

Sculpted, formal gardens (*jardins*) ringed by a low stone wall evoke 18th-century Parisian gardens and are a soothing respite from the busyness of Place Jacques-Cartier, a few steps away. A café overlooks the gardens in the summer.

Between October and May, the château invites families to join in on the last Sunday of the month for an old-timey bread-making session using its 18th-century hearth. In the summer, there are workshops in the garden on how to make soap and beeswax candles, paper marbling, and more. Dates and details are listed on the website.

280 rue Notre-Dame est. ⓒ 514/861-3708. www.chateauramezay.qc.ca. Admission C$8 (US$6.95/£3.45) adults, C$6 (US$5.20/£2.60) seniors, C$5 (US$4.35/£2.15) students, C$4 (US$3.50/£1.70) ages 5–17, free for children under 4, C$17 (US$14/£7.10) families. MC, V. June to late Nov daily 10am–6pm; late Nov to May Tues–Sun 10am–4:30pm. Métro: Champ-de-Mars.

MONT-ROYAL & PLATEAU MONT-ROYAL

To explore these areas, try the walking tours in chapter 8.

L'Oratoire St-Joseph ⭐   This huge Catholic church—consecrated as a basilica in 2004 and dominating the north slope of Mont-Royal—is seen by some as inspiring, by others as forbidding. At 236m (856 ft.), it is the highest point in Montréal. It came into being through the efforts of Brother André, a lay brother in the Holy Cross order who enjoyed a reputation as a healer. By the time he had built a small wooden chapel in 1904 on the mountain, he was said to have performed hundreds of cures. His powers attracted supplicants from great distances, and Brother André performed his work until his death in 1937. In 1982, he was beatified by the pope—a status one step below sainthood—and his dream of building a shrine to honor St. Joseph, patron saint of Canada, became a completed reality in 1967.

The church is largely Italian Renaissance in style, its giant copper dome recalling the shape of the Duomo in Florence, but of greater size and less grace. Inside is a sanctuary and museum where a central exhibit is the heart of Brother André. His original wooden chapel, with its tiny bedroom, is on the grounds and open to the public. Two million pilgrims visit annually, with many guests seeking intercession from St. Joseph and Brother André by climbing the middle set of 99 steps on their knees. Guided tours are offered in French and English and can be arranged in other languages. There is a modest 14-room hostel on the grounds; rooms at the Jean XXIII Pavilion start at C$45 (US$39/£19).

3800 chemin Queen Mary (on the north slope of Mont-Royal). ⓒ 514/733-8211. www.saint-joseph.org. Free admission, donations requested. Crypt and votive chapel daily 6am–10:30pm; basilica and exhibition on Brother

André daily 7am–9pm. The 56-bell carillon plays Thurs–Fri noon–3pm, Sat–Sun noon–2:30pm. Métro: Côtes-des-Neiges. Bus: 166.

Parc La Fontaine   The European-style park in Plateau Mont-Royal is one of the city's oldest and most popular. Illustrating the traditional dual identities of the city's populace, half the park is landscaped in the formal French manner, the other in the more casual English style. The central lake is used for pedal boating in summer and ice-skating in winter. Snowshoe and cross-country trails wind through trees in winter, as do bike paths in the warmer months, and there are tennis courts on the premises. An open amphitheater, the **Théâtre de Verdure,** features free outdoor theater, movies, and tango dancing in summer. The northern end is more pleasant than the southern end (along rue Sherbrooke), which seems to attract a seedier crowd.

Bounded by rue Sherbrooke, rue Rachel, av. Parc LaFontaine, and av. Papineau. © **514/872-2644.** Free admission; fee for use of tennis courts. Park daily 24 hr.; tennis courts (© 514/872-3626 reservations). Métro: Sherbrooke.

ILE STE-HELENE ☆

The small Ile Ste-Hélène and adjacent Ile Notre-Dame sit in the St. Lawrence River near Montréal Vieux-Port waterfront. Connected by two bridges, they now comprise the recently designated **Parc Jean-Drapeau,** almost entirely car-free and accessible by Métro, bicycle, or foot.

La Biosphère *(Kids)*   Not to be confused with the **Biodôme de Montréal** at Olympic Park (see listing earlier in this chapter), this interactive science facility is located in a geodesic dome designed by Buckminster Fuller to serve as the American Pavilion for Expo '67. A fire destroyed the acrylic skin of the sphere in 1976, and it served no purpose other than as a harbor landmark until 1995. The motivation behind the Biosphère is unabashedly environmentalist, with exhibition areas, a theater, an amphitheater, and, since 2007, two wind turbines, all devoted to promoting awareness of the St. Lawrence–Great Lakes ecosystem. Multimedia shows and hands-on displays invite the active participation of visitors, and "Planète Bucky" highlights Fuller's forward-thinking inventions for sustainable development. There is a preaching-to-the-choir quality to all this that slips over the edge into zealous philosophizing. But displays and exhibits are put together thoughtfully and will engage and enlighten most visitors, at least for a while. Don't make a special trip, but if you're on the island, stop by.

160 chemin Tour-de-l'Isle (Ile Ste-Hélène). © **514/283-5000.** www.biosphere.ec.gc.ca. Admission C$9.50 (US$8.25/ £4.10) adults, C$7.50 (US$6.50/£3.25) seniors and students, C$5 (US$4.35/£2.15) ages 7–17, free for children under 7. June–Sept daily 10am–6pm; Oct–May Mon and Wed–Fri noon–5pm, Sat–Sun and holidays 10am–5pm. Métro: Parc Jean-Drapeau, then a short walk.

Musée David M. Stewart ☆ *(Kids)*   If you're in downtown Montréal and hear what sounds like a gun salute, check your watch: If it's just before noon, the sound is coming from here. After the War of 1812, the British prepared for a possible future American invasion by building a moated fortress, which now houses the David M. Stewart Museum. The duke of Wellington ordered the fort's construction as another link in the chain of defenses along the St. Lawrence. Completed in 1824, it was never involved in armed conflict. The British garrison left in 1870, after confederation of the former Canadian colonies. Today the low stone barracks and blockhouses contain the museum and staff in period costume performing firing drills, tending campfires, attempting to recruit visitors into the king's army, and generally doing all they can to bring this piece of history alive.

The museum displays maps and scientific instruments that helped Europeans explore the New World, military and naval artifacts, and related paraphernalia from the time of Jacques Cartier (1535) through 1763, the end of the colonial period. Useful labels appear in French and English. From late June to late August, though, the fort really comes to life with daily reenactments of military parades and retreats by La Compagnie franche de la Marine and The Olde 78th Fraser Highlanders. (The presence of the French unit is an unhistorical bow to Francophone sensibilities; New France had become English Canada almost 65 years before the fort was erected.) If you absolutely must be photographed in stocks, they are provided on the parade grounds.

Vieux-Fort, Ile Ste-Hélène. (C) **514/861-6701.** www.stewart-museum.org. Admission C$10 (US$8.70/£4.30) adults, C$7 (US$6.10/£3) seniors and students, free for children under 7. Summer daily 10am–6pm; fall to late spring Wed–Mon 10am–5pm. Métro: Parc Jean-Drapeau, then a 15-min. walk. By car: Take the Jacques-Cartier Bridge to the Parc Jean-Drapeau exit, then follow the signs.

3 Especially for Kids

In addition to the 3 Bs—the **Biodôme de Montréal** (p. 115), **La Biosphère** (p. 120), and **boat tours** (p. 125)—and the other attractions flagged in this chapter as especially appealing to children, here are some spots that cater primarily to the under-18 crowd.

Atrium Le 1000 *(Kids)*   This indoor ice-skating rink in the heart of downtown Montréal is open year-round. Skate rentals are available on-site, and restaurants ring the rink. There is a "Tiny Tot" hour for children 12 and under and their parents from 10:30 to 11:30am weekends in summer and Sunday mornings in winter. Saturdays feature "DJ nites" after 7pm for ages 13 years and older.

1000 rue de la Gauchetière ouest, downtown. (C) **514/395-0555.** www.le1000.com. Admission C$5.75 (US$5/£2.45) adults, C$3.75 (US$3.25/£1.60) children 12 and under. Skate rental C$5 (US$4.35/£2.15). MC, V. Daily from 11:30am (10:30am some weekend days for children); closed Mon in summer. Métro: Bonaventure.

IMAX Theater *(Kids)*   The images and special effects are larger than life, always visually dazzling and often vertiginous, thrown on a five-story screen in the renovated theater of the **Centre des Sciences de Montréal** (the Montréal Science Centre, p. 114). Recent movies have brought both mountain climbing in the Alps and dinosaurs to vivid life. Running time is usually under an hour, and about a quarter of the screenings are in English. Tickets can be ordered online.

Quai King Edward, Vieux-Port. (C) **877/496-4724** or 514/496-4724. www.montrealsciencecentre.com. Admission from C$10 (US$8.70/£4.30) adults, C$9 (US$7.85/£3.90) seniors and ages 13–17, C$7 (US$6.10/£3) ages 4–12, free for children under 4. MC, V. Shows 10am–10pm. Métro: Place d'Armes or Champ-de-Mars.

Insectarium de Montréal *(Kids)*   Live exhibits featuring scorpions, tarantulas, hissing cockroaches, assassin bugs, praying mantises, and other "misunderstood creatures, which are so often wrongly feared and despised," as the Insectarium puts it, are displayed in this two-level structure near the rue Sherbrooke gate of the **Jardin Botanique** (Botanical Garden, p. 116). Needless to say, kids are delighted especially by the creepy critters. More than 3,000 mounted butterflies, beetles, scarabs, maggots, locusts, and giraffe weevils also are featured, and during the summer, the Butterfly House is full of beautiful live specimens fluttering among the nectar-bearing plants. In September, visitors can watch monarch butterflies being tagged and released for their annual migration to Mexico. The annual award-winning **"Insect Tasting"**

Moments   **Cirque du Soleil: Montréal's Hometown Circus**

Cirque du Soleil began as street performance in Baie-St-Paul, a river town an hour north of Québec City (p. 281). Stilt-walkers, fire-breathers, and musicians, the artists raised a small ruckus with one pure intention: to entertain. The troupe formally founded as Cirque du Soleil ("circus of the sun") in 1984.

With no animals, this circus has grown into a spectacle like no other. Using human-size gyroscopes, trampoline beds, trapezes suspended from massive chandeliers, and the like, Cirque creates worlds that are spooky, sensual, and otherworldly. Over 900 acrobats, contortionists, jugglers, clowns, dancers, and singers work for it, touring the world in companies simultaneously. Resident shows are established in Las Vegas and Orlando, Florida.

The company's offices are in Montréal in the northern Saint-Michel district, not far beyond the Mile End neighborhood. But they're not just offices: The Cirque has been developing a small campus of buildings in an industrial zone since 1997. All new artists come here to train for anywhere from a few weeks to a few months and live in residences on-site. The complex has acrobatic training rooms, a dance studio, production workshops to make the elaborate costumes and props, and a space large enough to erect a circus tent indoors. Some 1,600 staffers are employed at the Montréal facility, including 300 who work on costumes alone. The Cirque celebrates its 25th year in 2009.

Performances have taken place in Montréal from April to June in recent years, in the Cirque's signature yellow and blue tents that it erects temporarily on the Quays (piers) of Vieux-Port. Tickets aren't cheap—they start at C$60 (US$52/£26) for adults—but the effect is transporting. For more information, call (C) **800/361-4595** or visit www.cirquedusoleil.com.

(*Croque-insectes*) dinner seems to have been suspended, which is a shame. But you can still buy lollipops with scorpions inside at the gift shop.

4581 rue Sherbrooke est. (C) 514/872-1400. www.ville.montreal.qc.ca/insectarium. Admission includes access to the Botanical Garden next door. May 15–Oct C$16 (US$14/£6.90) adults, C$12 (US$10/£5.15) seniors and students, C$8 (US$6.95/£3.45) children 5–17, C$2.50 (US$2.20/£1.10) children 2–4. Rates drop about 15% rest of the year. See p. 112 for info about combination tickets with the Stade Olympique and Biodôme de Montréal. MC, V. Nov 1–May 14 daily 9am–5pm; May 15–Sept 6 daily 9am–6pm; Sept 7–Oct 31 daily 9am–9pm. Métro: Pie-IX or Viau.

La Ronde Amusement Park *(Kids* Montréal's amusement park, opened in 1967 as part of the Expo '67 (World's Fair), was run for its first 34 years by the city. It was sold to the American-owned Six Flags theme park empire in 2001 and at first seemed pretty much the same-old same-old, minus the threat of insolvency. But new rides have now been delivered, and like hot sauces, they're categorized by "thrill rating": moderate, mild, or max. There are 14 rides in the "max thrill" category, including Le Vampire, a suspended coaster where riders experience five head-over-heels loops at over 80kmph (50 mph). There are also Ferris wheels, carnival booths, and plenty of places to eat and drink. An antique carousel, Le Galopant, was added in 2007; it was built by Belgian artisans in 1885 and served as part of the Belgian Pavilion at the 1964–65 New York World's Fair. The Minirail, an original from La Ronde's 1967 opening, is an elevated train that circles the park. Young children have ample selection including the Tchou Tchou Train and *Bob l'éponge 3D*, a 10-minute SpongeBob SquarePants simulated ride. A section called **Le Pays de Ribambelle** opened in 2005, incorporating family-friendly rides and daily concerts.

Parc Jean-Drapeau Ile Ste-Hélène. (C) **514/397-2000.** www.laronde.com. Admission C$37 (US$32/£16) for patrons 1.37m (54 in.) or taller, C$25 (US$21/£11) for patrons shorter than 1.37m (54 in.), free for children under 3. Parking C$13 (US$11/£5.65). June–Aug daily 10:30am–10:30pm; spring and fall weekends only noon–7pm. Closed winter. Métro: Papineau then bus no. 169, or Parc Jean-Drapeau then bus no. 167.

Planétarium de Montréal *(Kids)* A window on the night sky, with mythical monsters and magical heroes, Montréal's planetarium is right downtown, in the heart of the city. Shows under the 20m (66-ft.) dome dazzle and inform kids at the same time. Multimedia presentations change with the seasons, exploring time and space travel and collisions of celestial bodies, and up to five different shows are screened daily. The special Christmas show, "Season of Light," can be seen November through early January. Shows in English alternate with those in French.

1000 rue St-Jacques ouest (at Peel). (C) **514/872-4530.** www.planetarium.montreal.qc.ca. Admission C$8 (US$6.95/£3.45) adults, C$6 (US$5.20/£2.60) seniors and students, C$4 (US$3.50/£1.70) children 5–17. MC, V. Hours vary according to show schedule; call for details. Métro: Bonaventure (exit toward rue de la Cathédrale).

4 Special-Interest Sightseeing

Centre Canadien d'Architecture (CCA) The understated but handsome Canadian Center of Architecture building occupies a city block, joining a contemporary structure with an older building, the 1875 Shaughnessy House. The CCA functions as both a study center and a museum, with changing exhibits devoted to the art of architecture and its history, including architects' sketchbooks, elevation drawings, and photography. The collection is international in scope and encompasses architecture, urban planning, and landscape design. Texts are in French and English. Opened in 1989, the museum has received rave reviews from scholars, critics, and serious architecture buffs. That said, it is only fair to note that the average visitor is likely to find it somewhat less enthralling. The bookstore has a special section on Canadian architecture with an emphasis on Montréal and Québec City. A **sculpture garden** tucked away across from boulevard René Lévesque is part of the CCA, designed by Montréal artist/architect Melvin Charney and a quiet retreat in the center of downtown.

1920 rue Baile (at rue du Fort). (C) **514/939-7026.** http://cca.qc.ca. Admission C$10 (US$8.70/£4.30) adults, C$7 (US$6.10/£3) seniors, C$5 (US$4.35) students, C$3 (US$2.60/£1.30) children 6–12, free for ages 5 and under and for those with limited mobility. Free Thurs after 5:30pm. Wed–Sun 10am–5pm (until 9pm Thurs). 1-hr. guided tour available for no extra fee. Métro: Atwater or Guy-Concordia.

Centre d'Histoire de Montréal Built in 1903 as Montréal's Central Fire Station, this red-brick-and-sandstone building is now the Montréal History Center, which traces the development of the city from its first residents, the Amerindians, to the European settlers who arrived in 1642, to the present day. Throughout its 14 rooms, carefully conceived presentations chart the contributions of the city fathers and mothers and subsequent generations. Imaginative exhibits, videos, and slide shows trace the development of the railroad, Métro, and related infrastructure. On the second floor, reached by a spiral staircase, is memorabilia from the early 20th century. A recent

exhibit re-created the trial of a woman accused of setting the massive fire that destroyed much of Vieux-Montréal in April 1734. Allow about an hour for a visit.

335 Place d'Youville (at rue St-Pierre). © 514/872-3207. www.ville.montreal.qc.ca/chm. Admission C$4.50 (US$3.90/£1.95) adults, C$3 (US$2.60/£1.30) seniors and children 6–17, free for children under 6. May–Aug Tues–Sun 10am–5pm; Sept–Apr Wed–Sun 10am–5pm. Métro: Square Victoria.

Musée de la Banque de Montréal Facing the **Basilique Notre-Dame** (p. 113) and Place d'Armes is Montréal's oldest bank building, with a classic facade beneath a graceful dome, a carved pediment, and six Corinthian columns. The outside dimensions and appearance remain largely unchanged since the building's completion in 1847. Pop in for 10 minutes to see the small museum just inside and to the left featuring a replica of the bank's first office, gold nuggets from the Yukon, a collection of 100-year-old mechanical banks, and a display on how to spot a forged bill. Take a look at the sumptuous interior, too: It was renovated from 1901 through 1905 by the famed U.S. firm McKim, Mead, and White, and features Ionic and Corinthian columns of Vermont granite, walls of pink marble from Tennessee, and a counter of Levanto marble.

119 rue St-Jacques ouest (at Place d'Armes). © 514/877-6810. Free admission. Mon–Fri 10am–4pm. Métro: Place d'Armes.

Musée Redpath This quirky natural history museum, housed in an 1882 building with a grandly proportioned and richly appointed interior, is on the McGill University campus. The main draws—worth a half-hour visit—are the mummies and coffin that are part of its collection of Egyptian antiquities, the second largest in Canada, and skeletons of whales and prehistoric beasts. If the unusual name seems slightly familiar, it could be because you've seen it on the wrappings of sugar cubes in many Canadian restaurants: John Redpath was a 19th-century industrialist who built Canada's first sugar refinery.

859 rue Sherbrooke ouest (rue University). © 514/398-4086. www.mcgill.ca/redpath. Free admission. Mon–Fri 9am–5pm; Sun 1–5pm. Closed Fri in summer and public holidays. Métro: McGill.

Pavillon de la TOHO Adjacent to the Cirque du Soleil training complex on reclaimed industrial land, TOHO is many things: a performance facility that brings small circus companies to its intimate in-the-round theater, an exhibit space with over 100 circus artifacts ringing the performance hall, and a model for green architecture. Built with recycled pieces of an amusement park bumper-car ride and wood from a dismantled railroad, the space is heated by biogas from a landfill next door and uses an "ice bunker" for cooling in the summer. Both processes produce zero greenhouse-effect gases and are explained in free brochures. It's worth a special trip only if you're a circus nut or environmental architecture fan—guided tours are available with advance reservations—but certainly check if there's a show playing and build a trip around that. The Pavilion is well north of tourist areas, above the Mile End neighborhood in the lower-income Saint-Michel district, but accessible by Métro and bus.

2345 rue Jarry est (corner of rue d'Iberville, at Autoroute 40). © 888/376-TOHU. www.tohu.ca. Free to view facility and exhibits; fee for tours. Daily 9am–5pm. Performances from C$23 (US$20–£9.70) adults, C$14 (US$12/£5.80) children 12 and younger. 8km (5 miles) from downtown, up rue St-Denis and east on rue Jarry to where it meets Autoroute 40. Métro: Jarry or Iberville and bus.

5 Organized Tours

An introductory guided tour is often the best—or, at least, most efficient—way to begin explorations of a new city. Even a mediocre tour with a guide can give you a good lay of the land and overview of Montréal's history. You'll also pass many of the attractions listed in this chapter and get a better sense of which you will want to spend more time exploring on your own.

For a complete listing of tours and tour operators, check under "Guided Tours" in the annually revised *Montréal Tourist Guide,* available at the downtown **Infotouriste Centre** at 1255 rue Peel (✆ 877/266-5687 or 514/873-2015; Métro: Peel). Most of the land tours leave from the Square Dorchester, just around the corner from the tourist office. Most boat tours depart from Vieux-Port (Old Port), at the waterfront bordering Vieux-Montréal. There's parking at the dock, or take the Métro to the Champ-de-Mars or Square Victoria station and walk toward the river.

BOAT TOURS

Among numerous opportunities for experiencing Montréal and environs by water, here are a few of the most popular:

Le Bateau-Mouche (✆ 800/361-9952 or 514/849-9952; www.bateau-mouche. com) is an air-conditioned, glass-enclosed vessel reminiscent of those on the Seine in Paris. It plies the St. Lawrence River from mid-May to mid-October. Cruises depart for 60-minute excursions at 1:30pm, 3pm, and 4:30pm; for a 90-minute cruise at 11:30am; and for a 3½-hour dinner cruise at 7pm (boarding at 6:30pm). The shallow-draft boat takes passengers on a route inaccessible by traditional vessels. It passes under several bridges and provides sweeping views of the city, Mont-Royal, and the St. Lawrence and its islands. Daytime snacks are available onboard. The 60-minute tours cost C$21 (US$18/£9.05) adults, C$19 (US$17/£8.15) students and seniors, C$11 (US$9.60/£4.75) children 2 to 12. The 90-minute tour costs C$25 (US$22/£11) adults, C$23 (US$20/£9.90) students and seniors, and C$11 (US$9.55/£4.75) children 6 to 16. Dinner cruises, with meals prepared by the kitchen of the Fairmont Queen Elizabeth, cost C$84 or C$149 (US$73 or US$130/£36 or £64) and reservations are essential. The tour departs from the Jacques-Cartier Pier, opposite Place Jacques-Cartier.

Croisières AML Cruises (✆ 800/563-4643 or 514/842-3871; www.croisieresaml. com) also travels the harbor and the St. Lawrence. The boats depart up to seven times a day, with options for a 1½-hour sightseeing tour, 4-hour "Love Boat" dinner cruise, and 3-hour Latin Fiesta dance parties that leave at midnight. Fares, not including dinner, are C$26 to C$42 (US$23–US$37/£23–£18) adults, C$24 to C$39 (US$21–US$34/£10–£17) students and seniors, C$13 to C$28 (US$11–US$24/£5.60–£12) children 6 to 16. The tour also departs from the Jacques-Cartier Pier, opposite Place Jacques-Cartier.

Croisière historique sur le canal de Lachine (✆ 866/846-0448 or 514/846-0428) is a leisurely Parks Canada trip up the Lachine Canal, which was inaugurated in 1824 so ships could bypass the Lachine Rapids on the way to the Great Lakes. The canal was reopened for recreational use in 1997 after much renovation, and is lined with 19th century industrial buildings, many of which are being converted into high-end apartments. The guided tours, which take 1 to 2 hours, are by a glass-topped *bateau-mouche,* which carries up to 49 passengers. From May 20 to June 23 and early September to mid-October, departures are at 1 and 3:30pm on Saturday, Sunday, and holidays; from late June to early September daily departures are at 1 and 3:30pm. Reservations required. Fares are C$17 (US$15/£7.20) adults, C$14 (US$12/£5.90) seniors and students, C$9.75 (US$8.50/£4.20) children, and C$42 (US$37/£18) families. The tour departs from a dock near the Marché Atwater farmer's market (Métro: Lionel-Groulx).

Les Sautes-Moutons (© 514/284-9607; www.jetboatingmontreal.com) is the option you want if you're looking for an exciting—and wet—experience. Their wave-jumper powerboats take on the roiling Lachine Rapids of the St. Lawrence River. The streamlined hydrojet makes the 1-hour trip from May to mid-October daily, with departures every 2 hours from 10am to 6pm. It takes half an hour total to get to and from the rapids, which leaves 30 minutes for storming up the river. Reservations are required, and plan to arrive 45 minutes early to obtain and don rain gear and a life jacket. Bringing a change of clothes is a good idea, because you almost certainly will get splashed or even soaked through. Fares are C$60 (US$52/£26) adults, C$50 (US$44/£22) ages 13 to 18, C$40 (US$35/£17) children 6 to 12. Boats depart from the Clock Tower Pier (Quai de l'Horloge; Métro: Champ-de-Mars).

Les Descentes sur le St-Laurent (© 514/767-2230; www.raftingmontreal.com) is another organization that provides hydro-jet rides on the rapids several times a day, 7 days a week from May to September. This operation is a little farther out than the others, so a little bit more of an adventure. Trips take 75 minutes and cost C$48 (US$42/£21) for adults, C$38 (US$33/£16) ages 13 to 18, C$28 (US$24/£12) for ages 8 to 12. Take to Métro to the Angrignon station and take bus no. 110, or pick up a free shuttle at the downtown Infotouriste Centre at 1255 rue Peel (Métro: Peel). Reservations are required.

The ferry (© 514/281-8000; www.navettesmaritimes.com) from Jacques-Cartier Pier in Vieux-Montréal to Ile Ste-Hélène is a much milder water voyage, but one that still offers great views. It's a great way to begin and end a picnic outing or visit to the old fort at Musée David M. Stewart or La Ronde Amusement Park. The ferry operates from mid-May to mid-October, with daily departures every hour in the high season, and costs C$4.50 (US$3.90/£1.95).

LAND TOURS

Gray Line de Montréal (© 514/934-1222; www.coachcanada.com) offers commercial guided tours in air-conditioned buses daily year-round. The basic city tour takes 3 hours and costs C$36 (US$31/£16) for ages 12 and up, C$30 (US$26/£13) ages 5 to 11. Tours depart from 1255 rue Peel in downtown.

Amphi-Bus (© 514/849-5181; www.montreal-amphibus-tour.com) is something a little different: It tours Vieux-Montréal much like any other bus, until it waddles into the waters of the harbor for a dramatic finish. Reservations are required; check the website for current times, prices, and departure sites.

Montréal's romantic *calèches* (© 514/934-6105; www.calechesluckyluc.com) are horse-drawn open carriages whose drivers serve as guides. These carriages operate year-round. In winter some steeds are hitched to old-fashioned sleighs for a ride around Parc Mont-Royal, the horses puffing steam clouds in the cold air, the passengers bundled in lap rugs. Carriages also depart from Square Dorchester in downtown and, in Vieux-Montréal, Place Jacques-Cartier and rue de la Commune, and Place d'Armes opposite the Notre-Dame Basilica.

WALKING & CYCLING TOURS

Walking tours of Vieux-Montréal, the underground city, or any other section that piques interest are available through **Guidatour** (℗ **514/844-4021;** www.guidatour. qc.ca), which developed its circuit in collaboration with the Centre d'Histoire de Montréal.

Bicycling tours from 1½ hours to 4 hours in length are available from **CaRoule/ Montréal on Wheels** (℗ **514/866-0633;** www.caroulemontreal.com). Located at 27 rue de la Commune est in Vieux-Port, CaRoule also rents bikes (see "Bicycling & In-Line Skating" below).

If you're interested primarily in the city's architecture, landscaping, and urban planning, **Heritage Montréal** (℗ **514/286-2662;** www.heritagemontreal.qc.ca) conducts most of its "Architectours" on foot or on bicycles, and in French and English. Heritage Montréal's summer schedule generally begins in mid-June and goes until late September, but check with them for a current schedule.

6 Spectator Sports

Montréalers are as devoted to ice hockey as other Canadians are, with plenty of enthusiasm left over for U.S.-style football, soccer, and the other distinctive national sport, curling. (They liked baseball too, but not enough: In 2005, the Montréal Expos, plagued by poor attendance, left for Washington, D.C., where the team became the Nationals.) The biggest single event on the Montréal sports calendar is its version of the Indy 500, the Grand Prix car race that roars into town for 3 days every summer.

AUTO RACING

For 3 days—in 2007, it was June 8, 9, and 10—Montréal's entire focus is on the Grand Prix, the FIA's only stop in Canada. Over 110,000 people pour each day onto the island of Ile Notre-Dame, where a permanent track is installed (the rest of the year the circuit is used by cyclists and walkers) and watch race cars make 70 laps at up to 318km (198 miles) an hour. In the rest of city, particularly rue Crescent in downtown, Formula 1 cars are on display, streets shut down, and revelers party deep into the night. Hotel prices typically double and most require 3-night stays. Three-day Grand Prix tickets cost C$90 to C$495 (US$78–US$431/£39–£213). Details and tickets sales are at ℗ **514/350-0000** and www.grandprix.ca.

FOOTBALL

You might not expect U.S.-style professional football in Canada, but the **Montréal Alouettes** (French for "larks") claim, somewhat dubiously, that "Montréal is synonymous with football." No matter; the team does enjoy considerable success, frequently appearing in the Grey Cup, the Canadian Football League's version of the U.S. Super Bowl. The Als play at McGill University's Percival-Molson Memorial Stadium on a schedule that runs from June into November. Tickets start at C$22 (US$19/£9.45); more details can be found at ℗ **514/871-2255** and www.montrealalouettes.com.

GOLF

In September 2007, the Royal Montréal Golf Club welcomed the PGA's Presidents Cup Tournament to the city for the first time. Check the PGA Tour schedule at www.pgatour.com and www.rmgc.org for future PGA events.

The Second Greatest Canadian Pastime? Name That Sport!

"With Ontario leading 6-4 in the 10th end, Manitoba skip Jennifer Jones prepared for her last shot. Manitoba had three rocks in the house, but Ontario had shot rock and had two guards sitting near one another, high atop the house, toward Jones; another guard sat just outside the rings. Jones was left with one option: She hit and rolled off the lone Ontario stone outside the rings to remove Ontario's shot rock near the button."

So was the verbatim report in *The Globe & Mail* of the Canadian women's championship game in February 2005. Manitoba won, 8 to 6. The sport: curling.

HOCKEY

The beloved **Montréal Canadiens** play downtown at the Centre Bell arena. The team has won 23 Stanley Cup championships since 1918, but hasn't enjoyed much success in recent years. The season runs from October to April, with playoffs continuing into June. Tickets are usually priced from C$22 to C$192 (US$19–US$167/£9.45–£83). Check www.canadiens.com for schedules and ticketing or call ✆ **514/790-1245.**

HORSE RACING

Popularly known as Blue Bonnets Racetrack, the **Hippodrome de Montréal** (✆ **514/ 739-2741;** www.hdem.com) celebrated its 100th birthday in 2007. It's the host facility for international harness-racing events, including the Coupe des Elevers (Breeders Cup). Parimutuel betting and free admission makes for a satisfying evening or Sunday afternoon outing. The Hippodrome is located in the northwest of the city at 7440 bd. Décarie (corner of rue Jean-Talon); take the Métro to Namur, then take a shuttle bus.

7 Outdoor Activities

After long winters, city locals pour outdoors to take sun and warm air at every possible opportunity. Even if you come to Montréal without your regular outdoor gear or a solid sense of direction, it's easy to get outside and join in.

BICYCLING & IN-LINE SKATING

Both bicycling and rollerblading are hugely popular in Montréal, and the city helps people indulge that passion: It boasts an expanding network of more than 350km (217 miles) of cycling paths and year-round bike lanes. In warm months, car lanes in heavily biked areas are blocked off with concrete barriers and turned into two-way lanes for people-powered vehicles.

If you're serious about cycling, get in touch with the nonprofit biking organization **Vélo Québec** (✆ **800/567-8356** or 514/521-8356 in Montréal; www.velo.qc.ca). Vélo (which means bicycle) was behind the development of a 4,000km (2,485-mile) bike network called *Route verte* **(Green Route)** that stretches from one end of the Québec province to the other. The route was officially inaugurated in the summer of 2007. The Vélo website has the most up-to-date information on the state of the paths, the Montréal Bike Fest, road races, new bike lanes, and more. (*Tip:* Several taxi companies have bike racks and charge just C$3/US$2.60/£1.30 extra for each bike. They're listed at the Vélo Québec website—search for "taxi"—or call the Vélo office.)

If you're looking just to rent a bike or pair of skates for an afternoon, you've got several options, depending on where you're based. In Vieux-Montréal, the shop

CaRoule/Montréal on Wheels (© 514/866-0633; www.caroulemontreal.com) at 27 rue de la Commune est, the waterfront road bordering the Vieux-Port, rents bikes and skates from April to October (and by appointment in Mar and Nov). Bikes cost C$9 (US$7.85/£3.90) an hour and C$30 (US$26/£13) a day on the weekend, rollerblades a little less. Helmets are included and a deposit is required. The staff will set you up with a map (also downloadable for their website) and likely point you toward the peaceful **Lachine Canal,** a nearly flat 11km (6.8-mile) bicycle path that travels alongside locks and over small bridges. The canal starts just a few blocks away. (The path is open year-round and maintained by Parks Canada from mid-Apr to the end of Oct.) Other options for short bike tours from Vieux-Port are Ile Notre-Dame, where the Grand Prix auto-racing track is a biker's dream less than 20 minutes away, or simply out to the 2.5km (1.5-mile) promenade that runs along the piers.

Also for rent at Vieux-Port in the spring and summer season are **Quadricycles,** or Q-cycles—4-wheeled roofed bike/buggies that can hold two to six people. They can only be used along Vieux-Port. The rental booth is in the heart of the waterfront area, next to the Pavillian Jacques-Cartier. Rentals are by the half-hour and cost C$6.50 (US$5.65/£2.80) for adults, C$5.50 (US$4.80/£2.35) for teens ages 13 to 17, and C$5 (US$4.35/£2.15) for children ages 6 to 12.

BOATING & KAYAKING

It's easy to rent kayaks, pedal boats, and small eco-friendly electric boats on the quiet **Lachine Canal,** just to the west of Vieux-Port. The company **H2O Adventures** (© 514/842-1306; www.h2oadventures.com) won a 2007 *Grand Prix du tourisme Québécois* award for being a standout operation and has rentals starting at C$10 (US$8.70/£4.30) an hour. It also offers 2-hour introductory kayak lessons for C$35 (US$30/£15) on weekdays (C$4/US$3.50/£1.70 more on weekends). It's open daily. Find it at the **Marché Atwater** farmer's market, where you can pick up lunch from the inside *boulangerie* and *fromagerie,* adjacent to the canal (Métro: Lionel-Groulx).

CROSS-COUNTRY SKIING

Parc Mont-Royal has an extensive cross-country course, as do many of the other city parks. Skiers have to supply their own equipment. Just an hour from the city, north in the Laurentides and east in the Cantons de l'Est, there are numerous options for skiing and rentals. See chapter 11.

HIKING

The most popular hike is to head to the top of **Parc Mont-Royal.** They call it a mountain here, but it's really more of a large hill. There are a web of options for trekking through it, from using the broad and handsome pedestrian-only **chemin Olmsted** (a bridle path named for Frederick Law Olmsted, the park's landscape architect) to using smaller paths and sets of stairs. The park is well-marked and small enough that you can wander without fear of getting too lost, but our walking tour in chapter 8 suggests one place to start and a number of options once you've headed in.

ICE-SKATING

In the winter, outdoor rinks are set up in Vieux-Port, Lac des Castors (Beaver Lake), and other spots around the city; check tourist offices for your best options. One of the most agreeable venues for skating any time of the year is the **Atrium Le 1000 de la Gauchetière** in the downtown skyscraper at that address. For one thing, it's indoors and warm. For another, it's surrounded by cafés to relax at after twirling around the big rink. And yes, it's even open in the summer. Admission is C$5.75 (US$5/£2.45) for adults 18 and up, C$4.75 (US$4.10/£2.05) for seniors, C$3.75 (US$3.25/£1.60) for children 12 and under. Skates rentals are C$5 (US$4.35/£2.15). Call © **514/395-0555** or log on to www.le1000.com for hours and more information.

JOGGING

There are many possibilities for running. In addition to the areas described above for biking and hiking, consider heading to either of the city's most prominent parks: **Parc La Fontaine** in the Plateau Mont-Royal neighborhood (p. 120), or **Parc Maison-neuve** in the east side of the city, adjacent to the **Jardin Botanique** and across the street from **Olympic Park** (p. 115). Both parks are formally landscaped and well-used for recreation and relaxation.

SWIMMING

The downtown **Hôtel Omni Mont-Royal** (p. 74) features a terrific health club, spa, and outdoor pool complex, with exercise machines, yoga classes, massages, steam rooms and saunas, and a year-round outdoor pool accessible from the inside on cold days. Nonguests can use it for C$25 (US$22/£11) adults and C$7 (US$6.10/£3) children, and it's open weekdays 6am to 9pm and weekends 7am to 8pm. The hotel is at 1050 rue Sherbrooke ouest, at rue Peel (© **514/284-1110**).

8

Montréal Strolls

Cities best reveal themselves on foot, and Montréal is one of the most pedestrian-friendly locales in North America. There's much to see in the concentrated districts—the cobblestoned "Old Town" of Vieux-Montréal, the downtown district and its luxurious "Golden Square Mile," the "The Mountain" of Mont-Real, and the bustling neighborhood of Plateau Mont-Real. The city's layout is straightforward and mostly simple to navigate, and the extensive Métro system gets you to and from the neighborhoods with ease. These strolls will give you a taste of what's best about old and new Montréal, and send you off to discover highlights of your own.

WALKING TOUR 1	VIEUX-MONTRÉAL

Start:	Place d' Armes, opposite the Notre-Dame Basilica.
Finish:	Vieux-Port.
Time:	2 to 3 hours.
Best Times:	Almost any day the weather is decent. Vieux-Montréal is lively and safe day or night. Note, however, that most of the museums are closed on Mondays. On warm weekends and holidays, Montréalers and visitors turn out in full force, enjoying the plazas, the 18th- and 19th-century architecture, and the ambience of the most picturesque part of their city.
Worst Times:	Evenings, and when museums and historic places are closed.

If you're coming from outside Vieux-Montréal, take the Métro to the Place d'Armes station, which lets off next to the expanded Palais des Congrès convention center. Follow the signs up the short hill 2 blocks toward Vieux-Montréal (Old Montréal) and the Place d'Armes. Turn right on rue St-Jacques. On your immediate right is the domed, colonnaded:

❶ Banque de Montréal

Montréal's oldest bank building dates from 1847. From 1901 to 1905, American architect Stanford White was in charge of extending the original building, and in this enlarged space he created a vast chamber with high, green-marble columns topped with golden capitals. The public is welcome to stop in for a look. Besides being lavishly appointed inside and out, the bank also houses a **small banking museum** (p. 124) illustrating early operations—go in the front door, turn left, then left again to find it. Admission is free.

Exiting the bank, cross the street to the:

❷ Place d'Armes

The centerpiece of this square is a monument to city founder Paul de Chomedey, sieur de Maisonneuve (1612–76). It marks the spot where the settlers defeated Iroquois warriors in bloody hand-to-hand fighting, with de Maisonneuve himself locked in combat with the Iroquois chief.

De Maisonneuve won and lived here another 23 years. The inscription on the monument reads (in French): YOU ARE THE BUCKWHEAT SEED WHICH WILL GROW AND MULTIPLY AND SPREAD THROUGHOUT THE COUNTRY. The sculptures at the base of the monument represent prominent citizens of early Montréal: Charles Lemoyne, a farmer; Jeanne Mance, the woman who founded the first hospital in Montréal; Raphael-Lambert Closse, a soldier and the mayor of Ville-Marie; and an unnamed Iroquois brave. Closse is depicted with his dog, Pilote, whose bark once warned the early settlers of an impending Iroquois attack.

Facing the Notre-Dame Basilica from the square, look over to the left. At the corner of St-Jacques is the:

❸ Edifice New York Life

This red-stone Richardson Romanesque building, with a striking wrought-iron door and clock tower, is located at 511 Place d'Armes. At all of eight stories, this was Montréal's first skyscraper back in 1888, and it was equipped with a technological marvel—an elevator.

Next to it, on the right, stands the 23-story Art Deco:

❹ Edifice Aldred

If the building looks somehow familiar, there's a reason: Built in 1931, it clearly resembles the Empire State Building in New York, also completed that year. The building's original tenant was Aldred and Co. Ltd., a New York–based multinational finance company with offices in New York, London, and Paris.

From the square, cross rue Notre-Dame, bearing right of the Basilica to the:

❺ Vieux Séminaire de St-Sulpice

The city's oldest building, surrounded by equally ancient stone walls. This seminary was erected by the Sulpician priests who arrived in Ville-Marie in 1657, 15 years after the colony was founded (the Sulpicians are part of an order founded in

Paris by Jean-Jacques Olier in 1641). The clock on the facade dates from 1701 and has gears made almost entirely of wood. Unfortunately, the seminary is not open to the public.

After a look through the iron gate, head east on rue Notre-Dame to the magnificent Gothic Revival:

❻ Basilique Notre-Dame

This brilliantly crafted church was designed in 1824 by James O'Donnell, an Irish Protestant architect living in New York. Transformed by his experience, he converted to Roman Catholicism and is the only person buried here. The main altar is made from a hand-carved linden tree. Behind the altar is the Chapel of the Sacred Heart (1982), a perennially popular choice for weddings. The chapel's altar, 32 bronze panels by Montréal artist Charles Daudelin, represents birth, life, and death. Some 4,000 people can attend at a time, and the bell, one of the largest in North America, weighs 12 tons. There's a small museum beside the chapel. See p. 113 for more about the church. (Come back at night for a romantic take on the city, when more than a score of buildings in the area, including the Basilica, are illuminated.)

Exiting the Basilica, turn right (east) on rue Notre-Dame, crossing rue St-Sulpice. Walk 4 blocks, and then face left to see the:

❼ Vieux Palais de Justice (Old Court House)

Most of this structure was built in 1856. The third floor and dome were added in 1891, and the difference between the original structure and the addition can be easily discerned with a close look. The city's civil cases were tried here until a new courthouse, the Palais de Justice, was built next door in 1978. Civic departments for the city of Montréal are housed here now. The statue beside the Old Court House, called *Homage to Marguerite Bourgeoys* (a teacher and nun), is by sculptor Jules LaSalle.

Walking Tour: Vieux-Montréal

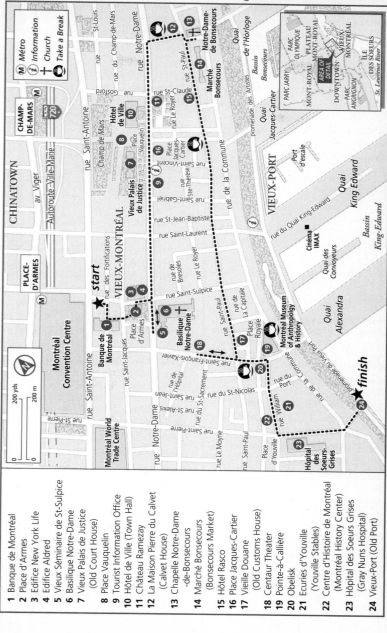

1 Banque de Montréal
2 Place d'Armes
3 Edifice New York Life
4 Edifice Aldred
5 Vieux Séminaire de St-Sulpice
6 Basilique Notre-Dame
7 Vieux Palais de Justice
  (Old Court House)
8 Place Vauquelin
9 Tourist Information Office
10 Hôtel de Ville (Town Hall)
11 Château Ramezay
12 La Maison Pierre du Calvet
  (Calvet House)
13 Chapelle Notre-Dame
  -de-Bonsecours
14 Marché Bonsecours
  (Bonsecours Market)
15 Hôtel Rasco
16 Place Jacques-Cartier
17 Vieille Douane
  (Old Customs House)
18 Centaur Theater
19 Pointe-à-Callière
20 Obelisk
21 Ecuries d'Youville
  (Youville Stables)
22 Centre d'Histoire de Montréal
  (Montréal History Center)
23 Hôpital des Soeurs Grises
  (Gray Nuns Hospital)
24 Vieux-Port (Old Port)

Also on your left, just past the Court House, is:
⑧ Place Vauquelin

This small public square, with a splashing fountain and view of the Champ-de-Mars park, was created in 1858. The statue is of Jean Vauquelin, commander of the French fleet in New France. The statue stares across rue Notre-Dame at Vauquelin's counterpart, the English Admiral Horatio Nelson. The two statues are symbols of Montréal's French and British duality.

On the opposite corner is a small but helpful:
⑨ Tourist Information Office

A bilingual staff is ready to answer questions and hand out many useful brochures and maps (daily in warmer months, Wed–Sun in winter). The famed Silver Dollar Saloon once stood on this site, though it has long since been torn down. The tavern was named for the 350 silver dollars embedded in its floor.

Around the corner, on the right, is a focus of activity in Vieux-Montréal, a magnet for both citizens and visitors year-round, the Place Jacques-Cartier, which we will visit later in the tour. Rising on the other side of rue Notre-Dame, opposite the top of the square, is the impressive:
⑩ Hôtel de Ville (Town Hall)

Built between 1872 and 1878 in the florid French Second Empire style, the edifice is seen to particular advantage when it is illuminated at night. In 1922, it barely survived a disastrous fire. Only the exterior walls remained, and after substantial rebuilding and the addition of another floor, it reopened in 1926. Do take a minute to look inside at the generous use of Italian marble, the Art Deco lamps, and the bronze-and-glass chandelier. The sculptures at the entry are *Woman with a Pail* and *The Sower*, both by Québec sculptor Alfred Laliberté.

Exiting Town Hall, cross rue Notre-Dame once again and turn left, continuing east. The small terraced park, with its orderly ranks of trees,

has a statue honoring the controversial long-time mayor of Montréal, Jean Drapeau. Next is:
⑪ Château Ramezay

Built by Claude de Ramezay between 1705 and 1706 in the French Regime style of the period, this was the home of the city's French governors for 4 decades, starting with de Ramezay, before being taken over and used for the same purpose by the British.

In 1775, an army of American rebels invaded and held Montréal, using the house as their headquarters. Benjamin Franklin was sent to persuade Montréalers to join the American revolt against British rule. He stayed in this château but failed to sway Québec's leaders to join his cause.

The house had a number of uses before becoming a museum in 1895. Today, it shows off furnishings, oil paintings, costumes, and other objects related to the economic and social activities of the 18th century and the first half of the 19th century. See p. 119 for more about the museum.

Continue in the same direction (east) along rue Notre-Dame to the corner of rue Bonsecours. Turn right. Near the bottom, on the left, is a house with a low maroon roof and an attached stone building on the corner. This is:
⑫ La Maison Pierre du Calvet (Calvet House)

Built in the 18th century and sumptuously restored between 1964 and 1966, this house would have been inhabited by a fairly well-to-do family in its first years. Pierre du Calvet, believed to be the original owner, was a French Huguenot who supported the American Revolution. Calvet met with Benjamin Franklin here in 1775 and was imprisoned from 1780 to 1783 for supplying money to the Americans. With a characteristic sloped roof meant to discourage snow buildup and raised end walls that serve as firebreaks, the building is constructed of Montréal graystone. It is now a *hostellerie* and restaurant (see review on p. 77), with an entrance at no. 405. Visitors are invited to come in for a look.

TAKE A BREAK
There is a voluptuously appointed dining room inside the **Hostel-lerie Pierre du Calvet** (405 rue Bonsecours), but in the warm months, lunches are served in an outdoor courtyard that opened to the public in 2007 (before then, it was privately used by the owner). Take a peek to see the indoor greenhouse and songbirds that lead to the stone-walled terrace.

The next street, rue St-Paul, is the oldest thoroughfare in Montréal, dating from 1672. Across the way is the small:

⓭ Chapelle Notre-Dame-de-Bon-Secours Chapel

Called the Sailors' Church because so many seamen come to worship here, this chapel was founded by Marguerite Bourgeoys, a nun and teacher who was made a saint in 1982. Although recent excavations have unearthed foundations of her original 1675 church, the building has been much altered, and the present facade was built in the late 18th century. A museum (entrance on the left) tells the story of Bourgeoys' life and incorporates the archaeological site, where discoveries dated to 400 B.C. (See p. 118 for more museum information.) Sailors saved at sea have made pilgrimages to the church to give thanks. Climb up to the tower for a view of the port and Old Town.

Just beyond the Sailor's Church, heading west down rue St-Paul, is an imposing building with a colonnaded facade and silvery dome, the limestone:

⓮ Marché Bonsecours (Bonsecours Market)

Completed in 1847, this building was used first as the Parliament of United Canada and then as the City Hall, the central market, a music recital hall, and finally the home of the municipality's housing and planning offices. It was restored in 1992 for the city's 350th birthday celebration to house temporary exhibitions and musical performances. It continues to be used for exhibitions, but it is more of a retail center now, with small art shops inside and sidewalk cafés near the entrance (p. 118).

When the Bonsecours Market was first built, the dome could be seen from everywhere in the city and served as a landmark for seafarers sailing into the harbor. Today it is lit at night.

Continue down rue St-Paul. At no. 281 is the former:

⓯ Hôtel Rasco

An Italian, Francisco Rasco, came to Canada to manage a hotel for the Molson family (of beer brewing fame) and later became successful with his own hotel on this spot. The 150-room Rasco was the Ritz of its day, hosting Charles Dickens and his wife in 1842, when the author was directing his plays at a theater that used to stand across the street. The hotel lives on in legend if not in fact, as it's devoid of much of its original architectural detail. Between 1960 and 1981 the space stood empty, but the city took it over and restored it in 1982. It has contained a succession of restaurants on the ground floor and now is home to the standout Mediterranean restaurant **Version Laurent Godbout** (p. 95).

Continue heading west on rue St-Paul, turning right when you hit:

⓰ Place Jacques-Cartier

Opened as a marketplace in 1804, this is the most appealing of the Old Town's squares, despite its obviously touristy aspects. Its cobbled cross streets, gentle downhill slope, and ancient buildings set the mood, while outdoor cafés, street entertainers, itinerant artists, and fruit and flower vendors invite lingering in warm weather. *Calèches* (horse-drawn carriages) depart from both the lower and the upper ends of the square for tours of Vieux-Montréal.

Walk slowly uphill, taking in the old buildings that bracket the plaza. Plaques in French and English describe some of them: the **Vandelac House** (no. 433), the **del Vecchio House** (nos. 404–410), and the **Cartier House** (no. 407). All these houses were well suited to the rigors of life in the raw young settlement. Their steeply pitched roofs shed the heavy winter snows rather than collapsing under the burden, and small windows with double casements let in light while keeping out wintry breezes. When shuttered, the windows were almost as effective as the heavy stone walls in deflecting hostile arrows or the antics of trappers fresh from raucous evenings in nearby taverns.

At the upper (northern) end of the plaza stands a monument to Horatio Nelson, hero of Trafalgar, erected in 1809. This monument preceded the much larger version in London by several years. After years of vandalism, presumably by Québec separatists, the statue had to be temporarily replaced for restoration; the original Nelson is now back in place at the crown of the column.

TAKE A BREAK
Most of the old buildings in and around the inclined plaza harbor restaurants and cafés. For a drink or snack, try to find a seat in **Le Jardin Nelson** (no. 407), near the bottom of the hill. Sit in the courtyard in back when the weather is good—there often is live music—or on the terrace overlooking the activity of the square.

Return to rue St-Paul and continue west. Take time to window-shop the many art galleries that have sprung up alongside the loud souvenir shops on the street. The street numbers will get lower as you approach the cross street of boulevard St-Laurent, the north-south thoroughfare that divides Montréal into its east and west

halves. Numbers will start to rise again as you move onto St-Paul ouest (west). At 150 rue St-Paul ouest is the neoclassical:

⑰ Vieille Douane (Old Customs House)

Erected from 1836 to 1838, the building was doubled in size to its present proportions when an extension to the south was added in 1882; walk around to the other side of the building to see how it's different. That end of the building faces Place Royale, the first public square in the 17th-century settlement of Ville-Marie (Montréal). It's where Europeans and Amerindians used to come to trade.

Continue on rue St-Paul to the cross street rue St-François-Xavier. Turn right for a short detour; up rue St-François-Xavier, on the right, is the stately:

⑱ Centaur Theater

The home of Montréal's principal English-language theater is a former stock-exchange building. The Beaux Arts architecture is interesting in that the two entrances are on either side rather than in the center of the facade. American architect George Post, who was also responsible for designing the New York Stock Exchange, designed this building, erected in 1903. It served in its original function until 1965, when it was redesigned as a theater with two stages.

Return back down rue St-François-Xavier, and cross St-Paul. At the next corner, the gray wedge-shaped building is the:

⑲ Pointe-à-Callière

Housing the Museum of Archaeology and History, with artifacts unearthed here during more than 10 years of excavation, this site was where Ville-Marie was founded in 1642. The museum also incorporates, via an underground connection, the Old Customs House you just passed. See p. 114 for more on this top-notch museum.

A fort stood here in 1645. Thirty years later, this same spot became home to the château of a monsieur de Callière, from whom the building and triangular square take their names. At that time, the St. Pierre River separated this piece of land from the mainland. It was made a canal in the 19th century and later filled in.

TAKE A BREAK
One possibility for lunch or a pick-me-up is the glass-walled second-floor **L'Arrivage Café** at the Pointe-à-Callière museum. Another is the moderately priced **Stash**, which you just passed back at 200 rue St-Paul ouest at the corner at rue St-François-Xavier. It specializes in Polish fare and opens at 11:30am on weekdays and noon on weekends.

Proceeding west from Pointe-à-Callière, near rue St-François-Xavier, stands an:

⑳ Obelisk

Commemorating the founding of Ville-Marie on May 18, 1642, the obelisk was erected here in 1893 by the Montréal Historical Society. It bears the names of the city's early pioneers, including de Maisonneuve and Jeanne Mance.

Continuing west from the obelisk 2 blocks to 296–316 Place d'Youville, you'll find the:

㉑ Ecuries d'Youville (Youville Stables)

Despite the name, the rooms in the iron-gated compound, built in 1825 on land owned by the Gray Nuns, were used mainly as warehouses, rather than as horse stables (the actual stables, next door, were made of wood and disappeared long ago). Like much of the waterfront area, the U-shaped Youville building was run-down and forgotten until the 1960s, when a group of enterprising businesspeople bought and renovated it. Today the compound contains offices and a popular steakhouse, **Gibby's.** Go through the passage to the right of the restaurant for a look at the inner courtyard if the gates are open, as they usually are.

Continue another block west to the front door of the brick building on your right, 335 rue St-Pierre and the:

㉒ Centre d'Histoire de Montréal (Montréal History Center)

Built in 1903 as Montréal's central fire station, this building now houses exhibits, including many audiovisual ones, about the city's past and present. Visitors will learn about the early routes of exploration, the fur trade, architecture, public squares, the railroad, and life in Montréal from 1920 to 1950. See p. 123 for details.

Head down rue St-Pierre toward the water. Less than a block away, on the right at no. 138, is the former:

㉓ Hôpital des Soeurs Grises (Gray Nuns Hospital)

The hospital was in operation from 1693 to 1871 and served as a novitiate for future nuns. The order, founded by Marguerite d'Youville in 1737, is officially known as the Sisters of Charity of Montréal. The present building incorporates several additions and was part of the city's General Hospital, run by the Charon Brothers but administered by d'Youville, who died here in 1771. The wing in which she died was restored in 1980. The wall of the original chapel remains. Visits inside must be arranged in advance by calling ℂ **514/842-9411.**

From here, walk down rue St-Pierre and cross the main street rue de la Commune and then the railroad tracks to enter the final stop on this tour:

㉔ Vieux-Port (Old Port)

Montréal's historic commercial wharves have been reborn as a waterfront park frequented in good weather by cyclists, in-line skaters, joggers, walkers, strollers, lovers, and picnickers. Across the water is the distinctive modular housing project **Habitat '67,** built by famed architect Moshe Safdie for the 1967 Expo. It is now a high-end apartment complex.

If you walk to your right, the little triangular building is the entry to **Parc des Ecluses (Locks Park),** a canal-side path where the first locks on the St. Lawrence River are located.

From here, you can walk north along the broad boulevard of rue McGill to reach **Square-Victoria** and its Métro station, the staircase to which is marked by an authentic Art Nouveau portal, designed by Hector Guimard for the Paris subway system. You might also want to return to the small streets parallel to rue St-Paul that house boutique clothing stores, one of the highest concentrations of art galleries in Canada, and more.

Another option if the weather is nice is to enter the Parc des Ecluses and follow the path along the **Lachine Canal.** In an hour or less you'll arrive at Montréal's colorful indoor/outdoor Atwater Market.

WALKING TOUR 2	DOWNTOWN

Start:	Bonaventure Métro stop.
Finish:	Musée McCord.
Time:	1½ hours.
Best Times:	Weekdays in the morning or after 2pm, when the streets hum with big-city vibrancy but aren't too crowded.
Worst Times:	Weekdays from noon to 2pm, when the streets, stores, and restaurants are crowded with businesspeople on lunch-break errands; Monday, when museums are closed; and Sunday, when most stores are closed and the area is nearly deserted (museums, however, are open).

After a tour of Vieux-Montréal, a look around the heart of the 21st-century city will highlight the ample contrast between these two areas. To see the city at its contemporary best, take the Métro to the Bonaventure stop to start this tour.

Take the Métro to the Bonaventure stop. Emerging from that station, the dramatic skyscraper immediately to the west is:

❶ 1000 rue de la Gauchetière

This young contribution to the already memorable skyline is easily identified by its copper-and-blue pyramidal top, which rises to the maximum height permitted by the municipal building code. Inside, past an atrium planted with live trees, is an indoor skating rink bordered by cafés.

Walk west for 1 block on rue de la Gauchetière. On the left is:

❷ Le Marriott Château Champlain

The hotel's distinctive facade of half-moon windows inspired its nickname: the "Cheese Grater."

Walk 1 more block and turn right on rue Peel, heading north. When you hit boulevard René-Lévesque, bear right and you'll arrive at:

❸ Square Dorchester

The square's tall old trees and benches invite lunchtime brown-baggers. This used to be called Dominion Square, but it was renamed for Baron Dorchester, an early English governor, when the adjacent street, once named for Dorchester, was changed to boulevard René-Lévesque. Along the east side of the square is the **Sun Life Insurance building,** built in three stages between 1914 and 1931, and the tallest building in Québec from 1931 until the skyscraper boom of the post–World War II era. This is a gathering point for tour buses and calèches. In winter, the calèche drivers replace their carriages with sleighs and give rides around the top of Mont-Royal.

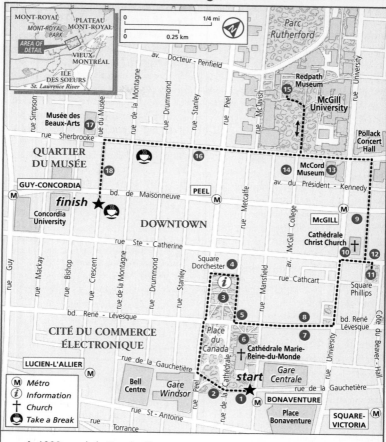

1. 1000 rue de la Gauchetière
2. Le Marriott
   Château Champlain
3. Square Dorchester
4. Infotouriste Centre
5. Boulevard René-Lévesque
6. Basilique-Cathédrale
   Marie-Reine-du-Monde
7. Fairmont The Queen Elizabeth
   (Le Reine Elizabeth)
8. Place Ville-Marie
9. Tour KPMG
10. Cathédrale Christ Church
11. Carré Phillips (Square Phillips)
12. Rue Ste-Catherine
13. Musée McCord
14. McGill University
15. Musée Redpath
16. Maison Alcan
17. Musée des Beaux-Arts
    (Museum of Fine Arts)
18. Rue Crescent

At the northeast corner of the square is the main office of:

④ Infotouriste Centre

Many useful maps and brochures are in stock here, most of them free for the taking. Visitors can ask questions of bilingual attendants, purchase tour tickets, change money, make hotel reservations, or rent a car. Open daily.

From that office, go back to the other end of the square and turn left (east) on:

⑤ Boulevard René-Lévesque

Formerly Dorchester Boulevard, this primary street was renamed in 1988 following the death of René-Lévesque, the Parti Québécois leader who led the movement in favor of Québec independence and the use of the French language. Boulevard René-Lévesque is the city's broadest downtown thoroughfare, and the one with the fastest traffic.

On the right is the:

⑥ Basilique-Cathédrale Marie-Reine-du-Monde

Suddenly get the feeling you're in Rome? This cathedral is a copy of St. Peter's Basilica, albeit at roughly one-quarter scale, built between 1875 and 1894 as the headquarters for Montréal's Roman Catholic bishop. The statue in front is of Bishop Ignace Bourget (1799–1885), the force behind the construction. It was sculpted in 1903 by Louis-Philippe Hébert, who is also responsible for the statue of de Maisonneuve in the Place d'Armes in Vieux-Montréal. See p. 117 for more details.

Continue past the cathedral. In the next block, on also on the right, is:

⑦ Fairmont The Queen Elizabeth (Le Reine Elizabeth)

Montréal's largest hotel (p. 68) stands above **Gare Centrale,** the main railroad station, and buses leave for Dorval and Mirabel airports from here. Opened in 1958, this is where John Lennon and Yoko Ono had their weeklong "Bed-In for Peace" in 1969.

On your left, directly across from Fairmont Le Reine Elizabeth, is:

⑧ Place Ville-Marie

Known as PVM to Montréalers, this glass box of a building was considered a gem of the postwar urban redevelopment efforts in Montréal. Architect I. M. Pei (best known for his glass Pyramid at the Louvre in Paris) gave the skyscraper and indoor shopping mall a cross-shaped floor plan, recalling the cross planted by Cartier atop Mont-Royal that claimed the island for France. Completed in 1962, the complex has a fountain in its plaza called *Feminine Landscape* (1972), by Toronto artist Gerald Gladstone.

Continue on boulevard René-Lévesque to the end of the block and turn left on rue Université. As you're walking, look up to the top of the skyscraper a few blocks down:

⑨ Tour KPMG

Pink and postmodern, this glass office building was completed in 1987 at the Place de la Cathédrale. The two-peaked top is meant to resemble a bishop's *mitre,* or cap, but many see the ears of a certain DC Comics superhero's mask instead.

Walk 2 blocks to rue Ste-Catherine. Across the street is:

⑩ Cathédrale Christ Church

Built from 1856 to 1859, this neo-Gothic building is the seat of the Anglican bishop of Montréal. The church garden is modeled on a medieval European cloister. The cathedral donated the land for the Tour KPMG office building and the shopping complex underneath it, Promenades de la Cathédrale, in return for eventual ownership of both. During construction, the church was elevated on cement piles, making it look like it was floating on air. See p. 117 for more.

Turn right on rue Ste-Catherine and walk just past avenue Union, where you'll see:

⑪ Carré Phillips (Square Phillips)

This plaza contains a statue of Edward VII and, during much of the year, a farm stand selling Québec maple products.

If you're in the mood for shopping, take some time to stroll west on this main shopping drag:

12 Rue Ste-Catherine

Many of Montréal's department stores are on this street, including, just across from Carré Phillips, **La Baie**—or "The Bay," short for Hudson's Bay Company, successor to the famous fur-trapping firm (see "Department Stores" on p. 156 for a list of other highlights). Head west of the Cathédrale Christ Church for the center of Montréal's shopping district. Be aware that several adult shops are housed alongside the stores and cafés.

To continue the walking tour, get to the corner of Ste-Catherine and avenue Union and go north on Union 3 blocks, to rue Sherbrooke. You'll be in front of McGill University's Schulich School of Music. Turn left and go 1 block. On your left is:

13 Musée McCord

This private museum of Canadian history first opened in 1921 and was substantially renovated in 1992. Named for its founder, David Ross McCord (1844–1930), the museum has an eclectic and often eccentric collection of over a million objects, images, and manuscripts. Folk art, beaded costumes, photographs, fine-china place settings, and more reveal elements of city and rural life from the 18th to the 20th century, and Amerindians are well represented. Opening hours and other details are on p. 112.

Continue west on rue Sherbrooke. On your right is:

14 McGill University

The gate is usually open to this, Canada's most prestigious university, home to over 33,000 students. It was founded after a bequest from a Scottish-born fur trader, James McGill. This central campus mixes modern concrete and glass structures alongside older stone buildings.

Also on the campus is the:

15 Musée Redpath

Housed in a building dating from 1882, this museum's main draws are the mummies that are part of its Egyptian antiquities collection, the second largest of its kind in Canada (p. 124).

Continue down rue Sherbrooke. About 30 feet past the front gate of McGill, note the large stone on the lawn. This marks the site of the Amerindian Horchelaga settlement that existed here before the arrival of the Europeans. Two blocks farther, on your left, is:

16 Maison Alcan

The street you're now on, rue Sherbrooke, is the heart of what's known as the "Golden Square Mile." This is where the city's most luxurious residences of the 19th and early 20th century were located, and where the vast majority of the country's wealthy lived. The Maison Alcan is an example of an office building that has nicely incorporated one of those 19th-century houses into its late-20th-century facade. Step inside the lobby to see the results over to the right.

Continue on rue Sherbrooke and:

> **TAKE A BREAK**
> If you're dressed nicely—sophisticated casual is recommended, which means no jeans or shorts—pop into **The Ritz-Carlton Montréal** (no. 1228), the city's "Grande Dame," for high tea at the Café de Paris. In warm weather it opens an outdoor terrace alongside its famous duck pond, complete with a family of ducklings. The Ritz Bar is another option, for cocktails and light snacks.

Continue another block on rue Sherbrooke, passing, on your left, the Holt Renfrew department store, identified on the side of its marquee only as HR. At the corner of rue Crescent you'll be at the:

17 Musée des Beaux-Arts (Museum of Fine Arts)

This is Canada's oldest and Montréal's most prominent museum. The modern annex on the left side of rue Sherbrooke was added in 1991 and is connected to the original stately Beaux Arts building (1912) across the street by an underground tunnel that doubles as a gallery.

Both buildings are made of Vermont marble. Additional details are on p. 109.

You've got a couple options here. If you're in the mood for the museum, by all means take this opportunity—a visit to the Museum of Fine Arts should be part of any trip to Montréal. For high-end shopping, drinking, or eating, turn left onto:

⑱ Rue Crescent

This and nearby streets are the locus of the social and dining district of downtown, largely yuppie Anglo in character, if not necessarily in strict demographics. The first block of Crescent has pricey boutiques and jewelers. The next 2 blocks are a gumbo of inexpensive pizza joints, upscale restaurants, and dozens of bars and dance clubs, drawing enthusiastic consumers looking to spend money and,

come darkness, party the night away. This center of gilded youth and glamour was once a run-down slum area slated for demolition. Luckily, buyers with a good aesthetic sense saw the possibilities of these late-19th-century row houses and brought them back to life.

TAKE A BREAK
Lively spots for coffee, snacks, and drink are abundant along rue Crescent. **Thursday's** (no. 1449, in L'Hôtel de la Montagne) is one, if you can find a seat on the balcony. Or head down a few steps into the unassuming Lebanese joint **Boustan** (no. 2020) for a filling shawarma sandwich. Yes, that's former Prime Minster Pierre Trudeau's photo at the register; he was a regular.

WALKING TOUR 3   PLATEAU MONT-ROYAL

Start: The corner of avenue du Mont-Royal and rue St-Denis.

Finish: Square St-Louis or Parc LaFontaine.

Time: At least 2 hours, but allow more time if you want to linger in the shops, restaurants, or major park of this intriguing neighborhood.

Best Times: Monday through Saturday during the day, when the shops are open. Most of this area is at its liveliest on Saturday. For barhopping, evenings work well.

Worst Times: Sunday, if shopping is important to you, because many stores are closed.

This is essentially a window-shopping, browsing, and grazing tour, designed to provide a sampling of the sea of ethnicities that make up Plateau Mont-Royal, north of downtown Montréal and due east of Mont-Royal Park. The largely Francophone neighborhood has seen an unprecedented flourishing of restaurants, cafés, clubs, and shops in recent years. It's bounded on the south by rue Sherbrooke and on the north by boulevard St-Joseph, where the **Mile End** neighborhood begins and continues farther north, and on the east by avenue Papineau and on the west by boulevard St-Laurent. Monuments are few along these commercial avenues, and the residential side streets are filled with row houses that are home to students, young professionals, and immigrants old and new. This walk is a glance into the lives of both established and freshly minted Montréalers and the way they spend their leisure time. Be aware that stores and bistros open and close with considerable frequency in this neighborhood, so some of the highlights listed below may not exist when you visit.

Walking Tour: Plateau Mont-Royal

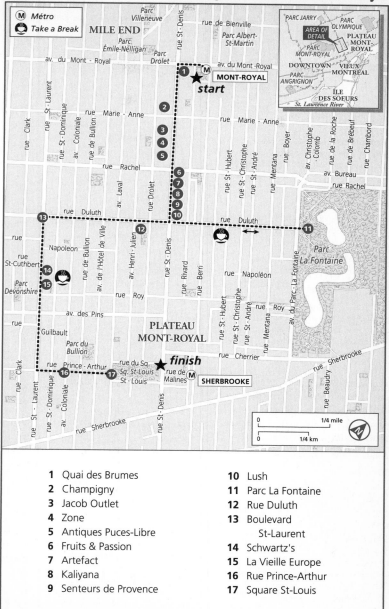

1 Quai des Brumes
2 Champigny
3 Jacob Outlet
4 Zone
5 Antiques Puces-Libre
6 Fruits & Passion
7 Artefact
8 Kaliyana
9 Senteurs de Provence
10 Lush
11 Parc La Fontaine
12 Rue Duluth
13 Boulevard St-Laurent
14 Schwartz's
15 La Vieille Europe
16 Rue Prince-Arthur
17 Square St-Louis

To begin, take the Métro to the Mont-Royal station. Turn left out of the station and, walking west on avenue du Mont-Royal to St-Denis. Turn left again. On the left side of the street, at 4481 rue St-Denis, is:

❶ Quai des Brumes

This popular jazz, blues, and beer gathering spot, offers live music most evenings, and even some afternoons. Its name means "Foggy Dock."

Continue down rue St-Denis, where you'll find a block of shops and cafés on two stories of the small buildings. Toward the end of the block, on the other side of the street, is no. 4380:

❷ Champigny

A large bookstore with mostly French stock, it also carries travel guides and literature in English, as well as CDs, magazines, and newspapers from all over the world. Most of the books are upstairs. There's an extensive children's section, as well. The store is open daily from 9am until 10pm.

If you didn't cross over for Champigny, cross over at the next street corner. Continue on rue St-Denis and in the next block, at no. 4268, is:

❸ Jacob Outlet

With pop music through the speakers and a steady stream of locals, this clothing store is an outlet to the popular Jacob chain (there's one next door). You'll find inexpensive T-shirts, denim jackets, and other casual clothes for the under-25 set.

A little farther, at no. 4246, is:

❹ Zone

This shop is part of a small Montréal-based chain; there are two other stores in the city and one each in Québec and Ottawa. Its specialty is contemporary housewares, sleekly monochromatic and brightly hued.

Next door, at 4240 rue St-Denis, is the wonderfully cluttered:

❺ Antiques Puces-Libre

Poke through three floors of 19th-century French-Canadian country collectibles here—pine and oak furniture, lamps, clocks, vases, and the like.

Continue to rue Rachel, and cross to the left side of rue St-Denis. Continue south to no. 4159A for:

❻ Fruits & Passion

This high-end Québec-based company has thousands of shops in Canada and outposts in Abu Dhabi, Kuwait City, and Paris, but it has just begun to distribute in the U.S. and Europe. It uses "natural extracts" in a line of fruit-scented soaps and shampoos and actual foods. It also sells dog-care items, including its HOT-dog Eau de toilette.

Just down the street, at 4117 rue St-Denis, is:

❼ Artéfact

Québécois designers sell clothing and paintings at this bright little boutique, where a slip of a summer dress runs about C$250 (US$218/£107).

After that, find no. 4107:

❽ Kaliyana

More women's clothes from a Canadian designer: This shop's natural fiber outfits are flowing, angular, and bordering on the avant-garde—like an Asian-influenced Eileen Fisher. It also stocks contemporary footwear including Arche from France and Trippen from Germany.

A little farther down the block, at 4077 rue St-Denis, you'll come upon:

❾ Senteurs de Provence

One of a small chain, this store displays hand-painted pottery and printed linens, as well as bath soaps, shower gels, and lotions of high order, all from France.

Shortly, stop in at no. 4067 and take a whiff of:

❿ Lush

On the ground floor of one of the prettiest Queen Anne Victorian row houses on the street, Lush sells soaps presented and wrapped as if they were aromatic, bubble-gum-colored hunks of cheese.

At the corner of St-Denis and rue Duluth, you have options. If you want to spend some time at the city's grand Parc La Fontaine, turn left and walk east. If you want to skip the park, turn right and jump to no. 12.

TAKE A BREAK
Walking east on rue Duluth toward Parc La Fontaine, you'll pass the delectable **Au Pied de Cochon** at no. 536, at the corner of rue St-Hubert. It opens at 5pm every day but Monday, so if it's late afternoon consider making a stop for your big meal of the day. Maybe a bowl of *poutine,* the classic Québécois comfort food? Or one of the restaurant's seven variations of pork, perhaps?

⑪ Parc La Fontaine

Strolling this park, particularly if you're visiting on a warm day, is an enormously satisfying way to see Montréal at play. This northwestern end of La Fontaine is well-used by people (and puppies) of all ages. The two ponds are linked and turned into a skating rink in the winter (skate rentals available). In the summer, the 2,500-seat **Théâtre de Verdure,** near where rue Duluth runs into the park, is an open-air venue for dance, music, theater, and film.

If you're happy exploring the park, consider this tour done. The Sherbrooke Métro will be the closest if you leave the park on its west side (see the "finish here" star on the walking tour map). To continue the stroll, retrace your steps on rue Duluth heading west.

⑫ Rue Duluth

Along with several small antiques shops, this street is dotted with ever-changing Greek, Portuguese, Italian, North African, Malaysian, and Vietnamese eateries. Many of the restaurants state that you can *"apportez votre vin"* (bring your own wine). Some are fresh and attractive, others not.

Continue along rue Duluth until it arrives at the boulevard St-Laurent, the north-south thoroughfare that marks where the east side of the city ends and the west side begins. Turn left.

⑬ Boulevard St-Laurent

St-Laurent is so prominent in the cultural history of the city that it's known to Anglophones, Francophones, and Allophones alike simply as "The Main." Tra-ditionally a beachhead for immigrants to the city, St-Laurent has increasingly become a street of chic bistros and clubs. The late-night section runs for several miles, roughly from rue Laurier in the north all the way down to rue Sherbrooke in the south. The bistro and club boom was fueled by low rents and the large number of industrial lofts in this area, a legacy of St-Laurent's heyday as a garment-manufacturing center. Today these cavernous spaces are places for the city's hipsters, professionals, artists, and guests to eat and play. Many spots have the life spans of fireflies, but some pound on for years.

At 3895 bd. St-Laurent you'll find:

⑭ Schwartz's

The language police insisted on the exterior sign with the French mouthful CHEZ SCHWARZ CHARCUTERIE HEBRAIQUE DE MONTRÉAL, but everyone just calls it Schwartz's (p. 102). This narrow, no-frills Hebrew deli might appear completely unassuming, but it serves a product called smoked meat against which all other smoked meats must be measured. Vegetarians and those who require some distance from their neighbors' elbows will hate it.

TAKE A BREAK
Pop in to **Schwartz's** for some of its famous smoked meat. Plates are listed either as small (meaning large) or large (meaning humongous). Don't forget a side of fries and a couple of garlicky pickles.

Next, a few steps along at no. 3855, is:

⑮ La Vieille Europe

This "Old Europe" delicatessen sells aromatic coffee beans from around the world, plus sausages and meats, cheeses, and cooking utensils. Stock up here if you're thinking of a picnic in the next day or two.

Continue down boulevard St-Laurent 1 more block and turn left (east) into:

16 Rue Prince-Arthur

Named after Queen Victoria's third son, who was governor-general of Canada from 1911 to 1916, this pedestrian street is filled with bars and restaurants, most of which add more to the liveliness of the street than to the gastronomic reputation of the city. The older establishments go by such names as La Cabane Grecque, La Caverne Grec, Casa Grecque—no doubt you will discern an emerging theme—but the Greek stalwarts are being challenged by Latino and Asian newcomers. Their owners vie constantly with gimmicks to haul in passersby, including two-for-one drinks and dueling tables d'hôte prices that plummet to C$10 (US$8.70/£4.30) or lower for three courses. Beer and sangria are the popular drinks at the white resin

tables and chairs set out along the sides of the street. In the warmer weather, mimes, vendors, street performers, and caricaturists also compete for the tourist dollar.

Five short blocks later, rue Prince-Arthur ends at:

17 Square St-Louis

This public garden plaza is framed by attractive row houses erected for well-to-do Francophones in the late 19th and early 20th centuries. People stretch out on the grass to take the sun, or sit bundled on benches willing March away. Among them are usually a few harmless derelicts. On occasional summer days, there are impromptu concerts. The square ends at rue St-Denis.

To pick up the Métro, cross rue St-Denis and walk east on rue des Malines. The Sherbrooke station is just ahead at the corner of rue Berri.

WALKING TOUR 4   MONT-ROYAL

Start:	At the corner of rue Peel and avenue des Pins.
Finish:	At the cross (la Croix du Mont-Royal) on top of the mountain.
Time:	1 hour to ascend directly to the Chalet du Mont-Royal and its lookout over the city and come back down; 3 hours to take the more leisurely chemin Olmstead route and see all the sites listed below. It's easy to leave out some stops to truncate the walk.
Best Times:	Spring, summer, and autumn mornings.
Worst Times:	Winter, when snow and slush make a sleigh ride to the top of the mountain much more enticing than a hike, and during the high heat of midday in summer.

Join the locals: Assuming a reasonable measure of physical fitness, the best way to explore the jewel of Parc Mont-Royal is simply to walk up it from downtown. They call it a mountain but it's really more of a very large hill, and a broad pedestrian-only road and smaller footpaths form a web of options for strollers, joggers, cyclists, and in-line skaters of all ages. Anyone in search of a little greenery and space heads here in warm weather, while in winter, cross-country skiers follow miles of paths and snowshoers tramp along trails laid out especially for them. The 200-hectare (494-acre) urban park was created in 1876 by American landscape architect Frederick Law Olmsted, who also designed Central Park in New York City and parks in Philadelphia, Boston, and Chicago (although in the end, relatively little of Olmsted's full design actually came into being). For more about the history of the park, as well as the most current events and happenings, go to **www.lemontroyal.qc.ca**.

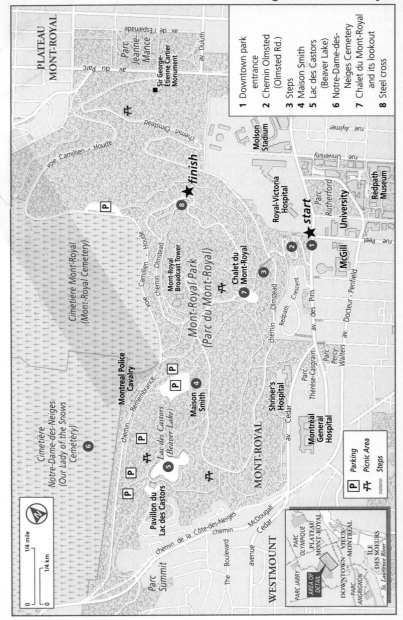

1 Downtown park entrance
2 Chemin Olmsted (Olmsted Rd.)
3 Steps
4 Maison Smith
5 Lac des Castors (Beaver Lake)
6 Notre-Dame-des-Neiges Cemetery
7 Chalet du Mont-Royal and its lookout
8 Steel cross

PLATEAU MONT-ROYAL

Parc Jeanne-Mance

av. de l'Esplanade

av. Duluth

Sir George-Étienne Cartier Monument

av. du Parc

voie Camillien – Houde

chemin Olmstead

finish

Cimetière Mont-Royal (Mont-Royal Cemetery)

Molson Stadium

Royal-Victoria Hospital

Parc Rutherford

Redpath Museum

rue Aylmer

rue University

University

McGill

rue Peel

start

Mont-Royal Broadcast Tower

Chalet du Mont-Royal

Mont-Royal Park (Parc du Mont-Royal)

chemin Olmstead

voie Camillien – Houde

chemin Olmstead

Redpath Crescent

av. des Pins

av. Docteur-Penfield

Cimetière Notre-Dame-des-Neiges (Our Lady of the Snows Cemetery)

Montreal Police Cavalry

chemin Remembrance

Maison Smith

Lac des Castors (Beaver Lake)

Pavillon du Lac des Castors

Parc Summit

chemin de la Côte-des-Neiges

McDougall

Cedar

The Boulevard

avenue

Parc Percy Walters

Parc Thérèse-Casgrain

Shriner's Hospital

av. Cedar

Montréal General Hospital

MONT-ROYAL

WESTMOUNT

N

1/4 mile
1/4 km
0

P Parking
⚘ Picnic Area
Steps

AREA OF DETAIL

PARC JARRY
PARC OLYMPIQUE
PLATEAU MONT-ROYAL
VIEUX-MONTRÉAL
ÎLE DES SŒURS
DOWNTOWN
PARC ANGRIGNON
St. Lawrence River

Start this tour at the corner of rue Peel and avenue des Pins, at the:

❶ Downtown park entrance

A map at the site helps to set bearings. From here, it's possible to reach the top of this small mountain by a variety of routes. Hearty souls can choose the quickest and most strenuous approach—taking the steepest sets of stairs at every opportunity, which go directly to the **Chalet du Mont-Royal and its lookout** at the top (no. 7, below). Those who prefer to take their time and gain altitude slowly can use the switchback bridle path. It's possible to mix and match the options as you go along. Don't be too worried about getting lost; the park is small enough that it's easy enough to regain your sense of direction no matter which way you head.

Head up either foot path from the entrance, and in a few steps you'll reach the broad bridle path:

❷ Chemin Olmsted (Olmsted Rd.)

Frederick Law Olmsted designed this road at a gradual grade for both pedestrians and horse-drawn carriages. Horses could pull their loads up the hill at a steady pace, and on the way down would not be pushed from behind by the weight of the carriage.

Chemin Olmsted is closed to automobiles. Early on, it passes some beautiful stone houses off Redpath Circle, to the left. If you want to bypass some of the switchbacks, you can use any of a number of paths for a shortcut (please stay only on established paths to prevent erosion, though).

After about the fourth switchback, you'll reach an intersection with the option to go left or right. Turn left. Following this shaded and pleasant road in the woods will get you to Maison Smith (no. 4, below) in about 45 minutes.

Another option to taking chemin Olmstead is to follow the:

❸ Steps

There are numerous sets of stairs through the woods that let you bypass the broad and flatter switchbacks of chemin Olmstead. They get walkers to the Chalet du Mont-Royal and its lookout (no. 7) more quickly. Fair warning: The last 100 or so steps go almost straight up. On the plus side, you'll get to share sympathetic smiles with strangers. Taking the steps bypasses sites no. 4, 5, and 6.

If you're taking the chemin Olmsted, you eventually arrive at a:

❹ Maison Smith

Built in 1858, this structure has been used as a park rangers' station and park police headquarters. From 1983 to 1992 it served as a small nature museum. It currently houses an information center with a small exhibit on the park and a gift shop. Nearby is the 90m-high (295-ft.) Radio Canada Tower.

From the Maison Smith, walk through the field of sculptures, away from the radio tower, until you reach:

❺ Lac des Castors (Beaver Lake)

The name refers to the once-profitable fur industry, not to the actual presence of the long-gone animals. In summer, it's surrounded by sunbathers and picnickers and filled with boaters. In the cold winter, before the snow sets in, it becomes an ice skater's paradise.

There's a small concession stand in the pavilion here, but if you're looking for something to eat, you might want to wait for the snack bar at the chalet (no. 7). Both the pavilion and chalet have restrooms and telephones.

Walk across the road, called chemin de la Remembrance (Remembrance Rd.) behind the pavilion, to enter:

❻ Notre-Dame-des-Neiges Cemetery

This is the city's predominantly Catholic cemetery, and from here you can visit the adjacent Protestant Mount Royal graveyard, and then behind it (to the north), if you're up for a longer walk, the small adjoining Jewish and Spanish-Portuguese cemetery. Notre-Dame-des-Neiges Cemetery reveals much of the ethnic mix in Montréal: there are headstones, some with likenesses in photos or tiles, for Montréalers with surnames as diverse as Zagorska, Skwyrska, De Ciccio, Sen, Lavoie, O'Neill, Hammerschmid, Fernandez, Müller, Haddad, and Boudreault.

If you've had enough walking, you can find a bus on chemin de la Remembrance that heads east toward the Guy Métro station. To continue the tour, head back to the Maison Smith and follow the signs on the main path for:

❼ Chalet du Mont-Royal and its Lookout

The front terrace here offers the most popular panoramic view of the city and the river. The chalet itself was constructed from 1931 to 1932 at a cost of $230,000 and has been used over the years for receptions, concerts, and various other events. Inside the chalet, note the 17 paintings hanging just below the ceiling, starting to the right of the door that leads into the snack bar. They relate the history of the region as well as the story of the French explorations of North America. In winter, there's a warming room for skiers here.

> **TAKE A BREAK**
> The concession stand in the **Chalet du Mont-Royal** is usually open from 9am to 5pm daily and sells sandwiches, fruit, ice cream, and beverages. Heed the signs that ask patrons to refrain from feeding the squirrels, no matter how adorably they're begging.

Facing the chalet from the terrace, locate the path running off to the right, marked by the sign CROIX. Follow it for about 10 minutes to a giant:

❽ Steel cross

Legend has it that Paul de Chomedey, sieur de Maisonneuve (1612–76) erected a wooden cross here in 1643 after the young colony survived a flood threat. The present incarnation of the **Croix du Mont-Royal,** installed in 1924, is lit at night and visible from all over the city.

Beside the cross is a plaque marking where a time capsule was placed in August 1992, during Montréal's 350th-birthday celebration. Some 12,000 children ages 6 to 12 filled the capsule with messages and drawings depicting their visions for the city in the year 2142, when Montréal will be 500 years old and the capsule will be opened.

To return to downtown Montréal, go back along the path to the chalet terrace. On the left, just before the terrace, is another path. It leads to the staircase described in no. 3 and descends to where the tour began. The walk down by this route takes about 15 minutes. The no. 11 bus also runs from the summit to the Mont-Royal Métro, and there are buses at Beaver Lake and along the chemin de la Remembrance.

9

Montréal Shopping

You can shop in Montréal until your feet swell and your eyes cross. Whether you view shopping as the focus of your travels or simply as a diversion, you won't be disappointed. Shopping ranks right up there with dining out as a prime activity among the natives. Most Montréalers are of French ancestry, after all, and seem to believe that impeccable taste bubbles through the Gallic gene pool. The city has produced a thriving fashion industry, from couture to ready-to-wear, with a history that reaches back to the earliest trade in furs and leather. There are more than 1,700 shops in the underground city alone, and many more than that at street level and above. It is unlikely that any reasonable consumer need—or even outlandish fantasy—cannot be met here.

The one dark cloud is that the Visitor Rebate Program, which used to allow nonresident visitors to apply for a rebate on tax they paid on most items purchased in Québec, was eliminated in April 2007. See "Taxes" at the end of chapter 2; additional details are available at **www.cra-arc.gc.ca/visitors**.

1 The Shopping Scene

When you're making purchases with a credit card, the charges are automatically converted at the going bank rate before appearing on your following monthly statement. In most cases, this is the best deal of all for visitors. Visa and MasterCard are the most popular credit cards in this part of Canada, while shops less frequently accept Discover. American Express is only accepted reluctantly and sometimes not at all.

Most stores are open from 9 or 10am to 6pm Monday through Wednesday, to 9pm on Thursday and Friday, and 9 or 10am to 5pm on Saturday. Many stores are now also open on Sunday from noon to 5pm.

THE BEST BUYS

While not cheap, **Canadian Inuit sculptures** and 19th- to early-20th-century **country furniture** are handsome and authentic. Less expensive crafts than the intensely collected Inuit works are also available, including quilts, drawings, and carvings by Amerindian and other folk artists.

The province's daring **clothing designers** produce some appealing fashions at prices that are often reasonable. And while demand has diminished somewhat, superbly constructed **furs and leather goods** are high-ticket items.

Ice cider (*cidre de glace*) and **ice wines** made in Québec province from apples and grapes left on trees and vines after the first frost are inexpensive and delightfully unique products to bring home. They are sold in duty-free shops at the border in addition to the stores listed at the end of this chapter.

Most international clothing items are priced at approximately the same costs as in their countries of origin, including such big names as Burberry and Ralph Lauren. Exceptions are British products, including **tweeds, porcelain,** and **glassware,** which tend to cost less here.

THE BEST SHOPPING AREAS

In downtown, **rue Sherbrooke** is a major shopping street, with international and domestic designers, luxury items such as furs and jewelry, art galleries, and the Holts department store. **Rue Crescent,** off of Sherbrooke, has a number of upscale boutiques scattered on its northern end, plus numerous cafés for a break from shopping.

Also downtown, **rue Ste-Catherine** is home to the city's top department stores and myriad satellite shops. Most of Montréal's big department stores were founded when Scottish, Irish, and English families dominated the city's mercantile class, and most of their names are identifiably English, albeit shorn of their apostrophes. The principal exception is La Baie, French for "The Bay," itself a shortened reference to an earlier name, the Hudson's Bay Company. Nearby, **rue Peel** is known for its men's fashions.

In Vieux-Montréal, the western end of **rue St-Paul** has a growing number of art galleries, clothing boutiques, and jewelry shops.

In Plateau Mont-Royal, **boulevard St-Laurent** sells everything from budget practicalities to off-the-wall handmade fashions. Look along **avenue Laurier** between boulevard St-Laurent and avenue de l'Epée for French boutiques, home furniture and accessories shops, and young Québécois designers. **Rue St-Denis** north of Sherbrooke has strings of shops filled with fun, funky items.

SHOPPING COMPLEXES

A unique shopping opportunity in Montréal is the **underground city,** a warren of passageways connecting more than 1,700 shops in 10 shopping malls that have levels both above and below street level (see p. 61 in chapter 4). Typical is the **Complexe Desjardins** (© 514/845-4636), a downtown destination bounded by rues Ste-Catherine, St-Urbain, and Jeanne-Mance and boulevard René-Lévesque. It has waterfalls and fountains, trees and hanging vines, music, lanes of shops going off in every direction, and elevators whisking people up to one of the four tall office towers.

You're also likely to end up in downtown's **Place Ville-Marie,** opposite Fairmont Le Reine Elizabeth hotel, between boulevard René-Lévesque and Cathcart (© 514/ 861-9393), which was Montréal's first major postwar shopping complex and is known locally simply as "PVM." It has more than 80 boutiques and eateries. A plaque honoring Vincent Ponte, who designed the underground city and died in 2006, is on the PVM esplanade.

The Montréal tourist office's *Official Tourist Guide* lists the other complexes at your service. The main thing to remember is that when you're in Montréal and you enter a street-level shopping emporium, it's likely that you'll be able to head to a lower level and connect to the maze of tunnels and shopping hallways that will lead you to another set of stores.

2 Shopping from A to Z

ANTIQUES

Antiques can be found along rue Sherbrooke near the Musée des Beaux-Arts and on the little side streets near the museum. More antiques and collectibles, in more than

50 tempting shops one after another, can be found along the lengthening "Antiques Alley" of rue Notre-Dame, especially concentrated between rue Guy and avenue Atwater.

Antiques Puces-Libres   Three fascinatingly cluttered floors are packed with pine and oak furniture, lamps, clocks, vases, and more, most of it 19th- and early-20th-century French-Canadian Art Nouveau. 4240 rue St-Denis (near rue Rachel), Plateau Mont-Royal. © **514/842-5931.**

ARTS & CRAFTS

In warmer months, stroll Vieux-Montréal: Artists display and sell their unremarkable but nevertheless competent works along short **rue St-Amable,** just off Place Jacques-Cartier. From there, meander into a walkway called **Le Jardin Amable** to find a court-yard filled with kiosks stocked with eye-catching costume jewelry and items crafted in silver and gold.

Some of the best stores in Montréal are found in city museums. Tops among them are shops in **Pointe-à-Callière** (the Montréal Museum of Archaeology and History), which is in Vieux-Montréal; shops in the **Musée des Beaux-Arts** and the **Musée McCord,** both on rue Sherbrooke in the center city; and the shop at the **Musée d'Art Contemporain** in the Place-des-Arts, on rue Ste-Catherine ouest, also downtown. See "Museum Stores," later in this chapter.

Guilde Canadienne des Métier d'Art Québec ★   A small but choice collection of craft items is displayed in a meticulously arranged gallery setting. Among the objects are blown glass, paintings on silk, pewter, tapestries, and ceramics. The store is particularly strong in avant-garde jewelry and Inukjuak sculpture. A small carving might be had for C$100 to C$300 (US$80–US$240/£43–£129), while the larger, more important pieces go for hundreds, even thousands, more. 1460 rue Sherbrooke ouest (near rue Mackay), downtown. © **514/849-6091.** www.canadianguild.com.

La Guilde Graphique   Nearly two dozen contemporary artists are represented here, working in a variety of media and with a variety of techniques, but primarily producing works on paper, including drawings, serigraphs, etchings, lithographs, and wood-cuts. Some of the artists can often be seen working in the upstairs studio. 9 rue St-Paul ouest (at bd. St-Laurent), Vieux-Montréal. © **514/844-3438.** www.guildegraphique.com.

L'Empreinte   This is a *coopérative artisane* (a craftspersons' collective). The ceramics, textiles, glassware, and other items on sale often occupy that vaguely defined territory between art and craft. Quality is uneven but usually tips toward the high end. 272 rue St-Paul est (next to the Marché Bonsecours), Vieux-Montréal. © **514/861-4427.** www.lempreinte coop.com.

Les Artisans du Meuble Québécois   A mix of crafts, jewelry, and other objects—some noteworthy, others mediocre—makes this an intriguing stop in Vieux-Montréal. Among the possibilities are clothing and accessories for women, greeting cards, woven goods, items for the home, and handmade quilts. 88 rue St-Paul est (near Place Jacques-Cartier), Vieux-Montréal. © **514/866-1836.**

Poterie Manu Reva   Abandoning a PhD program in biochemistry, the owner opened this shop to sell her work and that of fellow potters. The results are mostly attractive. On a recent visit, Montréal artist Hugo Didier's porcelain cups and bowls stamped on all sides with "Not made in China" were appealing. 5141 bd. St-Laurent (near av. Laurier), Plateau Mont-Royal. © **514/948-1717.** www.poteriemanureva.com.

BATH & BODY

Fruits & Passion   Like The Body Shop, Lush, and other shops full of good smells and a natural aesthetic, this Québec-based chain trades in its own variation of funky soaps, creams, and more (avocado body butter, vegetable soap with shavings of panama wood, and so forth). With only limited inroads to the U.S. and Europe so far, the shop's products make for simple gifts. 4159A rue Saint-Denis (near rue Rachel), Plateau Mont-Royal. ℂ 514/282-9406. www.fruits-passion.com.

Lush   Freshly installed on the ground floor of a pretty Queen Anne Victorian in the heart of the Plateau's St-Denis shopping district, this U.K.-based chain displays its rough-hewn chunks of soap like wheels of cheese. They're scented with olive oil, fig, mint, coriander, and orange. A fist-size chunk is about C$7 (US$6.10/£3). 4067 rue St-Denis (near av. Duluth), Plateau Mont-Royal. ℂ 514/849-5333. www.lush.com.

Spa Dr. Hauschka   A chichi spa for high-end pampering and getting "in touch with your inner beauty," as the materials put it. On-site treatments include facials, lavender baths, mud baths and more, but you can also buy the Dr. Hauschka products and indulge at home. 1444 rue Sherbrooke ouest (at rue Redpath), downtown. (ℂ 514/286-1444. www. spadrhauschka.com.

BOOKS

Check out the shops in Vieux-Montréal's **Pointe-à-Callière** (the Montréal Museum of Archaeology and History) and downtown's **Musée des Beaux-Arts**, **Musée McCord,** and the **Musée d'Art Contemporain;** as is the case with arts and crafts, some of the best bookstores in Montréal are in these city museums. See "Museum Stores," later in this chapter.

Canadian Centre for Architecture Bookstore   This bookstore may be the Centre's most engrossing department. It features a comprehensive selection of books on architecture, with an emphasis on Montréal in particular and Canada in general. Volumes are also available on landscape and garden history, photography, preservation, conservation, design, and city planning. 1920 rue Baile (at rue du Fort), downtown. ℂ 514/939-7020. www.cca.qc.ca/Bookstore.

Champigny *(Kids*   For those who know the language or want to brush up, this two-level bookstore with a primarily French-language stock is a valuable resource. It also sells tapes, CDs, and newspapers and magazines from all over the world. Most English-language books are on the upper floor. There's a large children's section. 4380 rue St-Denis (at rue Marie-Anne), Plateau Mont-Royal. ℂ 514/844-2587.

Chapters   This is the flagship store of a chain with many branches, the result of a merger between Smithbooks and Coles booksellers. Thousands of titles are available in French and English on both general and specialized subjects. 1171 rue Ste-Catherine ouest (at rue Stanley), downtown. ℂ 514/849-8825. www.chapters.indigo.ca.

Indigo Livres, Musique & Café   Occupying a street-level space in the Place Montréal Trust, this very complete store sells music, books, magazines, and gifts, and has a café upstairs. 1500 rue McGill College (near rue St-Catherine), downtown. ℂ 514/281-5549.

Paragraphe   This long storefront is popular with students from the McGill campus, which is a block away. The store hosts frequent autograph parties and author readings, and occasional musical performances. 2220 av. McGill College (south of rue Sherbrooke). ℂ 514/845-5811. www.paragraphbooks.com.

CLOTHING
FOR MEN

Boutique Hugo   Hugo Boss, that is, with stylings for those with the fit frames to carry off these clothes and the discretionary income to purchase them. 1407 rue Crescent (at rue Ste-Catherine), downtown. ℭ 514/843-5476. www.hugoboss.com.

Eccetera & Co.   Favoring ready-to-wear from such higher-end manufacturers as Hugo Boss and Canali, this store lays out its stock in a soothing setting with personalized service. As it says on the door: GOOD CLOTHES OPEN ALL DOORS. 2021 rue Peel (near bd. de Maisonneuve), downtown. ℭ 514/845-9181.

Harry Rosen ℛ   For over 50 years, this well-known retailer of designer suits and accessories has been making men look good in Armani, Versace, and the "Harry Rosen Made in Italy" line. (The store's website features a nifty "what not to wear" interactive page.) Les Cours Mont-Royal, 1455 rue Peel (at bd. de Maisonneuve), downtown. ℭ 514/284-3315. www.harryrosen.com.

Kamkyl   High-style with an Asian influence for "young moderns," presented in 186 sq. m (2,000 sq. ft.) nearly empty save for two black sofas, a coffee machine, and suspended steel racks displaying suits, jackets, and slacks. The owners of this spare Vieux-Montréal boutique are also the clothing's designers. 439 rue St-Pierre, Vieux-Montréal. ℭ 514/281-8221. www.kamkyl.com.

L'Uomo Montréal ℛ   A top men's clothing boutique, L'Uomo mostly deals in Italian and other European menswear by such forward-thinking designers as Kiton, Prada, Avon Celli, and Borrelli. 1452 rue Peel (near rue Ste-Catherine), downtown. ℭ 514/844-1008. www.luomo-montreal.com.

FOR WOMEN

Ambre   Fashionable suits, cocktail dresses, and dinner and casual wear made of linen, rayon, and cotton. To go with the clothes, there are bold complementary accessories. 201 rue St-Paul ouest (at rue St-François-Xavier), Vieux-Montréal. ℭ 514/982-0325.

Artéfact Montréal   Browse moderate to expensive articles of clothing by up-and-coming Québécois designers and artists. 4117 rue St-Denis (near rue Rachel), Plateau Mont-Royal. ℭ 514/842-2780.

Collection Méli Mélo *(Finds*   This shop used to focus on a mix of exotica and furniture from Morocco to Thailand down into sub-Saharan Africa. There's still some of that here, but a shift in spring 2007 brought a new concentration: women's clothes by Montréal's chic designers. The collection includes Helmer, Anastasia Lomonova, and Eugenia Design. During our last visit, a Montréal actress found just the right dress to wear to the Cannes Film Festival. 205 St-Paul ouest (at rue St-François-Xavier), Vieux-Montréal. ℭ 514/285-5585.

Kaliyana ℛ   Vaguely Japanese and certainly minimalist, these free-flowing garments are largely asymmetrical separates. Made by a Canadian designer, they come in muted tones of solid colors, with simple complementary necklaces. Also available is contemporary footwear including Arche from France and Trippen from Germany. Husbands and partners will be thankful for the couch. 4107 rue St-Denis (near rue Rachel), Plateau Mont-Royal. ℭ 514/844-0633. www.kaliyana.com.

Kyoze   The eye-catching creations of Québécois and other Canadian designers, including jewelry and accessories, are featured here. Prices are moderate to expensive. 380 St-Antoine ouest (near rue de Bleury), downtown. ℭ 514/847-7572.

La Cache   Clothes designed and manufactured in India are among the offerings of this national chain, augmented by housewares and bedding. Girls' outfits and vintage-styled jewelry are on offer as well. 3941 rue St-Denis (near rue Roy), Plateau Mont-Royal. © 514/842-7693. www.lacache.ca.

Mango   This is the first downtown outlet of a Spanish-owned international chain. Much of its merchandise is upmarket jeans and tees, but the dressier separates intrigue with quiet tones and jazzy cuts—very Euro. 1000 rue Ste-Catherine ouest (at rue Metcalfe), downtown. © 514/397-2323. www.mango.com.

Ms. Emma Designs *(Finds*   This shop is unassuming in the extreme, with little in the way of stylish fixtures. But as a new Montréal branch of a Toronto original, it's worth seeking out. Its stock is one-of-a-kind dresses and jackets, made from flowing hand-painted silks, and linen and wool from Italy. What's more, clothes will be custom-altered to fit each patron—common for men's clothing, rare for women's. 123 rue Laurier ouest, Mile End. © 514/270-9123. www.msemma.com.

FOR MEN & WOMEN

Montréal's long history as a center for the fur trade buttresses the many wholesale and retail furriers, which have outlets downtown and in Plateau Mont-Royal. Nowhere are fur shops more concentrated than on the "fur row" of **rue Mayor,** downtown between rue de Bleury and rue City Councillors.

Aritmetik   This fun shop features sportswear created by young, forward-looking Italian and other European designers. In Les Cours Mont-Royal shopping complex, 1455 rue Peel (north of rue Ste-Catherine), downtown. © 514/286-0565.

Club Monaco   Awareness of this expanding Canadian-owned international chain is growing, as is appreciation of its minimalist, largely monochromatic garments for men and women, along with silver jewelry, eyewear, and cosmetics. Think Prada but affordable, with a helpful young staff. In Les Cours Mont-Royal shopping complex, 1455 rue Peel (north of rue Ste-Catherine), downtown. © 514/499-0959. www.clubmonaco.com.

Le Château   The merchandizing philosophy here is to move it in then move it out fast. Inveterate shoppers drop by regularly to see what's arrived each week. What they find are affordable shirts, pants, dresses—mostly sportswear, but also suits and ties for businesspeople. 1310 rue Ste-Catherine ouest (near rue de la Montagne), downtown. © 514/866-2481.

Roots   The company whose berets and uniforms were such a hit at the 2006 Winter Olympics has a three-floor store here, in addition to other locations throughout Canada. Along with clothing, the store sells table settings, perfume, books, and CDs. 1035 rue Ste-Catherine ouest (at rue Peel), downtown. © 514/845-7995. www.roots.com.

Terra Nostra   Part of a small Québec chain, this spiffy shop features casual ware for men and women in deceptively simple shapes—a sort of upscale Gap. 900 rue Ste-Catherine ouest (at rue St-Marc), downtown. © 514/861-6315.

COFFEES & TEAS

Brûlerie St-Denis   This enticingly aromatic shop has an international selection of coffees from more than two dozen countries, whole or ground to order. There are tables inside and on the terrace at which to try a cup of the selections, with a sandwich or dessert if you want. There are about a half-dozen locales throughout the city. 3967 rue St-Denis (south of av. Duluth), Plateau Mont-Royal. © 514/286-9158. www.brulerie.com.

DEPARTMENT STORES

Montréal's major downtown shopping emporia stretch along rue Ste-Catherine from rue Guy eastward to Carré Phillips at Aylmer (department store Holt Renfrew is north on rue Sherbrooke ouest, parallel). An excursion along the 12-block stretch of Ste-Catherine can keep a diligent shopper busy for hours, even days. Also look for these stores' branches in the underground city.

Henry Birks et Fils ⊛   Across from Christ Church Cathedral at the corner of rue Ste-Catherine stands Henry Birks et Fils, a highly regarded jeweler since 1879. This beautiful old store, with its dark-wood display cases, stone pillars, and marble floors, is a living part of Montréal's Victorian heritage. Valuable products on display go well beyond jewelry to encompass pens and desk accessories, watches, ties, leather goods, belts and other personal accessories, glassware, and china. 1240 Phillips Square (at rue Ste-Catherine), downtown. ℂ **514/397-2511.** www.birks.com.

Holt Renfrew ⊛   This store began as a furrier in 1837, and is now a showcase for the best in international style, displayed in mini-boutiques and focusing on fashion for men and women. Brands including Giorgio Armani, Prada, Gucci, and Chanel are displayed with a tastefulness bordering on solemnity. The marquee outside reads only HR. 1300 rue Sherbrooke ouest (at rue de la Montagne), downtown. ℂ **514/842-5111.** www. holtrenfrew.com.

La Baie ⊛   No retailer has an older or more celebrated name than that of the Hudson's Bay Company, a name shortened in recent years to "The Bay," then transformed into "La Baie" by the language laws that decreed French the lingua franca. The company was incorporated in Canada in 1670. Its main store focuses on clothing, but also offers crystal, china, and Inuit carvings, and its Hbc Signature line features variations on the famous Hudson's Bay blankets. The company was bought by an American investor in 2006, an event that understandably caused consternation among some Canadians. 585 rue Ste-Catherine ouest (near rue Aylmer), downtown. ℂ **514/281-4422.** www.hbc.com.

Maison Simons   This branch was the first foray out of its home area for Québec City's long-established family-owned department store. Most Montréalers had never heard of it, but that changed fast given the fairly-priced fashions that fill the refurbished floors of a building that once housed the venerable Simpson's department store. 977 rue Ste-Catherine ouest (at rue Mansfield), downtown. ℂ **514/282-1840.** www.simons.ca.

Ogilvy ⊛⊛   This is the most vibrant of a classy breed of department store that appears to be fading from the scene. Established in 1866, Ogilvy has been at this location since 1912. A bagpiper still announces the noon hour and special events, and glowing chandeliers and wide aisles enhance the shopping experience. Ogilvy has always had a reputation for quality merchandise and now contains more than 50 boutiques, including such high-profile purveyors as Louis Vuitton, Anne Klein, Burberry, Aquascutum, and Jones New York. It's also known for its eagerly awaited Christmas windows. The basement-level Café Romy has quality sandwiches, salads, and desserts. 1307 rue Ste-Catherine ouest (at rue de la Montagne), downtown. ℂ **514/842-7711.** www.ogilvycanada.com.

EDIBLES

The food markets described in "Picnic Fare" at the end of chapter 6 carry abundant assortments of cheeses, wines, and packaged food products that can serve as gifts or delicious reminders of your visit when you get home.

Canadian Maple Delights *(Kids)*   Everything maple-y is presented here by a consortium of Québec producers of pastries, gelati, gift baskets, truffles, and, of course, every grade of syrup. A cute café serves gelato and sweets. 84 rue St-Paul est (near Place Jacques-Cartier), Vieux-Montréal. © 514/765-3456. www.mapledelights.com.

La Tomate   Inside a brick building painted on the outside with a two-story tomato, this shop is filled with quirkily packaged pastes, jellies, sauces, salsas, and ketchups, all made from the most humble of fruits. 4347 rue de la Roché (2 blocks north of rue Rachel), Plateau Mont-Royal. © 514/523-0222. www.tomateonline.com.

La Vieille Europe   In this compact storehouse of culinary sights and smells, you can choose from wheels of pungent cheeses, garlands of sausages, pâtés, cashews, honey, fresh peanut butter, or dried fruits. Coffee beans are roasted in the back, adding to the mixture of maddening aromas. 3855 bd. St-Laurent (north of rue Roy), Plateau Mont-Royal. © 514/842-5773.

Les Chocolats de Chloé *(Finds)*   If you approach chocolate the way others approach wine or cheese—that is, on the lookout for the best of the best—then this teeny shop will bring great delight. Chocolates are made on-site, and tastes can be had for as little as C$2.50 (US$2.15/£1.05). Especially adorable: a hollow chocolate fish filled with three little chocolate fishes, for C$9 (US$7.85/£3.90). 375 rue Roy est (at St-Denis), Plateau Mont-Royal. © 514/849-5550.

HOME DESIGN & HOUSEWARES

Also see "Arts & Crafts," earlier in this chapter, and "Department Stores," above.

Arthur Quentin *(star)*   Doling out household products of quiet taste and discernment for over 25 years, this St-Denis stalwart is divided into departments specializing in tableware, kitchen gadgets, and home decor. That means lamps and Limoges china, terrines and tea towels, mandolins and mezzalunas, and just about any related items that might be imagined. Clay jugs for making vinegar? *Naturellement.* 3960 rue St-Denis (south of av. Duluth), Plateau Mont-Royal. © 514/843-7513. www.arthurquentin.com.

Les Touilleurs   Kitchenware of the highest order, meticulously arranged like museum pieces in a minimalist setting, earned this shop design honors in 2003, soon after it opened. The stock includes only superior versions of cooking essentials, including small appliances that strike high new standards. Now it has doubled its size, incorporating a full kitchen where **cooking classes** are conducted by local chefs. 152 rue Laurier ouest (near rue St-Urbain), Mile End. © 514/278-0008. www.lestouilleurs.com.

Senteurs de Provence   The sunny south of France is evoked in pottery that's hand-painted in the creamy-bright colors of Provence, complemented by cunning collections of bath soaps and gels, printed linens, and lightly perfumed lotions and creams. Several locations. 363 rue St-Paul est (near Marché Bonsecours), Vieux-Montréal. © 514/395-8686.

12° en Cave   This store is dedicated to the good life, with an emphasis on the passions of wine aficionados. Reidel crystal, Laguiole cutlery, and a variety of decidedly high-end wine-related paraphernalia are for sale, and if you need a custom wine cellar built anywhere in North America, they'll do that, too. 367 rue St-Paul est (near Marché Bonsecours), Vieux-Montréal. © 514/866-5722. www.12encave.com.

JEWELRY & ACCESSORIES

Also see "Arts & Crafts" and "Clothing: For Women," earlier in this chapter.

bleu comme le ciel Costume jewelry here is flashy, often startling, and decidedly worth a visit for women looking to shake up their image. There are strings of fat faux pearls, often with tiny ceramic pigs attached, but the bulk of the stock reveals a clear Middle Eastern/North African influence with silvery strands of orange stones. Prices for most objects are in the reasonable C$100-to-C$300 (US$80–US$240/£43–£129) range. 2000 rue Peel (near bd. de Maisonneuve), downtown. ℂ 514/847-1128.

Clio Blue This rue Peel outlet features spare displays in a narrow modernist storefront, a design-competition winner. The custom jewelry tastefully incorporates Middle Eastern and South Asian motifs, often with carefully spaced semiprecious stones on silver strands and more festively designed bracelets. 1468 rue Peel (near bd. de Maisonneuve), downtown. ℂ 514/281-3112. www.clioblue.com.

LEATHER GOODS
Cuir Tag (Cuir et Peau de Mouton Tag) *(Finds* You have to check this out: *suede* jeans that are *washable!* They're made in Canada. Also on display are bomber jackets and other leather items. 1325 rue Ste-Catherine ouest (at rue Crescent), downtown. ℂ 514/499-1180.

MUSEUM STORES
Musée d'Art Contemporain Boutique The boutique of the contemporary art museum sells much of what might be expected, including poster-size reproductions of paintings and prints, postcards, and art books. Added to the mix are tasteful design pieces and unusual gifts as well as souvenirs that eschew the lowest-common-denominator standards of too many Vieux-Montréal shops. The museum's bookstore, Oliveri, has a wide selection, in both French and English, of monographs on Canadian and international artists since the 1950s. 185 rue Ste-Catherine ouest (at rue Jeanne-Mance), downtown. ℂ 514/847-6904. www.macm.org.

Musée des Beaux-Arts Boutique Next to the annex of the Museum of Fine Arts, this unusually large and impressive shop sells everything from folk art to furniture. The expected art-related postcards and prints are at hand, along with ties, watches, scarves, address books, toys, games, clocks, jewelry, and other crafts, with special focus on work by Québec artisans. The boutique is to the right of the entrance, and a large bookstore is to the left. 1390 rue Sherbrooke ouest (at rue Crescent), downtown. ℂ 514/285-1600. www.mbam.qc.ca.

Musée McCord Boutique Part of the newly expanded museum that relates the history of the province, this shop has a small, carefully chosen selection of Native and Canadian arts and crafts, china and rustic pottery, books with an emphasis on history, cards, and coloring books. 690 rue Sherbrooke ouest (at rue Victoria), downtown. ℂ 514/398-7100, ext. 274. www.mccord-museum.qc.ca.

Pointe-à-Callière Gift Shop Located in the Old Customs House at the end of the underground tour of the Museum of Archaeology and History (but with a separate entrance on rue St-Paul), this boutique sells collectibles for the home, gift items, paper products, souvenirs, toys, and books (in French). Particularly nice are the maple spoons and spatulas made by Québec artist Tom Littledeer. 150 rue St-Paul ouest (at Place Royale), Vieux-Montréal. ℂ 514/872-9150. www.pacmusee.qc.ca.

MUSIC

Archambault Musique   A premier spot to find CDs by French-Canadian singers, the Montréal Symphony Orchestra, Ensemble I Musici, and others. Many of the recordings can be difficult to get outside of Québec, so stock up here. 500 rue Ste-Catherine est (at rue Berri), downtown. © 514/849-6201. www.archambault.ca.

Inbeat   The decor is plain, but the stock includes CDs and vinyl that just aren't available anywhere else. The staff describes the store's offerings as "deep house, progressive, tribal, techno, trance, old skool, Afro-Latin nu jazz, US & UK garage," and there are things that don't even fit into *those* categories. 3814 bd. St-Laurent (near rue Roy), Plateau Mont-Royal. © 514/499-2063.

SHOES

Moka   This small shop features high-tech, super-comfort Geox-brand shoes. 224 rue St-Jacques (near rue St-François-Xavier), Vieux-Montréal. © 514/843-3333.

TOYS

Franc Jeu *(Kids*   Expectant parents (and new grandparents) will want to make a detour to browse through this store's expansive collection of Corolle dolls, which are known for their realistic look. The store also sells the clothes, jewelry, and accessories with which to dress the dolls. 4152 rue St-Denis (near rue Rachel), Plateau Mont-Royal. © 514/849-9253.

WINES & SPIRITS

The food markets described in "Picnic Fare" at the end of chapter 6 carry a good variety of wines, which are also sold in supermarkets and convenience stores (along with beer).

Liquor and other spirits, on the other hand, can only be sold in stores operated by the provincial **Société des Alcools du Québec (SAQ).** Though it was once as bureaucratic as most state-run agencies, successful upgrade efforts have made its stores more inviting and given differently named stores different personalities. The SAQ website, **www.saq.com,** has a ton of information about Québec wines and also lists all the area outlets. One of the largest is the downtown **SAQ Selection** at 440 bd. de Maisonneuve ouest west of rue de Bleury (© **514/873-2274**), a virtual supermarket of wines and liquors, with thousands of labels. Prices run from C$10 (US$8.70/£4.30) to way, way up for some bordeaux vintages.

The downtown **SAQ Signature** at 677 Ste-Catherine west in the Complexe Les Ailes (© **514/282-9445**) is one of SAQ's boutique shops, featuring a smaller selection of rarer wines, fine liquors, and gift items. Also downtown, the **SAQ Express** at 1108 rue Ste-Catherine ouest at the corner of rue Peel (© **514/861-7908**) is less fancy and meant for quick in-and-out purchases; it's open daily and later than the other stores, 11am to 10pm.

The VQA logo, for Vintners Quality Alliance, is given to wines that meet the state's quality standards.

Québec's unique **ice cider (*cidre de glace*),** made from apples left on trees after the first frost, can be purchased in duty-free shops at the border in addition to the stores listed above. One top producer is **Domaine Pinnacle,** made about an hour and a half from the city and a regular gold medalist in international competitions.

10

Montréal After Dark

Montréal's reputation for effervescent nightlife reaches back to the Roaring Twenties—specifically to the United States' 13-year experiment with Prohibition from 1920 to 1933. Americans streamed into Montréal for temporary relief from alcohol deprivation (while Canadian distillers and brewers made fortunes—few of them with meticulous regard for legalistic niceties). Montréal already enjoyed a sophisticated and slightly naughty reputation as the Paris of North America, which added to the allure.

Nearly a century later, clubbing and barhopping remain popular activities, with nightspots keeping much later hours in Montréal than in arch-rival Toronto, which still heeds Calvinist notions of propriety and early bedtimes.

Nocturnal pursuits are often as cultural as they are social. The city boasts its own outstanding symphony, dozens of French- and English-language theater companies, and the incomparable performance company Cirque du Soleil. It's also on the standard concert circuit that includes Chicago, Boston, and New York, so internationally known entertainers, music groups, and dance companies pass through frequently. A decidedly French enthusiasm for film, as well as the city's ever-increasing reputation as a movie-production center, ensures support for cinemas showcasing experimental, offbeat, and foreign films.

A new discount ticket office for Montréal cultural events opened in summer 2007. Called **Vitrine culturelle de Montréal** ("cultural window of Montréal"; ⓒ **514/285-4545;** www.vitrineculturelle. com), it's located at 145 rue Sainte-Catherine ouest in Place des Arts. It includes a central information office and full-price tickets as well as last-minute deals.

In summer, the city becomes even livelier than usual. Many of the events and festivals are listed in chapter 2 on p. 13. The biggest of the bunch is the 3-day Grand Prix du Canada, the country's only Formula 1 auto race that roars onto Ile Notre-Dame and brings the partying into downtown in June.

Concentrations of pubs and discos underscore the city's linguistic dichotomy. While there's a great deal of crossover, the parallel blocks of **rue Crescent,** rue Bishop, and rue de la Montagne north of rue Ste-Catherine have a pronounced Anglophone (English-speaking) character, while Francophones (French speakers) dominate the **Quartier Latin,** with college-age patrons most evident along the lower reaches of rue St-Denis and their yuppie elders gravitating to the nightspots of the slightly more uptown blocks of the same street. **Vieux-Montréal (Old Montréal),** especially along rue St-Paul, has a more universal quality, and many of the bars and clubs there feature live jazz, blues, and folk music. In the **Plateau Mont-Royal** area, boulevard St-Laurent, parallel to St-Denis and known locally as "The Main," has become a miles-long haven of hip restaurants and clubs, roughly from rue Sherbrooke up to rue Laurier. It's a good place to wind up in the wee hours, as there's always someplace with the welcome mat still out, even after the official 3am closings.

Tips **Checking What's On**

For details on performances or special events when you're in town, pick up a free copy of **Montréal Scope** (www.montrealscope.com), a weekly ads-and-events booklet usually available in hotel receptions, or the free weekly papers **Mirror** (www.montrealmirror.com) and **Hour** (www.hour.ca), both in English, or **Voir** (www.voir.ca) and **Ici** (www.icimontreal.com), both in French, available all over town. Also in French is the free monthly **Nightlife** magazine (www.night lifemagazine.ca). **Fugues** (www.fugues.com), available at the tourist information office in the Gay Village, provides news and views of gay and lesbian events, clubs, restaurants, and activities. Extensive listings of largely mainstream cultural and entertainment events are posted at **www.canada.com** and **www.montrealplus.ca.**

Most bars and clubs don't charge cover, and when they do, it's rarely more than C$10 (US$8.70/£4.30). Beer is usually in the C$4-to-C$7 (US$3.50–US$6.10/£1.70–£3) range, while cocktails are typically C$7 to C$12 (US$6.10–US$10/£3–£5.15).

Smoking has been banned in bars and restaurants throughout the province since 2006.

1 The Performing Arts

CIRCUS

Cirque du Soleil ★★★ *Kids*   Through the exposure generated by its frequent tours across North America, Europe, and Australia, the Montréal-based Cirque du Soleil enjoys an ever-widening following, and with good reason. Partly it's because of the absence of animals in the troupe, which means no one need be troubled by the possibility of mistreated lions and elephants. But mostly it's because of what *does* happen under the big tent, and linear descriptions and even photographs can't begin to do justice. Nothing less than magical, each show is a celebration of pure skill and theater. There are plenty of acrobats, clowns, trapeze artists, tightrope walkers, and contortionists, but there is dance, too, and people costumed to look like creatures not of this world—iguanas crossed with goblins, or peacocks born of trolls. There are even story lines, of a sort. This is truly for children of all ages. The troupe is so much in demand it's difficult to track how long it will alight in its hometown, although most recently it has performed from April to June in temporary tents erected directly in Vieux-Port on the water. Check ahead to find out current plans. © **800/361-4595.** www.cirquedusoleil. com. Tickets from C$60 (US$52/£26) adults.

Pavillon de la TOHO *Value*   Next door to the Cirque du Soleil's training complex and company offices, TOHO is a performance facility devoted to the circus arts. Acrobats and performers from the National Circus School, Québec's Productions à Trois Têtes, and the Imperial Acrobats of China have all put on recent shows here. TOHO features an intimate in-the-round hall done up like and old-fashioned circus tent and an exhibit space with over 100 circus artifacts. It's also a green building, built with recycled pieces of an amusement park bumper-car ride and wood from a dismantled railroad and heated by biogas from the adjacent landfill. The venue is located in the lower-income Saint-Michel district well north of downtown, but accessible by Métro and bus. 2345 rue Jarry est (corner of rue d'Iberville, where Jarry crosses Autoroute 40). ✆ **888/376-TOHU.** www.tohu.ca. Free to view the facility and exhibits daily 9am–5pm. Performance tickets from C$23 (US$20/£9.70) adults, C$14 (US$12/£5.80) children 12 and younger. 8km (5 miles) from downtown, north on rue St-Denis to where it meets Autoroute 40. Métro: Jarry or Iberville and bus.

CLASSICAL MUSIC & OPERA

L'Opéra de Montréal ✶✶✶   Founded in 1980, this outstanding opera company mounts six productions a year in Montréal, with artists from Québec and abroad participating in such shows as *La Traviata, Don Giovanni, Aida,* and *Otello.* Video translations are provided from the original languages into French and English. Performances are held from September to June in theaters at Place des Arts and occasionally at other venues. Place des Arts, Salle Wilfrid-Pelletier, 260 bd. de Maisonneuve ouest, downtown. ✆ **514/985-2258** for tickets. www.operademontreal.com. Tickets from C$44 (US$38/£19). Métro: Place des Arts.

L'Orchestre Symphonique de Montréal (OSM) ✶✶   Kent Nagano was brought on as conductor in 2005 and has focused the repertoire of this world-famous orchestra on programs featuring works by Franck and Bruckner in addition to Ravel, Mozart, and Bach. All is not staid: The orchestra has also partnered with local rockers Les Respectables for Pops events. It performs at Place des Arts and the Notre-Dame Basilica. Place des Arts, Salle Wilfrid-Pelletier, 260 bd. de Maisonneuve ouest, downtown. ✆ **514/842-9951** for tickets. www.osm.ca. Tickets from C$25 (US$21/£11). Métro: Place des Arts.

Orchestre Métropolitain du Grand Montréal   This orchestra performs during its regular season at Place des Arts, with a 2008 schedule that includes symphonies by Bruckner, Mahler, and Haydn, and a celebration of Glenn Gould. In the summer, it puts on free outdoor concerts at the Théâtre de Verdure in Parc La Fontaine. Place des Arts, Maisonneuve Theatre, 260 bd. de Maisonneuve ouest, downtown. ✆ **514/842-2112.** www. orchestremetropolitain.com. Tickets from C$21 (US$18/£9.05). Métro: Place des Arts.

CONCERT HALLS & AUDITORIUMS

Montréal has a score of venues, so check papers, magazines, and websites to see who's playing where during your stay. Big-name rock bands and pop stars that used to play at the Forum now show up at the downtown arena, Centre Bell.

Centre Bell   Seating up to 21,500, Centre Bell is the home of the Montréal Canadiens hockey team and host to big international rock and pop stars on the order of Justin Timberlake, the White Stripes, The Police, and Beyoncé, as well as such dissimilar attractions as Disney On Ice and Meat Loaf (not together, alas). 1260 rue de la Gauchetière ouest, downtown. ✆ **514/989-2841.** www.centrebell.ca. Métro: Bonaventure.

Metropolis   Starting life as a skating rink in 1884, the Metropolis is now a prime showplace for traveling rock groups, especially for bands on the way up or retracing their steps down. It has recently hosted Joss Stone, Ween, and Medeski, Scofield, Martin & Wood. While it is primarily a concert venue that can hold up to 2,300 customers, it is also home to a small attached lounge, Le Savoy. 59 Ste-Catherine est, downtown. ✆ **514/844-3500.** www. montrealmetropolis.ca/metropolis. Métro: St-Laurent or Berri-UQAM.

Place des Arts ✶✶   Since 1992, Place des Arts has been the city's central entertainment complex, mounting performances of musical concerts, opera, dance, and theater in five halls: **Salle Wilfrid-Pelletier** (2,982 seats), where the Orchestre Symphonique de Montréal often performs; the **Théâtre Maisonneuve** (1,458 seats), where the Orchestre Métropolitain de Montréal and Les Grands Ballets Canadiens, perform; the

Théâtre Jean-Duceppe (755 seats); the **Cinquième Salle** (417 seats); and the small **Studio-Théâtre Stella Artois** (138 seats). Portions of the city's many arts festivals are staged in the halls and outdoor plaza here, as are traveling productions of Broadway shows. 260 bd. de Maisonneuve ouest, downtown (ticket office). ✆ **514/842-2112** for information and tickets. www.pda.qc.ca. Métro: Place des Arts.

Pollack Concert Hall   In a landmark building dating from 1899 and fronted by a statue of Queen Victoria, this McGill University venue is in nearly constant use, especially during the school year with concerts and recitals by university students and professionals from the music faculty. Recordings of some concerts are available on the university's label, McGill Records. Concerts are also given in the campus's smaller **Redpath Hall,** 861 Sherbrooke St. ouest (✆ **514/398-4547**). On the McGill University campus, 555 rue Sherbrooke ouest, downtown. ✆ **514/398-4547**. www.music.mcgill.ca. Performances are usually free. Métro: McGill.

Théâtre de Outremont   Opened in 1929, the Outremont started a new life in 2001, with a larger stage and terraced seating. Its calendar incorporates all manner of French-language music, comedy, theater, and film, but non-Francophones will enjoy the dance shows, especially performances during the Montréal International Festival of Tango. 1248 av. Bernard ouest (at av. Champagneur), Mile End. ✆ **514/495-9944**. www.theatre outremont.ca/outremont. Métro: Outremont.

Théâtre de Verdure *Value*   Tango nights are popular at this open-air theater nestled in a popular park in Plateau Mont-Royal. Everything is free: music, dance, and theater, often with well-known artists and performers. Many in the audience pack picnics. Performances are held from June to August; check with the tourism office for days and times. Parc La Fontaine, Plateau Mont-Royal. Métro: Sherbrooke.

Théâtre St-Denis   Recently refurbished, this theater complex in the heart of the Latin Quarter hosts a variety of shows by the likes of Norah Jones and B. B. King, as well as segments of the Juste pour Rire (Just for Laughs) comedy festival in July. One hall seats 2,218 and the other 933. 1594 rue St-Denis (at Emery), Quartier Latin. ✆ **514/849-4211**. www. theatrestdenis.com. Métro: Berri-UQAM.

DANCE

Frequent appearances by notable dancers and troupes from other parts of Canada and the world—among them Paul Taylor, the Feld Ballet, and Le Ballet National du Canada—augment the accomplished resident companies.

Les Grands Ballets Canadiens ⭐⭐   This prestigious touring company, performing both a classical and a modern repertoire, has developed a following far beyond national borders in its 50 years (it was founded in 1957). In the process, it has brought prominence to many gifted Canadian choreographers and composers. The troupe's production of *The Nutcracker* is always a big event each winter in Montréal. Performances are held October through May. Place des Arts, 175 Ste-Catherine ouest (main entrance), downtown. ✆ **514/842-2112**. www.grandsballets.qc.ca. Tickets from C$25 (US$22/£11) and way up. Métro: Place des Arts.

THEATER

Centaur Theatre   The city's principal English-language theater is housed in a former stock-exchange building (1903). A mix of classics, foreign adaptations, and works by Canadian playwrights is presented; playwright Michel Tremblay's *Forever Yours, Marie-Lou,* for instance, is scheduled for its first staging in English in April 2008. 453 rue

St-François-Xavier (near rue Notre-Dame), Vieux-Montréal. ℭ **514/288-3161**. www.centaurtheatre.com. Tickets from C$31 (US$27/£13). Métro: Place d'Armes.

Saidye Bronfman Centre for the Arts   Montréal's Yiddish Theatre, founded in 1937, is based here. The Centre is a branch of the YM-YWHA Montréal Jewish Community Centres and host to dance and music recitals, occasional lectures, and plays in both Yiddish and English. Recent productions have included Noel Coward's *Fallen Angels* and the Dora Wasserman Yiddish Theatre's production of *Those Were the Days*. Note that the Centre is at a considerable distance from downtown, and the taxi fare is substantial. 5170 Côte-Ste-Catherine (near bd. Décarie), Plateau Mont-Royal. ℭ **514/739-2310**. www.saidyebronfman.org. Tickets from C$34 (US$30/£15). Métro: Côte-Ste-Catherine. Bus: 29 ouest.

2 The Club & Music Scene
COMEDY

The once red-hot market for comedy clubs across North America may have cooled, but it lives on in Montréal, mostly because the city is the home to the highly regarded **Juste pour Rire (Just for Laughs) Festival** (ℭ **888/244-3155;** www.hahaha.com) held every summer. Those who have so far avoided the comedy-club experience should know that profanity, bathroom humor, and ethnic slurs are common fodder for performers. To avoid becoming objects of the comedians' barbs, it's wise to sit well back from the stage. Check before buying tickets whether the show is in French or English.

Comedyworks   There's a full card of comedy at this long-running club situated on a jumping block of rue Bishop south of rue Ste-Catherine. Shows here are in English; Monday is open-mic night, Tuesday and Wednesday are improv nights with a comedy troupe working off the audience's suggestions, and Thursday through Saturday nights feature international headliners. No food is served, just drinks. Reservations are recommended, especially on Friday, when it may be necessary to arrive early to secure a seat. Shows are nightly at 9pm with additional 11:15pm shows on Fridays and Saturdays. 1238 rue Bishop (at rue Ste-Catherine), downtown. ℭ **514/398-9661**. www.comedyworksmontreal.com. Cover C$3–C$12 (US$2.60–US$10/£1.30–£5.15). Métro: Guy-Concordia.

DANCE CLUBS

As elsewhere, Montréal's dance clubs change in popularity in the blink of an eye and new ones sprout like toadstools after a heavy rain, withering just as quickly. For the latest, quiz concierges or waiters—whoever looks as if they might follow the scene. Here are a few that appear more likely to survive. At some, you may encounter steroid abusers with funny haircuts guarding the doors. Usually they'll let you inside; the admittance game is rarely as strict as the "hipper than thou" criteria at some Los Angeles clubs. Also see the clubs listed in "The Gay and Lesbian Scene," later in this chapter.

Club Balattou   An infectious, sensual tropical beat issues from this club-with-a-difference on The Main, a hot, happy variation from the prevailing grunge and murk that seeps out of what might be described as mainstream clubs. Things get going about 10pm every night but Monday. 4372 bd. St-Laurent (at rue Marie-Anne), Plateau Mont-Royal. ℭ **514/845-5447**. Métro: Mont-Royal.

Hard Rock Cafe   No surprises here, not with clones around the world. The formula still works, and this outpost in the heart of the rue Crescent party strip gets crowded at lunch and on weekend evenings. There's a terrace seating about 30 patrons. Open

Sunday through Thursday from 11am to 11pm, Friday and Saturday 11am to midnight, with a big dance floor that's hopping in the evenings. 1458 rue Crescent (near bd. de Maisonneuve), downtown. ② 514/987-1420. Métro: Guy-Concordia.

Les Foufounes Electriques   From the outside, it's like something out of a *Mad Max* movie: a multilevel disco–rock club that features hard-core rock and industrial bands like Agnostic Front and Gang Green. It's marked by a spider the size of a Toyota over the front gate. If you're within 2 blocks, you'll hear it. Open daily from 4pm to 3am. 87 Ste-Catherine est (near bd. St-Laurent), Quartier Latin. ② 514/844-5539. www.foufounes.qc.ca. Métro: St-Laurent.

Newtown   Huge fanfare trumpeted the 2001 opening of this tri-level club in the white-hot center of rue Crescent nightlife. One of the owners is Formula 1 race car driver and local hero Jacques Villeneuve, whose last name can be translated as "New Town." Adjoining town houses were scooped out to make one big trendy nightspot at a reported cost of C$6 million (US$5.3 million/£2.6 million) at the time, with a disco in the basement, big barroom on the main floor, restaurant one floor up, and rooftop terrace in summer. Reservations are usually required for the restaurant, but admission to the bar and dance floor shouldn't be a problem. The bar and restaurant are open daily, and the disco is open Friday and Saturday. 1476 rue Crescent (at de Maisonneuve), downtown. ② 514/284-6555. www.newtown.ca. Métro: Peel.

Orchid   An R&B and hip-hop nightclub with a 30,000-watt sound system, Orchid pulls in a mixed crowd of young professionals and college kids. The dress code states no runners (sneakers), hats, jerseys, or baggy jeans. Things get started around 10pm, and ladies drink for free before midnight on Fridays. 3556 bd. St-Laurent (north of rue Sherbrooke), Plateau Mont-Royal. ② 514/848-6398. Métro: Sherbrooke.

Time Supper Club   Though food is served, it isn't the prime attraction—Time gives its fabulous crowd a chance to get up from the tables and work off the calories to rock, house, and hip-hop that thumps on 'til closing at 3am. The waitstaff is startlingly attractive—okay, downright sexy. Dress well, look good, and approach the door with confidence. It's located in a dreary industrial neighborhood south of the downtown core, so you might want to arrive by car or taxi. 997 rue St-Jacques ouest (near rue Peel), downtown. ② 514/392-9292. Métro: Bonaventure.

FOLK, ROCK & POP

Montréal has a strong showing of innovative alternative rock; homegrown outfits include Arcade Fire, Wolf Parade, and Godspeed You! Black Emperor. (The band Of Montreal, by the way, is actually from Athens, Georgia.) Scores of bars, cafés, theaters, clubs, and even churches present live music on at least an occasional basis, even if only at Sunday brunch. The performers, local or touring, draw from every idiom, from metal to funk to folky vocals. Here are a few places that focus their energies on music.

Brutopia   This pub pulls endless pints of its own microbrews to go with rock/pop most nights a week. With several rooms on two levels, a terrace in back, and a street-side balcony, it anchors the raucous southern end of rue Crescent. Chances are you haven't heard of any of the bands, but they keep the tempo up. Sunday is open mic and Monday "Trivia Night." 1219 rue Crescent (north of bd. René-Lévesque), downtown. ② 514/393-9277. Métro: Lucien L'Allier.

Café Campus/Petit Campus   Ensconced here for 40 years, this bleak club on touristy rue Prince-Arthur has hosted The Von Bondies and Galaxie 500 over the years, and these days there are events such as The Johnny Cash Tribute Show. A smaller room,

Petit Campus, usually has DJ'd hip-hop. Folks over 35 are probably parents of the musicians. 57 rue Prince-Arthur est (near bd. St-Laurent), Plateau Mont-Royal. ⓒ **514/844-1010**. www. cafecampus.com. Cover from C$10 (US$8.70/£4.30). Métro: Sherbrooke.

Club Soda   This long-established club's current quarters in a seedy part of the Latin Quarter are even larger than its old location on avenue du Parc. It remains one of the prime destinations for performers just below the megastar level, including U.S. rockers Dinosaur Jr. and jazz-guy Mark Murphy, and also hosts several of the city's comedy festivals and acts for the annual jazz festival. 1225 bd. St-Laurent (at rue Ste-Catherine), Quartier Latin. ⓒ **514/286-1010**. www.clubsoda.ca. Tickets from C$15 (US$13/£6.45). Métro: St-Laurent.

Hurley's Irish Pub   The Irish have been one of the largest immigrant groups in Montréal since the famine of the 1840s, and their musical tradition thrives here. In front is a street-level terrace, with several semi-subterranean rooms in back. Celtic instrumentalists perform every night of the week, usually starting around 9:30pm. 1225 rue Crescent (at rue Ste-Catherine), downtown. ⓒ **514/861-4111**. www.hurleysirishpub.com. Métro: Guy-Concordia.

Le Divan Orange   This is a *cooperative de travail,* or worker's cooperative, which means, in part, that it is a not-for-profit operation, with the "suggested" cover charge going into the pot to pay the musicians. Bands and combos include jazz, country, indie rock, traditional North African, and events best described as performance art. Shows start around 9:30pm. It's open every night. 4234 bd. St-Laurent (near rue Rachel), Plateau Mont-Royal. ⓒ **514/840-9090**. www.ledivanorange.org. Cover C$5–C$10 (US$4.35–US$8.70/£2.15–£4.30) Métro: Mont-Royal.

Les Bobards   Why call this heavy-duty music venue "Tall Stories"? You'll get no good answer, but there's music here 6 days a week in a wide variety of forms—jazz, blues, salsa, sync-pop, Brazilian. Live shows start around 9:30pm. Foosball and pool can fill the time until then, and happy hour runs a l-o-o-n-g time, from 3 to 8pm. 4328 bd. St-Laurent (at rue Marie-Anne), Plateau Mont-Royal. ⓒ **514/987-1174**. www.lesbobards.qc.ca. Cover up to $5 (US$4.35/£2.15). Métro: Mont-Royal.

Les Deux Pierrots 🅡   This is perhaps the best known of Montréal's *boîtes-à-chansons* (song clubs). The main section is an intimate French-style cabaret, with a couple of attached rooms, La Boîte à Spectacles and Le Resto-Bar Le Pierrot. The singers interact animatedly with the crowd, often bilingually, from 8pm until 3am. 104 rue St-Paul est (west of place Jacques-Cartier), Vieux-Montréal. ⓒ **514/861-1270**. www.lespierrots.com. Cover from C$5 (US$4.35/£2.15). Métro: Place d'Armes.

JAZZ & BLUES

The respected and heavily attended **Festival International de Jazz,** held every summer in the city, caters to the public's interest in this original American art form. During the 11 days of the event, close to 150 indoor shows are scheduled, and there are countless outdoor performances as well. Wynton Marsalis, Harry Connick, Jr., Keith Jarrett, and even Bob Dylan have been featured in recent years, although it costs serious money to hear stars of such magnitude and tickets sell out months in advance. Fortunately, hundreds of other concerts are free. "Jazz" is broadly interpreted to include everything from Dixieland to reggae, world beat, and the unclassifiable experimental. For information on the festival, call ⓒ **888/515-0515** or visit www.montrealjazzfest.com.

Casa del Popolo   Kind of the CBGB of the Montréal jazz and indie music scene, this scruffy storefront might seem an unlikely place to launch an increasingly visible summer music festival, but that it has. While jazz and blues dominate the regular schedule, there's plenty of room for percussion specialists, bagpipe, calypso, reggae, and whatever else grabs their attention. The sister performance space **La Sala Rossa,** across the street at 4848 bd. St-Laurent, brings in strong acts like The Sea and Cake and Marc Ribot. Food is available—strictly vegetarian—and draft beer by the pint is the beverage preferred by the leftie bohemian clientele. Don't overdress. 4873 bd. St-Laurent (near bd. St-Joseph), Plateau Mont-Royal. ℂ **514/284-3804.** www.casadelpopolo.com. Cover C$6–C$15 (US$5.20–US$13/£2.60–£6.45). Métro: Laurier.

Maison de Jazz ✪   Right downtown, this New Orleans–style jazz venue has been on the scene for decades. Lovers of barbecued ribs and jazz, most of them well past the bloom of youth, start early in filling the room, which is decorated in mock Art Nouveau style with tiered levels. Live music starts around 7:30pm and continues until closing time. The ribs are okay and the jazz is of the swinging mainstream variety, with occasional digressions into more esoteric forms. 2060 rue Aylmer (south of rue Sherbrooke), downtown. ℂ **514/842-8656.** www.houseofjazz.ca. Cover C$5 (US$4.35/£2.15). Métro: McGill.

Modavie   In the winter, set aside Friday or Saturday night for dinner with jazz at this popular Vieux-Montréal bistro-bar-lounge (food information, p. 94); come in any night during the summer at 7pm for dinner and jazz. Single-malt scotches and cigars are at the ready. Music is usually mainstream jazz, by duos or trios. It's a friendly place, and the food is good, too. 1 rue St-Paul ouest (corner of rue St-Laurent), Vieux-Montréal. ℂ **514/287-9582.** Métro: Place d'Armes.

Upstairs Jazz Bar & Grill   Name aside, the club is *down* a few steps from the street. Big names are infrequent, but the jazz groups appearing every night are more than competent. Performances usually begin at 9pm. Decor is largely vintage record-album covers and fish tanks. Pretty good food ranges from bar snacks to more substantial meals, including table d'hôte offerings. Most patrons are edging toward their middle years or are already there. 1254 rue Mackay (near rue Ste-Catherine), downtown. ℂ **514/931-6808.** www.upstairsjazz.com. Cover usually about C$10 (US$8.70/£4.30). Métro: Guy-Concordia.

3 The Bar & Café Scene

An abundance of restaurants, bars, and cafés line the streets near the downtown commercial district, from rue Stanley to rue Guy between rue Ste-Catherine and boulevard de Maisonneuve. **Rue Crescent,** in particular, hums with activity from late afternoon until far into the evening, especially after 10pm on summer weekend nights, when the street swarms with people careening from bar to restaurant to club. In the Plateau Mont-Royal neighborhood, **Boulevard St-Laurent,** or The Main, as it's known, is another nightlife strip, abounding in bars and clubs, most with a distinctive European—particularly French—personality, as opposed to the Anglo flavor of the rue Crescent area. **Rue St-Paul,** west of Place Jacques-Cartier in Vieux-Montréal, falls somewhere in the middle on the Anglophone-Francophone spectrum. In all cases, bars tend to open around 11:30am and stay open late. Many of them have *heures joyeuses* (happy hours) from as early as 3pm to as late as 9pm, but usually for a shorter period within those hours. At those times, two-for-one drinks are the rule. Otherwise, given the high taxes on alcoholic beverages, the beverage of choice is most often beer. Look for a sign reading BIERES EN FUT—beer on draft. Last call for orders is 3am, but patrons are often allowed to dawdle over those drinks until 4am.

DOWNTOWN/RUE CRESCENT

Le Cabaret   In L'Hôtel de la Montagne and within sight of the trademark lobby fountain with its nude bronze sprite sporting stained-glass wings, this appealing piano bar draws a crowd of youngish to middle-aged professionals after 5:30pm. In summer, there's a terrace bar on the roof by the pool for sunbathing, swimming, meals, drinks, and dancing; it's open to nonguests, too. 1430 rue de la Montagne (north of rue Ste-Catherine). ℂ **514/288-5656.** Métro: Guy-Concordia.

Le Tour de Ville   Memorable and breathtaking. We're talking about the view, that is, from Montréal's only revolving restaurant and bar (the bar part doesn't revolve, but you still get a great view). The best time to go is when the sun is setting and the city lights are beginning to blink on. Open daily from 5:30pm, and on Sunday mornings for brunch. In the Delta Centre-Ville Hôtel, 777 rue University. ℂ **514/879-4777** for reservations. Métro: Square Victoria.

Ritz Bar   A mature, prosperous crowd seeks out the quiet Ritz Bar in the Ritz-Carlton, adjacent to the semi-legendary Café de Paris restaurant. Anyone can take advantage of the tranquil room and the professionalism of its staff, but because the atmosphere is rather formal, most men will be more at ease with a jacket. The bar is just off the hotel lobby, to the right. In the Ritz-Carlton Hôtel, 1228 rue Sherbrooke ouest (at rue Drummond). ℂ **514/842-4212.** Métro: Peel.

Sir Winston Churchill Pub ⚑   The three levels of bars and cafés incorporated in the Sir Winston Churchill Pub have been operating for over 40 years and are rue Crescent landmarks. The New Orleans–style sidewalk- and first-floor terraces (open in summer and enclosed in winter) make perfect vantage points for checking out the pedestrian traffic. Inside and down the stairs, the pub, with English ales on tap, attempts to imitate a British public house. The burgers and such have to look up to see mediocrity, but the mixed crowd of questing young professionals doesn't seem to mind. Mondays are retro night, Tuesdays "Create Your Own Drink" night, and Wednesdays Ladies' Night. Open daily 11:30am to 3am. 1459 rue Crescent (near rue Ste-Catherine). ℂ **514/288-3814.** Métro: Guy-Concordia.

Thursday's   In existence too long to be considered "hot," this remains a prime watering hole for Montréal's young professional set. The pubby bar spills out onto a terrace that hangs over the street, and there's a glittery disco in back. Both the bar and the disco are in L'Hôtel de la Montagne. Voted "Best Pick-Up Spot" by the *Montréal Mirror* in 2007 for its third year running. In L'Hôtel de la Montagne, 1449 rue Crescent (north of rue Ste-Catherine). ℂ **516/288-5656.** Métro: Guy-Concordia.

W Hotel   With its Le Plateau Lounge, W Bartini, and Wunderbar open daily until 3am, W attracts some of the best-looking partiers in town. 901 Victoria Square (at rue McGill). ℂ **516/395-3100.** Métro: Square-Victoria.

VIEUX-MONTREAL

Aszú *Finds*   This classy wine bar features a selection of 450 labels—all private import. Better still, on any night, between 60 and 70 are available by the glass. A menu of oysters, tartar trio, seasonal mushrooms, and the like provides accompaniment to the main event. With room for about 30 people at the bar, 40 at inside tables, and 75 on a cute side terrace, this is a cozy find—get here before the crowds catch on. A café upstairs is open from 7am to 4pm daily. 212 rue Notre Dame ouest (at rue St-François-Xavier). ℂ **514/845-5436.** Métro: Place d'Armes.

Le Jardin Nelson   Near the foot of Place Jacques Cartier, the main plaza in Vieux-Montréal, a passage leads into a tree-shaded garden court in back of a stone building dating from 1812. A pleasant hour or two can be spent listening to jazz every noontime and evening, and afternoons from Thursday to Sunday. Food takes second place, but the kitchen does well with its pizzas and crepes, the latter with both sweet and savory fillings (including lobster). There's a covered people-watching porch in front, and dining rooms and a bar inside. When the weather's nice, it's open until 2am. Closed November through mid-April. 407 Place Jacques-Cartier (at rue St-Paul). © 514/861-5731. Métro: Place d'Armes or Champ de Mars.

Suite 701   When the Hôtel Place d'Armes converted its old lobby and wine bar to a spiffy lounge, yuppies young and not-so got the word fast. They crowd in nightly, but especially Thursdays, when Montréalers single and not-really try to pair up for the upcoming weekend. They can practice their approaches and rejections while sampling such upscale bar food as mac-'n'-cheese with chipotle peppers, and beef short rib *poutine*. Happy hour is from 5 to 8pm. At the corner of rue St-Jacques and côte de la Place d'Armes. © 514/904 1201. Métro: Place d'Armes.

PLATEAU MONT-ROYAL

Bifteck   Even on the most dismal of Mondays, this perennially popular bar jumps, with a grunge crowd aging from barely legal to early 30s. Most of them quaff beer by the pitcher, but attention is also given to shooters, including classy evergreens such as Kamikazi and Windex. Despite the name, food isn't served, apart from popcorn. 3702 bd. St-Laurent (near rue Prince Arthur). © 514/844-6211. Métro: Sherbrooke.

Champs   Montréalers are no less enthusiastic about sports, especially hockey, than other Canadians, and fans both avid and casual drop by this three-story sports emporium to catch up with their teams and hoist a few. Games from around the world are fed to walls of TV monitors, and the bar can screen up to 14 events. Food is what you expect—burgers, steaks, and such. 3956 bd. St-Laurent (near rue Duluth). © 514/987-6444. Métro: Sherbrooke.

Laïka   Amid the plethora of St-Laurent watering stops, this bright little boîte stands out for its open front in summer and the fresh flowers on the bar and some of the tables. Tasty sandwiches and tapas are served, and the Sunday brunch is popular. DJs spin house, funk, and whatnot from mid-evening to 3am for the mostly 18- to 35-year-old crowd. 4040 bd. St-Laurent (near rue Duluth). © 514/842-8088. Métro: Sherbrooke.

Le Pistol   Get here early, because this spot on The Main gets packed in no time. Catering to the collegiate set as opposed to the chichi club-goer, this bar offers ample attractions, including high-definition plasma TVs to follow hockey, and tasty food, including sandwiches named for Bond flicks—Goldfinger, Moonraker. A stereo system moves from jazz to house to rock. The ground-floor front is thrown open in decent weather. Drinks and eats are mostly under C$8 (US$6.95). 3723 bd. St-Laurent (near rue Prince Arthur). © 514/847-2222. Métro: Sherbrooke.

Shed Café   When you want to get your goth on, head to this bar/restaurant, in a lively stretch of The Main near rue Sherbrooke. There's a good crowd 7 days a week, noshing on local *bières en fût* as well as good fries and oversize portions of cake. The crowd skews young, but with enough diversity to make an hour or two interesting. 3515 bd. St-Laurent (north of rue Sherbrooke). © 514/842-0220. Métro: Sherbrooke.

MILE END

Mile End Bar   Walk into this designer bar before 10pm and you might be drinking in scant company. While food isn't its *raison d'etre*, there's a compact menu of nibbles categorized as tapas, pinchos (skewered tapas), and *amuses gueles*. By 10pm, though, the three floors start to fill up, and DJs work the crowds into a lather. 5322 bd. St-Laurent (south of rue St-Viateur). © 514/279-0200. Métro: Laurier.

Whisky Café   Those who enjoy scotch, particularly single-malts like Laphraoig and Glenfiddich, will find over 150 different labels to sample here. (Because the Québec government applies stiff taxes for the privilege, many of the patrons—suits to grad students—seem to stick to beer.) The decor is sophisticated, with exposed beams and vents, handmade tiled tables, and large wood-enclosed columns. Another decorative triumph: The men's urinal has a waterfall acting as the *pissoir*. Attached is a separate cigar lounge, with leather armchairs and Cubans on sale until 3am. 5800 bd. St-Laurent (at rue Bernard). © 514/278-2646. Métro: Laurier.

QUARTIER LATIN

Jello Bar   Lava lamps and other fixtures make it look like the rumpus room of a suburban ranch house in the 1960s, but central to the rep of this goofy throwback that draws folks from 25 to 40 years old is the menu of more than 50 kinds of martinis. Most are flavored excuses for people who don't really like liquor, but the classic gin and vodka versions are stalwarts to be savored. Live music—merengue, salsa, swing—usually played Wednesday through Saturday helps fuel dancing and the rollicking good mood that pervades the bar. Other times, there's a DJ. 151 rue Ontario est (near bd. St-Laurent). © 514/285-2621. Métro: St-Laurent.

4 The Gay & Lesbian Scene

The city's lively **Quartier Gai (Gay Village),** or simply The Village, comprises a stretch of rue Ste-Catherine from rue St-Hubert to rue Papineau. One of the largest gay and lesbian communities in North America, it is action central for both natives and visitors. That's true on any night, really, but especially during such annual events as the weeklong celebration of sexual diversity known as **Divers/Cité** in late July and early August (www.diverscite.org) and the **Black & Blue Festival** (www.bbcm.org), probably the world's largest circuit party with a week of entertainment and club dancing held for a week in October. In 2006, Montréal added another pink feather to its cap by hosting the first World Outgames, attracting more than 16,000 athletes.

If you're looking for a more low-key time without all the muscle, disco, and traces of seediness that surround the edges of the neighborhood, you'll find the city overall to be tolerant of same-sex couples. The official **Tourisme Montréal** website at **www. tourisme-montreal.org** offers a "Montréal Gay to Z" mini-site that includes listings of gay-friendly accommodations, links, and more. **The Village Tourism Information Centre** at 576 Ste-Catherine Street est, Suite 200 (© **888/595-8110** or 514/522-1885) is open daily in the summer and weekdays the rest of the year. In addition, the **Québec Gay Chamber of Commerce** has a website at **www.ccgq.ca.**

Of several local publications, the most useful magazine is *Fugues,* describing current and future events as well as listing gay-friendly lodgings, clubs, saunas, and other resources. Get a copy at the tourist office mentioned above or from the free racks around the city, or check www.fugues.com.

Chez Mado   The glint of the sequins can be blinding! Relatively new on the Village scene and inspired by 1920s cabaret theater, this determinedly trendy place has both performances and dancing and is considered a premiere venue these days. Every night of the week has a different theme, from Monday's karaoke and Wednesday's variety events to Friday and Saturday's festive drag shows. Happy hour is from 4 to 9pm. Look for the massive pink-haired drag queen on the retro marquee. 1115 rue Ste-Catherine est (near rue Amherst). ⓒ **514/525-7566.** Métro: Beaudry.

Club Unity Montréal   The former dance club Unity II was one of the biggest and most popular discos in town before it was severely damaged in an April 2006 fire. It reopened as Club Unity Montréal a few months later and once again draws well-dressed, friendly, mixed crowds Fridays and Saturdays to its three-rooms, top-of-the-line lighting and sound systems, and large outdoor roof terrace. 1171 Ste-Catherine est. ⓒ **514/523-2777.** www.clubunitymontreal.com. Métro: Beaudry.

Gotha Salon Bar Lounge   For a quieter venue in the Village, this cozy lounge for both men and women has a fireplace, live piano on Sunday night, and a relaxed vibe. It's at street level below the Aubergell Bed & Breakfast on rue Amherst, a road with antiques shops chockablock with vintage and collectible goodies from the 1930s to 1980s. 1641 rue Amherst ⓒ **514/526-1270.** Métro: Beaudry.

Sky Club & Pub ⚐   A complex that includes a pub serving dinner Monday through Saturday and brunch on weekends, the Nirvana male strip club, and a spacious dance floor, Sky is thought by many to be the city's hottest spot for the young and fabulous. It continues to thrive after expensive recent renovations, and the spiffy decor and pounding (usually house) music in the disco contribute to the popularity. There are also drag performances in the cabaret room and a roof terrace. 1474 rue Ste-Catherine est (near rue Amherst). ⓒ **514/529-6969.** www.complexesky.com. Métro: Beaudry.

Stéréo   One of a growing number of after-hours clubs, this hyper-hip disco doesn't crank up the jaw-dropping sound system until 2am and then roars until noon. Club kids, drag queens, hipsters, and students gay and straight all come out to play on Friday, Saturday, and Sunday nights. Passionate devotees have been known to tattoo the club's audio-wave logo on their person. Cover C$20 (US$17/£8.60) and up. 858 rue Ste-Catherine est (near rue Berri). ⓒ **514/286-0325.** www.stereo-nightclub.com. Métro: Berri-UQAM.

5 More Entertainment

CINEMA

In Montréal, English-language films are usually presented with subtitles in French. However, when the initials "VF" (for *version française*) follow the title of a non-Francophone movie, it means that the movie has been dubbed into French. Policies vary on English subtitles on non–English-language films—the best idea is to ask at the box office. Besides the many first-run movie houses that advertise in the daily newspapers, Montréal is rich in "ciné-clubs," which tend to be slightly older and show second-run, foreign, and art films at reduced prices.

Admission to films is usually about C$10 (US$8.70/£4.30) for adults, and less for students, seniors, children, and afternoon shows.

Foreign-language and independent films are the menu at **Ex-Centris,** 3536 bd. St-Laurent (ⓒ **514/847-2206;** www.ex-centris.com), and the architectural surroundings are at least as interesting—sort of a post–machine-age spaceship. Go inside and try to find the ticket booth to ask about showtimes just to see what we mean. A casual and nifty bar-café, Café Méliès (p. 101), is on the premises. The films are in English about half the time.

The **National Film Board of Canada (Cinema ONF)** at 1564 rue St-Denis (© **514/ 496-6887**), shows Canadian and international films, primarily in English and French, particularly classics. Also at the theater/office is the unique CinéRobothèque, a high-tech screening center that lets visitors browse a multimedia catalog and then watch a film at a personal viewing station.

Imposing, sometimes visually disorienting images confront viewers of the five-story screen in the **IMAX Theatre** in the Centre des Sciences de Montréal in the Vieux-Port (© **877/496-4724**). Many of the films are suitable for the entire family. See "Especially for Kids," in chapter 7.

GAMBLING

The **Casino de Montréal** (© **800/665-2274** or 514/392-2746; www.casino-de-montreal.com), Québec's first, is housed in recycled space: The complex re-uses what were the French and Québec Pavilions on Ile Notre-Dame during Expo '67 (the World's Fair that Montréal hosted). Asymmetrical and groovy, the buildings provide a dramatic setting for games of chance. Four floors contain more than 115 game tables, including roulette, craps, blackjack, baccarat, and varieties of poker, and there are more than 3,200 slot machines. Its four restaurants get good reviews, especially the elegant **Nuances** (p. 106). There are also live shows in the Cabaret, a 500-seat performance hall. No alcoholic beverages are served in the gambling areas, and patrons must be 18 and dressed neatly (the full dress code is posted online). Open 24 hours a day, 7 days a week, the Casino is entirely smoke-free, with outside smoking areas. Overnight packages are available.

To get there you can drive or take the Métro to the Parc Jean-Drapeau stop and then walk or take the Casino shuttle bus (no. 167). From May through October, there's also a free shuttle bus *(navette)* that leaves on the hour from the downtown Infotouriste Centre at 1001 rue du Square-Dorchester. Call © **514/392-2746** for information on the shuttle and its other downtown stops.

11

Side Trips from Montréal

You don't have to travel far from Montréal to reach mountains, parks, or bike trails; in fact, nature is just a 30-minute drive either to the north or east of the city. The resort regions of the Laurentians (to the north) and the Cantons-de-l'Est (to the east) have both seen the development of year-round vacation retreats, with skiing in the winter, biking and boating in the summer, maple sugaring in the spring, and vineyard touring and leaf-peeping in the fall.

The pearl of the Laurentians (also called the Laurentides) is Mont-Tremblant, the highest peak in eastern Canada and a mecca in the winter for skiers and snowboarders from all over North America. Development has been particularly heavy in the resort town here, for both better and worse. The region has dozens of other ski centers, too, with scores of trails at every level of difficulty, and many are less than an hour from Montréal. The area loses none of its charm in the summer (and in fact gains some of it back with thinned-out traffic). That's when ski resorts become attractive green mountain rental properties close to biking, fishing,

and golfing. It's even possible to participate in cattle roundups.

The bucolic Cantons-de-l'Est to the southeast of Montréal were known as the Eastern Townships when they were a haven for English Loyalists and their descendants. The region is still referred to by that name by some Anglophones today. It's blessed with memorable country inns that used to be the homes of early-1900s aristocracy and the beautiful Lake Massawippi. As with the Laurentians, many of the same trails developed for winter sports are used for parallel activities in summer. The mountain of Bromont, for example, has marked paths for mountain biking, and Mont-Orford Park is the focal point for hiking trails linking six regional parks. Rock climbing, white-water kayaking, sailing, and fishing are additional options, with equipment readily available for rent.

Because the people of both regions rely heavily on tourism for their livelihoods, knowledge of at least rudimentary English is widespread, even outside such obvious places as hotels and restaurants.

1 North into the Laurentians (Laurentides)

55–129km (34–80 miles) N of Montréal

Don't expect spiked peaks or high ragged ridges. The rolling hills and rounded mountains of the Laurentian Shield are among the oldest in the world, worn down by wind and water over eons. They average between 300m and 520m (984 ft. and 1,706 ft.) in height, with the highest being Mont-Tremblant, at 968m (3,176 ft.). In the lower area, nearer to Montréal, the terrain resembles a rumpled quilt, its folds and hollows cupping a multitude of lakes large and small. Farther north the summits are higher and craggier, with patches of snow persisting well into spring, but these are still not the Alps or the Rockies. They're welcoming and embracing rather than awe-inspiring.

Half a century ago the first ski schools, rope tows, and trails began to appear. Today there are 14 ski centers within a 64km (40-mile) radius, and cross-country skiing has as enthusiastic a following as downhill (many enthusiasts say some of the best cross-country trails are on the grounds of a monastery called Domaine du St-Bernard in Mont-Tremblant). Sprawling resorts and modest lodges and inns are packed in winter with skiers, some of them through April. Trails for advanced skiers typically have short pitches and challenging moguls, with broad, hard-packed avenues for beginners and the less experienced.

But skiing is only half the story. As transportation improved, people took advantage of the obvious opportunities for watersports, golf (courses in the area now total over 30), tennis, mountain-biking, hiking, and every other kind of summer sport. Before long, the region had gained a sometimes-deserved reputation for fine dining and a convivial atmosphere that survives to this day.

Bird-watchers of both intense and casual bent can be fully occupied. Loon lovers, in particular, know that the lakes of Québec province's mountains are home to an estimated 16,000 of the native waterfowl that gives its name to the dollar coin. Excellent divers and swimmers, the birds are unable to walk on land, which makes nesting a trial. They're identified by a distinctive call that might be described as an extended mournful giggle.

At any time of the year, a visit to any of the villages and resorts in the Laurentians is likely to yield pleasant memories. The busiest times are in February and March for skiing, July and August for summer vacation, and during the Christmas-to–New Year holiday period. At other times of the year, reservations are easier to get, prices for virtually everything are lower, and crowds are thinner. May and September are often characterized by warm days, cool nights, and just enough people that the streets don't seem deserted.

March and April are the months when the maple trees are tapped, and *cabanes à sucre* ("sugar shacks") open up everywhere, some selling just maple syrup and candies, others serving full meals and even staging entertainment.

July and August bring glorious summer days to the Laurentians, and during the last 2 weeks in September the leaves put on a stunning show of autumnal color. Skiers can usually expect reliable snow from early December to mid-April.

In May and June, it must be said, the indigenous black flies and mosquitoes can seem as big and as ill-tempered as buzzards, so be prepared. Some of the resorts, inns, and lodges close down for a couple of weeks in the spring and the fall; a handful are open only for a few weeks in the winter months.

Prices can be difficult to pin down. The large resorts have so many types of rooms, suites, cottages, meal plans, discounts, and packages that you may need a travel agent to pick through the thicket of options. In planning, remember that Montréalers fill the highways when they "go up north" on weekends, particularly during the top skiing months, so plan ahead if you'll be there with them and make reservations early. Check websites for deals, and show your AAA card for discounts. An unfortunate note for pet owners: Few Laurentian resorts accept animals.

See p. 66 in chapter 5 for general information about hotel rates and the Frommer's star system.

The Laurentians (Laurentides)

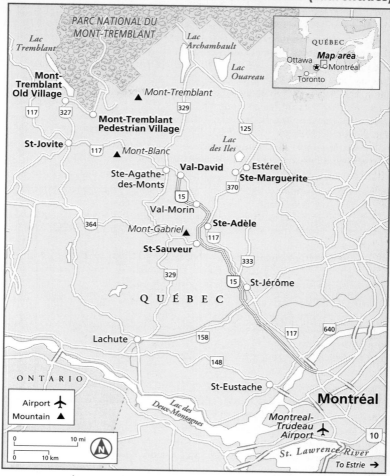

ESSENTIALS
GETTING THERE

BY CAR   The fast and scenic Autoroute des Laurentides, also known as Autoroute 15, goes straight from Montréal to the Laurentian mountains. Just follow the signs to St-Jérôme. The exit numbers are actually the distance in kilometers that the village is from Montréal.

Although the pace of development is quickening, crowding the highway with water parks, condos, and chain restaurants, this is still a pretty drive once you're past St-Jérôme and out of the clutches of the tangle of expressways surrounding Montréal. You'll quickly get a sweeping, panoramic introduction to the area, from the rolling hills and forests of the lower Laurentians to the mountain drama of the upper range.

Those with the time to meander can exit at St-Jérôme and pick up the older, parallel Route 117, which plays tag with the autoroute all the way to Ste-Agathe-des-Monts. Most of the region's more appealing towns are strung along or near Route 117. (Beware in the winter, however, when parts of 117 can become riddled with potholes large enough to do serious damage to your car.) North of Ste-Agathe, the autoroute ends and Route 117 becomes the major artery for the region, continuing well past Mont-Tremblant and deep into Québec's north country, finally ending at the Ontario border hundreds of miles from Montréal.

Québec's equivalent of the Highway Patrol maintains a presence along the stretch of Autoroute 15 between St-Faustin and Ste-Adèle. While enforcement of speed limits is loose, if you are pulled over, remember that radar detectors are illegal in the province (even if they're not turned on) and can be confiscated.

BY BUS   Groupe Galland buses depart Montréal's **Terminus Voyageur,** 505 bd. de Maisonneuve est, stopping in the larger Laurentian towns, including Ste-Sauveur, Ste-Adèle, and Mont-Tremblant; call © **514/333-9555** or check www.galland-bus.com for schedules. The ride to Mont-Tremblant takes just under 3 hours. Some of the major resorts provide their own bus service from Montréal at an additional charge, so ask when booking.

The tourist office recommends the nonprofit **Allo Stop,** an alternative program that coordinates ride-shares to help reduce the numbers of cars on the road. Guests help pay for gas. Call © **514/985-3032** for the Montréal office.

BY LIMOUSINE   Taxis and limousines await arrivals at Trudeau Airport in Montréal, where all domestic and international commercial flights arrive, and will take you to any Laurentian hideaway—for a price. While the fare for the 1-hour trip by limo from Trudeau is steep, four or five people can share the cost and lessen the pain. Ask for the standard fare to your inn or lodge when making accommodations reservations. The inn will often arrange for a taxi or limo to meet you and may even help to find other guests arriving at the same time to share the cost.

BY PLANE   Aéroport International Pierre-Elliot-Trudeau de Montréal (airport code YUL; © **800/465-1213** or 514/394-7377; www.admtl.com), known more commonly as Montréal-Trudeau Airport, is 30 to 60 minutes from the Laurentians, depending on your destination. The newly renovated **Mont-Tremblant International Airport** (© **877/425-7919;** www.mtia.ca), 24 miles north of Mont-Tremblant, has direct flights from Toronto and accommodates charter flights from North America and Europe. The airport is a former military base.

VISITOR INFORMATION

Tourist offices are plentiful throughout the Laurentians. Look for the blue ? signs along the highways or in towns. For an orientation to the entire region, there is a major tourist information center, well-marked from the highway, at Exit 51 off Autoroute 15. It shares a building with a 24-hour McDonald's restaurant, and there is a gas station next door. Called **Tourisme Laurentides** (© **800/561-6673;** www.laurentides.com), it has racks of brochures and a helpful staff who can make reservations for lodging throughout the Laurentides for free. It's open every day of the year, from 8:30am to 5pm (until 9pm in summer).

ST-SAUVEUR

Only 60km (37 miles) north of Montréal, the village of St-Sauveur (pop. 8,470) can easily be visited on a day trip. The area is flush with outlet malls and the carloads of

> **Tips** **On the Road: A Quick Guide**
>
> Canada is on the metric system, so distances are measured in kilometers (1 kilometer = .62 miles). Many U.S. cars have a secondary speedometer that gives speed in kilometers. The maximum posted speed limit on most highways is 100kmph (62 mph). Few drivers observe it.
>
> At service stations, *AVEC SERVICE* means FULL SERVICE, and *LIBRE SERVICE* means SELF SERVICE. The directions on the pump are usually in both French and English, especially at name-brand stations. Gas is sold by the liter, and 3.78 liters equals 1 gallon. It's comparatively expensive by U.S. standards, with recent prices of C$1.15 a liter (US$1/49p) translating to about US$4.35 a gallon.
>
> Road signs are always in French, and only sometimes in English as well. *ARRET* means STOP, while *CONTROLE RADAR* means what you think. *DEMI TOUR* means U-TURN. The mysterious green-and-white signs declaring only *CLSC* refer to the presence nearby of a CENTRE LOCALE DE SERVICES COMMUNAUTAIRES, or Local Center of Community Services, where you can go for assistance with any problems on the road.

shoppers they attract, but a few blocks farther north, the older village square is dominated by a handsome church, and the streets around it bustle with a less frenzied activity much of the year. Be prepared to have difficulty finding a parking place in season (try the large lot behind the church). Dining and snacking on everything from crepes to hot dogs are big activities here, evidenced by the many beckoning cafés. In season, there's a tourist kiosk on the square.

The area is well-known for its night skiing—there are nearly two dozen well-lit trails. In summer, the **Parc Aquatique du Mont St-Sauveur,** 350 rue St-Denis (© 450/227-4671; www.mssi.ca), Canada's largest water park, features rafting, a wave pool, a "tidal wave" river, and slides, including a mountain slide where you go up in chairlifts and ride down in tubes.

Ten days in early August are dedicated to St-Sauveur's annual **Festival des Arts** (© 450/227-0427; www.artssaintsauveur.com), with an emphasis on music and dance, including jazz and chamber concerts and ballet troupes.

WHERE TO STAY & DINE

If the idea of a picnic appeals—and in this town of ordinary restaurants, it well might—drive west on the main street to **Chez Bernard,** 411 rue Principale (© 450/240-0000). Inside the pretty little house behind the iron fence, you'll find a store selling fragrant cheeses, crusty breads, wines, savory tarts, pâtés, sausages, smoked meats, and a variety of prepared meals. There are three small tables. Prices range from C$4 to C$15 (US$3.50–US$14/£1.70–£6.45). The store opens daily at 10am.

Le Petit Clocher At the end of a residential cul-de-sac at the top of a hill, tucked in the woods and looking out to the ski mountains in the distance, this converted monastery is an intriguing new B&B. The decor is a riot of styles: English country-cottage braided rugs and wood roosters meet medieval tapestries and knights' armor. Each room has a French-Catholic theme (La Chapelle, La Divine), with La Cardinale featuring a red double whirlpool in the bedroom corner. In the winter, the antique piano in the main room is covered entirely with miniature houses to make a multi-leveled village tableau. Six of the seven rooms look out at the mountains beyond; the last room faces the woods where deer wander by. Have a light dinner to take full advantage of the opulent breakfast put on by the chatty owner: fresh croissants, French cheeses, asparagus quiche, warm grapefruit, maple water just tapped from the trees outside, and individual soufflés. This could be the best breakfast in all the Laurentians.

216 av. de l'Eglise, St-Sauveur, PQ J0R 1R7. ℂ 450/227-7576. Fax 450/227-6662. www.bbcanada.com/lepetit clocher. 7 units. C$185–C$215 (US$161–US$187/£80–£92) double. Rates include huge breakfast. Packages available. AE, MC, V. Take Exit 60 off Autoroute 15, turn left at the traffic light (364 West), right on Chemin de la Gare, right on rue Principale and left on av. de l'Eglise. Look for sign for after 1km and turn left up driveway. **Amenities:** Outdoor hot tub. In room: A/C, TV, Wi-Fi, Internet access, hair dryer.

Manoir Saint-Sauveur Just minutes off the autoroute and in the heart of the outlet shopping frenzy, this is one of the region's several large resort hotels. It has a monster outdoor pool and a comprehensive roster of four-season activities. A large on-site spa, **Le Spa du Manoir,** offers a broad range of body treatments and massage therapy. Rooms are spacious and comfortable, blandly modern with light-wood furnishings that hint vaguely of 19th-century Gallic inspirations. Units in the condo section have kitchenettes. The main building, with its green roof and many dormers, is easily spotted from the road. The front desk adjusts room prices up or down according to season, demand, and the occupancy rate on any given night, so ask if they have anything cheaper when you book or arrive.

246 Chemin du Lac Millette, St-Sauveur, PQ J0R 1R3. ℂ 800/361-0505 or 450/227-1811. Fax 450/227-0780. www.manoir-saint-sauveur.com. 242 units. C$149–C$269 (US$130–US$234/£64–£116) double. 2 children 17 and under stay free in parent's room. Children 6–12 eat for half price; children under 6 eat for free. Packages available. AE, MC, V. Take Exit 60 off Autoroute 15. **Amenities:** 2 restaurants (Continental and café); bar; large indoor and outdoor pools; golf nearby; substantial health club; spa; Jacuzzi; sauna; limited room service; babysitting; laundry service; same-day dry cleaning. In room: A/C, TV, Wi-Fi, Internet access, hair dryer, iron.

STE-ADELE & MONT-GABRIEL

In the winter, the ski mountain of Mont-Gabriel is a popular destination. To get there, follow Autoroute 15 to Exit 64 and turn right at the stop sign. In addition to offering downhill skiing, the mountain is wrapped in cross-country trails that range through the surrounding countryside.

The village adjacent, Ste-Adèle (pop. 10,662), only 67km (42 miles) north of Montréal, is a near-metropolis compared to the other Laurentian villages. What makes it seem big are its services: police, doctors, ambulances, a shopping center, cinemas, art galleries, and a larger collection of places to stay and dine. As rue Morin mounts the hill to Lac Rond, Ste-Adèle's resort lake, it's easy to see why the town is divided into a lower part *(en bas)* and an upper part *(en haut)*.

To get there, either take Route 117, which swings directly into its main street, boulevard Ste-Adèle, or get off Autoroute 15 at Exit 67.

EXPLORING STE-ADELE

The main street of Ste-Adèle, **rue Valiquette,** is a busy one-way thoroughfare lined with cafés, galleries, and bakeries, but **Lac Rond** is the center of activities during the summer. Canoes, sailboats, and *pédalos* (pedal-powered watercraft), which can be rented from several docks, glide over the placid surface, while swimmers splash and play near shoreside beaches. In winter, downhill ski equipment can be rented at **Le Chantecler** resort (see below), which has 25 trails.

WHERE TO STAY & DINE

Hôtel Le Chantecler ✦ *Value*   Sprawled across steep slopes cupping Lac Rond, this resort is comprised of two- and three-story stone buildings, their roofs bristling with steeples and dormers. It has 25 runs (17 lit at night) on four mountains for all levels of skiers, including a 190m (623-ft.) vertical drop, plus a ski school. Cross-country skiing and ice-skating are available. A chalet up top has a cafeteria and bar. There's a disco in the main lodge in winter and a vast dining terrace for sunset drinks and frequent barbecues. Warm weather brings the possibilities of windsurfing and boating on the lake, as well as rounds on two golf courses. Rooms renovated in 2006 have pine furniture; most have air-conditioning. Many rooms have whirlpools. A bountiful buffet breakfast is served in the glass-enclosed dining room, which overlooks the slopes and the lake, with its small beach. Regular upgrading takes care of most of the dings and dents that routinely afflict family resorts.

1474 Chemin Chantecler, Ste-Adèle, PQ J8B 1A2. © **888/916-1616.** Fax 450/229-5593. www.lechantecler.com. 215 units. From C$92 (US$80/£40) double. Rates include breakfast, taxes, and tips. Children under 18 stay free in parent's room. Packages and meal plans available. AE, DC, DISC, MC, V. Take Exit 67 off Autoroute 15, turn left at the 4th traffic light onto rue Morin, then turn right at the top of the hill onto Chemin Chantecler. **Amenities:** Restaurant (regional); bar; indoor pool; lake beach; 6 lit tennis courts; golf; racquetball and badminton; watersports equipment; bike rental; hiking trails; horseback riding; health club w/squash; whirlpool; saunas; limited room service; free Wi-Fi in lobby; babysitting; dry cleaning. *In room:* A/C (most rooms), TV w/pay movies, Wi-Fi, free high-speed Internet, coffeemaker, hair dryer, iron.

Hôtel Mont-Gabriel ✦ *Kids*   Perched high atop the ski mountain of Mont-Gabriel and looking like the rambling log "cottages" of the turn-of-the-20th-century wealthy, this desirable, kid-friendly resort is only 45 minutes from Montréal's Trudeau Airport. Set on a 480-hectare (1,186-acre) forest estate, the complex features golf and tennis programs in summer and ski and spa packages in winter. The spacious rooms in the Tyrol section are the most desirable and modern, many with views of the surrounding hills. All were renovated in 2006. Those called Rustique are constructed of logs and have views of either the pool or the mountains. The rooms in the Marquise section were scheduled to be updated in fall 2007. Some units have fireplaces and/or whirlpool tubs. The hotel is a ski-in–ski-out facility, with 18 ski runs all lit for night skiing. Dogsledding and snowmobiling are also available in season.

1699 Chemin Mont-Gabriel, Ste-Adèle, PQ J8B 1A5. © **800/668-5253** or 450/229-3547. Fax 450/229-7034. www. montgabriel.com. 128 units. From C$96 (US$84/£41) double. Meal plans and packages available. AE, MC, V. Take Exit 64 from Autoroute 15. **Amenities:** Restaurant (Continental); bar; heated indoor and outdoor pools; 18-hole golf course; 6 night-lit clay tennis courts; health club; spa; Jacuzzi; sauna; alpine skiing on-site, ice-skating, small business center; massage; babysitting. *In room:* A/C, TV, Wi-Fi, Internet, coffeemaker, hair dryer, iron.

L'Eau à la Bouche ✦   The owners leave no doubt where their priorities lie. While the hotel is entirely satisfactory, the restaurant is their beloved baby, and it has the glowing reviews to prove its prowess (the star up there is for the dining). False modesty isn't a factor—*l'eau à la bouche* means "mouthwatering"—and the kitchen mostly delivers. Native ingredients and ample portions are meshed with nouvelle presentations, and the menu changes often. Full advantage is taken of seasonal products, as with one summer starter of a poached half-lobster with chanterelles and gathered wild vegetables. Game dishes arrive in fall. Desserts are impressive, but the cheese plate—pungent nubbins delivered with warm baguette slices—is truly special. There are two meal options, and both are pricey: the C$150 (US$130/£65) Discovery Menu, and the C$67 (US$58/£29) table d'hôte, with extra charges for potatoes (C$6/US$5.20/£2.60) and vegetables (C$10/US$8.70/£4.30).

> **Tips Biker's Paradise: The New 4,000km *Route Verte***
>
> Québec is bike-crazy. In summer 2007, the Québec province officially inau-
> gurated the new *Route verte* **(Green Route),** a 4,000km (2,485-mile) bike
> network that stretches from one end to the other and links up all regions
> and cities. The idea started in 1995 and is modeled on the Rails-to-Trails pro-
> gram in the U.S. and cycling routes in Denmark, Great Britain, and along the
> Danube and Rhine rivers. It was initiated by the nonprofit biking organiza-
> tion **Vélo Québec** (www.velo.qc.ca) with support from the Québec Ministry
> of Transportation.
>
> Included in the network is the long-popular **P'tit Train du Nord bike trail**
> that goes north into the Laurentians to Mont-Tremblant and beyond. It's
> built on a former railway track and passes through the villages of Ste-Adèle,
> Val David, and Ste-Agathe-des-Monts. Cyclists can get food and bike repairs
> at renovated railway stations along the way and hop on for just a day trip
> or a longer tour. Access fees are C$5 (US$4.35/£2.15) a day for adults, C$3
> (US$2.60/£1.30) ages 6 to 17, and free for children under 6. Season passes
> are available.
>
> The *Route verte* website (www.routeverte.com) has maps of all the paths
> and links to bed-and-breakfasts, campsites, and hotels that are especially
> focused on serving bikers. Accredited accommodations have a **"Bienvenue
> cyclistes!" sticker** and provide a covered and locked place for overnight
> bicycle storage, access to high-carb meals with lots of fruits and veggies, a
> bike pump and tools, and information about where to make repairs nearby.
> *Cycling in Québec: Official Guide to Bicycling on Québec's Route Verte* is
> available from the site.
>
> Also look for the free *Official Tourist Guide to The Laurentians,* published
> by regional tourist office (www.laurentides.com). It has a 32-page section
> on biking. The company **Transport du parc linéaire** (𝄇 **888/686-1323** or 450/
> 569-5596; www.transportduparclineaire.com) provides baggage transport
> from inn to inn.

Bedrooms in the hotel have reproductions of Québec country furniture, and six
have fireplaces and balconies or patios. A spa with massage rooms and a pretty outdoor hot tub and small waterfall is new. Chef and owner Anne Desjardins has also
added a package that includes 2 days working alongside her in the kitchen.

3003 bd. Ste-Adèle (Rte. 117), Ste-Adèle, PQ J8B 2N6. 𝄇 **888/828-2991** or 450/229-2991. Fax 450/229-7573. www.
leaualabouche.com. 17 units. C$185–C$245 (US$161–US$213/£80–£105) double. Packages and meal plans available.
AE, DC, MC, V. **Amenities:** Restaurant (contemporary French); heated outdoor pool in summer; golf nearby; spa; limited room service; babysitting; laundry service; dry cleaning. *In room:* A/C, TV, Wi-Fi, Internet access, hair dryer, iron, safe.

STE-MARGUERITE
Ste-Marguerite (pop. 2,250) is alongside the large Lac Masson and home to **Bistro à
Champlain,** one of the prime restaurant destinations in the region. To get there, take
Exit 69 off of Autoroute 15. Or, if driving from Ste-Adèle, look for a street heading
northeast named Chemin Pierre-Péladeau (Rte. 370). It becomes a narrow road that

crosses the 30-foot-wide Rivière du Nord and then winds through evergreen forests past upscale vacation homes. The road dead-ends at the lake, with the restaurant at the intersection. Ste-Marguerite is 96km (60 miles) north of Montréal.

In summer, information about the area is available from **Pavillon du Parc,** at 74 Chemin Masson, in Ste-Marguerite-du-Lac-Masson (℃ **514/228-3525**). The pavilion is alongside Lac Masson and across from the restaurant.

The resort **L'Estérel** (℃ **888/378-3735** or 450/228-2571) is just 2 miles from the center of Ste-Marguerite, in the village of Estérel. It borders a lake that the hotel grooms into an 8km (nearly 5-mile) ice-skating rink and dogsled run in the winter.

WHERE TO DINE IN STE-MARGUERITE

Bistro à Champlain 𝄐𝄐 FRENCH   On the shore of Lac Masson is one of the most honored restaurants in the Laurentians. Its 1864 building used to be a general store, and it retains the exposed beams and cash register. Abstract paintings and prints, some of them by prominent artists, adorn the rough-hewn board walls. The 35,000-bottle cellar is the reason that many people make gastronomic pilgrimages here from Montréal. In fact, it can be fairly said that the tail wags the dog—this is a place to have some food with your wine. The wine list is as thick as the A-to-D volume of an encyclopedia (a PDF of all 162 pages is posted on the restaurant's website), and everyone is invited to visit the cellar. If you're feeling giddy, try a 2-ounce pour of Château d'Yquem with a serving of seared duck foie gras for C$79 (US$69/£34). Waiters are ready and equipped to discuss even the humblest bottles at length.

75 Chemin Masson, Ste-Marguerite-du-Lac-Masson. ℃ **450/228-4988.** www.bistroachamplain.com. Reservations recommended. Main courses C$19–C$44 (US$17–US$38/£8.15–£19); table d'hôte C$46 (US$40/£20); menu degustation C$82 (US$71/£35). AE, DC, MC, V. Summer daily from 6pm; fewer days the rest of year, so call to check.

VAL-DAVID

At Exit 76 of Autoroute 15 (and also along Route 117) is Val-David, the faintly bohemian enclave (pop. 3,800) of the area. At 80km (50 miles) north of Montréal, it conjures up images of cabin hideaways set among hills rearing above ponds and lakes, and creeks tumbling through fragrant forests.

The **tourist office** is on the main street at 2501 rue de l'Eglise (℃ **888/322-7030,** ext. 235 or 819/322-2900, ext. 235; www.valdavid.com). It's open June 20 to Labour Day daily 9am to 7pm, and September 5 to June 19 daily 10am to 4pm. Another possibility for assistance is **La Maison du Village,** a cultural center that mounts art exhibits in a two-story wooden building at 2495 rue de l'Eglise (℃ **819/322-7474**). It's right next door to the tourist office.

Note that this far north into the Laurentians, the telephone area code changes to 819.

EXPLORING VAL-DAVID

Val-David is small, so park anywhere and meander at leisure. There are many artist studios, and the village sponsors a huge **ceramic art festival** from mid-July to mid-August. Sculptors and ceramicists, along with painters, jewelers, pewter smiths, and other craftspeople display their work. There are concerts and other outdoor activities at the same time. See www.1001pots.com for information. Also look for the **organic farmer's market** every Saturday morning from late June to late September.

Val-David is one of the villages along the bike way called the **Parc Linéaire le P'Tit Train du Nord,** a former railroad right of way (see box, p. 180). Get picnic fixings at the Metro Supermarket across from the tourist office and turn left onto the bike path just around the corner from the tourist office. Walk 5 minutes to the North River in the **Parc des Amoureax.** There are plenty of benches, as well as some parking spaces if you drive. Watch for the sign SITE PITTORESQUE.

WHERE TO STAY & DINE

Edelweiss ⧉★   Business is good at this intimate hostelry hidden in the woods east of town, enough to underwrite the new building next to the original Tyrolean structure. That makes a total of 13 bedrooms that stay full of admirers of the inn's kitchen. Despite the Austro-Germanic appearance of the place, the Belgian chef and co-owner (his wife, the manager, is from Québec) draws from the French canon. His graceful touch is drawing more and more notice from serious eaters. Don't miss his foie gras terrine. Waterzooi (fish stew) and lamb are other specialties, with main courses from C$16 (US$14/£6.90) and a seven-course degustation menu for C$65 (US$57/£28). All of the rooms have gas fireplaces and Jacuzzis. Deer are kept in a pen behind the inn. Room prices include a five-course table d'hôte dinner and breakfast.

3050 Chemin Doncaster, Val-David, J0T 2N0. ℂ 866/355-7800 or 819/322-7800. Fax 819/322-1550. www.ar-edelweiss.com. 13 units. C$190–C$240 (US$165–US$209/£82–£103). Rates include table d'hôte dinner and breakfast. Packages available. AE, MC, V. From downtown, the main street becomes Chemin Doncaster; watch for hotel sign on left, at 2.8km (1¾ miles). **Amenities:** Restaurant (French); heated outdoor pool w/Jacuzzi; massage; free bikes. *In room:* TV, hair dryer.

STE-AGATHE-DES-MONTS

With a population of 9,024, Ste-Agathe-des-Monts, 103km (64 miles) north of Montréal, has surpassed St-Adele for the title of largest town in the Laurentians. It marks the end of Autoroute 15.

The town dock on the lake, Lac des Sables, and pretty surrounding **waterfront park** make Ste-Agathe a good place to pause. One possibility is to rent a bicycle from **Intersport Jacques Champoux,** 74 rue St-Vincent (ℂ 819/326-3480), for the 5km (3-mile) ride around the lake. Lake cruises, beaches, and watercraft rentals seduce many visitors into lingering for days.

Croisières Alouette (ℂ 819/326-3656; www.croisierealouette.com) offers cruises on the lake that depart from the dock at the foot of rue Principale from mid-May to mid-October. It's a 50-minute trip on a boat equipped with a bar. There is a running commentary on the sights that you'll observe, and a discussion of the water-ski competitions and windsurfing that Ste-Agathe and the Lac des Sables are famous for. The cost for the Alouette cruise is C$12 (US$10/£5.15) for adults, C$10 (US$8.70/£4.30) for seniors and students, and C$5 (US$4.35/£2.15) for children 6 to 15. Children under 6 go free.

VILLE DE MONT-TREMBLANT

The Mont-Tremblant region is a kind of Aspen-meets-Disneyland. It's beautiful country, with good skiing in the winter, while a fast-growing resort village on the slope makes the area a destination in all four seasons.

In 2005, the villages of St-Jovite and Mont-Tremblant and the pedestrian village at the mountain, which had all been independent, combined to become the single Ville de Mont-Tremblant. Most maps, hotels, restaurants, and residents, however, still refer to the areas as distinct "sectors," which can cause some confusion to first-time visitors.

To get there, follow Route 117 about 37km (23 miles) north from Ste-Agathe to the St-Jovite exit. That's 122km (76 miles) north of Montréal. To get to Mont-Tremblant mountain from St-Jovite, turn right on Route 327 just before the church. Most vacationers make their base at one of the resorts or lodges at the mountain or on or near Route 327. Mont-Tremblant is 130km (81 miles) north of Montréal.

To get directly to the mountain from Route 117, drive 5km (3 miles) north of the St-Jovite exit and take Montée Ryan. Follow the blue signs for 10km (6¼ miles). Also look for signs with the resort's logo, which turns the "A" in "Tremblant" into a kind of ski mountain.

A few more words of clarification about the abundant use of the name Tremblant. There is Mont-Tremblant, the mountain. At the base of its slope is Tremblant, the growing resort village described below (it's sometimes called Mont-Tremblant Station). Just adjacent is Lac (Lake) Tremblant. And there is the small former village of Mont-Tremblant, known as the old village, about 5km (3 miles) northwest of the resort. Clear as mud?

In any case, **St-Jovite,** about 12km (7½ miles) south of the mountain, is the district's commercial center. A pleasant community, it provides most of the expected services. The small-town main street, **rue Ouimet,** is lined with cafés and shops, including **Le Coq Rouge,** which sells folk art and country antiques.

Tourist information, including maps of local ski trails, is available at the **Tourisme de Mont-Tremblant,** 5080 Montée Ryan (© **877/425-2434** or 819/425-2434), open daily 9am to 5pm; and **Tourisme de Saint-Jovite/Mont-Tremblant,** 48 Chemin de Brébeuf (© **819/425-3300**), also open daily 9am to 5pm. You can also log on to www.tourismemonttremblant.com.

SKIING, WATERSPORTS & MORE

Mont-Tremblant, the mountain, is the highest peak in the Laurentians at 875m (2,871 ft.). In 1894, the provincial government began setting aside land for a "government forest preserve," establishing **Parc Mont-Tremblant.** The foresight of this early conservation effort has afforded outdoor enjoyment to hikers, skiers, and four-season vacationers ever since: The park is the largest in the province, at 1,510 sq. km (583 sq. miles). It has 400 lakes and 6 rivers in its boundaries, along with 196 bird species and a forest primarily of sugar maple and yellow birch as far as the eye can see. The mountain's name comes from a legend of the area's first inhabitants: Amerindians named the peak after the god Manitou, and say that when humans disturbed nature in any way, Manitou became enraged and made the great mountain tremble—*montagne tremblante.*

The **Mont-Tremblant ski resort** (www.tremblant.ca) draws the biggest downhill crowds in the Laurentians, and is repeatedly voted the top resort in eastern North America by *Ski Magazine.* Founded in 1939 by the Philadelphia millionaire Joe Ryan, it's one of the oldest in North America. It pioneered creating trails on both sides of a mountain and was the second mountain in the world to install a chairlift. The vertical drop is 650m (2,133 ft.). When the snow is deep, skiers here like to follow the sun around the mountain, making the run down slopes with an eastern exposure in the morning and down the western-facing ones in the afternoon. There are higher mountains with longer runs and steeper pitches, but something about Mont-Tremblant compels people to return time and again.

Today the resort has snowmaking capability to cover 253 hectares (625 acres). Of the 94 total downhill runs and trails, half are expert terrain, about a third are intermediate, and the rest beginner. The longest trail, Nansen, is 6km (almost 4 miles). There is plenty of cross-country action on maintained trails and another 112km (70 miles) of ungroomed trails in the adjacent national park.

Watersports in summer are almost as popular as the ski slopes and trails in winter, because the base of Mont-Tremblant is surrounded by opportunities. They include Lac Tremblant, a gorgeous stretch of lake, and another dozen lakes, as well as rivers and streams. From June to October, **Croisières Mont-Tremblant,** 2810 Chemin du village (© **819/425-1045;** www.croisierestremblant.com), offers a 70-minute narrated cruise of Lac Tremblant, focusing on its history, nature, and legends. Fares are C$15 (US$13/£6.45) for adults, C$12 (US$10/£5.15) for seniors, C$6 (US$5.20/£2.60) for children ages 6 to 15, and free for children under 6.

Other summer options include golf at the renowned **Le Diable** and **Le Géant** courses, tennis, boating, swimming, biking, and hiking. Right at the pedestrian village, the **Tremblant Film Festival** takes place for 5 days in June.

A new summer diversion is the downhill **dry-land luge run** right at the pedestrian village. The engineless sleds are gravity-propelled, reaching speeds of up to 30 mph (48kmph) if you choose. Rides cost C$10 (US$8.70/£4.30). The resort has other games and diversions right in the village to keep occupied for days.

One unusual activity is the opportunity to participate in a real cattle roundup. The adventure lasts 5 hours and takes place at the **Ranch Mont-Tremblant,** 40 minutes from the mountain. Cost is C$120 (US$104/£52) and young teens and adults love it. Call © **819/681-4848.**

WHERE TO STAY

There are abundant options for housing in the area. In addition to the listings below, bed-and-breakfast lodgings are listed at www.bbtremblant.com. For camping options within **Parc national du Mont-Tremblant,** visit www.parcsquebec.com. Also see the sidebar "Soaring Through Mont-Tremblant's Pedestrian Village," p. 188.

Of the accommodations listed below, these are in or just adjacent to the pedestrian village: Ermitage du Lac, Fairmont Mont Tremblant, Homewood Suites by Hilton, Le Westin Resort Tremblant, and Quintessence.

Of the accommodations listed below, these are in the old village: Auberge La Porte Rouge and Hôtel Mont-Tremblant.

And of the accommodations listed below, these are a short driving distance from both the pedestrian village and old village: Château Beauvallon, Gray Rocks, Hôtel du Lac, Le Grand Lodge, and Wyndam Cap Tremblant.

Auberge La Porte Rouge *(Value* This unusual motel is located in the old village of Mont-Tremblant. Wake to a view of Lake Mercier through the picture window (every unit has one), or gaze at the lake from your little balcony. Some rooms have both fireplaces and whirlpool tubs. Later in the day, take lunch on the terrace facing the lake or wind down in the cocktail lounge. Deluxe rooms accommodate two to three people, while the cottages have room for 10 people. The dining room serves two meals a day. Rowboats, canoes, and pedal boats are available, and the motel is directly on the regional bike and cross-country ski linear park, Le P'tit Train du Nord. The motel is run by a third-generation owner. Rates include dinner and breakfast.

1874 Chemin du Village, Mont-Tremblant. J8E 1K4. © **800/665-3505** or 819/425-3505. Fax 819/425-6700. www.aubergelaporterouge.com. 26 units. C$138–C$234 (US$120–US$204/£59–£101) double. Rates include dinner and breakfast. Packages available. MC, V. **Amenities:** Restaurant (European); heated outdoor pool; watersports equipment; bike rental. *In room:* A/C, TV, free Wi-Fi, coffeemaker, iron (on request).

Château Beauvallon *★ Kids* Open since December 2005, this 70-suite three-story property has positioned itself as an affordable luxury retreat for seasoned travelers.

Croissant-shaped around a pool and year-round outdoor hot tub, this newest member of the region's high-end resorts has a relaxed elegance that caters to both couples and families or groups of friends. Every suite has two bathrooms, a gas fireplace, a small bedroom with a plush California king-size bed, a queen-size Murphy bed and a pullout couch, a patio, a 32-inch high-definition flatscreen TV (with a smaller flatscreen TV in the bedroom), and a fully equipped kitchenette. A large central lounge with fireplace provides a warm gathering place. Beauvallon is located directly at the famed Le Diable golf course, and is a member of the "Small Luxury Hotels of the World" group.

6385 Montée Ryan, Mont-Tremblant, PQ J8E 1S5. ℂ 888/245-4030 or 819/681-6611. Fax 819/681-6499. www.chateaubeauvallon.com. 70 units. C$179–C$329 (US$156–US$286/£77–£141) suite. Packages available. AE, DC, MC, V. Free valet parking and self-parking. **Amenities:** Restaurant (international); bar; 2 pools (outdoor heated pool with terrace, indoor heated); golf adjacent; small exercise room; all-year outdoor hot tub; concierge; 24-hr. room service; in-room massage; babysitting; same-day laundry service; same-day dry cleaning. *In room:* A/C, TV, free Wi-Fi, kitchenette, hair dryer, safe.

Ermitage du Lac 🌟🌟 *Kids*   Find this recent entry in the pedestrian resort's lodging-go-round slightly to the right and behind the 19th-century church located at the main entrance. It's just the place for families on long vacations, with all of its units large studios or one- to three-bedroom suites, and its locale directly next to Parc Plage, the beach on Lac Tremblant. Fireplaces and balconies are standard, as are kitchens fully equipped with oven-ranges, microwaves, unstocked fridges, and necessary cookware and crockery (only some have dishwashers, though). There is a secure underground parking garage, which is free.

150 Chemin du Curé-Deslauriers, Mont-Tremblant, PQ J8E 1C9. ℂ 800/461-8711 or 819/681-2222. Fax 819/681-2223. www.tremblant.ca. 67 units. From C$155 (US$135/£67) double. Rates include breakfast. AE, MC, V. **Amenities:** 4 restaurants (2 French, Japanese, bistro); outdoor pool and hot tub in summer; exercise room; concierge; business center; laundry facilities; dry cleaning. *In room:* A/C, TV w/pay movies, Wi-Fi, free high-speed Internet, kitchen, coffeemaker, hair dryer, iron.

Fairmont Mont Tremblant 🌟🌟   This 1996 luxury lodging stands on a crest above the village, as befits its stature among the Tremblant hostelries. Although young compared with the Fairmont chain's Château Frontenac in Québec City and Le Reine Elizabeth in Montréal, it hews closely to the high standards of its siblings across Canada. Inside the plain exterior, the enlarged lobby area has a north-woods look, with a wood-burning fireplace and antiques and folk art prominent in public areas. Guests use the outdoor pool right through the winter, and they can ski out and ski in to the hotel, which is close to the bottom of the chairlift. Even visitors staying elsewhere in the resort troop past the tantalizing buffet lines of in-house restaurant **Windigo** for nightly dinner. The concierge can arrange bike, blade, and ATV rentals, as well as golf, tennis, fishing, tubing, and horseback rides.

3045 Chemin de la Chapelle, Mont-Tremblant, PQ J8E 1B1. ℂ 800/441-1414 or 819/681-7000. Fax 819/681-7099. www.fairmont.com. 314 units. From C$199 (US$173/£86) double. Packages available. AE, DC, DISC, MC, V. Pets accepted. **Amenities:** Restaurant (international); café; bar; indoor lap pool and heated outdoor pools; health club; spa; concierge; business center; shopping arcade; limited room service; babysitting; laundry service; same-day dry cleaning. *In room:* A/C, TV w/in-house movies and video games, high-speed Internet, minibar, coffeemaker, hair dryer, iron, safe.

Gray Rocks 🌟 *Kids*   Having celebrated its 100th anniversary in 2006, the area's dowager resort continues to hold its charm. Rooms are in a huge rambling main building, while condo units—which feature full kitchens, air-conditioning, and washers and dryers—are in a forested village across the lake, a short walk from the lodge. The family-friendly resort covers most of the recreational bases, including, for summer, an exceptionally large number of tennis courts (22), junior and adult tennis schools, two 18-hole golf courses, horseback riding at its own stables, boating, movies, live entertainment, and an outdoor barbecue along the lake. In winter, it has its *own mountain*, with 22 trails, 4 lifts, and a ski school. The on-site **Oceano Spa** was added in 2005. In the summer there's a supervised kids club for younger children and teens Monday through Friday with kayaking, riding, crafts, and scavenger hunts. Also in the warm months, the lounge has a piano and entertainment.

2322 rue Labelle, Mont-Tremblant, PQ J8E 1T8. ℂ **800/567-6767** or 819/425-2771. Fax 819/425-9156. www.gray rocks.com. 161 units, including 56 condos. C$230–C$370 (US$200–US$322/£99–£159) double; from C$165 (US$144/£71) condo. Dinner and breakfast for 2 is included in room rate, but not in condo rate. Children 5 and under eat for free. Packages available. AE, DISC, MC, V. **Amenities:** Restaurant (Continental); bar; large indoor pool; 36 holes of golf; 22 tennis courts; on-site ski mountain; health club; spa; sauna; watersports equipment; business center; babysitting; coin-op laundry; laundry service; dry cleaning. *In room:* A/C, TV, coffeemaker, hair dryer.

Homewood Suites by Hilton   Taking up the interiors of several buildings meant to look like separate candy-colored row houses, the most desirable rooms are those that overlook the Place St-Bernard, the central gathering space of the pedestrian village: Many of the resort's restaurants and shops form the perimeter of the plaza. All accommodations are crisply furnished suites, with fireplaces and equipped kitchens. Ski lockers are available to guests, who have ready access to the slopes.

3035 Chemin de la Chapelle, Mont-Tremblant, PQ J8E 1E1. ℂ **888/288-2988** or 819/681-0808. Fax 819/681-0331. www.homewoodsuites.hilton.com. 103 units. C$159–C$595 (US$138–US$518/£68–£256) suite. Rates include breakfast and afternoon snack (Mon–Thurs). AE, DC, DISC, MC, V. **Amenities:** Restaurant (buffet); ski-in-ski-out; access to health club; babysitting; coin-op laundry facilities; same-day dry cleaning. *In room:* A/C, TV, Internet access, kitchen, fridge, coffeemaker, hair dryer, iron.

Hôtel du Lac 𝕂𝕂 *Kids*   Terraced into a hillside sloping steeply to the shore of Lac Tremblant a few miles outside the resort village hubbub, this attractive property first developed nearly 100 years ago now consists of several lodges in muted alpine style. Essentially a concentration of privately owned apartments operated by a single management, the accommodations represent excellent value and that greatest of luxuries: space. Most of the rental units are suites of one or two bedrooms, which go for prices about equivalent to a single room at many other resorts in the region. A typical suite has a fireplace, balcony, sitting room with TV and a dining table, full kitchen with cookware and dishwasher, and two bathrooms. (In 2005, 25 units were renovated, so ask for one of them.) Nearly all accommodations have views of the lake and the slopes of Mont-Tremblant, which rises from the opposite shore. This is a family resort, with a for-fee day camp in the summer, so expect childish squeals in the dining rooms in peak months—July, August, February, and March. During ski season, a free bus shuttles between the lodge and the slopes; during summer, there is dancing Saturday nights.

121 rue Cuttle, Mont-Tremblant, PQ J8E 1B9. ℂ **800/567-8341** or 819/425-2731. Fax 819/425-5617. www.club tremblant.com. 122 units. C$199–C$239 (US$173–US$208/£86–£103) suite. Packages available. AE, DC, MC, V. Take Lac Tremblant North and follow signs for less than a mile. **Amenities:** 3 restaurants (French, Continental, bistro); heated indoor and outdoor pools; 3 tennis courts; health club; spa with massage; watersports equipment; children's playground and day camp in summer; babysitting; boutique. *In room:* A/C, TV, Internet access, kitchen, fridge, coffeemaker, hair dryer, iron, washing machine.

Hôtel Mont-Tremblant *Value*   This modest hotel down the block from the Auberge La Porte Rouge (see above) is in the former village of Mont-Tremblant. It's popular both with skiers who want to avoid the resort village's higher prices (there's a shuttle bus stop to the mountain across the street) and, in summer, with cyclists who like the location directly on Le P'tit Train du Nord cycling path (see "Biker's Paradise: The New 4,000km *Route Verte*," p. 180). Rooms all have private bathrooms, most have twin or double beds, and a few have sitting areas. What's more, this 1902 inn houses the popular restaurant **Le Bernardin**, which has a covered front terrace. All meals are served, with dinner main courses from C$15 to C$35 (US$13–US$30/£6.45–£15). Room prices include dinner and breakfast for two.

1900 Chemin du Village, Mont-Tremblant, PQ J8E 1K4. ℭ **888/887-1111** or 819/425-3232. Fax 819/425-9755. www.hotelmonttremblant.com. 25 units. C$140–C$190 (US$122–US$165/£60–£82) double. Rates include dinner and breakfast. MC, V. **Amenities:** Restaurant (Mediterranean); bar; beach nearby; bike storage. *In room:* A/C, TV, hair dryer.

Le Grand Lodge ⭑⭑

Replacing the old Villa Bellevue on the bank of Lake Ouimet, this handsome all-suites hotel was built with the palatial log construction of the north country. The atmosphere is adult and sophisticated. The suites leave little to be desired—all come with full kitchens, fireplaces, and balconies—and they haven't yet had the battering of many ski seasons. Dog-sledding directly from the hotel, snow-shoeing, and snowmobiling flesh out the more obvious winter skiing pursuits, and in the summer, there is horseback riding and canoeing and kayaking on the lake. With lodgings this comfortable, though, you might pass much of the time with a bottle of wine in front of the fire. This is a highly desirable addition to Mont-Tremblant's housing stock, at a quiet distance from the frequent clamor of the main resort. Like it enough and you can buy one of the condos in the complex.

2396 rue Labelle (Rte. 327), Mont-Tremblant, PQ J8E 1T8. ℭ **800/567-6763** or 819/425-2734. Fax 819/425-9725. www.legrandlodge.com. 112 units (101 suites, 11 studios with 2 queen-size beds). C$120–C$640 (US$104–US$557/£52–£275) suite; C$100–C$380 (US$87–US$331/£43–£163) studio. Children 17 and under stay free in parent's room; children 5 and under eat free. Packages available. AE, DC, MC, V. Small pets accepted. **Amenities:** Restaurant (international); bar; large heated indoor pool; private lake beach; 4 tennis courts; spa; exercise room; sauna; watersports equipment; children's playground; concierge; limited room service; in-room massage; babysitting; coin-op laundry; dry cleaning. *In room:* A/C, TV w/pay movies, free Wi-Fi, kitchen, fridge, coffeemaker, hair dryer, iron.

Le Westin Resort Tremblant ⭑⭑⭑

Easily one of the most attractive hotels in the pedestrian resort, this turn-of-this-century addition competes for king of the hill. Restrained, elegant corporate decor in rich blues and reds prevails, applied to rooms that have every convenience you might expect and some you might not. In the latter category are gas fireplaces, wet bars, in-room video games, Internet access through the television, and what the hotel calls its Heavenly Bed, featuring an exclusive 10-layer mattress. All units have at least small kitchenettes with microwaves, toasters, fridges, and enough plates and flatware for four. Many have balconies. The outdoor pool, ringed by the hotel, is open all year.

100 Chemin de Kandahar, Mont-Tremblant, PQ J8E 1E2. ℭ **800/461-8711** or 819/681-8000. Fax 819/681-8001. www.westin.com/tremblant. 126 units. From C$179 (US$156/£77) double. Packages available. AE, DC, MC, V. **Amenities:** 2 restaurants (Japanese, international); bar; heated outdoor pool w/whirlpool; bike rental; miniature golf; health club; spa; watersports equipment; children's programs; concierge; business center; 24-hr. room service; massage; laundry service; same-day dry cleaning. *In room:* A/C, TV w/pay movies and video games, Internet access, kitchen/kitchenette, fridge, coffeemaker, hair dryer, iron, safe.

Quintessence ⭑⭑⭑

Go in assuming that virtually every service you might find in a much larger deluxe hotel will be available to you . . . then concentrate on the extras. Check-in is in your room—make that "suite"—so you don't have to stand around at

Soaring Through Mont-Tremblant's Pedestrian Village

The pedestrian-only resort village on the slope of Mont-Tremblant is the social hub of winter tourism in the Laurentians. From the bottom of the village near the parking lots and bus shuttle, small lanes lead up past cute shops and more than three dozen restaurants and bars. Along the paths and spread off in all directions are hotels, the most prominent of which are described in this chapter.

The village has the prefabricated look of a theme park, but at least planners used the Québécois architectural style of pitched or mansard roofs in bright colors, not ersatz Tyrolean or Bavarian Alpine flourishes. For a sweeping view, take the free gondola from the bottom of the village to the top; it zips over the walkways, candy-colored hotels, and outdoor swimming pools.

In both winter and summer the village hosts outdoor concerts and barbecues and events like the goofy spring Caribou "Splash" Cup, where skiers dress in Halloween costumes, ski down an alpine trail into a pool of cold water, and then run through the village, stopping for shooters and a full glass of beer. Dude!

Few restaurants in the village rise above mediocrity and are fine for the après-ski thing or a casual evening, but take most serious meals off the premises.

The resort is owned by Intrawest, a real estate giant headquartered in Vancouver. It plans to add two additional villages, a conference center, and 1,200 housing units to the resort within the next 10 years.

Reservations for lodgings in the resort can be made by contacting the establishments directly or through a central number (© **888/738-1777** or 514/876-7273) or www.tremblant.ca. In addition to hotel rooms, there are options to rent fully equipped condos and single-family residences.

a reception desk. Discover the hugely comfortable bed with the 4-inch-thick feather mattress cover. Note that the bathroom floor is heated, that the jets in the tub are controlled by a remote, and that the shower is of the drenching rainforest variety. Maybe order a massage in your room, in front of a blazing wood-burning fireplace. Take in the view of the lake, and if it's warm, book a picnic and a ride on the hotel's gorgeous 1910 mahogany powerboat. Float in the outdoor infinity pool, followed by a steam and a sauna. Anticipate a lavish dinner with a goblet of wine from the 18m-long (60-ft.) wine cellar. There is a separate honeymoon cottage, although no sacrifice is made by booking one of the less expensive units.

3004 Chemin de la Chapelle, Mont-Tremblant, PQ J8E 1E1. © **866/425-3400** or 819/425-3400. Fax 819/425-3480. www.hotelquintessence.com. 30 units. Suites from C$299 (US$260/£129) and way up.. Packages available. AE, DC, MC, V. **Amenities:** Restaurant (contemporary French); bar; heated outdoor pool and hot tubs; health club; spa; massage; concierge; business center; 24-hr. room service; babysitting; laundry service; same-day dry cleaning. *In room:* A/C, TV w/pay movies, Wi-Fi, high-speed Internet access, CD player, minibar, hair dryer, iron, safe.

Wyndam Cap Tremblant   The Wyndham is a sprawl of condos, both residential and rental, built into a mountainside with terrific views of Mont-Tremblant, Lake

Mercier below, and distances far into the horizon; sunsets are striking. At press time there were 20 buildings, with a plan to build three to four new ones a year until they reach 40. That means that the rental units, all suites with one to five bedrooms, are likely to stay new and sleek and clean, as additional ones get built. It also means that the property will be in a state of constant construction, so be sure to ask for a unit not directly overlooking a hole in the ground. The suites are large and have all the amenities needed for an extended stay: a kitchen, a fireplace, a washer and dryer, a private balcony with a barbecue in summer, a locker for skis or golf clubs. The two outdoor pools include one with a long slide that's popular with kids, and there's an indoor virtual golf center. The resort's restaurant, **Il Pinnacolo,** is surprisingly good. A shuttle picks up every half-hour to take skiers or shoppers to the Mont Tremblant resort.

205-9, du Mont-Plaisant, Mont-Tremblant, QC J8E 1L2. (C) **888/425-3777** or 819/681-0990. Fax 819/681-0015. www.captremblant.com. 175 units. From C$159 (US$138/£68) suite. Packages available. AE, DC, MC, V. **Amenities:** Restaurant (international); bar; outdoor pools in summer; hot tubs; 3 tennis courts; exercise room; virtual golf room; concierge; business center. *In room:* A/C, TV/DVD, CD player, free Wi-Fi, kitchen, washer/dryer, hair dryer.

WHERE TO DINE

Although most Laurentian inns and resorts have their own dining facilities and often require that guests use them (especially in winter), Ville de Mont-Tremblant does have several decent independent dining options for casual lunches or the odd night out. Restaurants in the area open and close with irritating unpredictability, but the ones recommended below are among the more reliable.

Antipasto ITALIAN   Housed in an old train station moved to this site in downtown St-Jovite, there is the expected railroad memorabilia on the walls, but the owners have resisted the temptation to play up the theme aspect to excess. Captain's chairs are drawn up to big tables with green Formica tops. Almost everyone orders the César salad (their spelling), which is dense and strongly flavored—the half-portion is more than enough as a first course. Individual pizzas are cooked in brick ovens with an enormous range of toppings including scallops and crabmeat on a choice of regular or whole-wheat crust. Pastas are available in even greater variety; those with shellfish are among the winners. There are outdoor tables in summer.

855 rue de Saint-Jovite (in the St-Jovite sector). (C) **819/425-7580.** Main courses C$11–C$36 (US$9.55–US$31/ £4.75–£16). AE, MC, V. Daily 11am–10pm.

Aux Truffes *✮* FRENCH CONTEMPORARY   The management and kitchen here are more ambitious than just about any on the mountain, evidenced by a wine cellar that sails through Canadian, Californian, Argentine, Australian, Spanish, and many admirable French bottlings, up to a Château Latour '86 for C$900 (US$783/£387). (*Wine Spectator* magazine gave Aux Truffles its award of excellence for its wine list in 2006.) Put yourself in the hands of the knowledgeable wine steward and go from there. Meals proceed from a heartier-than-usual *amuse-bouche* to imaginative mains such as caribou chop marinated in black currant and cocoa, or roasted duck breast *magret* stuffed with foie gras and a black truffle sauce. Close with selections from the *plateau* of raw-milk Québec cheeses.

688 rue de Saint-Jovite (in the resort village). (C) **819/681-4544.** www.auxtruffes.com. Main courses C$29–C$46 (US$25–US$40/£12–£20). AE, MC, V. Daily 6–10pm.

Le Cheval de Jade FRENCH   Chef Oliver Tali is what is known in the culinary world as a "maître canardier," or master chef in the preparation of duck. In fact there is only one maître canardier in all of Canada recognized by France's *l'ordre des canardiers*, and he's the one. Normally that would mean that at this modest-looking roadside restaurant with a dozen tables and country decor at the end of Saint-Jovite's main street, there's really only one choice: the house specialty, "Caneton des Laurentides à la Rouennaise" (regional duckling). But surprise: the bouillabaisse and salmon tartar are also standouts. If you are interested in the duck, you have to call in advance and make a special reservation.

688 rue de Saint-Jovite (in the St-Jovite sector). ☎ 819/425-5233. www.chevaldejade.com. Reservations recommended. Main courses C$29–C$34 (US$25–US$30/£12–£15); table d'hôte from C$29 (US$25/£12); 7-course gastronomic menu C$173 (US$151/£74) for 2. AE, MC, V. Tues–Sat 5:30–10pm.

Patrick Bermand ☆ MEDITERRANEAN   If you cherish seafood and have been disappointed by the paucity of finned offerings by local restaurants, reserve for dinner here on Friday or Saturday night. Other nights you'll still find a marked improvement over other eateries in the lackluster Tremblant dining scene (the restaurant is also more likely to be open during slow off-season periods). Appetizers are especially satisfying and have included garlicky, buttery escargot served in individual ceramic pots and cool chunks of tuna rolled in black sesame seeds accompanied by cold sesame noodles. Main courses are good, too, but large—a lot of leftovers walk out the door. Opened in 2003 in a roadside log cabin–style house, the restaurant is in the former village of Mont-Tremblant, a short drive from the splashy pedestrian village.

2176 Chemin du Village (Rte. 327 in the old village). ☎ 819/425-6333. www.patrickbermand.com. Main courses C$26–C$43 (US$23–US$37/£11–£19). AE, MC, V. Daily 5–10pm; sometimes closed Mon in off season.

2 The Cantons-de-l'Est Region

20–160km (12–99 miles) SE of Montréal, toward Sherbrooke

The rolling countryside of Cantons-de-l'Est has long served as breadbasket to Montréal and the rest of the Québec province. Still referred to by some Anglophones as the Eastern Townships (and, less frequently, as Estrie), the region is largely pastoral, marked by billowing hills, small villages, a smattering of vineyards, and the 792m (2,598-ft.) peak of Mont-Orford, centerpiece of a provincial park. The southern edge of Cantons-de-l'Est borders Vermont, New Hampshire, and Maine, and just past the exit for Knowlton, at kilometer 100, there's an especially beguiling vista of the rolling Appalachian Mountains that stretches toward New England, not far over the horizon.

Serene glacial lakes attract summer swimmers, boaters, and fishing enthusiasts. Bicyclists zip along rural roads, passing day-trippers touring the region's wine and cider orchards. Except for a few disheartening signs for fast-food stops, the region is largely advertising-free. In the winter, skiers who don't head north to the Laurentians come this direction; the Ski Bromont ski center, just 45 minutes from Montréal, offers a full 50 illuminated trails for night skiing. Sherbrooke is the gritty, industrial capital at the center of the region, but the highlights noted below are located before you reach it, in an upside-down triangle approximately bordered by the villages of **Bromont** and **North Hatley** on the north (with 62km, or 38 miles, between them) and **Dunham** in the south.

Unlike the Laurentides, which becomes like a ghost-town in mud season, the Cantons-de-l'Est kick into another kind of gear when spring warmth thaws the ground, as crews penetrate every stand of sugar maples to tap the sap and "sugar off." The result is maple festivals and farms hosting sugaring parties, with guests wolfing down prodigious country repasts capped by traditional maple syrup desserts. Montréal newspapers and local tourist offices keep up-to-date lists of what's happening and where during the sugaring; most spots are within an hour's drive from the city.

Autumn has its special attractions, too, for in addition to the glorious fall foliage (usually best from early Sept to early Oct), the orchards of Cantons-de-l'Est sag under the weight of apples of every variety, and cider mills hum day and night to produce Québec's "wine." Particularly special are the ice cider aperitifs produced by vineyards such as Domaine Pinnacle from apples that have frosted over. Visitors are invited to help with the harvest, paying a low price to pick their own baskets of fruit. Cider mills open their doors for tours and tastings.

English town names such as Granby, Sutton, and Sherbrooke are vestiges of the time when Americans loyal to the Crown migrated here during and shortly after the Revolutionary War. Now, however, the Cantons-de-l'Est are about 90% French-speaking, with a name to reflect that demographic. A few words of French and a little sign language are sometimes necessary outside hotels and other tourist facilities, since the area draws fewer Anglophone visitors than do the Laurentides.

Best of all for tourists, the Cantons are one of Québec's best-kept secrets: It's mostly Québécois who occupy rental houses here. Follow their lead. For extended stays in the region, consider making your base in one of the several luxury inns along the shores of Lac Massawippi and take day trips from there.

ESSENTIALS
GETTING THERE
BY CAR   Leave Montréal by the Pont Champlain bridge, which funnels into arrow-straight Autoroute 10. Go east in the direction of Sherbrooke, and within a half-hour you'll be passing silos and fields, clusters of cows, and meadows strewn with wildflowers. Exits are numbered by how many kilometers you've traveled.

BY BUS   **Limocar** (which is actually a bus service) offers about 10 trips a day from Montréal through Cantons-de-l'Est as far as Sherbrooke. Most of the trips are express, with some making local stops at Granby, Bromont, in Magog. Call © **866/692-8899** or 514/842-2281 or visit www.limocar.ca for schedules and prices.

VISITOR INFORMATION
A **tourist information office** at Exit 68 off Autoroute 10 (© **866/472-6292** or 450/375-8774; fax 450/375-3530; www.granby-bromont.com) is open Monday through Friday 8:30am to 4:30pm and Saturday and Sunday 9am to 5pm (shorter hours in winter). You can also contact **Tourisme Cantons-de-l'Est,** 20 rue Don-Bosco sud, Sherbrooke, PQ J1L 1W4 (© **800/355-5755;** fax 819/566-4445; www.cantons delest.com) for more information.

Telephone area codes are 450 and 819, depending on the part of the region that you're calling. Towns with a 450 area code are closer to Montréal.

EXPLORING CANTONS DE L'EST
GRANBY
North of Autoroute 10 at Exit 68, about an hour out of Montréal, this largely mundane city (pop. 58,390) does have a few fun surprises.

First is the **Zoo de Granby,** 525 rue St-Hubert (© **877/472-6299** or 450/372-9113; www.zoodegranby.ca). Take Exit 68 or 74 off Autoroute 10 and follow the signs. New are a hippo's river, outside gorilla park, "Mayan Temple" with jaguars and spectacled bears, lemur's island, and tiger's habitat—which can be toured by elevated train. There is also a shark petting area (called a "touch tank" and overseen by an educator), an aviary with multicolored lorikeets, free bumper cars and Ferris wheel, and an attached water park with massive wave pool. Open daily June through early September, and weekends through early October, from 10am to 7pm in high season and until 5pm in shoulder periods. Admission is C$27 (US$23/£11) for 13 and older, C$21 (US$18/£8.80) for seniors, and C$17 (US$14/£7.10) for children 3 to 12, and includes entry to both the zoo and the water park.

Granby is also home to **Parc de la Yamaska** (© 800/665-6527; www.sepaq.com), with swimming on the longest beach in the area; watersports including kayaking, pedal boating, windsurfing, and canoeing. This is the northern part of the Appalachian mountain range, lush and verdant in the summer season.

BROMONT

Founded in 1964 primarily to accommodate an industrial park and other commercial enterprises, this town of 5,528 is now a popular destination for day and night skiing at **Ski Bromont** (www.skibromont.com) in the winter and mountain biking (rent bikes at the entrance to the town opposite the tourist office), hiking, and horseback riding in the warmer months. Shoppers have the area's largest **flea market** (*marché aux puces*) to take in, with more than 1,000 vendors set up in the local drive-in from 9am to 5pm weekends from April to October. There are several golf courses in the area, one of them associated with the resort described below.

Where to Stay & Dine

Château Bromont ℱ ⅋ℛⅈⅆℛ   A landscaped panoramic terrace looks up at the ski mountain across the way, giving this hotel a most attractive setting. The Château is one of a trio of properties built adjacent to the Royal Bromont golf course, making this a particularly choice spot for a golf getaway. Because the rooms all have Nintendo games and the hotel coordinates family packages with horseback riding or a day at the Granby Zoo, this is also a good choice for families. In addition to squash and racquetball courts, there's a European spa featuring mud and algae baths for those who just want to relax. About a third of the rooms have a fireplace. The interior decor gets a trifle gaudy here and there, but it's not jarring.

90 rue Stanstead, Bromont, PQ J2L 1K6. © 888/BROMONT or 450/534-3433. Fax 450/534-0514. www.chateau bromont.com. 152 units. From C$156 (US$136/£67) double. Rates include breakfast. Some dates require 2-night minimum stay. Children under 12 stay free in parent's room. Packages available. AE, DC, DISC, MC, V. **Amenities:** 2 restaurants; bar; heated indoor and outdoor pools; hot tubs; golf; racquetball court; spa; exercise room; massage; babysitting. *In room:* A/C, TV w/pay movies, Internet access, Nintendo, minibar, coffeemaker, iron, safe.

KNOWLTON

For a good confluence of countryside, cafés, and antiquing, head to the town of Knowlton, located at the southeast corner of Brome Lake and part of the seven-village municipality known as **Lac Brome** (pop. 5,078). Get there by taking Autoroute 10 to Exit 90 and heading south on Route 243 toward Lac Brome.

In the summer season, you can pick up maps at the **Lac Brome tourist center** on Route 243 shortly after you've left Autoroute 10. Knowlton is about 8km (5 miles) past the tourist center, and you'll hug the eastern side of the lake for most of the trip. (Be careful; bikers share the roads with nary a shoulder to fall back on.) There is a public parking area and **lake beach** (Plage Douglass) about 5km (3 miles) into the route, just before Knowlton. You can park to take a dip or do some or simple lakeside hiking.

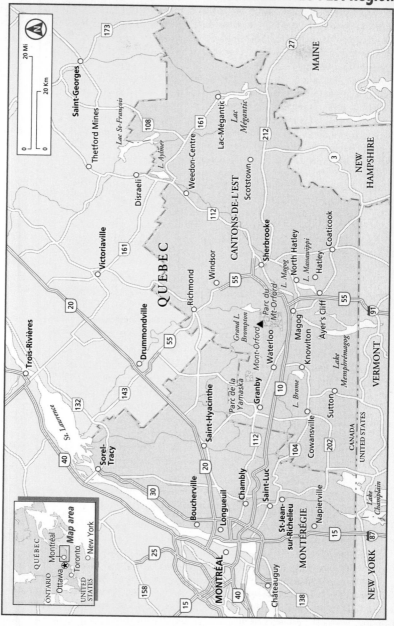

Knowlton is compact, but its two main shopping streets (Lakeside and Knowlton) have 35 boutiques and antiques stores that reveal a creeping chic influenced by refugees and day-trippers from Montréal. They sell toys, gourmet items, quilts, jewelry, pottery, gifts, and clothing. One shop sells outdoor gear and whimsically refers to itself as "L.L. Brome."

Knowlton is one of the last towns in the region where a slim majority of the residents have English as their mother tongue. Paul Holland Knowlton, a Loyalist from Vermont, settled here in the early 1800s, establishing a farm, general store, and sawmill. He was a Member of Parliament for Lower Canada from 1830 to 1834.

The major local sight is the **Musée Historique du Comté de Brome (Brome County Historical Museum)** at 130 rue Lakeside (Rte. 243) (© **450/243-6782**). It occupies five historic buildings, including the town's first school. Exhibits focus on various aspects of town life, with re-creations of a general store and courthouse. The Martin Annex (1921) is dominated by a 1917 Fokker single-seat biplane, the foremost German aircraft in World War I. Also on premises are collections of old radios and 18th- to early-20th-century weapons. The museum sells books about the area. Admission is C$5 (US$4.35/£2.15) adults, C$3 (US$2.60/£1.30) seniors, and C$2.50 (US$2.15/£1.10) children. It's open mid-May through mid-September Monday to Saturday 10am to 4:30pm, Sunday 11am to 4:30pm, and closed the rest of the year, and takes about an hour to tour.

For a quick snack, the funky, barn-like **Station Knowlton Country Store** at 7 Mount Echo Road (© **450/242-5862**) sells fruit smoothies and healthy sandwiches for under C$4 (US$3.50/£1.70). You can also buy a variety of handmade soaps and pick up free copies of the English language paper "The Outlet," whose tag line is "Linking the Eastern Townships' 41,000 English-speaking community."

Where to Stay & Dine

Auberge & Spa West Brome   Out in the country, beyond the town limits, drivers approaching this quiet property first notice the creamy yellow 1898 farmhouse at roadside. That's where reception and the restaurant are located. About 100 yards back are three gray modern structures where the bedrooms are located. A spa with therapeutic baths, massage rooms, pedicure chairs, and more was added in 2005. Rooms are in three categories: Classic, on the small side but not cramped; Deluxe, with full kitchens, fireplaces, and decks; and Suite, with or without whirlpool tubs. The suites can accommodate four. All beds are new, with feather mattresses.

Tips   **Biking the Cantons-de-l'Est: Easy On, Easy Off**

The Québec province's new *Route verte* (Green Route), a 4,000km (2,485-mile) bike network, stretches southeast into the Cantons-de-l'Est on a new 200km (124-mile) circuit called the *Véloroute des Cantons* (© **800/355-5755**).

Bikers can find information and maps of the route at www.cantonsdelest. com/velo. Included is where to find picnic areas, restaurants, and bathrooms near the trail; accommodations catering to cyclists; parking areas; and bike rental and repair shops. Day tripping is easy, but there are also all-inclusive 3- and 4-day bike tours for beginners and more advanced bikers. The tours are offered by the company **Ekilib** (© **888/713-3311**; www.ekilib.com) in partnership with Tourism Eastern Townships.

Finds   Cantons-de-l'Est: Wine (and *Cidre de Glace*) Country

Canada is generally known more for its beers and ales than its wines, but that hasn't stopped agriculturists from planting vines and transforming the fruit into drinkable clarets, chardonnays, and sauternes. So far, the most successful efforts have blossomed along the Niagara Frontier in southern Ontario and in the relatively warmer precincts of British Columbia.

The Cantons-de-l'Est enjoys the mildest microclimates in the province, and where apples grow, as they do in these parts, so will other fruits, including grapes. Most vintners and orchards are concentrated around **Dunham,** about 103km (64 miles) southeast of Montréal, with several vineyards along Route 202. A stop for a snack or a tour of facilities makes for a pleasant afternoon. If you're really gung-ho, you can follow the established *route des vins* wine route that passes a dozen area vintners (find the map at www.brome-missisquoi.ca).

Ice cider and ice wine are two regional products that may be new to visitors: They're beverages made from apples and grapes left on the trees and vines past the first frost, and served ice-cold with foie gras, cheeses, or dessert. One top producer is **Domaine Pinnacle,** at 150 Richford Rd. in Frelighsburg (© **450/298-1226;** www.icecider.com), just a few minutes from Dunham. Its *cidre de glace* is regularly a gold medalist in international competitions: It's delightfully smooth and not cloyingly sweet. Its tasting room and boutique are open daily from 10am to 5pm May through December.

The family-owned and -run **Les Blancs Coteaux,** at 1046 Rte. 202 in Dunham (© **450/295-3503;** www.blancscoteaux.com) serves picnic baskets and offers guided tours for C$5 (US$4.35/£2.15) per person for groups of four or more; call to make a reservation. The vineyard's shop sells its La Vieille Grange red wine, Seyval Blanc white, apple liqueur, and *cidre de glace.*

The most credible wines in the region come out of **Le Cep d'Argent,** at 1257 Chemin de la Rivière in Magog (© **819/864-4441;** www.cepdargent. com). The partners here produce several wines including prizewinners Le Cep d'Argent dry white and Le Délice du Chai, made from maréchal Foch and de Chaunac grapes. They offer several tour options, including a "privilege tour" of the champagne cellar that gets into the *méthode champenoise* and includes tastings of six wines with regional products. Cost is C$15 (US$13/£6.45) for the 90-minute exploration. Reservations are required.

128 Rte. 139, West Brome, PQ J0E 2P0. © **888/902-7663.** Fax 450/266-2040. www.aubergewestbrome.ca. 25 units. C$145–C$195 (US$126–US$170/£62–£84) double; suites from C$195. Rates include breakfast. Packages available. High-season weekends 2-night minimum stay. AE, MC, V. **Amenities:** Restaurant (regional); bar; heated outdoor pool and hot tub; fitness room; spa. *In room:* A/C, TV, Internet, coffeemaker, coffeemaker, hair dryer.

Auberge Lakeview   The core structure of this Victorian inn dates from 1874, and a 19th-century flavor has been sustained through many renovations. Leather chairs are arranged around the fireplace in the lobby, tin ceilings prevail, and Spencer's, the brass-and-mahogany pub that is a replica of the London original, is a cozy spot to settle in for an evening. If you're lucky, you'll be there on the occasional night when there's dancing to live music. The bedrooms come in four categories of relative comfort—go for the best ("deluxe studio") and get two robes, a sitting area, access to the veranda, and a heart-shaped whirlpool bathtub. Much of the furniture is crafted in Québec country style. Since rates include dinner, this is the place to sample the area's important gourmet treat, Lake Brome duck. Make sure to try the duck wings served as a bar snack.

50 rue Victoria, Knowlton (Lac Brome), PQ J0E 1V0. (C) 800/661-6183 or 450/243-6183. Fax 450/243-0602. www.aubergelakeviewinn.com. 28 units. May–Dec C$312–C$462 (US$271–US$360/£134–£199) double; Nov–Apr C$272–C$400 (US$237–US$348/£117–£172) double. Rates include dinner, breakfast, and gratuities for 2. Packages available. AE, MC, V. 1 block south of the town hall. **Amenities:** Restaurant (Continental); bar; heated outdoor pool. *In room:* A/C, TV, Internet access, hair dryer.

MONT-ORFORD

Exit 115 north off Autoroute 10 leads into one of Québec's most popular provincial parks. From mid-September to mid-October, **Parc du Mont-Orford** blazes with autumn color. Visitors come to try the 18-hole golf course and 80km (50 miles) of short and long hiking trails in summer; in winter, they flock to the ski and snowboarding slopes or the network of cross-country ski and snowshoe trails.

Mont-Orford is a veteran **ski area** compared to Bromont (p. 192) and has long provided slopes of choice for the moneyed families of the Cantons-de-l'Est and Montréal in the snowy months. The resort is composed of contiguous Mont-Giroux, Mont-Desrochers, and Mont-Orford itself, the second-highest peak in Québec after Mont-Tremblant. Combined, they provide 4 faces with 7 lifts and 56 trails. Information is at (C) **866/673-6731** and www.orford.com.

The area's other ski resorts—**Owl's Head** ((C) **800/363-3342;** www.owlshead.com) and **Mont-Sutton** ((C) **450/538-2545;** www.montsutton.com)—are more family-oriented and less glitzy than Mont-Orford.

Orford has another claim to fame in the warm months in the **Centre d'Arts Orford,** 3165 Chemin du Parc ((C) **800/567-6155** or 819/843-3981; www.arts-orford.org), set on a 222-acre estate within the park and providing music classes for talented young musicians every summer. From late June to the middle of August, a series of classical and chamber music concerts is given in connection with **Festival Orford.** Prices are C$32 to C$35 (US$28–US$30/£14–£15) for professional concerts, C$5 (US$4.35/£2.15) for student ("rising star") performances. Concert and dinner packages are available. Guided tours for the "artistic path" garden walk featuring 20 sculptures by international artists cost C$5 (US$4.35/£2.15).

Where to Stay

Manoir des Sables ★★   This contemporary facility is one of the most complete resort hotels in the region, serving business groups, couples, families, golfers, skiers, skaters, fitness enthusiasts, tennis players, and kayakers. And, as the pitchmen say, that's not all! Add snowshoeing trails, snowmobiling, toboggan rides, and Saturday-night horse-drawn sleigh rides in the winter, and tube slides and fishing in the hotel's lake to the list of activities. An 18-hole expert golf course and 9-hole par-3 executive course are both on-site, as is a spa offering algae wraps, "pressotherapy" detoxification, and more. Bedrooms have all the big-city gadgets and niceties, which is to be expected since the hotel began life as a Sheraton. Rooms have either one queen-size or two double beds, and about third have fireplaces. The new Château section contains 24 upscale suites and its own lounge.

Moments   Maple Heaven in *Cabanes à Sucre*

For a purely Québec experience that shouldn't be missed, get yourself to a sugar shack. Called *cabanes à sucre* or *érablières* in French, they were once places that merely processed sap from maple trees. Once producers realized that they were drawing large audiences, some began to offer wider experiences to keep the customers reaching for their wallets, putting in bars and dining rooms where bountiful spreads of simple country food are served at long communal tables. Some even put in dance floors and live entertainment. Originally open only during sugaring-off season, roughly February through April, a few now stay open much longer, even all year. There are hundreds across the province, with small directional signs often positioned at roadsides or on highways.

At most shacks you can see the rendering room, where sap gathered from taps in maple trees is boiled in a trough called the evaporator, and then cooked further on a stove. After that, the syrup is filtered and poured into cans or bottles.

Tastes are often offered by setting up a long narrow tray of snow and pouring a wiggly stream of syrup down the middle. This forms a sort of maple taffy, which is rolled up onto Popsicle sticks for lollipop-like eating.

At the restaurants, there usually isn't a menu. If there's not a buffet, just sit down at a table and food will start coming. Thick pea soup is standard, as are baked beans, loaves of fragrant bread, sausages, ham slices, home fries, coleslaw, and stacks of pancakes. At the ready are preserves, pickles, and all the maple syrup you can ingest. Total cost rarely exceeds C$25 (US$22/£11).

Signature products are available in a variety of sizes and forms, primarily syrup and candy. Some folks consider the best syrup to be the clearer and lighter Grade A from the first run of sap, while others prefer the darker and denser Grade B from later in the season.

90 av. des Jardins, Orford, PQ J1X 6M6. (C) **800/567-3514** or 819/847-4747. Fax 819/847-3519. www.manoirdes sables.com. 141 units. C$126–C$250 (US$110–US$217/£54–£107) double. Children under 17 stay free in parents' room. AE, DC, MC, V. Packages and meal plans available. Take Exit 118 from Autoroute 10 and follow Rte. 141 north to the hotel, on the right. **Amenities:** 2 restaurants (international); bar; indoor and outdoor pools; 27-hole golf course on property; tennis courts; health club; spa; bike rental; children's programs; game room; secretarial services; limited room service; babysitting; dry cleaning. *In room:* A/C, TV w/pay movies and Nintendo, free Wi-Fi, coffeemaker, hair dryer, iron.

MAGOG & LAC MEMPHREMAGOG

Orford is where people visit, but Magog (pop. 23,386) is where people live. As with countless other North American place names, Magog came by its handle through corruption of a Native Canadian word. The Abenaki name *Memrobagak* (Great Expanse of Water) somehow became Memphrémagog, which was eventually shortened to Magog (pronounced *May*-gog).

Confusingly, the town of Magog is *not* adjacent to Lac Magog, which is about 13km (8 miles) north of town. Instead, it's positioned at the northernmost end of the large, long Lac Memphrémagog (pronounced Mem-*phree*-may-gog), which spills across the U.S.-Canadian border into Vermont on its southern end.

The helpful **Bureau d'Information Touristique Memphrémagog,** at 55 rue Cabana (via Rte. 112), in Magog (© **800/267-2744** or 819/843-2744; www.tourisme-memphremagog.com), is open daily: 8:30am to 8pm in summer, and 9am to 5pm the rest of the year.

Magog has a fully utilized waterfront, and in late July to early August each year the **Lac Memphrémagog International Swimming Marathon** (© **818/847-3007;** www. traversee-memphremagog.com) creates a big splash. From 1979 to 2003, competitors would start out in Newport, Vermont, at 6am and swim 42km (26 miles) to Magog, arriving in midafternoon around 3:30 or 4pm. Since 2004, the event has become a 34km (21-mile) race, beginning and ending in Magog.

To experience the lake without such soggy exertion, take a 1¾-hour **lake cruise** aboard the 70-passenger *Aventure I* or 100-passenger *Aventure II* © **819/843-8068;** www.croisiere-memphremagog.com). A daylong cruise is also available. The boats leave from Point Merry Park, the focal point for many of the town's outdoor activities. Cruises off-season depend upon demand; call ahead for times and prices.

Several firms rent sailboats, motorboats, kayaks, and windsurfers, among them **Boutique Nautique 30 Degrés,** 201 rue Merry sud (© **819/843-2102;** www. 30degres.com) and **Marina Le Merry Club,** 201 rue Merry sud (© **819/843-2728;** www.lemerryclub.com.

Abbaye de Saint-Benoît-du-Lac   There's no mistaking the abbey, with its granite steeple that thrusts into the sky above Lac Memphrémagog and with Owl's Head Mountain in the background. Although Saint-Benoît-du-Lac dates only from 1912, the serenity of the site is timeless. Some 50 monks live here largely in silence, keeping the art of Gregorian chant alive in their liturgy, which can be attended by outsiders. For the 45-minute service, walk to the rear of the abbey and down the stairs; follow signs for the *oratoire* and sit in back to avoid the otherwise obligatory standing and sitting during the service.

A blue cheese known as L'Ermite, among Québec's most famous, is produced at the monastery, along with a creamy version and Swiss and cheddar types. They are on sale in a little shop, which also sells honey, books, tapes of religious chants, and a

---

(*Fun Fact* **Québec's Own Nessies?**

Lac Memphrémagog is known locally for more than just its annual international swimming marathon: Eagle eyes scan the ripples for Memphre (pronounced Mem-*phree*), the lake's legendary sea creature. Like the Loch Ness monster, which was first spotted in the Scottish waters in the year 565, Memphre supposedly surfaced for the first time in 1798 but left no hard evidence. Other sightings, it will come as no surprise, have been claimed since then.

Locals in North Hatley whisper about a creature of their own in Lake Massawippi, who they have dubbed Wippi. Like Loch Ness, Lake Massawippi has pockets that go very deep—up to 500 feet in some spots. Unlike Loch Ness, neither Memphrémagog nor Massawippi has been subjected to teams of scientists bouncing sonar signals to search out the water's depths. Memphre and Wippi, you are free to surface and retreat again in peace.

nonalcoholic cider produced from fruit of the orchard on the property. Visitors in the last 2 weeks of September or the first 2 weeks of October may want to help pick apples. And visitors will want to peek into the tiny stone chapel to the left at the entrance to the property, opposite the small cemetery.

The abbey maintains hostels (separate) for men and women (✆ **819/843-4080** for men, ✆ **819/843-2340** for women). Suggested price is C$40 (US$35/£17) per person for room and board; find out more at www.st-benoit-du-lac.com. Room reservations must be in advance by phone.

Saint-Benoît-du-Lac. ✆ **819/843-4080.** Free admission; donations accepted. Daily 5am–9pm; Mass with Gregorian chant daily at 11am; vespers with Gregorian chant at 5pm (7pm Thurs). No vespers Tues July–Aug. Shop: Mon–Sat 9–10:45am and 11:50am–4:30pm; from 1:15pm in the afternoons in winter and spring. Driving west from Magog on Rte. 112, watch for the 1st road on the left on the far side of the lake; take Chemin Bolton est 19km (12 miles) south to the turnoff to the abbey.

Where to Stay

Lodging choices in Magog aren't beguiling. However, if you must spend the night here, there are a number of modest B&Bs and small hotels located along the blocks of rue Merry, immediately north and south of its intersection with the main street, rue Principale. Otherwise, our recommendation is to look for accommodations in one of the nearby towns described in this section.

LAKE MASSAWIPPI

Set among rolling hills and fertile farm country, the 19km-long (12-mile) Lake Massawippi, with its scalloped shoreline, is easily the most desirable resort area in the Cantons-de-l'Est. It was settled in the late years of the 19th century by people of wealth and power, including many U.S. Southerners trying to escape the sultry summers of Virginia and Georgia (they came up by train and are said to have pulled down their window shades while they crossed through Yankee territory). They built grand estates with verandas and formal gardens on slopes along the lakeshore, with enough bedrooms to house their friends and extended families for months at a time. Several homes have been converted into inns, including the lavish **Manoir Hovey** (see below). For an escape from intensive travel or work, it's difficult to do better than here.

The jewel of Lake Massawippi (which means "deep water" in Abenaki) is the town of **North Hatley** (pop. 780). Only 148km (92 miles) from Montréal and just half an hour from the United States border, it has a river meandering through it that empties into the lake. Apart from impressive sunsets over the lake, the town has some very fine restaurants, access to 54km (33 miles) of good bike paths, and a summertime program of Sunday-afternoon public band concerts. A listing of activities is online at www.northhatley.net.

Horse lovers will want to know about **Randonnées J. Robidas** at 32 Chemin McFarland (✆ **888/677-8767** or 819/563-0166). Guides lead trail rides through forest and meadow beside the Massawippi in summer, with rates starting at C$37 (US$32/£16) for an hour and a half of group riding. Buggy and winter sleigh rides are possibilities as well, and there's a discovery farm and nature school on-site.

Where to Stay

The acclaimed gastronomic resort Auberge Hatley, a longtime Frommer's favorite, burned to the ground in early 2006. The Groupe Germain, which owned the property (along with the Dominion 1912 in Québec City and Hôtel Le Germain in Montréal) announced later that year that it will not be rebuilding. There are, however, over a dozen other lodging options, including the three listed here. These full-service inns won't refuse children, but they have serious dining rooms that can test youngsters' patience. Other meal arrangements should be made for children under 13.

Auberge Ripplecove & Spa 🅴🅴🅴   A warm welcome is extended by the staff of this handsome inn, and impeccable housekeeping standards are observed throughout. With 4.8 hectares (12 acres) directly on the southern end of Lake Massawippi, the hotel is a grand mini-resort, with private beachfront and equipment for sailing, sailboarding, water-skiing, canoeing, and kayaking. In the winter, there are cross-country skiing on the property and horse-drawn sleigh rides on Saturday afternoons. The core structure dates from 1945, but subsequent expansions have added well-appointed rooms, suites, cottages, and, in 2003, a spa with a full range of body therapies and 4-season outdoor hot tub overlooking the lake. Check out the elegant lobby lounge and its ornate 4.2m-high (14-ft.) breakfront built in 1880. About half the 35 rooms have gas fireplaces, private balconies, and whirlpools. The inn's award-winning lakeside restaurant fills up most nights in season with diners drawn to the kitchen's reputation for creativity. "Tuna steak with saffron risotto" or "Ducs de Montrichard duck confit with apple cider," anyone? Innkeeper Jeffrey Stafford is the brother Steve Stafford, owner of **Manoir Hovey,** below. Taste and energy run in the family, as does partnership: The properties offer a 4-night biking package to stay in and travel between the two inns.

700 Chemin Ripplecove, Ayer's Cliff, PQ J0B 1C0. 🅒 **800/668-4296** or 819/838-4296. Fax 819/838-5541. www.ripple cove.com. 35 units. June–Oct C$306–C$576 (US$266–US$501/£132–£248) double; Nov–May C$258–C$454 (US$224–US$395/£111–£195). Rates include dinner, breakfast, and gratuities for 2, and the use of most recreational facilities. AE, MC, V. Take Rte. 55 to Exit 21; follow Rte. 141 SE and watch for signs. **Amenities:** Restaurant (contemporary French); pub; heated outdoor pool; golf nearby; lit tennis court; exercise room; spa; free bikes; concierge; limited room service. *In room:* A/C, TV (most with cable), Internet access, coffeemaker, hair dryer, iron.

Le Tricorne   At the end of a long dirt and gravel road deep in the countryside, this family-run inn offers spectacular views of Lake Massawippi and the rolling Canadian Appalachians. While the core of the main house is 145 years old, it looks as if it could have been erected only a few years ago—the exterior is dusty rose and white, and the interior decked out in *Good Housekeeping* manner, with equestrian-print wallpaper and tartans. A newer building 45m (148 ft.) up the hill has five larger bedrooms decorated in a more sophisticated corporate style. With 92 acres of land, three small ponds, and a heated outdoor pool, this hotel offers the peace and quiet of being tucked away in the woods. No phones or TVs, but those are available in common rooms. Some of the units have wood fireplaces, and about half have jet bathtubs.

50 Chemin Gosselin, North Hatley, PQ J0B 2C0. 🅒 **819/842-4522.** Fax 819/842-2692. www.manoirletricorne.com. 17 units (some with shower only). Summer C$115–C$250 (US$100–US$217/£49–£107) double; winter C$95–C$195 (US$83–US$170/£41–£84) double. Rates include full breakfast. AE, MC, V. Take Rte. 108 W out of North Hatley and follow the signs. Children over 8 years are welcome. **Amenities:** Heated outdoor pool; golf nearby. *In room:* A/C, no phone.

Manoir Hovey 🅴🅴🅴   Built in 1898 by the owner of Georgia Pacific in Atlanta, this lakeside manor house, with its broad veranda and ivy-covered white pillars, was inspired by George Washington's home in Mount Vernon, Virginia. Aristocratic touches today include tea and scones in the afternoon, a carefully manicured English garden with fresh herbs and flowers used by the kitchen, and a massive stone hearth in a library lounge with deep chairs and sofas and floor-to-ceiling bookshelves bearing works from the original owner's collection. Manoir Hovey manages to create the magical balance of feeling like both a genteel, private estate for a private getaway and a grand resort for a weekend's pampering.

Sumptuously appointed rooms are ravishingly luxurious: Even the oldest units have been given recent touches like Italian bathroom tiles or antique sink basins, and all feature high-end bedding with goose-down duvets, plush robes, and CD players with classical discs. Each room is differently appointed and there are five price categories depending on view, size, and features; some mid-priced superior rooms, for instance, feature a fireplace and Jacuzzi. Dinner is included in the cost with a spectacular option of caribou with crystallized "foie gras taboulé" bits that melt when sprinkled onto the meat. Free touring bikes, two beaches, and the use of canoes, kayaks, and rowboats add to the appeal, and in winter you can take a turn at ice fishing.

575 Chemin Hovey, North Hatley, PQ J0B 2C0. ✆ **800/661-2421** or 819/842-2421. Fax 819/842-2248. www.manoir hovey.com. 39 units. June–Oct and Christmas C$300–C$580 (US$261–C$505/£129–£249) double; Nov–May C$260–C$470 (US$226–C$409/£112–£202) double; suites from C$265 (US$231/£114) per person. Rates include 3-course dinner, full breakfast, tax, gratuities, and use of most recreational facilities for 2. Packages available. AE, DC, MC, V. Take Exit 29 off Autoroute 55 and follow Rte. 108 E, watching for signs. **Amenities:** Restaurant (contemporary French); bar; heated outdoor pool; golf nearby; lit tennis court; free bikes; fitness room; concierge; limited room service; massage; dry cleaning. *In room:* A/C, TV, free Wi-Fi, coffeemaker, hair dryer, iron.

Where to Dine

Café Massawippi ⚜ FRENCH CONTEMPORARY   It took daring to open an ambitious restaurant in the same small town as the multi-starred inns described above, but chef-owner Dominic Tremblay has pulled it off. Contained in a small roadside house with a plain, unassuming interior hung with inept abstract paintings, the restaurant might inspire low expectations at first glance. The true art, though, appears on the plate. The declared house specialties—foie gras and venison tartare—might be bypassed, but how to choose between roasted salmon with wild mushroom crumble and white truffle oil, and rack of lamb glazed with rosemary honey and Yukon gold blinis? Appetizers are equally appealing, including prosciutto and roasted scallop with spicy guacamole and a mango and Tequila dressing. Although the menu is short (and changes frequently), you will be forgiven if you change your mind two or three times. All evening meals are served as six-course table d'hôte, and served leisurely over 2½ to 3 hours.

3050 Chemin Capelton. ✆ **819/842-4528**. www.cafemassawippi.com. Reservations recommended. Table d'hôte dinner C$40–C$54 (US$35–US$47/£17–£23). AE, DC, MC, V. Late May to early Oct daily 5:30–10pm; July–Aug daily 11:30am–3pm; rest of year Wed–Sun 6–10pm.

Pilsen Restaurant & Pub INTERNATIONAL   For food less grand and less expensive than that at the entries described above, check out Pilsen in the center of North Hatley. Housed in a former horse-carriage manufacturing shop from 1900, the restaurant has a narrow deck with tables overhanging the river that feeds the lake. The place fills up quickly on warm days, the better to watch boats setting out or returning. Patrons snaffle up renditions of quesadillas and burgers, pastas, and fried calamari, as well as more adventurous fare, such as the Ploughman's Platter with wild game terrine, St-Benoit-du-Lac blue cheese pâté, onion confit, and apples. There's an extensive choice of beers, including local microbrew Massawippi Blonde and the Czech Pilsner Urquel, for which Pilsen was named. Park behind the restaurant.

55 rue Principale. ✆ **819/842-2971**. Reservations recommended on weekends. Main courses C$10–C$29 (US$8.70–US$25/£4.30–£13); AE, MC, V. Daily 11:30am–10:30pm. The bar stays open well past midnight most nights.

STANSTEAD, ROCK ISLAND & BEEBE PLAIN

For a brief detour on the way south to Vermont, follow Route 143 as far as possible without actually crossing into the United States, and turn west to explore the three border villages that compose the town of Stanstead.

Stanstead (pop. 3,162) was settled in the 1790s and, as a border town, became a commercial center for the Québec-Boston stagecoach route. Many of the society homes from the late 1800s have been preserved. Fans of geographical oddities will love the **Haskell Opera House** (© **802/873-3022**). Dating from 1904, it's literally and logistically half Canadian and half American: The stage and performers are in Canada, and the audience is in the United States. There are still shows performed in the hall; call for the current schedule.

In 1995, Stanstead incorporated the village of **Rock Island,** which is the commercial center of the area. Also gathered into the township was **Beebe Plain,** west of Rock Island, a center for quarrying granite.

What makes Beebe Plain notable is 1km-long (⅔-mile) **Canusa Street.** The north side is in Canada, the south side in the United States—thus its name, CAN-USA. Check the car license plates on either side. Here, it's long distance to call a neighbor across the street, and, while folks are free to walk across the street for a visit, they are expected, at least technically, to report to the authorities if they decide to drive.

12

Getting to Know Québec City

Few municipalities are as breathtaking on approach as Québec City. Situated along the majestic St. Lawrence River, much of the oldest part of the city—Vieux-Québec—sits atop Cap Diamant, a rock bluff that once provided military defense. Fortress walls still encase the upper portion of the old city, and the soaring Château Frontenac, a hotel with castle-like turrets, dominates the landscape. Hauntingly evocative of a coastal town in the motherland of France, the tableau is as romantic as any in Europe.

Québec City is the soul of New France and holds that history dear. It was the first significant settlement in Canada, founded in 1608, 400 years ago, by Samuel de Champlain. Much of 2007 was spent sprucing up the city for its 400th-anniversary celebrations in 2008, adding more access to the waterfront and an entirely new pavilion called Espace 400^e that will open in spring 2008 and be the central location for celebrations throughout the year. After 2008, it will become a Parks Canada discovery center.

The city is almost entirely French in feeling, spirit, and language, and 95% of the population is Francophone, or French-speaking. But many people do know some English, especially those who work in hotels, restaurants, and shops, and thousands of resident college students study English as a second language. Although it is often more difficult in Québec City than in Montréal to get by without French, the average Québécois goes out of his or her way to communicate—in halting English, sign language, simplified French, or a combination of all three. Most of the Québécois are uncommonly gracious, even with the city being the capital of the politically prickly Québec province.

Because of its beauty, history, and unique stature as the only walled city north of Mexico, the historic district of Québec City was named a UNESCO World Heritage Site in 1985—the only area so designated in North America.

Ile d'Orléans, an agricultural and resort island within sight of Vieux-Québec, is less than a half-hour from downtown and an easy day- or overnight-trip. Consider, too, a trip along the northern coast of the St. Lawrence past the shrine of Ste-Anne-de-Beaupré, the waterfalls near Mont Ste-Anne, and on to pastoral Charlevoix and the Saguenay River, where whales come to play.

1 Orientation

Almost all of a visit to Québec City can be spent on foot in the old Lower Town—which hugs the river below the bluff—and in the old Upper Town—atop the Cap Diamant (Cape Diamond)—because many accommodations, restaurants, and tourist-oriented services are based there. The colonial city was first built right down by the St. Lawrence; it was here that the earliest merchants, traders, and boatmen earned their

Québec City Orientation

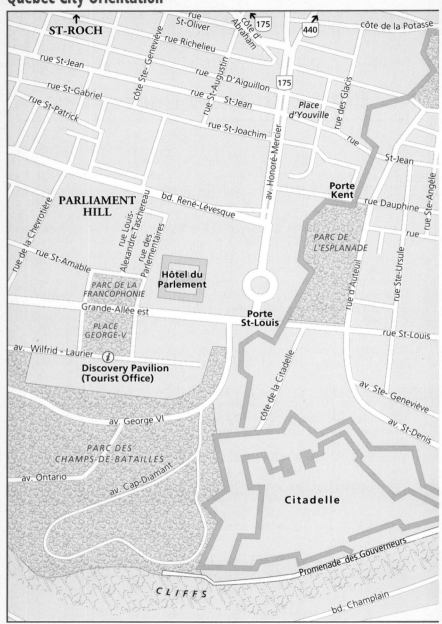

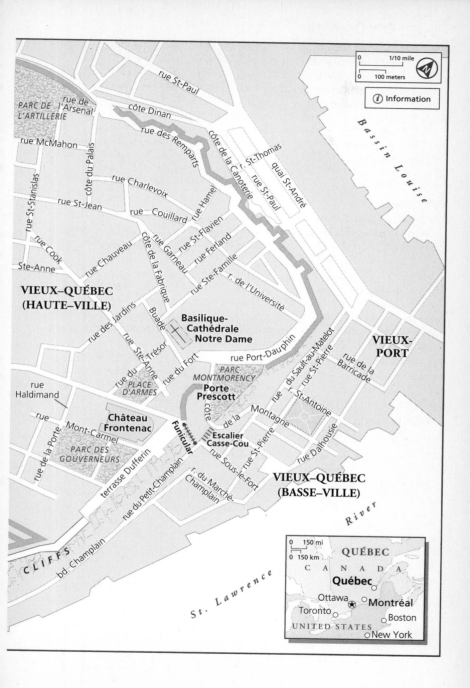

livelihoods. Unfriendly fire from the British and Amerindians in the 1700s moved residents to safer houses atop the cliffs that form the rim of the Cap.

Basse-Ville (Lower Town) became primarily a district of wharves and warehouses. That trend has been reversed, with new *auberges* (inns) and small hotels and many attractive bistros and shops bringing new life to the area. The area maintains the architectural feel of its origins, with narrow cobbled streets.

Haute-Ville (Upper Town) turned out to not be immune to cannon fire either, as the British General James Wolfe was to prove in 1759 when he took the city from the French. Nevertheless, the division into Upper and Lower Towns persisted for obvious topographical reasons. The Upper Town remains enclosed by fortification walls, with a cliff-side elevator *(funiculaire)* and several steep streets connecting it to Lower Town.

ARRIVING

BY PLANE   Jean-Lesage International Airport (airport code YQB; ✆ **418/640-2700;** www.aeroportdequebec.com) is small, despite the grand name. Bus service is no longer available between the airport and the city. A taxi to downtown Québec City is a fixed-rate C$30 (US$26/£13).

BY TRAIN   The handsome train station in Québec City, **Gare du Palais,** 450 rue de la Gare-du-Palais, was designed by Bruce Price, who is also responsible for the Château Frontenac. The Lower Town location isn't central, though, so plan on a strenuous uphill hike or a C$6-to-C$9 (US$5.20–US$7.85/£2.60–£3.85) cab ride to the Upper Town or other areas of the Lower Town. That's per trip, incidentally, not per passenger, as an occasional cabbie may pretend.

BY BUS   The bus terminal, at 320 rue Abraham-Martin (✆ **418/525-3000**), is just next to the train station. As from the train station, it is an uphill climb or quick cab ride to the Upper Town or other parts of the Lower Town. A taxi should cost about the same as from the train station.

BY CAR   For driving directions to Québec City, see "Getting There," in chapter 2.

VISITOR INFORMATION

The Greater Québec Area Tourism and Convention Bureau operates two useful provincial information centers in and near the city. The most convenient is in the Discovery Pavilion at 835 av. Wilfrid-Laurier (✆ **877/783-1608** or 418/641-6290), near La Citadelle, just outside the walls of the old city. There's another in suburban Ste-Foy, at 3300 av. des Hôtels (✆ **877/783-1608** or 418/641-6290). They have rack after rack of brochures and attendants who can answer questions and make hotel reservations. Both offices are open daily 8:30am to 7:30pm from June 24 to Labour Day; 8:30am to 6:30pm Labour Day to mid-October; the rest of the year 9am to 5pm Monday through Saturday, 10am to 4pm Sunday. The website for the bureau is www.quebecregion.com.

The Québec Government's tourism department operates a **Centre Infotouriste de Québec** on Place d'Armes, across from the Château Frontenac, at 12 rue Ste-Anne (✆ **877/266-5687;** www.bonjourquebec.com). It's open from 8:30am to 7:30pm daily from June 21 to early September, and from 9am to 5pm the rest of the year. The office has brochures, information about cruise and bus tour operators, a 24-hour ATM *(guichet automatique),* a currency-exchange office, and a free lodging reservation service. Also in front of the Château is the independent **Kiosque Frontenac**

(© **418/692-5483**), which sells walking, bus, and boat tours and does currency exchange. It's open daily from 9am until 8 or 9pm in summer.

From early June to Labour Day, student staff of the tourist office pilot motor scooters through the tourist districts of the Upper and Lower Towns, making themselves available for questions. (They are also in force on foot during the Winter Carnival season.) In French, they're called the *service mobile,* and their blue mopeds bear flags with a large "?". Just hail them as they approach; they're bilingual.

CITY LAYOUT

MAIN AVENUES & STREETS   Within the walls of the **Haute-Ville (Upper Town),** the principal streets are rues St-Louis (which becomes the Grande-Allée outside the city walls), Ste-Anne, and St-Jean, and the pedestrians-only Terrasse Dufferin, which overlooks the river in front of the Château Frontenac. In the **Basse-Ville (Lower Town),** major streets are St-Pierre, Dalhousie, St-Paul, and, parallel to St-Paul, St-André. There are good maps of the Upper and Lower Towns and the metropolitan area available at any tourist office.

FINDING AN ADDRESS   If it were larger, the historic district, with its winding and plunging streets, might be confusing to negotiate. However, it's very compact, so most visitors have little difficulty finding their way around. Most streets are only a few blocks long, making it is fairly easy to find a specific address.

THE NEIGHBORHOODS IN BRIEF

Vieux-Québec: Haute-Ville   The Upper Town of Old Québec, surrounded by thick ramparts, occupies the crest of Cap Diamant and overlooks the *Fleuve Saint-Laurent* (St. Lawrence River). It includes many of the sites for which the city is famous, among them the Château Frontenac, Place d'Armes, Basilica of Notre-Dame, Québec Seminary and Museum, and Terrasse Dufferin. At a still higher elevation, to the south of the Château and along the river, is the Citadelle, a partially star-shaped fortress begun by the French in the 18th century and augmented often by the English well into the 19th century. With most buildings at least 100 years old and made of granite in similar styles, the Haute-Ville is visually harmonious, with few jarring modern intrusions. When they added a new wing to the Château Frontenac a few years ago, for instance, they modeled it after the original—standing policy here. The Terrasse Dufferin is a pedestrian promenade that attracts crowds in all seasons for its magnificent views of the river and its water traffic, which includes ferries gliding back and forth, cruise ships, and Great Lakes freighters putting in at the harbor below.

Vieux-Québec: Basse-Ville and Vieux-Port   The Lower Town part of Old Québec encompasses Vieux-Port, the old port district; the impressive Museum of Civilization, a highlight of any visit; Place Royale, perhaps the most attractive of the city's many squares and where the small Notre-Dame-des-Victoires church resides; and the restored Quartier du Petit-Champlain, including pedestrian-only rue du Petit-Champlain. Petit-Champlain is undeniably touristy, but not unpleasantly so, and has many agreeable cafés and shops. Most visitors travel between Lower and Upper Towns by the cliff-side elevator *(funiculaire)* at the north end of rue du Petit-Champlain, or by the adjacent stairway.

Parliament Hill Once you pass through the walls at the St-Louis Gate, you're still in Haute-Ville (Upper Town), but no longer in the old city of Vieux-Québec. Rue St-Louis becomes Grande-Allée, a wide boulevard that passes the stately Parliament building on the right and runs parallel to the broad expanse of the Plains of Abraham off to the left, where one of the most important battles in the history of North America took place between the French and the British for control of the city and where the lively Carnaval de Québec is held each winter. Two blocks after the Parliament, the Grande-Allée becomes lined on both sides with terraced restaurants and cafés. The city's large modern hotels are in this area, and the Musée des Beaux-Arts is a pleasant 20-minute walk up the Allée from the Parliament. Moving southwest on Grande-Allée, the area becomes more residential and flows into the Montcalm district.

St-Roch Northwest of Parliament Hill and enough of a distance from Vieux-Québec to warrant a cab ride, this newly revitalized neighborhood has some of the trendiest restaurants and bars in the city. A dreary indoor pedestrian mall on the central rue St-Joseph est has been gutted—with the roof removed, sidewalks widened, and new benches added—and money has been given to artists to renovate the interior and exterior of their industrial buildings. All this adds up to a neighborhood with a youthful pop and an influx of new technology and media companies. Much of St-Roch, including what's referred to as Québec's "downtown" shopping district, remains nondescript and a little grubby. But the blocks gravitating from the corner of rue St-Joseph and rue du Parvis (where Hugo Boss moved in with a massive store) are increasingly home to top-notch restaurants and cute boutiques. (On older maps, rue du Parvis was called rue de l'Eglise.)

2 Getting Around

Once you're within or near the walls of the Haute-Ville, virtually no place of interest, hotel, or restaurant is beyond walking distance. In bad weather, or when you're traversing between opposite ends of Lower and Upper Towns, a taxi might be necessary, but in general, walking is the best way to explore the city.

BY BUS

Local buses run quite often and charge C$2.50 (US$2.15/£1.10) in exact change. One-day passes cost C$5.95 (US$5.20/£2.55), and discounts are available for seniors and students with proper ID. Bus stops have easy-to-follow signs that state the bus numbers and direction of travel for each route. Flag down the bus as it approaches so the driver knows to stop. The Québec City museum card includes 2 days of unlimited public transport in addition to free entrance to 24 museums for 3 days.

Bus routes are listed online at **www.rtcquebec.ca**. Buses in the most touristed areas include no. 7, which travels up and down rue St-Jean, and nos. 10 and 11, which shuttle along Grande-Allée/rue St-Louis.

BY FUNICULAR

To get between the Upper Town and Lower Town, there are streets, staircases, and a cliff-side elevator, which has long operated along an inclined 64m (210-ft.) track. It was closed for a couple of years after a fatal accident in 1996. Repaired now, the **upper**

station is near the front of the Château Frontenac and Place d'Armes, while the **lower station** is at the northern end of rue du Petit-Champlain, inside the Maison Louis-Jolliet. The funicular offers excellent aerial views of the historic Lower Town on both the short trip up and the trip down, and runs daily from 7:30am until 11pm all year, and up to midnight in high season. Wheelchairs are accommodated. The one-way fare is C$1.75 (US$1.50/75p). Read more about its history at **www.funiculaire-quebec.com**.

BY TAXI

Taxis are everywhere, cruising and parked in front of the big hotels and in some of the larger squares of the Upper Town. In theory, they can be hailed, but they are best obtained by locating one of their stands, as in the Place d'Armes or in front of the Hôtel-de-Ville (City Hall). Restaurant managers and hotel bell captains will also summon them if you ask. Fares are the same as in Montréal, meaning they're somewhat expensive given the short distances of most rides. The starting rate is C$3.15 (US$2.75/£1.35), and each kilometer costs C$1.45 (US$1.25/60p). Tip 10% to 15%. A taxi from the train station to one of the big hotels is about C$6 to C$9 (US$5.20–US$7.85/£2.60–£3.90) plus tip. To call a cab, try **Taxi Coop** (© **418/525-5191**) or **Taxi Québec** (© **418/525-8123**).

BY CAR

See "By Car" under "Getting Around," in chapter 4, for information on gasoline and driving rules in Canada. Unlike in Montréal, drivers in Québec City are permitted to turn right at red traffic lights, but only after coming to a full stop and yielding to pedestrians in the crosswalk.

RENTALS   The phone numbers listed here are for car-rental companies' general information and their desks at the airport terminal: **Avis** (© **800/437-0358** or 418/872-2861); **Budget** (© **800/268-8900** or 418/872-9885); **Hertz** (© **800/263-0600** or 418/871-1571).

The basic map you get from the rental agency should suffice for Québec City, which is compact if a little tricky to navigate because of there are so few roads between Upper Town and Lower Town and because many streets are one-way.

PARKING   On-street parking is very difficult in the cramped quarters of old Québec City. When you find a rare space on the street, be sure to check the signs for the hours when parking is permissible. When meters are in place, the charge is C50¢ (US45¢/20p) per 15 minutes. Some meters go up to 5 hours. Metered spots generally have to be paid for Monday through Saturday from 9am to 9pm, and Sunday 10am to 9pm. But be sure to check: Spots along the Parc des Champs-de-Bataille (Battlefields Park), for instance, are in effect all 24 hours.

Many of the smaller hotels have special arrangements with local garages, with discounts for guests of three or four dollars less per day than the usual C$12 (US$10/£5.15) or more per day. Check with your hotel first before parking in any lot or garage.

If a particular hotel or *auberge* doesn't have access to a garage or lot, plenty are available and are clearly marked on the foldout city map available at tourist offices. Several convenient lots include, in Upper Town, the one next to the Hôtel-de-Ville (City Hall); on Parliament Hill, in the office building Complexe Marie-Guyart (Complexe G), at 1058 rue Louis-Alexandre-Taschereau off boulevard René-Lévesque; and, in Lower Town, across the street from the Musée de la Civilisation, on rue Dalhousie, where discounts are often offered on weekends.

Long May They Wave: The Flags of Canada and Québec

With a relatively small population spread over a territory larger than the continental United States, Canadians' loyalties have always tended to be directed to the cities and regions in which they live, rather than to the nation at large. Part of it comes from the semi-colonial relationship the nation retained with England (Queen Elizabeth II is still on all the currency), and part from the fact that its citizens speak two different major languages. It wasn't until 1965 that the now-familiar red-and-white maple leaf version of the Canadian flag was introduced, replacing the red ensign with a Union Jack in the upper-left corner, and Canadians didn't even have a national anthem until *O, Canada!* was given the title in 1980.

Regional pride and identification grew after World War II. Québécois began asserting themselves and officially adopted their new "national" flag, the *Fleurdelisé,* in 1950. The flag employs the traditional blue and white of France with four fleurs-de-lis.

In the face of decades of hurt and outright hostilities between French and English Canada, there must be occasional sighs of longing in some quarters for the diplomatic display that is the flag of the city of Montréal. Adopted way back in 1832, it has red crossbars on a white background. The resulting quadrants have depictions of a rose, a fleur-de-lis, a thistle, and a shamrock. They stand, respectively, for the founding groups of the new nation—the English, French, Scots, and Irish.

BY BICYCLE

Given the hilly topography and tight quarters of the Upper Town of Vieux-Québec, cycling isn't a particularly attractive option. But outside of the Upper Town walls is another story. In Lower Town, **Cyclo Services,** at the Marché du Vieux-Port at 160 rue du Quai St-André (℡ **418/692-4052;** www.cycloservices.net), rents bicycles for C$12 (US$10/£5.15) an hour or C$20 (US$17/£8.60) for 4 hours. It also rents electric bikes, tandems, and bike trailers.

Like Montréal, Québec City has a good network of cycling paths called the ***Route Verte*** **(Green Route).** There are both shorter local paths as well as access to long-distance paths. **Promo-Vélo** (www.promo-velo.org) has information in French.

13

Where to Stay in Québec City

Staying in one of the small hotels within or below the walls of Vieux-Québec can be one of your trip's most memorable experiences. That isn't a guarantee, however, that it will be comfortable. Standards of amenities and prices fluctuate so wildly from one small hotel to another—even within a single establishment—that it is wise to examine any rooms offered before registering. From rooms with private bathrooms, minibars, cable TVs, and wireless Internet connections, to walk-up budget accommodations with linoleum floors and toilets down the hall, Québec City has a wide enough variety of lodgings to suit most tastes and wallets.

If cost is a prime consideration, note that prices drop significantly from November to May, except for such events as the winter Carnaval de Québec in February. As a rule, the prices given in the listings below are rack rates for a double occupancy room. That means that you'll rarely, if ever, have to pay that much, unless it's Carnaval or one of the big days of the city's 400th-anniversary celebrations. Many hotels offer special deals through their websites or AAA discounts. The higher rates given apply during the warmer months, the Christmas season, and Carnaval.

In the budget category, even with an advance reservation, always ask to see two or three rooms before making a choice. Unless otherwise noted, all rooms in the lodgings listed below have private bathrooms—*en suite,* as they say in Canada. Note that some properties use the word

"spa" to mean an outdoor hot tub; when used in the listings below, it means an indoor facility offering massages and the like. Also, many of the hotels listed here are completely nonsmoking; if you are a smoker, check before booking.

Similar in atmosphere and price range to these small hotels are the more than 40 bed-and-breakfasts in and around Vieux-Québec. With rates mostly in the C$70-to-C$120 (US$61–US$104/£30–£52) range, they don't represent substantial savings over the small hotels, but will give you the opportunity to get to know some of the city dwellers.

When calling to make arrangements at a B&B, be very clear about your needs and requirements. A deposit is often required, and minimum stays of 2 nights are common. Credit cards may not be accepted. A very useful *Official Accommodation Guide,* put out by Québec City Tourism and revised annually, is available at the tourist offices. It lists every member of the Greater Québec Area Tourism and Convention Bureau, from B&Bs to five-star hotels, providing details about number of rooms, prices, and facilities.

If you prefer the conveniences of large chain hotels and the Fairmont Le Château Frontenac is fully booked, you can go outside the ancient walls to the younger part of town, Parliament Hill. High-rise hotels out there are within walking distance or a quick bus or taxi ride away from the attractions in the old city. In recent years, as well, a clutch of new boutique hotels and small inns in the

Lower Town has greatly enhanced the lodging stock.

See p. 66 in chapter 5 for information about the Frommer's star rating system, price rates, categories, and taxes.

1 Best Hotel Bets

- **Best Historic Hotel: Fairmont Le Château Frontenac,** 1 rue des Carrières (*©* **800/441-1414** or 418/692-3861), is more than a century old. It was one of the first hotels built to serve railroad passengers and to encourage tourism at a time when most people stayed close to home—and it still rewards a visit. See below.
- **Most Romantic Boutique Hotel (Tie):** The **Auberge Saint-Antoine,** 8 rue St-Antoine (*©* **888/692-2211** or 418/692-2211) features a grand new wing and archaeological displays from lobby to bedside, and it's hard to beat curling up with a glass of wine beside the fire in one of the cozy lobby alcoves. See p. 219. The sleek **Dominion 1912,** 126 rue St-Pierre (*©* **888/833-5253** or 418/692-2224) is also a favorite, infusing a pre–World War I building with cunning modernist flavor, continuing a trend in designer hotels and inns in the Basse-Ville. See p. 220.
- **Best Hotel Location:** Where else? For tourists, nothing can beat **Fairmont Le Château Frontenac** for proximity to all the sights. In fact, "The Château" *is* one of the sights. See below.
- **Best Hotel for Business Travelers:** The **Hilton Québec,** 1100 bd. René-Lévesque est (*©* **800/445-8667** or 418/647-2411), has a central location, a good fitness center, and executive floors with concierges and business services. See p. 217.
- **Best Hotel Health Club and Pool:** Even if you're not staying at the **Hilton Québec,** you can come for the Sunday brunch, which includes free admission to the year-round heated outdoor pool. See p. 217.
- **Most Memorable Hotel:** How many chances do you get to sleep in a hotel built completely of ice, on a bed of ice, near a chandelier and disco and front hallway all made of ice, ice, ice? The **Hôtel de Glace,** Station Touristique Duchesnay, 30 minutes outside the city (*©* **877/505-0423;** www.icehotel-canada.com), is open from January to April or the first thaw, whichever comes first. See p. 216.

2 Vieux-Québec: Haute-Ville (Upper Town)

VERY EXPENSIVE

Fairmont Le Château Frontenac ✦✦✦ *Kids*   Québec's magical "castle" opened in 1893 and has been wowing visitors ever since. The turreted hotel has hosted Queen Elizabeth and Prince Philip, and during World War II, Winston Churchill and Franklin D. Roosevelt had the entire place to themselves for a conference. It was built in phases, following the landline, so the wide halls take crooked paths (on the hotel's 100th birthday in 1993, management added a 66-room wing, and because "The Château" serves as the very symbol of the city, care was taken to replicate the original architectural style throughout). Luxurious rooms are outfitted with regal decor and elegant château furnishings, bathrooms have marble touches, every mattress was replaced in 2006 and 2007, and some 400 rooms were renovated in the same period as well. Anyone can stay on the more princely (and pricey) Fairmont Gold floors, which have a separate concierge and reception and a lounge with an honor bar in the afternoons and breakfast in the mornings. Highly variable room prices depend on size, location, how recently the room was renovated, and view, with river views garnering top dollar. But lower-priced rooms overlooking the inner courtyard can be eminently appealing: The gabled view is quite romantic, and children might imagine Harry Potter swooping by in a Quidditch match. The **Véranda Saint-Laurent** is a casual piano bar with dancing on the weekends. An archaeological excavation of parts of the Terrace Dufferin will continue through 2008, so ask for a room not directly on top of the work.

1 rue des Carrières (at Place d'Armes), Québec City, PQ G1R 4P5. ℂ 800/441-1414 or 418/692-3861. Fax 418/692-1751. www.fairmont.com/frontenac. 618 units. May–Oct from C$249 (US$217/£107) double; Nov–Apr from C$199 (US$173/£86) double; suites from C$499 (US$434/£215) and way up. Children under 18 stay free in parent's room. Children 5 and under eat free, 6–12 get 50% off meals. AE, DC, DISC, MC, V. Valet parking C$31 (US$27/£13). Pets accepted. **Amenities:** 3 restaurants (fusion, international); bar; indoor pool and kiddie pool with outdoor terrace; expansive health club; spa; whirlpool; concierge; business center; Wi-Fi in lobby and bar; shopping arcade; salon; limited room service; in-room massage; babysitting; same-day dry cleaning; executive floors. *In room:* A/C, TV w/pay movies and some Web access, high-speed Internet, minibar, coffeemaker, hair dryer, iron.

EXPENSIVE

L'Hôtel du Vieux-Québec *Kids*   This century-old brick hotel has been renovated with care. Some guest rooms are equipped with sofas and two double beds, and six have kitchenettes. With these homey layouts, the hotel is understandably popular with families, skiers, and the groups of visiting high-school students who descend upon the city in late spring. In addition to **Les Frères de la Côte** on the ground floor, there are many moderately priced restaurants and nightspots nearby. Six rooms were renovated in 2007. In the summer, the hotel offers complimentary walking tours of the area.

1190 rue St-Jean (at rue de l'Hôtel Dieu), Québec City, PQ G1R 1S6. ℂ 800/361-7787 or 418/692-1850. Fax 418/692-5637. www.hvq.com. 44 units. July to mid-Oct C$184–C$300 (US$160–US$261/£79–£129) double; late Oct to June C$94–C$154 (US$82–US$134/£40–£66) double. Packages available. AE, MC, V. *In room:* A/C, TV, hair dryer, iron.

Manoir Victoria *🐾*   The sprawling lobby isn't especially beguiling, even though a C$4-million renovation was completed in 2004. But there is a new wing (ask for a room there) and two serviceable restaurants on the premises, and the proximity to the rue St-Jean restaurant-and-bar scene is a plus for many. An added extra is the indoor pool, rare in this city. The hotel, which with its lobby of stained glass and maroon curtains has an air of a grand old-timer, sprawls all the way from the main entrance on Côte de Palais to adjacent St-Jean, zigzagging around a couple of stores. A long staircase reaches the lobby, but elevators make the trip to most of the rooms. All 156 rooms were redecorated in 2002. Upping its appeal, the hotel installed a spa in 2004, with packages including body wraps in mud or algae or chocolate (!), Swedish massages, exfoliations with sea salt, and "pressotherapy." Prices start at C$40 (US$35/£17).

44 Côte du Palais (rue St-Jean), Québec City, PQ G1R 4H8. ℂ 800/463-6283 or 418/692-1030. Fax 418/692-3822. www.manoir-victoria.com. 156 units. May–Oct C$159–C$219 (US$138–US$191/£68–£94) double; Nov–Apr C$109–C$169 (US$95–US$147/£47–£73) double. Packages available. AE, DC, DISC, MC, V. Valet parking C$18 (US$16/£7.75). **Amenities:** 2 restaurants (French); bar; heated indoor pool; exercise room; expansive spa; concierge; Internet lounge; limited room service; babysitting; same-day laundry service; same-day dry cleaning. *In room:* A/C, TV w/pay movies, free Wi-Fi, free high-speed Internet, minibar, coffeemaker, hair dryer, iron.

MODERATE

Château Bellevue   Occupying several row houses at the top of the Jardin des Gouverneurs, this mini-hotel has a helpful staff as well as some of the creature comforts that smaller inns in the neighborhood lack. Although the rooms are small and often suffer from unfortunate decorating choices, they are quiet for the most part, have private bathrooms, and offer one or two double beds, or a queen-size. A few higher-priced units overlook the park. The hotel's private parking is directly behind the

Where to Stay in Québec City

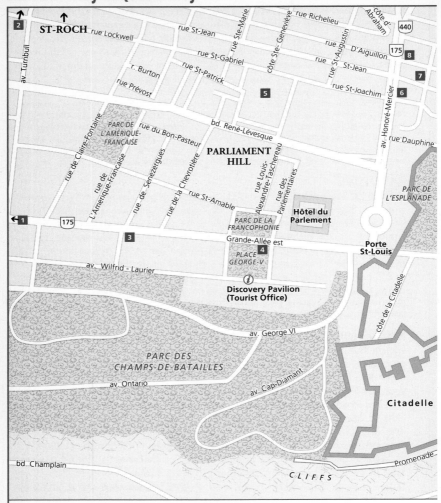

Auberge Le Vincent **2**
Auberge Saint-Antoine **19**
Auberge Saint-Pierre **18**
Château Bellevue **12**
Château Laurier **4**

Courtyard by Marriott **6**
Dominion 1912 **16**
Fairmont Le Château Frontenac **14**
Hilton Québec **5**
Hôtel Le Priori **15**

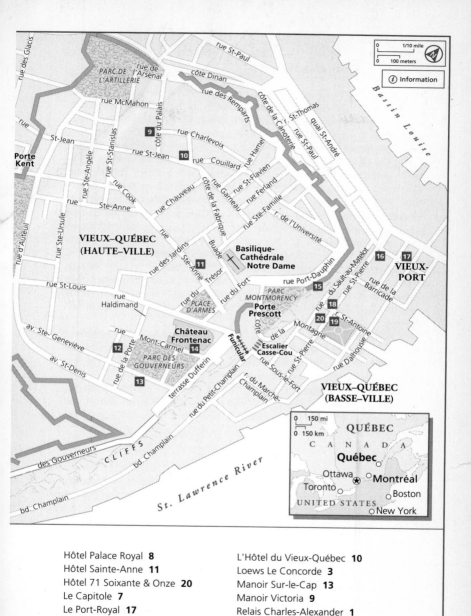

Hôtel Palace Royal **8**
Hôtel Sainte-Anne **11**
Hôtel 71 Soixante & Onze **20**
Le Capitole **7**
Le Port-Royal **17**

L'Hôtel du Vieux-Québec **10**
Loews Le Concorde **3**
Manoir Sur-le-Cap **13**
Manoir Victoria **9**
Relais Charles-Alexander **1**

Moments   Québec's Ice Hotel: The Coldest Reception in Town

For C$15 (US$13/£6.45) you can visit, but for C$199 per person (US$173/£86) you can spend the night. Tempted? Québec's Ice Hotel (℡ **877/505-0423; www.icehotel-canada.com**) is built each winter at the Station Touristique Duchesnay, a woodsy resort a half-hour outside of Québec City. It's crafted from 500 tons of ice, and everything is clear or white, from the ice chandelier in the 18-foot vaulted main hall to the thick square ice shot glasses in which vodka is served, to the pillars and arches and furniture. That includes the frozen slabs they call beds (deer skins and sleeping bags provide insulation). Nighttime guests get their rooms after visitors leave at 8pm and have to clear out before the next day's arrivals at 10am. Some rooms are themed and vaguely grand: The chess room, for instance, has solid-ice chess pieces the size of small children at each corner of the bed. Other rooms bring the words "monastic" or "cell block" to mind. Bear in mind that except for in the hot tub, temperatures everywhere hover between 23° and 28° Fahrenheit (–5 to –2 Celsius); refrigerators are used not to keep sodas cold but to keep them from *freezing*. And whoever dreamed up the luxury suite with a real fireplace that somehow *emits no heat:* There is a special circle in hell for you.

In 2007, the hotel had 36 rooms and suites, a wedding chapel, 2 small art galleries, and a disco where guests could shake the chill from their booties. Open each January, the Hôtel de Glace takes guests until April or the first thaw, whichever comes first—at that point it's destroyed.

Locals have a bemused reaction to all the fuss. As a waitress down the road told one guest: "I would have charged you half as much and let you sleep in a snowbank behind the pub."

building, a notable convenience in this congested part of town, although there are only a few spaces. Free coffee and a wine machine (think soda machine, but classier) are available in the lobby. If you're searching for a room on the spot and this place is full, there are some dozen other small lodgings within a block in any direction. A sister hotel, the **Château Laurier** (p. 218), is located outside the walls on Parliament Hill.

16 rue de la Porte (at av. Ste-Geneviève), Québec City, PQ G1R 4M9. ℡ **800/463-2617** or 418/692-2573. Fax 418/692-4876. www.oldquebec.com. 58 units. May–Oct 15 C$109–C$239 (US$95–US$208/£47–£103) double; Oct 16–Apr C$94–C$174 (US$82–US$151/£40–£75) double. Children under 18 stay free in parent's room. Packages available. AE, DC, DISC, MC, V. Valet service. **Amenities:** Concierge; small business center. *In room:* A/C, TV w/pay movies, free Wi-Fi, hair dryer, iron (on request).

Hôtel Sainte-Anne   Housed in a 19th-century row house that fronts on a pedestrian block of rue Ste-Anne, in the very center of the historic district of the Upper Town, this is a European-style design hotel, economy division. Exposed stone and brick walls are common, and each room has a tall, narrow, free-standing cabinet containing a TV near the top, an unstocked fridge, a coffeemaker, and a wardrobe. The effect is quite spare, but unusual light fixtures add drama. Beds are comfortable and bathrooms feature satisfyingly drenching showers (most rooms have just showers; ask if you want one of the few with a bathtub). Breakfast and room service are provided from the adjacent restaurant Le Grill, and parking is at City Hall down the block, for C$12 (US$10/£5.15) with in-and-out privileges.

32 rue Ste-Anne (near rue des Jardins), Québec City, PQ G1R 1X3. ✆ 877/222-9422 or 418/694-1455. Fax 418/692-4096. www.hotelste-anne.com. 28 units. June 15–Oct 15 from C$169 (US$147/£73) double; rest of year from C$129 (US$112/£55) double. AE, DISC, MC, V. **Amenities:** Limited room service; in-room massage; laundry service. *In room:* TV, free Wi-Fi, free high-speed Internet, fridge, coffeemaker, hair dryer.

INEXPENSIVE
Manoir Sur-le-Cap   All was fresh, painted, and shellacked a few years ago at this inn on the south side of the Parc des Gouverneurs, opposite the Château Frontenac. It still looks good, with gleaming floors and many exposed stone or brick walls. The price is right, although if you require air-conditioning be sure to request one of the seven units that have it. (Know, too, that these four floors have no elevator). Upgrade to what they call their "condo"—an apartment in a separate building in back—and get a balcony, a fireplace, and a kitchenette with microwave oven and basic crockery.

9 av. Ste-Geneviève (near rue de la Porte), Québec City, PQ G1R 4A7. ✆ 866/694-1987 or 418/694-1987. Fax 418/627-7405. www.manoir-sur-le-cap.com. 14 units. C$85–C$185 (US$74–US$161/£37–£80) double. AE, MC, V. *In room:* TV, Wi-Fi, Internet, hair dryer, iron.

3 Parliament Hill/On or Near the Grande-Allée
EXPENSIVE
Courtyard by Marriott ✿   By sidestepping the conventional template of the parent chain, this fresh entry makes a substantial contribution to the ongoing enhancement of Place d'Youville as a day-and-night gathering place for visitors and natives alike. A handsome building from the 1930s was converted into Marriott's first hotel in Québec City. The lobby impresses with a balustraded second floor above a fireplace flanked by leather sofas. Beyond the bar is the full-service restaurant. Rooms got a luxe upgrade in 2006 in bedding, with five pillows per bed and sheet covers on the duvets. All rooms have either an oversize chair that pulls out into a single bed or a sofa bed. Washing machines for guest use stand ready next to the small exercise room.

850 Place d'Youville (near rue St-Jean), Québec City, PQ G1R 3P6. ✆ 800/321-2211 or 418/694-4004. Fax 418/694-4007. www.marriott-quebec.com. 111 units. C$199–C$299 (US$173–US$260/£86–£129) double. Packages available. AE, DC, DISC, MC, V. Valet parking C$20 (US$17/£8.60), self-parking C$17 (US$15/£7.30). **Amenities:** Restaurant (French); bar; exercise room w/Jacuzzi; concierge; business center; free Wi-Fi in lobby; limited room service; babysitting; self-service laundry; dry cleaning. *In room:* A/C, TV w/pay movies, free high-speed Internet, fridge, coffeemaker, hair dryer, iron.

Hilton Québec ✿✿   Superior on virtually every count to the other mid-rise contemporary hotels outside the old town, this Hilton is entirely true to the breed, the clear choice for executives and those leisure travelers who can't bear to live without their gadgets. The location—across the street from the city walls and near the Parliament—is excellent. Public rooms are big and brassy, Hilton-style, while guest rooms are tasteful in light blues and mustard golds. It helps if you like mirrors, because in some units they make up entire walls in the bathroom, along the closet doors, and above the minibar. Ask for an upper-floor room on the side facing the St. Lawrence River and Old Québec, and see the sunrise over the Citadelle. The busy boulevard René-Lévesque outside provides a steady hum of cars but is not overly distracting.

Nonguests can come for a Sunday brunch that includes free admission to the heated outdoor pool. The hotel is connected to the Place Québec shopping complex.

1100 bd. René-Lévesque est, Québec City, PQ G1K 7K7. © **800/HILTONS (445-8667)** or 418/647-2411. Fax 418/647-6488. www.hiltonquebec.com. 571 units. Summer from C$169 (US$147/£73) double and way up; winter C$109–C$225 (US$95–US$196/£47–£97) double. Children stay free in parent's room. Packages available. AE, DC, DISC, MC, V. Valet parking C$21 (US$18/£9.05). Pets accepted. **Amenities:** Restaurant (international); bar; heated outdoor pool (year-round); well-equipped health club w/sauna and massage; concierge; car-rental desk; business center; limited room service; babysitting; laundry service; same-day dry cleaning; executive floors. *In room:* A/C, TV w/pay movies, high-speed Internet, minibar, coffeemaker, hair dryer.

Le Capitole ❤   Le Capitole is as gleefully eccentric as the business hotels it competes with are conventional. Rooms are all curves and obtuse angles, borrowing from Art Deco, and feature stars on the carpets and painted clouds on the ceiling. Beds have down duvets, and some rooms feature bathtubs in the corner. Mostly this all works to its advantage, although some of the angles and funky furniture are tests to practicality. The hotel's owner runs the adjacent music and theater venue (also called Le Capitole) and **Ristorante Il Teatro,** which often becomes an after-hours hangout for visiting musicians. The hotel's entrance, near the heart of Place d'Youville, is squeezed almost to anonymity between the theater and restaurant—just head for the theater marquee. Note that unlike many business hotels nearby, prices are higher on the weekends than midweek during the off season because of the proximity to the theater.

972 rue St-Jean (1 block outside the old city walls), Québec City, PQ G1R 1R5. © **800/363-4040** or 418/694-4040. www.lecapitole.com. 40 units. May 27–Oct 13 C$199–C$219 (US$173–US$191/£86–£94) double; rest of the year C$135–C$175 (US$117–US$152/£58–£75); suites from C$175 (US$152/£75). Packages available. AE, DC, DISC, MC, V. Valet parking C$19 (US$17/£8.15). **Amenities:** Restaurant (Italian/international); bar; concierge; limited room service; in-room massage; laundry service; dry cleaning. *In room:* A/C, TV/VCR, CD player, CD and video library, free Wi-Fi, free high-speed Internet, minibar, coffeemaker, hair dryer.

Loews Le Concorde ❤   From outside, the skyscraper that houses this hotel is something of a visual insult to the skyline, rising from a neighborhood of late-Victorian town houses. But its height means that it offers spectacular views of the river and the old city, even from the lower floors. **L'Astral,** a revolving rooftop restaurant with a bar and live piano music on weekends, has better food than usually can be expected of such sky-high venues. Standard rooms have marble bathrooms, plush robes, and three phone lines. Of all the hotels listed here, this is the farthest from Vieux-Québec, about a 10-minute walk to the walls and then another 10 minutes to the center of the Haute-Ville.

1225 cours du Général de Montcalm (at Grande-Allée), Québec City, PQ G1R 4W6. © **800/463-5256** or 418/647-2222. Fax 418/647-4710. www.loewshotels.com. 406 units. May–Oct C$199–C$299 (US$173–US$260/£86–£129) double; Nov–Apr C$139–C$239 (US$121–US$208/£60–£103) double. 2 children under 18 stay free in parent's room. Packages available. AE, DC, DISC, MC, V. Self-parking C$21 (US$18/£9.05); valet parking C$23 (US$20/£9.90). Pets accepted. **Amenities:** Restaurant (international); 2 bars; heated outdoor pool (in season); well-equipped health club w/sauna; concierge; business center; limited room service; babysitting; laundry service; same-day dry cleaning. *In room:* A/C, TV w/pay movies, high-speed Internet, minibar, coffeemaker, hair dryer, iron, safe.

MODERATE

Château Laurier ❤❤   Anchoring the east end of the action-filled Grande-Allée, this property has perked up considerably from the dowdy old-timer it used to be. A new saltwater pool and Finnish sauna opened in 2007, with a spa, health center, and landscaped garden to follow. There are now nine categories of rooms and suites, thanks to nearly continual expansion in recent years. Some have working fireplaces, whirlpools, and king-size beds; all enjoy the comforts and doodads of a first-class hotel. The new rooms are clearly more desirable than those in the plainer and more cramped original wing, with good-size desks and leather sitting chairs with reading lamps. Many rooms on the higher floors have views of the Citadelle and St. Lawrence River. At press time, the restaurant was closed for renovations but expected to open again by 2008. The hotel is 2 blocks west of the fortress wall and St-Louis Gate.

1220 Place Georges V ouest (at Grande-Allée), Québec City, PQ G1R 5B8. © **800/463-4453** or 418/522-8108. Fax 418/524-8768. www.oldquebec.com. 291 units. May–Oct 28 C$114–C$309 (US$99–US$269/£49–£133) double; Oct 29–Apr C$94–C$269 (US$82–US$234/£40–£116) double; suites C$159–C$939 (US$138–US$817/£68–£404). Children under 18 stay free in parent's room. Packages available. AE, DC, MC, V. Parking C$19 (US$17/£8.15). **Amenities:** Restaurant; indoor saltwater pool; sauna; concierge; business center; limited room service; babysitting; laundry service; dry cleaning. *In room:* A/C, TV w/pay movies, CD player, free Wi-Fi, high-speed Internet, coffeemaker, hair dryer, iron, safe.

Hôtel Palace Royal 🏰🏰   The newest and most luxurious addition to a small, family-owned Québec hotel group, this property elevates the standards of the business hotels outside the city walls. Admittedly, it lacks a distinctive personality, perhaps because it's still young (it opened in 2000). Lots of bronze statuary and marble are lavished on the lobby areas, while room balconies overlook a kidney-shaped indoor pool at the heart of a sort-of-tropical garden. Two-thirds of the units are suites, with fridges, microwave ovens, and, in four rooms, whirlpool bathtubs big enough for two.

775 av. Honoré-Mercier (at Place d'Youville), Québec City, PQ G1R 6A5. © **800/567-5276** or 418/694-2000. Fax 418/380-2553. www.jaro.qc.ca. 234 units. From C$134 (US$117/£58) double; from C$154 (US$134/£66) suite. Packages available. AE, DC, DISC, MC, V. Valet parking C$19 (US$17/£8.15). **Amenities:** Restaurant (steakhouse); bar; indoor pool; whirlpool; exercise room; sauna; concierge; business center; limited room service; babysitting; same-day dry cleaning on weekdays. *In room:* A/C, TV, high-speed Internet, fridge, coffeemaker, hair dryer, iron, microwave.

INEXPENSIVE

Relais Charles-Alexander (Value   On the ground floor of this attractive brick-faced small hotel is an art gallery, which also serves as the breakfast room. This stylish use of space extends to the bedrooms as well, which are crisply maintained and decorated with eclectic antique and wicker pieces and reproductions. Rooms in front are larger, and most have showers (three have tubs). They are quiet, for the most part, given that the inn is just outside the orbit of the sometimes-raucous Grande-Allée terrace bars. The fortress walls and St-Louis Gate are less than a 15-minute walk away, and the pleasant residential shopping street avenue Cartier is just around the corner.

91 Grande-Allée est (2 blocks east of av. Cartier), Québec City, PQ G1R 2H5. © **418/523-1220.** Fax 418/523-9556. wwww.quebecweb.com/rca. 23 units. June–Oct and Carnaval C$124–C$134 (US$108–US$117/£53–£58) double; Nov–May C$89–C$99 (US$77–US$86/£38–£43). Rates include breakfast. MC, V. Parking C$7 (US$6.10/£3). **Amenities:** Breakfast room; dry cleaning. *In room:* A/C, TV, hair dryer.

4 Vieux-Québec: Basse-Ville (Lower Town)/Vieux-Port

EXPENSIVE

Auberge Saint-Antoine 🏰🏰🏰   There isn't enough space here to chart the evolution of this uncommonly attractive property from charming waterfront inn to landmark luxury hotel. It began with an 1830 maritime warehouse with a soaring ceiling, dark beams, and a stone floor. A modern wing and a remodeled 1727 annex then were added, connected by a copper-mansard central structure. During the course of excavation, ancient walls were uncovered and remain in view, and artifacts unearthed in the process are now on display throughout the hotel—in public areas, at the door to each room as an identifier, and at bedside, lit with an underwater-like blue glow. Rooms are modern and sleek: seafoam-tiled bathrooms feature bathing nooks with rainshower nozzles directly overhead, and details include luxury linens, plush robes, a Bose sound system, heated bathroom floors, and no-fog mirrors. Many of the rooms have balconies or terraces, six have fireplaces, and a few suites have kitchenettes. The auberge even offers a small cinema to watch movies in. A striking new lounge serves breakfast, lunch, snacks, and drinks, and the high-end restaurant, **Panache** (p. 231), took over the original warehouse lobby.

8 rue St-Antoine (next to the Musée de la Civilisation), Québec City, PQ G1K 4C9. © **888/692-2211** or 418/692-2211. www.saint-antoine.com. 94 units. C$159–C$379 (US$138–US$330/£68–£163) double; C$299–C$549 (US$260–US$478/£129–£236) suite. Children under 12 stay free in parent's room. AE, DC, MC, V. Valet garage parking C$23 (US$20/£9.90). **Amenities:** Restaurant (new Québécois); bar; concierge; business center; Wi-Fi in public areas; limited room service; in-room massage; babysitting; same-day laundry service weekdays; same-day dry cleaning weekdays. *In room:* A/C, TV, free high-speed Internet, coffeemaker, hair dryer, iron, safe.

Dominion 1912 🏨🏨🏨 Old Québec meets new in one of the most romantic boutique hotels in the city. The owners stripped the inside of the 1912 Dominion Fish & Fruit building down to the studs and pipes and started over, keeping the angular lines and adding soft touches. If you require a rock-hard mattress, look elsewhere; these Québec-made beds are deep, soft, and enveloping, heaped with linen-covered pillows and covered with feather duvets. (Like them enough and you can buy them from the Dominion's online boutique.) Custom-made bedside tables swing into place or out of the way; room tones are gray-green and champagne-white; black-and-white photos of architectural details provide subtle decor. Even the least expensive rooms are large, and modem outlets are at handy desktop level. About a third of the rooms have only showers, while the rest include tubs. Room no. 206 is a dandy, with a shower that shares a glass wall with the bedroom, and views of the city's centuries-old former-industrial buildings. A hearty continental breakfast is set out near the fireplace in the handsome lobby along with morning newspapers, and you can relax at a large group table, in linen-covered easy chairs, or on the terrace in back. A basement fitness room has been added.

126 rue St-Pierre (at rue St-Paul), Québec City, PQ G1K 4A8. © **888/833-5253** or 418/692-2224. Fax 418/692-4403. www.hoteldominion.com. 60 units. May–Oct C$205–C$375 (US$178–US$326/£88–£161) double; Nov–Apr C$169–C$239 (US$147–US$208/£73–£103) double. Rates include breakfast. AE, DC, MC, V. Valet parking C$16 (US$14/£6.90). Pets accepted. **Amenities:** Espresso bar; exercise room; concierge; computer with Internet in lobby for guests; limited room service; babysitting; laundry service; same-day dry cleaning. *In room:* A/C, TV, free Wi-Fi, high-speed Internet, CD player, minibar, coffeemaker, hair dryer, iron, safe.

Hôtel 71 Soixante & Onze 🏨🏨 The latest entry in the roster of Basse-Ville boutique hotels, this is owned by the same people as the adjacent **Auberge Saint-Pierre** (see below). They share a bar, but that's the end of the similarities. Where the auberge is faux-country in style, 71 is super-slick and ultra-contemporary. It used to be a bank, and it retains those lofty ceilings and capacious dimensions while being distinctly mellower. Room no. 620, for instance, has 15-foot cream-colored walls, putty-colored curtains that extend nearly ceiling to floor, blonde-wood floors, and charcoal tile in the bathroom—cool without being chilly. It's warmed up with deep-red velveteen chairs and cloth panels that serve as closet doors. Bathrooms are in the open style common to the boutique hotels of the area, with just seafoam-green glass separating the shower from the sink area and shower nozzles of the fashionable big-disk, rainforest variety, flooding straight down (all rooms have showers, and four have bathtubs as well). All rooms are on floors four to seven and many feature bird's-eye views of the tops of the 19th-century buildings of Old Québec, the St. Lawrence River, the ramparts of the fortress wall, or the Château Frontenac. Café 71, on the first floor, is open for breakfast, snacks during the day, and espresso 24 hours.

71 rue St-Pierre (near rue St-Antoine), Québec City, PQ G1K 4A4. ℭ 888/692-1171 or 418/692-1171. Fax 418/692-0669. www.hotel71.ca. 40 units. C$165–C$295 (US$144–US$257/£71–£127). Rates include a complimentary cocktail and breakfast. Packages available. AE, MC, V. Valet parking C$18 (US$16/£7.75). **Amenities:** Restaurant; bar; exercise room w/spectacular river view; concierge; 24-hour business center w/river view; room service; massage; babysitting; laundry service; dry cleaning. *In room:* A/C, TV/DVD, CD player, free Wi-Fi, free high-speed Internet, coffeemaker (on request), hair dryer, iron (on request), safe.

MODERATE

Auberge Saint-Pierre ℱ   This is one of the city's country-cozy auberge options. Most rooms are surprisingly spacious, and the even more commodious suites are a luxury on a longer visit, especially since they have modest kitchen facilities. The made-to-order furnishings are meant to suggest, rather than replicate, traditional Québec styles, although in some rooms the furniture is a bit crowded. Most units have original brick or stone walls, and some rooms on the fourth to seventh floors have a river view. Most (35) have whirlpool tubs but only a few have showers. New paint spiffed up all the rooms in early 2007. The full breakfasts, included in the price, are special, cooked to order by the chef in an open kitchen.

79 rue St-Pierre (behind the Musée de la Civilisation), Québec City, PQ G1K 4A3. ℭ 888/268-1017 or 418/694-7981. Fax 418/694-0406. www.auberge.qc.ca. 41 units. May–Aug C$119–C$275 (US$104–US$239/£51–£118) double; Sept–Apr C$99–C$239 (US$86–US$208/£43–£103) double. Rates include full breakfast. AE, DC, DISC, MC, V. Valet parking C$16 (US$14/£6.90). **Amenities:** Bar; concierge; in-room massage; babysitting; laundry service; dry cleaning. *In room:* A/C, TV, free Wi-Fi, coffeemaker, hair dryer, iron.

Hôtel Le Priori   A forerunner of the burgeoning Basse-Ville hotel scene, Le Priori provides a playful Art Deco ambience behind the somber facade of a 1726 house. Designer Philippe Starck inspired the original owners, who installed versions of his conical stainless-steel sinks in the bedrooms and sensual multi-nozzle showers in the small bathrooms. In four rooms, claw-foot tubs sit beside the queen-size beds, which are covered with duvets. New table lamps help enliven the formerly dim lighting. Suites have sitting rooms with wood-burning fireplaces, kitchens, and Jacuzzis, and several, including no. 10, are quite masculine, with brown walls in the bedroom, an animal skin rug, and fur throws. Several suites are up stairs with no elevator. Rooms face either the small street out front or the leafy inner courtyard. The inventive restaurant **Toast!**, off the lobby and in the courtyard in summer, draws good notices, including ours (p. 232).

15 rue Sault-au-Matelot (at rue St-Antoine), Québec City, PQ G1K 3Y7. ℭ 800/351-3992 or 418/692-3992. Fax 418/692-0883. www.hotellepriori.com. 26 units. Summer C$169–C$229 (US$147–US$199/£73–£98) double; winter C$129–C$189 (US$112–US$164/£55–£81); suites from C$229 (US$199/£98). Rates include breakfast. Packages available. AE, MC, V. Self-parking C$15 (US$13/£6.45) per day. **Amenities:** Restaurant (fusion); bar; concierge; limited room service; in-room massage; babysitting; dry cleaning. *In room:* A/C, TV/DVD, free Wi-Fi, CD player, coffeemaker, hair dryer, iron.

Le Port-Royal *Kids*   This bright newcomer near to the water is giving serious competition to the best boutique hotels of the Basse-Ville. (The first customers arrived in mid-spring 2005.) The preexisting 18th-century structure was hollowed out to make a total of 40 suites, the smallest of which is 37 sq. m (398 sq. ft.). They all have well-equipped kitchenettes with microwave ovens and range tops; some have dishwashers as well. Four to six people can be accommodated in each unit, making this an excellent

choice for families as well as long-stay businesspeople. From May through October the hotel operates at near total capacity, so book early. A fitness center and roof garden are planned for 2009. **Le 48,** a restaurant under separate management with an entrance from the lobby, provides room service and a snack-y menu of tapas, burgers, wraps, and such. Pets are allowed as long as they're not left alone in the room, and the hotel has a free walking service.

1144 rue St-Pierre (rue St-Andre), Québec City, PQ G1K 4A8. ℭ **418/692-2777.** Fax 418/692-2778. www.hotelport royalsuites.com. 40 units. Nov–Apr C$159–C$259 (US$138–US$225/£68–£111) suite; May–Oct C$189–C$349 (US$164–US$304/£81–£150) suite. AE, MC, V. Parking C$15 (US$13/£6.45). Pets accepted. **Amenities:** Restaurant (international); bar; limited room service; laundry service; same-day dry cleaning. In room: A/C, TV/DVD, free Wi-Fi, CD player, coffeemaker, hair dryer, iron.

5 St-Roch

Until about 2000, there were few reasons for locals, let alone travelers, to include Québec's St-Roch neighborhood in their plans. All that is changing. Young restaurateurs, artists, and media techies have settled in and dubbed the area "Le Nouvo St-Roch" (proper spelling would be too traditional).

MODERATE

Auberge Le Vincent *R* *Value*   Within a few blocks of the epicenter of the emerging "Le Nouvo St-Roch" neighborhood at rue du Parvis are restaurants worth going out of your way for—including the four listed in chapter 14. Plunked at the edge of this orbit of technology companies, skateboard punks, and well-heeled hipsters is the van Gogh–inspired Le Vincent, which opened its 10 rooms in August 2006. Housed in a renovated 100-year-old building, the sophisticated rooms are a good value for all the luxe features: goose-down duvets, 400-thread-count sheets, plush towels, custom-made dark cherrywood furniture, artwork by locals, generous lighting options, and Kohler bath fixtures. Breakfasts are made to order in a brick-walled seating area off the lobby, whose floor is painted in Vincent-style sunbursts and roiling blue curves. Bike storage and repair are available. Rooms are up either one or two flights of stairs. The hotel is a short walk from rue St-Jean, with its boutiques and restaurants, and Place D'Youville.

295 rue St-Vallier est (corner of rue Dorchester), Québec City, PQ G1K 3P5. ℭ **418/523-5000.** Fax 418/523-5999. www.aubergelevincent.com. 10 units. C$119–C$149 (US$104–US$130/£51–£64) double; C$150–C$179 (US$130–US$156/£64–£77) suite. Rates include breakfast. Packages available. AE, MC, V. Valet parking C$15 (US$13/£6.45). **Amenities:** Concierge; in-room massage; laundry service; dry cleaning. In room: A/C, TV/DVD, free Wi-Fi, free high-speed Internet, CD player, fridge, coffeemaker, hair dryer, iron (on request).

6 A Resort Hotel in the City

MODERATE

Château Bonne Entente *RR* *Kids*   Cast a line for trout in the pond in front in summer, twirl around the skating rink in winter, get swaddled in seaweed year-round—and still be only a 15-minute drive from Vieux-Québec. Bushels of dollars have elevated this hotel far beyond the folksy boardinghouse that it was a half-century ago, and it has been accorded membership in the prestigious consortium The Leading Hotels of the World. For romantics, the choice has to be the Art Deco room (in the "Distinctive" suite category) with a monster tub for two beneath a fresco of a country lane. An on-site **AmeriSpa** with 22 treatment rooms offers massages, scrubs, and even an apple-ice-cider body wrap and maple-sugar body scrub. There's a supervised "Fun Club" play area for children with toys, videos, and a nap space. The tennis courts, alas, have been lost to the expanded man-made lake. Golfers have access to a private course 15 minutes away. Aiming to get a "5 Green Key rating" by 2008, the hotel is converting to water-saving toilets and organic detergents.

3400 Chemin Ste-Foy, Québec, PQ G1X 1S6. ℂ 800/463-4390 or 418/653-5221. Fax 418/653-3098. www.chateau bonneentente.com. 165 units. C$159–C$184 (US$138–US$160/£68–£79) double; suites from C$359 (US$312/£154). Packages available. AE, DC, DISC, MC, V. Free parking. Rte. 40 west, take the exit onto Autoroute Duplessis, shortly turning onto Chemin Ste-Foy; at the light, turn right into the main hotel entrance. **Amenities:** 2 restaurants (California, Québécois); bar; large outdoor pool in summer; golf nearby; extensive health club and spa; concierge; business center; room service; babysitting; laundry service; dry cleaning; CD and DVD library. *In room:* A/C, TV, Wi-Fi, CD player, minibar, coffeemaker, hair dryer, iron, safe.

14

Where to Dine in Québec City

Not long ago, it was fair to say that this gloriously scenic city had no *temples de cuisine* comparable to those of Montréal or Manhattan. That has changed. There are now restaurants comparable in every way to the most honored establishments of any North American city. What's more, surprising numbers of creative and ambitious young chefs and restaurateurs are bidding to achieve similar status. It is now easy to eat well in the capital—quite well, in an increasing number of cases.

By sticking to any of the many competent bistros, the handful of *nuovo Italiano* trattorie, and a couple of jazzy fusion eateries, you will likely be more than content. Another step up, a half-dozen ambitious enterprises tease the palate with hints of higher achievement.

Even the blatantly touristy restaurants along rue St-Louis in Upper Town and around the Place d'Armes, many of them with hawkers outside and accordion players and showy tableside presentations inside, can produce decent meals. The less extravagant among them, in fact, are entirely satisfactory for breakfast or simple lunches, particularly useful if you're staying in one of the many old town guesthouses that serve no meals.

The best dining deals are the *table d'hôte* (fixed-price) meals. Nearly all full-service restaurants offer them, if only at lunch. As a rule, they include at least soup or salad, a main course, and a dessert. Some places add in an extra appetizer and/or a beverage. The total price is approximately what you'd pay for the main course alone.

Game is popular, including venison, quail, goose, caribou, and wapiti (North American deer). Many menus feature emu and lamb raised just north of the city in Charlevoix. Mussels and salmon are also standard, but you might want to look beyond those staples.

At the better places, and even at some that might seem inexplicably popular, reservations are all but essential during traditional holidays and the festivals that pepper the social calendar. Other times, it's usually necessary to book ahead only for weekend evenings. In the listings below, where no mention is made of reservations, they aren't necessary. Dress codes are rarely stipulated, but "dressy casual" works almost everywhere.

Remember that for the Québécois, *dîner* (dinner) is lunch, and *souper* (supper) is dinner, though the word dinner below is used in the common American sense. Also note that an *entrée* in Québec is an appetizer, while a *plat principal* is a main course. The evening meal tends to be served earlier in Québec City than in Montréal, at 6 or 7pm rather than 8pm.

Smoking in restaurants, bars, and most other public places in the Québec province has been banned since 2006.

1 Best Dining Bets

- **Best Bistros:** In a city that specializes in the informal bistro tradition, **L'Echaudé,** 73 rue Sault-au-Matelot, near rue St-Paul (© **418/692-1299**), is a star. Classic dishes are all in place, from confit de canard to steak frites. The dining terrace just a block from the waters of Vieux-Port is on a street that is pedestrian-only in the summer. See p. 231. The spiffed-up **Le Clocher Penché,** 203 rue St-Joseph est (© **418/640-0597**), offers a 187-bottle wine list and a cozy atmosphere and is a good reason to explore the trendy St-Roch neighborhood. See p. 233.
- **Best New Restaurant:** Amid the cluster of innovative new restaurants that have blessed the city in the past few years, St-Roch's **Utopie,** 226½ rue St-Joseph est (© **418/523-7878**), is the one most likely to equal the current champs. See p. 233.
- **Best Rockin' Hot Spot with Good Food:** You don't have to be young and gorgeous to get into the **VooDoo Grill,** 575 Grande-Allée est (© **418/647-2000**), but there seems to be a lot of self-selection going on. As part of a complex that includes two bars and the Maurice disco, the noise level gets brutal and the pace frantic, making the surprisingly good food all the more remarkable. See p. 227.
- **Best Seafood:** The owner of **Le Marie-Clarisse,** 12 rue du Petit-Champlain (© **418/692-0857**), selects all the just-off-the-boat seafood served at his comfortable bistro at the bottom of Breakneck Stairs, next to the funicular. There's a fireplace inside, 300-year-old walls, and a terrace outside. See p. 230.
- **Best Sugar Pie:** Québec's favorite dessert reaches its apogee at **Aux Anciens Canadiens,** 34 rue St-Louis (© **418/692-1627**), in central Upper Town. Think smooth maple sugar with a crust. An ideal end to a traditional meal. See p. 226.
- **Best View:** Revolving rooftop restaurants rarely dish out food as elevated as their lofty venues. **L'Astral** in the Loews Le Concorde hotel, 1225 Cours du Général de Montcalm (© **418/647-2222**), on Parliament Hill is an exception. The food is above average and the cost is reasonable. See p. 270 in "Québec City After Dark."
- **Best People-Watching:** The few outdoor tables at **Le Marie-Clarisse**—perched above the main pedestrian intersection of Quartier du Petit-Champlain—monopolize an unsurpassed observation point. See p. 230.
- **Most Idyllic Terrace:** The main room, all crimson glow and retro lighting, is nice enough, but try to get out onto the leafy enclosed back terrace of Lower Town's **Toast!,** 17 rue Sault-au-Matelot (© **418/692-1334**). It's a haven from the bustle. See p. 232.
- **Best Place for a Family Holiday Meal:** The large (it seats over 200) and jovial **Le Café du Monde,** 84 rue Dalhousie (© **418/692-4455**), right on the water of Vieux-Port, manages the near-impossible: fast service without compromising quality even on crowded holiday weekends. See p. 233.
- **Best Breakfast with Locals:** Just outside the tourist centers in the residential neighborhood of Montcalm, the outdoor-terraced **Café Krieghoff** at 1091 av. Cartier © **418/522-3711**) gets a mix of families, singles, and artsy folks of all ages. See p. 227.
- **Best Restaurants, Period:** Laurie Raphaël, 117 rue Dalhousie (© **418/692-4555**), has given itself a total physical overhaul and now is both sophisticated *and* endlessly eclectic; see p. 230. However, **Initiale,** 54 rue St-Pierre (© **418/694-1818**), can no longer be denied equal status. It is more hushed and classic of the two; see p. 230. Visitors might have the best meals of their lives at these stellar restaurants, just blocks from each other in Lower Town/Vieux-Port.

2 Restaurants by Cuisine

FRENCH BISTRO

L'Ardoise (Basse-Ville/Vieux-Port, $$,
p. 232)

L'Echaudé ✿ (Basse-Ville/Vieux-Port,
$$$, p. 231)

Le Clocher Penché ✿ (St-Roch, $$,
p. 233)

FRENCH CONTEMPORARY

Initiale ✿✿✿ (Basse-Ville/Vieux-Port,
$$$$, p. 230)

Le Paris-Brest ✿ (Parliament Hill,
$$$, p. 227)

Panache ✿✿ (Basse-Ville/Vieux-Port,
$$$$, p. 231)

FRENCH/INTERNATIONAL

Le Café du Monde ✿ (Basse-Ville/
Vieux-Port, $$, p. 233)

FUSION

Laurie Raphaël ✿✿✿ (Basse-Ville/
Vieux-Port, $$$$, p. 230)

Toast! ✿ (Basse-Ville/Vieux-Port, $$$,
p. 232)

Utopie ✿ (St-Roch, $$$, p. 233)

Versa (St-Roch, $$, p. 234)

VooDoo Grill ✿ (Parliament Hill,
$$$, p. 227)

LIGHT FARE

Café Krieghoff (Parliament Hill, $,
p. 227)

QUÉBÉCOIS

Aux Anciens Canadiens ✿ (Haute-
Ville, $$$, see below)

SEAFOOD

Le Marie-Clarisse ✿ (Basse-Ville/
Vieux-Port, $$$, p. 231)

Poisson d'Avril (Basse-Ville/Vieux-
Port, $$$, p. 232)

SUSHI/JAPANESE

Yuzu ✿ (St-Roch, $$, p. 234)

3 Vieux-Québec: Haute-Ville (Upper Town)

EXPENSIVE

Aux Anciens Canadiens ✿ QUEBECOIS   Smack in the middle of the tourist
swarms and inundated by travelers during peak months, this venerable restaurant is in
what is probably the oldest (1677) house in the city. (The windows are small because
their original glass came over from France packed in barrels of molasses.) Surprisingly,
the food at this famous establishment is both fairly priced (at least at lunch) and well
prepared. In addition, it's one of the best places in La Belle Province to sample cook-
ing that has its roots in the earliest years of New France; don't count on ancient
Québécois recipes tasting this good anywhere else. Caribou figures into many of the
dishes, as does maple syrup (with the duckling, goat cheese salad, and luscious sugar
pie). Servings are large enough to ward off hunger for a week. Servers are in costume,
and there are carved wooden bas-reliefs of regional scenes. Watch for the many menu
supplements (additional prices for certain choices) on the table d'hôte meals.

34 rue St-Louis (at rue des Jardins). © **418/692-1627.** www.auxancienscanadiens.qc.ca. Reservations recommended.
Main courses C$26–C$50 (US$23–US$44/£11–£22); table d'hôte dinner C$39–C$62 (US$34–US$54/£17–£27), lunch
C$15 (US$13/£6.45). AE, DC, MC, V. Daily noon–10pm.

Key to Abbreviations: $$$$ = Very Expensive $$$ = Expensive $$ = Moderate $ = Inexpensive
The prices within each review refer to the cost in Canadian dollars of individual main courses, using the fol-
lowing categories: Very Expensive ($$$$), main courses at dinner average more than C$35; Expensive
($$$), C$25 to C$35; Moderate ($$), C$12 to C$25; and Inexpensive ($), C$12 and under.
Restaurants are listed alphabetically at the end of the index in the back of this book.

4 Parliament Hill/On or Near the Grande-Allée

EXPENSIVE

Le Paris-Brest ⚜ FRENCH CONTEMPORARY   Named for a French dessert, this is one of the best restaurants outside the walls, tendering a polished performance from greeting to check. Within minutes after the doors are opened at lunchtime, a happy noise ensues, drowning out the cellphone users. Dinner is quieter, with jazz on the sound system and honey-amber lighting. A fashionable crowd comes in wearing everything from bespoke suits to designer jeans. A comely waitstaff dressed in black conveys as much warmth as the rushed process permits. The menu doesn't change much, so pay attention to the daily specials, which are more likely to demonstrate the kitchen's creativity. Wapiti with raspberry sauce and spiced pear was a recent highlight, as was roasted salmon with tomatoes and balsamic vinaigrette. Find the entrance on rue de la Chevrotière. There are outdoor tables, and valet parking is available after 6pm.

590 Grande-Allée est (at rue de la Chevrotière). ✆ 418/529-2243. Reservations recommended. Main courses C$15–C$32 (US$13–US$28/£6.45–£14); table d'hôte lunch C$12–C$17 (US$10–US$15/£5.15–£7.30), dinner C$18–C$35 (US$16–US$30/£7.75–£15). AE, DC, MC, V. Mon–Fri 11:30am–2:30pm; daily 5:30–11:30pm.

VooDoo Grill ⚜ FUSION   Of all the unlikely places to expect a decent meal, let alone one that surpasses most of what can be found at more conventional local restaurants, this takes the laurels. Waitstaff are clad in all-black (women in sleeveless halter tops even when temperatures are arctic outside), African carvings adorn the walls, thumping music sets the pace, and conga drummers circulate nightly, beating out rapid, insistent rhythms—a tremendous distraction. It is all loud, young, and casual. The menu is divided into three categories: "Air," "Water," and "Land," with features such as a filet mignon from Québec's Charlevoix region grilled with mushrooms and asparagus and a plate featuring shrimps, scallops, and Chinese ravioli stuffed with seafood. If you're interested, the cover charge for the disco upstairs is waived with proof that you ate at VooDoo. There's also an attached cigar lounge, the Société Cigare, with 200 offerings.

575 Grande-Allée est (corner of rue de la Chevrotiére). ✆ 418/647-2000. www.voodoogrill.com. Reservations recommended. Main courses C$17–C$48 (US$14–US$42/£7.10–£21). AE, DC, MC, V. Mon–Fri 11am–2am; Sat–Sun 5pm–2am.

INEXPENSIVE

Café Krieghoff LIGHT FARE   Walk down Grande-Allée about 10 minutes from the Parliament, and turn right on avenue Cartier. This 5-block strip is the heart of the Montcalm residential neighborhood, with bakeries, boutiques, restaurants, and bars.

⌒Finds Picnic Fare

Les Halles du Petit-Cartier is, in effect, a mall for foodies, containing a collection of merchants in open-fronted shops purveying fresh meats and fish, cheeses, sushi, pâtés and terrines, glistening produce, deli products, pastries, confections, and fancy picnic items. There are a few fast-food counters and delis that make up sandwiches to order. How about a cooked lobster for your picnic? It's open 7 days a week and located just outside the tourist orbit: west of the Parliament Hill district, in the Montcalm residential neighborhood, at 1191 av. Cartier (1 block north of Grande Allée).

Where to Dine in Québec City

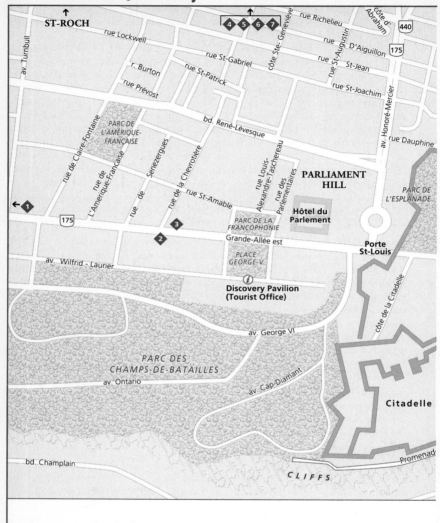

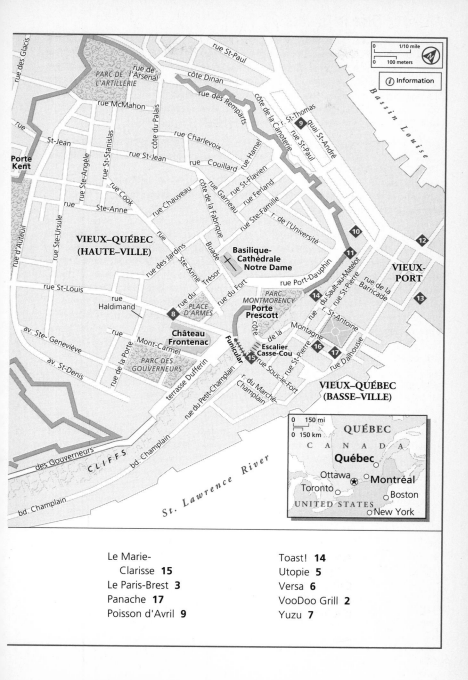

Le Marie-
  Clarisse **15**
Le Paris-Brest **3**
Panache **17**
Poisson d'Avril **9**

Toast! **14**
Utopie **5**
Versa **6**
VooDoo Grill **2**
Yuzu **7**

In the middle of it all is this cheerful café, which features an outdoor terrace a few steps up from the sidewalk. On weekend mornings it's packed with artsy locals of all ages, whose tables get piled high with bowls of café au lait and huge plates of egg dishes, sweet pastries, or classics like steak frites. Service is efficient and good-natured. There's also a modest auberge upstairs with seven rooms.

1091 av. Cartier (north of Grande-Allée). (©) 418/522-3711. www.cafekrieghoff.qc.ca. Most items under C$10 (US$8.70/£4.30). MC, V. Sun–Thurs 7am–11pm; Fri–Sat 7am–midnight.

5 Vieux-Québec: Basse-Ville (Lower Town)/Vieux-Port

VERY EXPENSIVE

Initiale *⟨⟨⟨* FRENCH CONTEMPORARY   No more waffling: Initiale is not only one of the capital's elite restaurants, but it holds that status among the best of the entire province. The palatial setting of tall windows, columns, and a deeply recessed ceiling sets a gracious tone, and the welcome is both cordial and correct. Subdued lighting and the muffled noise level help, too. Cast economy to the winds, choosing from prix-fixe menus of three to six courses. They are changed often, because the chef values freshness of ingredients over novelty. As an example, one dinner started with a buckwheat crepe folded around an artichoke, a round of crabmeat with a creamy purée of onions, and a flash-fried leaf of baby spinach that added a delicate crackle, all arrayed on the plate as on an artist's palette. It continued with grilled tuna supported by sweet garlic, salsify, and lemon marmalade, and a swirl of pasta with marguerite leaves. The veal is tender, young, pink beef, selected on the hoof by the chef at "Matal-ick's Farm." Québec cheeses are an impressive topper. This is a place to celebrate important events. Men should wear jackets; women can pull out the stops.

54 rue St-Pierre (corner of Côte de la Montagne). (©) 418/694-1818. www.restaurantinitiale.com. Reservations rec-ommended on weekends. Main courses C$38–C$45 (US$33–US$39/£16–£19); table d'hôte dinner C$64 or C$94 (US$56 or US$82/£28 or £40). AE, DC, MC, V. Tues–Fri 11:30am–2pm; Tues–Sat 6–9pm.

Laurie Raphaël *⟨⟨⟨* FUSION   Energized by the emergence of a challenging cadre of sharp young chefs and restaurateurs in the city, the owners of this smashingly creative restaurant tinker relentlessly with their handiwork. An overhaul of the space a couple of years ago made it a suitable arena for what has long been one of the city's most accomplished kitchens. Living up to its more sophisticated setting (which is tem-pered by decorating dashes of eye-popping red and electric pink), the platings are pret-tier than ever. Silky-smooth foie gras arrives on a teeny ice cream paddle, drizzled with a port and maple syrup reduction. Alaskan snow crab is accompanied by a bright-pink pomegranate terrine. Rabbit is served two ways: as a braised leg atop a traditional cas-soulet, and trimmed like a rack of lamp. An egg yolk "illusion" of thickened orange juice encapsulated in a skin of pectin is served in a puddle of maple syrup in an Asian soup spoon. And so on. Service falls within the friendly/correct range, and the pace of the meal is spot-on. With all the vigorous new competition, this is still top of the order. The renovations, by the way, added a fancy public kitchen (they call it a "labo-ratory with a domestic touch") where chef/owner Daniel Vézina gives cooking classes twice a week.

117 rue Dalhousie (at rue St-André). (©) 418/692-4555. www.laurieraphael.com. Reservations recommended. Main courses C$38–C$49 (US$33–US$43/£16–£21); gourmet dinner menu C$94 (US$82/£40); 3-course chef's inspiration C$60 (US$52/£26); table d'hôte lunch C$23 (US$20/£9.90). AE, DC, DISC, MC, V. Tues–Fri 11:30am–2pm; Tues–Sat 5:30–10pm.

Panache ✦✦ FRENCH CONTEMPORARY   The restaurant of the superb **Auberge Saint-Antoine** (p. 219) started life in 2004 with a big advantage: It is housed in a former 19th-century warehouse delineated by massive wood beams and rough stone walls. A wrought-iron staircase winds up to a second dining level, creating the feel of a secret attic with tables tucked into its eves. Flickering candles, a center fireplace, velvet couches, generous space between tables, and excellent acoustics—not loud, not churchlike—enhance the inherent romantic aura. Aiming to serve up *cuisine Québécoise revisitée*—French Canadian cuisine with a twist—the frequently changing menu is heavy on locally sourced game, duck, fish, and vegetables. Appetizers have included "Mushrooms from my friend, Michel," served with duck confit, foie gras, and celery ravioli, and emu tartare, folded with capers and a lightly flavored vinaigrette. The Angus beef prepared two ways—grilled rumpsteak and rib tips—coupled with turnip and shitake gnocchi, is a knockout. A slip of a bar inside the restaurant seats about a dozen. The **Café Artefact,** a separate lounge just off the main lobby of the Auberge, provides a casual pre-meal meeting spot.

10 rue St-Antoine (in Auberge Saint-Antoine). ✆ **418/692-1022.** www.saint-antoine.com. Reservations recommended at dinner. Main courses C$37–C$45 (US$32–US$39/£16–£19); tasting menu C$149 (US$130/£64). AE, DC, MC, V. Breakfast Mon–Sat 6:30–10:30am; lunch Mon–Fri noon–2pm; brunch Sun 11am–2pm; dinner daily 6–10pm.

EXPENSIVE

L'Echaudé ✦ FRENCH BISTRO   The most polished of the necklace of restaurants adorning this Vieux-Port corner, L'Echaudé is like a well-worn cashmere sweater, going well with either silk trousers or 10-year-old jeans. Sit at either the stainless steel bar or at tables covered with butcher paper. Two walls of mirrors reflect the bright amber light, and the businessman's lunch is written on the mirror, Parisian style. Grilled meats and fishes and the seafood stews are very satisfying and an excellent value, even if they blaze no new trails. Good lunch deals range from cheese omelets to steak tartare, served with appetizer, dessert, and coffee. Among classics on the menu are steak frites, lobster bisque, duck confit, and salmon tartare. Less expected are the lobster and scallops cannelloni in a white-wine sauce, or the wild deer medaglioni pasta with cranberry sauce. The owner keeps an important cellar, with 150 varieties of wine, about a dozen available by the glass. The bistro is frequented mostly by locals, aged from their 20s to forever, attended by a highly efficient staff. In the summertime, the small street in front of the patio is closed off to car traffic.

73 rue Sault-au-Matelot (near rue St-Paul). ✆ **418/692-1299.** www.echaude.com. Reservations suggested on weekends. Main courses C$18–C$38 (US$16–US$33/£7.75–£16); table d'hôte dinner cost of the main plus C$15 (US$13/£6.45). AE, DC, MC, V. Mon–Fri and Sun 11:30am–2:30pm; daily 5:30–10pm.

Le Marie-Clarisse ✦ SEAFOOD   This spot, at the bottom of Breakneck Stairs and perched just overlooking the pedestrian-only rue du Petit-Champlain, sits where the streets are awash with day-packers and shutterbugs. It serves what many consider to be the best seafood in town, chosen by a finicky owner who makes his selections personally at the market. The result of daily fish deliveries is a menu that changes often, so look closely at the long list of specials posted on chalkboards. A more pleasant hour cannot be passed anywhere in Québec City than here, over a platter of shrimp or pâtés, out on the terrace on a summer afternoon. In winter, on the other hand, cocoon by the stone fireplace inside, indulging in the dense bouillabaisse—a stew of mussels, scallops, tuna, tilapia, and shrimp, with a boat of saffron mayo to slather on croutons. Try a Québec wine to wash it down, maybe the l'Orpailleur from Dunham. The inside rooms are formed of rafters, brick, and stone walls that are over 300 years old, evoking the feel of a small country inn.

12 rue du Petit-Champlain (at the Funiculaire). (C) **418/692-0857**. www.marieclarisse.qc.ca. Main courses C$30–C$33 (US$26–US$29/£13–£14); table d'hôte dinner from C$38 (US$33/£16). AE, MC, V. Mon–Sat 11:30am–10pm; terrace Apr–Oct daily.

Poisson d'Avril SEAFOOD   Whoever christened this place was having a little joke: Its name means both "April Fool" and "April Fish." Nevertheless, nautical trappings of the three rooms that include model ships, marine prints, and mounted sailfish make the real intent clear. The menu is packed with seafood, including some combinations of costly crustaceans responsible for the stiffer prices noted below. The crowded Provençal bouillabaisse has calamari, scallops, shrimp, mussels, and rouille, while a special platter called *L'assiette du commodore* is laden with snow crabs, half a lobster, and the fish of the day. Mixed grill and pastas are also available. In good weather, there's a covered dining terrace. With the restaurant located almost directly next to Espace 400e, the new exhibition pavilion opening in June 2008, this will be a crowded location, so make reservations for weekend meals.

115 quai Saint-André (in Vieux-Port, near Espace 400e). (C) **418/692-1010**. www.poissondavril.net. Reservations recommended. Main courses C$13–C$67 (US$11–US$58/£5.60–£29); table d'hôte the price of your main plus C$13 (US$11/£5.60). AE, DC, MC, V. Daily 5–10pm.

Toast! 👗 FUSION   This zesty restaurant adjoins **Hôtel Le Priori** and occupies the space where Laurie Raphaël started before it went on to become the city's gastronomic flag bearer. There must be good karma, because Toast! has all the signs of following the same trajectory. As is true of most important restaurants in the province, the kitchen has its base in the French idiom, but takes off in many directions. See that in a pecan-crusted rack of rabbit with a cold purée of potato, cream, and horseradish, perked with a basil foam and Parmesan. Or fennel soup followed by chopped tuna, spiced with ginger and lemon zest, shaped into a burger and then grilled—but on just one side. Every dish is like that: audacious, sprightly, and attentive to joined tastes and textures. The interior room has a crimson glow from a wall of fire-engine-red tiles, retro-modern lights, and red Plexiglas paneling in the windows. Try for the outdoor dining terrace out back, if it's warm enough: With wrought-iron furniture and big leafy trees overhead, it's an oasis.

17 rue Sault-au-Matelot (at rue St-Antoine). (C) **418/692-1334**. www.restauranttoast.com. Reservations recommended on weekends. Main courses C$27–C$45 (US$23–US$39/£12–£19). AE, DC, MC, V. Mon–Fri 11:30am–2pm; daily 6–10:30pm (until 11pm Thurs–Sun); Sun 10:30am–2pm.

MODERATE

L'Ardoise FRENCH BISTRO   This is one of several appealing bistros that wrap around the intersection of rues St-Paul and Sault-au-Matelot. A new owner took over in the fall of 2006 but the decor is still the same, with the van Gogh–bright orange swirls and cobalt blue ceiling, and jaunty Piaf- and Sinatra-style vocals and accordion on the stereo. The menu, though, is a little different. Mussels are staples at Québec restaurants, prepared in the Belgian manner, with bowls of fries on the side. L'Ardoise no longer offers the all-you-can-eat plate, but instead offers a still-reasonable mussels and fries *(moules et frites)* for C$16 (US$14/£6.90), with seconds for C$7 (US$6.10/£3). There are 11 sauce options for the mussels, from Dijon mustard to curry. On a recent chilly day, a bowl of penne pasta with salmon, broccoli pesto, and aged cheddar hit the spot just right. There's an additional brunch menu from 10:30am to 3pm on weekends. This is a place to sip a double espresso, leaf through a book, and maybe meet the neighbors.

71 rue St-Paul (near rue du Sault-au-Matelot). © **418/694-0213**. www.lardoiseresto.com. Reservations recommended at dinner. Main courses C$15–C$36 (US$13–US$31/£6.45–£16); table d'hôte the price of your main plus C$15 (US$13/£6.45). AE, DC, MC, V. Mon–Fri 11:30am–3pm; Sat–Sun 10:30am–3pm; daily 5:30–10pm (closing earlier in winter).

Le Café du Monde ☆ *Value* FRENCH/INTERNATIONAL   A longtime and entirely convivial eating venue, the Café du Monde moved in 2002 to its current location adjoining Le Terminal de Croisières—the cruise terminal. It's a larger, jovial Parisian-style space, seating 135 inside and another 75 on a terrace overlooking the St. Lawrence River and Ile d'Orléans. The staff is as amiable as ever, the food a touch more creative but still within bistro conventions. The short menu continues to feature classic French preparations of pâtés, duck confit, onion soup, smoked salmon tartare, and four versions of mussels with frites. A recent brunch plate—scrambled eggs with salmon, dill, potatoes, fruit, and a croissant, for C$9 (US$7.85/£3.90)—was serviced fast and with a smile, even on a busy holiday weekend.

84 rue Dalhousie (next to the cruise terminal). © **418/692-4455**. www.lecafedumonde.com. Reservations recommended. Main courses C$12–C$27 (US$10–US$23/£5.15–£12); table d'hôte C$12–C$16 (US$10–US$14/£4.95–£6.65). AE, DC, MC, V. Mon–Fri 11:30am–11pm; Sat–Sun and holidays 9:30am–11pm.

6 St-Roch

EXPENSIVE

Utopie ☆ *Finds* FUSION   It's still young, but Utopie has proven so far to have the essential ingredients for its considerable success. The clientele has a stylish sheen, the interior is almost painfully chic, the food isn't same-old, and the location is sufficiently out-of-the-way to require that customers are those in the know. Stands of birch trunks march down the middle of the high-ceilinged space, and blown-up photos of bark are aligned on one wall. The chef is an owner, along with three others who run the front; all are young and clearly ambitious. Sautéed *lotte* (monkfish) was joined with translucent baby bok choy and wild asparagus no thicker than bean sprouts one night, with garlic cream another. One menu staple is the duck confit with braised endive and onion compote. All is calm and refined, leaving some dishes somewhat listless, but with no startling clashes of flavor. The all-out meal is the six-course degustation menu with a wine pairing for C$105 (US$91/£45).

226½ rue St-Joseph est (near rue Caron). © **418/523-7878**. www.restaurant-utopie.com. Reservations recommended on weekends. Main courses C$22–C$27 (US$19–US$23/£9.45–£12); table d'hôte dinner C$29–C$65 (US$25–US$57/£12–£28). AE, MC, V. Tues–Fri noon–2pm; Tues–Sun 6–9pm.

MODERATE

Le Clocher Penché ☆ *Finds* FRENCH BISTRO   Open since 2000 and owned by two self-styled "artisan chefs," the development of this unpretentious neighborhood bistro parallels the polishing-up this neighborhood has seen during the same period. With its caramel-toned woods, tall ceilings, and walls serving as gallery space for local artists, Le Clocher Penché has a laid-back European sophistication. And the wine list features 187 choices, with 96% private importation and 73% organic or "biodynamic"; about 10 wines are sold by the glass. If your timing is lucky, you'll be in town for the special dinner held every 3 or 4 months that includes six wine tastings for C$70 (US$61/£30). The short menu changes regularly and can include duck confit and wild boar. The rich blood sausage *(boudin noir)* was served on a delicate pastry bed with caramelized onions and yellow beets, and the tamer but still marvelous risotto had mushrooms and big chunks of asparagus. The menu touts that much of the food is sourced locally. Service reflects the food—amiable and without flourishes.

203 rue St-Joseph est (at rue Caron). © 418/640-0597. Reservations recommended. Main courses C$16–C$23 (US$14–US$20/£6.90–£9.90); weekend brunch C$14 (US$12/£6). AE, DC, MC, V. Mon–Fri 11:30am–3pm; Sat–Sun 9am–3pm; daily 5–10pm.

Versa FUSION   Looking more like a club than a restaurant, this is a destination to remember when with a group in a partying mood. A communal table sits beneath a teak oval ceiling illuminated by pin lights and a basketball-size disco ball, just the arena for friendly extroverts. Seatings have a '60s Swedish mien, and the windows along the front open in good weather. The translucent panels behind the back bar pulse with a rainbow of colors, highlighting the pride of the barkeeps, their inventive roster of cocktails—over a dozen martinis, yes, but also some eye-popping specials. One begins with muddled grapes and fresh ginger before 2 ounces of icy vodka are poured over. Dinners might feature mussels four ways, soufflé of black crab, leg of lamb with maple syrup, or, for the less hungry or demanding, a "Diablo dog" or tartare burger. The after-dinner action floats between here and the **Boudoir Lounge** across the street, the hottest nightspot in St-Roch (p. 268).

432 rue du Parvis (at rue St-Françoise). © 418/523-9995. www.versarestaurant.com. Main courses C$12–C$32 (US$10–US$28/£5.15–£14); table d'hôte dinner C$21–C$35 (US$18–US$30/£9.05–£15), lunch C$9–C$18 (US$7.85–US$16/£3.85–£7.75). MC, V. Mon–Fri 11am–midnight; Sat–Sun 5pm–midnight.

Yuzu 🍴 SUSHI/JAPANESE   For just a while, this was the hottest restaurant in town, offering evenings of astonishingly good food. Chefs have come and gone, but the restaurant is still worth seeking out. It's at the epicenter of the renovated portion of St-Roch, an area that's slowly getting a youthful pop amid otherwise dreary office buildings and low-key retail. Sushi and Japanese preparations are the focus, but authenticity isn't sought, not with foie gras on the card (and as expensive as you expect). Individual sushi run C$4 to C$15 (US$3.50–US$13/£1.70–£6.45) each, and there are tasting menus of C$65 (US$57/£28) for five courses and C$85 (US$74/£37) for seven. The restaurant, we were told, is putting more of a focus on wine, with more private importation.

438 rue du Parvis (at bd. Charest). © 418/521-7253. www.yuzu.ca. Reservations recommended. Main courses C$12–C$22 (US$10–US$19/£5.15–£9.45). AE, DC, MC, V. Mon–Fri 11:30am–2:30pm; Sun–Wed 5–10pm; Thurs–Sat 5pm–midnight.

15

Exploring Québec City

Wandering at random through the streets of Vieux-Québec is a singular pleasure, comparable to exploring a provincial capital in Europe. On the way, you can happen upon an ancient convent, blocks of gabled houses with steeply pitched roofs, a battery of 18th-century cannons in a leafy park, and a bistro with a blazing fireplace on a wintry day. The Old City, Upper and Lower, is so compact that it's hardly necessary to plan precise sightseeing itineraries. Start at the Terrasse Dufferin alongside the Château Frontenac and go off on a whim, down Breakneck Stairs (Escalier Casse-Cou) to the Quartier du Petit-Champlain and Place-Royale, or out of the walls to the military fortress of the Citadelle that overlooks the mighty St. Lawrence River and onto the Plains of Abraham, where Generals James Wolfe of Britain and Louis-Joseph, Marquis de Montcalm of France fought to their mutual deaths in a 20-minute battle that changed the destiny of the continent.

Most of the historic sights are within the city walls of Vieux-Québec's Haute-Ville (Upper Town) and Basse-Ville (Lower Town). It's all fairly easy walking. While the Upper Town is hilly, with sloping streets, it's nothing like, say, San Francisco, and only people with physical limitations are likely to experience difficulty. Other sights are outside the walls of the Upper Town, along or just off of the grand boulevard called Grande-Allée. If rain or ice discourages exploration on foot, tour buses and horse-drawn *calèches* are options.

If you're planning to hit up several museums, consider getting a **Québec City Museum Card.** Good for 3 consecutive days, the pass gives entry to 24 museums and attractions, including many mentioned in this chapter, and includes two 1-day bus passes. The price is C$40 (US$35/£17); there are no discounts for seniors or children. The pass is available at all participating attractions and at the Québec City Tourism Information Bureau at 835 av. Wilfrid-Laurier, in the Discovery Pavillion. To find out more, call © **418/641-6172** or visit www. museocapitale.qc.ca/cartema.

1 The Top Attractions

VIEUX-QUEBEC: BASSE-VILLE (LOWER TOWN)

Musée de la Civilisation ✿✿✿ *Kids*   Try to set aside at least 2 hours for a visit to this special museum, one of the most engrossing in all of Canada—or anywhere, for that matter. Designed by the McGill University–trained Moshe Safdie and opened in 1988, the Museum of Civilization is an innovative presence in the historic Basse-Ville, near Place-Royale and the waterfront. A dramatic atrium-lobby sets the tone with a representation of the St. Lawrence River with an ancient ship beached on the shore. Through the glass wall in back you can see the 1752 Maison Estèbe, now restored to contain the museum shop. It stands above vaulted cellars, which can also be viewed.

Québec City Attractions

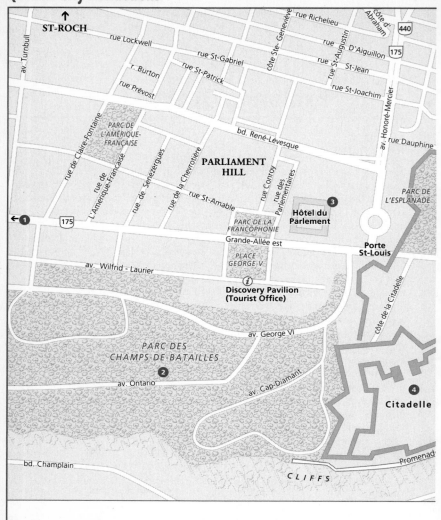

Basilique Notre-Dame **8**

Chapelle/Musée
   des Ursulines **5**

Château Frontenac **6**

Espace 400e **13**

Hôtel du Parlement **3**

La Citadelle **4**

Maison Chevalier **10**

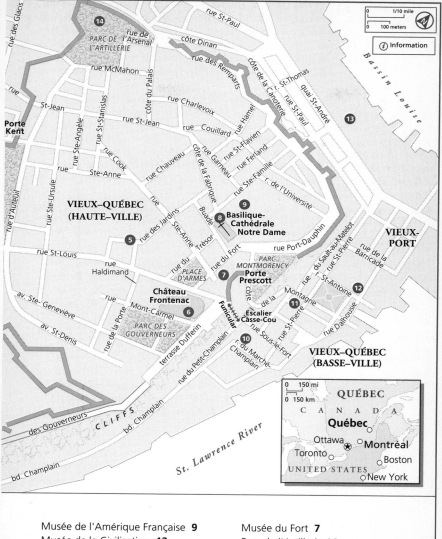

Musée de l'Amérique Française **9**
Musée de la Civilisation **12**
Musée des Beaux-Arts
   du Québec **1**

Musée du Fort **7**
Parc de l'Artillerie **14**
Parc des Champs-de-Bataille **2**
Place-Royale **11**

The precise mission of the museum has never been entirely clear. For example, recent temporary exhibits have included the science and fiction of dragons, 110 years of Québec cinema, the cultural origins of money, and the opportunity to solve a faux murder. But nevermind: Through highly imaginative display techniques, hands-on devices, computers, holograms, videos, and even an ant farm, the curators have ensured that visitors will be so enthralled by the experience that they won't pause to question its intent.

If time is short, definitely use it to take in "Memoires," a permanent exhibit that is a sprawling examination of Québec history, moving from the province's roots as a fur-trading colony to the present. Furnishings from frontier homes, tools of the trappers' trade, religious garments from the 19th century, and 20th-century posters endow visitors with a rich sense of Québec's daily life from generation to generation. Another permanent exhibition called "Encounter with the First Nations" examines the products and visions of the aboriginal tribes that inhabit Québec. Exhibit texts are in French and English, and there's a café on the ground floor.

85 rue Dalhousie (at rue St-Antoine). ✆ **418/643-2158.** www.mcq.org. Admission C$10 (US$8.70/£4.30) adults, C$9 (US$7.85/£3.85) 65 and over, C$7 (US$6.10/£3) students over 16, C$4 (US$3.50/£1.70) children 12–16, free for children under 12; free to all on Tues Nov 1–May 31 and Sat 10am–noon Jan–Feb. Late June to Labour Day daily 9:30am–6:30pm; day after Labour Day to late June Tues–Sun 10am–5pm.

Place-Royale ⭐⭐⭐ *Kids*   This small but picturesque plaza is considered by Québécois to be the literal and spiritual heart of Basse-Ville—in grander terms, the birthplace of French America. Royal Square is a short walk from the bottom of the funicular and Breakneck Stairs, via rue Sous-le-Fort. In the 17th and 18th centuries, it was the town marketplace and the center of business and industry. Today, folk dances and other festive gatherings are often held near the **bust of Louis XIV** in the center.

The **Eglise Notre-Dame-des-Victoires** dominates the plaza. The oldest stone church in Québec, it was built in 1688 after a massive fire in Lower Town destroyed 55 homes in 1682, and then was restored in 1763 and 1969. Its paintings, altar, and large model boat suspended from the church ceiling were votive offerings brought by early settlers to ensure safe voyages. The church is open daily to visitors May through October. Sunday Masses are held at 10:30am and noon.

All the buildings on the square have been restored, although some of the walls are original. For years, there was only an empty lot behind the stone facade on the northeast side, but now it is a whole building again. On the ground floor is the **Centre d'Interprétation de Place-Royale.** Inside, a 20-minute multimedia show and other exhibitions detail the city's 400-year history and the development of the plaza. Guided tours of the area are available from the interpretation center in both English and French. Walk past the Centre on your left and at the end of the block turn around to view a *trompe l'oeil* mural depicting citizens of the early city.

Centre d'Interprétation de Place-Royale, 27 rue Notre-Dame. ✆ **418/646-3167.** Admission to the Place-Royale and Eglise Notre-Dame-des-Victoires is free; Center d'Interprétation admission C$5 (US$4.35/£2.15) adults, C$4.50 (US$3.90/£1.95) seniors, C$2 (US$1.75/85p) ages 12–16, free for children under 12. June 24–Sept 6 daily 9:30am–5pm; Sept 7–June 23 Tues–Sun 10am–5pm.

VIEUX-QUEBEC: HAUTE-VILLE (UPPER TOWN)

La Citadelle ⭐⭐   The duke of Wellington had this partially star-shaped fortress built at the south end of the city walls in anticipation of renewed American attacks after the War of 1812. Some remnants of earlier French military structures were

Tips 2008: Québec Throws Itself a Party

In 1608, Samuel de Champlain founded a settlement at Kebec, at the foot of Cape Diamond. That settlement became the city of Québec. For the last few years, the city has been sprucing itself up and planning blowout celebrations for 2008, to commemorate its 400th anniversary. Among the happenings:

- **The June opening of Espace 400ᵉ**, a new pavilion on the waterfront where the Centre d'Interprétation du Vieux-Port used to be. It will host special 400th-anniversary exhibits, performances, conferences, and shows from June to September. After 2008, it will become a Parks Canada discovery center.

- **Four days of "exceptional events" from July 3 to July 6**, including an official ceremony, Mass at the Basilique Notre-Dame, tie-in concerts with the Québec City Summer Festival, and an aerial photograph of the Plains of Abraham that everyone is invited to join.

- **Nightly projections of video onto the silos** across the water from Espace 400ᵉ—what organizers say will be one of the largest projections of its kind.

- **Major international meetings,** including the IIHF World Hockey Championship, usually held in Europe, in May; the 49th International Eucharist Congress, a major gathering of Catholic hierarchy, in June; the 4th World Youth Congress in August; and the 12th Summit of French-Speaking Countries in October.

- **Special exhibits at museums** and tourist venues across the city, including "Québec: A City and its Artists" and an exhibit of works from The Louvre, both at the Musée des Beaux-Arts du Québec.

- **A spectacular closing event** featuring Cirque du Soleil on October 19.

For the most up-to-date information about events and tickets, visit **www. myquebec2008.com.**

incorporated into the Citadelle, including a 1750 magazine. Dug into the Plains of Abraham high above Cap Diamant ("Cape Diamond"), the rock bluff adjacent to the St. Lawrence River, the fort has a low profile that keeps it all but invisible until walkers are actually upon it. The facility has never actually exchanged fire with an invader but continues its vigil for the state. It's now a national historic site, and since 1920 has been home to Québec's Royal 22e Régiment, the only fully Francophone unit in Canada's armed forces. That makes it the largest fortified group of buildings still occupied by troops in North America.

As part of a 55-minute guided tour only, the public may visit the Citadelle and its 25 buildings, including the small regimental museums in the former powder house and prison. Despite a couple of spectacular overlooks, the length of the tour and the dry narration are likely to test the patience of younger visitors and the legs of many older people. In those cases, it might be better simply to attend the ceremonies of the changing of the guard (daily at 10am in summer) or beating the retreat (Fri at 7pm in summer). Walk or drive up the Côte de la Citadelle; there are many parking spaces inside the walls.

Côte de la Citadelle (enter off rue St-Louis). © **418/694-2815.** www.lacitadelle.qc.ca. Admission C$10 (US$8.70/£4.30) adults, C$9 (US$7.85/£3.85) seniors and students over 17, C$5.50 (US$4.80/£2.35) age 17 and younger. Apr daily 10am–4pm; May–June daily 9am–5pm; July to Labour Day daily 9am–6pm; Sept (after Labour Day) daily 9am–4pm; Oct daily 10am–3pm; Nov–Mar 1 bilingual tour a day at 1:30pm. Changing of the guard (30 min.) June 24 to Labour Day daily at 10am; beating the retreat (20 min.) July to early Sept Fri at 7pm, and Sat–Sun at 7pm at the Esplanade Park. May be canceled in the event of rain.

PARLIAMENT HILL / NEAR THE GRANDE-ALLEE

Musée des Beaux-Arts du Québec 🎨🎨 *Kids* Toward the southern end of the Parc des Champs-de-Bataille (Battlefields Park), just off the Grande-Allée and a half-hour walk or a short bus ride from the Haute-Ville, the Musée du Québec (as it's known in shorthand) is the city's major art museum. It occupies two buildings, one a former prison, linked together by a soaring glass-roofed "Grand Hall" housing the reception area, a stylish café, and a shop.

The original 1933 Gérard-Morisset Pavilion houses much of the permanent collection—the largest aggregation of Québécois art in North America, filling eight galleries with works from the beginning of the colony to the present. The museum tilts to the modern in addition to the indigenous; there's a permanent exhibition of works by famed Québec abstract expressionist/surrealist Jean-Paul Riopelle. Included is his *L'Hommage à Rosa Luxemburg,* a triptych made up of 30 individual paintings that include spray-painted ghosts of birds and handyman tools. The museum acquired in 2005 the important Inuit art collection assembled over many years by Québécois Raymond Brousseau. Much of the work has been produced in the last 20 years, and about 300 works from the 2,635-piece collection are on display. Look for the small whimsical statue called *Woman Pulling Out Grey Hairs.*

The second building is the 1867 Charles-Baillairgé Pavilion, a former prison, which in the 1970s became a youth hostel nicknamed the "Petite Bastille." One cellblock has been left intact as an exhibit. Make sure to keep climbing until you get to the tower room; it's the highest point in the museum, a small widow's walk accessible only by spiral staircase. In addition to housing the massive wooden sculpture of a body in motion by Irish artist David Moore, it offers terrific views of the city in every direction. There are several spots in the museum focused on children, including a craft projects room. An accomplished café-restaurant serves table d'hôte lunches Monday through Friday, brunch on Saturday and Sunday, and dinner Wednesday evenings.

Parc des Champs-de-Bataille, near where av. Wolfe-Montcalm meets Grande Allée © **418/643-2150.** www.mnba.qc.ca. Free admission to permanent collection. Admission for special exhibitions C$12 (US$10/£5.15) adults, C$10 (US$8.70/£4.30) seniors, C$5 (US$4.35/£2.15) students over 16, C$3 (US$2.60/£1.30) ages 12–16, free for children under 12. June 1 to Labour Day daily 10am–6pm (until 9pm Wed); day after Labour Day to May 31 Tues–Sun 10am–5pm (until 9pm Wed). Bus: 11.

Parc des Champs-de-Bataille 🎨🎨 *Kids* Covering 108 hectares (267 acres) of grassy hills, sunken gardens, monuments, fountains, and trees, Québec's Battlefields Park is Canada's first national urban park. It stretches over the Plains of Abraham, where Britain's General James Wolfe and France's Louis-Joseph, Marquis de Montcalm engaged in their short but crucial battle in 1759, resulting in the British defeat of the French troops (and the death of both military leaders). Today it is a favorite place for all Québécois when they want some sunshine or a bit of exercise.

From the spring through the fall, be sure to see the Jardin Jeanne d'Arc (Joan of Arc Garden), just off avenue Wilfrid-Laurier between Loews le Concorde Hôtel and the Ministry of Justice. This spectacular garden combines French classical style with British-style flower beds. Close to 6,000 trees representing more than 80 species blanket the fields. Prominent among these are sugar maple, silver maple, Norway maple, American elm, and American ash. Within the park are also two Martello towers, cylindrical stone defensive structures built between 1808 and 1812, when Québec feared an invasion from the United States.

Free concerts are given during the summer at a bandstand here, the Kiosque Edwin-Bélanger. Theatrical events are also presented in the park during the summer. Fittingly, perhaps, the national anthem "O Canada" was first performed here.

The **Discovery Pavilion of the Plains of Abraham,** at 835 av. Wilfrid-Laurier, at the far northeastern end near the Citadelle (© **418/648-4071**), has a gift shop, Internet station, bathrooms, and, in winter, cross-country ski rentals. The tourism bureau also has an office here. A multimedia exhibit called "Odyssey: A Journey Through History on the Plains of Abraham" is presented in English, French, Spanish, and Japanese.

Park open 24 hr. www.ccbn-nbc.gc.ca. Discovery Pavilion, 835 av. Wilfrid-Laurier © **418/648-4071**. Odyssey show C$10 (US$8.70/£4.30) adults, C$8 (US$6.95/£3.45) seniors and ages 13–17, free for 12 and under. Open year-round; summer daily 8:30am–5:30pm; winter Mon–Fri 8:30am–5pm, Sat 9am–5pm, Sun 10am–5pm.

2 More Attractions

VIEUX-QUEBEC: HAUTE-VILLE (UPPER TOWN)

Basilique Notre-Dame ✦   Notre-Dame Basilica, representing the oldest Christian parish north of Mexico, has weathered a tumultuous history of bombardment, reconstruction, and restoration. Parts of the existing basilica date from the original 1647 structure, including the bell tower and portions of the walls, but most of today's exterior is from the reconstruction completed in 1771. The interior, a re-creation undertaken after a fire in 1922, is flamboyantly neo-baroque, with shadows wavering by the fluttering light of votive candles. Paintings and ecclesiastical treasures still remain from the time of the French regime, including a chancel lamp given by Louis XIV. Over 900 people are buried in the crypt, including 4 governors of New France (Frontenac, Vaudreuil, Callières and Jonquière). The basilica is connected to the group of old buildings that make up Québec Seminary. There is an organ concert the first Sunday of every month at 3:30pm.

16 rue Buade (at Côte de la Fabrique). © **418/692-2533**. Cathedral fee C$2 (US$1.75/£85p) adults, free for ages 16 and younger. Crypt and guided tour fees C$2 (US$1.75/85p) adults, C$1 (US85¢/45p) ages 16 and younger. Organ concert suggested donation C$5 (US$4.35/£2.15). Free admission for those who come for prayers and services. Mon–Sat 7:30am–6pm in summer (closing at 4pm the rest of the year), Sun 8:30am–6pm. Guided tours May–Oct daily.

Chapelle/Musée des Ursulines   This chapel is notable for the sculptures in its pulpit and two richly decorated altarpieces. They were created by Pierre-Noël Levasseur between 1726 and 1736. Although the present building dates only from 1902, much of the interior decoration is nearly 200 years older. The tomb of the founder of the Ursulines teaching order, Marie de l'Incarnation, who arrived in Québec City in 1639 at the age of 40, is to the right of the entry. The Ursuline convent, built originally as a girls' school in 1642, is the oldest in North America, and Marie de l'Incarnation was beatified by Pope John Paul II in 1980. The museum tells the story of the nuns, who were also pioneers and artists. Included are vestments woven with gold thread by the Ursulines and a cape made of the drapes from the bedroom of Anne of Austria, which was given to Marie de l'Incarnation when she left for New France in 1639. There are also musical instruments and Amerindian crafts, including the *flèche*, or arrow sash, which is still worn during the winter carnival. Some of the docents are nuns of the still-active order.

12 rue Donnacona (des Jardins). ⓒ 418/694-0694. www.patrimoine-religieux.com. Free admission to chapel. Museum C$6 (US$5.20/£2.60) adults, C$5 (US$4.35/£2.15) seniors, C$4 (US$3.50/£1.70) students 17 and over, C$3 (US$2.60/£1.30) ages 12–16, free for children under 12. Museum May–Sept Tues–Sat 10am–noon and 1–5pm, Sun 1–5pm; Oct–Apr Tues–Sun 1–5pm. Chapel May–Oct Tues–Sat 10–11:30am and 1:30–4:40pm.

Château Frontenac ⚜ Opened in 1893 to house railroad passengers and encourage tourism, this monster version of a Loire Valley palace is Québec City's emblem, its Eiffel Tower. The hotel can be seen from almost every quarter, commanding its majestic position atop Cap Diamant, the rock bluff that once provided military defense. (See p. 212 in chapter 13 for more details.) Visitors curious about the interior can take a 50-minute guided tour; reservations are recommended.

1 rue des Carrières, at Place d'Armes. ⓒ 418/691-2166. Tours C$8.50 (US$7.40/£3.65) adults, C$7.75 (US$6.75/ £3.35) for seniors, C$6 US$5.20/£2.60) children ages 6–16. May 1–Oct 15 daily 10am–6pm; Oct 16–Apr 30 Sat–Sun 1–5pm (departures on the hour).

Musée de l'Amérique Française Located at the Québec Seminary, which dates from 1663, the Museum of French America focuses on the evolution of French culture in North America. Its extensive collections include paintings by European and Canadian artists, engravings from the early French regime, rare books, early scientific instruments, and even mounted animals and an Egyptian mummy. The mix makes for a mostly engrossing visit, although parts of the museum can be rather dry. The museum is located in three parts of the large seminary complex, and the beautiful François-Ranvoyze section has extensive *trompe l'oeil* ornamentation and served as a chapel for the seminary priests and students. Recent construction has added an annex to the chapel, an underground passage, and a new entrance lobby. Concerts are often held in the chapel, which was visited by Pope Jean-Paul II in 1984.

2 Côte de la Fabrique (next to Basilique Notre-Dame). ⓒ 418/692-2843. www.mcq.org. Admission C$6 (US$5.20/ £2.60) adults, C$5 (US$4.35/£2.15) seniors, C$3.50 (US$3.05/£1.50) students 17 and older, C$2 (US$1.75/85p) children 12–16, free for children under 12, free to all Tues from Nov 1–May 31. Late June to Labour Day daily 9:30am–5pm; Sept to mid-June Tues–Sun 10am–5pm. Guided tours (call for reservations) of exhibitions and buildings 10am and 3:30pm in summer; call for times the rest of the year.

Musée du Fort A long-running but still effective multimedia show combines film, light, stirring music, and a 36-sq.-m (400-sq.-ft.) scale model of the city and environs to tell the story of the several battles that flared here in the 18th century. At less than 25 minutes, it is a sufficiently engrossing presentation during which only the very young are likely to grow restless. Check in advance when shows in English are scheduled.

10 rue Ste-Anne, Place d'Armes. ⓒ 418/692-2175. www.museedufort.com. Admission C$7.50 (US$6.50/£3.25) adults, C$6 (US$5.20/£2.60) seniors, C$5 (US$4.35/£2.15) students. Apr 1–Oct 31 daily 10am–5pm; Nov 1–Mar 31 Thurs–Sun 11am–4pm; Dec 26–1st Sun in Jan daily 11am–4pm. Open to groups with reservations in winter months.

Parc de l'Artillerie Fortifications erected by the French in the 17th and 18th centuries enclose Artillery Park. In addition to protecting the garrison, the defensive works contained an ammunition factory that was functional until 1964. On view are the old officers' mess and quarters, an iron foundry, and a scale model of the city created in 1806. Costumed docents give tours. In July and August, there are twice-daily musket demonstrations; hours vary. (It may be a blow to romantics and history buffs to learn that the nearby St-Jean Gate in the city wall was built in 1940, the fourth in a series that began with the original 1693 entrance, which was replaced in 1747, and then replaced again in 1867.)

2 rue d'Auteuil (near Porte St-Jean). ℂ 418/648-4205. www.pc.gc.ca/artillerie. Admission C$3.95 (US$3.45/£1.70) adults, C$3.45 (US$3/£1.50) seniors, C$1.95 (US$1.70/85p) ages 6–16, free for children under 6. Additional fees for audio guide, special activities, and tea ceremony. Apr 1–Oct 7 daily 10am–5pm; by reservation only the rest of the year.

VIEUX-QUEBEC: BASSE-VILLE (LOWER TOWN)

The **Escalier Casse-Cou** connects the Terrasse Dufferin at the top of the cliff with rue Sous-le-Fort at the base. The name translates to "Breakneck Stairs," which is self-explanatory as soon as you see them. They lead—very steeply—from Haute-Ville to the Quartier du Petit-Champlain in Basse-Ville. A stairway has existed here since the settlement began. In fact, in 1698 the town council forbade citizens from taking their animals up or down the stairway. If they didn't comply they were punished with a fine.

Espace 400ᵉ   Occupying what used to be the Centre d'Interprétation du Vieux-Port on the waterfront, this newly renovated and expanded pavilion is set to open in May 2008 as the central location for Québec's 400th-anniversary celebrations. From June to September 2008, Espace 400ᵉ will host exhibits, performances, conferences, and shows. From 2009 on, it will become a Parks Canada discovery center.

100 quai St-Andre (at rue Rioux). www.myquebec2008.com.

Maison Chevalier   Built in 1752 for ship owner Jean-Baptiste Chevalier, the existing structure incorporated two older buildings, dating from 1675 and 1695. It was run as an inn throughout the 19th century, and after the Québec government restored the house it became a museum in 1965. The interior has exposed wood beams, wide-board floors, and stone fireplaces. A permanent exhibit, "A Sense of the Past," shows how people lived in the 18th and 19th centuries. While exhibit texts are in French, guidebooks in English are available at the sometimes-unattended front desk. The house also serves as an air-conditioned refuge on hot days.

50 rue du Marché-Champlain (near rue Notre-Dame). www.mcq.org. Free admission. Late June to Labour Day daily 9:30am–5pm; Sept to mid-Oct and Dec 19–Jan 1 Tues–Sun 10am–5pm; the rest of the year Sat–Sun 10am–5pm.

PARLIAMENT HILL / NEAR THE GRANDE-ALLEE

Hôtel du Parlement   Since 1968, what the Québécois choose to call their "National Assembly" has occupied this imposing Second Empire château constructed in 1886. Twenty-two bronze statues of some of the most prominent figures in Québec's tumultuous history gaze out from the facade. Highlights are the Assembly Chamber, and the Legislative Council Chamber, where parliamentary committees meet. Throughout the building, representations of the fleur-de-lis and the initials VR (for Victoria Regina) remind visitors of Québec's dual heritage. The building can be toured unaccompanied, but there are free 30-minute guided tours in both French and English (as well as Spanish and Italian). Call for tour times in the language you want.

The grand Beaux-Arts style restaurant **Le Parlementaire** (ℂ 418/643-6640) is open to the public. Featuring Québec products and cuisine, it serves breakfast and lunch Monday through Friday most of the year.

Entrance at corner of Grande-Allée est and av. Honoré-Mercier. ℂ 418/643-7239. www.assnat.qc.ca. Free admission. Guided tours in summer Mon–Fri 9am–4:30pm; Sat–Sun and holidays 10am–4:30pm; in winter Mon–Fri 9am–4:30pm.

3 Especially for Kids

Children who have responded to Arthurian tales of fortresses and castles or to the adventures of Harry Potter often delight in simply walking around this storybook city. As soon as possible, head for **Terrasse Dufferin** in the Upper Town, which has those coin-operated telescopes that kids find so engaging. In decent weather, there are always street entertainers, ranging from Peruvian musical groups to men who play saws or wineglasses. Archaeological digs under the northern end of the Terrasse that started in 2005 will still be underway into 2008, although they may include some new viewing stations put in for the city's 400th-anniversary celebrations.

A few steps away at Place d'Armes are **horse-drawn carriages,** and not far in the same direction is the **Musée du Fort,** at 10 rue Ste-Anne (p. 242). Also at Place d'Armes is the top of **Breakneck Stairs.** Halfway down, across the road, are giant **cannons** ranged along the battlements on rue des Ramparts. The gun carriages are impervious to the assaults of small humans, so kids can scramble over them at will. At the bottom of the Breakneck Stairs, on the left, is a **glass-blowing workshop,** the Verrerie la Mailloche. It's somewhat less impervious to the assaults of small humans but still kid-friendly: In the downstairs room, craftsmen give intriguing and informative glass-blowing demonstrations. The glass is melted at 2,500°F (1,350°C) and is worked at 2,000°F (1,100°C).

Also in the Lower Town, at 86 rue Dalhousie, the terrific **Musée de la Civilisation** (p. 235) keeps kids occupied for hours in its exhibits, shop, and café. The **ferry** across the St. Lawrence to Lévis, which leaves from Lower Town not far from the museum, is inexpensive and can be thrilling for kids. The crossing, over and back, takes less than an hour (p. 245).

If military sites are appealing, **La Citadelle** has tours of the grounds and buildings, although the distances covered and the dry narration are apt to give kids the fidgets. You might be better off taking them to the colorful changing of the guard and beating retreat ceremonies (p. 238). To run off some excess energy, head for **Battlefields Park (Parc des Champs-de-Bataille),** also called the **Plains of Abraham,** directly next to the Citadelle. Acres of grassy lawn give children room to roam and provide the perfect spot for a family picnic (p. 241).

On Wednesdays and Saturdays from late July to mid-August, the city hosts a grand fireworks competition, **Les Grands Feux Loto-Québec.** It takes place at the highly scenic Montmorency Falls 15 minutes north of city center, with international pyrotechnical teams presenting their own program each evening. Tickets get you admission to the base of the falls. Call (C) **888/523-3473** for details; tickets are available online at www.quebecfireworks.com. If you're visiting around Halloween, the city hosts a 3-day **Festival d'Automne** October 30 through November 1. There are ice-skating performances, concerts by the National League of Musical Improvisation of Québec, light-and-sound shows, and more. Check www.infofestival.com/faq.

When in doubt, though, just head to the water. The **Village Vacances Valcartier** ((C) **418/844-1239;** www.valcartier.com) at 1860 bd. Valcartier in St-Gabriel-de-Valcartier, is about a half-hour drive northwest of downtown. In summer, it has 35 slides, a huge wave pool, two "theme rivers," and diving shows. In winter, those same facilities are put to use for snow rafting on inner tubes, sliding down ice slides, and skating. The **Canyon Ste-Anne** ((C) **418/827-4057;** www.canyonste-anne.qc.ca) about 45 minutes northeast, offers thrilling bridge walks over a rushing waterfall, particularly spectacular in spring when the snow begins to melt. See p. 278 in chapter 19.

4 Organized Tours

Québec City is small enough to get around quickly and easily with a good map and a guidebook, but a tour is helpful for getting background information on the history and culture of the city, grasping the lay of the land, and seeing those attractions that are a bit of a hike or require wheels to reach. Directly in front of the Château Frontenac, the **Kiosque Frontenac** (② **418/692-5483**) can make reservations for most city tours, whether by bus, boat, or foot. Below are some agencies and organizations that have proved reliable in the past.

BUS TOURS

Buses are obviously convenient if extensive walking is difficult for individual visitors, especially in the hilly and steeply sloping Upper Town. Among the established tour operators, **Dupont** (② **888/558-7668** or 418/649-9226) offers English-only tours, which are preferable since twice as much information is imparted in the same amount of time as on a bilingual tour. The company's city tours are in small coaches, while day trips out of the city, to the casino at Charlevoix and along the south shore, for example, are in full-size buses. Dupont also offers a 10-hour whale-watching excursion by bus to Baie-Ste-Catherine and cruise boat into the St. Lawrence River. **La Tournée du Québec Métro** (② **800/672-5232** or 418/836-8687) has tours of Old Québec and excursions to Ile d'Orléans, Montmorency Falls, and Ste-Anne-de-Beaupré, with free hotel pickup. City tours usually last 2 to 2½ hours and cost about C$30 (US$26/£13) for adults, about half that for children.

HORSE-DRAWN CARRIAGE TOURS

A romantic but expensive way to tour the city is in a horse-drawn carriage, called a *calèche.* There are three companies that operate in the city. Carriages will pick you up or can be hired throughout the city, including at Place d'Armes. The 40-minute rides of **Calèches du Vieux-Québec** (② **418/683-9222**) and **Calèches de la Nouvelle-France** (② **418/692-0068**) cost C$75 (US$65/£32) plus tip for four people maximum. The other company is **Calèches Royales du Vieux-Québec** (② **418/687-6653**). Carriages operate all summer, rain or shine.

RIVER CRUISES

A variety of cruise possibilities are offered by **Croisières AML** (② **800/563-4643** or 418/692-1159 in season; www.croisieresaml.com). Weighing in at 900 tons, M/V *Louis Jolliet* is a three-deck 1930s ferry–turned–excursion vessel. It can carry 1,000 passengers, and has bilingual guides, full dining facilities, and a bar. The basic cruise lasts 1½ hours, and has three daily departures in high season. There's also a full-dinner evening "Love Boat" cruise with dancing as part of the experience. Prices for the 1½-hour "Discoverer" cruises are C$28 (US$24/£12) for adults, C$26 (US$23/£11) for seniors and students, and C$14 (US$12/£6) for children 6 to 16. Fares on the "Love Boat" cruises are C$33 (US$29/£14) for adults, C$31 (US$27/£13) for seniors and students, and C$16 (US$14/£6.90) for ages 6 to 16, but meals are extra, from C$28 to C$49 (US$24–US$43/£12–£21) per person extra, tax and tip not included. Board the boats at quai (pier) Chouinard, 10 rue Dalhousie, near Place-Royale in the Lower Town.

   Croisères Dufour (② **800/463-5250** or 418/692-0222; www.groupedufour.com), also offers a variety of cruises within the city for similar prices, as well as tours down to Montréal.

For **whale-watching cruises,** you need to first drive north about 2 hours along the St. Lawrence River into the Charlevoix region. Whale-watch boats leave from the towns of Baie Ste-Catherine and Tadoussac and typically spend 2½ hours looking for whales. There are packages that include a night at the famed Hotel Tadoussac, buffet dinner, and breakfast. See the last section of chapter 19 for information.

WALKING TOURS
Times and points of departure for walking tours change, so get up-to-date information at any of the tourist offices or at the kiosk on Terrasse Dufferin near the Château Frontenac and beside the funicular entrance. Many tours leave from there. If you want to go at your own pace, see if the kiosk is still renting "audio-guide" CD players for C$10 (US$8.70/ £4.30). The recorded narration leads past most of the major sites, taking anywhere from 1 to 3 hours. The **Association des guides touristiques de Québec** (✆ **418/683-2104**) can provide guides for any length of time, on foot or in your car or theirs.

5 Spectator Sports
Québec has not had a team in any of the major professional leagues since the NHL Nordiques left in 1995, but since 1999 it has been represented by the **Les Capitales de Québec (Québec City Capitales) baseball club** of the Northern League (www. capitalesdequebec.com). Home games are played in Stade Municipal (Municipal Stadium), 100 rue du Cardinal Maurice-Roy (✆ 418/521-2255), not far beyond the St-Roch neighborhood. Tickets cost from C$9 to C$16 (US$7.85–US$14/£3.85–£6.90).

Harness races take place at the **Hippodrome de Québec,** 250 bd. Wilfrid-Hamel ExpoCité (✆ **418/524-5283;** www.hdeqc.com/hq). Races are typically held year-round at 1:25 or 7:25pm (times vary from season to season). Call or check the website for the latest status.

6 Outdoor Activities
The waters and hills around Québec City provide countless opportunities for outdoor recreation, from swimming, rafting, and fishing, to skiing, snowmobiling, and sleigh rides. There are three centers in particular to keep in mind for most winter and summer activities, both within easy drives from the capital. All are within a 45-minute drive. The provincial **Parc de la Jacques-Cartier** (✆ **418/848-3169** in summer, 418/528-8787 in winter; www.sepaq.com/pq/jac/en) is off Route 175 north; **Station Touristique Duchesnay** (✆ **877/511-5885** or 418/875-2122; www.sepaq.com/ duchesnay) is a resort in the town of Ste-Catherine-de-la-Jacques-Cartier; and **Parc Mont Ste-Anne** (✆ **888/827-4579** or **418/827-4561;** www.mont-sainte-anne.com) is northeast of the city toward Charlevoix. All three are mentioned in the listings below. See p. 279 in chapter 19 for details about Parc Mont Ste-Anne.

From about mid-November to late March, the **HiverExpress** shuttle service picks up passengers at over a dozen hotels in the morning to take them to Parc Mont Ste-Anne and Station Stoneham (where Parc de la Jacques-Cartier is) and returning them to Québec City in later afternoon. Round-trip fare the same day is C$25 (US$22/ £11). Call ✆ **418/525-5191** to make a reservation or ask if your hotel participates when booking a room.

In season, the HiverExpress shuttle service to the mountain that picks up from downtown hotels. The cars or minivans are equipped to carry ski gear and cost C$25

(US$22/£11) round-trip (the same day) per person. For information call © **418/ 525-5191.**

BIKING

Given the hilly topography of the Upper Town, biking isn't a particularly attractive option inside the walls. But there are lots of places to go for a couple hours right in the city, either along the river or up in Parliament Hill in the Parc des Champs-de-Bataille (Battlefields Park). Rentals are available at a shop next to the Marché du Vieux-Port (Old Port Market) in the flatter Lower Town: **Cyclo Services,** 160 rue du Quai St-André (© **418/692-4052**) rents bikes for C$16 (US$14/£6.90) for 2 hours and C$25 (US$22/£11) for 12 hours, with other increments available. Bike trailers and electric bikes are available. The company also conducts guided tours on bicycle with several routes in the immediate environs of the city. It's open daily in summer. A marked path for cyclists (and in-line skaters) along the waterfront follows the second half of the route described in the Lower Town Walking Tour 2 (p. 256). Tourist information centers have bicycle trail maps and can point out a variety of routes depending on your time and interests.

CAMPING

There are over 20 campgrounds in the greater Québec City area, some with as few as 25 individual campsites and others up to about 250 (one even has 703 sites). Most have showers and toilets available. One of the largest (they even accept credit cards) is in the **Parc Mont Ste-Anne** (p. 246). One of the smaller grounds, with 161 sites and chalet rentals, is **Camping La Loutre** (© **418/528-6868**) on Lac Jacques-Cartier in the park of the same name. The tourist site www.quebecregion.com has details.

CANOEING

The several lakes and rivers of **Parc de la Jacques-Cartier** are fairly easy to reach, yet still seem to be in the midst of virtual wilderness. Canoes are available to rent in the park itself. The **Station Touristique Duchesnay** resort is directly on the shores of Lac Saint-Joseph and has canoeing, kayaking, and pedal boats for rent.

CROSS-COUNTRY SKIING

In the city, the **Parc des Champs-de-Bataille (Battlefields Park),** where the Carnaval de Québec establishes its winter playground during February, has a network of groomed cross-country trails. Equipment can be rented at the Discovery Pavilion at 835 av. Wilfrid-Laurier, near the Citadelle (© **418/648-2586**). The **Station Touristique Duchesnay** offers extensive trails on the grounds along with ski rentals. This is where the Ice Hotel is built each winter, making it well worth the trip out. There's also a spa, nightly accommodations, and a good bistro, Le Quatre-Temps, on the resort's campus. The **Association of Cross-Country Ski Stations** (www.rssfrq.qc.ca) has a list of maps and other options.

DOG SLEDDING

Aventure Inukshuk (© **418/875-0770;** www.aventureinukshuk.qc.ca), at 143 route de Duchesnay in Ste-Catherine-de-la-Jacques-Cartier, is located in Station Touristique Duchesnay, near where the Ice Hotel is built each winter. Guides show you how to lead a sled pulled by six dogs. Even on the short 1-hour trip, you go deep into the hushed world of snow and thick woods, past rows of Christmas trees, and over a beaver pond. The company's 200-plus dogs live in a field of individual pens and houses under evergreen trees, and they work up an enormous cacophony of howls whenever a team of dogs is harnessed up and set to go. Guides work with the same dogs every day, training and caring for their teams themselves. Overnight trips with camping are available. The 1-hour trip, which includes an additional half-hour of training, is C$88 (US$76/£38). Children ages 6 to 12 are half price, and ages 2 to 5 go free. It's expensive, especially for families, but the memory stays with you.

Aventures Nord-Bec (℗ 418/889-8001; www.aventures-nord-bec.com), at 4 chemin des Anémones in Stoneham, is also about a half-hour from the city. It's a different direction, though, so dog sledding and a trip to the Ice Hotel can't be bundled into the same visit. You do, though, get a longer ride for your dollar. One-and-a-half to 2 hours of dog sledding in addition to a 20-minute lesson costs C$83 adult (US$72/£36) and C$25 (US$22/£11) ages 5 to 11.

DOWNHILL SKIING

Foremost among the nearby downhill centers is **Mont Ste-Anne,** containing the largest total skiing surface in eastern Canada, with 65 trails (17 lit for night skiing). In season, the Hiver Express shuttle service to the mountain that picks up from downtown hotels. Farther away—about an hour and a half north in the Charlevoix region—**Le Massif** is a mountain almost directly on the St. Lawrence River. See p. 282 in chapter 19.

FISHING

Anglers can wet their lines in the river that flows through the **Parc de la Jacques-Cartier.** The catches are mostly trout and salmon. Permits are required and can be purchased at many sporting-goods stores. Information on regulations for fishing is available from the **Minstère des Ressources naturelles et de la Faune** (℗ 866/248-6936; www.mrnf.gouv.qc.ca/faune).

GOLF

Le Grand Vallon (℗ 888/827-4579 or 418/827-4653; www.legrandvallon.com) at Parc Mont Ste-Anne, is an 18-hole, par 72 course with tree-lined stretches, wide-open mid-course sections, four lakes, and 40 sand traps. Rates are C$36 to C$85 (US$31–US$74/£16–£37) and include golf cart, access to the driving range, and practice balls. Club rental is available.

ICE-SKATING

In the wintertime, outdoor rinks (with skate rentals) are set up in the Place d'Youville just outside the Upper Town walls.

SWIMMING

Those who want to swim during their visit should plan to stay at one of the handful of hotels with pools. **Fairmont Le Château Frontenac** has one, as do **Manoir Victoria, Château Laurier, Hilton Québec, Loews Le Concorde,** and **Château Bonne Entente.** See chapter 13 for details. **Village Vacances Valcartier,** an all-season recreational center in St-Gabriel-de-Valcartier (1860 bd. Valcartier; ℗ 418/844-1239) a half-hour from the city, has an immense wave pool and water slides.

TOBOGGANING

An old-fashioned toboggan run is created every winter down a steep staircase at the south end of the Terrasse Dufferin. It runs nearly all the way to the Château Frontenac. Tickets are sold at a temporary booth near the end of the run and include the use of toboggans.

16

Québec City Strolls

The many pleasures of walking in picturesque Québec are entirely comparable to walking in similar *quartiers* in northern European cities. Stone houses rub shoulders; carriage wheels creak behind muscular horses; sunlight filters through leafy canopies, falling on drinkers and diners in sidewalk cafés; and childish shrieks of laughter echo down cobblestone streets. Not common to other cities, however, is the bewitching vista of river and mountains that the Dufferin promenade bestows.

In winter especially, Old Québec takes on a Dickensian quality, with lamp glow flickering behind curtains of falling snow. A man who should know—Charles Dickens himself—described the city as having

"splendid views which burst upon the eye at every turn."

An alternative to these guided strolls is to simply **"walk the walls"** of the city. It takes about an hour. In some sections you are literally on top of the fortress wall; in most spots you're on a path alongside it. There's a little creative guesswork involved in figuring out how to follow the route. Because of the number of stairs and occasional two-foot gap to traverse, walking the wall rates as moderately strenuous and is not for young children or strollers. But it's easy to get on and off the path, and the trek offers wonderful views of the city.

WALKING TOUR 1	THE UPPER TOWN (VIEUX-QUEBEC: HAUTE-VILLE)
Start:	Terrasse Dufferin, the boardwalk in front of the Château Frontenac.
Finish:	Hôtel du Parlement, on Grande-Allée just outside the walls of the old city.
Time:	2 hours.
Best Times:	Anytime, although early morning when the streets are emptier is most atmospheric.
Worst Times:	None.

The Upper Town (Haute-Ville) of Old Québec (Vieux-Québec) is surrounded by fortress walls. This section of the city overlooks the St. Lawrence River and includes much of what makes Québec so beloved, including the Château Frontenac, Place d'Armes, and Basilica of Notre-Dame. Buildings and compounds along this tour have been carefully preserved, and most are at least 100 years old. We start at the grand Terrasse Dufferin, a pedestrian promenade that attracts romantics in all seasons for its magnificent views of the river and its water traffic.

Walking Tour: The Upper Town

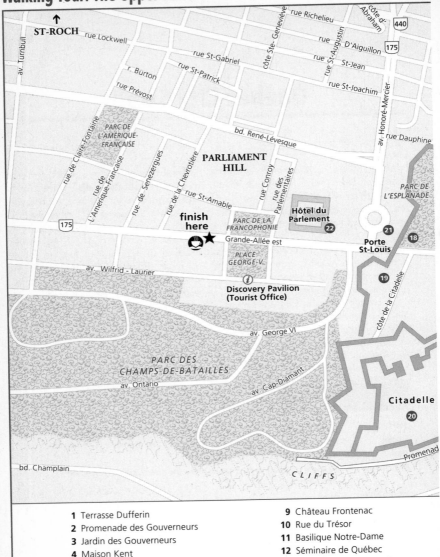

1 Terrasse Dufferin
2 Promenade des Gouverneurs
3 Jardin des Gouverneurs
4 Maison Kent
5 Maison Jacquet
6 Maison Maillou
7 Québec Ministry of Finance
8 Place d'Armes
9 Château Frontenac
10 Rue du Trésor
11 Basilique Notre-Dame
12 Séminaire de Québec
13 Hôtel-de-Ville (City Hall)
14 Anglican Cathedral of
   the Holy Trinity

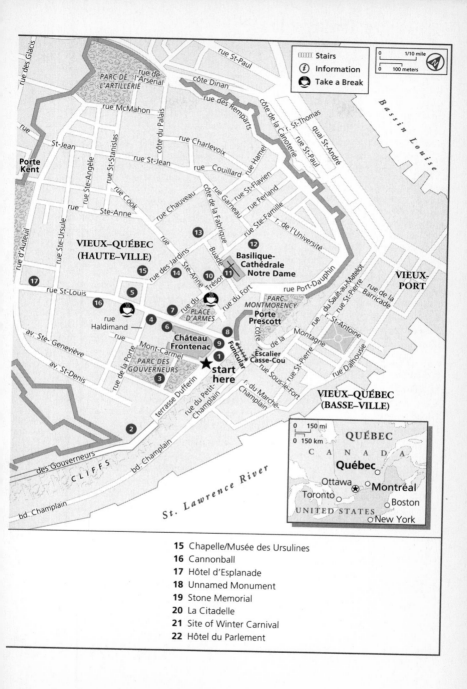

Stairs
ⓘ **Information**
☕ **Take a Break**

1/10 mile
100 meters

rue St-Paul
rue de l'Arsenal
côte Dinan
rue des Remparts
côte de la Canoterie
Bassin Louise

PARC DE L'ARTILLERIE
rue McMahon
côte du Palais
St-Thomas
quai St-André
rue St-Paul

Porte Kent
rue St-Jean
rue Ste-Angèle
rue Ste-Stanislas
côte du Palais
rue Charlevoix
rue Hamel
rue St-Jean
rue Couillard
rue St-Flavien

rue Ste-Ursule
rue Cook
rue Ste-Anne
rue Chauveau
côte de la Fabrique
rue Garneau
rue Ferland
rue Ste-Famille
r. de l'Université

rue d'Auteuil
VIEUX–QUÉBEC (HAUTE–VILLE)
rue des Jardins
⑬
⑫
Basilique-Cathédrale Notre Dame
VIEUX-PORT

⑰
rue St-Louis
⑮
⑭
Ste-Anne
⑩
Trésor
⑪
rue du Fort
rue Port-Dauphin
rue du Sault-au-Matelot
rue St-Pierre
rue de la Barricade

⑤
⑯
rue Haldimand
④
⑦
⑥
PLACE D'ARMES
☕
⑧
PARC MONTMORENCY
Porte Prescott
rue St-Antoine
côte de la Montagne
rue St-Pierre

av. Ste-Geneviève
rue
Mont-Carmel
Château Frontenac
⑨
①
Escalier Casse-Cou
rue Sous-le-Fort
rue Dalhousie

av. St-Denis
⑬
PARC DES GOUVERNEURS
terrasse Dufferin
★ **start here**
Funicular
r. du Marché-Champlain
rue Champlain
VIEUX–QUÉBEC (BASSE–VILLE)

rue du Petit-Champlain
②
bd. Champlain
des Gouverneurs
CLIFFS
bd. Champlain
St. Lawrence River

150 mi
150 km
QUÉBEC
C A N A D A
Québec
Ottawa
Montréal
Toronto
Boston
UNITED STATES
New York

15 Chapelle/Musée des Ursulines
16 Cannonball
17 Hôtel d'Esplanade
18 Unnamed Monument
19 Stone Memorial
20 La Citadelle
21 Site of Winter Carnival
22 Hôtel du Parlement

Start the walk at the:

❶ Terrasse Dufferin

This boardwalk promenade, with its green-and-white–topped gazebos, looks much as it did 100 years ago, when ladies with parasols and gentlemen with top hats and canes strolled along it on sunny afternoons, with the Château Frontenac as a backdrop. It offers vistas of river, watercraft, and distant mountains.

Stroll south on the Terrasse Dufferin, past the château. If possessed of sufficient energy and leg strength, some people may want to continue up the stairs at the end of the boardwalk and then walk south to the:

❷ Promenade des Gouverneurs

This path, renovated in 2007, skirts the sheer cliff wall and climbs up past Québec's Citadelle, a 20-minute uphill walk away. Return to the Terrasse Dufferin, walking as far as the battery of ancient (but not original) cannons set up as they were in the old days.

From the middle of Terrasse Dufferin, climb the stairs toward the obelisk to the:

❸ Jardin des Gouverneurs

This park, located just west of the Château Frontenac, is so named because it stands on the site of the mansion built to house the French governors of Québec. The house burned in 1834, and the ruins lie buried under the great bulk of the Château.

In summer, the park, also known as the Parc des Gouverneurs, is the scene of various shows and musical programs sponsored by the municipal government. Small hotels border it on three sides.

The obelisk monument at the lower end of the sloping park is dedicated to both generals in the momentous battle of September 13, 1759, when Britain's General James Wolfe and France's Louis-Joseph, Marquis de Montcalm fought for what would be the ultimate destiny of Québec (and, quite possibly, all of North America). The French were defeated and both generals died; Wolfe, wounded in the fighting, lived only long enough to hear of England's victory. Montcalm died a few hours after Wolfe. Told that he was mortally wounded, Montcalm replied, "All the better. I will not see the English in Québec."

Walk up rue Mont-Carmel, which runs between the park and the Château Frontenac, and turn right onto rue Haldimand. At the next corner, at rue St-Louis, stands a white house with blue trim called:

❹ Maison Kent

Built in 1648, this might be the oldest building in Québec. Although it's most famous for being the place in which France signed the capitulation to the British forces, its name comes from the duke of Kent. The duke, Queen Victoria's father, lived here for a few years at the end of the 18th century, just before he married Victoria's mother in an arranged liaison. His true love, it is said, had lived with him in Maison Kent. Today, the building houses the consulate general of France, as the tricolor over the door attests.

To the left and diagonally across from Maison Kent, at rue St-Louis and rue des Jardins, is:

❺ Maison Jacquet

This small white dwelling with crimson roof and trim dates from 1677, and now houses a popular restaurant. Among the oldest houses in the province, it has sheltered some prominent Québécois, including Philippe Aubert de Gaspé, the author of *Aux Anciens Canadiens,* who lived here from 1815 to 1824. Gaspé's book recounts the history and folklore of Québec.

TAKE A BREAK
Try Québécois home cooking right here at the restaurant named for de Gaspé's book, **Aux Anciens Canadiens**, 34 rue St-Louis. Consider caribou in blueberry-wine sauce or duckling baked in maple syrup, but don't forget the sugar pie floating in cream.

Leaving the restaurant, turn left toward the river and walk along attractive, if commercialized, rue St-Louis, to no. 17, the:

❻ Maison Maillou

This house's foundations date from 1736, though the house was enlarged in 1799 and restored in 1959. Note the metal shutters used to thwart weather and unfriendly fire. The building now houses the Québec Board of Trade and Industry.

The large building across the street from Maison Maillou is the impressive:

❼ Québec Ministry of Finance

This place started out in 1799 as a courthouse, was renovated between 1927 and 1934, and was restored again from 1983 to 1987. Since then it has been Québec's Ministry of Justice, the name on the facade notwithstanding. The architect of the exterior was Eugène-Etienne Taché, minister of public works at that time. The interior of the building is largely Art Deco. The street fronting the Ministry of Finance building is a popular parking spot for *calèches,* the horse-drawn carriages that tour the city.

Continue on rue St-Louis to arrive, on your left, at the central plaza called:

❽ Place d'Armes

This plaza was once the military parade ground outside the governors' mansion (which no longer exists). In the small park at the center is the **Monument to the Faith,** which recalls the arrival of the Recollet monks from France in 1615. They were granted a large plot of land by the king of France in 1681 for their church and monastery. Facing the square is the **monument to Samuel de Champlain,** who founded Québec in 1608. Created by French artists Paul Chevre and Paul le Cardonel, the statue has stood here since 1898. The statue's pedestal is made from stone that was also used in the Arc de Triomphe and Sacré-Coeur Basilica in Paris.

Near the Champlain statue is the diamond-shaped **monument designating Québec City as a UNESCO World Heritage Site,** the only city in North America with that distinction. Placed here in 1985, it is made of bronze, granite, and glass. A **tourist information center** (with restrooms) is also at Place d'Armes, at 12 rue Ste-Anne.

Again, up to the right, is the:

❾ Château Frontenac

This famous edifice defines the Québec City skyline. The first, lower part was built as a hotel from 1892 to 1893 by the Canadian Pacific Railway Company. The architect, Bruce Price of New York, raised his creation on the site of the governor's mansion and named it after Louis de Buade, Comte de Frontenac. Monsieur le Comte was the Governor General of New France who, in 1690, was faced with the threat of an English fleet under Sir William Phips during King William's War. Phips sent a messenger to demand Frontenac's surrender, but Frontenac replied, "Tell your lord that I will reply with the mouths of my cannons." Which he did. Phips sailed away. Known locally simply as "the Château," the hotel today has 618 rooms (p. 212). There are guided tours inside.

TAKE A BREAK
This is a great part of town to sit and watch the world go by. Grab a sidewalk table and enjoy something to drink or a bite to eat at **Restaurant Le Relais,** a red-roofed building with a mock-Tudor facade at 16 rue Ste-Anne.

Just adjacent to the Restaurant Le Relais is the narrow pedestrian lane called:

❿ Rue du Trésor

Artists hang their prints and paintings of Québec scenes on both sides of the walkway. In decent weather, it's busy with browsers and sellers. Most prices are within the means of the average visitor.

Follow rue du Trésor from rue Ste-Anne down to rue Buade and turn left. On the right, at the corner of rue Ste-Famille is the:

⓫ Basilique Notre-Dame (1647)

The basilica has suffered a tumultuous history of bombardment and repeated reconstruction. Its interior is ornate, the air rich with the scent of burning candles. Many artworks remain from the time of the French regime. The chancel lamp was a gift from Louis XIV, and the crypt is the final resting place for most of the bishops of Québec.

Downhill from the basilica on rue Ste-Famille, on the right with the green window frames, is the historic:

⓬ Séminaire de Québec

Founded in 1663 by Bishop Laval, the first bishop in North America, the seminary had grown into Laval University by 1852, and for many years, it occupied the expanded seminary campus. By the middle of the 20th century, however, a new university was constructed west of the city in Ste-Foy. During summer only, tours are given of the old seminary's grounds and some of its stone and wood buildings, revealing lavish decorations of stone, tile, brass, and gilt-framed oil paintings. Call ☎ **418/694-1020** for tour details. **The Musée de l'Amérique Française,** tucked inside the seminary, has one entrance at 9 rue de la Vieille-Université and another adjacent to the basilica (p. 242). It's open year-round.

This area is still known as the Latin Quarter—after the language that once dominated university life. An animated neighborhood at night, many visitors will want to return to rues Couillard, Garneau, and St-Jean after the sun goes down. To continue the tour, head back to the basilica. Directly across the small park from the church is the:

⓭ Hôtel-de-Ville (City Hall)

The building's lower level, with an entrance around to the right at 43 Côte de la Fabrique, houses the **Centre d'Interpretation de la Vie Urbaine (Urban Life Interpretation Center),** with a large-scale model of Québec City and its suburbs as they were in 1975. It helps strangers to get their bearings, and it might be surprising to see how spread out the city actually is. While the historic Upper and Lower Towns are compact, the city actually covers 92 sq. km (36 sq. miles). The center also houses a fair-trade boutique-café.

The park next to the City Hall is often converted into an outdoor show area in summer, especially during the **Festival d'Eté (Summer Festival)** with concerts and other programs staged here.

Facing the front of the Hôtel-de-Ville, go left on rue des Jardins and cross rue Ste-Anne. On the left are the spires of the:

⓮ Anglican Cathedral of the Holy Trinity

Said to be modeled after St-Martin-in-the-Fields in London, the building dates from 1804 and is the first Anglican cathedral to be built outside of the British Isles. The interior is simple but spacious and bright, with pews of solid English oak from the Royal Windsor forest and a latticed ceiling in white with a gilded-chain motif. Visitors may happen upon an organ recital or choral rehearsal.

One block up rue des Jardins, turn right at the small square (triangle-shaped, actually) and go a few more steps to 12 rue Donnacona, to the:

⓯ Chapelle/Musée des Ursulines

The museum displays the handiwork of the Ursuline nuns from the 17th, 18th, and 19th centuries. There are also Amerindian crafts and a cape that was made for Marie de l'Incarnation, the reverend mother and a founder of the convent, when she left for New France in 1639.

Be sure to peek into the restored chapel if it's open (May–Oct). It shelters the remains of General Montcalm, who was buried here after he fell in the battle that marked the end of French rule in Québec in 1759. Montcalm's tomb is under the chapel and not accessible to the public. His skull, on the other hand, is on display in the Ursuline Museum next door. The tomb of Marie de l'Incarnation, who died in 1672, is here. The altar, created by sculptor Pierre-Noël Levasseur between 1726 and 1736, is worth a look.

From the museum, turn right on rue Donnacona and walk to the entrance of the Ursuline Convent, built originally in 1642. The present complex is actually a succession of different buildings added and repaired at various times up to 1836, because frequent fires took their toll. A statue of founder Marie de l'Incarnation is outside. The convent is now a private girls' school and is not open to the public.

Continue left up the hill along what is now rue du Parloir to rue St-Louis. Cross the street and turn right. At the next block, rue du Corps-de-Garde, note the tree with a:

⓰ Cannonball

Lodged at the base of the trunk, one story says that the cannonball landed here during the War of 1759 and over the years became firmly embraced by the tree. Another story says that it was placed here on purpose to keep the wheels of horse-drawn carriages from bumping the tree when making tight turns.

Continue along St-Louis another 1½ blocks to rue d'Auteuil. The house on the right corner is now the:

⓱ Hôtel d'Esplanade

Notice that many of the windows in the facade facing rue St-Louis are blocked by stone. This is because houses were once taxed by the number of windows they had, and the frugal homeowner found this way to get around the law, even though it cut down on his view.

Continue straight on rue St-Louis toward the Porte St-Louis, a gate in the walls. Next to it is the Esplanade powder magazine, part of the old fortifications. Just before the gate on the right is an:

⓲ Unnamed monument

This monument commemorates the 1943 meeting in Québec of U.S. President Franklin D. Roosevelt and British Prime Minister Winston Churchill. It's a soft-pedaled reminder to FrenchQuébécois that it was English-speaking nations that rid France of the Nazis.

Cross back over St-Louis and go up the hill along Côte de la Citadelle. On the right are headquarters and barracks of a militia district, arranged around an inner court. Near its entrance is a:

⓳ Stone memorial

This marks the resting place of 13 soldiers of General Richard Montgomery's American army, felled in the unsuccessful assault on Québec in 1775. (Obviously, the conflicts that swirled for centuries around who would ultimately rule Québec didn't end with the fateful 1759 battle between the British and the French.)

Continue up the hill to:

⓴ La Citadelle

The impressive star-shaped fortress keeps watch from a commanding position on a grassy plateau 108m (354 ft.) above the banks of the St. Lawrence. It took 30 years to complete, by which time it had become obsolete. Since 1920, the Citadelle has been the home of the French-speaking Royal 22ᵉ Régiment, which fought in both world wars and in Korea. A new pedestrian walkway on the left (tunneling into the hill) has posted historical information. With good timing, it is possible to both visit the regimental museum and watch **the changing of the guard** or the ceremony called "beating the retreat," weather permitting (see p. 239 for ceremony times).

Return to rue St-Louis and turn left through Porte St-Louis, which was built in 1873 on the site of a gate dating from 1692. Here the street broadens to become the Grande-Allée. To the right is a park that runs alongside the city walls. This is the:

㉑ Site of Winter Carnival

One of the most captivating events in the Canadian calendar, the 17-day **Carnaval de Québec** takes place every February and includes outdoor games, snow-tubing, dog-sled races, canoe-races, and more. A palace of snow and ice rises on this spot just outside the city walls, with ice sculptures throughout the field. Colorfully clad Québécois come to admire the palace and dance the night away at Friday and Saturday night outdoor parties. On the other side of Grande-Allée, a carnival park of games, food, and music is set up on the Parc des Champs-de-Bataille. Teams of artists from around the world participate in the International Snow Sculpture Competition. See p. 13 in chapter 2 for more about the festivities.

Fronting the park, on your right, stands Québec province's stately:

㉒ Hôtel du Parlement

Constructed in 1884, this government building houses what Québécois are pleased to call their "National Assembly." Along the facade are 22 bronze statues of prominent figures in Québec's tumultuous history. There are tours of the sumptuous Parliament chambers inside, where symbols of the fleur-de-lis and the initials VR (for Victoria Regina) are reminders of Québec's dual heritage. If the crown on top is lit, Parliament is in session.

The massive fountain in front of the building, La Fontaine de Tourny, was originally commissioned by the mayor of Bordeaux, France, in the 19th century. Sculptor Mathurin Moreau created the dreamlike figures on the fountain's base. It was installed in 2007 as a gift from the Simons department store to the city for its 400th anniversary in 2008.

TAKE A BREAK
The **Le Parlementaire** restaurant in the Hôtel du Parlement is open to the public for breakfast and lunch Monday through Friday most of the year. If this is not the right day or time, go 1 more block down the Grande-Allée to find plenty of options, including outdoor cafés in summer. One possibility is the chain **Au Petit Coin Breton**, at 655 Grande-Allée est, known for its many crepe options. Another possibility is **Chez Ashton**, at 640 Grande-Allée est. It makes what many consider the town's best *poutine*—french fries with fresh cheese curds and brown gravy. In the winter, you get a discount: If it's −20 degrees Celsius, you get 20% off!

To return to the old city, walk or take the no. 10 bus back along Grande-Allée. For another half-hour of scenic strolling, continue along the stately Grande-Allée, past three- and four-story houses built for English shipbuilders at the end of the 19th century. You'll get to the **Parc des Champs-de-Bataille** (**Battlefields Park;** p. 240), which runs parallel and then joins up with the Grande-Allée. Turn left into the park and the left again behind the **Musée des Beaux-Arts** (p. 240). Continue along the park's boulevards or foot paths. To the right of the Citadelle, pick up Promenade des Gouverneurs. This walkway will return you to the Terrasse Dufferin and the Château Frontenac.

| WALKING TOUR 2 | THE LOWER TOWN (VIEUX-QUEBEC: BASSE-VILLE & VIEUX-PORT) |

Start:	In Upper Town at the Terrasse Dufferin, the boardwalk in front of the Château Frontenac.
Finish:	Place-Royale, the restored central square of Lower Town.
Time:	1½ hours.
Best Times:	Anytime during the day. Early morning lets you soak up the visual history, although shops won't be open.
Worst Times:	Very late at night or when it's very cold.

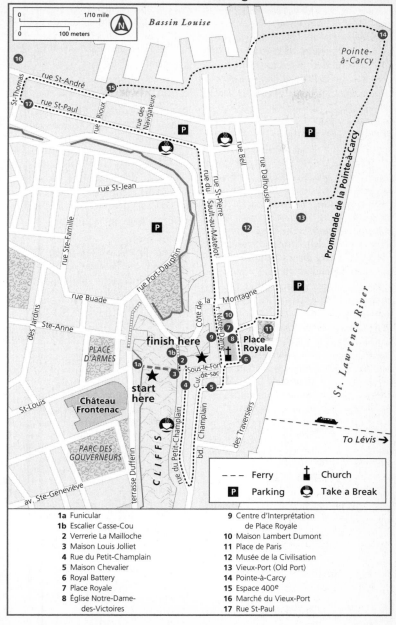

Bassin Louise

0   1/10 mile

0   100 meters

N

rue St-André

rue St-Paul

St-Thomas

rue Rioux

rue des Navigateurs

Pointe-
à-Carcy

Promenade de la Pointe-à-Carcy

rue St-Jean

rue du Sault-au-Matelot

rue St-Pierre

rue Bell

rue Dalhousie

rue Ste-Famille

rue Port-Dauphin

rue Buade

Côte de la Montagne

r. Notre-Dame

des Jardins

Ste-Anne

finish here

Place
Royale

PLACE
D'ARMES

start
here

Sous-le-Fort

Cul-de-sac

Château
Frontenac

St. Lawrence River

St-Louis

rue du Petit-Champlain

bd. Champlain

des Traversiers

PARC DES
GOUVERNEURS

terrasse Dufferin

C L I F F S

To Lévis →

av. Ste-Geneviève

– – – Ferry   ✝ Church

P Parking   ☕ Take a Break

1a Funicular	**9** Centre d'Interprétation
1b Escalier Casse-Cou	de Place Royale
2 Verrerie La Mailloche	**10** Maison Lambert Dumont
3 Maison Louis Jolliet	**11** Place de Paris
4 Rue du Petit-Champlain	**12** Musée de la Civilisation
5 Maison Chevalier	**13** Vieux-Port (Old Port)
6 Royal Battery	**14** Pointe-à-Carcy
7 Place Royale	**15** Espace 400ᵉ
8 Église Notre-Dame-	**16** Marché du Vieux-Port
des-Victoires	**17** Rue St-Paul

The Lower Town (Basse-Ville) part of Old Québec (Vieux-Québec) encompasses both the oldest residential area of the city—now flush with boutique hotels, high-end restaurants, and touristy shops and cafés—and Vieux-Port, the old port district. The impressive Museum of Civilization is here, and if you have time, you may want to take a pause from the tour for a visit. We start at the cliff-side elevator *(funiculaire)* that connects the Upper and Lower towns.

If you're in the Upper Town, descend to the Lower Town by the:

❶ Funicular (Option A)

This cable car's upper terminus is on Terrasse Dufferin near the Château Frontenac. As the car descends the steep slope, its glass front provides a broad view of the Basse-Ville. The mammoth grain elevators down by the harbor have a capacity of 8 million bushels. Beyond them is the river, with its constant boat traffic, and over to the left, the Laurentides Mountains rise in the distance.

Or, if you prefer a more active (and free) means of descent, use the stairs to the left of the funicular, the:

❶ Escalier Casse-Cou (Option B)

"Breakneck Stairs" is the self-explanatory name given to this stairway. Stairs have been in place here since the settlement began. In fact, in 1698, the town council forbade citizens from taking their animals up or down the stairway.

Both Breakneck Stairs and the funicular arrive at the intersection of rues Petit-Champlain and Sous-le-Fort. At the bottom of the stairs on the left is the:

❷ Verrerie La Mailloche

In the downstairs room, craftsmen give glass-blowing demonstrations—intriguing and informative, especially for children who haven't seen that ancient craft. The glass is melted at 2,500°F (1,350°C) and is worked at 2,000°F (1,100°C). There are displays of the results and a small shop in which to purchase them.

Exit and glass-blowing shop and walk straight ahead. On your right is the building that funicular passengers exit from:

❸ Maison Louis Jolliet

Built in 1683, this home belonged to the Québec-born explorer who, with a priest, Jacques Marquette, was the first person of European parentage to explore the upper reaches of the Mississippi River. Jolliet's former house is now the lower terminus for the funicular and full of tourist trinkets and geegaws.

Continue down:

❹ Rue du Petit-Champlain

Allegedly the oldest street in North America, in the warm months, this pedestrian-only lane swarms with restaurant-goers, café sitters, strolling couples, and gaggles of schoolchildren. (See chapter 17 for shopping suggestions.) In the winter, it's a snowy wonderland with ice statues and twinkling white lights.

TAKE A BREAK
Although it's early in the stroll, there are so many eating and shopping options here that you might want to pause here for a while. Look for the sign with the flying rabbit for **Le Lapin Saute,** at 52 rue du Petit-Champlain, for a country-cozy bistro with solid, hearty food in generous portions. The smoked mackerel salad and grilled pork chop with maple syrup are both terrific if you're not up for the signature rabbit.

At the end of Petit-Champlain, turn left onto boulevard Champlain. A lighthouse from the Gaspé Peninsula used to stand just across the street, but it has been returned to its original home, leaving just an anchor and cannons to stand guard over the river.

Following the curve of the street, there are nice boutiques and cafés in this block. At the corner is the crimson-roofed:

❺ Maison Chevalier

Dating from 1752, this was once the home of merchant Jean-Baptiste Chevalier. Note the wealth of windows in the house, more than 30 in the facade alone. In 1763, the house was sold at auction to ship owner Jean-Louis Frémont, the grandfather of Virginia-born John Charles Frémont (1813–90). John Charles was an American explorer, soldier, and politician who mapped some 10 Western and Midwestern territories. This notable workaholic of French-Canadian heritage was also a governor of California and Arizona, a candidate for president of the United States in 1856, and a general during the Civil War.

The Chevalier House was sold in 1806 to an Englishman, who in turn rented it to a hotelier, who then transformed it into an inn. From this time to the end of the century, under various owners, it was known as the London Coffee House. In 1960, the Québec government restored the house, and it became a museum about 5 years later, overseen by the Musée de la Civilisation, which mounts temporary exhibitions here. Entrance is free. (See p. 243 for more details.)

Just past the Maison's front door, turn left and walk up the short block of rue Notre-Dame to rue Sous-le-Fort. Turn right, and walk 1 more block to the:

❻ Royal Battery

Fortifications were erected here by the French in 1691 and the cannons added in 1712 to defend the Lower Town from the British. The cannons got their chance in 1759, but the English victory silenced them and the exodus to the Upper Town left them to rust. Sunken foundations were all that remained of the battery by the turn of the 20th century, and when the time came to restore this area, it had to be rebuilt from the ground up.

From the Royal Battery, walk back up rue Sous-le-Fort. You'll find a good photo opportunity: Up the street, the imposing Château Frontenac is framed between ancient houses.

Turn right rue Notre-Dame. Half a block up the grade is the heart of Basse-Ville, the:

❼ Place-Royale

Occupying the center of the first permanent colony in New France, this small and still very much European feeling enclosed square served as the town marketplace. The square went into decline around 1860 and by 1950 had become a derelict, run-down part of town. Today it has been restored to very nearly recapture its historic appearance. The prominent bust is of Louis XIV, the Sun King, a gift from the city of Paris in 1928 that was installed here in 1931. The striking 17th- and 18th-century houses once belonged to wealthy merchants. Note the ladders on some of the steep roofs used to fight fire and remove snow. See p. 238 for more about the square.

Facing directly onto the square is the small:

❽ Eglise Notre-Dame-des-Victoires

Named for French naval victories over the British in 1690 and 1711, the oldest stone church in Québec was built in 1688 after a massive fire in Lower Town destroyed 55 homes in 1682. The church was restored in 1763 after its partial destruction by the British in the 1759 siege. The white-and-gold interior has a few murky paintings and a large model boat suspended from the ceiling, a votive offering brought by early settlers to ensure safe voyages. On the walls, 14 small prints depict the stages of the Passion. The church is open to visitors 9am to 5pm from May through October (p. 238).

Walk straight across the plaza, passing the:

❾ Centre d'Interprétation de Place-Royale

For decades, this space was nothing but a propped-up facade with an empty lot behind it, but it has now been rebuilt to serve as an interpretation center with shows and exhibitions about the history of this district, good for kids as well as adults (p. 238).

At the corner on the right is the:

⑩ Maison Lambert Dumont

This building now houses Geomania, a store selling rocks and crystals. In earlier years, though, it was home to the Dumont family and part of row of residences. To the right as you're facing it once stood a hotel where U.S. President William Taft would stay as he headed north to vacation in the picturesque Charlevoix region.

Walk past the last building on your left about 15m (49 ft.) and turn around. The entire end of that building is a *trompe l'oeil* mural of streets and houses and depictions of citizens from the earliest colonial days to the present, an amusing splash of fool-the-eye trickery.

Return to Place-Royale and head left toward the water, down two small sets of stairs to the:

⑪ Place de Paris

This plaza contains an undistinguished white sculpture that resembles three stacked Rubik's Cubes, a gift from the city of Paris.

Continue ahead to rue Dalhousie and turn left. A few short blocks and on the left is the:

⑫ Musée de la Civilisation

This wonderful museum, which opened in 1988, may be housed in a nondescript gray-block building and situated among the cobblestone streets in the historic Basse-Ville, but there is nothing bland or traditional about it once you enter the space. Spacious and airy, with ingeniously arranged multidimensional exhibits, it is one of the most innovative museums in Canada, if not in all of North America. If there is no time now, put it at the top of the must-see list for later. See p. 235 for museum details.

Across the street from the museum is the:

⑬ Vieux-Port (Old Port)

In the 17th century, this 29-hectare (72-acre) riverfront area was the port of call for European ships bringing supplies and settlers to the new colony. With the decline of shipping and the shifting of economic power to Montréal by the early 20th century, the port fell into precipitous decline. But since the mid-1980s, it has experienced a rebirth, becoming the summer destination for international cruise ships. It got additional sprucing up in 2007 for Québec's 400th anniversary in 2008.

TAKE A BREAK

If you're doing this stroll in the colder months, you might want to head indoors at this point. **Le 48 Saint-Paul**, at that same address, is just steps from the corner of rue Dalhousie and rue St-Paul, 1 block from the museum. With a black-on-white interior, this restaurant is both sleek and affordable, with creative burgers and pizzas and a good selection of local beers. If you're still game to continue, head back to rue Dalhousie and cross over toward the Terminal de Croisières.

From the museum, head across the parking lot to the river and turn left at the water's edge. After the Terminal de Croisières, you'll pass the Agora, an outdoor theater that has been under renovation, and, behind it, the city's Customs House, built between 1830 and 1839.

Continue along the river's promenade, past the Agora, to the small, landscaped:

⑭ Pointe-à-Carcy

The bronze statue of a sailor here is a memorial to Canadian merchant seamen who lost their lives in World War II. From the point, look out across Louise Basin to the Bunge of Canada grain elevator, which stores wheat, barley, corn, and soybean crops that are produced in western Canada before they are shipped to

Europe. The bridge to rural **Ile d'Or-léans** can also be seen. Ile d'Orléans is the island that supplies Québec with much of its fresh fruits and vegetables, and is an easy day-trip from the city (see chapter 19). The water below is the launch area for the canoe race across the ice floes during **Carnaval de Québec** (p. 13).

Follow the walkway left from Pointe-à-Carcy along the Louise Basin. You'll pass the free **Musée Naval de Québec,** renovated in 2007, and the city's Navy School. On the right in the warm months are ticket offices and boarding docks for whale-watching and scenic river cruises.

At the end of the basin, take a short jog left, then right along the water's edge. Up ahead, at 100 rue St-André and rue Rioux, is a modern gray building with two large port holes, the:

⑮ Espace 400ᵉ

Occupying what used to be the Vieux-Port Interpretation Center, this new and expanded pavilion is the central location for Québec's 400th-anniversary celebrations. From June to October 2008, Espace 400ᵉ will host exhibits, performances, conferences, and shows. From 2009 on, it will become a Parks Canada discovery center.

From Espace 400ᵉ, go to rue St-André, turn right, and walk 1 block to the:

⑯ Marché du Vieux-Port

The market has jaunty teal roofs and blue banners. Farther down the street is the 1916 train station, designed by New York architect Bruce Price, who designed the Château Frontenac in 1893 and used his signature copper-turned-green spires here, too.

During the summer season, the colorful farmer's market has rows of booths heaped with fresh fruits and vegetables, honey, relishes, jams, and handicrafts. Above each booth hangs a sign with the name and telephone number of the seller. A lot of them bear the initials I.O., meaning they come from Ile d'Orléans, an island 16km (10 miles) outside the city. The market is enclosed, and the central part of it, with meats and cheeses for sale, is heated. There are cafés and kiosks inside to get a cup of coffee or a meal, as well as an ice-cream stand and a bakery.

Leaving the market, cross rue St-André at the light and gas station and walk 1 short block to:

⑰ Rue St-Paul

Turn left onto this street, home to a burgeoning number of antiques and artisan shops here, such as the stained glass and model ship studio at no. 152. There's a real sense of unspoiled neighborhood here.

TAKE A BREAK
The busy **Café le Saint Malo,** at 75 rue St-Paul and rue du Sault-au-Matelot, has low ceilings, rough stone walls, and storefront windows that draw patrons inside. Come for a full meal or, on sunny days, a drink or coffee and dessert at a sidewalk table.

From here, return to the heart of Lower Town—Place-Royale and the funicular—by turning right off of rue St-Paul onto either rue du Sault-au-Matelot or the parallel rue St-Pierre. Both are quiet streets with galleries, restaurants, and posh shops. Meander along and adjust to the relaxed pace of this nook of the city.

17

Québec City Shopping

The compact size of Vieux-Québec, with its upper and lower sections, makes it especially convenient for browsing and shopping. Though similar from one place to the next, much of the merchandise is generally of high quality. There are several art galleries deserving of attention, including an outdoor version in the Upper Town (Haute-Ville). Antiques shops are proliferating along rue St-Paul in the Lower Town (Basse-Ville).

1 The Shopping Scene

Vieux-Québec's Lower Town, particularly the area known as **Quartier du Petit-Champlain,** offers many possibilities—clothing, souvenirs, gifts, household items, collectibles—and is avoiding (so far) the trashiness that often afflicts heavily touristed areas. Find it just off Place-Royale and encompassing rue du Petit-Champlain, boulevard Champlain, and rue Sous-le-Fort (opposite the funicular entrance).

In the Upper Town, wander along **rue St-Jean,** both within and outside the city walls, and on **rue Garneau** and **Côte de la Fabrique,** which branch off the east end of St-Jean. There's a shopping concourse on the lower level of the Château Frontenac. For T-shirts, postcards, and other souvenirs, myriad shops line **rue St-Louis.**

If you're heading to St-Roch to eat, build in a little time to stroll **rue St-Joseph,** which for a few blocks has new boutiques alongside cafés and restaurants.

Outside the walls, just beyond the strip of cafés that line Grande-Allée, **avenue Cartier** has shops and restaurants of some variety, from clothing and ceramics to housewares and gourmet foods. The 5 blocks attract crowds of youngish and middle-aged locals, and the hubbub revs up on summer nights and weekends. The area remains outside the tourist orbit, but it's an easy walk: Head up the wide, tree-lined Grande-Allée and turn right onto Cartier.

Most stores are open Monday through Wednesday from 9 or 10am to 6pm, Thursday and/or Friday from 9am to 9pm, and Saturday from 9am to 5pm. Many stores are now also open on Sunday from noon to 5pm.

THE BEST BUYS

Indigenous crafts, handmade sweaters, and **Inuit art** are among the desirable items not seen everywhere else. An official igloo trademark identifies authentic Inuit (Eskimo) art, although the differences between the real thing and the manufactured variety become apparent with a little careful study. Inuit artwork, which usually means carvings in stone or bone, is a "best buy" not because of low prices, but because of its high quality. Expect to pay hundreds of dollars for even a relatively small piece.

Maple syrup products make sweet gifts, and **ice cider** (*cidre de glace*) and **ice wines** made in Québec province from apples and grapes left on trees and vines after the first frost can be had for around C$25 (US$22/£11). They are sold in duty-free shops at the border in addition to the state liquor stores (SAQ) listed at the very end of this chapter.

Apart from a handful of boutiques, Québec City does not offer the high-profile designer clothing often showcased in Montréal.

SHOPPING COMPLEXES

In the Upper Town, next to the Basilique Notre-Dame, there's a small complex filled with upscale shops called **Les Promenades du Vieux-Québec,** at 43 rue Buade. You'll find a perfumery, shops selling Inuit carvings, cafés, a currency exchange, an Internet café, and clothing for men and women. Just outside the city walls, **Place Québec** incorporates dozens of shops, a cinema, restaurants, a convention center, and the Hilton hotel, an easy-to-spot landmark. Place Québec is accessible from boulevard Réne-Lévesque and the Hilton.

Shopping malls on a grander scale aren't found in or near the Old Town. For mall shopping, it's necessary to travel to the neighboring municipality of **Sainte-Foy.** The malls there differ little from their cousins throughout North America, in layout and available products. For sheer size, however, you can't beat **Place Laurier,** at 2700 bd. Laurier (© **418/651-5000**), with 350 shops, including 40 restaurants. More than 12 millions people visit each year—a fact which will either make your eyes sparkle with excitement or glaze over in stupor.

THE ANTIQUES DISTRICT

Dealers in antiques have gravitated to rue St-Paul in the Lower Town. To get there from the Place-Royale, follow rue St-Pierre and turn left on rue St-Paul. There are more than 20 shops, with more likely to open, filled with knickknacks, Québec country furniture, candlesticks, brass beds, old clocks, Victoriana, Art Deco and Art Moderne objects, and even the increasingly sought-after kitsch and housewares of the early post–World War II period.

2 Shopping from A to Z

The neighborhood for each shop below is listed with the address: Lower Town and Upper Town in Vieux-Québec, and Montcalm, the residential neighborhood just west of Parliament Hill.

ARTS & CRAFTS

Artisans du Bas-Canada   Crafts predominate here, all a little on the expensive side. There are plenty of fur hats, moccasins, lumberjack coats, jewelry, toy soldiers, soapstone carvings, and Canada-themed books. Or perhaps a chess set of Generals Montcalm and Wolfe, so you can reenact the battle that left both men dead? 30 Côte de la Fabrique, Upper Town. © **418/692-2109.** www.artisanscanada.com.

Aux Multiples Collections   Inuit, vernacular, and modern Canadian art are on offer in this gallery. The most appealing items, and those given prominence in display, are the Native Canadian carvings in stone, bone, and tusk. The shop ships purchases. Prices are high, but competitive for merchandise of similar quality. Check out, too, its sibling, the new private museum called **Galerie Brousseau et Brousseau,** nearby at 35 rue St-Louis (© **418/694-1828**). 69 rue Ste-Anne (opposite the Hôtel-de-Ville), Upper Town. © **418/692-1230.** www.sculpture.artinuit.ca.

Boutique Claude Berry, Inc Here you'll find hand-painted porcelains from Limoges, jacquard replicas of medieval tapestries, and religious articles—a grab bag that might produce that elusive gift. 6 Côte de la Fabrique, Upper Town. ✆ **418/692-2628.**

Boutique Métiers d'Art In a stone building at the corner of Place-Royale, this carefully arranged store displays works by over 100 Québécois craftspeople, at least some of which are likely to appeal to almost any customer. Among these objects are sculptures, dolls, masks, jewelry, graphics, and a variety of gifts. When departing, be sure to turn left, walk past the end of the building and turn around—it's a surprise! 29 rue Notre-Dame, Lower Town. ✆ **418/694-0267.** www.boutiquemetiersdart.fr.

Boutique Sachem Galerie Fur hats, baby moccasins (from C$14/US$12/£6), T-shirts, and dresses are all packed into this compact boutique. Foremost, though, is the wide variety of miniature "Inukshuk" human figurines, which look like they've been made of stacked rocks. The Inukshuk is part of the logo of the 2010 Winter Olympics being held in Vancouver, so stock up now and be ahead of the curve. 17 rue des Jardins (near Hôtel-de-Ville), Upper Town. ✆ **418/692-3056.** www.liroquois.com.

Canadeau Defying easy classification, this store purveys a wide range of Canadian crafts, handicraft jewelry, Inuit carvings, furs, watches, handmade knives, and sweaters in uncommon designs. 1124 rue St-Jean (near Côte du Palais), Upper Town. ✆ **418/692-2265.** www.canadeau.com.

Dugal The owners have their ateliers in Montréal but maintain their only shop here. He works in wood, carving sinuous and remarkably comfortable rocking chairs, while his wife creates jewelry featuring black pearls set in gold and silver. 15 rue Notre-Dame, Lower Town. ✆ **418/692-1564.**

Galerie d'Art du Petit-Champlain This shop features the superbly detailed carvings of Roger Desjardins, who applies his skills to meticulous renderings of waterfowl. The inventory has been expanded to show lithographs, paintings, and some Inuit art. 88½ rue du Petit-Champlain (near bd. Champlain), Lower Town. ✆ **418/692-5647.** www.quartierpetit champlain.com.

Galerie d'Art Trois Colombes Québécois and other Canadian artisans, including Inuits and Amerindians, produce these weavings, carvings, snowshoes, and duck decoys. The store also sells handmade hats, coats, sweaters, moccasins, moose T-shirts, and rag dolls. They ship worldwide. 46 rue St-Louis, Upper Town. ✆ **418/694-1114.**

Rue du Trésor Outdoor Gallery Sooner or later, everyone passes this alley near the Place d'Armes. Artists gather along here much of the year to exhibit and sell their work, much like the artists on rue St-Amable in Vieux-Montréal. Most of the prints on view are of Québec scenes, and one or two might make attractive souvenirs. The artists seem to enjoy chatting with interested passersby. Rue du Trésor (between rues Ste-Anne and Buade), Upper Town. No phone.

BATH & BODY
Fruits & Passion Like The Body Shop, this Québec-based chain features body lotions, shampoos, candles, foods, and even dog-care items. Its Cuchina hand care line uses olive oil and olive leaf extract, and foods include fig-aromatized balsamic vinegar. 75 rue du Petit-Champlain, Lower Town. ✆ **418/692-2859.** www.fruits-passion.com.

BOOKS, MAGAZINES & NEWSPAPERS

Librairie du Nouveau Monde   This store has a wide variety of books, mostly in French, including the *Historical Guide to Québec,* by Yves Tessier (available in English), a good read about the city's past, filled with illustrations, photographs, and a foldout map. 103 rue St-Pierre (behind the Musée de la Civilisation), Lower Town. (*C*) **418/694-9475.** www.total.net/~linomond.

Maison de la Presse Internationale   As the name says, this large store in the midst of the St-Jean shopping and nightlife bustle stocks magazines, newspapers, and paperbacks from around the world, in many languages. It's daily at 7am (except Sun, at 8am) until 11pm or midnight, and carries the *New York Times, Wall Street Journal, International Herald Tribune,* and many U.S. periodicals. There's another branch in the Place Québec, the mall between the Hilton and Radisson hotels on Parliament Hill. 1050 rue St-Jean (at the corner of rue Ste-Angèle), Upper Town. (*C*) **418/694-1511.**

Un Coin du Monde   On avenue Cartier a few blocks from the Musée des Beaux-Arts du Québec, this shop carries a wide variety of English-language magazines as well as housewares, cards, and emu soap from the Charlevoix region northeast of Québec City. 1150 av. Cartier (corner of rue Aberdeen), Montcalm. (*C*) **418/648-1562.**

CLOTHING

Also see **Artisans du Bas-Canada** and **Galerie d'Art Trois Colombes,** under "Arts & Crafts," above.

Fourrures du Vieux-Port   The fur trade underwrote the development and exploration of Québec and the vast lands west, and it continues to be highly important to this day. This merchant in the Basse-Ville has as good a selection as any, including knit furs and shearlings, along with designer coats by Christ, Louis Féraud, and Zuki, among others. 55 rue St-Pierre, Lower Town. (*C*) **418/692-6686.** www.quebecfourrure.com.

La Maison Darlington   The popular emporium in this ancient house comes on strong with both tony and traditional clothing for men and women produced by such makers as Ballantyne, Dale of Norway, and Geiger Austrian. Better still are the hand-smocked dresses produced by Québécois artisans for babies and little girls. 7 rue de Buade (near the Hôtel-de-Ville), Upper Town. (*C*) **418/692-2268.**

La Maison du Hamac   Although this shop does indeed carry a wide selection of hammocks, as its name asserts, it also has clothing from Latin America—colorful hats, shirts, belts, vests, bags, and jewelry from Mexico, Nepal, Guatemala, Indonesia, and Brazil. Masks and kites, too. 91 rue Ste-Anne, Upper Town. (*C*) **418/692-1109.** www.maisondu hamac.com.

Marie Dooley   A teeny boutique shop featuring the chic, youthful women's clothing of Dooley, a Québec-born designer. 3B bd. René-Lévesque est (1 block east of av. Cartier), Montcalm. (*C*) **418/522-7597.** www.mariedooley.com.

Murmure   Off the tourist track on avenue Cartier, this small boutique features casual, middle-end dresses, jackets, and skirts, catering primarily to 30- to 50-something women. (For designer jeans and skimpy jackets for younger women, visit **Urbain,** directly across the street.) 989 av. Cartier (at bd. René-Lévesque), Montcalm. (*C*) **418/522-1016.**

Zazou   This little shop focuses primarily on casual and dressy fashions from Québécois designers, including wool sweaters with nature motifs. 31 Petit-Champlain (near the funicular), Lower Town. (*C*) **418/694-9990.** www.quartierpetitchamplain.com.

A DEPARTMENT STORE

La Maison Simons   The only department store in Old Québec opened here in 1840. Small by modern standards, Simons has two floors for men's and women's clothing, emphasizing sportswear for both adults and slouchy teens. Most of it is pretty basic. Tommy Hilfiger products are much in evidence. 20 Côte de la Fabrique (near the Hôtel-de-Ville), Upper Town. ℂ **418/692-3630.** www.simons.ca.

FOOD

La Petite Cabane à Sucre   Canada is the biggest producer of maple syrup in the world, and Québec is the source of 75% of it. "The little sugar shack" sells ice cream, honey, maple syrup, maple candy, and related products, including tin log cabins that pour syrup from their chimneys. 94 rue du Petit-Champlain (near bd. Champlain), Lower Town. ℂ **418/692-5875.** www.quartierpetitchamplain.com.

Marché du Vieux-Port   By the water near the train station, this year-round market blossoms in spring and summer with farmers' bounty from Ile d'Orléans and beyond. In addition to fresh fruits and vegetables, you'll find relishes, jams, honey, meats, cheeses, and handicrafts. 160 Quai Saint-André (near Espace 400ᵉ), Lower Town. ℂ **418/692-2517.** www.marchevieuxport.com.

HOUSEWARES

Zone   In a more residential area, Zone is a nifty housewares store featuring a wide variety of colorful bowls and plates for the kitchen, clocks and frames for the office, and small lamps and vases for the rest of the house. 999 av. Cartier (at the corner of bd. René-Lévesque), Montcalm. ℂ **418/522-7373.** www.zonemaison.com.

LEATHER GOODS

Ibiza   Replacing a shop that sold toys and kids' things, this leather store sells coats, hats, gloves, slippers, handbags and, oddly enough, knives. 57 Petit-Champlain (in mid-block), Lower Town. ℂ **418/692-2103.** www.quartierpetitchamplain.com.

MUSIC

Archambault   This shop, part of a Canadian chain of a dozen stores, has two large floors of recorded music, mostly CDs, arranged under French and English categories. The helpful staff goes to some lengths to find what you want. 1095 rue St-Jean, Upper Town. ℂ **418/694-2088.** www.archambault.ca.

WINES

Société des Alcools de Québec   Liquor and other spirits can only be sold in stores operated by this provincial agency. The SAQ outlets are virtual supermarkets of wines and spirits, with thousands of bottles in stock. The avenue Cartier outlet has about 20 kinds of imported beers. Québec's unique **ice cider** *(cidre de glace),* made from apples left on trees after the first frost, can be purchased here as well as at duty-free shops at the border. Look for the VQA logo, for Vintners Quality Alliance, on wines that have received the state seal of approval for quality. There is another SAQ outlet at the Château Frontenac. 1059 av. Cartier (near rue Fraser), Montcalm. ℂ **418/643-4334.** www.saq.com.

18

Québec City After Dark

Although Québec City can't pretend to match the volume of nighttime diversions of exuberant Montréal, there is more than enough after-dark activity to occupy your evenings during an average stay. Apart from theatrical productions, almost always in French, knowledge of the language is rarely necessary to enjoy nighttime entertainment.

On Wednesdays and Saturdays from late July to mid-August, the city hosts a grand fireworks competition, **Les Grands Feux Loto-Québec,** at the scenic Montmorency Falls 15 minutes north of city center (p. 244).

The neighborhood for each venue below is listed with the address: Lower Town and Upper Town in Vieux-Québec; Vieux-Port, adjacent to Lower Town; Parliament Hill; Montcalm, the residential neighborhood just west of Parliament Hill; and St-Roch.

1 The Performing Arts

CLASSICAL MUSIC, OPERA & DANCE

The premier classical groups are **L'Orchestre Symphonique de Québec** (© 418/643-8486; www.osq.org), Canada's oldest symphony; the **Québec Opéra** (© 418/529-0688; www.operadequebec.qc.ca); and **Les Violons du Roy** (© 418/692-3026; www.violonsduroy.com). The orchestra and opera both play at the Grand Théâtre de Québec (see below). Les Violons du Roy is a string orchestra established in 1985 that features young musicians in the early stages of their careers. They perform at the Raoul-Jobin hall in the Palais Montcalm, which reopened in 2007 after renovations. The venue is centrally located in Place d'Youville (see below).

CONCERT HALLS & PERFORMANCE VENUES

Many of the city's churches also host sacred and secular music concerts, as well as special Christmas festivities.

Colisée Pepsi   Rock concerts by name acts on the order of Bob Dylan and Rush are held here, with events such as dog shows and wedding expositions filling in other days. The stadium is located in a park about a 10-minute drive northwest of Parliament Hill. 250 bd. Wilfrid-Hamel (ExpoCité), north of St-Roch. © 418/691-7110. www.expocite.com.

Grand Théâtre de Québec 🎭🎭🎭   Classical music concerts, opera, dance, jazz, blues, klezmer, and theatrical productions are presented in two halls, one of them containing the largest stage in Canada. Visiting conductors, orchestras, and dance companies often perform here when resident organizations are away. In addition to **L'Orchestre Symphonique de Québec** and the **Québec Opéra** performing here, **The Trident Theatre** troupe performs in French in the Salle Octave-Crémazie. 269 bd. René-Lévesque est (near av. Turnbull), Parliament Hill. © 418/643-8131. www.grandtheatre.qc.ca.

Kiosque Edwin-Bélanger *(Value)*   The bandstand at the edge of Battlefields Park is home to a summer music season, from about mid-June to late August. The outdoor performances are Thursday through Sunday evenings at 8pm and range from chorales and classical recitals to jazz, pop, and blues. All concerts are free. 390 av. de Bernières (at the Plains of Abraham), Parliament Hill. *(C)* **418/648-4050.**

Le Capitole   Various shows are offered on an irregular schedule in this historic 1,262-seat theater. Dramatic productions and comedic performances are in French, but the theater also hosts rock groups and occasional classical recitals. An ongoing production, from June to July, is the *Elvis Story.* 972 rue St-Jean (near Porte St-Jean), Parliament Hill. *(C)* **800/261-9903** for tickets, or 418/694-4444 for information. www.lecapitole.com.

Palais Montcalm *(R)*   Reopened after renovations in 2006 and 2007 to make it more modern and bigger, this venue is home to the well-regarded Les Violons du Roy. The main performance space is the 979-seat Raoul-Jobin theater, which presents a mix of dance programs, classical music concerts, and plays. More intimate recitals and jazz groups are found in a 125-seat café/theater. 995 Place d'Youville (near Porte Saint-Jean), Parliament Hill. *(C)* **418/641-6411** for tickets. www.surscene.qc.ca/montcalm.htm.

2 The Club & Music Scene

Québec City's **Festival d'Eté (Summer Festival),** what organizers say is the largest cultural event in the French-speaking world, is held in the heart of Vieux-Québec for about 2 weeks each July. Highlights include the free jazz and folk combos who perform in an open-air theater next to City Hall. Since 2007, some of the action has also shifted into the St-Roch neighborhood. The festival brings in artists from Africa, Asia, Europe, and North America for more than 500 programs showcasing theater, music, and dance. For details, call *(C)* **888/992-5200,** or check www.infofestival.com.

DANCE CLUBS

Boudoir Lounge *(R)*   The hottest club so far in trendy St-Roch (and the bar of choice for much of the city's restaurant staff), Boudoir has two bars on the main floor and a disco downstairs. DJs work the fine sound systems in both rooms to 3am, with live jazz on Sundays and bands on Wednesdays. The dramatic decor, including a fireplace in the front, is far more diverting than some of the dismal black holes popular elsewhere in town. 441 rue du Parvis (at bd. Charest est), St-Roch. *(C)* **418/524-2777.**

Chez Dagobert   Long one of the top discos in Québec City, this three-story club has an arena arrangement on the ground floor for live bands, with raised seating around the sides. There's also a large dance floor and TV screens to keep track of sports events. The sound system is just a decibel short of bedlam; more than a few habitués don earplugs. Things don't start jamming until well after 11pm, and the party goes to 3am nightly. The crowd divides into students and their more fashionably attired older brothers and sisters. A whole lot of eyeballing and approaching goes on. 600 Grande-Allée est (near rue de la Chevrotiére), Parliament Hill. *(C)* **418/522-0393.**

Maurice   Successfully challenging **Chez Dagobert** (across the street and listed above) at the top rung of the nightlife ladder, this triple-tiered enterprise occupies a converted mansion at the thumping heart of the Grande-Allée scene. It includes a surprisingly good restaurant (**VooDoo Grill;** p. 227), a couple of bars, and music that tilts heavily toward Latin. In the wintertime, there's a sidewalk-level "Icecothèque" with a bar made completely of ice, ice sculptures, and roaring music. Theme nights are frequent, and crowds of nearly 1,000 20- and 30-somethings are not unusual. 575 Grande-Allée est, Parliament Hill. © 418/647-2000. www.mauricenightclub.com.

ROCK, FOLK, BLUES & JAZZ CLUBS

Most bars and clubs stay open until 2 or 3am, closing earlier if business doesn't warrant the extra hour or two. There are three principal streets to choose among for nightlife, all near or just beyond Parliament Hill: the Grande-Allée, rue St-Jean, and avenue Cartier.

Bar Les Voûtes Napoléon   Down a flight of stairs tucked behind the outdoor cafés and away from the general bustle on the Grande-Allée, this amicable *boîtes à chansons* has music 7 nights a week starting at 10:30pm, and is always free. The stone arches and low ceiling give the front room a cavelike feel, with small tables, a bar, and a postage-stamp stage for the Québec singer-songwriters passing through town. 680 Grande-Allée, Parliament Hill. © 418/640-9388.

Chez Son Père ⍟   A musical institution in Québec since 1960, this stage is where French-Canadian folk singers (of both traditional and contemporary folk music) often get their start. Québécois music is featured on Fridays and Saturdays, with traditional French and folk music the other nights. The stage has the usual brick walls and sparse decor. During the school year there is a young, friendly college crowd, and at other times there are more tourists. 24 rue St-Stanislas (near rue St-Jean), Upper Town. © 418/692-5308. http://barchezsonpere.qc.ca.

Largo *(Finds)*   This attractive restaurant-club, which opened in 2004, is one of a growing number of clubs, restaurants, and shops sprucing up a several-blocks-long strip of St-Joseph street in the emerging St-Roch district. The space combines the old and the new: High ceilings and chandeliers give it an old-time class, while blond-wood floors, clean angles, and contemporary art make it modern. There's jazz on Thursdays, Fridays, and Saturdays, starting at 8pm. Food prices are a little steep, with main courses from C$17 to C$39 (US$15–US$34/£7.30–£17). 643 rue St-Joseph est, St-Roch. © 418/529-3111.

Pub St-Patrick   This Irish pub just keeps on getting on. Pints of Guinness are the steadiest pour, of course, and food is available, but the music of the Ould Sod is the big draw. For that, show up on Friday and Saturday starting at 9:30pm. 45 rue Couillard (near rue St-Jean), Upper Town. © 418/694-0618.

Théâtre du Petit-Champlain   Québécois and French singers alternate with jazz and rock groups in this roomy café-theater in the Lower Town. Have a drink on the patio before the show. The box office is open Monday through Friday from 1 to 5pm, to 7pm the night of a show. Performances are usually Tuesday through Saturday. 68 rue du Petit-Champlain (near the funicular), Lower Town. © 418/692-2631. www.theatrepetitchamplain.com. Tickets C$15–C$30 (US$13–US$26/£6.45–£13), depending on the artist.

3 The Bar & Café Scene

In addition to the bars listed below, also check out the strip of the **Grande-Allée** between Place Montcalm and Place George V, just beyond the St-Louis Gate of the old wall, where a beery collegiate atmosphere can sometimes rule as the evening wears on. The bars reviewed in this section are removed from the Grande-Allée melee.

Note that smoking has been banned in bars throughout the province since 2006.

Aviatic Club A favorite for after-work drinks since 1945, this bar is located in the front of the city's restored train station. The theme is aviation (odd, given the venue), signaled by two miniature planes hanging from the ceiling. There's food, ranging from sushi to Tex-Mex, along with local and imported beers. 450 de la Gare-du-Palais (near rue St-Paul), Lower Town. ✆ **418/522-3555.**

D'Orsay Visitors who are well into their mortgages will want to keep this dark but chummy pub-bistro in mind. Most of the clientele is on the far side of 35, and they strike up conversations easily. In summer afternoons and evenings, music is piped to the decidedly unprecious terrace out back. There is a full menu of conventional international dishes, from onion soup and fajitas to burgers and mussels. 65 rue de Buade (opposite Hôtel-de-Ville), Upper Town. ✆ **418/694-1582.**

L'Astral ⊛ Spinning slowly above a city that twinkles below like tangled necklaces, this restaurant and bar atop the Hôtel Loews le Concorde unveils a breathtaking 360-degree panorama. Many people come for dinner at the high-quality restaurant, but you can also just come for drinks and the view. 1225 Cours du Général de Montcalm (at the Grande-Allée), Parliament Hill. ✆ **418/647-2222.**

Le Pape-Georges *Finds* This cozy wine bar in a 325-year-old stone-and-beamed room features *chanson* (a French cabaret singing style), along with other music genres, usually Thursday through Sunday at 10pm. Light fare—plates of mostly Québec cheeses, assorted cold meats, and smoked salmon—is served, along with up to 15 choices of wine by the glass (it's open from noon daily). Although it's in the middle of a tourist district, most of the patrons appear to be locals. 8 rue Cul-de-Sac (near bd. Champlain), Lower Town. ✆ **418/692-1320.**

Saint Alexandre Pub ⊛ Roomy and sophisticated, this is one of the best-looking bars in town. It's done in British pub style, with polished mahogany, exposed brick, and a working fireplace that's a particular comfort during the 8 cold months of the year. It serves 40 single-malt scotches and more than 200 beers, along with hearty victuals that complement the brews. (Stick to beer—the cocktails are skimpy.) Live music—rock, blues, sometimes jazz or Irish—is occasionally presented, usually Friday and Saturday nights, but check before planning your night around it. 1087 rue St-Jean (near St-Stanislas), Upper Town. ✆ **418/694-0015.**

GAY BARS & CLUBS

The gay scene in Québec City is a small but vibrant one, centered in the Upper Town just outside the city walls, on **rue St-Jean** and the parallel **rue d'Aiguillon,** starting from where they cross **rue St-Augustin** and heading west. The restos and clubs in the popping St-Roch quartier are also gay-friendly.

Le Drague Cabaret Club ("The Drag"), at 815 rue St-Augustin (✆ **418/649-7212;** www.ledrague.com), just off rue St-Jean, has a cabaret and two dance rooms. The cabaret features drag shows on Sunday nights, with live shows, karaoke, country-music dancing, and theater improv on other nights.

Lesbians make up most of the clientele at the cute **Amour Sorcier Café Bar** at 789 Côte Ste-Geneviève (✆ **418/523-3395**), but it gets a mixed crowd of women and men, gay and straight. There is a low-pressure bar inside the old building and a terrace out front for drinks and snacks. It's about 3 blocks west of Place d'Youville.

At the end of August, there's a 3-day gay fest, **Fête Arc-en-Ciel** (www.fetearcenciel. qc.ca).

19

Side Trips from Québec City

The first four excursions described below can be combined and completed in a day. Admittedly, it will be a morning-to-night undertaking, especially if much time is taken to explore each destination, but the farthest of the four destinations is only 42km (26 miles) from Québec City. The shrine of Ste-Anne-de-Beaupré is a religious destination, while the waterfalls of both Montmorency and Canyon Ste-Anne are dazzling fun, especially in the spring when the winter thaws make them thunder. Just over a bridge near Montmorency, bucolic Ile d'Orléans, with its maple groves, orchards, farms, and 18th- and 19th-century houses, is an unspoiled mini-oasis.

With 2 or more days available, you can continue along the northern shore to Charlevoix, where inns and a gambling casino invite an overnight stay, and consider taking the ferry across the river and driving toward Québec City along the St. Lawrence's southern bank, exploring different riverside villages as you make your way back.

Although it is preferable to drive in this region, tour buses go to Montmorency Falls and the shrine of Ste-Anne-de-Beaupré, and circle the Ile d'Orléans.

For more information, log on to **www. quebecregion.com**.

1 Ile d'Orléans

16km (10 miles) NE of Québec City

Ile d'Orléans was long inhabited by Native Indians and settled by the French as one of their first outposts of New France in the 17th century. Long isolated from the mainland, the island's 7,000 current residents keep a firm resistance to development, so far preventing it from becoming just another sprawling bedroom community. Many of the island's oldest houses are intact, and it remains a largely rural farming area.

Until 1935, the only way to get to Ile d'Orléans was by boat (in summer) or over the ice in sleighs (in winter). The highway bridge that was built that year has allowed the island's fertile fields to become Québec City's primary market-garden. During harvest periods, fruits and vegetables are picked fresh on the farms and trucked into the city daily. In mid-July, hand-painted signs posted by the main road announce *FRAISES: CUEILLIR VOUS-MEME* (STRAWBERRIES: YOU PICK 'EM). The same invitation is made during apple season, August through October. Farmers hand out baskets and quote the price, paid when the basket's full. Bring along a bag or box to carry away the bounty.

Thousands of migrating snow geese, ducks, and Canada geese stop by in April and May and again in late October. It's a spectacular sight when they launch themselves into the air in flapping hordes so thick that they almost blot out the sun.

ESSENTIALS

GETTING THERE

BY CAR   It's a short drive from Québec City to the island. Get on Autoroute 440 east, in the direction of Ste-Anne-de-Beaupré. In about 15 minutes, the Ile d'Orléans bridge is on the right. If you'd like a guide, **Maple Leaf Guide Services** (© **418/ 622-3677**) can provide one in your car or theirs.

While it's possible to bike over the bridge, it's not recommended: The sidewalk is narrow and precarious. But cyclists can park their cars at the tourist office (see below) for C$5 (US$4.35/£2.15) a day.

BY BUS   There are no local buses, but there are organized bus tours. **Dupont** (© **418/649-9226;** www.tourdupont.com) offers a 6-hour tour with stops at a sugar shack, apple orchard, and *chocolaterie*. **La Tournée du Québec Métro** (© **800/672- 5232** or 418/836-8687) and **Old Québec Tours** (© **418/664-0460**) offer shorter tours of the bottom southern edge of the island.

VISITOR INFORMATION

After arriving on the island, follow the "?" signs and turn right on Route 368 East toward Ste-Pétronille. The **Bureau d'Accueil Touristique** (© **418/828-9411;** www. iledorleans.com) is in the house on the right corner, and it has a useful guidebook (C$1/US87¢/43p). It's open late June to mid-October Sunday through Thursday 8:30am to 7:30pm, and Friday and Saturday 8:30am to 8pm; the rest of the year Monday through Friday 9am to 5pm, Saturday 10am to 5pm, and Sunday 11am to 3pm. The *Québec City and Area Guide,* available from Québec City tourism offices, describes a short tour of Ile d'Orléans. A driving-tour CD can be rented at the tourist office, and cycling maps are available.

The three lodgings recommended below for Ile d'Orléans are all of the *auberge* type, meaning they have six or more rooms and full-service restaurants open to both guests and nonguests. But there are also many bed-and-breakfast inns and *gîtes* (homes with a room or two available to travelers), which are cheaper and less elaborate. You can see very brief details about many of these offerings on the tourist office's website, **www.iledorleans.com**. Many lodgings also provide leaflets to the tourist office.

EXPLORING THE ISLAND

A coast-hugging road—Route 368, also called *chemin Royal* and, in a few stretches, *chemin de Bout-de-l'Ile*—circles the island, 34km (21 miles) long and 8km (5 miles) wide, and another couple of roads bisect it. Farms and picturesque houses dot the east side, and abundant apple orchards enliven the west side.

There are six tiny villages, originally established as parishes, and so each has a church as its focal point. Some are **stone churches** that date from the days of the French regime, and with fewer than a dozen such churches left in all of Québec province, this is a particular point of pride. It's possible to do a circuit of Ile d'Orléans in half a day, but you can justify a full day if you eat a good meal, visit a sugar shack, do a little gallery hopping, or just skip stones from the beach. If you're strapped for time, loop around as far as St-Jean then drive across the island on Route du Mitan ("Middle Road"). You'll get to the bridge by turning left onto Route 368 West.

For much of the year you can meander around the island at 40kmph (25 mph), having to pull over only occasionally to let a car pass. There is no bike path, which means bikers share the narrow rural roads. Cars need to drive with care in the busiest summer months, and cyclists might want to visit any month but July or August.

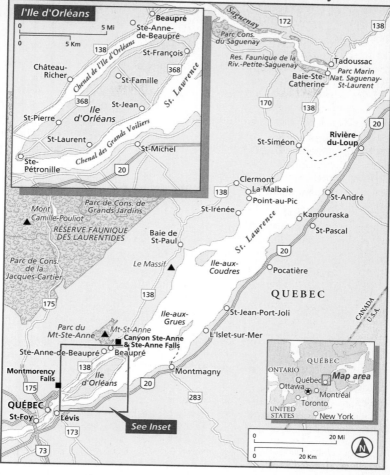

Important navigational note: Street numbers on the ring road "chemin Royal" start anew in each village, so that you could pass a no. 1000 chemin Royal in one stretch and then another no. 1000 chemin Royal a few minutes later. Be sure you know not just the number of your destination but which village it's in as well.

STE-PETRONILLE

The first village reached on the recommended counterclockwise tour is Ste-Pétronille, only 3km (1¾ miles) from the bridge (take a right turn off the bridge). When the British occupied the island in 1759, General James Wolfe had his headquarters here before launching his successful attack on Québec City. The village is best known for its Victorian inn, **La Goéliche** (see below), and also claims the northernmost stand of **red oaks** in North America, dazzling in autumn. The houses were once the summer homes of wealthy English in the 1800s; the church dates from 1871. Even if you don't stay at the inn, drive down to the water's edge, where there's a small public area with benches and views of Québec City. Strolling down the picturesque **rue Laflamme** is another pleasant way to while away an hour.

Where to Stay & Dine

La Goéliche 🛏 On a rocky point of land at the southern tip of Ile d'Orléans stands this country inn and restaurant with a wraparound porch. This building is a virtual replica of the 1880 Victorian house that stood here until 1996. That one burned to the ground, leaving nothing but the staircase. This one manages to retain the period flavor with tufted chairs, Tiffany-style lamps, and a few antiques. All rooms are individually furnished and face the water, and first-floor units have small terraces. There are two apartments for groups or longer stays. The river slaps at the foundation of the glass-enclosed terrace dining room, which is a grand observation point for watching cruise ships and Great Lakes freighters steaming past.

22 chemin du Quai, Ste-Pétronille, PQ G0A 4C0. ☎ **888/511-2248** or 418/828-2248. Fax 418/828-2745. www. goeliche.ca. 16 units. C$128–$208 (US$111–US$181/£55–£89) double. Rates include breakfast. Packages available. AE, DC, MC, V. Free parking. **Amenities:** Restaurant (contemporary French); bar; heated outdoor pool; golf and tennis nearby; babysitting. *In room:* Wi-Fi, minibar, coffeemaker, hair dryer.

ST-LAURENT

From Ste-Pétronille, continue on Route 368, which is called "chemin de Bout-de-l'Ile" for a few minutes here. After 7km (4⅓ miles), you'll arrive at St-Laurent, founded in 1679, once a boat-building center turning out ships for Glasgow shipowners that could carry up to 5,300 tons. To learn more about the town's maritime history, head down to the water and visit **Le Parc Maritime de St-Laurent** (☎ **418/828-9672**), an active boatyard from 1908 to 1967. Before the bridge was built, islanders journeyed across the river to Québec City by boat from here. The Maritime Park incorporates the old Godbout Boatworks and offers demonstrations of the craft. It's open daily from 10am to 5pm mid-June through early September.

Where to Stay & Dine

Auberge Le Canard Huppé A roadside inn reminiscent of those found in the motherland, this tidy establishment takes considerable pride in its kitchen. A four-course dinner, made up almost entirely of local products, is served from 5 to 8pm and costs C$38 (US$33/£16); reservations required. Guests can have their breakfast in the bistro/bar or on the terrace under the linden tree. Just one room has a TV, but all are attractively decorated. Practice your French: The prickly owner/chef, who took over the auberge in 2004, speaks English well but begrudges each syllable.

2198 chemin Royal (Rte. 368), St-Laurent, PQ G0A 3Z0. ☎ **418/828-2292**. Fax 418/828-0966. www.canard-huppe. com. 10 units. From C$125 (US$109/£54) double. Rates include full breakfast. Packages available. AE, DC, MC, V. **Amenities:** Restaurant (contemporary French); bar. *In room:* A/C, hair dryer.

Le Moulin de Saint-Laurent 🛏 COUNTRY FRENCH This former flour mill, in operation from 1720 to 1928, has been transformed into one of the island's most romantic restaurants. Rubble-stone walls and hand-wrought beams form the interior, with candlelight glinting off hanging copper and brass pots. On a warm day, sit on the shaded terrace beside the waterfall tumbling down a small hill, and be sure to wander upstairs to see the Québécois antiques. Lunch can be light—maybe an omelet or a plate of assorted pâtés or cheeses—and the ice cider made on the island is a refreshing alternative to wine. There's music on Sunday nights in the summer. Main courses at dinner range from C$16 to C$26 (US$14–US$23/£6.90–£11), and reservations are recommended. The restaurant is closed from November to April, but the owners rent nine cottage chalets at the shore year-round. Each has a fully equipped kitchen and some have a fireplace and washing machine, particularly appealing for bikers. Pets are allowed in most units.

754 chemin Royal (Rte. 368), St-Laurent, PQ G0A 3Z0. (✆ **888/629-3888** or 418/829-3888. Fax 418/829-3716. www. moulinstlaurent.qc.ca. 9 units. Summer, from C$180 (US$156/£77) double. Rates include dinner and breakfast. Packages available. AE, DC, MC, V. **Amenities:** Restaurant (contemporary French); terrace next to waterfall; small outdoor heated pool in summer. *In room:* TV, stereo, kitchen.

ST-JEAN

St-Jean, 6km (3¾ miles) from St-Laurent, was home to sea captains. That might be why the houses in the village appear more luxurious than others on the island. The creamy yellow "Scottish brick" in the facades of several of the homes was ballast in boats that came over from Europe. The village church was built in 1734, and the walled cemetery is the final resting place of many fishermen and seafarers.

On the left as you enter St-Jean is the stately and well-preserved **Manoir Mauvide-Genest,** 1451 chemin Royal (✆ **418/829-2630**). Jean Mauvide was a French surgeon who settled here in 1720. He went on to acquire much of the western part of the island and built this small estate in 1752, becoming one of the leading figures in New France. The manor house is unlike any other building on the island and filled with authentic and reproduction furnishings of Mauvide's era; it's classified as a historic monument. Guided tours are available by reservation. Extensively restored in the past 10 years, the manor is open daily from 10am to 5pm May through November 1, and by reservation the rest of the year. Admission is C$5 (US$4.35/£2.15) for adults, C$2 (US$1.75/85p) for children under 12.

The manor also has a **restaurant** with an outdoor terrace and river views serving light meals—soups and salads, assorted pâtés and cheeses, smoked trout, a quiche du jour, antipasto plates—as well as formal repasts of three to five courses starting at C$14 (US$12/£6). It's open Tuesday through Sunday from 11:30am to well into the evening, depending on business. Call (✆ **418/829-2630** for reservations.

Also in St-Jean is the **La Sucrerie Blouin,** 2967 chemin Royal (✆ **418/829-2903**), a *cabane à sucre* (the traditional "sugar shack"), where maple syrup is made and casual all-you-can-eat meals are available. A family of bakers who have lived on the island for 300 years runs this place. See demonstrations of the syrup-making equipment and get debriefed on the process that turns the sap of a tree into syrup.

If you're pressed for time, this is where you can pick up **Route du Mitan,** which crosses Ile d'Orléans from here to St-Famille on the west side of the island. Route du Mitan is marked with a small sign on the left just past the church in St-Jean. Even if you're continuing the full loop, a detour down the road is a diverting tour through farmland and forest; return to St-Jean and proceed east on Route 368 to St-François.

ST-FRANÇOIS

The 9km (5⅔-mile) drive from St-Jean to St-François exposes vistas of the Laurentian Mountains off to the left on the western shore of the river. Just past the village center of St-Jean, **Mont Ste-Anne** can be seen in the distance, its slopes scored by ski trails. The St. Lawrence River, a constant and mighty presence, is 10 times wider here than when it flows past Québec City, and can be viewed especially well from the town's observation tower. Regrettably, the town's original church (1734) burned in 1988. It was replaced in 1992.

After you've looped around the northern edge of the island, the road stops being Route 358 East and becomes Route 368 West.

STE-FAMILLE

Founded in 1661, Ste-Famille is the oldest parish on the island and 8km (5 miles) from St-François. Across the road from the triple-spired church (1743) is the convent of **Notre-Dame Congregation,** founded in 1685 by Marguerite Bourgeoys, one of Montréal's prominent early citizens.

Also here is the **Maison de nos Aïeux,** 3907 chemin Royal (© **418/829-0330**) a genealogy center with mini-movies about some of the island's oldest families and information about the island's history. It's open 10 months a year (closed Dec and Jan), daily in the summer from 10am to 6pm, and costs C$3 (US$2.60/£1.30). Adjacent is the **Parc des Ancêtres,** a riverside green space with picnic tables.

ST-PIERRE

When you reach St-Pierre, you're nearly back to where you started. Its central attraction is the island's oldest church (1717). Services are no longer held there, but there's a large handicraft shop in the back, behind the altar, which is even older than the church (1695).

The orchard **Bilodeau** at 2200 chemin Royal (© **418/828-9316**) makes for a satisfying final stop on the island. It produces some of Ile d'Orléans's regular ciders and *cidre de glace,* or ice cider, an after-dinner drink made from apples left on the trees until after the first frost. Visitors can partake of samples, guided tours of the facility, apple picking from mid-August to mid-October, and a shop. Open May through December and by appointment the rest of the year.

If you're still hungry, the **Buffet d'Orléans,** 1025 route Prévost (© **418/828-0013**) just at the bridge, is an old-time diner where the waitresses wear white skirts and black aprons, the bread comes in plastic, and the walls are faux stone. Get the *tourtière maison,* a homemade meat pie in a crust, served with two scoops of mashed potatoes and vegetables, for about C$10 ($8.70/£4.30). Open daily 7am to 9pm year-round, and to 11pm in the summer.

2 Montmorency Falls

11km (7 miles) NE of Québec City

Back on the mainland, **Montmorency Falls,** which were named by Samuel de Champlain for his patron, the duke of Montmorency, are 83m (272 ft.) tall. That's 30m (98 ft.) higher than Niagara—a boast no visitor is spared. They are, however, far narrower. On summer nights the plunging water is illuminated, and from late July to mid-August there is an international fireworks competition overhead 2 nights a week, **Les Grands Feux Loto-Québec** (p. 244). The yellow cast of the falls results from the high iron content of the riverbed.

ESSENTIALS

GETTING THERE

BY BUS   Tour companies **La Tournée du Québec Métro** (© **800/672-5232** or 418/836-8687), **Old Québec Tours** (© **418/664-0460**), and **Dupont** (© **418/649-9226**) all have tours to the falls. Schedules and programs are subject to frequent change, so check by phone.

BY CAR   Take Autoroute 440 east out of Québec City. After 10 minutes, watch for the exit for the falls and the parking lot. If you miss the exit, you'll see the falls on your left and will be able to U-turn.

VIEWING THE FALLS

The falls are surrounded by the provincial **Parc de la Chute-Montmorency** (© 418/663-3330; www.sepaq.com/chutemontmorency), where visitors can take in the view and have a picnic. The grounds are accessible year-round. In winter, there's a particularly impressive sight, as the freezing spray sent up by crashing water builds a mountain of white ice at the base called the *pain de sucre* (sugarloaf). It sometimes grows as high as 30m (98 ft.) and attracts ice climbers.

There are a variety of platforms from which the falls can be viewed, including a footbridge that spans the river just where it flows over the cliff. There are also stairs that ascend one side from the bottom to near the top, and a cable car (not for the vertiginous) that runs from the parking lot off Autoroute 440 to a terminal above the falls near **Manoir Montmorency,** a villa that contains an interpretation center, a café-bar, and a restaurant. The restaurant serves good-quality lunches and dinners and a popular Sunday buffet brunch. Call (© **418/663-3330**) for meal reservations, which are suggested. The dining room and porch have a side view of the falls.

Admission to the falls is free, although parking costs C$9 (US$7.85/£3.85). Round-trip fares on the cable car cost C$8.25 (US$7.20/£3.55) for adults, C$4 (US$3.50/£1.70) for ages 6 to 16. The cable car operates every day from late April to late August, and on a more limited schedule the rest of the year. Packages are available that include parking and cable rides.

3 Ste-Anne-de-Beaupré

33km (21 miles) NE of Québec City, 22km (14 miles) NE of Montmorency Falls

The village of Ste-Anne-de-Beaupré is a religious destination, centered on a two-spired basilica that is one of Canada's most famous shrines. More than a million and a half people make the pilgrimage each year to a complex that includes the church, a hillside Station of the Cross, a chapel, the museum of Ste-Anne, and the church store. The church has housing for temporary guests and a plot of land for RV campers.

Legend has it that French mariners were sailing up the St. Lawrence River in the 1650s when they ran into a terrifying storm. They prayed to their patroness, St. Anne, to save them, and when they survived they dedicated a wooden chapel to her on the north shore of the St. Lawrence, near the site of their perils. Not long afterward, a chapel laborer was said to have been cured of lumbago, the first of many documented miracles. Since that time, believers have made their way here to pay their respects to St. Anne, the mother of the Virgin Mary and grandmother of Jesus.

The route to the town is along the river, and the river is tidal. At low tide, the beach is sometimes speckled with hundreds of birds pecking for food. You can see them behind the houses, gas stations, and garages that pepper the road.

ESSENTIALS
GETTING THERE
BY BUS   La Tournée du Québec Métro (© **800/672-5232** or 418/836-8687) and **Old Québec Tours** (© **418/664-0460**) both have tours that include Ste-Anne-de-Beaupré.

BY CAR Autoroute 440 turns into Autoroute 40 at Montmorency Falls and then becomes Route 138 almost immediately. Continue on 138 to Ste-Anne-de-Beaupré. The church and exit are visible from the road.

EXPLORING THE BASILICA

The towering **basilica** is the most recent building raised on this spot in St. Anne's honor. After the sailors' first modest wooden chapel was swept away by a flood in the 1600s, another chapel was built on higher ground. Floods, fires, and the ravages of time dispatched later buildings, until a larger structure was erected in 1887. In 1926, it, too, lay in ruins, gutted by fire. The present basilica is constructed in stone, following an essentially neo-Romanesque scheme, and was consecrated on July 4, 1976. Inside the front doors, look for the two columns dressed with racks of canes—presumably from people cured and no longer in need of assistance—that go 9m (30 ft.) high.

The church and the whole town of Ste-Anne-de-Beaupré are particularly busy on days of saintly significance: the first Sunday in May, mid- through late July, the fourth Sunday in August, and early September. In the summer, there is a daily candlelight procession at 8:15pm.

Other parts of the shrine include the **Way of the Cross,** lined with life-size bronze figures, on the hillside opposite the basilica; the **Scala Santa Chapel** (1891); the **Memorial Chapel** (1878), with a bell tower and altar from the late 17th and early 18th centuries, respectively; and the **Musée Sainte-Anne** (contributions accepted).

Also in the village is a building called the **Cyclorama,** which houses a 14m-high (45-ft.), 360-degree painting depicting old Jerusalem at the moment of Christ's crucifixion ("relive the sight," says the brochure). Open from mid-April to October, admission is C$8 (US$6.95/£3.45) for adults, C$7 (US$6.10/£3) for seniors 65 and older, and C$5 (US$4.35/£2.15) for children 6 to 16.

WHERE TO STAY & DINE

Auberge La Camarine ⚘ This inn has a kitchen that is equaled by only a handful of restaurants in the region. The cuisine is of that variety of fusion cookery that joins French, Italian, and Asian techniques and ingredients. Roasted pheasant and its salsa of caramelized apples is illustrative, and Québécois cheeses are offered for the meal's close. Guests have a choice of a four-course menu starting at C$28 (US$24/£12) or a degustation menu for C$60 (US$52/£26), and weekend brunches are C$18 (US$16/£7.70). While the locale on Route 138 isn't particularly scenic, guest rooms blend antique and contemporary notions, and some have fireplaces and/or balconies.

10947 bd. Ste-Anne (Rte. 138), Beaupré, PQ G0A 1E0. ℂ 800/567-3939 or 418/827-5703. Fax 418/827-5430. www.camarine.com. 31 units. From C$95 (US$83/£41) double. Packages available. AE, DC, MC, V. **Amenities:** Restaurant (fusion); bistro-bar; access to nearby health club. *In room:* A/C (some rooms), TV.

4 Canyon Ste-Anne, Ste-Anne Falls & Parc Mont Ste-Anne

42km (26 miles) NE of Québec City, about 9km (6 miles) NE of Ste-Anne-de-Beaupré

After Ste-Anne-de-Beaupré, you're finally in thick evergreen woods, and the busyness of urban life begins to slip away. A short drive off Route 138 is the deep gorge and powerful waterfall created by the Ste-Anne-du-Nord River. Unseen from the main road, the Canyon Ste-Anne and its falls are an exhilarating sight to experience and only take about an hour and a half to visit. Nearby is the Parc Mont Ste-Anne, which surrounds an 800m-high (2,625-ft.) peak. Summertime invites camping, hiking, and biking (rentals available), while wintertime turns it into Québec City's busiest ski area.

ESSENTIALS

GETTING THERE

BY BUS From about mid-November to the end of April, the **Hiver Express** (© 418/525-5191) shuttle service from Québec City carries passengers to a variety of ski slopes, including Mont Ste-Anne, making it possible to stay in the city at night and ski the mountain by day. The cars or minivans are equipped to carry ski gear, and the round-trip fare is C$25 (US$22/£11).

BY CAR Continue along Route 138 from Ste-Anne-de-Beaupré. To get to the Parc, follow the signs; the resort entrance is easy to spot from the highway. To get to the waterfalls, turn onto the secondary Route 360. The marked entrance is on the left.

VIEWING THE STE-ANNE FALLS

The dirt road from Route 360 leads through the trees to a parking lot, picnic grounds, and building containing a cafeteria, a shop, and the ticket booth. The falls are less than a 10-minute walk from the entrance, but an open-sided shuttle bus is available. It takes you to the top of the falls, where there are trails that go down both sides of the water. Three footbridges go directly across the falls, too: The first goes over the narrow river just before the water starts to drop, and the second crosses right over the canyon, from the top of the rock walls that drop straight down to the water. Proximity to the unending, thundering water crashing over massive rocks is likely to induce vertigo in even the most stable of nerves. The final bridge is at the base of the gorge, just 9m (30 feet) above the water where it starts to flatten out again, and ends at an observation platform. Along both trails are eight platforms that jut over the water and well-written information plaques.

The falls are 75m (243 ft.) high and at their most spectacular in the spring, when melt-off of winter snows bloats the rivers above and sends 100,000 liters of water over *per second.* (The volume drops to 10,000 liters in Aug and Sept.) From 1904 to 1965, the river was used to float logs from lumbering operations, and part of the dramatic gorge was created by dynamiting in 1917, to cut down on the literal log-jams. So voluminous is the mist coming from the fall that it creates another wall of mini-waterfalls on the side of the gorge. Management has wisely avoided commercial intrusions along the trails, letting the awe-inspiring natural beauty speak for itself.

There is an option for visitors to zip across the canyon directly over the water harnessed onto a cable wire (an extra fee, for the very brave-hearted only). Visitors who have difficulty walking can see the falls without going too far from the bus, and those who suffer acrophobia can stay on the side trails, strolling amid the hemlock and poplar trees, avoiding the bridges. A minor claim to fame: Scenes from the 2000 John Travolta film *Battlefield Earth* were filmed here.

Admission is C$10 (US$8.70/£4.30) adults, C$7.50 (US$6.50/£3.25) ages 13 to 17, C$4.50 (US$3.90/£1.95) ages 6 to 12. The site is open daily May through late October. Hours are 9am to 4:45pm, with an extra hour to 5:45pm from June 24 to Labour Day. It's closed the rest of the year. Confirm the hours, which are subject to change due to weather, by calling © **418/827-4057.**

PARC MONT STE-ANNE

Parc du Mont Ste-Anne (© **888/827-4579** or 418/827-4561; www.mont-sainte-anne.com) is a wilderness resort surrounding an 800m-high (2,625-ft.) peak and an outdoor enthusiast's dream. In summer and early fall, it offers camping, hiking, golfing, in-line skating, paragliding, and canyoning. It's well known for its huge network of trails for both **hard-core mountain biking** and milder day-tripping (bikes can be rented at the park). A panoramic gondola to the top of the mountain operates daily between mid-June and mid-October and on weekends for about a month on either end, weather permitting.

General admission to the park is C$8.85 (US$7.70/£3.80) for a family in a car, C$3.55 (US$3.10/£1.50) for adults, and C$1.75 ($1.55/75p) for children 7 to 17 years old. Gondola ticket prices are C$15 (US$13/£6.45) for adults, C$12 (US$10/£5.15) for ages 7 to 17, and C$13 (US$11/£5.60) for seniors, with a variety of family rates.

In winter, **skiing on Mont Ste-Anne** is terrifically popular. Just 40 minutes from Québec City, this is the region's largest and busiest mountain. There are 65 trails on three sides of the mountain, with a 625m (2,050-ft.) vertical drop. At night, 17 trails are lit. Full-day lift tickets are C$55 (US$48/£24) for adults, C$45 (US$39/£19) for seniors, C$42 (US$37/£18) for ages 13 to 17, and C$29 (US$25/£12) for ages 7 to 12.

Also in the winter, the park offers the largest network of cross-country ski trials in Canada, at 212km (131 miles). There are seven heated rest huts, three of which can accommodate overnight guests. A day ticket is C$18 (US$16/£7.75) for adults, C$13 (US$11/£5.60) for seniors, C$12 (US$10/£5.15) for ages 13 to 17, and C$7 (US$6.10/£3) for children 7 to 12. The park also offers dog-sledding, snowshoeing, snowmobiling, ice-canyoning, and winter paragliding.

The park is an easy commute from the city, which is what most people do. Its entrance is easy to spot from the highway. For information about what's happening at the resort, hours, and rates, call ℭ **418/827-4561** or visit www.mont-sainte-anne.com.

WHERE TO STAY & DINE

Château Mont Sainte-Anne ⑇ 𝒦ids   Tucked into the base of its namesake mountain, this resort opened in 1979 and continues to grow, with additional renovations in 2005 and 2006. While the management is succeeding in its efforts to increase summer business, with two golf courses and a strong network of mountain biking trails, its real identity is as a ski center. It is well suited in its role as a winter ski lodge, with ski-in–ski-out accessibility at the base of the gondola lift. All rooms have either kitchenettes or full kitchens, and 40 have fireplaces. The menu in the main dining room is unusually inventive for a mass feeding operation, and the bar provides satisfying pub grub. The hotel has a game room for young children and organizes family programs every day. A free shuttle van carries guests to and from Québec City.

500 bd. Beau-Pré, Beaupré, PQ G0A 1E0. ℭ **866/900-5211** or 418/827-5211. Fax 418/827-5072. www.chateau msa.ca. 240 units. From C$289 (US$251/£124) double in winter; from C$179 (US$156/£77) double in summer. Children under 17 stay free in parent's room. Children ages 7 to 12 eat for half price; children 6 and under eat for free. Packages available. AE, DC, MC, V. Pets accepted in 10 units. **Amenities:** 2 restaurants (eclectic, international); bar/bistro; indoor and outdoor pools; outdoor hot tubs; golf; health club; spa; children's programs; game room; babysitting; laundry service; dry cleaning. In room: A/C, TV w/pay movies, Wi-Fi, kitchenette, fridge, coffeemaker, hair dryer.

5 Central Charlevoix: Baie-St-Paul, St-Irénée & La Malbaie

Baie-St-Paul: 93km (58 miles) NE of Québec City; St-Irénée: 125km (78 miles) NE of Québec City; La Malbaie: 140km (87 miles) NE of Québec City

The Laurentians move closer to the shore of the St. Lawrence River as they approach what used to be called Murray Bay at the mouth of the Malbaie River. U.S. President William Howard Taft, who had a summer residence in the area, once said that the air here was "as intoxicating as champagne, but without the morning-after headache."

In 1988, Charlevoix was named a UNESCO World Biosphere Reserve, a protected area for cross-disciplinary research into conservation. Development here is balanced against environmental concerns. This was one of the first designated areas with a human population. Grand vistas over the St. Lawrence abound, and there are many farms in the area. The rolling, dark green mountains with their white ski slope scars offer numerous places to hike and bike in the warm months and ski when there's snow.

Baie-St-Paul is an artists' colony, and good-to-memorable country inns dot the countryside up to La Malbaie. La Malbaie has a casino, a smaller offshoot of the one in Montréal. It's not unheard of, by the way, for the region to still have snow in May.

ESSENTIALS
GETTING THERE
BY CAR   Take Route 138 as far as Baie-St-Paul. Turn onto Route 362 to go into downtown Baie. To continue northeast, take either 138 or 362, which runs closer to the water and lets you visit St-Irénée on the way to La Malbaie.

VISITOR INFORMATION
Baie-St-Paul has a year-round **tourist office** on Route 138 (© **418/435-4160**), open daily from 8:30am to 4:30pm in the winter, until 7pm in the summer. It's before the village on a hill above it and well marked from the highway (it's a sharp turnoff), and offers a grand vista of the river and town below. There are also offices throughout the region including one in La Malbaie directly on the water at 495 bd. de Comporté, Route 362 (© **800/667-2276** or 418/665-4454). It's open daily until 9pm in the summer months, and 4:30pm off-season. Regional information is also at **www.tourisme-charlevoix.com**.

BAIE-ST-PAUL & ISLE-AUX-COUDRES
The first town of any size reached in Charlevoix via Route 138, this attractive community of 7,365 holds on to a reputation as an artists' retreat that began at the start of the 20th century. More than two dozen boutiques and galleries and a couple of small museums show the work of local painters and artisans. Given the setting, it isn't surprising that many of the artists are landscapists, but other styles and subjects are represented. Although some of their production is of the hobbyist level, much is highly professional. Options include the **Maison de René-Richard,** at 58 rue St-Jean-Baptiste (© **418/435-5571**) and **Carrefour culturel Paul-Médéric,** 4 rue Ambroise-Fafard (© **418/435-2540**).

For **bicycling,** pop off the mainland by taking the free 15-minute car ferry to the small island of **Isle-aux-Coudres.** Popular paths offer a 26km (about 16-mile) loop around the island. Single bikes, tandems, and quadricycles for two adults and two small children can be rented from **Centre Vélo-Coudres** (© **418/438-2118**). The island also has a smattering of boutiques and hotels. The ferry leaves from the town of St. Joseph-de-la-Rive, along Route 362 just east of Baie-St-Paul.

Foodies will want to consider a driving tour of the *circuit agroalimentaire,* a **tour of 11 working farms and shops.** They include **La Ferme Basque de Charlevoix,** 813 rue St-Edouard in St-Urbain (© **418/639-2246;** lafermebasque.ca), a small-scale family-run duck farm that makes foie gras sold throughout the province, and **La Maison d'Affinage Maurice Dufour,** 1339 bd. Mgr-de-Lavel (Rte. 138) Baie-St-Paul (© **418/435-5692;** www.fromagefin.com), a *fromagerie* that makes the highly regarded artisanal cheese Le Ciel de Charlevoix and serves dinner Wednesdays through Sundays.

Many of Canada's elite skiers train at **Le Massif** (© **877/536-2774** or 418/632-5876; www.lemassif.com), the largest ski mountain in the area. It has a network of 43 trails that give skiers the illusion that they're heading directly into the adjacent St. Lawrence.

There are rumblings of a major project for the area: Daniel Gauthier, a founder of the Cirque du Soleil, has said he wants to further develop Le Massif, adding housing to the mountain and a 180-room hotel on a farm near downtown Baie-St-Paul. He also wants to refurbish a train line to allow travelers to travel to the area without their cars. At press time, none of these projects had broken ground yet.

A LOCAL MUSEUM

Centre d'Exposition   This brick-and-glass museum has three floors of work primarily by regional artists. Photography and Inuit sculptures are included, and temporary one-person and group shows are mounted throughout the year.

23 rue Ambroise-Fafard, Baie-St-Paul. © **418/435-3681**. www.centredexpo-bsp.qc.ca. Admission C$4 (US$3.50/£1.70) adults, C$2.50 (US$2.20/£1.10) students, free for children 12 and under. Tues–Sun 11am–5pm (until 6pm in summer).

WHERE TO STAY & DINE

La Maison Otis   Slip into this rambling collection of connecting buildings as into a pair of favorite old jeans. Combinations of fireplaces, whirlpools, stereo systems, VCRs, four-poster beds, and suites that sleep four are all available. A long porch fronts the colorful main street, and a small indoor pool and sauna are on the premises. Meals are no sacrifice, served in a room with a stone fireplace and shaded candlesticks on pink tablecloths. Smoked "Basque" filet of duck with honeyed figs and leg of lamb steamed with garlic and cumin have been excellent in the past. Rates include dinner and breakfast; room-only rates are available for stays of more than 1 day. The hotel also runs the attached **Café des Artistes,** open all day, where the pizzas with wafer-thin crusts are exceptional. It does busy business with the town's casual art community.

23 rue St-Jean-Baptiste, Baie-St-Paul, PQ G0A 1B0. © **800/267-2254** or 418/435-2255. Fax 418/435-2464. www.maisonotis.com. 30 units. C$182–C$355 (US$158–US$309/£78–£153) double. Rates include 5-course dinner and breakfast. Packages available. MC, V. Pets accepted. **Amenities:** 2 restaurants (regional; café); bar; indoor pool; attached spa; sauna; free Wi-Fi in lobby and café; massage; babysitting. *In room:* A/C in 18 units, TV, Internet, coffeemaker, hair dryer, iron.

Le Saint-Pub BISTRO   This casual bistro is part of the town's Micro-Brasserie. There's a small bar and small, neat area with tables, and the kitchen serves up solid renditions of bar food, Québecois-style. House specialties are barbecue chicken (C$16/US$14/£6.90) and a variety of foods cooked with beer (beer and onion soup, chocolate and stout pudding). The *traditionnel cigare au chou et sa sauce tomate* (ground pork wrapped in cabbage leaves with tomato sauce) is tasty. Five beers on tap and four in bottles are all made on-site. There's a patio in summer.

2 rue Racine, Baie-St-Paul. © **418/240-2332**. www.microbrasserie.com. Main courses C$16–C$25 (US$14–US$22/£6.90–£11). MC, V. Mon–Thurs 11:30am–2pm and 5–9pm; Fri–Sat 11:30am–9pm; Sun noon–8pm.

ST-IRENEE

From Baie-St-Paul, take Route 362 northeast toward La Malbaie. The air is scented by sea salt and rent by the shrieks of gulls, and Route 362 roller-coasters over bluffs above the river, with wooded hills interrupted by narrow riverbeds. It can be treacherous in the ice, though, so if you're heading straight to La Malbaie you might want to opt for the flatter Route 138, which runs more or less parallel.

In 32km (about 20 miles) is St-Irénée, a cliff-top hamlet of just 685 year-round residents. Apart from the setting, the best reason for dawdling here is the 60-hectare (148-acre) property and estate of **Domaine Forget** (✆ 888/336-7438 or 418/452-3535 for reservations; www.domaineforget.com). The facility is a performing arts center for music and dance and offers an International Music Festival and a Music and Dance Academy. Concerts are mostly staged in a 604-seat concert hall, with summertime Sunday musical brunches on an outdoor terrace with spectacular views of the river. The program emphasizes classical music with solo instrumentalists and chamber groups, but is peppered with jazz combos, dance recitals, and world music events. Most tickets are C$20 to C$35 (US$17–US$30/£8.60–£15).

From September to May, Domaine **rents its student dorms** to the general public. They're clean and well-appointed studios, with cooking areas and beds for 3 to 5 people. They cost C$60 to C$90 (US$52–US$78/£26–£39), with discounts for longer stays, and include access to studio work areas.

Sea kayaking tours from a half-day to 4 days can be arranged through several companies in the area. **Katabatik** (✆ 800/453-4850 or 418/665-2332; www.katabatik.ca), based in La Malbaie, offers ecotouring that combines kayaking with information about the bays of the St-Lawrence estuary. A half-day tour is C$50 (US$43/£22) for adults, C$40 (US$35/£17) for children 14 to 17, and C$30 (US$26/£13) for children 9 to 13. Tours start in St-Irénée as well as other spots along the coast.

LA MALBAIE: POINTE-AU-PIC & CAP-A-L'AIGLE

From St-Irénée, Route 362 starts to bend west after 10km (6¼ miles), as the mouth of the Malbaie River starts to form. La Malbaie (or "Murray Bay," as it was called by the wealthy Anglophones who made this their resort of choice from the Gilded Age through the 1950s) is the collective name of five former municipalities: Pointe-au-Pic, Cap-à-l'Aigle, Rivière-Malbaie, Sainte-Agnès, and Saint-Fidèle. At its center is a small and scenic bay. Inhabitants of the region justifiably wax poetic about their wildlife and hills and trees, the place "where the sea meets the sky." They also have something quite different to preen about these days, as well: a casino.

A CASINO & A MUSEUM

Casino de Charlevoix   This is the second of Québec's gambling casinos (the first is in Montréal) and it is about as tasteful as such establishments get. Cherrywood paneling and granite floors enclose the ranks of more than 800 slot machines, a keno lounge, and over 20 tables, including blackjack, roulette, stud poker, and minibaccarat. Only soft drinks are allowed at the machines and tables, so players have to go to an adjacent bar to mourn (or celebrate) their losses. There is a dress code that keeps out sloppy or gang-related ware. Parking is free.

183 av. Richelieu (follow the many signs). ✆ 800/665-2274 or 418/665-5300. www.casino-de-charlevoix.com. Free admission (18 and over only). Daily 9am–3am on summer weekends; somewhat shorter hours other days.

Musée de Charlevoix   Located on the Pointe-au-Pic Harbour, the museum features folk art, sculptures, and paintings by regional artists in both its permanent collection and frequent temporary exhibitions.

10 chemin du Havre (at the corner of Rte. 362). ✆ 418/665-4411. Admission C$5 (US$4.35/£2.15) adults, C$4 (US$3.50/£1.70) seniors and students. June to mid-Oct daily 9am–5pm; mid-Oct to May Mon–Fri 10am–5pm, Sat–Sun 1–5pm.

WHERE TO STAY & DINE

Fairmont Le Manoir Richelieu ★★ (Kids)   The grand resort of the region. Since 1899, there has been a hotel here, first serving the swells who summered in this aristocratic haven. After waves of renovations, the decor of this "castle on the cliff" is reminiscent of its posh heritage, with Queen Anne furniture and light blue hues—tasteful and elegant. Many rooms are at deluxe standards, with bathrobes, two or three phones, and easy Internet connections. The Fairmont Gold floor has a lounge serving complimentary breakfasts and evening hors d'oeuvres. The hotel offers spectacular views of the St. Lawrence River. A C$15-million (US$13-million/£6.5-million), 4-year project molded the golf course into a glorious 27-hole expanse overlooking the St. Lawrence on one side and the hills and mountains of Charlevoix on the other. Guests include young couples, elderly folks who have been coming here since they were youngsters, gamers visiting the **Casino de Charlevoix** next door, and families who take advantage of the region's many child-friendly activities.

181 rue Richelieu, La Malbaie, PQ G5A 1X7. ℂ **800/441-1414** or 418/665-3703. Fax 418/665-8131. www. fairmont.com. 405 units. Summer C$259 (US$225/£111) double; Nov–May C$159 (US$138/£68) double; suites from C$379 (US$330/£163]). Packages available. AE, DC, MC, V. Valet parking C$19 (US$17/£8.15) with in/out privileges; self-park for free. **Amenities:** 4 restaurants (international); bar; indoor and outdoor pools; Jacuzzi; sauna; golf; 3 tennis courts; health club; spa w/22 treatment rooms; watersports equipment; game room; concierge; business center; shopping arcade; limited room service; babysitting; laundry service; same-day dry cleaning; executive rooms. In room: A/C, TV w/pay movies, fax, high-speed Internet, minibar, coffeemaker, hair dryer, iron, safe.

La Pinsonnière ★★★   It takes real confidence to close a property for 7 months, spend over a million dollars, and end up with just 18 units—7 *fewer* than you had when you started. But Valérie Andrée Authier set her sights on making everything just a little more luxe when she took over this top-notch inn from her parents. The 2006 renovation created six deluxe rooms (up from one) which feature spectacular river views, princely linens, private terraces, and spa bathrooms with oversize whirlpools, private saunas, or steam showers. The newer rooms are in contemporary, streamlined decor, while the older ones are more classic Queen Anne. Each room has a fireplace, either gas or wood. There is a three-room on-site spa and an unspoiled beach at the end of the property. La Pinsonnière was one of the first hostelries in Canada to be invited into the prestigious Relais & Châteaux organization. Dinners are C$68 (US$59/£29) and menus change daily. Wines are a particular point of pride here, evidenced by the impressive 12,000-bottle cellar with 750 different labels (tours nightly).

124 rue St-Raphaël, La Malbaie (secteur Cap-à-l'Aigle), PQ G5A 1X9. ℂ **800/387-4431** or 418/665-4431. Fax 418/665-7156. www.lapinsonniere.com. 18 units. C$285–C$485 (US$248–US$422/£123–£209) double. Packages available. Minimum 2-night stay on weekends, 3 nights on holiday weekends. AE, MC, V. Pets accepted. **Amenities:** Restaurant (creative French); bar; heated indoor pool; tennis court; beach; access to nearby health club; sauna; spa; nature trail; concierge; limited room service; massage; babysitting; laundry service; dry cleaning. In room: A/C, TV, free Wi-Fi, free high-speed Internet, hair dryer, minibar, iron, safe.

Vices Versa REGIONAL   Here's the nifty premise: Two chefs, married, team up to create their own restaurant. Only instead of combining their palates into one menu, they create his-and-hers menus and cook on separate stoves. As they say on the website, "He likes butter, cream, and bacon, she likes herbs and spices. He is a sauce type, she is more of an emulsion type. He sees potatoes and mushrooms everywhere, she cherishes the whole garden patch." Both, though, feature locally-grown foie gras, guinea fowl, cheeses, vegetables, and ciders. They only plan one seating per evening, which means the meal is leisurely, with no pressure to go anywhere.

216 St-Etienne, La Malbaie. © **418/665-6869.** www.vicesversa.com. Reservations recommended. Main courses from C$40 (US$35/£17); table d'hôte C$60 or C$100 (US$52/£26 or US$87/£43). MC, V. Thurs–Sat 6–9:30pm all year, with additional days seasonally; call for exact days.

6 Upper Charlevoix: St-Siméon, Baie Ste-Catherine & Tadoussac

St-Siméon: 173km (107 miles) NE of Québec City; Baie Ste-Catherine: 207km (129 miles) NE of Québec City; Tadoussac: 214km (133 miles) NE of Québec City.

St-Siméon is where travelers catch the ferry to the southern shore of the St. Lawrence. The northern end of Charlevoix, at Baie Ste-Catherine, is marked by the confluence of the Saguenay River and the St. Lawrence, and these waters attract a half-dozen species of whales, many of which can be seen from shore mid-June through late October. **Whale-watching cruises** are popular. Tadoussac is just across the Saguenay and the southernmost point of the tourist region called Manicouagan.

ESSENTIALS
GETTING THERE
BY CAR   Take Route 138 to reach the ferry at St-Siméon, and continue on 138 up to Baie Ste-Catherine. Tadoussac is across the Saguenay River. There is a free car ferry for the 10-minute crossing.

VISITOR INFORMATION
St-Siméon has a year-round **tourist office** at 494 rue St-Laurent, open daily between late June and Labour Day. Visit www.tourisme-charlevoix.com for more information.

ST-SIMEON
After visiting La Malbaie, you have several options. You can return back to Québec City the same way you came—it's only 140km (87 miles) along the north shore. Or, you can continue up Route 138 for 33km (20 miles) to St-Siméon and cross the St. Lawrence by ferry, landing at Rivière-du-Loup a little over an hour later and return-ing to Québec City along the south shore. If it's the summer season and you have more time—a full afternoon, or an extra day to stay overnight—consider either tak-ing the St-Siméon ferry for a 3-hour round-trip ride, or continuing on to Baie-Ste-Catherine and Tadoussac to go on a whale-watching cruise. You also could simply soak in the striking views offered by the free ferry crossing at Saguenay River, and then turn around and retrace your steps. (Note that in the winter and early spring, most of the few establishments you'll drive past between St-Siméon and Tadoussac are closed.)

To get to **the ferry in St-Siméon,** follow the signs that direct cars and trucks down to the terminal. Capacity is 100 cars; boarding is on a first-come, first-served basis. Departures vary substantially from month to month, so check at © **418/638-2856** or www.travrdlstsim.com for the schedule on the day you're traveling. One-way fares are C$37 (US$32/£16) for a car, C$15 (US$13/£6.25) for each passenger age 12 to 64 years, less for seniors and children. Arrive at least 90 minutes before departure during the summer and holidays. Voyages take about an hour.

From late June to September, passengers may enjoy a bonus on the trip: That's when the **whales** are most active. They are estimated at more than 500 in number when pelagic (migratory) species join the resident minke and beluga. The ferry steams through the area they most enjoy, so summer sightings are an ever-present possibility.

BAIE STE-CATHERINE

To enhance your chances of seeing whales, continue northeast from St-Siméon on Route 138, arriving 30km (19 miles) later in Baie-Ste-Catherine (pop. 254), near the estuary of the Saguenay River. In season, companies offer cruises to see whales or cruise the majestic Saguenay Fjord.

The cruise companies use different sizes and types of watercraft, from powered inflatables called Zodiacs that carry 10 to 25 passengers up to stately catamarans and cruisers that carry up to 500. The Zodiacs don't provide food, drink, or narration, while the larger boats have snack bars and naturalists onboard to describe the action. Zodiaks, though, are more maneuverable, darting about at each sighting to get closer to the rolling and breaching behemoths.

Zodiac passengers are issued life jackets and waterproof overalls, but should expect to get wet anyway. It's cold out there, too, so layers and even gloves are a good idea. People on the large boats sit at tables inside or ride the observation bowsprit, high above the waves. Big boats are the wimp's choice for whale-watching. Ours, too.

One of the most active companies offering trips is **Croisières AML,** whose main office is in Québec City (© **800/563-4643** all year, 418/692-1159 in season; www.croisieresaml.com). From June to mid-October, they have up to six whale-watching departures daily. Fares for the 3-hour "Whales and Fjord" tours on the larger boats are C$57 (US$50/£25) for adults, C$52 (US$45/£22) for seniors and students, and C$25 (US$22/£11) for children 6 to 16. Two-hour Zodiac "Adventure" fares are C$52 (US$45/£22) for adults, C$47 (US$41/£20) for seniors and students, and C$37 (US$32/£16) for children 6 to 16. Excursions of comparable duration and with similar fares are provided by **Group Dufour Croisières** (© **800/463-5250;** www.dufour.ca). Both companies have departures from both the Baie-Ste-Catherine and Tadoussac wharves. Most cruises last 2 to 3 hours.

TADOUSSAC

From Baie Ste-Catherine, take the free 10-minute ferry, **Traverse Tadoussac** (© **877/787-7483** or 418/235-4395), to get to Tadoussac, which sits directly on the water. The ferry crosses at the mouth of the dramatic Saguenay River, and palisades with evergreens poking out of rock walls rise sharply from both shores, the reason this area is often referred to as a fjord. The ferry can board up to 75 vehicles. Departure times vary according to season and demand, but in summer figure every 20 minutes from 8am to 8pm, and less frequently the other 12 hours and in low season. (The ferry is also the reason that trucks travel in convoys on the highway after each ferry crossing.)

Tadoussac is known as "The Cradle of New France." The oldest permanent European settlement north of Florida, it was established in 1600. Missionaries followed and stayed until the middle of the 19th century. The hamlet might have vanished soon after, had a resort hotel—now the **Hôtel Tadoussac,** below—not been built there in 1864. A steamship line brought vacationers from Montréal and points farther west and deposited them here for stays that often lasted all summer.

Apart from the hotel, just a few small support businesses, a marina, and some dozen small motels and B&Bs constitute the town. The sight of a beaver waddling up the hill from the ferry terminal in broad daylight is met with only mild interest. **Whale-watching** companies have departures from here as well as from Baie Ste-Catherine (above). There's also golfing at the 9-hole public **Club de Golf Tadoussac** (© **418/235-4306**), which has been in operation since 1890.

For 4 days in June, the town hosts a **Festival de la Chanson,** a festival of French song with more than a two dozen performers. Call ℂ **866/861-4108** or 418/235-2002 or check www.chansontadoussac.com.

A WHALE CENTER

Centre d'Interprétation des Mammifères Marins   This small interpretation center, directly on the river's edge, offers information about whales, which can often be seen from the shores starting in mid-April each year. It offers a 15-minute film and whale experts on-site. It is run by the nonprofit GREMM, which is dedicated to scientific research on the marine mammals of the St. Lawrence. It posts updates about whale activity at www.whales-online.net.

108 rue de la Cale Sèche (on the waterfront). ℂ **418/235-4701.** Admission C$8 (US$6.95/£3.45) adults, C$6 (US$5.20/£2.60) seniors, C$4 (US$3.50/£1.70) children 6–12. Family and group rates. Closed mid-October to mid-May.

WHERE TO STAY & DINE

Hôtel Tadoussac   From the opposite shore, you might glimpse the bright-red mansard roof of this sprawling hotel, which dominates the land sloping to the river. (Once you're in front of it, you might also recognize it as the centerpiece in the film *Hotel New Hampshire.*) First established in 1864, the hotel's current building was erected in 1942. Balconies and a large front lawn overlook the river and the comings and goings of boats and Zodiacs. Inside, the public spaces and bedrooms have a shambling, country-cottage appearance—there's no pretense of luxury here (although there is free Wi-Fi in the sprawling lobby). Maple furnishings and hand-woven rugs and bedspreads are all made in Québec. There is no air-conditioning, although all bedrooms have overhead fans and the 50 river-view rooms get a good breeze. Meals in the large dining room are better than might be expected, while falling well short of impressive. The hotel is open from early May through mid-October. In 2005, it was bought by a Vancouver hotel company, but no renovations are planned for 2008.

165 rue Bord de l'Eau, Tadoussac, PQ G0T 2A0. ℂ **800/561-0718** or 418/235-4421. Fax 418/235-4607. www.hotel tadoussac.com. 149 units. C$154–C$239 (US$134–US$208/£66–£103) double. Children under 18 stay free in parent's room. Packages available. AE, DC, MC, V. Closed mid-Oct to early May. **Amenities:** 3 restaurants (regional; buffet; casual); bar; heated outdoor pool; tennis court; spa; concierge; babysitting; children's programs. *In room:* TV, coffeemaker, hair dryer, iron.

Appendix: Montréal & Québec City in Depth

Deciding where to eat, where to stay, what to see, and how to play can make trip-planning fun, but seeking out and beginning to understand another culture and society are the most enriching experiences of travel. Here's a bit of background on Montréal and Québec City.

1 A Look at French Canada: Now & Then

Québec is immense, the largest province in the second-largest country in the world (after Russia) at 1,667,926 sq. km (643,819 sq. miles)—more than three times as large as France. It stretches from the northern borders of New York, Vermont, and New Hampshire up north to almost the Arctic Circle. To the east of it lie Maine and the province of New Brunswick; to the west, the province of Ontario and James and Hudson bays. Its substantial fund of natural resources includes 16% of the world's supply of fresh water.

Most of the province's population lives in its lower regions—the St. Lawrence lowlands and parts of the Appalachians and the Laurentians. More than 80% of its 7.5 million residents live within an area 322km (200 miles) long and 97km (60 miles) wide, one of the highest concentrations of people in sparsely populated Canada.

The greater Montréal metropolitan area is home to nearly half of the province's population. The city itself is on an island that is part of the Hochelaga Archipelago. The island is situated in the St. Lawrence (St-Laurent) River near where it joins the Ottawa River. At the city's center is a 232m (761-ft.) hill (which natives like to think of as a mountain) called Mont-Royal, from which the city takes its name. Real mountains rise nearby: the Laurentides (the Laurentians) are the oldest range in the world and the playground of the Québécois. The northern foothills of the Appalachian mountains separate Québec from the United States and add to the beauty of the Cantons-de-l'Est, the bucolic region on the

Dateline

- **1534** Jacques Cartier sails up the St. Lawrence, claiming the territory for France and marking the first European discovery of Canada.
- **1608** Motivated by the burgeoning fur trade, Samuel de Champlain founds a settlement at Kebec, at the foot of Cape Diamond. It will become the city of Québec.
- **1642** Paul de Chomedey, sieur de Maisonneuve, establishes a colony called Ville-Marie that will become Montréal.
- **1668** Québec Seminary is founded in Québec City, later to become Laval University in 1852.
- **1682** A massive fire on August 4 in Québec's Lower Town destroys 55 buildings in 7 hours. Rules established afterward require the use of stone walls to limit fire jumps.
- **1759** British General Wolfe defeats French General Montcalm on the Plains of Abraham in Québec City.
- **1760** Montréal falls to the British.

opposite side of the St. Lawrence once known as the Eastern Townships, where many Montréalers have country homes. Québec City, 263km (163 miles) northeast of Montréal, commands a stunning location on the rim of a promontory overlooking the river, which is at its narrowest point here.

THE EUROPEANS ARRIVE The Vikings landed in Canada more than 1,000 years ago, probably followed by Irish and Basque fishermen. English explorer John Cabot stepped ashore briefly on the east coast in 1497, but it was the French who managed the first meaningful European toehold in the wilderness. When **Jacques Cartier** sailed up the St. Lawrence in 1535, he recognized at once the tremendous strategic potential of **Cape Diamond,** "the Gibraltar of the North." But he was exploring, not empire building, and after stopping briefly on land he continued on his trip upriver.

Cartier continued past the spot that would become Québec City under Champlain to what was then a large island with a fortified Iroquois village called **Hochelaga** and composed of 50 longhouses. As usual, he didn't linger but pushed onward in his search for the sea route to China. His progress was halted by the fierce rapids just west of what is now the Island of Montréal. In a demonstration of mingled optimism and frustration, he dubbed the rapids "La Chine" on the assumption that China was just beyond them (today, they're known as the Lachine). He then decided to check out the Indian settlement after all, landing at a spot in what is now Old Montréal, and paid his respects to the Native people before moving on. That was the extent of Cartier's contribution to the future city.

Samuel de Champlain arrived 73 years later, in 1608, determined to settle at Québec, a year after the Virginia Company founded its fledgling colony of Jamestown, hundreds of miles to the south. The British and French struggle for dominance in the new continent focused on their explorations, and there the French outdid the English. Their far-ranging fur trappers, navigators, soldiers, and missionaries opened up not only Canada but also most of what eventually became the United States, moving all the way south to the future New Orleans and claiming most of the territory to the west. This vast region later comprised the **Louisiana Purchase.** At least 35 of the subsequent 50 states were mapped or settled by Frenchmen, who left behind thousands of names to prove it, among them Detroit, St. Louis, New Orleans, Duluth, and Des Moines.

Champlain's first settlement, or *habitation,* grew to become Québec City's

---

- **1763** The king of France cedes all of Canada to the king of England in the Treaty of Paris.
- **1775** Montréal is occupied by American Revolutionary forces who withdraw after a few months, when an attempted siege of Québec City by Benedict Arnold fails.
- **1821** English-speaking McGill University is founded in Montréal.

- **1845** Cholera! With the increased number of immigrants from Ireland, Scotland, and England to Québec City, cholera breaks out.
- **1867** The British North America Act creates the federation of the provinces of Québec, Ontario, Nova Scotia, and New Brunswick.
- **1883** *"Je me souviens"* becomes the official motto

of Québec—an ominous "I remember."
- **1900–10** Three hundred twenty-five thousand French Canadians emigrate to the United States.
- **1922** Armand Bombardier invents the prototype for the Ski-Doo, the first snowmobile, which will make him famous and wealthy in the late 1950s.

continues

Basse-Ville, or Lower Town, on the flat riverbank beneath the cliffs of Cap Diamant (Cape Diamond). But almost from the beginning there were attacks, first by the Iroquois, then by the English, and later by the Americans. To better defend themselves, the Québécois constructed a fortress on the cape, and gradually the center of urban life moved to the top of the cliffs.

THE FOUNDING OF MONTREAL

Paul de Chomedey, sieur de Maisonneuve, arrived in 1642 to establish a colony and to plant a crucifix atop the hill he called Mont-Royal. He and his band of settlers came ashore and founded Ville-Marie, dedicated to the Virgin Mary, at the spot now marked by Place-Royale. They built a fort, a chapel, stores, and houses, and the energetic Jeanne Mance made her indelible mark by founding the hospital named Hotel-Dieu-de-Montréal, which still exists today.

Life was not easy. Unlike the friendly Algonquins who lived in nearby regions, the Iroquois in Montréal had no intention of living in peace with the new settlers. Fierce battles raged for years, and the settlers were lucky that their numbers included such undaunted souls as la Salle, du Luth, de la Mothe Cadillac, and the brothers Lemoyne. At Place d'Armes today there's a statue of de Maisonneuve, marking the spot where the settlers defeated the Iroquois in bloody hand-to-hand fighting.

From that time the settlement prospered. Until the 1800s, Montréal was contained in the area known today as Vieux-Montréal. Its ancient walls no longer stand, but its long and colorful past is preserved in the streets, houses, and churches of the Old City.

ENGLAND CONQUERS NEW FRANCE

In the 1750s, the struggle between Britain and France had escalated, after a series of conflicts, beginning in 1689, that had embroiled both Europe and the New World. The latest episode was known as the French and Indian War in North America, an extension of Europe's Seven Years' War. Strategic Québec became a valued prize. The French appointed Louis Joseph, Marquis de Montcalm, to command their forces in the town. The British sent an expedition of 4,500 men in a fleet under the command of a 32-year-old general, James Wolfe. The British troops surprised the French by coming up and over the cliffs of Cap Diamant. The ensuing battle for Québec, fought on the Plains of Abraham just southwest of the city center on September 13, 1759, is one of the most important battles in North American history: It resulted in a continent that was under British influence for

- **1925** The Seagram Company is founded in Montréal.
- **1940** Women are granted the right to vote in provincial elections in Québec, having obtained that right in federal elections in 1917.
- **1948** The Québec flag, bearing four fleurs-de-lis, is adopted.
- **1962** Montréal's underground city is born, with the construction of Place Ville-Marie.

- **1967** Montréal hosts the successful Expo '67.
- **1968** The Parti Québécois is founded by Reneé Lévesque, and the separatist movement begins in earnest. Québécois Pierre Elliott Trudeau is elected prime minister of Canada, and he holds that office for most of the following 18 years.
- **1976** The Parti Québécois comes to power in Québec and remains in office until

1985, when the Liberal Party succeeds it. Montréal hosts the Olympics.
- **1984** Québécois Brian Mulroney becomes prime minister of Canada.
- **1989** The North American Free-Trade Agreement goes into effect, gradually removing most tariffs on goods of national origin moving between the United States and Canada.

over a century. (That influence carries on to today: The face of Queen Elizabeth II is still on all Canadian currency.)

The battle lasted just 18 to 25 minutes, depending on which historian you read, and resulted in 600 casualties. Both generals perished as a result wounds received. Wolfe lived just long enough to hear that the British had won. Montcalm died a few hours later. Today a memorial to both men overlooks Terrasse Dufferin in Québec City, the only statue in the world commemorating both victor and vanquished of the same battle. The inscription, in neither French nor English but Latin, says, simply, COURAGE WAS FATAL TO THEM.

THE UNITED STATES INVADES

The capture of Québec determined the course of the war, and the **Treaty of Paris** in 1763 ceded all of French Canada to England. In a sense, this victory was a bane to Britain, however. If the French had held Canada, the British government might have been more judicious in its treatment of the American colonists. As it was, the British decided to make the colonists pay the costs of the French and Indian War, on the principle that it was their homes being defended. They slapped so many taxes on all imports that the infuriated U.S. colonists openly rebelled against the Crown.

But if the British misjudged the temper of the colonists, the Americans were equally wrong about the mood of the Canadians. **George Washington** felt sure that French Canadians would want to join the revolution, or at least be supportive. He was mistaken on both counts. The Québécois detested their British conquerors, but they were also staunch Royalists and devout Catholics, and saw their contentious neighbors as godless Republicans. Only a handful supported the Americans, and three of Washington's most competent commanders came to grief in attacks against Québec. Thirty-eight years later, in the **War of 1812,** another U.S. army marched up the banks of the Richelieu River where it flows from Lake Champlain to the St. Lawrence. And once again, the French Canadians stuck by the British and drove back the invaders. The war ended essentially in a draw, but it had at least one encouraging result: Britain and the young United States agreed to demilitarize the Great Lakes and to extend their mutual border along the 49th parallel to the Rockies.

MONTREAL & QUEBEC CITY TODAY

The ancient walls that protected Québec City over the centuries are still in place today, and the town within their embrace has changed little, preserving for posterity the heart of New France.

- **1990** The Meech Lake Accord, recognizing Québec as a "distinct society" within Canada, is voted down, and separatist agitation increases.
- **1992** Montréal celebrates its 350th birthday.
- **1993** Mulroney resigns with public approval ratings in the single digits. He is succeeded by Kim Campbell, the first female prime minister. She and the Tories are soundly defeated by Jean Chrétien and the Liberals in October.
- **1994** Québec's separatist Parti Québécois wins provincial elections, ending 9 years of Liberal rule.
- **1995** Despite seemingly unstoppable momentum toward independence, a referendum on separation from the rest of Canada is narrowly defeated.
- **1996** Sharp cuts in federal contributions to Canada's cherished universal health-care system provoke job actions by doctors. Accounts of unsanitary hospitals, outdated equipment, and delays for treatment cause mounting unease in the face of governmental demands for even greater efficiencies and cost-cutting procedures.

continues

Montréal, though, has gone through a metamorphosis. It was "wet" when the United States was "dry" due to Prohibition from 1920 to 1933. Bootleggers, hard drinkers, and prostitutes flocked to this large city situated so conveniently close to the American border and mixed with rowdy people from the port, much to the distress of Montréal's mainly upstanding citizenry. For half a century the city's image was decidedly racy, but in the 1950s a cleanup began, with a boom in high-rise construction and eventual restoration of much of the derelict Old Town. In 1967, Montréal welcomed the world to Expo '67, the World's Fair. The great gleaming skyscrapers and towering hotels, the superb Métro system, and the highly practical underground city date mostly from the 40 years since the Expo.

All this activity helped to fuel a phenomenon later labeled the **"Quiet Revolution."** The movement was to transform the largely rural, agricultural province into an urbanized, industrial entity with a pronounced secular outlook. French Canadians, long denied access to the upper echelons of desirable corporate careers, started to insist upon equal opportunity with the powerful Anglophone minority.

Inevitably, a radical fringe movement of separatists emerged, signaling its intentions by bombing Anglophone businesses.

The **FLQ** (Québec Liberation Front), as it was known, was behind most of the terrorist attacks, reaching its nadir with the kidnapping and murder of a cabinet minister, Pierre Laporte.

Most Québécois separatists, though, were not violent, and most French-speaking Québécois were not even separatists. **Pierre Trudeau,** a bilingual Québécois, became prime minister in 1968. More flamboyant, eccentric, and brilliant than any Canadian who ever held the post, he necessarily devoted much of his time to trying to placate voters on both sides of the issue. In 1969, the **Official Languages Act** mandated that all federal agencies provide services in both French and English. But succession remained a dream for many people; in 1980, a provincial referendum on separation from the confederation was defeated by only 60% of the vote. Subsequent attempts to assuage the chafed sensibilities of French Québécois failed again and again, as often at the hands of other provincial premiers as by the Québécois, hounding at least three prime ministers from office.

In 1993, the governing Tories were defeated by the opposition Liberals. The new Prime Minister, **Jean Chrétien,** a federalist, was not aided in his task of national reconciliation by representation in the House of Commons of the

- **1998** The governing provincial Parti Québécois wins reelection in November, beating off the resurgent Liberals, headed by Jean Charest. Still, the margin of victory is narrower than expected, and Premier Lucien Bouchard shelves plans for an early referendum on independence.
- **1999** By changing the definition of spouse in 39 laws and regulations, the government of Québec eliminated all legal distinctions between same-sex and heterosexual couples, becoming the first province in Canada to recognize the legal status of same-sex civil unions.
- **2000** Despite signs of Québec's emergence from a decade-long recession, by some measures surpassing the rest of Canada, support for Bouchard and separation falls below 40% of the electorate.
- **2001** Premier Bouchard resigns unexpectedly, throwing his separatist Parti Québécois into disarray. Polls show increasing disaffection with the idea of Québec sovereignty. He is succeeded by Bernard Landry.

militantly separatist **Bloc Québécois,** which became the largest opposition party in the same election.

On a regional level, the issue continued to simmer. In Québec the following year, the **Parti Québécois** won provincial elections to end 9 years of Liberal control. The new premier, **Jacques Parizeau,** vowed to hold an early referendum on sovereignty. In October 1995, the referendum lost by a mere 1% of the total vote. Parizeau resigned the next day, after making intemperate remarks about the negative role of ethnic voters in the results.

An unsettled mood prevailed in the province, thanks to a recession and general uncertainty over the future. But by 2000 things began to change. The Canadian dollar strengthened against the U.S. dollar. Unemployment, long in double digits, shrank to under 6%, the lowest percentage in more than 2 decades. Crime in Montréal (already one of the safest cities in North America) hit a 20-year low.

Nationally, the Liberal Party was racked by an ongoing corruption scandal. A vote of confidence was held in May 2005. The governing Liberals won by a single vote, but redemption was short-lived. In January 2006, the opposition Conservatives led by **Stephen Harper** ousted the long incumbent Liberals.

Meanwhile, the presence of skilled workers made much of Canada a favored site for Hollywood film and TV production. The rash of FOR RENT and FOR SALE signs that disfigured Montréal in the 1990s continued evaporating, replaced by a welcome shortage of store and office space.

Today, the quest for separatism seems to be fading. Conversations with ordinary Québécois suggest they are weary of the argument. As significantly, in provincial elections in March 2007, the Liberal Party, headed by **Jean Charest,** won just a minority government, with an out-of-nowhere second-place victory for the new **Action démocratique du Québec** party and its young leader **Mario Dumont.** The separatist Parti Québécois placed a distant third with just 28% of the vote marking, many think, the beginning of the end of the PQ's 40-year political movement and campaign for independence.

2 The Politics of Language

The defining dialectic of Canadian life is language, the thorny issue that has long threatened to tear the country apart.

Many Québécois believe that a separate independent state is the only way to maintain their culture in the face of the

■ **2002** The 28 towns and cities on Montréal Island are merged into one megacity with a population of 1.8 million inhabitants. Prime Minister Jean Chrétien, until then enjoying excellent approval ratings, runs afoul of an ethics scandal in midyear over favors exchanged for campaign donations. In August, he announces that he won't seek a fourth term.

■ **2003** In regional elections, Landry and the Parti Québécois lose in a landslide to the Liberals and their leader Jean Charest, an avowed federalist. Nationally, Paul Martin takes over as prime minister in December.

■ **2004** Martin calls for a new June election in the face of another financial scandal. He wins, but there are substantial Liberal losses in Parliament. In Montréal, 15 of the boroughs vote to de-merge from the megacity imposed in 2002.

■ **2005** Continued revelations in the corruption scandal bring about a vote of confidence in the House of Commons in May. The Liberals win by only one vote and lose to the Tories in a January 2006 election. Gay marriage is made legal in all of Canada's provinces and territories.

continues

Anglophone (English-speaking) ocean that surrounds them. The role of Québec within the Canadian federation has long been the most debated and volatile issue in Canadian politics.

There were reasons for the festering intransigence, of course—about 240 years' worth. A kind of linguistic exclusionism prevailed for much of the region's early history, with wealthy Scottish and English bankers and merchants denying French-Canadians access to upper levels of business and government.

The French language, though, was only the most tangible aspect to what many in Québec remain committed to. There is a kind of bedrock loyalty held by many to the province's Gallic roots. France may have relinquished control of Québec in 1763, but its influence, after its century and a half of rule, remains powerful. Many Québécois continue to look across the Atlantic for inspiration in fashion, food, and the arts. Culturally and linguistically, it is that tenacious French connection that gives the province its special character.

One attempt to smooth ruffled Francophones (French-speakers) was made in 1969, when federal legislation stipulated that all services were henceforth to be offered in both English and French, in effect declaring the nation bilingual. That didn't long assuage militant Québécois. They undertook to guarantee the primacy of French in their own province. To prevent dilution by newcomers, the children of immigrants are required to enroll in French-language schools, even if English or a third language is spoken in the home. Bill 101 was passed in 1977, which all but banned the use of English on public signage. Stop signs now read ARRET, a word that actually refers to a stop on a bus or train route. (Even in France, the red signs read STOP.) The bill funded the establishment of enforcement units, virtual language police who let no nit go unpicked.

The resulting backlash provoked the flight of an estimated 400,000 Anglophones to other parts of Canada. Canadian Prime Minister Brian Mulroney met with the 10 provincial premiers in April 1987 at a retreat at Québec's Meech Lake to cobble together a collection of constitutional reforms. The Meech Lake Accord, as it came to be known, addressed a variety of issues, but most important to the Québécois it recognized Québec as a "distinct society" within the federation. In the end, however, Manitoba and Newfoundland failed to ratify the accord by the June 23, 1990, deadline. As a result, support for the secessionist cause burgeoned in Québec, fueled by an election that firmly placed the separatist Parti Québécois in

---

■ **2006** The television show *Little Mosque on the Prairie* gives a peek into the religious and cultural issues faced by Québec's large immigrant population.

■ **2007** Jean Charest and his Liberal Party win just a minority number of seats in provincial elections. In second place is the new Action démocratique du Québec party, led by

Mario Dumont. The separatist Parti Québécois's anemic third-place showing is perceived as a crushing defeat for both the PQ and the separatist movement.

control of the provincial government. A referendum, held in 1995, was narrowly won by residents who favored staying within the union, but the vote settled nothing. The issue continued to divide families and dominate political discourse.

The year 2007 may have seen the death blow to the issue, however. In provincial elections, once-reigning separatist Parti Québécois placed third with just 28% of the vote. The election was perceived by many as the first step in closing the door on the campaign for independence.

None of this debate should deter visitors. The Québécois are exceedingly gracious hosts. Montréal may be the largest French-speaking city outside Paris, but most Montréalers grow up speaking both French and English, switching effortlessly from one language to the other as the situation dictates. Telephone operators go from French to English the instant they hear an English word out of the other party, as do most store clerks, waiters, and hotel staff. This is less the case in country villages and in Québec City, but there is virtually no problem that can't be solved with a few French words, some expressive gestures, and a little goodwill.

3 Recommended Books, Music & Film

Canadian writers whose sense of place infuses their work include short-story author Alice Munro and novelists Douglas Coupland and Margaret Atwood. Playwright Michel Tremblay, an important dramatist, grew up in Montréal's Plateau Mont-Royal neighborhood and uses that setting for much of his work. His *Les Belles-Sœurs,* written in 1965, introduced the lives of working-class francophone Québécois to the world. The openly gay writer continues to live and work in Montréal. (Meanwhile, Atwood has even branched out into product invention to help far-flung writers: She has come up with something called a "LongPen," which allows authors to have book signings from a distance, using a robot to "sign" a book after the author makes a signature on a computer screen. The gizmo debuted at the Nicholas Hoare bookstore in Montréal in 2006.)

Writing from the perspective of a minority within a minority, the late Jewish Anglophone Mordecai Richler inveighed against the excesses of Québec's separatists and language zealots in a barrage of books and critical essays in newspapers and magazines. Montréal journalist Taras Grescoe's *Sacré Blues* (Macfarlane Walter & Ross, 2001), which carries the subtitle "An Unsentimental Journey Through Québec," presents an affectionate but balanced assessment of his adopted province.

Montréal has a strong showing of innovative alternative rock bands, including Arcade Fire, Wolf Parade, and Godspeed You! Black Emperor. (The band Of Montreal, however, is from Athens, Georgia.) Singer-songwriter Rufus Wainwright grew up in Montréal and got his start at city clubs, while singer-songwriter Leonard Cohen grew up in the city's Westmount neighborhood and attended McGill University.

Many U.S. films are made across the border for financial reasons, even when their American locales are important parts of the stories (see, for instance, *Brokeback Mountain,* which was filmed in Alberta). Québécois films—made in the province, in French, for Québec audiences—can be difficult to track down outside the country. A new initiative announced in spring 2007 called "Eléphant: mémoire du cinéma québécois" (www.elephant.canoe.ca) should help with that: It plans to provide extensive information on all 800 Québec-made feature films at a website, and to make them available on Canadian television on-demand. Recent features worth seeking out are Jean-Marc Vallée's box-office hit *C.R.A.Z.Y.,* a gay coming-of-age story; Louise Archambault's *Familia,* about mothers and daughters; and Sarah Polley's *Away From Her,* with Julie Christie as a woman with Alzheimer's.

Index

See also Accommodations and Restaurant indexes, below.

CLOSED
due to
accidental demolition

WEGEN BISSIGEN
EICHHÖRNCHEN GESCHLOSSEN

CERRADO
CABRAS

Κλειστό
Μετεωρίτες

POOL CLOSED
プール
も
閉
鎖
中
ELECTRIC EELS

Hotel
closed for
facelifting

FERMÉ POUR
RAISON
DE GRÈVE
DES BONNES

FECHADO!
POR CAUSA DE
ATAQUES DOS CROCODILOS

— I don't speak
sign language.

A hotel can close for all kinds of reasons.
Our Guarantee ensures that if your hotel's undergoing construction, we'll
let you know in advance. In fact, we cover your entire travel experience.
See www.travelocity.com/guarantee for details.

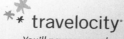

travelocity
You'll never roam alone.

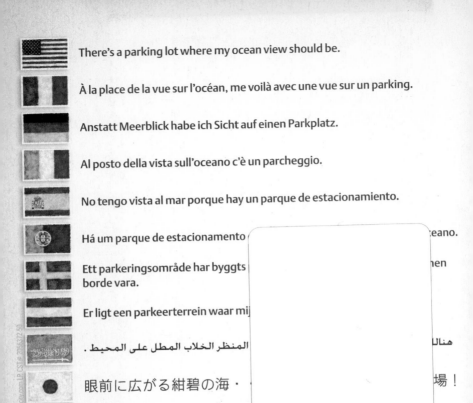